The War for Korea, 1945–1950

MODERN WAR STUDIES

Theodore A. Wilson
General Editor

Raymond A. Callahan
J. Garry Clifford
Jacob W. Kipp
Jay Luvaas
Allan R. Millett
Carol Reardon
Dennis Showalter
David R. Stone
Series Editors

The War for Korea, 1945–1950

A House Burning

Allan R. Millett

 University Press of Kansas

© 2005 by the University Press of Kansas
All rights reserved

Published by the University Press of Kansas (Lawrence, Kansas 66045), which was
organized by the Kansas Board of Regents and is operated and funded by Emporia State
University, Fort Hays State University, Kansas State University, Pittsburg State
University, the University of Kansas, and Wichita State University

Library of Congress Cataloging-in-Publication Data

Millett, Allan Reed.
    The war for Korea, 1945–1950 : a house burning / Allan R. Millett.
        p.   cm. — (Modern war studies)
    Includes bibliographical references and index.
    ISBN 978-0-7006-1393-9 (cloth : alk. paper)
    1. Korea—History—20th century.   2. Korea—History—Allied occupation,
1945–1948.   3. Communism—Korea—History—20th century.   4. World politics—
1945–1955.   5. Korean War, 1950–1953—Causes.   I. Title.   II. Series.
    DS916.M465 2005
    951.904′1—dc22   2005009166

British Library Cataloguing-in-Publication Data is available.

Printed in the United States of America

10 9 8 7 6 5 4 3

The paper used in this publication meets the minimum requirements of the American
National Standard for Permanence of Paper for Printed Library Materials Z39.48-1984.

To two veterans of the Korean War:
Brig. Gen. Edwin Howard Simmons, USMC (Ret.)
Director Emeritus, History and Museums Division,
Headquarters Marine Corps
and
The late Dr. Horace Grant Underwood
Professor Emeritus, Yonsei University, Republic of Korea
Lieutenant Commander, USNR
and
To the memory of Dr. Kim Chull-Baum,
my colleague at the Korean National Defense College and
founder of the Korean War Studies Association

"This world is a burning house. The people, unaware that the house is on fire, are in danger of being burned to death so Buddha in his compassion devises ways of saving them."

Contents

(photo inserts follow pp. 42 and 158)

Acknowledgments   ix

List of Abbreviations   xvii

Introduction   1

1. The Years of Division, 1919–1945   16

2. Defeat and Division: Korea on the Brink, 1945–1946   43

3. Putting Korea Together Again: The Rise and Fall of the US-USSR Joint Commission, 1946–1947   72

4. The Moscow Agreement Is Abandoned, 1947   92

5. The United Nations Enters the Struggle, 1947–1948   122

6. The Republic of Korea Enters the World and Almost Dies Stillborn, 1948–1949   159

7. "We Are Fighting for Our Lives!" 1949–1950   186

8. The Once and Future Invasion, 1949–1950   229

Epilogue and Prologue, June 1950   254

Appendix: The Romanization of Korean and Chinese   259

Notes   265

Bibliographical Essay   311

Index   325

Acknowledgments

There is an ancient Korean proverb that advises one not to put the burden of a donkey on the back of a grasshopper. I am a grasshopper when it comes to Korean history. Undertaking a comprehensive history of the Korean War, a donkey's load of fifteen years, has shown me the wisdom of another Korean proverb: a theft will be successful if it involves the participation of many skilled thieves. If any thefts have been performed in this study of the Korean War, I alone am responsible for the crimes of literary and historical commission and omission. The study's successes, however, represent the contributions of an international gang of advisers and supporters. I am keenly aware of the handicaps I brought to this project, especially in the area of foreign language competence and cultural sensitivity for Asia, which I had not even visited until 1986. I have done my best to make up for the donkey's load of learning I lacked when I began the serious study of the Korean War in 1993. I can only hope that I became a stronger grasshopper with the help of all those whose assistance I acknowledge here. This homage is not exhaustive, since some of it already appeared in an earlier book, *Their War for Korea* (Brassey's, 2002), or will follow, more appropriately, in volume II of this study.

My largest debt is to my wife, Martha E. Farley-Millett, and my daughter, Eve Noelle Farley Millett, whose love of the Korean people and appreciation of their joys and sufferings gave my research an affective dimension it otherwise would have lacked. Martha and I visited the Republic of Korea for the first time in 1986. We returned with Eve, then seven months old, in 1991 for what proved to be a series of visits that allowed all of us to live in Seoul for an accumulated time of more than two years by 2003. Martha and Eve have actually spent more time in Korea than I have, nurturing our friendships and thinking about how one can do justice to the Korean people in writing.

Martha's favorite headstone in the Seoul Foreigners Cemetery on the north bank of the Han River, known as Yanghwajin, belongs to Homer B. Hulbert. A pioneer in Western education in Korea in the last days of the Chosun dynasty (1886–1907), Hulbert chose to leave Korea, whose independence he had championed, rather than work under Japanese rule. He did not return to Korea until it was free again. He lived only six days after returning to Seoul in 1949, the stress of travel apparently too much for a man of eighty-six to endure. Buried at Yanghwajin with all the honors the Republic of Korea could bestow on a foreigner, Hulbert had composed his own epitaph: "I would rather be buried in Korea than in Westminster Abbey." Without fail, Martha visits the Hulbert grave site during every visit to Seoul. Eve simply regards Korea as her second home.

Not far from the Hulbert grave site now rest the remains of our greatest patron, teacher, and friend in Korea, Dr. Horace G. Underwood, who died on January 15, 2004. I am consoled that Horace read most of this book in manuscript form before his death at Severance Hospital on the campus of Yonsei University—that great institution created as Chosun Christian College by his grandfather, Rev. Horace G. Underwood. We met Horace and his wife Dorothy in 1991 and lived in their home for several months in 1994–1995 while they were home on leave in the United States. My academic education in Korean history began in Horace's personal library as well as the library of Yonsei University, to which Horace arranged access. Summer after summer for the next decade, the Underwoods took us in as boarders and included us in their rich social and intellectual life in Seoul, as well as days of sun and storms at their Taechon Beach cottage. The younger generation of Underwoods, Horace H. and Nancy Underwood and Peter Underwood, graciously accepted us as extended family, as did Carol and Richard F. Underwood of Urbana, Illinois. Dick had served as headmaster of Seoul Foreign School and, like his older brother Horace, was a former officer of the American armed forces and veteran of the Korean War. He became another counselor on things Korean past and present.

We might never have learned of Horace Underwood's historical stature or personal magnetism had we not met Betsy Fletcher of Columbus, Ohio, who had grown up in Korea in a missionary family. Learning that we were going to Korea in early March 1991, Mrs. Fletcher encouraged us to meet Dr. Underwood, perhaps the most important bit of advice I ever received.

Our family education in Korean history actually started in the United States before we visited Seoul for an international military history conference. Our earliest instructors were two of my graduate students and their wives—then-Capt. Donald M. Bishop and Jemma Kim Bishop, and then-Maj. and Mrs. Huh Nam-sung (Barbara). Don and Jemma left the air force for the more exciting life of U.S. foreign service officers specializing in Chinese and Korean affairs. Huh Nam-sung returned to Korea, doctorate in hand, to become director of operations of the Presidential Security Service, director of the Korean Institute for National Security Affairs, and dean of faculty at the Korean National Defense University (KNDU). Both Don and Nam-sung have dedicated themselves to seeing that my writing about Americans in Asia and about Koreans remains rooted in reality. They have regarded my education as a personal project for twenty years, including important trips to and in China and Korea.

As both a friend and a shrewd historian, Dr. Mark C. Monahan has no equal, except Horace Underwood. He developed his perceptiveness as the ultimate survivor of service in the United Nations Partisan Infantry Regiment Korea (1951–1953), the South Korean army, the U.S. Army, and the U.S. Marine Corps, from which he retired as a lieutenant colonel and intelligence specialist. With a doctorate in Chinese language and literature from Georgetown University, Mark (born Chung Il-yong) is the beloved professor of international education and Asian history at Yonsei University and the University of Maryland–Asia. Our neighbor in Seoul, he is a *chingu* (friend) without parallel.

During that first trip to Seoul in 1986, we met another of our godfathers for the study of the Korean War: Thomas Ryan, who was then chief of the history office that served the United Nations Command, the U.S. Forces Korea, and the U.S. Eighth Army. An archaeologist by education, Tom became my principal instructor on Korean terrain, historic sites, battlefields, Korean War bibliography, and the rich and underutilized files held by his office at the U.S. Army base in Yongsan, Seoul. In addition to his ties to the U.S. Army, in which he still serves as a reserve lieutenant colonel, Tom had wide contacts in the United Nations community and the South Korean army, and he shared them without reservation. In the history office I got to know two of Tom's partners, Ronnie V. Miller and Kim In-hwa, both former army officers, who shared Tom's love of human history (as opposed to command chronologies) and became my companions on many a "staff ride" along the Demilitarized Zone (DMZ) from coast to coast and to the battlefields south of the DMZ. Although Tom left Korea for a Stateside assignment in 1996, which eventually took him to Kuwait and Iraq, his successors extended the courtesies of their office to me as a friend and a historian. They are Dr. Richard A. Gorell, Robert Collins, and Dr. Richard G. Davis. I also profited from the expertise of two air force historians with extensive Korean service, John Sullivan and Deryl D. Danner.

Beginning with our first extended stay in Korea in 1991, we enjoyed the tutelage of many Koreans and Americans who freely gave their time to advance our education: Sue Bae, Royal Asiatic Society; Frederick Carriere, Korean-American (Fulbright) Educational Association; Lt. Col. Stephen M. Tharp, USA, secretariat, Military Armistice Commission; Steven Bradner, political adviser to the commanding general, Combined Forces Command (CFC); Ambassadors Donald Gregg, James T. Laney, and Stephen Bosworth; the late Dr. Donald S. Macdonald, whose experience in Korea began in the U.S. Army Military Government in Korea (USAMGIK) in 1946; Gen. Paik Sun-yup; Tim Long, a China specialist for "another government agency"; Dr. Suh Yong-sun, researcher at the Korean Military History Institute, which is now known as the Korean Institute for Military History Compilation (KIMHC); John A. Nowell and George D. Kim of the U.S. Forces Korea public affairs office at Yongsan; Dr. Cho Sung-hun, KIMHC; Chi Kap-chong, chairman, UN Korean Allies Association; and Dr. Eom Ik-sang, Korean and

Chinese linguist, Sookmyung Women's University. I am also indebted to the members past and present of two of my institutional hosts: the Neutral Nations Supervisory Commission and Headquarters, Marine Forces Korea, whose administrative support and advice have been indispensable. Maj. Gen. and Mrs. William P. Eshelman, USMC, established the "aid to the Milletts program" in 1991.

In addition to the Underwoods and Mark Monahan, four other veterans of the Korean War have influenced my understanding of that conflict and Korean history. My primary guide to the history of Korean-American military relations from the Korean perspective is Maj. Gen. Lim Sun-ha, ROKA (Ret.), who in terms of actual service may be the first officer of the Korean Constabulary, which became the army of the Republic of Korea. I told General Lim's personal story in *Their War for Korea,* but I acknowledge my indebtedness to him here because he introduced me to many of his contemporaries, including Gen. Kang Yong-hoon, Maj. Gen. Kim Ung-soo, and Brig. Gen. Lee Chi-op. Sun-ha and his wife Sandy have been stalwart champions of better Korean-American relations and the memorialization of the officers of the Korean Constabulary, who served the USAMGIK in good faith and at some risk of alienation from their own political elite. Some of their fellow officers in the Korean army resented their professionalism, including general-turned-president Park Chung-hee. I owe a similar debt to the late Lt. Col. James H. Hausman, USAR, the acknowledged de facto leader of the U.S. Army advisers from 1946 to 1950. Jim died in Austin, Texas, on October 6, 1996. Although he never saw this book, he read my earlier writings on the Korean army and the Korean Military Advisory Group (KMAG), and he provided access to his own papers and introduced me to other KMAG veterans.

Although they have never met, Cho Sung-kyu, professor emeritus of English at Yonsei University, and Brig. Gen. Edwin Howard Simmons, USMC (Ret.), director emeritus of the Marine Corps History and Museums Division, Headquarters Marine Corps, share a great deal more than advanced age, honorable military service in Korea, and dedication to my continuing education. They are devoted students of the English language and its application to the expression of human values. They both have advanced degrees from American universities to which I have personal ties—Miami University and Ohio State University. Professor Cho serves the cause of Korean-American friendship as executive director of the Korean American Cultural Foundation. An accomplished historian and novelist, General Simmons still gives freely of his stylistic expertise, honed as editor of the *Marine Corps Gazette* and the hands-on historical director of the Marine Corps for almost thirty years. Serving as General Simmons's reserve deputy in the twilight of my Marine Corps career was one of my most rewarding military experiences. The second volume of *The War for Korea* (1950–1954) will bear his obvious imprint.

I want to pay special tribute to my colleagues at the Korean National Defense University, an institution with which I have been associated for more than a decade. They have been gracious hosts during our visits to Korea, and we were happy to arrange an in-residence program for KNDU faculty members at the Mershon Center, Ohio State University. In addition, Korean academics with graduate degrees in international relations and military history from Ohio State have been key faculty members at the Korean Military Academy, the Korean Naval Academy, the Korean Institute for Defense Analysis, the Sejong Institute, and several civilian universities. In addition to Col. Huh Nam-sung, the core members of the "mafia" are Col. Yoon Jung-ho, Dr. Kim Young-ho, Col. Jung Byung-ho, Col. Kim Hyun-ki, Dr. Lee Choon-kun, Dr. Kim Tae-hyun, Dr. Kim Taeho, Lt. Cmdr. Cho Duk-hyun, Maj. Gen. Kim Kook-hun, Maj. Park Il-song, Dr. Rhee Kang-suk, Maj. Gen. Kim Hyun-soo, Lt. Col. Lee Chang-hoon, Col. Yoo Yoon-sik, and Capt. Mun Hwei-mok (ROKN). Of this group, my closest associate (other than Colonel Huh) is Park Il-song, whose own research and willingness to be my translator during his years as my doctoral student have given him "adopted son" status — an honor not taken lightly in Korean society.

One of my goals in this book was to tell the story of the Korean Military Advisory Group in its formative years, 1946–1950. In addition to General Lim and Colonel Hausman, my point man for the history of KMAG became Col. Harold S. Fischgrund, USA (Ret.), historian of the KMAG veterans association and Jim Hausman's close friend. Through Colonel Fischgrund's good offices, I collected original documents, reports, letters, maps, and oral histories of lasting importance from the following contributors: Lt. Gen. W. H. Sterling Wright, Brig. Gen. H. F. Mooney, Col. James C. Holland, Col. F. Foster Cowey Jr., Lt. Col. Charles L. Wesolowsky, Lt. Col. Ralph Bliss, Lt. Col. Minor Kelso Jr., Lt. Col. Edwin M. Joseph, and Robert Shackleton. All these KMAG veterans read my earlier pieces on the creation of the South Korean army, but with the exception of Colonel Fischgrund, they have not read this book. Katherine Roberts gave me access to the official records of her father, Brig. Gen. William L. Roberts, KMAG's commander from 1948 to 1950. Mrs. Carl B. Nerdahl provided copies of letters from her late husband written from Korea in 1949–1950.

The papers of other American officers who served in the U.S. Army Forces in Korea (USAFIK) and USAMGIK are described in the bibliographical essay, but I wish to acknowledge the special contribution of Susan Bertsch Cull (Columbus, Ohio) and David Bertsch (Akron, Ohio), who allowed me access to the papers, still in family hands, of their late father, Capt. Leonard M. Bertsch, AUS. Bertsch played a key role in the political activities of the USAMGIK, although he was hardly the evil genius portrayed by scholars critical of that government. Bertsch was a skilled political operative (a Democratic civil service commissioner for Summit County, Ohio) before entering the army as a military government officer. The deft, experienced Bertsch, honor graduate of Holy Cross and Harvard Law School, became the "agent" of the commanding general, USAFIK, and the military governor, USAMGIK. I also want to thank Col. John D. Herren, USA (Ret.), for access to the family-held papers of his father, the late Lt. Gen. Thomas W. Herren, who served two Korean tours (1946–1948 and 1951–1953).

The Department of History and the Mershon Center at Ohio State University, my institutional homes for thirty-five years, have played a critical part in supporting all my research projects. The study of the Korean War is no exception. In addition to released time, my department colleagues provided wise counsel from their own specializations: Dr. Peter L. Hahn (U.S. diplomatic history), Dr. David L. Stebenne (U.S. political history), Dr. William R. Childs (U.S. business history), Dr. James Bartholomew (modern Japanese history), and Dr. Samuel Chu (modern Chinese history).

Three directors of the Mershon Center—Dr. Charles F. Hermann, Dr. Richard Ned Lebow, and Dr. Richard K. Herrmann—generously supported my research with time, money, and solitude. My most immediate benefactor for this project has been Maj. Gen. Raymond E. Mason Jr., USAR (Ret.), who allows me to spend his money and bear his name (he endows my chair). On a number of occasions I have consulted with my former graduate students with special expertise on the Korean War: Dr. Charles J. Gross (air operations), Dr. Andrew J. Birtle (U.S. Army counterinsurgency operations), Dr. Richard B. Meixsel (Filipino participation in the Korean War), Dr. William Donnelly (National Guard mobilization), Col. David R. Gray (special operations), Lt. Col. Kelly Jordan (U.S. Army in the Far East), Maj. Bryan Gibby (KMAG), Maj. Thomas Hanson (U.S. Eighth Army), and Maj. C. J. Horn (helicopter operations). During their in-residence study at Ohio State University, several students provided me with their skilled services as research assistants: William B. Feis, Mark R. Jacobson, Katherine Becker, Leo J. Daugherty III, Peter Schrijvers, Paul Jussel, Bryan Gibby, Maj. Son Hyung-ki, and John M. Stapleton Jr. Dr. Robert Rush made short sojourns for me into the Center of Military History files. Dr. James G. Hogue took time from his study of the Civil War to do research for me in the John Foster Dulles Papers, Princeton University Library. As she has for so many of my projects large and small, Beth Russell of the Mershon Center provided essential administrative support.

My benefactors and advisers represent much of the Korean-American studies community in the United States and abroad. At one time or another I talked about this project and received the guidance of Dr. Li Xiao-bing, Carole Cameron Shaw, Dr. Stephen Shaw, Dr. Richard Immerman, Dr. James I. Matray, Ambassador William Sherman, Don Oberdorfer, Dr. Paul Pierpaoli, Dr. Paul Edwards, Dr. Spencer Tucker, the late John Toland, Sir Max Hastings, the late Clay Blair, Col. S. M. W. Hickey, Gen. Sir Anthony Farrar-Hockley, Lt. Gen. Michael V. Hayden (USAF), Niles Bond, Dr. Bruce Cumings, Dr. B. C. Koh, Dr. Bonnie B. C. Oh, Dr. John K. C. Oh, Dr. Conrad Crane, Dr. Edward Marolda, Lt. Col. Thomas Fairful, Lt. Col. Duane E. Biteman (USAF), Dr. Lee Chung-min, Dr. Baek Jong-chun, and the research team of the Cheju 4.3 Research Institute.

Peer reviews are essential to the process of writing history and often mean the difference between a book riddled with avoidable factual errors and wrongheaded interpretations and a book that approaches the perfection we seek but cannot achieve. The official readers of this manuscript for the University Press of Kansas were Dr. William Stueck, University of Georgia–Athens, and Dr. Carter J. Eckert, former director of the Korea Institute, Harvard University. Their own works set a high standard in Korean-American history, and they read this manuscript with the professional attentiveness I expected. I did not accept all their suggested revisions, but I certainly considered them. Of equal value for the expertise they brought to their criticisms and recommendations were Dr. Donald Clark, Trinity University, San Antonio, Texas, and Col. Jiyul Kim, USA, both of whom provided detailed recommendations and corrections. Professor Clark is the historian of the Protestant missionary experience in Korea and the grandson and son of missionaries. Colonel Kim has just completed his doctoral studies at Harvard. He is another historian of KMAG, having served in its successor, the Joint United States Military Assistance Group Korea. His wife, Sheila Miyoshi Jaeger Kim, is a professor of modern Korean social and cultural history. No one could have better friends and tutors than the Kims. I also received valuable criticism of the entire manuscript from Huh Ho-joon, chief researcher for the Korean government's investigating committee for the Cheju 4.3 incident. Both General Simmons and General Lim also read the entire manuscript and offered sound advice. So, too, did Professor Jeffrey Grey, a historian of Commonwealth military operations in Korea and my "mate" in Australia, and Professor Peter Maslowski from the University of Nebraska–Lincoln, my longtime collaborator on a book on American military history. Another collaborator, Professor Yu Bin, Wittenberg University, remains my valued expert on Chinese history, and he, too, read the entire manuscript. Professor Yu and I have profited from the advice of Dr. Song Zhongyue (Beijing). I provided copies of the manuscript to other experts who helped with my research: Dr. Kathryn Weathersby (Korea Project, the Woodrow Wilson Center Cold War International History Project), Col. Victor A. Gavrilov (Institute of Military History, Russian Federation Ministry of Defense), Dr. James H. Grayson (School of Asian Studies, University of Sheffield), Dr. John Merrill (Department of State), Professors Melvyn P. Leffler and Chen Jian (University of Virginia), Professor Mark C. Monahan, Dr. Richard G. Davis (CFC-USFK-UNC History Office), Dr. Ronald H. Spector (George Washington University), and my many friends at the Japanese National Institute of Defense Studies.

The documentary sources for Korean War history can be found around the world, although the number of people who do research in Moscow, Beijing, and Pyongyang is limited, and I am not one of them. However, some of my friends are. The archives, collections, and repositories I searched provided the material that gives the texture of truth to historical writing on the Korean War. I cannot thank everyone who assisted me at these institutions, but I want to name the repositories and indicate a few of the people who provided timely, continuing, and important assistance: the Harry S. Truman Presidential Library, Independence, Missouri (Dennis Bilger and Elizabeth Safly); the Dwight D. Eisenhower Presidential Library, Abilene, Kansas (David Haight); the Douglas MacArthur Memorial Library and Museum, Norfolk, Virginia (William J. Davis and James Zobel); the U.S. Army Military History Institute (Richard Sommers, Dave Keogh, and Louise Arnold-

Friend); the George C. Marshall Library (Marti Gansz); the Air Force Historical Research Agency, Maxwell Air Force Base, Alabama; the Hoover Institution on War, Revolution, and Peace; the National Security Agency; the Central Intelligence Agency; the U.S. Army Center of Military History; the National Archives and Records Administration (Timothy K. Nenninger and Richard Boylan); the Korean Language Institute, Yonsei University; the Franklin D. Roosevelt Presidential Library, Hyde Park, New York; the Defense Prisoner of War/Missing Personnel Office; the Naval Historical Center; the Marine Corps History and Museums Division (Dan Crawford and Robert Aquilina); the Citadel Archives and Museum; the Princeton University Library; the U.S. Military Academy Library; the U.S. Naval Academy Library; and the U.S. Air Force Academy Library.

A variety of educational hosts gave me the opportunity to broaden my knowledge of Korean history and to test my ideas on their faculty and students: the Korea Foundation, Yonsei University, the Korean National Defense University, Temple University, the University of Nebraska–Lincoln, Kansas State University, the Eisenhower Historical Site at Gettysburg, Pennsylvania, the U.S. Naval Academy, the Korean Military Academy, the University of Tennessee at Knoxville, Hawaii Pacific University, the Truman Library, the D-Day National Museum and the University of New Orleans, the Japanese National Institute of Defense Studies, Wittenberg University, the College of Wooster, the Wisconsin Veterans Museums, the Douglas MacArthur Library and Memorial and Old Dominion University, the Second Marine Division and Marine Corps Base Camp Lejeune, the Australian Defense Force Academy and the Army History Unit, the Australian Department of Defence, the University of North Texas, Texas A&M University, the University of Illinois at Champaign-Urbana, the U.S. Military History Institute and the Army War College, the Marine Corps Command and Staff College, Harvard University, the First Infantry Division Museum and Foundation, the Royal Asiatic Society of Korea, the University of Missouri–Kansas City, Tel Aviv University, the Korean Association of International Studies, and the Korean War Studies Association.

If I have overlooked or slighted any person or organization that has contributed to my education in Korean history, I am comforted by the fact that I can correct the oversight in the second volume of this project. Although I share the strengths of this study with many, I alone bear the responsibility for its errors and shortcomings, the usual disclaimer of an author who does not really believe that there are such errors and that the shortcomings are neither numerous nor important. I hope others will enjoy the challenge of reading this book as much as I enjoyed the challenge of writing it.

Abbreviations

AUS	Army of the United States
CFC	Combined Forces Command
CIA	Central Intelligence Agency
CIC	Counterintelligence Corps
CIG	Central Intelligence Group
CINC	commander in chief
DAC	Department of the Army civilian employee
DMZ	Demilitarized Zone
DNP	Democratic National Party
DPI	Department of Public Information
ECA	U.S. Economic Cooperation Administration
FACC	Foreign Assistance Correlation Committee
FECOM	Far East Command
GARIOA	Government Aid and Relief in Occupied Areas
GRU	Main Intelligence Directorate (USSR)
JCS	Joint Chiefs of Staff
JSPOG	Joint Strategic Plans and Operations Group
KC	Korean Constabulary
KDP	Korean Democratic Party
KGB	State Security Committee (USSR)
KIMHC	Korean Institute for Military History Compilation
KLO	Korean Liaison Office
KMAG	Korean Military Advisory Group
KNDU	Korean National Defense University
KNP	Korean National Police
KNYM	Korean National Youth Movement
KPA	Korean People's Army

MDAP	Mutual Defense Assistance Program
NATO	North Atlantic Treaty Organization
NCO	noncommissioned officer
NEAJUA	Northeast Anti-Japanese United Army
NEB	National Economic Board
NSC	National Security Council
NSRRKI	National Society for the Rapid Realization of Korean Independence
OPC	Office of Policy Coordination
OSS	Office of Strategic Services
PLA	People's Liberation Army
PMAG	Provisional Military Advisory Group
POW	prisoner of war
RCT	Regimental Combat Team
RG	Record Group
ROKA	Army of the Republic of Korea
ROKAF	Air Force of the Republic of Korea
ROKN	Navy of the Republic of Korea
RVA	Revolutionary Volunteer Army
SANACC	State–Army–Navy–Air Force Coordinating Committee
SCAP	Supreme Commander Allied Powers
SIC	Special Investigating Committee
SIGINT	signals intelligence
SKLP	South Korean Labor Party
SWNCC	State-War-Navy Coordinating Committee
UN	United Nations
UNC	United Nations Command
UNCOK	United Nations Commission on Korea
UNTCOK	United Nations Temporary Commission on Korea
USA	U.S. Army
USAF	U.S. Air Force
USAFIK	U.S. Army Forces in Korea
USAMGIK	U.S. Army Military Government in Korea
USAR	U.S. Army Reserve
USFK	U.S. Forces Korea
USMC	U.S. Marine Corps
USNR	U.S. Navy Reserve
YMCA	Young Men's Christian Organization

Introduction

Like the proverbial shrimp caught between two whales, the Korean War is trapped between World War II and the Vietnam War in American remembrance. Americans tend to recall wars for their domestic impact, not their international effect. This is not a uniquely American phenomenon, but it dulls the understanding of the long-term impact of such "small wars" on the rest of the world and on Americans themselves. The wars with Mexico (1846–1848) and Spain (1898) demonstrated the large consequences of splendid little wars. The war in Korea was neither splendid nor little, and its impact on American foreign policy—particularly the cold war with the Soviet Union and especially outside Europe—made it one of the formative events of the post–World War II world. The changes the war wrought in the newborn Western alliance system were dramatic, making the North Atlantic Treaty Organization (NATO) the foundation of forward, collective defense. The change in the political climate toward defense spending in the United States was so dramatic that critics of the "militarization" of "containment" have asserted for fifty years that the administration of President Harry S. Truman provoked the war.[1]

Although the analysis of the causes, conduct, and consequences of the Korean War will continue as long as there are two Koreas, the war is now at least partially detached from the history of United States–Soviet relations from 1945 to the 1990s. This historiographical surgery should encourage more research and less polemical argument, at least outside of Korea. Americans should not be surprised that Koreans and their Western champions feel passionately about a conflict that resembles the War of the Rebellion and the War between the States. Feeling passionately does not guarantee thinking wisely. Whether authors approve or disapprove of the Korean War, they have written a good deal of nonsense about the war in several languages. Yet the history of the Korean War, in all its complexity, continues to come into sharper focus with the publication of books and articles based on archival research, now predominantly from Russian and Chinese sources. The work of a new generation of Japanese and Korean historians has enriched the study of the war in ways that will continue to elude North American, British, and European historians. The besetting sins of Korean War history are the inability of academic historians to deal with military affairs, the inability of official historians to deal with political and institutional failures, the inability of secular humanists to deal with the power of faith systems, and the inability of military historians to deal with anything but the combat performance of their favorite armed forces.[2]

This study of the Korean War will appear in two volumes, the first covering the period between August 1945 and June 1950. The second volume will begin in May 1950 and end in 1954, when the last prisoners had been processed, the political conference required by the armistice had failed, and the competing regimes of Syngman Rhee and Kim Il-sung had eliminated their domestic opponents and tied their patrons to the once and future aid of their war-torn countries. This first volume is not limited to the "causes" of the Korean War, because the war had already killed tens of thousand of Koreans (but only three Americans) before June 25, 1950. On that day, the war took on a new form and sent Korean and American—as well as Russian and Chinese—casualties soaring into the millions. Selecting a starting date for the war is a matter of judgment, but it surely falls in the period February–October 1948, with the general strike of February and March, the insurgency on Cheju-do island or the Cheju 4.3 incident in April, and the mutiny of the Fourteenth Regiment, Korean Constabulary, in Yosu and Sunchon. All these events occurred in the American occupation zone (the Republic of Korea after August 15, 1948), which meant that southern Koreans were fighting other southern Koreans.

The southern Korean insurgency drew its leaders and most persistent partisans from the South Korean Labor (or Communist) Party, which sought to unify Korea as a revolutionary socialist state in collaboration with its comrades in Pyongyang. The Korean Communists abandoned any serious attempt at peaceful unification in 1948, in a desperate attempt to prevent the establishment of the Republic of Korea. Since they sought to impose their revolutionary program—such as the confiscation of farmlands—by violence, the Communists chose war, a war that followed the same pathology as the civil wars in China and Vietnam. Unlike the wars of decolonization won by other Asian Communists, the Korean revolutionaries ran into opponents unwilling to concede civic virtue and military prowess to the Communists. These Koreans—American supported—represented a coalition of ultra-nationalist authoritarians, traditional conservatives with vested property rights, free-market entrepreneurs, reformers who in Europe would have been Christian Democrats or Christian Socialists, humanitarian liberals, and apostate Communists. Both sides had a fair share of adventurers, opportunists, romantics, and profiteers, too. Nevertheless, they envisioned themselves as the founders of a new Korea, for which they were prepared to die and kill without compromise. Their war for Korea was neither limited nor forgotten.[3]

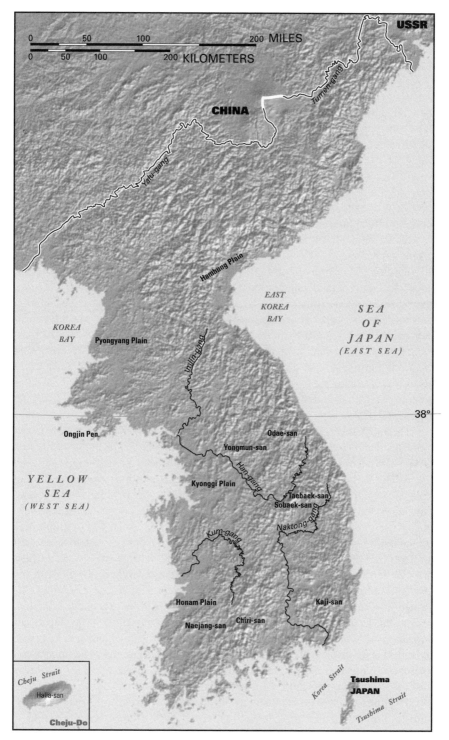

Map 1. Korea: Topography

A Cuban nationalist and a Mexican president once despaired about the future of their native lands: so far from God, so close to the United States. The history of Korea is thrice confounded: so far from Buddha, Confucius, and God; so close to Russia, China, and Japan. Perhaps one should add that Korea is too far from the United States. The history of modern Korea, defined as the past two centuries, has been shaped by the struggle of the Korean people to preserve their national identity and culture while trying to define just what that identity and culture are. The clash of three of the world's five great systems of value and faith (Islam and Judaism excluded) has not made this task easy, and the political conflict of four large and messianic nation-states over the fate of the Korean peninsula has made the life of the Koreans a never-ending struggle for survival. It is no accident that Koreans often compare themselves to the Jews, Poles, and Irish.

Korea's modern history is shaped by three epochs of war and revolution. The first is the decline of the Chosun dynasty from the middle of the nineteenth century until the establishment of the Japanese protectorate in 1905. During this era of political and social disintegration, Korea lost its status as the Hermit Kingdom and became—often by invitation—a stewpot of imperialism extended through various agencies by imperial and nationalist China, the Japan of the Meiji Restoration, czarist Russia, and a Protestant Christian–commercial United States. Britons, French, Canadians, and Germans added their more limited influence to the mix of modernizing models that diverted Korea from its traditional rural Asian society built on the teachings of Confucius and Buddha. Two wars ended the regional competition over Korea and Manchuria—the Japanese defeat of China in 1895, and the Japanese defeat of Russia in 1905.[4]

The Japanese epoch (1905–1945) redirected the tensions between Korean traditionalism and modernity into a parallel struggle for national liberation while preserving the economic modernity brought by the Japanese. In 1910 Japan annexed Korea. The diaspora of Koreans to Manchuria dramatized this tension; the Korean refugees who flooded Manchuria after 1910 wanted to fight the Japanese as partisans, work for the Japanese in government and business, and avoid the Japanese in Christian villages and urban enclaves. Within Korea, the Japanese authorities stamped out resistance with violence and assimilation, both of which were often untimely and immoderate but always effective. After Japan went to war in China in 1937, Japanese control tightened; the imperial administration saw the Koreans as cheap industrial labor and exploitable farmers in a desperate war effort. Although Koreans of varied political persuasions fought the Axis far afield—one Korean in the U.S. Army served as a battalion operations officer in the Japanese-American 442d Regimental Combat Team in Italy, while another served as chief of staff of a Soviet army division in Germany—the Koreans produced no national liberation movement that created a dominant postwar national leader. There was no Korean Charles de Gaulle, Tito, or Ho Chi Minh.

The third epoch of modern Korean history began with the collapse of the Japanese empire in 1945 and stretches into the twenty-first century. It is the period of the "two Koreas," not unlike an earlier epoch of the three kingdoms of Koryo, Paekche, and Shilla. In 2003, during one of the Republic of Korea's periodic bouts of anti-Americanism, a Korean television crew interviewed a stylish young woman who asserted that Americans were murderous brutes, but that Koreans did not kill Koreans. One wonders where her family has lived since 1945. The two Koreas may have been the accidental product of the Soviet and Allied rush to liquidate the Japanese imperial presence, but they also represented the political expression of two different visions of a modern Korea, built on the wreckage of the colonial experience and the resistance to Japanese imperialism in all its forms. The revolutionaries would have fought one another in some form even if not a single American or Russian soldier had set foot in Korea.

The bloody civil war of 1948–1954, in which Koreans helped kill more than two million of their countrymen, hardened the division of the two Koreas. Reunification still seems distant—unless there is another war, in which case the "winners" will be only slightly less ruined (again) than the "losers." The Democratic People's Republic of Korea exchanged colonialism for *juche,* or self-determination, and in doing so impoverished its people and created a Stalinist version of the Hermit Kingdom. It worries its neighbors with its special combination of unworldliness and bellicosity. It gives special meaning to the term *rogue state* through its export of weapons, narcotics, and counterfeit money. The Republic of Korea still fights its own battles of identity and independence within an international security and economic context shaped by its relationships with Japan, China, Russia, and the United States. This Korea is still too close and too far from its global neighbors to be too comfortable.[5]

Of all the nations that affected Korean history, the most distant, the United States of America, has been the most puzzling and inconstant. In its first treaty with Korea in 1882, the United States offered its "good offices" to help Korea "if other powers deal unjustly or oppressively" with either government. Yet not until September 1945 and then again in June 1950 did the United States challenge, at any risk to itself, the designs of other states to absorb Korea. The great American villain in Korean history is Theodore Roosevelt, who won a Nobel Peace Prize for appeasing Japan at Korea's expense in 1905; the great American hero (at least in Seoul) is Douglas MacArthur, the liberator and unifier of Korea in 1950. Many Koreans are not sure whether the American intervention of 1950 was a noble expiation of past sins or just another catastrophe visited on them by the Great Powers. Koreans share others' confusion and exasperation with the United States: how can a nation of such great wealth, all forms of power, moral commitment to justice and liberty, and global influence be so fickle, inattentive, ambivalent, and often cowardly in support of its declaratory values and interests? The Communists need not ponder such puzzlements, since they have all the answers about the global class struggle. American inconstancy allowed imperial Japan to become a regional hegemon in Asia despite American interest in the independence of Korea and China; this appeasement of Asian imperialism was eventually reversed at the cost of millions of lives, one hundred thousand of them in the American armed forces.[6]

A small story from the lives of real Koreans illuminates the yin and yang of Korean-American relations, as well as the woes of the Korean people in the twentieth century. The adventures of Peter Kim are not unique, but representative. Peter, the oldest son of Dr. Kim Chang-sei and Lee Chung-sil, was born in Soonan, South Pyongan Province, Korea, in 1912. He immigrated with his parents to Shanghai, China, in 1917, shortly after the birth of his brother David. Technically, the Kims remained citizens of Japan, but they stayed in China just long enough to qualify for resident status, which allowed them to travel to the United States as visitors but did not qualify them as potential naturalized citizens under U.S. immigration laws. The Kim family odyssey, however, took them to Los Angeles (1920–1926), where Peter attended American schools between the ages of eight and fourteen. He notes: "My early American background . . . has so influenced my life as to permanently identify me with Americans and American interests." The Kims were also Christians. During the Los Angeles years, Peter and David became the older brothers of James (born in 1921) and Betty Marie (born in 1923). The two youngest Kims were American citizens, registered as such by their parents. The Kims guarded James's and Betty's citizenship by following all the residence and registration rules required by U.S. law. The family, however, could not take up permanent residence in the United States and returned to Korea (1926–1928), where Peter continued his American-Christian education at Seoul Foreign School. The difficulties of life in colonial Korea, however, drove the Kim family back to Shanghai, a city with a large expatriate Korean community as well as thousands of American and European diplomats, businessmen, and missionaries and their families.[7]

For thirteen years the Kims lived a more or less normal life in Shanghai. However, a family tragedy occurred when Dr. Kim, who had traveled alone to the United States in 1930, died in Los Angeles in 1933. He had been working on a religious-medical assignment that would have allowed the whole family to join him that same year. Having completed high school at the English-language Shanghai Public School for Boys, Peter Kim had already become an employee of an American real estate investment company in Shanghai. His ability to speak English ("I cannot recall when I did not speak English") as well as Chinese and Korean made him a valuable employee, although not unique in Shanghai in the 1930s. Much of his business success, on which his family now depended, required his complete Americanization. With total conviction that his adopted country would reward his service, Peter joined the American infantry company of the Shanghai Volunteer Corps (1932) under the sponsorship of an officer of the U.S. Army. He served in the unit in the mobilization of 1937–1938 and dropped out in 1938 "only because I considered the international situation too delicate to continue risking an incident with the Japanese while not enjoying formal recognition as an American." Peter thought that his comrades and employers believed he was an American citizen. Whether he was a Chinese or Japanese citizen was arguable, but an American citizen he certainly was not.[8]

The Depression and permanent Japanese occupation of Shanghai in 1937 made the Kim family's position even more perilous, but Peter persisted in making himself invaluable. When the American electric company for which he worked (1933–1935) went bankrupt, he became a member of Getz Brothers and Company, San Francisco, which sold American building supplies to Chinese and expatriate construction companies in Shanghai. Peter's clients included Masonite, Owens-Illinois, Pittsburgh Plate Glass, ARMCO Steel, and Flinkote. Peter used his money and connections to send James and Betty (U.S. citizens) back to California, out of harm's way, to continue their education. Although Betty, ill and despondent, returned to Shanghai and her mother's care in 1939, James remained in the United States until he deployed to the South Pacific as a soldier in the U.S. Fortieth Infantry Division. When James Kim arrived in the land of his ancestors in late 1945, he was a first lieutenant in the U.S. 160th Infantry Regiment. In the meantime, Peter Kim faced a new crisis—the American-Japanese war that began on December 8, 1941. Peter immediately became an unpaid agent of the wartime American Association of Shanghai, which attempted to protect the lives and property of American citizens under the international laws governing the rights of civilian "innocents" stranded abroad by war within a belligerent or occupied nation. Peter worked for the American Association until the Japanese finally repatriated the last internees in 1943. In March 1943 he joined the staff of the Swiss consul general in order to have some income. His sister Betty, as a U.S. citizen, drew a small State Department allowance.

Peter Kim's welfare work made his own life more perilous, for he could hardly avoid contact with the Japanese, who probably thought that he was a U.S. citizen. Peter ran a food kitchen for the most impoverished internees, and a Japanese army camera crew, making a propaganda movie showing how well the Japanese treated Europeans, caught him on film. As he feared, Peter became an interest of the *kempeitai,* the dreaded Japanese military police. Peter assumed more risks when he helped the marines who had surrendered at Wake Island and Beijing. In 1943 he was the only member of the American Association executive committee who knew the repatriation regulations and could travel about Shanghai. When the last American departed, so did Peter's political cover. The *kempeitai* arrested him and subjected him to ten days of interrogation and beatings, during which he was accused of being a secret agent for the U.S. Navy, the U.S. Army, the State Department, and the Chinese Nationalists. At the end of Peter's detention, the Japanese tried to recruit him to spy on those Europeans who remained in Shanghai or to make multilingual propaganda radio broadcasts. The Swiss consul general promised to protect Mrs. Kim, Betty, and David while Peter and his youngest brother, Richard, escaped inland to Nationalist-controlled China, where they would join the U.S.

Army advisory mission and air expeditionary force, with headquarters in Chungking. The Kim brothers believed that wartime military service for the United States would make them citizens without difficulty. They were wrong.

With the help of the Swiss, the Kim brothers escaped Shanghai and reached the American air bases in Kweilin just ahead of the Japanese summer offensive of 1944. They managed to enlist in the U.S. Army as planned, but their scheme to rescue the rest of their family proved hopeless. A year later, both Kims had reached the rank of T-5, a technician equal to a sergeant. Richard worked as a purchasing agent clerk in the Services of Supply; Peter became a member of the theater joint intelligence staff and Lt. Gen. Albert C. Wedemeyer's civil affairs staff. On August 15, 1945, an auspicious day for all Koreans, he returned to Shanghai disguised as a first lieutenant to help rescue American prisoners of war, arrange the Japanese surrender to the Nationalists, protect American property, and reestablish the American consulate. Before he left on this mission, he appealed to his immediate superior, a civil affairs colonel, to help him with a continuing problem: his citizenship.

True to character, the careful and anxious Peter Kim had learned that his special case (and his brother Richard's) did not fall under the citizenship provisions for aliens in the Second War Powers Act of 1942. (In 2003 there were thirty-seven thousand aliens serving in the U.S. armed forces, and their naturalization still creates legal problems.) For example, an alien serviceman could become a naturalized citizen without ever being a resident of the United States or its territories. The problem was that the Kims were Japanese citizens, which made them *enemy* aliens. The State Department had never recognized the exiled Korean provisional government in China—even after Pearl Harbor—and there was no provision to naturalize Korean servicemen or any other "enemy alien" Koreans. Peter Kim thought that he would just take his chances with a new quota or policy that would cover Koreans, if he could return to the United States. The U.S. Army, however, would discharge him by law—probably within a few months—at the site where he enlisted. He and Richard would still be in China, Japanese citizens or stateless, and at the mercy of the Chinese authorities of whatever political ilk. Given the Kims' wartime service, the Japanese would do them no favors. The ultimate irony was that General Wedemeyer offered Peter Kim a reserve lieutenant's commission to keep him on active duty, but Peter could not be commissioned without citizenship, which Wedemeyer could not grant a Korean.

The only solution rested in a special act of Congress, a provision for personal redress, relief, and reward that became a matter of "private law." The person who opened this door was Col. Marshall Carter, a China-Burma-India staff officer of unusual intelligence and unique political leverage in Washington. With an understanding that cut to the quick of the issue, Carter supported a Peter and Richard Kim Act. Peter Kim's service was critical to the American presence in China, but he could not serve safely in China unless he became an American citizen, and his value would be enhanced if he became a U.S. Army lieutenant. Waiting for some ruling on Koreans was ridiculous, Carter believed, as all prior attempts to determine "the status of Korea as a nation" had proved futile. "It appears that the status [of Korea] cannot be determined locally at any reasonable date."⁹

Still serving as a temporary first lieutenant at the pleasure of the theater commander, Peter Kim continued to work hard for the American cause in China. Although the War Department had sent a Kim brothers bill to Congress, there had been no action when the special provisions of his "convenience" commission expired on February 19, 1946. Peter Kim again became a T-5 with the clock ticking toward his unwanted discharge. A commission warrant remained in his commander's desk drawer in the consulate. On February 24, 1946, the War Department, relatively certain of favorable congressional action on the Kims' case, allowed Peter Kim to be discharged from the wartime Army of the United States and then appointed a second lieutenant (Officer Reserve Corps, U.S. Army Reserve) on a two-year contract for extended active duty in China. Pursuant to Senate Bill No. 1607, passed and recorded as Private Law 808 (79th Congress, 2d Session), Peter Kim became a citizen of the United States on December 4, 1946, and continued on active duty in Shanghai until he was released in February 1948. The army even allowed him to claim California as his home of record, so Peter Kim, veteran and American by act of Congress, returned to the nation he had so loyally served and had not seen since 1926. Two years later he returned to Korea and another war.¹⁰

The moral of this story is that Koreans have a tradition of injustice and supplication to uncaring governments, both their own and the Japanese colonial administration. Because of their contacts with individual Americans and their thirsty study of the *ideals* of American liberalism and democracy, the Koreans came to believe that the U.S. government reflected the interests of a people who truly understood their material and spiritual poverty. Americans would help them escape Japanese rule and their own archaic traditionalism that placed individuals at the mercy of Confucian communalism. Peter Kim had a duty not only to improve his own condition but also to use his success for the benefit of his family. Such a sense of responsibility may not be unique to Koreans—and may indeed be the global norm—but it is less valued by Americans than by almost all other peoples. Time and again the U.S. government, perceived as a symbolic father, acted in ways that Koreans viewed as capricious at best and treacherous at worst. They found it hard to understand why such a rich and generous people—for such were the Americans they had met in Korea—could tolerate a government so mean-spirited, selfish, and alien to what Koreans believed was the fundamental goodness of the American people.¹¹

Peter Kim's desperate search for a new national identity dramatizes the search for collective identity in an Asia embroiled in revolutionary turmoil for more than a century. Like other Asian nationalists, the Koreans resisted colonialism. In fact, they developed a tradition of populist protest, the *minjung* ideal, that never fell to the pressures for accommodation inherent in the canons of Buddhism, Confucianism, and Christianity. The *minjung* ideal preached the ultimate responsibility of the common people *(yangmin)* to protest oppression, demand social justice, assert communal values, define moral correctness, and preserve the mystic bond between the Korean people and the spirits of the land and nature. *Minjung* idealism goes beyond Western populism because it stresses a spiritual redemption and salvation that transcends politics. It offers little guidance on governance of any sort; in Korean tradition, the questions of governance were answered by Chinese philosophers. A mix of hope, fear, and fatalism offers dissidents an unparalleled opportunity to ignite significant portions of the Korean people into mass political demonstrations against grievances large or small, real or imagined. The value of the protest is in the act itself, although a favorable governmental response is not unwelcome. Nevertheless, even today, a Korean demonstration retains a social communalism that sometimes seems more like a marching picnic and songfest than a serious political action.[12]

The use of the terms *right* and *left* to describe political philosophies in Korea can obscure more than they reveal when used by the Western press, American observers, and historians after the fact. The terms, of course, originated with the French Revolution and the seating pattern of the various factions that attended meetings of the Estates General. In the twentieth-century Anglo-American political world, influenced by the rise of Marxist socialism and its variants, *right* came to mean a political position associated with preservation of the existing political, social, and economic order, usually through the mechanism of a strong central government with broad interventionist powers exercised by the executive branch of the existing regime. *Right* also might suggest economic policies that build state power but do not endanger a fundamentally capitalist system rooted in the corporate and private ownership of land, real property, and the means of production for the principal benefit of owners and investors. It might also mean imposed social behavior, defined by government.

Left, in contrast, represented a philosophy that stressed the change of a society's core public and private institutions in order to redistribute existing or future wealth by governmental action; such a policy, if carried to its logical conclusion, would eventually destroy social classes and ensure the equitable treatment and protection of all citizens. The critical agencies for such changes were a powerful central government, the parallel power of a dominant socialist party, and state (communal) ownership of land and the means of production. Individual liberties and personal ownership always came second to the collective good of the entire polity, defined by the government and the socialist party.

The success of the Bolshevik Revolution in Russia and subsequent efforts to bring revolution to other nations such as France, Germany, and China gave an additional meaning to *right* and *left*. Rightists opposed Communism, and leftists advocated or sympathized with Communism, either Russian or some other variant. Depending on the society, the Right protected organized religion (especially the Catholic Church) and the power of private associations. The Left regarded religion as "the opiate of the masses" and denied the inherent right of private associations to function, protected by custom and law from government abolition or control.

Another contemporary concern was the emphasis on national rather than international values and institutions. Rightists favored traditional, nationalistic values in family behavior and relationships, language, education, religious practice, and all forms of high and popular culture and artistic expression, along with ethnic homogeneity. Leftists stressed the universal nature of humankind, the building of social organizations on a multiracial basis, the threat of nationalistic values and behaviors to peace and prosperity, and the incidence of wars caused by nationalist emotions, as well as the control of wealth and the historical class struggle.

The difficulty of applying *right* and *left* to Korean politics in 1945–1950 is that virtually all factions represented some elements of both positions. American officers and diplomats observed that all Koreans were Communists, by which they meant that all Koreans wanted revolutionary changes to occur in all or most aspects of Korean political and economic life. Almost all the political leaders believed in a strong, interventionist central government acting through a dominant executive branch; only the short-lived, local People's Committees of 1945–1946 represented a true departure from the central authoritarian model, and they only pushed authoritarianism down to the *myon* (county), city, and provincial levels. As Americans of many different political persuasions observed in 1945–1950, *democracy* was not a word that any Korean political leader understood in practice. Yet no one wanted to restore a Korean monarchy, the power of the *yangban* (educated landholder) class and the mandarinic bureaucracy, Japanese colonialism, Shintosim, or even the Western concept of the rights of individuals taking precedence over the rights of the polity and ascribed authority. Koreans of the postcolonial period wanted to be right and left at the same time, which confused many Americans then and now. The easiest way to solve the descriptive dilemma (then and now) was to call the Communists and any other group that advocated some aspect of socialism the Left, and to call the anti-Communist, authoritarian, xenophobic entrepreneurial factions the Right. This division, however, undervalued the role of Christianity, Buddhism, and Chondogyo in modern Korean politics. Another option is to deny (as some Korean authors do) that Korean politicians of the era represented any political philosophies at all. Instead, they were driven by social and personal connections, their desire to use government posts as a method of obtaining economic security for their families, and a cultural compulsion to wield arbitrary power over other Koreans. There is certainly much truth in this analysis, but it criticizes Koreans for political behavior on which they have no monopoly; it also ignores the fact that the postcolonial political parties represented goals shared by many Koreans, grew from a strong sense of Korean identity, and had as much claim to Korean authenticity as the Communists did.[13]

The collapse of the Japanese empire in 1945 created a vacuum of political power that extended from India through Southeast Asia and north along the international date line to Japan itself. Nowhere were the former European colonial powers, governments-in-exile, or resistance movements prepared to take power, except in the most superficial sense. The politics of postwar Korea should be understood within this crisis of legitimacy and succession, which affected all of Asia. Wars of postcolonial succession and social revolution became the rule, not the exception. The Koreans shaped their unique civil war among many civil wars.

The Asia-Pacific war (1937–1945) created revolutionary conditions in which native political leaders sought to replace the European and Japanese imperialists. In India, communal religious conflict between Muslims and Hindus led to partition and the creation of two states, India and Pakistan. In Burma, the non-Burmese hill tribes, which had provided the fighting heart of the Anti-Fascist People's Freedom League, fought one another (Communists versus non-Communists). Then, after the assassination of Aung San, the national resistance hero, they fought a central government established by the collaborationist Burmese. In Malaya, the anti-Japanese resistance, dominated by ethnic Chinese led by the Communist Chin Peng, reorganized to oppose the restoration of British-Malay rule.[14]

The pattern of political pause and renewed civil war was repeated almost everywhere in Asia. Within a year from the end of the war, Indonesian guerrillas had returned to the jungle to take up arms against the Dutch, with the leadership tilted slightly to the Muslim nationalists of Acmet Sukarno rather than the Communists, both of whom could claim resistance to the Japanese. In Indochina, the Vietnam Doc Lap Dong Minh (led by Ho Chi Minh) survived Japanese repression while the Vietnam Quoc Dan Dong fought itself into extinction with revolts against the French and the Japanese (1930–1945), leaving the field to the Communists. The Vietminh, however, did not begin their war against the French until they ensured that weak French colonial forces had replaced the British, Indian, and Chinese Nationalist divisions that had arrived to take the Japanese surrender in 1945. The anti-Japanese resistance in the Philippines, which included American servicemen and profited from external support from Gen. Douglas MacArthur's Southwest Pacific Command, produced two postcolonial political elites—the *americanistas,* represented by Ramon Magsaysay, and the Communist Hukbalahaps of Luis Taruc. In a war of succession that lasted from 1946 until the early 1960s, the *americanistas* held a slight edge, largely through economic and military assistance and the honored promise of Philippine independence in 1946.

In China, the final conflict between the Nationalists and Communists began before the end of 1945 as the Communists rushed into the cities of Manchuria and north China to claim Japanese arms and to petition for Soviet military aid. Despite the assistance of the U.S. Navy, which provided shipping, and two U.S. Marine Corps divisions, the Nationalist army never reached parity with its principal opponent, the Communist Fourth Field Army (Lin Biao). American assistance propped up the Nationalist armies until 1949, but diplomatic negotiations with the Communists and equipment and advisers for the Nationalists could not halt the Communist march south and the flight of the Nationalist government to Taiwan. The first U.S. serviceman to die in combat with a Chinese Communist patrol—a marine—fell in northern China on May 21, 1946, not four years later in Korea. Far to the south, the Nationalist government sent a military expedition to claim the right to govern Taiwan (Formosa), which had been annexed by Japan in 1895 after its successful war with China. After enduring more oppression from their new colonial masters, the Taiwanese rose in arms and mass protests in February 1947. They died by the thousands at the hands of the Nationalist army and thus established a thirst for freedom from mainland Chinese rule that did not discriminate between the vestiges of the Guomindang and the claims of the People's Republic of China.

The experience of Korea stands in contrast with that of other Asian nations, not because the Koreans did not seek liberation but because they received it at relatively low cost. Nationalism throughout Asia had been forged and tempered by the fires of fighting the European imperialists, then the Japanese, and even themselves between 1937 and 1945; in Korea, however, the sheer weight of Japanese oppression and economic co-option had eliminated all but passive resistance. Perhaps if more Koreans had fought and died between 1937 and 1945, fewer Koreans would have died in 1948–1953. Thousands of Koreans died in World War II, of course, but they did so as part of the Japanese armed forces or as victims of the American bombing of the Japanese home islands. Dying as a participant in the Japanese war effort, however unwillingly, is not the same as sacrificing one's life and liberty in the cause of national independence. If there is any lesson in postcolonial politics, it is that power grows from a partisan leader who remains in his homeland and fights, not from expatriate politicians.

The United States did not ignore the fevers of national liberation that flamed across the Middle East and Asia in 1945, built on the fires of anti-imperialism that had flared in the 1930s. World War II had sealed the fate of the two principal colonial powers, France and Great Britain. In five short years, France retreated from Morocco, Tunisia, Lebanon, and Syria, holding on to only Indochina and Algeria by force until its defeats of 1954 and 1962. The postwar British Labour Party turned the withdrawal east of Suez into a rout in Egypt, Palestine, Transjordan, Iraq, Iran, India, and Burma, while fighting for Malaya. Ironically, American influence flowed around the chaos into Turkey, Saudi Arabia, Iran, Pakistan, and Thailand. The intellectual heirs of Adam Smith, John Knox, Cecil Rhodes, and Halford J. Mackinder, speaking another English dialect, offered a new form of association that extended the benefits of colonialism in terms of military security and economic development without the onus of direct governance and social, religious, and racial discrimination. The American version of neocolonialism (the Russians had another) was neither quiet nor ugly, but it was distinctly peculiar and confusing to the people of the postcolonial Middle East and Asia. It was especially difficult to judge just what the Americans would and would not fight for when faced with "wars of national liberation" that served Communist purposes.

Measured by the postcolonial politics of Asia, the war in Korea began in 1948 and is not yet finished. There is one Germany, one Vietnam, one China, and many Yugoslavias, but there are still two Koreas. After the defeat of Japan, the leaders of two Korean revolutionary movements raced home from exile and established two competing "new" Koreas. In the writings of Mao Zedong and Ho Chi Minh, with a Hispanic variant produced by Fidel Castro and Che Guevara, the concept of "people's war" helps explain the politics of postwar Korea—with one very large exception. In Korea there were *two* revolutionary movements trying to replace the old order.[15]

In theory, a people's war progresses through three phases. The first is the period of organization and political mobilization during which the revolutionary vanguard creates a shadow government and forces the most humble people into making political choices, voluntary or coerced. The goal of this phase is to create a broad foundation of popular support and legitimacy for the revolution and an image of inevitable victory and irreversible, fundamental changes in society. The revolutionaries must then progress to a second phase (although the organizational work continues), which is the use of terrorism and partisan warfare to destroy the existing social order. The most hated representatives of government are the obvious targets: administrators, police, soldiers, and tax collectors. But within the public service sector, the death list expands to include any representative of authority: teachers, social workers, public health technicians, public works engineers, and mail carriers. The proscribed occupations do not end with civil servants but include any representative of institutions that might challenge the revolution: social aristocrats, clergy, businesspeople and bankers, foreign welfare workers, and heads of powerful families, clans, and villages. Although one might be tempted to brand Communism alone with such a thirst for public service pogroms, one should also remember that the Terror in France and the American Revolution cast a very wide net well before the birth of Karl Marx.

The third and final phase of people's war brings the final victory and domestic and international recognition of the revolution's success. The shadow government enters the light (usually of the foreign media) as the only legitimate regime within the country; it proves its right to govern ("the mandate of heaven") by fielding an army capable of defeating its opponents in conventional battles. It finds patrons abroad, and it can borrow money and negotiate international agreements for security and economic development. For the revolutionary leadership, the tricky problem in this phase is not to exchange one foreign master for another. For the Koreans, the end of Japanese colonialism marked the rebirth of two competing revolutionary movements, neither of which quite succeeded or failed. The Communists sought to use a people's war against the "puppet" southern Koreans, and the ultranationalist revolutionaries used their own people's war variant to replace an American military occupation. They then applied their new political power to defeat the southern Communists and challenge the northern Communists with the reluctant help of the United States and the United Nations.

Outside isolated rural villages in central Korea, the enterprising traveler can still find an occasional pair of carved figures that, to an American, look suspiciously like totem poles. The GIs called them "devil posts." They are *changsung,* the symbols of the dualistic relationship of good and evil and a plea to the mystical forces of the universe to protect the village. Carved and painted to represent a male spirit and a female spirit, the *changsung* do not look entirely friendly, even to each other, but their power is supposed to work in concert to protect the people. Like the *changsung,* the two Korean revolutionary movements in 1945 needed each other as much as they hated each other. In ideological terms, each group despised the other as only true believers can hate heretics. Yet both shared a deep commitment to restore Korean sovereignty and to lead the nation into the modern, postcolonial world. Their own flaws and the accidents of history turned this hope into tragedy.

1

The Years of Division, 1919–1945

"Daehan Tongnip Manse!"
"Long Live Korean Independence!" or *"Korean Independence 10,000 [Years]"*

Nothing ever went quite right for the Korean nationalists. After almost ten years of oppressive Japanese rule, a coalition of Korean patriots in 1919 joined the wave of anticolonialism sweeping the Middle East and Asia in the wake of World War I. Self-determination had become the demand of the moment, loudest between the armistice of November 1918 and the signing of the Treaty of Versailles in May 1919. The Koreans understood that the Allies would carve up the carcasses of the Austro-Hungarian and Ottoman empires, and they were not unhappy to see Russia plunged into a civil war between the Bolsheviks and the White Russians. They could not admit to themselves that the victorious Allies had rejected President Woodrow Wilson's suggestion that self-determination apply to the British, French, Dutch, Belgian, and Italian colonies too. And the Japanese empire—hardly begun with the annexations of Formosa (1895) and Korea (1910)—was part of this winning coalition.

When some leaders of the independence movement in Korea met in February 1919, they knew that a delegation of their countrymen in exile in China and the United States had gone to the Paris Peace Conference. This delegation planned to pressure Japan to give up Korea, just as the Allies had pressured the Japanese not to control the former German colonies in China or czarist Russia's holdings in north Asia. The patriots wanted the Japanese government to loosen its draconian rule of Korea; between 1911 and 1916, the prison population of Korea had soared from 16,807 to 32,836. The Japanese national gendarmerie and the colonial police had rounded up political dissenters with enthusiasm under the direction of the governor-general, Count Terauchi Masatake. In 1916 Tokyo sent another general, Hasegawa Yoshimichi, to Seoul, but he simply continued the policy of forced assimilation. As the prison population doubled, so, too, did the size of the colonial police force. The Korean notables who started the independence movement thus saw nonviolent demonstrations and moral suasion as the only alternative to rebellion, terrorism, and assassination, all of which had only added to the ranks of Korean martyrs. Civil disobedience as envisioned by the protest leaders also reflected their belief in spiritual renewal and moral conversion.[1]

The leaders of the independence movement represented the two most powerful forces for spiritual revitalization in Korean society: Chondogyo and Protestant Christianity. The charismatic leader of Chondogyo, Son Pyong-hui, emerged as the single most important leader in bringing the Korean notables together in unified protest. His Christian counterparts were Kil Sun-ju, Yi Sang-jae, and Yi Sang-hun, who represented the core of the Christian protesters—the Methodists of Seoul and the Presbyterians of Pyongyang. The small group of Catholic dissidents refused to work with members of Chondogyo or followers of the "Teaching of the Heavenly Way," a synthesis of Buddhism, Confucianism, Taoism, and Shamanism that had ingested some forms of the Catholic faith, the first Christian religion to come to Korea in the late eighteenth century from China. In political terms, Chondogyo had become the refuge of the survivors and disciples of the Tonghaks, who had carried the principles of Korean nationalism, Eastern religions, social leveling, and economic justice into open warfare in 1871 and 1894. Much to their later dismay, the Japanese encouraged Chondogyo, since it might lure idealists and patriots away from the Korean Christian churches. Chondogyo might also be comfortably redirected toward Shintoism, and it had no powerful foreign sponsors such as Great Britain or the United States.[2]

The Korean nationalists seized on the death of the emperor of Chosun on January 20, 1919, to take their challenge to Japanese policy before a world audience. Kojong's death encouraged the usual rumors of conspiracy, suicide, and murder; he had died in protest—or so the rumors went. In the meantime, news of the Paris Peace Conference came to Tokyo from young men associated with the YMCA and the Korean student associations in Japanese universities. Believing that the nationalist notables in Korea would not act, a group of students drafted a petition for independence. Student associations in Korea, many with links to the Protestant churches and Christian-sponsored private schools, became inflamed by the prospect of a demonstration at the time of the emperor's funeral, something that their elders and the Chondogyo leaders regarded with anxiety. Although still divided about how to frame their protest, the nationalists agreed to draft their own document and assigned the task to Choe Nam-son, a gifted young journalist, literary figure, and former student leader. In the meantime, Son Pyong-hui forged a Chondogyo consensus on how the document should be presented: it would be a petition to the Japanese government and the Paris Peace Conference on behalf of all Korean political groups with the mass support of the Korean people. At a minimum, the document would receive mass circulation.

From the end of January until the fateful day that gave the protest its name— the March First, or Samil (3.1), Movement—the Chondogyo leaders continued meeting, maintaining contact with Choe Nam-son through their own young fire-brand, Choe In. They communicated with the Christian leaders through Choe Nam-son and his close friend, Song Chin-u, a charismatic teacher at the elite Chungang Preparatory School. Direct contact between the Chondogyo and Christian leaders began on February 20 in Seoul. Each group regarded the other with suspicion. The Chondogyo leaders—who had persuaded two Buddhist monks to join their group—feared that the Christians would take their cause into the streets, where an enraged people, led by student demonstrators, could turn any assembly into a violent confrontation with the Japanese police. Christians questioned whether the Chondogyo leaders were spiritually sound and politically trustworthy. Both groups, however, had a declaration to read and review, and the leaders faced two related decisions: whether to sign the document, and under what circumstances. On February 24 the leaders agreed that the document would be a declaration of independence and that they would sign it as such. They would not, however, read the document to a crowd and thus inflame passions. Those men most committed to the protest—twenty-nine of those present, plus four who consented to have their names used—agreed to hold one last meeting to sign the document at Son Pyong-hui's home on February 28, but not to authorize its release until March 1, three days before the emperor's state funeral in Seoul.

The thirty-three signers—sixteen Christians, fifteen Chondogyos, and two Buddhists—proclaimed the independence of "the Kingdom of Korea" and the liberation of the Korean people from Japanese rule. The Japanese and Korean people could work together to bring peace and prosperity to their nations in "an age of restoration and reconstruction" that would use Western learning without compromising Asian values:

> The age of Force is gone, and the Age of Reason and Righteousness has arrived. The spirit of moral law and humanity, nurtured and perfected during past centuries, is about to shed its light of new civilization upon the affairs of mankind. The arrival of the new spring to the earth calls for the revival of all creatures. If the forces of the past have suffocated the people like the cold snow and ice of winter, then the force of the present age is the revitalizing breeze and warmth of spring.[3]

After the inner secretariat of the March First Movement ensured that copies of the declaration would be distributed throughout Korea by March 1, many of the movement's younger leaders left the country for China, traveled to other cities in Korea to work with students' and women's groups that supported the declaration, or disappeared to escape arrest. The movement already showed signs of fracture at the top. There was no single signing event; the signers came and went, and some leaders (including Yi Sang-jae) refused to sign at the last minute.

The Chondogyos learned, to their dismay, that the Christian leaders had acceded to student groups' demand that mass rallies be held for a reading of the declaration. Most of the signers refused to address any rally. The Chondogyos urged the Buddhist signers to preach nonviolence at the first and largest rally at Independence Gate near Pagoda Park, a site symbolic of Korean liberty. The best the signers could do was to agree to meet for lunch at a fashionable Chinese restaurant nearby. The crowd in Pagoda Park expected one of the notables to read the declaration of independence, but those present at lunch (reported to be twenty-nine in number) did not even read the document to themselves on March 1, since they had already approved it and did not want to be associated with the rallies outside. Instead, they toasted ten thousand years of future Korean independence: "Daehan Tongnip Manse!" They then surrendered to the Japanese police, who had surrounded the restaurant. Instead, a schoolteacher from Haeju, Hwanghae Province, read the declaration to the crowd with difficulty, since he did not understand some of Choe Nam-son's Chinese characters. The crowd's roaring "Manse" needed no interpretation, nor did the columns of students and other young people who poured out of Pagoda Park toward other places where demonstrators had assembled to read and cheer the declaration of independence.

On the first day of the March First Movement, also known as the Manse Revolution, the protest remained relatively peaceful, and the Japanese police and soldiers acted with restraint. By day's end, only 134 people had been arrested in Seoul. In the Pyongyang area, however, the demonstrations produced fights between the police and protesters, and in two places a mob attacked police stations with rocks and torches. News of the movement spread rapidly in the north and more slowly in the south, but within two weeks, city dwellers all over Korea had seen the declaration. Within one week, Koreans in twenty-one cities had organized mass rallies and demonstrations, with participants numbering in the hundreds of thousands. The outlawed Korean flag—the *taegukki*—bloomed in every city like spring flowers; forbidden songs of patriotism and liberty filled the streets. The streets also filled with Japanese police and soldiers; fights broke out almost immediately and continued to do so from March 5 until the movement collapsed in May. A shadowy group called the "National Congress" urged violence. Were they Korean extremists or Japanese agents? The Japanese did not care. At a cost of 6 dead and 134 wounded, the Japanese security forces killed an estimated 1,200 Koreans, wounded an estimated 16,000 marchers of all ages and both sexes, and destroyed more than 1,000 churches, schools, and homes. Almost 20,000 Koreans went to jail, of whom 2,656 were convicted and either executed or imprisoned. This superficial clemency is misleading, since torture and deprivation short of an actual trial were standard practice in Korea, and the Japanese soldiers conducted their own field executions. The rank and file of the March First Movement became the target of retribution; only four signers died in 1919–1929, and only one of them died in jail—of illness. Eleven signers lived to see the liberation of Korea in 1945. None of the signers played a crucial role in the years of resistance that followed, although their average age in 1919 was only forty-eight. Like the March First Movement they created, these men unleashed disciples and critics who would take the cause of national liberation into a political winter of violence and frustration.[4]

THE CREATION OF TWO REVOLUTIONS

The March First Movement represented the latest and most dramatic demonstration of Korean rage against a historic role as the first-order victim of northern Asia. Through the millennia, invaders had come to the Korean peninsula from two directions—the Asian mainland and the islands of Japan. In the early nineteenth century, however, the pressure of visitors became more complicated with the introduction of foreign influence; the Korean response was to retreat into militant isolation, expelling or killing the occasional travelers who visited the Kingdom of Chosun. Having built a society founded on the precepts of Buddhism and Confucianism, the Koreans had no desire to change their agrarian society of highly formalized, rigidly structured communal values and premodern attitudes toward nature, economics, intellectual activity, and governance. Confucianism demanded prescribed and enforced social relationships. Korean society took on hierarchical characteristics that produced little individual social mobility. Monopolizing a standard Confucian examination that controlled entry to official positions, the *yangban,* the educated landholders, produced the political and military leaders who served the king.

With European influence growing in Japan and China during the nineteenth century, Korea could not have maintained its status as the Hermit Kingdom. What made Korea's political history unique is that its eroding isolation set off a court struggle over which foreign power should assume the role of Korea's protector against the other powers. This competition hastened the end of the Chosun dynasty and created the foundation of the two revolutions that attempted to build a new Korea. The problems started with a Chosun dynasty succession crisis when King Chol-chong died in 1863 without a direct heir. The throne went to a nephew, Yi Myong-bok, who became King Kojong, but he was not the real ruler, since he was only twelve years old. Instead, Kojong's father, Yi Ha-ung (1820–1898), took office as regent under the title Hungson Taewongun. Grand Prince Yi, known simply as the Taewongun, brought to his office a degree of energy and reform-mindedness that no recent king had shown. The Taewongun, however, only improved the efficiency and ruthlessness of an archaic central government, which alienated some of the *yangban* and much of the *chunmin* population, city and town dwellers who served the government and ran the service businesses. The farmers, freeholders and tenants alike, simply felt the yoke of more taxes. Although the Taewongun worried about the growing Russian, French, and British presence in China and the American, British, and German influence on Japan, he believed that imperial China was Korea's best partner to form an alliance that would hold the foreigners at bay. Even after Japan and China reluctantly made trading concessions to the Europeans in the 1850s, the Taewongun persecuted Chinese and French Catholics who had entered Korea and approved the harsh treatment of foreign merchant vessels, including the burning of an American vessel, the *General Sherman* (1866), and the execution of its crew, which included two Americans and an Englishman.[5]

The Taewongun continued his war of isolation by blunting a French punitive expedition to Seoul in 1866 and a similar American expedition in 1871. Although both Western forces won local battles, their commanders regarded the risk of running the forts that guarded the Han River estuary as prohibitive. King Kojong's wife, Queen Min Myong-song, and her talented and ambitious Min relatives forced the Taewongun to surrender power to his son in 1873, when Kojong came of age. Thereafter, Korea's fortunes declined with dramatic speed. After his retirement, the Taewongun waged war against the Min clan, often with the encouragement of Chinese and Japanese agents. Cowed by a Japanese naval expedition, Kojong signed the Treaty of Kanghwa (1876) with Japan, which recognized Korea's independence in exchange for commercial concessions and access. The Chinese court (still favored by the Taewongun) responded by demanding similar concessions and urging Korea to open its doors to the United States and Great Britain, both of which might check Japan's hegemonic instincts.

Between 1882 and 1886, the Chosun court negotiated treaties of amity and commerce with the United States, Great Britain, Germany, Russia, and France. In the meantime, the conflict between Queen Min and the Taewongun continued, with the deposed regent now looking to the Japanese for help as the Chinese, including Gen. Yuan Shi-kai and various diplomats from Beijing, threw their weight behind King Kojong. For a decade, a Japanese faction battled the Russian-Chinese faction for control of the government; palace revolts in 1883 and 1884 were followed by the rural Tonghak revolts of the 1890s. Although King Kojong and his son, Crown Prince Sunjong, escaped assassination, the king lost his modernized palace guard (American and Russian trained) and the support of the Min clan, including the queen, who was murdered by Japanese assassins in 1895. Korean nationalism, however, focused more on opposition to the Chinese influence, which was viewed as far more reactionary than the Japanese influence; the latter appealed to some Korean nationalists as a force for modernization based on the British and German models. The Japanese government simplified the problem of Chinese influence by defeating the Chinese armed forces in Korea and Manchuria in the war of 1894–1895. The Japanese completed the destruction of the Russian-Korean coalition ten years later in another war that left Korea a Japanese protectorate.

Korean opponents of the monarchy and the Chinese and Japanese influence in court often found a common bond in Christianity. With the treaties that opened Korea to European influence came a wave of Protestant missionaries, as well as an end to the persecution of Catholics, who emerged from their underground parishes to form a church organization governed by the bishopric of Seoul. The two most influential Protestant denominations, the Presbyterians and the Methodists, drew personnel from the United States, Great Britain, Canada, and Australia. The missionaries were not necessarily ordained ministers but included church-sponsored educators, doctors, nurses, and music teachers. The first church-sponsored Protestant missionary was Horace N. Allen, a Presbyterian medical doctor from Ohio; he arrived in 1884 as a legation physician and later became the American minister as well as a wealthy entrepreneur and champion of Japanese modernization. The first two regular missionaries, Horace Grant Underwood (Presbyterian) and Henry G. Appenzeller (Methodist), were ordained ministers; their wives, Lillias Horton Underwood and Ella Dodge Appenzeller, were a doctor and a teacher, respectively. These two couples arrived by plane on Easter Sunday 1885. By 1919, the number of Western residents of Korea numbered 1,143, of whom 709 were American citizens and 238 British, Canadian, and Australian. More than 400 Europeans were officially registered as church-sponsored missionaries representing the Methodists, Presbyterians, Church of Canada, and Seventh Day Adventists, as well as the Oriental Missionary Society and the Salvation Army. The dominant Methodists and Presbyterians worked reasonably well together; they even divided Korea into "missionary zones," with the American Presbyterians concentrating around Pyongyang, the Canadians and British of all denominations along the northeastern coast from the border to Wonsan, all denominations in Seoul and the Han River valley, and the Methodists throughout southern Korea.[6]

Although the Protestant missionaries attempted to reach the common people of Korea—mostly in the coastal cities—they found themselves embroiled in Seoul politics and the violence that led to the end of the Chosun dynasty. The missionaries risked harassment by antiforeign, anti-Christian forces, but their Korean converts suffered imprisonment, torture, and banishment, not for their religious convictions but because their new faith encouraged them to advance Western concepts of freedom of the press, liberal education, and democratic government. Church membership and the rate of conversion to Protestant Christianity showed an undeniable political rhythm. Between 1885 and 1895, Korean Christians numbered less than 1,000; they increased to 12,500 in the next decade as the Chosun dynasty faded away. The Christian population then soared to 200,000 in the first five years of Japanese domination (1905–1910), viewed as a "Great Awakening," Korean style. Once the Japanese took complete control, they immediately used their police to cow the Korean churches, many of which had native clergymen and supported themselves financially. Conversions slowed or stopped, and in some areas the Protestant churches lost members in the face of Japanese harassment. By 1912, the Japanese were bold enough to charge several American and British clergymen (including George McCune, Samuel A. Moffett, and Horace Grant Underwood) as part of a conspiracy to assassinate Terauchi Masatake, the governor-general. Virtually all of the 157 Koreans accused in this shadowy and uncertain plot were Presbyterians and Methodists. The American and British diplomatic missions offered what protection they could to the Korean Christians, which usually meant rescuing them from Japanese prisons and hustling them off into exile abroad.[7]

Although the Korean Christians used their religion as a form of political protest against Japan, some in the American and British missionary community believed that Japanese influence would spur economic development and advance modernization in Korea, thus opening a schism between the Christian oppositionists and the Christian accommodationists among both the European and the Korean faithful. Horace Allen argued for the positive economic benefits of Japanese influence, a position generally held by the American diplomatic community in Asia.

The British government, military allies with Japan after 1902, showed little interest in saving its missionary community in Korea, but Japanese authorities usually dealt with British subjects with care, in contrast to the treatment of their Korean coreligionists. In general, the missionaries tried to avoid confrontation with the Japanese and counseled the Koreans to focus on education and improved standards of living rather than to expend themselves in hopeless protests. Nevertheless, they encouraged the Koreans to attend progressive schools, publish newspapers, write about political theory, and learn about modern business management and engineering. Some younger Korean reformers took the heady broth of Western liberalism and positivism along with the Christian faith, while others turned away from Christianity because it seemed insufficiently militant in its anticolonialism and weakhearted on the use of violence against the Japanese. The apostates, however, often found it useful to develop alliances with the Christians for nationalist purposes. The same relationships influenced Chondogyo.

The nonreligious nationalists believed that Western-style reform in the 1890s had done nothing to revitalize Korean society and discourage the Japanese. The centers of progressive reform—the Paejae Boys School and Debating Society, the Independence Club, the *Independent* newspaper—had produced symbolic victories (a national flag and a national anthem) and pallid reforms in governmental administration. Leading reformers such as So Chae-pil moved from military action in the attempted coups of the 1880s (his Japanese phase) to exile in the United States, where he became a physician and American citizen before his return to Korea in the 1890s as Philip Jaisohn. He founded the *Independent* (the first newspaper printed in Korean) and the Independence Club before fleeing Korea again in 1898 because the monarchy viewed him as a dangerous subversive. The court's suppression of the Independence Club caught one of Jaisohn's disciples, a twenty-three-year-old firebrand from Pyongsan, Hwanghae Province, named Yi Sung-man—better known later by his Westernized name, Syngman Rhee. As a boy, raised in a slipping *yangban* family, Rhee had been cured of temporary blindness by Dr. Horace Allen, who later encouraged his education at the Paejae Boys School in Seoul. After six years in prison (1898–1904), during which successive beatings ruined his delicate hands and left his limbs stiff and painful, Rhee won his release on the promise that he leave Korea. Between 1905 and 1910, he earned degrees at George Washington, Harvard, and Princeton universities. He made a short return to Seoul as a YMCA secretary, but Japanese harassment sent him to Hawaii, where he organized the Korean agricultural laborers into a branch of Shinminhoe, or New People's Association, the principal nationalist secret society. By 1919, Rhee had become a Christian and well-known charismatic spokesman for Korean independence in Washington.[8]

The establishment of a Japanese protectorate administration (1905) and the abdication of King Kojong (1907) gave the non-Christian nationalists a new cause for open rebellion. The uprising of the Righteous Army *(uibyong)* consisted of idealistic youths, former Korean army soldiers, and rural traditionalists. The Japanese army crushed the *uibyong* at a cost of an estimated seventeen thousand Korean lives, but twice as many former rebels survived to carry on a terrorist program of assassination that took the lives of the first Japanese resident-general (Marquis Ito Hirobumi), an American agent of the Japanese government (D. W. Stevens), and a Korean nobleman who took a position in the colonial government. Measured by his later importance to Korean nationalism, the most prominent survivor of both the Tonghak rebellion and the uprising of the *uibyong* partisans was Kim Ku, aged twenty-four in 1900. Known as "the Assassin" for one actual killing and his constant involvement in terrorist plots, Kim Ku was a man of unpleasant looks and personality. He spent seven years in prison between 1898 and 1914 and then went underground as an agent of the Shinminhoe. In 1919 Kim Ku went to Shanghai to join a new association of nationalists to form a provisional Korean government.[9]

By 1919, the non-Christian nationalists had developed their own leaders and constituency, fed by disillusioned reformers who believed that the Christians had forfeited their right to lead by their failure to use violence and their insufficient influence on the British and American governments. Perhaps the revolutionaries in China and Russia would prove better allies for Korean independence; certainly, Chinese and Russian patriots had greater reason to resist Japan and revenge their defeats of 1895 and 1905. The Korean "independence and justice fighters" formed secret associations in China, Manchuria, Russia, and even Japan. Although seriously divided from the Christians on issues of violence and leadership, the nationalists had much the same vision of a new Korea. They wanted a market economy, a constitutional republic, personal liberties, and a modern, efficient centralized government that would not depend on foreign patronage or the approval of the *yangban*. They had a cadre of veteran leaders who could be as hard as the Japanese, and they would not shrink from another opportunity to challenge the Japanese colonial government and its police. Plotting in their apartments in China and Russia, the nationalist revolutionaries awaited a better time to rejoin the battle for Korean independence.

The tightening Japanese control in Korea proper (1905–1920) drove hundreds of thousands of Koreans from their homeland, and these expatriates founded the two Korean revolutionary movements. The Christians immigrated to the United States, especially the territory of Hawaii, and to China, where Protestant and Catholic congregations provided safe haven. The nationalist revolutionaries also went to China, Manchuria, Siberia, and the Maritime Territory of Russia, where the Manchurians and Russians (whether czarists or Communists) found the Koreans useful in subverting Japanese businesses and military forces. Korean guerrilla forces in the borderlands along the Yalu and Tumen rivers mounted raids into northern Korea, even after the defeat of the Righteous Army, and they won a battle at Chingshan-li (October 1920) over a Japanese army pursuit force. The Japanese colonial government actually encouraged Korean immigration to Manchuria and employment in Japanese-owned businesses, mines, and railroads, since Japanese settlers proved difficult to recruit, and Korean employees were available and willing to work for low wages. By 1920, the Korean population in Manchuria and Russia numbered over a million. In the meantime, Korean expatriates, principally students and young politicized professionals, formed another pool of potential revolutionaries in Japan itself. By 1920, the Korean population in Japan numbered forty-one thousand. These Koreans, denied real assimilation into Japanese society, formed their own secret societies and political clubs. Some of them became fascinated with the socialist solutions to colonialism.

The Korean Marxists started their separate organizational existence as an expatriate liberation movement in Russia and China, thus creating two loose factional groups that competed to form a clandestine party structure within Korea itself. The first Korean Communist Party began as the Korean Section, Russian Communist Party, in Irkutsk, Siberia, in January 1918 to conduct guerrilla warfare against the czarist White Guards and the Japanese expeditionary force sent to Russia to crush the Bolsheviks. Another group of socialists rallied around Yi Tong-hwi, a charismatic former Korean army officer and Righteous Army commander who had gone to war as a Christian ultranationalist but broke with the Christians over the issue of political violence. As a secular nationalist, Yi Tong-hwi founded the Korean Restoration Army (1914) in Manchuria to conduct guerrilla operations. The Japanese army soon broke up his organization, so he fled to Russia, where he founded the Korean People's Socialist Party in Khabarovsk, Siberia, in 1918.

Unwilling to fuse his party with the Irkutsk Communists, Yi Tong-hwi went to Shanghai, where he became the leading socialist and the prime minister of the first Provisional Government of Korea in Exile (October 1918). One of his closest disciples was an improbable Seoul socialist named Yo Un-hyong, whose radical politics sometimes took a backseat to his interest in clothes, sports, women, and parties. At age twenty-nine, he abandoned a university professorship in Seoul to join the expatriate leaders in Shanghai, where he organized the New Korea Youth Party, a prototypical young men's "direct action" association and vehicle of political indoctrination outside the law. Yo Un-hyong, a dapper Korean Ronald Coleman, used his genial personality and eloquence to recruit more reformers, but he avoided confrontations and decisions. His opponents called him the "Golden Axe," an instrument of alluring beauty that cannot cut.

Yi Tong-hwi and his disciples such as Yo Un-hyong (who always asserted that he was not a *real* Communist) felt secure and aggressive enough to form the Koryo Communist Party in Shanghai in 1920. The group immediately received recognition from Moscow as the official Korean Communist Party and a member of the Comintern, which qualified it for Russian funding. The non-Communist expatriate leaders of the provisional government rejected Yi Tong-hwi's party and Russian connections and drove him from office, which led to the collapse of the Koryo Communist Party in 1921 and Yi's return to Russia. Yo Un-hyong remained in Shanghai and became the darling of the Korean socialists. He built his own influence by maintaining good relations with the Chinese Communists and the Korean student associations in Japan. He managed to charm the Japanese into believing that he was not a threat, merely an idealistic youth leader who valued authoritarianism. He attended the Tokyo meeting that produced the first version of the declaration of independence, and his friends became the leaders of the North Star Society, the Korean branch of the clandestine Japanese Communist Party. Yo Un-hyong attended a Far East conference in Moscow in 1921 financed by the Comintern. He did not, however, take the lead in any of the organizational efforts that created a new Korean branch within the Chinese Communist Party, and he remained close to many of the Christian and non-Christian leaders at home and abroad. Yo became a champion of independence won without violence. The Japanese believed that he was one of the strongest nationalist leaders and imprisoned him for three years.[10]

The Korean independence and modernization movement, before and after the March First Movement, showed early and deep signs of schism. If one focuses on personalities, organizational titles, and temporary coalitions of parties, the Korean politicians of the era seem to have had only one area of agreement—the eventual elimination of the Japanese colonial regime and the creation of an independent Korean national government that was not a monarchy. In ideological terms, however, the revolutionaries started to polarize in 1919–1921 when the Communists began to show strength in their expatriate parties in Russia and China. Until the rise of Korean Communism, the principal point of division among the nationalists was the role of violence. The Christians, especially those who remained in Korea, chose the road of diplomacy, moral suasion, and passive resistance; they had the assistance of exiles such as Syngman Rhee, who enlisted American supporters to lobby on Korea's behalf, although without much success. The majority of the Chondogyo leaders also chose forms of passive resistance, although the movement lost its leverage when the Japanese abandoned it as an alternative to Christianity. The non-Christian nationalists, such as Kim Ku and other Righteous Army survivors, drew disaffected Christians and new xenophobes into their ranks. They believed that assassination and guerrilla warfare were essential to wear down the Japanese and attract Chinese allies to the battle. All the Chinese faced the imperialist peril, whether they were warlords like Chang Tso-lin, Nationalists, or Communists.

The nationalists—Christians or not, passive resisters or terrorists—held common views on economic development and the structure of civil society. Even though few of them had business experience, they were entrepreneur–market capitalists, although not necessarily free traders. Like their American Progressive counterparts, they saw a role for national government as a regulator and, perhaps, an investor in and manager of public services such as communications, roads, railroads, and the infant industries essential to industrial development, including steel and coal mining. Some of them admired and wanted to copy Japanese economic growth and modernization, a model of corporate consensus and government-business partnership camouflaged in Western business language and managerial forms. The nationalists envisioned a constitution that ensured a republican form of government with popular political participation (real democracy and full adult suffrage were other matters entirely) and the protection of individual liberties embodied in the American Bill of Rights. Obviously, there would have to be freedom of religion. Some of the nationalists came to admire the corporatist values of European fascism in the 1930s, but only when they became convinced by the Depression and the politics of hatred and division that if Western liberalism could not work where it was born, it could not work in Korea.[11]

The Korean Communists, whether their mentors were Russian or Chinese, came to see Marxism-Leninism as a true faith and the principles of the class struggle and socialism as a set of commandments: "The great miseries of inequity in societies, the increase in the distance between the rich and the poor, the uneasiness of the likelihood of the great unemployed masses, and the difficulties of a great many people are all products of the capitalist system." The Communists recognized that Christianity represented the greatest barrier to their revolutionary modernization of Korea: "The past events have amply proved that religious superstition is an obstacle to social emancipation. Therefore, we must carry on a scientific cultural movement and a religion-boycotting movement. The activity to degrade the faith of the believers should be avoided because it may, on the contrary, strengthen their religious belief."[12] Although the nationalist revolutionaries and the Communist revolutionaries focused their energies on their common Japanese oppressor, their inevitable struggle against each other was simply postponed.

THE STRUGGLE FOR KOREAN LIBERATION, 1921–1937

The collapse of the March First Movement did not kill the Koreans' campaign against Japanese colonialism, but it drove the independence leaders into exile or underground in two separate revolutionary movements. The nationalists who remained in Korea did so at Japanese sufferance. To others, their passive resistance through cultural activism looked suspiciously like collaborationism. The Japanese finally showed some subtlety in their administration of Korea, which was officially an imperial colony of Japan administered by a governor-general in Seoul. The Japanese administrators followed an imperial policy that allowed greater participation in public affairs and economic development for the Korean elite, a mix of dispossessed *yangban,* service workers and minor officeholders, and an emerging educated middle class. The Japanese government also sought to sever the Christians from their overseas protectors in Great Britain (which also represented Canada and Australia) and the United States and to drive a wedge between the Korean Christians and their European missionary mentors in Korea's educational system, theological seminaries, hospitals, and churches. Only during the 1930s did the Japanese abandon a "cultural policy" that advanced assimilation in an incremental way. As the war in China proved more frustrating and the possibility of war with Great

Britain and the United States increased, the Japanese threw away the carrots and went back to wielding big sticks to force the Koreans to become good Japanese. The result was to revive Korean anticolonialism abroad and draw Koreans into an Asian coalition opposing Japan.[13]

The Japanese policy of moderate accommodation and limited repression found its perfect instrument in a new governor-general, Adm. Saito Makoto, a modernizer who had studied politics as a naval attaché in America and who had the political skill to serve twice as navy minister until he was forced from office in 1914 in a wave of financial scandals. Admiral Saito demonstrated a new moderation when he refused to use an assassination attempt in Seoul Station upon his arrival from Tokyo in September 1919 as an excuse to extend the suppression campaign then under way against the March First Movement. He began a series of conciliatory meetings with the Korean elite, reduced the role of the *kempeitai* in law enforcement, lessened the pressure on Korean schools and newspapers to advance Japanese policies, and improved public administration and urban living conditions. Saito's reformism had strategic objectives that he and the cabinet in Tokyo had agreed on: to reduce the role of private (mostly Christian) schools; to protect public order by adding almost fifty-eight hundred policemen, most of whom were Koreans; and to subordinate the Korean churches to their weak Japanese counterparts. Happier Koreans within Korea would turn the independence movement into a foreign influence that would fade with time.

The Saito regime (1919–1931) may have been "happy times" compared with the colonial administrations that preceded and followed it, but it could not operate free of pressure from the Chosen Army—as the Japanese army of occupation was known—or the tension between the civilian ministers in Tokyo and the generals who challenged the cabinets of the 1920s as Western "appeasers" and subversive democrats. One major dispute between Saito and the army was the policy toward the guerrillas who had established themselves in the Korean communities across the Tumen and Yalu rivers in Manchuria. Survivors of the March First Movement and the earlier Righteous Army war (1906–1907), these Korean partisans of the Independence Army (Tongnip-gun) probably numbered only about two thousand fighters, but they could hide within a Manchurian-Korean population of more than a million. Halfhearted attempts by the Chinese warlord army of Gen. Chang Tso-lin did not disrupt the Korean raiders to the Japanese's satisfaction. The Japanese concluded that the partisans had received support from expatriate Korean Christians and the Russian Bolsheviks, thus giving them a chance to smite two subversive groups with one punitive expedition. Without Chang Tso-lin's blessing, a Japanese task force of division strength (roughly ten thousand soldiers) invaded Manchuria in October 1921, where they killed some three thousand Koreans and destroyed thirty villages, many of them Christian. Canadian missionaries made accurate and forceful reports on the extent of the Japanese atrocities in the Chientao incident. Despite missionary outrage that influenced British diplomats even in Beijing, the Foreign Office and the British ambassador to Japan made sure that the

British government did not protest the Chientao incident. The Japanese army saw the lesson clearly: the British, like the Americans, would do nothing to protect the Koreans, even their Christian coreligionists.[14]

The Korean nationalists understood their "betrayal" only too well and sought different ways to advance the cause of independence. Some, of course, simply abandoned the cause by leaving public life or accepting Japanese patronage. The internal resisters had much in common: Western education through the Christian schools, student activism in the 1910–1919 period, and dedication to Korean survivalism through education and nonviolent noncooperation. The most influential men in the group were Song Chin-u, headmaster of Chungang School and editor of the *Tong-a Ilbo,* the most vocal nationalist newspaper; Cho Man-sik, leading Presbyterian elder of Pyongyang and agricultural reformer; Kim Sung-su, philanthropist and head of a textile corporation; Cho Pyong-ok, a Columbia University Ph.D. (1925) and Chosun Christian College faculty member; Chang Taek-sang, a graduate of Waseda University with an Edinburgh University doctorate (1921); and An Ho-sang, educated in China, Japan, and Germany (Ph.D., Jena University, 1929) and a professor of philosophy and language. These leaders also shared another common experience: most of them served terms as political prisoners of Japan. Some, like An Ho-sang and Chang Taek-sang, leaned toward an authoritarian, corporatist state with limited civil liberties and forced economic development by a government-business alliance. Others stressed the development of a modern Korean culture based on free enterprise and Christian values. Although it became fashionable for their political opponents to call these men and their followers "collaborators" and "rightists," their claims as Korean patriots were real enough. Their greatest limitation was their unwillingness to subject the Korean people to more death and destruction through a guerrilla war against Japan. No Mao Zedong emerged from their polished, affluent, educated ranks.

The expatriate nationalists settled in two locations, separated as much by personalities and plans as by thousands of miles. One group rallied to Syngman Rhee and set up the Korean Commission, to lobby in Washington and New York, and the Korean National Association, a mass membership group for fund-raising, cultural education, and military training, with its largest membership in California and Hawaii. The Korean National Association was the creation of another venerated independence leader and intellectual, An Chang-ho, American educated and in exile since 1909 for subversive activities in Korea. Like Rhee, An Chang-ho had gone to Shanghai to help form the Korean provisional government but had become disillusioned and returned to the United States to pursue his plan for Korean spiritual rejuvenation through the Corps for the Advancement of Individuals, or Hungsandan. Almost by default, Syngman Rhee became the leading political spokesman for Korea in America. Rhee built a cadre of American-educated Koreans with strong ties to the Presbyterian and Methodist churches and who accepted Rhee as their leader, whatever his messianic view of his role in Korean history. They were John Chang (Chang Myon, a Catholic), Herbert Kim, Louise Yim, Ben C.

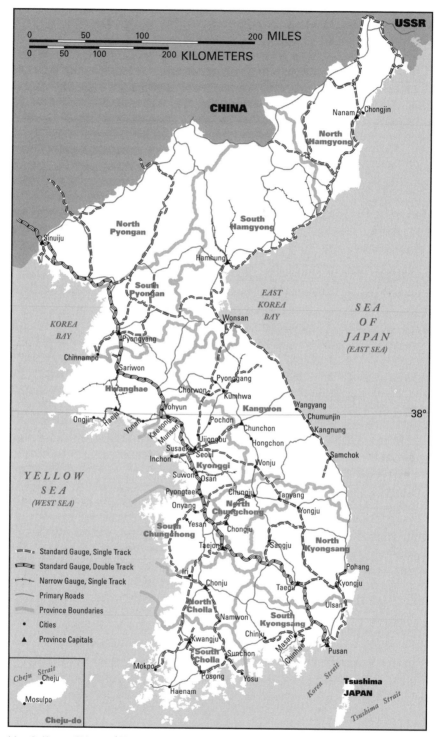

USSR

0   50   100   200 MILES
0   50   100   200 KILOMETERS

CHINA

Nanam ▲ Chongjin

North
Hamgyong

Sinuiju

North
Pyongan

South
Hamgyong

Hamhung

EAST
KOREA
BAY

SEA
OF
JAPAN
(EAST SEA)

South
Pyongan

Wonsan

KOREA
BAY

Pyongyang

Chinnampo

Sariwon

Hwanghae

Pyonggang

Chorwon

Kumhwa

Yohyun

Yangyang

Kangwon

Chumunjin

38°

Ongjin

Haeju

Yonan

Kaesong

Pochon

Chunchon

Kangnung

Munsan

Uijongbu

Hongchon

Susaek

Seoul

Samchok

Inchon

Kyonggi

Wonju

Suwon

Osan

YELLOW
SEA
(WEST SEA)

Pyongtaek

Chungju

Tanyang

Onyang

North
Chungchong

Yongju

Yesan

South
Chungchong

Chongju

Taejon

Sangju

North
Kyongsang

Iri

Pohang

Chonju

Taegu

Kyongju

North
Cholla

Ulsan

Namwon

South
Kyongsang

Kwangju

Chinju

Masan

South
Cholla

Sunchon

Chinhae

Pusan

Mokpo

═══ Standard Gauge, Single Track
▭▭▭ Standard Gauge, Double Track
┼┼┼ Narrow Gauge, Single Track
─── Primary Roads
─── Province Boundaries
•   Cities
▲   Province Capitals

Cheju Strait
Cheju

Mosulpo

Posong

Yosu

Haenam

Tsushima
JAPAN

Korea Strait

Tsushima Strait

Cheju-do

Map 2. Korea: Cities and Transportation Networks

Limb, Hugh Cynn, and Henry Chung. The "Americanists" were at least a generation younger than Rhee and depended on his patronage. They and their respected elder teacher had limited influence or visibility in Washington, but they could use their connections with the Methodist and Presbyterian mission headquarters in New York City to meet and cultivate American philanthropists and media giants such as Harold Issacs of *Newsweek,* William Randolph Hearst, and Henry Luce.[15]

Rhee himself spoke and traveled tirelessly in the cause of Korean independence. Although he made unrelenting financial demands on his Hawaiian constituents, he lived with comparative austerity and lack of corruption. He could claim with some justice that he had been imprisoned and tortured for his convictions, political and religious, although his listeners thought that he was accusing the Japanese of these horrors when, in fact, his tormentors had been King Kojong's police. He increased his access among the patrons of the victimized in 1935 by marrying an attractive Austrian named Francesca Donner, twenty-five years his junior and his lifelong confidante, political adviser, and supporter of all his prejudices and misjudgments of people and events. Mrs. Rhee believed that her husband had a monopoly on Korean patriotism and the corner on honesty and frugality, although they both proved to be innocents on the subject of capitalism and economic development. As little-known refugee politicians, their eccentric views affected no one but their close associates. In 1945, however, Rhee's romantic nationalism and inability to compromise or share power became matters of terrible significance to Americans and Koreans alike.

Although Korean students in Japan continued to form and reform secret patriotic societies into the 1930s, the major base for the expatriate Korean independence movement was China and the provisional government in exile in Shanghai. After the Japanese attacked the city in 1932 and 1937, the Korean exiles moved upriver to Nanjing and Chungking with the Nationalist government and the foreign diplomats who followed in its doleful wake. The Korean refugees organized parties—most tied to individual leaders—but they did use China to form occasional coalitions that even included the Communists. They also tried to form an exile army, and they sent agents into Korea and guerrilla bands into Manchuria.

The nationalists, however, never managed to fully engage the Chinese Nationalists in their cause, while the Korean Communists attached themselves to the Chinese Communist Party and the Soviet administrations in Siberia and the Maritime Territory. Even before the Sino-Japanese War became the Asia-Pacific war in 1941, the Korean Communists had made greater headway than the nationalists in preparing to ensure that *their* revolution would triumph after liberation. The nationalists failed to organize an effective disciplined party, a mass population base, and an armed force, and they failed to secure foreign patronage. These failures did not make them any less revolutionary in their intentions.

Although the first exile organization in Shanghai—the Korean Youth Association founded by Chang Tok-su and Yo Un-hyong—established an office in 1918, the provisional government of the Republic of Korea became the central organization around which almost one thousand Korean expatriates rallied in 1919 and 1920. No formula could accommodate a stable coalition, and Korean Communists and socialists faded away from the Shanghai group in the mid-1920s. By 1932, the Shanghai factions had coalesced into two groups outside the provisional government—the centrist-leftist Korean Anti-Japanese Front Unification League of Kim Kyu-sik and Kim Tu-bong, and Kim Ku's ultranationalist Korean Independence Party, which organized a military program and established good contacts with the large Korean population in Manchuria. All three of these Kims were destined to rise and finally fall in the struggle to dominate the liberation and reformation of Korea. Charismatic, violent, relatively uneducated, and a natural conspirator and terrorist, Kim Ku continued to deal with his rivals, real and imagined, through intimidation and duplicity. He had already killed a Japanese and feared nothing. Kim's reputation attracted protégés with an authoritarian bent such as Yi Pom-sok, aged twenty-two in 1922, who had attended a Chinese military academy and led raids against the Japanese in Manchuria. Yi became an officer in the Chinese Nationalist army and a key figure in organizing Kim Ku's Korean Restoration Army, a cadre of academy-trained Korean youths who planned to command a real army someday.[16]

Kim Ku's sometime rival and sometime partner, Kim Kyu-sik, had little of the terrorist appeal of Kim Ku or the charisma of playboy-orator Yo Un-hyong. He was a sickly, reclusive intellectual who had grown up in a Presbyterian orphanage under the protection of Dr. Horace Grant Underwood, the patron saint of Korean Presbyterianism. As a young man in Christian schools he fell under the influence of Philip Jaisohn, who encouraged him to go to the United States for a college education. Despite a series of illnesses, Kim Kyu-sik finished high school in America and then attended Roanoke College (Virginia), from which he graduated in 1903. He returned to Korea the next year, but the Japanese forced him to leave Seoul and the employ of the Underwoods and the Saemunan Presbyterian Church in 1913. Married with a young son, he went to Shanghai to join the independence movement, which he represented in Paris and Washington until he returned to China in 1919 and became the "foreign minister" of the provisional government and a coalition builder. Although cosmopolitan in many ways, Kim Kyu-sik had an obsessive concern for Korean cultural traditions and *yangban* values, which doomed him to serve or fall victim to stronger personalities. One of these was his sometime ally and the emerging leader of the expatriate Communists, Kim Tu-bong.

The Korean Communists had no better success in developing a single party and a single leader than did the nationalists, but by 1941, they had two firm bases in China and another in Russia. These concentrations of Communist organizers allowed terrorists and partisans to engage the Japanese in Manchuria and journey into Korea proper to build an underground party and guerrilla organization. The Japanese had defeated the Communists in both Manchuria and Korea by the late 1930s, but the dogged Communists survived in their sanctuaries in Russia and China. The Chinese faction became the power base of Kim Tu-bong. Fleeing to Shanghai in 1919, thirty-year-old Kim Tu-bong spent the next twenty years becoming a leading Communist propagandist, party official, and agent among the Manchurian Koreans. Although he moved in and out of shifting coalitions in Shanghai, he also developed good relations with the leadership of the Chinese Communist Party—such good relations, in fact, that he felt confident that he would become the party leader of a unified Korea. The owlish, intellectual Kim Tu-bong, a dedicated Marxist-Leninist and learned philologist, needed a military arm. He found a natural partner in another clansman, Kim Mu-chong, a Chinese academy–trained veteran of the Righteous Army and a professional artillery officer. Moreover, the rugged, outgoing Kim, known to his troops affectionately as "Mu Chong," had been part of the advance guard of the Eighth Route Army's Long March and thus was a comrade of two military giants of Communist China—Zhu De and Peng Dehuai.[17]

Kim Tu-bong made the critical strategic move to make himself and Kim Mu-chong the Communists of choice in China when he severed all contact with the nationalists and other Communist factions in 1942 and moved to Mao Zedong's headquarters in Yanan district, Shanxi Province. This move reflected his fear that the Shanghai-Nanjing Koreans favored another Communist leader with strong ties to the Manchurian Koreans, Kim Won-bong, who had moved his party faction south from Beijing in 1932 in order to receive recognition from the Chinese Nationalists (which meant money and arms) and to work with Kim Ku, Yo Un-hyong, and other nationalist leaders. The Chinese Nationalists recognized Kim Won-bong as "their Communist" and allowed him to form a small cadre of trained Koreans (the Korean Volunteer Corps) to organize more partisans in Manchuria.

Intense, cerebral, and exhausted by coalition politics, Kim Tu-bong found the revolutionary purity of Mao Zedong's Yanan Communists more to his liking. Upon his arrival in Yanan, he announced the creation of the North China Korean Independence League, dedicated to an unrelenting war against "the Alliance of the Four Blood-suckers," which were Great Britain, France, the United States, and Japan. He wanted war, not talk: "The Korean people will emerge to clear away all darkened, impoverished, estranged and enslaving colonial livelihoods."[18]

Using Kim Mu-chong's prestige as a draw, Kim Tu-bong subverted part of the Korean Volunteer Corps and brought it to Yanan to form a new organization, the Korean Volunteer Army, with Kim Mu-chong as commander and the trusted Pak Il-u as political commissar. This force joined the war against Japan in north China and served as a magnet for Korean deserters from the Manchukuo army, the multiethnic force the Japanese organized to conduct counterpartisan operations. Kim Tu-bong's fortunes improved as the Chinese Communists and their armies built their strength for the civil war to come.

The Korean Communists in Russia gave away nothing in militancy to their comrades in China, but the Soviets gave them less freedom than the Koreans of the Yanan faction enjoyed in the struggle against Japan. The Soviets gave the Irkutsk faction new advantages in 1921 when the Red Army attacked and scattered a non-Communist Korean force of two thousand in Siberia. The Soviets, however, denied the Irkutsk faction a monopoly position when they lured Yi Tong-hwi and his followers back from Shanghai in 1922 and gave him an office in Vladivostok to run an organization called the Far East Area Committee, Korean Bureau, Russian Communist Party. The Soviets refused to sanction the creation of a separate Korean Communist Party, but they would support guerrilla operations against the Japanese in Manchuria. The Red Army also accepted Koreans as volunteers (officers and enlisted) in the war against fascism. The coalition of Chinese and Korean Communists in Yanan and the remnants of the Shanghai Communist faction (Kim Won-bong) held the organizational initiative in fighting the complete Japanese occupation of Manchuria in 1931. The Soviet Koreans, however, had residual advantages: access to Soviet educational institutions and military training schools, experience in minor party administration, and training in operating state-owned industrial and transportation enterprises.

The Shanghai and Irkutsk divisions of the Korean Communist movement did not shrink from sending organizers into Korea proper, but the Japanese police and army, unrestrained by the limitations they had faced in Manchuria before 1931, kept the party from developing a grassroots organization and continuing leadership. The first concerted efforts to establish a party within Korea started in 1923 when the Irkutsk faction sent agents to Seoul, where they were joined by representatives of the Shanghai faction. One was a Communist Youth International officer, Cho Pong-am, and another was a young, dynamic recent graduate of Lenin University in Moscow, Pak Hon-yong. The Seoul Communists formed a secret group, the Tuesday Society, in 1924 and then persuaded Korean Communists from Japan to join them in forming the first Korean Communist Party in 1925. The Communists pledged to focus their recruitment among workers and farmers, but in truth, their best success was in organizing the volatile student population of Seoul and other major cities. Under Pak Hon-yong's directorship, the Korean Communist Youth Association claimed more than thirty thousand members in 1925. Thin and intense, with the round, black-rimmed glasses of the era magnifying his piercing eyes, twenty-six-year-old Pak Hon-yong had begun his rise to power and eventual tragedy. He was a pure revolutionary whose dedication aroused the respect of his enemies and the fear and loathing of his own colleagues, who eventually killed him. Pak Hon-yong was the Korean Kirov, too noble to survive the revolution he advanced with so much fervor and sacrifice.

The Japanese correctly judged the Communists to be the greatest threat to their control within Korea. Aided by captured documents, informers, and confessors, the police rounded up two groups of party leaders in 1925 and 1926. Pak Hon-yong went to prison for the first time and, under torture, suffered a nervous breakdown. Released in 1929, he returned to China a broken man. In the meantime, the Peace Preservation Law of 1925 and its amendments gave the Japanese authorities unlimited power to arrest and interrogate suspected political activists. The Koreans held a mass demonstration in 1926 (led by nationalists and members of the Tuesday Society) that gave them the confidence to form a coalition of nationalists and socialists called the Shinganhoe (New Shoot Society) in 1927. The Communist representative was Ho Hon, a Seoul attorney and a comrade of Cho Pong-am and Pak Hon-yong. The Communists immediately pushed Shinganhoe toward more radical positions until the coalition began to collapse. In 1929 and 1930 the Japanese arrested hundreds of leaders, including Ho Hon. The survivors suspected that they had been betrayed by other Communists. As the broad front collapsed, the Communists, led by a reborn Pak Hon-yong, reorganized themselves into a small, disciplined party no longer tainted with class compromises. Plagued by informers and ill-advised public demonstrations, this version of the Korean Communist Party collapsed under police pressure. Pak Hon-yong was jailed again (1933–1939), until his physical and mental state had deteriorated so badly that the Japanese turned him loose as mad and harmless. But Pak was angry, not mad, and he immediately started another Communist party, with the Japanese in hot pursuit. Pak fled to southern Korea, his home region, where he found anonymity as a brickyard worker near Kwangju, Chollanam-do (South Cholla Province), a traditional haven for radicals and rebels. Even in his internal exile, Pak Hon-yong stayed in touch with other comrades in hiding and vowed that he would return to Seoul someday to continue his revolution.[19]

After a decade of "benign" administration of Korea, the imperialist factions in the high command of the Japanese Imperial Army finally convinced the cabinet in 1931 to remove Admiral Saito and to crush Korean nationalism as part of the plan to eliminate the vestiges of Chinese and Russian control in Manchuria. Largely at the initiative of Chinese Communists, the resistance partisans in Manchuria rallied and enlarged their ranks with disaffected Manchurians and announced a loose federation of guerrilla columns. Estimated by the Japanese at about thirty thousand fighters, these scattered groups became the Northeast Anti-Japanese United Army (NEAJUA, 1932–1934). The Shanghai and Irkutsk factions sent men to join the NEAJUA, but the new army gave others a chance to rise to power—in this case, Manchurian Korean guerrillas who had been members of neither the nationalist nor the Communist military elite in the 1920s. One of these local leaders was Kim Song-ju, a rebellious middle school dropout who liked to stage antiteacher demonstrations. Born in 1912 in a peasant home near Pyongyang, Kim Song-ju grew up in northern Korea and Manchuria. Orphaned at the age of sixteen, Kim Song-ju became a "freedom fighter" after surviving his first and only imprisonment for political activity in 1929. He joined a guerrilla band that operated along the Korean-Manchurian border, but these fighters were more like bandits than dedicated Communist partisans. Most of their raids were directed toward Koreans that the band had decided were pro-Japanese, as measured by their relative wealth. Kim Song-ju advanced from private to junior leader (ranks were avoided) and fell under the influence of a Chinese guerrilla leader who introduced him to Marxism-Leninism sometime in the mid-1930s. As the NEAJUA took shape, Kim Song-ju worked his way into the command of the Sixth Division, Second Army, First Route Army, NEAJUA, a grand name for a column of 150 to 250 partisans. At the age of twenty-five, Kim Song-ju reached for the greatness he believed to be his destiny.

Despite two minor skirmishes that resulted in victories over unwary Japanese columns and a bold raid on the town of Pochonbo, Korea, Kim Song-ju's force faced the same fate as the rest of the guerrilla army—a relentless campaign of annihilation at the hands of the Japanese Kwantung army and its colonial counterpart, the Manchukuo army, a force of Chinese and Korean mercenaries. Kim Song-ju's shrinking band survived longer than most through guile and a well-advised retreat toward the Russian border. Nevertheless, Kim's band also fought when the odds favored an engagement. Kim showed a flair for leadership, spoke good Chinese, and commanded the loyalty of tough associates. During three years of marching and surviving, Kim Song-ju adopted a nom de guerre, and the self-appointed savior of Korea became Kim Il-sung.

The Japanese-Manchukuo counterguerrilla columns ran down the bands of the NEAJUA one by one, aided by defections, internal strife, cold, hunger, and hopelessness among the partisans. Kim Il-sung managed to keep his unit together despite casualties and key defections; the commander of the First Route Army switched sides and joined the pursuit of Kim's band, which shrank to fewer than one hundred fighters, even though Kim dragooned miners and woodcutters into his ranks and extorted supplies from Korean villages. Although the exact date that Kim's group crossed into Siberia is uncertain, Kim's ragged guerrillas probably made their first contact with Russian officers in January 1941. Kim's band was one of the last to escape the Japanese pursuers. The Russians already knew his name and his reputation for tenaciousness. When Kim Il-sung went into exile, he was the senior surviving officer of the entire First Route Army. Like so many other Korean revolutionaries, he, too, had to wait for a more favorable correlation of forces.[20]

THE ASIA-PACIFIC WAR AND THE FATE OF KOREA, 1937–1945

The incomplete war in China that began in 1937 and the second war of 1941–1945 accomplished the fragmentation of Korean society and the polarization of its independence factions. In terms of the whole Korean social structure, the two wars brought comprehensive economic deprivation and psychological despair. Population pressures and patterns of immigration produced many kinds of dislocation. Even with a wave of immigration to Manchuria and Japan, the population of Korea rose from around 20 million (1930) to 25 million (1944). Attracted or conscripted into essential war work in Japanese factories or mines, the Korean population in Japan reached 2.4 million by 1944. The Koreans in Japan, all of whom faced discrimination and exploitation, ranged from displaced noblemen to minor office workers to college students to industrial workers and coal miners. The Japanese lured or dragooned more than a million workers into their war effort. The Japanese army's "comfort women" program ruined the lives of more than 100,000 Korean girls. In addition, 365,000 Koreans entered the auxiliary services of the Japanese army, most of them working in rear-area construction and service units or as prison-camp guards. Subjected to relentless Allied bombing, land battles, and illness and starvation on isolated islands, 150,000 Koreans lost their lives in the war. The Korean industrial workforce in Korea and Japan supporting the war, plus those in military service, numbered around 6 million. In Korea proper, more than a million youths left their farms (or were conscripted) for urban-based industry and a life of regimented rootlessness, much like that in the Soviet Union. The Korean population of Manchuria reached over 2 million, also part of Japan's effort to conquer China.[21]

Within Korea, the demographic changes reflected the war-induced acceleration of fundamental social tensions. Like the fire-induced cracking of the finish on a celadon vase, the fissures of Korean society spread without quite shattering the Korean people. In terms of interprovincial movement, Koreans went to the northern provinces to work in the Japanese industrial enterprises that grew wherever the economic planners could find the right combination of raw materials (coal, minerals), hydroelectric power, railroad and seaborne transportation, and a pliant workforce. Tenant farmers—whose numbers had doubled since 1920—provided the workers. Forced urbanization was not just a phenomenon in northern Korea; other unskilled workers moved to Seoul, Taejon, Taegu, Chinju, Kwangju, and Pusan to become a volatile urban proletariat. Wage earners felt the ravages of inflation and food shortages. The per capita income of Koreans was one-third that of the Japanese and even lower than that of the Taiwanese. Japanese pricing and control of the rice harvest left all Koreans malnourished and impoverished; although rice production doubled in the 1940s, per capita rice consumption in Korea dropped by half, and rice prices declined for producers and climbed for consumers. Koreans were reduced to eating rough grains and *tubu* paste, traditionally regarded as the food of the poor. Deprivation spared no one except for Koreans who were completely committed to the Japanese cause.

Japanese policies to "amalgamate" the Koreans into Japanese culture—as second-class citizens, to be sure—increased in the late 1930s and reached new extremes in the 1940s. In 1935–1937 the Japanese officialdom began to enforce regulations on the observance of Shinto, the combination of emperor and ancestor worship that served as a state religion in Japan. In 1937 Governor-General Minami Jiro, a hard-line army general, ordered every Korean public event to begin with the "Pledge of the Imperial Subjects." The Ministry of Education in Tokyo attacked the Korean school system; teaching in the Korean language was abolished, and instruction in Japanese became mandatory. Failure to use Japanese to conduct official business meant the loss of privileges and employment in the colonial bureaucracy, an employer of choice in hard times. Korean-language newspapers disappeared, replaced by Japanese-censored journals. In 1940 the government decreed that all Koreans should have Japanese names, and in 1942 any instruction or publication in the Korean language became illegal. The political police and tax collectors enforced Japanization at the local level with baton-wielding enthusiasm.

As intended, the assimilation movement bore heavily on the Korean Christians and the American and British Protestant missionaries. The Korean Catholics won a reprieve when Pope Pius XII ruled that Shintoism was a secular civil observance that did not violate Christian concepts of idolatry. The Protestants found no such easy solution. The Korean Methodist Church, administered by a Korean bishop, accepted the Catholic concept of Shintoism in 1937, and late the next year the Presbyterians voted to comply. The Shinto shrine issue tended to divide the churches along ethnic lines, with the European missionaries opposed to Shintoism and the Koreans more accommodating. White missionaries soon became targets of Japanese police harassment, and by 1940, the American and British governments advised missionaries to leave Korea. Fewer than fifty missionaries stayed at their posts in Korea, and the men who did usually sent their families off to safer places. Church business was supposed to conform with Japanese regulations, and the cultural mavens in Tokyo advanced a plan for a new Japanese-language version of the Bible that would eliminate the Old Testament and all its idle chatter about chosen people and armed rebellion. The elders of the Saemunan Presbyterian Church told Horace Horton Underwood, whom the Japanese had removed from the presidency of Chosun Christian College, to stop attending their church services. The college and church had been founded by his family and supported by them for fifty years.

The widening of the conflict in China into the Asia-Pacific war in December 1941 sent shock waves through those groups dedicated to Korean liberation and revolution. For the European missionaries, the new war meant house arrest and eventual exchange in 1942; the Americans returned to the United States, and the Canadians, Australians, and British returned to their homelands, where many entered the armed services (usually in civil affairs and intelligence) or became government employees for the duration. Korean Christians shared the same (or greater) sacrifices as their fellow countrymen; those who wanted to fight for Korea usually headed to China if they escaped the Japanese police. The revived Korean Commission, clearly under Syngman Rhee's domination, raised funds from Americans who wanted to support Nationalist China's war on Japan, and Koreans could be part of that struggle. The Chinese Nationalists acknowledged their role as spokesmen for a free Korea and urged the Roosevelt administration to recognize the legitimacy of the provisional government of Korea as early as April 1942. Rhee himself went beyond the moral suasion of books and pamphlets. He contacted Millard Preston Goodfellow, a temporary army colonel who had joined the Office of Strategic Services (OSS) from the army's G-2 staff. Through his friendship with Brig. Gen. William Donovan, the "Wild Bill" of the Western Front and New York City politics, Goodfellow spent the war as one of Donovan's deputies.

Rhee's personal relationship with Goodfellow—which presumably allowed access to Donovan and perhaps *his* patrons—enhanced Rhee's prestige, at least with his fellow Koreans, and certainly in his own mind. Donovan's patron was Secretary of the Navy Frank Knox, and Knox also knew Goodfellow, who had been a newspaper correspondent in World War I and was a co-owner and editor of two newspapers (one in his native Brooklyn, the other in his adopted Idaho). Goodfellow relished backroom politics, conspiracies, and eccentric goals and methods. He claimed friendships with Herbert Hoover, Dean Acheson, and two news czars, William Randolph Hearst and Frank Gannett. Goodfellow's experience as director of the Boys Clubs of America probably proved to be perfect preparation for becoming director of the Special Activities Group, which specialized in forming OSS sabotage groups. Frozen out of the war of subversion in Europe by his enemies in the OSS, Goodfellow focused on OSS activities in the China-Burma-India theater, since General MacArthur had forbidden OSS agents to go anywhere near his own Southwest Pacific theater and his Allied Intelligence Bureau. Goodfellow's limited domain included the Asian expatriate groups in Washington, and Rhee became one of his most ardent admirers. The Goodfellow-Rhee partnership had one operational focus: to recruit young Koreans to return to Asia and set up resistance bands in Manchuria and Korea that could be used to rescue Allied pilots as the air war against Japan accelerated in early 1945. In the partisan war against Japan, however, the Rhee-Goodfellow team accomplished almost nothing.[22]

Other Korean expatriates with postwar plans rallied to the Communist cause in the Soviet Union in the 1940s. They, too, joined the war effort against Japan with limited effect, since their sponsors, the Russians, were officially neutral. After extensive and prolonged screening of the refugee Korean guerrillas who sought sanctuary in Siberia and the Maritime Territory, the Soviets offered the Korean Communists charter membership in a new Sino-Korean unit, the Eighty-eighth Special Operations Brigade, supervised by the Reconnaissance Bureau (the intelligence staff) of the Soviet Far East Military District. Composed of Koreans from three separate camps, the Eighty-eighth Brigade, commanded by a Chinese partisan but guided by a Russian chief of staff and political commissar, was formed at a camp near Khabarovsk, Siberia, probably sometime in 1942. The Korean recruits underwent military training and political indoctrination; most of the partisans had limited schooling. The military training had more results than all the tutorials in Marxism-Leninism as interpreted by Joseph Stalin. The brigade was really a skeletonized formation, consisting only of cadres who would presumably enter Korea and Manchuria someday and organize anti-Japanese partisans. The actual strength of the entire brigade numbered only around two hundred. Some of its officers, however, became the Kapsan, or partisan group, in Korean Communist politics. Their spiritual leader by 1945 was Kim Il-sung.

Kim Il-sung's leadership role in the partisan faction remains shrouded in mystery, not just because his activities in 1941–1945 are uncertain, but because his credentials as a Manchurian guerrilla of the NEAJUA were no stronger than those of several of his Eighty-eighth Brigade comrades. Three men especially could claim a leadership role, all of whom were older than Kim Il-sung and had more extensive records of party service and field operations: Choe Yong-gun, forty-five years old in 1945, an educated, veteran partisan who served as the brigade political commissar; Kang Kon, a hard-bitten but shrewd field commander who led one of the brigade's four battalions; and Kim Chaek, a battalion political commissar and veteran revolutionary. Kim Il-sung also commanded a battalion, estimated at forty to forty-five men. Also in the ranks as junior officers were Kim Il, An Kil, Choe Hyon, and Choe Yong-jin. Much of Kim Il-sung's power came from his cordial relations with the Soviet officials and army officers who dealt with the brigade. Kim enjoyed socializing, and his wife, the revolutionary heroine Kim Chong-suk, proved to be a hostess and party worker of note. Even three children (the eldest of whom was Kim Jong-il) did not divert her from her wifely socialist duties, but she died giving birth to her fourth child, who was stillborn, in 1949. Kim Il-sung helped his own cause by being an apt pupil of the commissars; he already knew Chinese and learned some Russian. In all, he was likable, eager to please, and completely dedicated to socialism and the destruction of the Japanese empire.

The Russians enlisted other Koreans in addition to the Kapsan faction. They were expatriates whose families had immigrated to Russia to escape the Japanese even before the Bolshevik Revolution. Those who had survived and persevered in the Soviet Union had found places for themselves in the party bureaucracy, educational system, military establishment, and limited technocracy. Those who came of age in the 1930s and 1940s were citizens of the Union of Soviet Socialist Republics, hence their collective identification as Soviet Koreans. Measured by their influence in Korean politics, the most notable was Ho Ka-i, born in Russia in 1904 and a veteran revolutionary and party organizer in the Republic of Uzbekistan. Educated at Sverdlovsk's University of the Toilers of the East, Ho spoke Korean as a second language and preached Stalin's socialism with fervor in both Russian and Korean. Other Soviet Koreans used the Red Army as an avenue to preferment. Nam Il, who became a Korean People's Army general and negotiator at Panmunjom as well as director of a guerrilla war against the Republic of Korea, saw Berlin before he saw Seoul. Born in Korea but raised in Uzbekistan, Nam Il, aged thirty-two in 1945, graduated from a teachers college in Tashkent and then went immediately into the Red Army as an officer candidate at Smolensk Military School. He served as an officer continuously through World War II and participated in the battles for Stalingrad and Warsaw. He returned to the Far East to participate in the war with Japan and arrived in Korea for the first time as a major in the Red Army. Among his comrades in the Red Army were future senior generals of the Korean People's Army Kim Il and Yu Song-chol and six other flag officers of 1950, all of them in specialist-technical positions or key roles in the training and indoctrination commands.[23]

The Korean partisans in China and Manchuria also used the war to build their strength for the war of liberation to come, but there was a difference between the nationalists of the provisional government and the two major Communist factions—one in alliance with the Kim Ku clique in Chungking, and the other the Yanan faction allied with Mao Zedong and the People's Liberation Army. The Kim Ku regime and its leftist collaborators believed that they would flourish under the patronage of the Chinese Nationalists and their distant patron, the United States of America. Their common enemy was Japan. The Yanan faction (Kim Tu-bong and Kim Mu-chong) saw Japan as an enemy but also distrusted all other Korean factions (including the Communists under Soviet protection) and every Chinese group except the Chinese Communist Party. The Chungking coalition trained young Korean men for the Korean Restoration Army and sent some of them north to join partisan groups; if these men did not die in battle, they usually ended up in the ranks of the People's Liberation Army, which formed its own Korean auxiliary, the Korean Volunteer Army, a force that numbered only five hundred to one thousand men in 1945. Most Koreans who joined the People's Liberation Army simply went into the army's regular formations, and by 1945, it had at least two Korean divisions and probably forty thousand Korean soldiers in its ranks. Many of them were Korean deserters from the Manchukuo army or service units of the Kwantung army. The Yanan faction, therefore, had the greatest military leverage among expatriate Koreans and the most loyal sponsor, the Chinese Communist Party.

The Yanan faction developed a skilled, dedicated, educated, and ruthless cadre of political and military leaders who shared a common dream of ruling a unified, socialist Korea. Kim Tu-bong remained the party and intellectual leader of the Yanan Koreans, and his protégé, Pak Il-u, became the political commissar of the Korean Volunteer Army, commanded by Kim Mu-chong. This triad of leaders ran the Anti-Japanese Military and Political College, the key Yanan training center for Koreans. Either in their own small cadre army or in the People's Liberation Army, the Yanan leaders produced a military elite of their own that was generally more experienced and better educated than their comrades in Russia: Yi Sang-cho, Kim Ung, Yi Kwon-mu, and Pang Ho-san, also future senior officers of the Korean People's Army. As a matter of policy, the Yanan faction separated the most promising Korean deserters from the Japanese forces opposing them in 1945 and put them in the Korean Volunteer Army rather than send them to the renewed civil war in China.[24]

The immediate focus of every expatriate Korean military unit was the Seventeenth Area Army, Imperial Japanese Army, which was the Korean occupation force, or Chosen Army. When the imperial headquarters rushed reinforcements from mainland Asia to the Philippines and the Marianas in 1944, four divisions left Korea. Three remaining depot divisions, a mere shadow of the Chosen Army, numbered only 32,000 officers and men. In the 1945 reorganization following the defeat in the Marianas and the continuing defense of Luzon, the Japanese army restored the Chosen Army to a formidable defense force, oriented to deny the Americans air and naval bases in southern Korea that would assist the strategic bombing campaign on the Japanese home islands. The Tumen River border with Russia became the responsibility of the Manchurian Kwantung army. The deployments in southern Korea matched the mission. The Fifty-eighth Army (three divisions) garrisoned Cheju-do, a large volcanic, subtropical island seventy miles from mainland Korea. Cheju-do became another Iwo Jima, with concrete coastal

The band of the U.S. Seventh Infantry Division leads the parade of U.S. troops through the streets of Seoul, September 9, 1945. (National Archives)

A U.S. Army captain meets a Soviet liaison team along the Thirty-eighth Parallel, September 1945. (National Archives)

Kim Ku: terrorist, patriot,
president of the Korean
Provisional Government
in China, rival to
Syngman Rhee, and
victim of political
assassination, 1949.
(Korean War Memorial)

Anti-trusteeship demonstrators mass for a rally and march in Seoul, December 1945.
(National Archives)

American and Soviet generals assemble on the steps of Marble Hall, Doksu Palace, Seoul, for the first meeting of the Joint Commission, January 1946. The two U.S. Army generals are Lt. Gen. John R. Hodge, commander of the U.S. Army Forces in Korea, and Maj. Gen. Archibald V. Arnold, the military governor and delegation head. The Red Army generals (left to right) are Maj. Gen. G. I. Shanin, Col. Gen. Terentii F. Shtykov (head of the delegation and occupation commander), Maj. Gen. N. Lebedev, and Maj. Gen. A. A. Romanenko. (U.S. Army)

Soldiers of the Sixth Regiment, Korean Constabulary, still wearing castoff Japanese army uniforms, enjoy a wrestling match at their camp near Pohang, 1946. (Maj. John R. Lloyd Jr.)

Dr. Syngman Rhee, president of the Republic of Korea (1948–1960), enjoys a rare moment of joy during the summer of 1948. (U.S. Army)

Three leaders of a liberated Korea meet in Seoul in July 1947 to form a moderate political coalition. They are (left to right) Kim Kyu-sik, Dr. Philip Jaisohn (So Chae-pil), and Yo Un-hyong. (National Archives)

Members of Division M, Korean National Police, muster outside police headquarters in Seoul, 1946. That division was the Seoul metropolitan police department, led by the controversial Dr. Chang Taek-sang. (National Archives)

Yi Pom-sok, prime minister and defense minister of the Republic of Korea, speaks at a rally in Seoul, 1948. Yi, a former officer in the Chinese Nationalist Army, based his power on the anti-Communist youth movement in southern Korea. (National Archives)

Voters in the American occupation zone choose National Assembly representatives in the first national election, Seoul, May 1948. (The Bertsch Family)

One of the few surviving fortified substations of the Korean National Police, Taechon City, North Chungchong Province, 2000. Police posts were special targets for guerrilla attacks in 1946 and 1948. (Horace G. Underwood)

A Korean National Police officer guards the wreckage of a bombed and looted police armory, May 1948. (National Archives)

Three founders of the Republic of Korea gather to watch the independence parade in Seoul on August 15, 1949. They are (left to right) Lt. Gen. John R. Hodge, USA; General of the Army Douglas MacArthur, USA; and President Syngman Rhee. (U.S. Army)

Kim Il-sung (unarmed) poses with four of his most trusted men, armed with the first Soviet-designed PPSh41 submachine guns manufactured in Pyongyang. The North Korean generals (left to right) are Chae Yong-gun, Kim Chaek, Kang Kon, and Nam Il. (National Archives)

Dr. Cho Pyong-ok lobbies with Bahadur Singh, UNTCOK, April 1948. Cho served as director of the Korean National Police, special representative to the United Nations, and leader of the conservative Democratic Party (1945–1950). (National Archives)

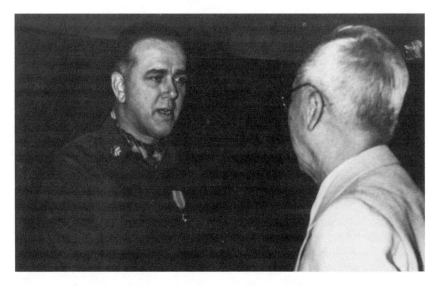

Lt. Col. Russell D. Barros, USA, chief of and then senior adviser to the Korean Constabulary (1946–1948), receives the Ulchi Distinguished Military Service Medal from President Syngman Rhee in March 1953 for his contributions to Korean defense. (Gen. Lim Sun-ha)

2

Defeat and Division:
Korea on the Brink, 1945–1946

With rising dismay, Governor-General Abe Nobuyuki realized in early August 1945 that the future of Japanese rule in Korea could be counted in weeks, if not days. When Japan surrendered to the Allies, General Abe's responsibility had one focus: protecting 163,255 Japanese servicemen and 378,714 civilians from the vengeance of the Koreans. The Soviet intervention in the war against Japan on August 8 tripled the number of Japanese in Korea as refugees from Manchuria flooded across the Yalu River. The Russian offensive made some sort of accommodation with the Koreans essential. Abe knew that the Russians' arrival would encourage anti-Japanese reprisals and would reproduce the massacres, rapes, and pillages the Soviet army had visited on the Germans and their Eastern European allies. Reduced to defend the Marianas and Philippines against the Americans and then stripped again to reinforce the home islands, the Kwantung army in Manchuria had no chance of sustained resistance against the Soviet army's First Far Eastern Front of four army groups, composed of eighty divisions of 1.5 million men. Like Japanese colonial governors all over Asia, General Abe wanted to turn over governmental authority and responsibility to a native elite with sufficient nationalist credentials to command popular obedience. The carrot in the negotiations was the de facto acceptance of Korean independence and the immediate surrender of Japanese public property; the stick was the willingness of the Japanese army to fight in the defense of Japanese civilians against the Koreans. The chaos of the transition might even allow the Japanese to escape if they had Korean help. Even as Abe started negotiations with Korean notables in Seoul, Japanese civilians flooded the railway for Pusan and the ferries for Shimonoseki, Honshu.[1]

Abe's counterparts all over the wreckage of the Japanese empire faced similar challenges, for in August 1945, 6.5 million Japanese remained outside the home islands. Half of the expatriate Japanese were civilians and their families, isolated in their colonial homes by the U.S. Navy's submarine force. When Emperor

Hirohito accepted the Allied terms in the Potsdam Declaration (July 26, 1945) on August 15, he demanded that his field commanders cooperate with the Allied military authorities, who would accept their surrender and arrange for the repatriation of the overseas Japanese as quickly and peacefully as possible. Local native loyalists could also join the reverse migration. General Abe had some distinct advantages in Korea. His charges were not far from home, and no well-established anti-Japanese partisan force lurked in the countryside or cellars to start a war against the hated occupiers. If he acted quickly enough, Abe might save not just lives but also Japanese-owned private property that could be transferred to cooperative Korean entrepreneurs or reclaimed later by legal action. Abe also had his own army to pacify. On August 16 part of the Seventeenth Area Army's Seoul garrison mutinied until its officers insisted that every Japanese soldier obey the emperor. Another explosive possibility was the Japanese massacre of Korean Christians, always viewed as the agents of American and British imperialism. The Japanese planned to defend Korea by executing or imprisoning twenty thousand Koreans identified as pro-Allied fifth columnists. If the Japanese-Korean colonial police put this plan into operation, the result would make the March First Movement repression look benign by comparison.[2]

General Abe found cooperative Koreans hard to locate. Abe dispatched his civil administrator, Endo Ryusaku, to find a Korean governor. His first candidate, the prominent nationalist Song Chin-u, had a recent record of accepting Japanese rule. For reasons personal and prudent, Song Chin-u refused four days of overtures during which he was asked to form a transitional government in Seoul and raise a militia that would work with the Japanese army and colonial police to keep order. Still without any Korean to whom he could surrender, Abe turned to the dapper Yo Un-hyong, like Song Chin-u, a longtime nationalist and sometime associate of the Provisional Government of Korea in Exile. On August 14 Yo Un-hyong, now a Seoul newspaper editor, learned that he was Abe's alternative savior. He already had a list of five nonnegotiable conditions for accepting the responsibility for forming a Korean government that would protect the Japanese. The Japanese went to Yo because they knew that he had influence over the militant Korean student associations in Seoul and that he had good contacts among the radical nationalists, which included the surviving Communists. Yo demanded that the Japanese accept his terms in exchange for their safety. Nothing about property could be guaranteed. Yo demanded that the Japanese release all the Korean political prisoners in their custody (some thirty thousand people), stop exporting food to Japan while Koreans went unfed, and not use the army or police to interfere with the new Korean government, student associations, and labor unions. Concerned that the Russians would occupy all of Korea, and unaware that the United States and the Soviet Union had just agreed to create two occupation zones north and south of the Thirty-eighth Parallel, General Abe accepted Yo Un-hyong's terms on August 15.

By the time General Abe and Yo Un-hyong had sealed their pact of convenience, the general outline of the Allies' terms had reached Japanese and Allied military headquarters throughout Asia. Part of that information included an agreement between President Harry S. Truman and Soviet premier Joseph Stalin that their armies would share the task of disarming and repatriating the Japanese in Korea. As an operational expedient, the Americans suggested that Korea be divided at the Thirty-eighth Parallel so that the American and Soviet soldiers would know what people and ground were within their jurisdiction. Similar methods had already been adopted in the occupations of Germany and Austria and would be applied in French Indochina and China for the same purpose: to process prisoners of war (POWs) and civilians of all nationalities and then send them home. No line on a map worked well in dividing Korea. Colonels Charles H. Bonesteel III, a career army officer, and Dean Rusk, a Georgia farm boy and Rhodes scholar turned university dean, assumed the task as part of their staff duties with the State-War-Navy Coordinating Committee. They selected the first major latitude line north of Seoul and the Han River valley, one of the two political centers of Korea and the site of the headquarters of the Japanese colonial government and the Seventeenth Area Army. That line was the Thirty-eighth Parallel. This division also meant that the U.S. Army could use the port of Inchon as well as Kunsan and Pusan to evacuate the Japanese. Stalin accepted the proposed division on August 16 without revision. Some of Truman's advisers believed that the Russians would not abide by the agreement, since the Soviet Twenty-fifth Army (Col. Gen. Ivan M. Chistiakov) was already in Korea and marching south without opposition. Two advisers, W. Averell Harriman and Edwin W. Pauley, expressed some concern that the Russian lust for nonnegotiated reparations in terms of machinery, food, raw materials, and human labor would take the Russians beyond the border town of Kaesong, but the Soviets withdrew from Kaesong to their zone without pressure.[3]

Yo Un-hyong wasted no time in forming the Committee for the Preparation of Korean Independence (August 15, 1945) from among the nationalist notables of Seoul. He called for all Koreans to avoid clashes with the Japanese and the colonial police while the committee put together a new constitution (based on the declaration of independence of 1919) and awaited the American occupation force, which would assume temporary peacekeeping duties until the Japanese went home. Emissaries went to other cities to form branches of the committee, to ensure the release of political prisoners, and to form local militia units that would protect lives and property, thus filling a growing vacuum created by the desertion of thousands of Japanese and Korean colonial police officers. Within a month, Yo's committee had spawned almost 150 local affiliates as well as hundreds of new labor unions, farmers cooperatives, and very active student associations. Along with Korean soldiers demobilized from Japanese service, student groups provided the manpower for the local defense units, the *chiandae*. Another force—composed almost exclusively of Korean veterans and commanded by former officers in the Japanese service—opened a headquarters in downtown Seoul and adopted the title of Korean Preparatory Army. By the end of August, it claimed fifteen thousand members under training. These varied units armed themselves with weapons abandoned by the police, looted from Japanese armories, or purchased from Japanese soldiers, who knew a market for rifles when they saw one.

The preparatory committee scared the Japanese, and it also scared moderate nationalists, who watched its demands for the confiscation of Japanese property and farmlands mount toward some sort of Korean socialism. The committee, a loose and shifting group of perhaps a hundred members in Seoul, had two major constituent groups: the Korean Independence League (Yo Un-hyong's personal political association) and the Communists. In European terms, members of the Korean Independence League might have qualified as populists and social democrats. The Communists were "beet" revolutionaries, Red all the way through, as they boasted and their critics charged. The first group of Communists met on August 15 in Seoul at the Changan building and thus became the Changan faction. Two days later, Pak Hon-yong, who had left his South Cholla brickyard for the smoke-filled rooms and embattled streets of Seoul, rallied old and new comrades and declared the rebirth of the Korean Communist Party with his group, the Seoul district. The Seoul district and Changan faction fought each other for dominance—a fight Pak Hon-yong won within a few months—but they collaborated to push Yo Un-hyong to the left. Yo did not need much convincing; on August 18 a group of unidentified street toughs beat him, and while he recovered, the preparatory committee drifted. On September 6 almost a thousand committee members rallied at a Seoul girls' high school and declared the creation of the Korean People's Republic. No American troop units had yet arrived, and the Japanese generals believed that they now faced a revolution.[4]

On balance, the creation of the Korean People's Republic bore the imprint of Pak Hon-yong's Seoul district of the Communist Party, grudgingly endorsed by Yo Un-hyong's group. It was also a preemptive strike against the Changan Communists. On September 8 the eighty-eight organizers of the Korean People's Republic (the title adopted at Pak Hon-yong's urging) published a list of officers and ministers who would presumably form the executive branch of the new government. The ten individual leaders identified with specific posts represented a wide range of political positions and factions, but they were all national figures with reputations for some sort of resistance to Japanese colonialism. A second concern may have been to form a government that the occupying Americans might accept for short-term expediency (the evacuation of the Japanese) and then allow to continue because there was no reasonable alternative in the face of popular pressure. Real power in the government would remain in the hands of the socialist revolutionaries. Four of the most prominent nationalists in the cabinet—Chairman Syngman Rhee, Minister of Interior Kim Ku, Minister of Foreign Relations Kim Kyu-sik, and Minister of Communications Shin Ik-hui—remained abroad; all but Rhee were members of the Korean provisional government. Minister of Finance Cho Man-sik, a favorite of the Christians, remained in Pyongyang to deal with the Russians and had no influence in the Korean People's Republic. An elderly apolitical jurist, Yi In, held the post of justice minister. Kim Sung-su, the textile entrepreneur and educational philanthropist, received the post of minister of education, but he had already shown no interest in associating with the new republic, for personal and political reasons. Although Pak Hon-yong kept himself out of the government, he believed that he could control Vice-Chairman Yo Un-hyong, who retained his popularity as a public orator but showed no flair for backroom politics. Prime Minister Ho Hon, a Seoul lawyer, and Minister of Security Choe Yong-dal, an organizer of paramilitary youth groups, were firmly in Pak's Seoul district of the Communist Party. No member of the Communist Changan faction received an appointment, and the only northern Korean other than Cho Man-sik who received any mention was "General" Kim Il-sung, claimed by the Changan faction, who was appointed legislative representative to the People's Republic. No expatriate Communists with Russian or Chinese ties were included.

On September 14 the Korean People's Republic published its political platform. Its central concern was the elimination of all vestiges of Japanese colonialism, with a special emphasis on the nationalization of major businesses, most of which were essentially Japanese public corporations such as the railroads, the telephone system, mining enterprises, banking, shipping, and some manufacturing businesses. Property held by "national traitors" or Japanese collaborators was also subject to confiscation. Korean agriculture would remain a private enterprise, but landlords could take no more than 30 percent of a crop's value as rent from their tenants. The new Korea would provide political and religious freedom, extend voting rights to males and females over age eighteen, and establish the right of unionization and collective bargaining.[5]

The preemptive politics of the Korean People's Republic did not go unchallenged, but the postliberation politics of August and September 1945, largely a function of Seoul-based factions, represented a conflict of personalities and programs. At the heart of the creation of the Korean Democratic Party (Hanguk Minjudang) was the issue of collaboration with the Japanese and the future of wealth and property forfeited by the Japanese. Formed after four days of intense negotiation at Chondogyo Hall, a favorite political meeting site in Seoul, the Korean Democratic Party rejected the representativeness of the preparatory committee and its successor, the Korean People's Republic. The leadership of the Korean Democratic Party regarded Yo Un-hyong as an unprincipled opportunist who had played into the hands of the Japanese as well as the Communists by severing any connection between the liberation movement and the Korean provisional government in exile. Certainly the nationalist notables who composed the elite leadership of the Korean Democratic Party were troubled by the "socialistic" economic program advertised by the People's Republic, but much of the republic's September 14 program was acceptable to the party. The most active leaders of the party, Kim Sung-su and Song Chin-u, did not have to prove their patriotism, nor did other party leaders such as Cho Pyong-ok, Chang Myon, Chang Taek-sang, An Ho-sang, George Paek, and Chang Tok-su. Although the Korean Democratic Party elite included members whose wartime relationship with the Japanese appeared too close, these

men exercised no special leverage. Party leaders could claim that they represented
a true break with the past, whereas the non-Communist members of the People's
Republic did not. The leaders of the Korean Democratic Party were highly educated in Western or elite Japanese universities, sometimes both. They were proven
organizational leaders in business and education; many of them were serious Christians and had suffered for their faith; they had a clear vision of how to balance economic development with public order and individual liberties. They were especially angry that the leaders of the Korean People's Republic had staked a false
claim as the true heirs to the goals of the March First Movement.[6]

The rapid postliberation appearance of the Korean People's Republic and the
Korean Democratic Party simply reflected the continuing struggle between two
competing revolutionary movements, both rooted in resistance to Japanese colonialism in the 1920s and 1930s. Both still reflected the personalism and court politics that had always plagued Korea; both carried the burden of some survivalism-
collaborationism with the Japanese and the fantasies of expatriate politics. Both
reflected top-down visions of reform and government, representative but not democratic. Although the leaders of the Korean People's Republic might pay lip service to the local liberation movements of the People's Committees outside Seoul,
the republic's September 14 manifesto was certainly a blueprint for a central government with strong executive powers. Both the Korean People's Republic and the
Korean Democratic Party, in terms of American postindependence politics, sought
Hamiltonian ends by Hamiltonian means, strong central government with broad
authority. There was nothing of the spirit of Thomas Jefferson, Samuel Adams, and
Patrick Henry in Song Chin-u, Kim Sung-su, Yo Un-hyong, Pak Hon-yong, Kim
Ku, An Ho-sang, Syngman Rhee, and their lesser associates. The only Korean
politician whom knowledgeable American observers thought was fully imbued
with democratic political values was Kim Kyu-sik, who was also the least effective member of the emerging elite. To question the democratic commitment of Korean politicians of 1945 does not, however, disqualify them as patriotic nationalists who wanted to build a new Korea that rejected the traditionalism of the Chosun
dynasty and the corrupting influence of Japanese colonialism.

THE RUSSIANS RETURN TO KOREA, 1945

Driven out of Korean politics in 1895–1905 by the Japanese, the Russians returned
with a vengeance in 1945 when the three divisions of the Twenty-fifth Army attacked across the Tumen River and conducted amphibious landings at the east coast
cities of Unggi and Najin on August 10. After five days of sporadic resistance, the
remaining 25,000 Japanese soldiers, facing a Soviet army almost five times as
large, capitulated. Many Japanese soldiers and colonial policemen left their units
and headed for safe haven south of the Thirty-eighth Parallel. The northern Koreans greeted the Russians with joy, until they learned that the Soviet soldiers, many

of them Muslim Asians, regarded the Koreans as a conquered people, not liberated victims of Japanese oppression. Although the Soviet troops' behavior did not reach the same scale of violence that it did in Manchuria, the Twenty-fifth Army conducted its share of rapes, beatings, murders, and looting that marked the advance of all Soviet armies into enemy territory. Japanese and Korean deaths in Manchuria and Korea were estimated at 50,000 to 80,000. The Soviets captured 2.7 million soldiers and civilians and then shipped about 400,000 Japanese and Korean POWs off to labor camps in Siberia, from which 95,000 survivors eventually returned. Supporting itself with confiscated food and fuels—much of it from private hands, as well as Japanese military supplies—the Twenty-fifth Army marched without opposition into Pyongyang and Wonsan on August 21–24 and immediately started to seize industrial machinery, fertilizer, stored minerals, coal, and timber, in addition to food.[7]

Although robbery and physical attacks on Koreans by Soviet soldiers did not end, the Russian generals had their troops under control by October 1945; however, the Soviet program of forced reparations continued for several more months. An American mission that visited northern Korean cities for a six-day period in December 1946 estimated that the Soviets had taken $1 billion in property and might have destroyed another $2 billion, although the mission head, Ambassador Edwin W. Pauley, admitted that some of the destruction had been accomplished by the Japanese. In the meantime, Soviet technicians took control of the transportation and communications systems, the numerous reservoirs and hydroelectric plants, textile and cement factories, forests, port facilities, and Korea's lone fertilizer plant. The Soviets had no immediate interest in agriculture, so they allowed the most radical tenant farmers to seize their landlords' land and not pay crop shares or taxes on the property or crops they confiscated. This instant land reform cast the Soviets as generous liberators and set off conflict among the Koreans, not directed at the Soviet army. Where the Soviets found functioning People's Committees, they turned the problems of peacekeeping over to a new native police force composed largely of demobilized Korean soldiers, uniformed in blue variants of Russian military uniforms. Crimes against Soviet military personnel and property were punished by the Soviet military police.

The horrors of the Soviet occupation were reported not just by frightened Korean refugees but also by Western journalists and a small U.S. Army liaison mission in Pyongyang. The driver and Korean-language interpreter for the two officers of the mission (Russian-speaking intelligence specialists) was Technician Grade 3 Richard F. Underwood, the youngest of the third-generation Underwoods of Chosun Christian College, Severance Hospital, and the Korean Presbyterian Church. In eight months of service in Pyongyang (October 1945–June 1946), Dick Underwood, a member of the Office of Strategic Services (OSS), established contacts with anti-Soviet Koreans, predominantly Christians and, more specifically, members of the Presbyterian Church in Korea, established by his grandfather during the Chosun dynasty. Underwood took testimony about oppression, collected documents, and accepted photographs of Soviet economic depredations. He also saw the Soviet army in its prime. For excitement, the Soviets tried to run over Koreans with their vehicles, and the Soviet soldiers amused everyone by using Western toilets as wash basins. Private theft went on constantly. Underwood watched Soviet soldiers cut down telephone poles for firewood and construction material. He warded off attacks from Korean street gangs by speaking profane street Korean, which proved that the tall, blond "Big Nose" was actually an American. He also watched the Soviet high commanders refuse to send water-purifying chlorine (the Russians controlled the only plant in Korea) to the American zone, which increased the virulence of a cholera epidemic, until the Americans threatened to stop rice shipments to Pyongyang. Leonard E. Barsdell, an Australian civilian public affairs officer in MacArthur's headquarters, accompanied an Allied POW rescue team that landed in Pyongyang in August 1945. Barsdell witnessed the same acts of violence and looting (individual and organized) that appalled Underwood. Barsdell reported broad approval and cooperation between the Koreans and the Allied rescue team, but he also predicted that the Soviets and their Korean agents would soon control Pyongyang.[8]

The Soviets also came to Korea to reestablish a Korean Communist Party in their own occupation zone and to support the southern Communists in their dealings with the Americans. At a minimum, building a cadre of Korean collaborators assisted the program of forced reparations by taking control of the People's Committees before they became a focal point of protest against the occupation. The Soviets did nothing to move directly against the People's Committees. Instead, they simply did nothing to support them—and the Soviets controlled the security forces. The best way to control the People's Committees was simply to place them under the supervision of the Five Province Administrative Bureau and place this bureau under the direction of the People's Committee of Pyongyang, chaired by none other than the elderly saint of the nationalists, Cho Man-sik. General Chistiakov and his principal assistants for political affairs and civil administration, Maj. Gen. Nikolai G. Lebedev and Maj. Gen. Alexei A. Romaneko, may have considered Cho Man-sik an authentic revolutionary with whom they could work, but his status as a leading Christian lay leader made him suspect from the start.

The Soviets had alternative comrades whose potential for cooperation was much greater than Cho Man-sik's. Following a proven formula for establishing a native Communist Party, Lebedev and Romaneko had their own candidate in tow, Capt. Kim Il-sung, accompanied by his trusted comrades of the Kapsan faction, the former Manchurian partisans. One of them, Choe Yong-gun, was a former student of Cho Man-sik, a happy coincidence. When the Russians first brought Kim Il-sung to meet Cho Man-sik on September 30 at the Club Hwabang, the elder patriot did not know the young man in the Red Army uniform, but he knew Choe Yong-gun, a true patriot in the war against Japan. The Soviets also ensured that other potential leaders did not disturb the flow of political events. When Kim Tu-bong and Kim Mu-chong attempted to cross the Yalu River with four thousand armed members of the Yanan faction, the Red Army kept them at bay for four months until Kim Tu-bong promised to disband his private army and cooperate with the approved four-party coalition government. The Russians made their point by allowing one of Kim Mu-chong's elite units to march into Sinuiju and then disarmed it at gunpoint. On October 12, 1945, General Chistiakov announced that he would permit the organization of formal political parties. These parties would vie in elections for seats in a multiparty legislative assembly that would represent the northern Koreans in any negotiations for a unified Korea, as well as establish a provisional government for the Five Province Administrative Region.

Within the next month, two Marxist-Leninist parties announced that they had received official recognition—the Communist Party of Korea and the New People's Party. These two parties soon merged to become the North Korean Workers' Party, with Kim Il-sung as the general secretary. His only local potential challenger, a charismatic schoolteacher with longtime Communist activity, Hyon Chunhyok, had been murdered by another Communist (later identified as a defector to the Kapsan faction) on September 28, 1945. Another party emerged from the followers of March First Movement veteran Kim Tal-hyon, who also served as the spiritual leader of 1.5 million Chondogyo members in northern Korea. The fourth party, the Democratic Party, was founded in early November and rallied to Cho Man-sik. The price of recognition, however, was the appointment of two Kapsan faction stalwarts, Choe Yong-gun and Kim Chaek, as Cho's principal administrative assistants. Symbolic of the drawing of irreconcilable political lines in Korea, Choe and Kim were generals in the Korean People's Army by 1950; the two brothers they replaced at Cho's side, Paik Sun-yup and Paik In-yup, became two of the most highly regarded generals of the army of the Republic of Korea.

With the Kapsan faction well placed within the new parties, Kim Il-sung and the Russians agreed that the Yanan faction might return to Korea and become members of the North Korean Workers' Party. Whether the multiparty system had any future remained to be seen, but it gave the Russians the facade of representative government while they waited to see how the Americans would deal with the fractious politicians south of the Thirty-eighth Parallel. As for the northern Koreans, they believed that their activism served the cause of immediate independence and unification for all Korea.

The formation of a Soviet-sponsored Communist Party in Pyongyang, which claimed no connection to Pak Hon-yong's southern Communists, reflected Kim Il-sung's confidence that the Kapsan faction would now control events. Under the Potemkin party system, his faction and the Soviet Koreans held real power. His young protégé, O Chin-u, held the post of Pyongyang police chief, and Choe Yong-gun became chief of security, Interim People's Committee. Kim and his Soviet advisers—whom he plied with drinking parties and the company of *kisaeng* women—agreed to a public rally to announce the creation of the "united democratic national front." On the afternoon of October 14, Kim Il-sung and the Soviet generals, with Cho Man-sik in tow, mounted a dais erected in a playground below Pyongyang's Moranbong Hill, a traditional site of Korean nationalist rallies. Kim harangued the curious crowd of 100,000 with a classic description of a future socialist Korea based on confiscated Japanese wealth. His utopian dream faced a threat from the neoimperialists of America and their Korean and Japanese lackeys. He repeated the same theme to a party gathering four days later. Although he was allowed to speak on October 14, Cho Man-sik stirred little interest or sympathy. Except for his most devoted disciples, the frail, small old man with the long beard and thick glasses evoked a past of political impotence. Kim Il-sung, in contrast, broke a student protest strike in Sinuiju in November 1945 by his personal intervention and persuasiveness. He turned the people against the strikers, who were protesting a principal's removal, by branding the student leaders as Cho Mansik's misguided provocateurs. A vigorous, young, self-confident leader, a hero in battles against the Japanese, had swept the March First Movement leaders into the dustbin of history.[9]

THE AMERICANS RETURN TO KOREA, 1945–1946

Although the soldiers of the U.S. Army's XXIV Corps knew little if anything about Korea, the Koreans—at least the educated political elite—knew a great deal about Americans. They regarded them as the most selfless and helpful foreigners—along with the British, Canadians, and Australians—to come to Korea. The United States had defeated Japan, and now it would reverse the betrayal of 1905 by becoming the enthusiastic midwife for the birth of a new, independent Korea.

Only the Washington Koreans—Syngman Rhee and his associates of the Korean Commission—knew that the U.S. government believed that the birth might be premature. The active representatives of Nationalist China in Washington, backed by champions in the State Department and the coalition of influential Americans known as the "China Lobby," kept Korean independence alive by linking it to Chiang Kai-shek's demand that China's "lost lands" taken by Japan should be returned after the inevitable Allied victory. All of the Japanese empire taken since 1895 would be forfeit. Manchuria, Formosa, and the Pescadores would revert to China; all other lands, including Korea, would be guided to some new (and indefinite) political status. The United States, Great Britain, and Nationalist China, "mindful of the enslavement of the Korean people," would ensure "that in due course Korea shall be free and independent." Franklin Roosevelt, Winston Churchill, and Chiang Kai-shek endorsed this position in their final communiqué after the Cairo Conference (November 22–25, 1943).

When FDR met with Churchill and Stalin at Yalta, the Crimea, in February 1945, the future of Korea did not receive serious attention, and there was no elaboration of the Cairo declaration. In a private conversation FDR proposed to Stalin that the United States, the Soviet Union, and Nationalist China provide some sort of interim administration for Korea, a trusteeship that would lead to an independent Korean state. Stalin had no objection to the proposal, except that he thought Great Britain should be included as a trusteeship power. He also thought that any interim administration should be short, and he agreed with FDR's afterthought that no foreign troops should occupy Korea. The issue drifted. At the next "Big Three" meeting in July 1945 at Potsdam, in a defeated Germany, a new president, Harry S. Truman, accepted the State Department's judgment that any policy should be based on "the probable inability of the Koreans to govern themselves." Reasserting the principles of the Cairo declaration, the Big Three simply agreed that Korean self-determination would come after a military government replaced the Japanese, then passed responsibility to "an international supervisory administration," which would usher in an independent, representative Korean government chosen by the Koreans. There was no implementing plan or timetable.[10]

There was still a war to be won before Korea became anything but a Japanese colony. For the American military planners, Korea had little strategic importance except as a potential (if limited) site for operations related to the bombing of the Japanese home islands and submarine attacks against Japanese shipping. The OSS had scant interest in Korea, whatever the illusions of Rhee and Preston Goodfellow. Gen. Douglas MacArthur's Allied Intelligence Bureau, so active in the Southwest Pacific theater, had no reason to see Korea as its responsibility, since the dual air-amphibious advance of the Pacific Ocean areas forces (under Adm. Chester W. Nimitz) was focused on the capture of either Formosa or the Ryukyu Islands as a prelude to a tightening economic assault or an amphibious landing on Kyushu. The lack of success of air and ground operations in China added to Korea's marginalization as a wartime concern. It had no monopoly on strategic neglect, but its future did concern the State Department, which shared the responsibility for postwar reconstruction with the army.[11]

In June 1945 the State Department circulated its assessment of postwar conditions in Asia, "An Estimate of Conditions in Asia and the Pacific at the Close of the War in the Far East and the Objectives and Policies of the United States." The diplomats foresaw an era of turmoil in Asia as the native political elites renewed their struggles for national liberation. The United States should not stand in the way of this inevitable political movement, but its freedom to act would be inhibited by its need to continue its wartime collaboration with the Great Powers. These nations included traditional European colonial powers (Great Britain, France, the Netherlands) and neocolonial powers such as Nationalist China and the Soviet Union, which sought redress for their historical territorial losses to Japan. Either group might assert some claim to Korea. Such claims were specious, however, because Korea had already been recognized by the international community as an independent nation in the nineteenth century. The Japanese colonial regime had only increased the stridency of Korean nationalism, and Korean hatred of Japan could hardly be exaggerated. A Japanese defeat could easily bring a wave of retributive violence to Korea, since two-thirds of the Koreans were underfed, employed in forced and underpaid Japanese war work or back-breaking rice growing, and

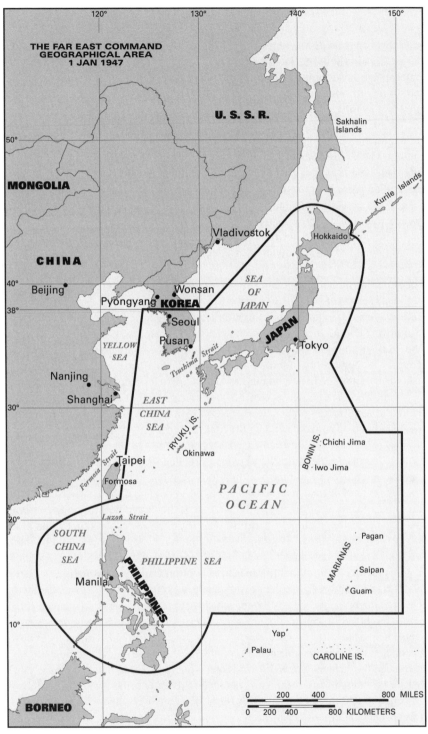

THE FAR EAST COMMAND
GEOGRAPHICAL AREA
1 JAN 1947

120° 130° 140° 150°

U. S. S. R.

Sakhalin
Islands

50°

MONGOLIA

Kurile Islands

CHINA

Vladivostok

Hokkaido

40°

Beijing

Wonsan

SEA
OF
JAPAN

Pyongyang KOREA

38°

Seoul

Pusan

JAPAN

Tokyo

YELLOW
SEA

Tsushima Strait

Nanjing

Shanghai

30°

EAST
CHINA
SEA

RYUKU IS.

BONIN IS. Chichi Jima

Okinawa

Iwo Jima

Formosa Strait

Taipei

Formosa

PACIFIC
OCEAN

20°

Luzon Strait

SOUTH
CHINA
SEA

PHILIPPINE SEA

Pagan

MARIANAS

Manila

PHILIPPINES

Saipan

Guam

10°

Yap

Palau

CAROLINE IS.

0   200   400   800 MILES

0   200   400   800 KILOMETERS

BORNEO

Map 3.

seething with resentment. "There will undoubtedly be considerable confusion and chaos . . . disorder may become general." There was no Korean government underground or in exile that was "truly representative" of the Korean people or qualified to govern. When the Soviet Union entered the war with Japan (as Stalin had promised at Yalta in March 1945), it could occupy all of Korea with relative ease. Yet, for all the problems, the United States should help Korea with "the early establishment of a strong, democratic, independent nation." Thus the United States could demonstrate its commitment to national self-determination in Asia.[12]

The barrier to shaping a policy toward an independent Korea remained the more pressing problem of dealing with a defeated Japan. Its surrender, as defined by the Allies since early 1943, would be unconditional, which meant that any bargaining would come after capitulation, if at all. The American position, first shaped by a planning committee of the Joint Chiefs of Staff, reflected Roosevelt's guidance and State Department views. Japan should be disarmed, its forces demobilized, its production of weapons halted, and its society purged of associations and educational agencies that exalted warrior values and war as an instrument of policy. To secure these goals might entail a revolutionary reordering of Japanese society, which would be faster and more peaceful if the Japanese would cooperate. Therein lay the dilemma of the status of Emperor Hirohito. Although Hirohito had been an active party to all the decisions that had brought war in China in 1937 and the Asia-Pacific war of 1941, he now appeared to be crucial to shaping a quick surrender and the rapid transformation of the "new" Japan. He might also retain some control over the Japanese armed forces, whose cooperation was essential to the peaceful process of capitulation and repatriation from the far reaches of the doomed Japanese empire.

Under the plans developed by the State-War-Navy Coordinating Committee, the interagency group that prepared policy recommendations for the three departments its members represented, the overseas Japanese forces would assume many postsurrender responsibilities: traveling to central locations to surrender to Allied representatives (but not local native leaders), collecting arms and munitions for surrender and destruction, dismantling active defenses and fixed weapons such as coast artillery and minefields, and providing for the safety and well-being of Allied POWs and internees. There were many "don'ts" in the surrender plan: don't harm the lives and property of local civilians, don't destroy Japanese military and private property in foreign lands that has economic value for peaceful use, don't force non-Japanese to go to Japan, don't take any form of wealth back to Japan, and don't meddle in local politics. To accomplish these demands, the Japanese armed forces could defend themselves, their civilian countrymen, and their local allies until Allied troops could assume full responsibility for the preservation of peace. To provide some continuity from war to peace—and withdrawal—Japanese civil servants should remain at their posts in critical agencies such as transportation, communications, public health services, and law enforcement related to pure criminal actions, but not the enforcement of Japanese laws against political dissent and economic activity.[13]

After much interagency debate and coordination with the Allies—which in-cluded the Soviet Union as of August 9, 1945—President Truman approved the basic surrender terms and postsurrender occupation and repatriation conditions on August 15 and September 6, 1945, even though the Soviet Union remained un-happy about its exclusion from the occupation of the Japanese home islands. The president also appointed his best available emperor-surrogate: General of the Army Douglas MacArthur, inclined by age, self-esteem, and military record to be a cred-ible American shogun for the military occupation and spiritual rebirth of Japan. With serious reservations about his political guidance, MacArthur went to Tokyo to preside over the central Japanese surrender aboard the battleship *Missouri* in Tokyo Bay on September 2, 1945, and assumed responsibility for the surrender plan, Operation Blacklist. Other Allied commanders took the responsibility for ac-cepting Japanese surrenders elsewhere, but Korea, as well as Japan, fell within MacArthur's jurisdiction as Supreme Commander Allied Powers (SCAP) and his parallel assignment as Commander in Chief U.S. Army Forces Pacific. Among his many talents and distressing shortcomings, MacArthur had a genuine concern for the future of Korea, which he knew from his forty-year association with Asian poli-tics. Even though he was best known for his commitment to the Philippines, MacArthur knew something about Japanese and Korean history and culture. He was not averse to listening to the counsel of Americans he regarded as real experts on north Asia, including missionaries, businessmen, journalists, and educators. MacArthur's claim to expertise about the Chinese was suspect, but he knew a great deal more about Korea than other senior army officers. Nevertheless, his first pri-ority remained the reconstruction of Japan.

In his new role as occupation commander, MacArthur issued Proclamation No. 1, Commander in Chief U.S. Army Forces Pacific, directed to "the People of Korea." This was his guidance for the surrender of Japanese forces in Korea, and the terms were identical to those MacArthur had issued for the occupation of Japan on September 2, with the addition of the phrase that "in due course Korea shall be-come free and independent." The Koreans were warned that attacks on American troops and the Japanese would be regarded as criminal acts. Japanese civil servants would remain at their posts for the time being, and this included the police. The American military occupation force, the army's XXIV Corps, would preserve the peace and arrange for the rapid repatriation of the Japanese, as well as protect lives, property, and freedom of religion. In truth, however, the Korean mission did not hold MacArthur's attention, since he had a larger task in Japan. In addition, the War Department had already assigned someone to command the army's Korean expeditionary force.[14]

Except for their taste in starched khaki uniforms, crushed army barracks caps, and aviator sunglasses, Lt. Gen. John R. Hodge and MacArthur had little in com-mon. In 1945 MacArthur was sixty-five, Hodge fifty-two. Like most of his World War II contemporaries, Hodge had entered the army in the World War I period.

He had been a captain in the postwar army when MacArthur was already a general. There were even more striking differences. MacArthur was a Military Academy graduate (1903), and a legendary one at that; Hodge had gone to the University of Illinois before dropping out to attend officer candidate school in 1917. MacArthur, the son of a distinguished general, had grown up on army posts. Hodge came from a farm near Golconda in downstate Illinois, a land of cornfields, scrub woods, and coal mines. Hodge was short and muscular but spare, vigorous, and fond of crewcuts. Unlike MacArthur, Hodge had no touch of the palace and stage about him, and his approach to people was close, personal, confrontational, and impatient. His army career showed a steady pattern of energetic, intelligent over-achievement and a love of soldiering. His World War I career as a communications officer in the U.S. Sixty-first Infantry Regiment in France brought him little recognition, but he had no trouble receiving a postwar regular commission and promotion to captain (1920) in the infantry. His interwar assignments included service in four different infantry regiments and an infantry brigade headquarters. After a four-year assignment as an instructor of military science and tactics at Mississippi Agricultural and Mechanical College, Hodge attended the Infantry School at Fort Benning (1925–1926) and performed with enough distinction to earn an assignment to the two-year course of the Army Command and General Staff College, Fort Leavenworth (1932–1934), and the Army War College (1934–1935), followed by a tour at the Air Corps Tactical School, Maxwell Field (1935–1936). After a short tour with troops, Hodge held a series of assignments on operations and training staffs in the War Department and in a field corps. In June 1942, as a temporary brigadier general, Hodge returned to Hawaii, where he had served earlier with the U.S. Twenty-seventh Infantry. He became the assistant division commander of the Twenty-fifth Infantry Division, commanded by a friend and admirer, Maj. Gen. J. Lawton "Lightning Joe" Collins, a future army chief of staff.

From the campaigns in the Solomons to the final bloodbath of Okinawa, John Hodge proved that the army had not wasted its investment in his field service and formal schooling. He proved an apt alter ego to Collins in the later stages of the battle of Guadalcanal (for which he won the Legion of Merit) and earned a promotion to major general and command of the Americal Division, a mix of regular army and National Guard regiments and battalions assigned separately to the South Pacific theater in 1942–1943. When the commander of the U.S. Forty-third Infantry Division faltered in the battle for New Georgia, Hodge replaced him for a week of intense combat and won the first of his three Distinguished Service Crosses. After commanding his own division on Bougainville, Hodge moved to command the XXIV Corps in the Leyte campaign, then took his corps headquarters north to take over the three army divisions that made the initial landings on Okinawa. He even earned an Air Medal by flying his own small aircraft on reconnaissance missions over enemy lines on Leyte. He wore a Purple Heart for a slight wound suffered on Bougainville. He attracted some attention from the press for his heroics, but Hodge had few of the graces of true media generals such as MacArthur and Collins. He was, however, no fool and a quick study, and he could see that his corps' occupation duties were not as simple as he originally believed.[15]

John Hodge approved his XXIV Corps order for the occupation of Korea ("Baker Forty" or Field Order 55) on August 28. His primary mission was to disarm the Japanese, enforce the anticipated surrender terms, keep order, and await instructions on how to pass power to the Koreans. Hodge's counterpart, Lt. Gen. Kozuki Yoshio, commander of the Seventeenth Area Army in Seoul, urged the Americans to hurry. Already facing the restless Koreans, Kozuki reported that the Russians had crossed the Thirty-eighth Parallel and occupied Kaesong, which was true. The Americans had to come quickly if the Japanese were to keep the transfer of power peaceful. Of course, the Japanese had already transferred power to the preparatory committee of Yo Un-hyong, but only the Americans' presence could ensure that the Russians would not march into the Han River valley.

MacArthur agreed with Kozuki and ordered Hodge to leave Okinawa and get to Seoul and Kaesong with his one available division, the U.S. Seventh Infantry. First, a group of Allied special operations troops would take custody of the 680 American, British, and Australian POWs gathered at Inchon, a task accomplished on September 6. In the meantime, Hodge's convoy got under way on September 5 and reached Inchon harbor on the morning of September 8. Before coming ashore from his headquarters transport, Hodge received reports from his own advance party, which had landed by plane at Kimpo airfield on September 3, from the operations officer of the Seventeenth Area Army, and from three Korean representatives of the preparatory committee and the Korean People's Republic, which was all of two days old. Hodge stuck with his orders: establish law and order and keep the Koreans and Japanese apart. He thanked the Koreans, led by Yo Un-hyong himself, for telling him which Koreans he could trust and which ones were Japanese collaborators unacceptable to the Korean people. Hodge made no commitments except to protect everyone—Japanese and Korean—who remained peaceful. With a sense of urgency and considerable uncertainty about conditions in Seoul—where clashes between the police and demonstrators had already resulted in casualties—Hodge sent a regiment of the Seventh Infantry Division to the capital the next day and appointed the division commander, Maj. Gen. Archibald V. Arnold, military governor of Seoul. Most of the Japanese remained at their posts even after the formal surrender on the afternoon of September 9, but not General Abe or his director of police.[16]

The first week of the American occupation brought Hodge more difficulty than solid achievement, but no major incidents in the Inchon-Kimpo-Seoul area tarnished the transition. Hodge, however, learned that some of his offhand remarks about the difficulty of dealing with the Koreans—"the same breed of cat" as the Japanese—and the cooperativeness of the Japanese did not play well with the American and Korean press, which branded him an insensitive racist and arrogant dictator. The furor reached Washington, and the State Department disavowed the policy of retaining Japanese officials in Korea. Even President Truman felt compelled to make two public statements to the effect that senior Japanese officials would go if they had not done so already. MacArthur did not have to wait for more guidance. On September 11 he ordered Hodge to terminate the Japanese civil government and replace it with a military governor, General Arnold, who took office the following day. In an act of more than symbolic importance, Arnold announced that English was now the official language of government in Korea.[17]

General Hodge now faced several complex and interacting missions that his corps and military government were ill prepared to perform simultaneously. He still did not have a definitive statement about his mission, other than to disarm and repatriate the Japanese. He decided that getting the Japanese out of office and on their way home took overriding priority. In late September Hodge's second force, the U.S. Fortieth Infantry Division (California and Utah National Guard), arrived from the Philippines and took over security and repatriation operations in the crucial port of Pusan. The Sixth Infantry Division, also from the Philippines, did not reach its posts in southwestern Korea until the last two weeks of October. The Japanese military and civilian personnel, limited to all the harmless and worthless possessions they could carry, flowed south by railroad to Pusan's Pier One for a final inspection and embarkation. By November 6, the last Japanese military unit had departed, and by the end of December, the U.S. Army had repatriated 394,089 Japanese. The Japanese employees of the military government dropped from 10,000 to 1,000 essential technicians in the national railroad and telephone-telegraph systems, along with utility workers and other skilled operators who had no Korean counterparts.[18]

The Russians and the American troops proved more difficult to control than the Japanese, who had real incentives to cooperate. Despite some menacing deployments and hard words, the Russians admitted that they had gone to Kaesong by mistake. They had indeed withdrawn, but they kept a motorized rifle division poised on the road to Seoul, which did not make the deployment of the Seventh Infantry Division any easier. The Russians also showed no inclination to provide any economic resources to the south; the only immediate export from the Soviet zone was thousands of refugees, who crossed into the American zone at the rate of 4,000 to 6,000 a week for twelve weeks. The military government estimated that it accepted responsibility for an estimated 400,000 refugees from northern Korea and almost a million Koreans returning home from Japan. Those who managed to slip through the cordon of border guards and thieves above the Thirty-eighth Parallel brought little of value with them; the Soviets were happy to have them bring in millions of Korean won and Japanese yen, since it only fueled inflation in the southern zone, but gold and jewels were fair game. The American troops along the repatriation pipeline began their duties with discipline and attentiveness, but their interest declined over time as they pondered their own delayed transfer home for demobilization. Hodge urged his division commanders to crack down on theft, drunkenness, and petty violence as winter approached, and he warned the army staff that his understrength, ill-trained soldiers, commanded by war-weary officers, were a growing liability in his relations with the Koreans.[19]

The issue of Korean independence and participation in government bedeviled Hodge and the senior officers of the military government. The central government in Seoul hired American civilians (many returning missionary family members) and Koreans, especially those who spoke English, to replace the Japanese as rapidly as possible. This policy received the support of Maj. Gen. John H. Hilldring, who administered the special army fund for Government Aid and Relief in Occupied Areas, which sent $4.9 million to Korea in 1945. Hodge received thirty-two military government companies, and by November, these companies (1,385 officers and men) had taken their posts in every province and major and minor city. With instructions to revive the Korean economy as quickly as possible, Hodge established a joint committee of Koreans and Americans, which placed some confiscated Japanese businesses into the hands of Korean managers while awaiting the final disposition of Japanese property. Japanese-owned landholdings, about one-third of all arable lands, went to new Korean owners. The military government reformed the renamed Korean National Police (Kyongchalchung) by releasing every Japanese official and most senior Korean colonial police officers, which reduced the force to nine thousand, or 40 percent of its preliberation strength. Recruitment then brought the force back to twenty-five thousand officers, many of whom were returning veterans or refugees from northern Korea, supervised by U.S. Army line and military police officers.[20]

Hodge received more precise guidance from Washington, endorsed by MacArthur, that made it clear that his reform program in Korea should essentially follow the same broad lines as MacArthur's in Japan. It did not deal with the fact that the Koreans did not see themselves like the Japanese did—a defeated society struggling to preserve its cultural identity and economic future through a mix of limited reform and cosmetic compliance. State-War-Navy Coordinating Committee Memorandum 176/8, "Basic Initial Directive to the Commander in Chief U.S. Army Forces Pacific for the Administration of Civil Affairs in Those Areas of Korea Occupied by U.S. Forces," reassured Hodge that he had almost absolute power to move Korea toward "a free and independent nation." He could manage the economy, expand or curtail civil liberties, bar collaborators and subversives from office, process refugees, free political and economic prisoners, dispose of Japanese property, recognize unions, publish and enforce regulations on censorship and freedom of movement, reform the banking system, protect religious freedom, and decide what level of political activity and organization was acceptable. What he could *not* do, imagined or real, was to establish the foundation of a Korean national government, which would require a great deal of Great Power negotiation. Yet this was the issue Hodge faced every day, because this was the issue the Koreans cared about most.[21]

Hodge inherited two broad coalitions of Korean nationalist politicians, and neither group appealed to him as the basis for a future Korean government. His political adviser since September 3, career foreign service officer H. Merrell Ben-ninghoff, agreed that the Communist Party and the People's Party could not be trusted to continue the process of reconciliation with Japan, on which the Korean economy would eventually depend. At worst, the Communists would carry out or-ders from the Soviets in Pyongyang. Even though Hodge's liaison mission in Pyong-yang could not get much information on the Russians, U.S. Army Forces in Korea had the advantage of a small communications intelligence unit that could intercept and decode Russian radio transmissions, and someone in the Russian consulate in Seoul was a spy for the Americans. In any event, Hodge accepted the Japanese warning that the Communists were a menace. He found no reason to change his hostility toward the Communists, although he maintained close contact with none other than Pak Hon-yong. As for Yo Un-hyong, Hodge believed that he was an ineffectual party organizer with no special constituency except some student groups. Like the Communists, he saw Yo as a "golden axe." The People's Party was nothing but Yo's undisciplined disciples.[22]

The other potential source of a government might have been the Korean Dem-ocratic Party, whose members could best be characterized as limited modernizers and free-market entrepreneurs. Based on their age, education, relative wealth, and social status, the leaders of the Korean Democratic Party appealed to the Ameri-cans, in part because so many of them spoke some English and took advisory roles or employment in the military government. At the same time, a faction of the Ko-rean Democratic Party had worked too closely with the Japanese and regarded any plan for redistributing non-Japanese wealth as simply Communism in the guise of social democracy. The Americans in Seoul had serious reservations about the democratic values of the Korean Democratic Party, enhanced by the autocratic manner and outspoken conservatism of party leaders. Another disability was that the Korean Democratic Party elite could be perceived as pro-Japanese and silent partners in the repression of the colonial administration. Hodge, Benninghoff, and their senior advisers thought that the Korean Democratic Party represented the best pool of potential Korean leaders, but they did not believe that this group *as a party* represented the majority of Koreans.[23]

The Americans looked for other alternatives. Hodge raised the unpopular issue (in Washington) of the status of the Korean provisional government, whose offi-cials desperately wanted to return to Seoul but could not do so without American approval and air transportation. Hodge considered Syngman Rhee, equally anx-ious to return to Korea, an apostate member of the provisional government and someone who could at least understand American perspectives. Hodge and MacArthur tried to persuade the War Department and State Department to give the provisional government a chance, but State's position was that Rhee, Kim Ku, Kim Kyu-sik, Shin Ik-hui, Yi Pom-sok, and all their compatriots could return only as individuals, although they would be free to serve on whatever advisory commis-sion Hodge established. The provisional government, however, whatever its claims, could not be regarded as a direct substitute for the People's Republic. The

OSS, nevertheless, declared that the provisional government was not a front for the Chinese Nationalists or for the Japanese and had real claims to Korean leadership. The issue was whether the leaders of the provisional government could ever negotiate with Korean leftists or curb their virulent hatred of the Soviet Union and Japan. With misgivings, the diplomats and generals in Washington gave Hodge approval to open the political arena to Syngman Rhee and Kim Ku.[24]

Hodge and Benninghoff profited by the active debate within the State Department about the relative importance of China and a reformed Japan for the future of Asia and about America's role in the historical tension between China and Japan. By late 1945, this continuing exchange strengthened the faction at State and MacArthur's headquarters that had saved Hirohito and shaped the dramatic reform program MacArthur was administering with such verve. The demilitarization of Japan would continue apace with the prosecution of Japanese war criminals and the crafting of a new constitution that would condemn war as an act of policy. The China experts, old and new, were divided among themselves as to the course of a new civil war between the Nationalists and the Communists, a war they hoped to halt or slow by military aid to the Nationalists, the presence of two U.S. Marine Corps divisions in north China, and the assistance of the Soviet Union, which had signed a treaty with Chiang Kai-shek in August 1945 that appeared to abandon the Chinese Communists. An independent Korea might at least remove that unhappy land as a potential battlefield and provide some support for Nationalist China and the new Japan. One potential alternative was to create a unified Korea that would be demilitarized and neutralized by international agreement, much as Austria would be. Almost any improvement in the Korean political scene seemed worth the risk.[25]

Syngman Rhee became the first expatriate Korean nationalist to reach Seoul at the invitation of the military government. Hodge, counseled by Koreans, thought that Rhee would be a force for unity. Rhee applied for a passport (he was technically an enemy alien), which was issued on a routine basis on September 5, but his travel to Korea could not begin until he received approval from MacArthur, who controlled travel in and out of Japan and Korea as part of his occupation powers. Moreover, the U.S. Army had to provide air transport into Japan, since there was no commercial air service yet. When MacArthur's office issued Rhee a travel permit, it identified him as a "high commissioner," which the State Department protested, since the permit suggested American approval of Rhee's political activities. The War Department replaced MacArthur's offensive permit, a State Department clerk fixed the passport, and the army sent Rhee on his way without fanfare or an escort. He reached Guam and found no aircraft headed for Tokyo; SCAP dispatched an aircraft for him. Assisted by Richard Underwood, who was also Korea-bound, Rhee and his baggage reached Haneda airport, where MacArthur's staff took him in tow. On October 11 Rhee finally reached Seoul, where Hodge booked him at the Chosun Hotel, guarded by American military police and assisted by American and Korean secretaries assigned by the military government. The public interest in Rhee—the news media were in full cry—forced Hodge to call a press conference the next day to welcome Rhee, which Hodge did with genuine (perhaps exaggerated) enthusiasm.[26]

If Hodge had expected Rhee to function as a trustworthy conciliator and fusionist statesman, his hopes quickly faded. Rhee at first acted as if he would try to create a moderate and reformist coalition that would accommodate the leaders of the provisional government when they arrived from China. The instrument of reconciliation might have been the advisory council that Hodge had created on October 5, but since half the members of the council were founders of the Korean Democratic Party, Yo Un-hyong refused to serve. Another member, Cho Man-sik, could not leave Pyongyang. Rhee rejected any role in the advisory council, and he also refused a leadership role in the Korean Democratic Party and the Korean People's Republic. He held a press conference on October 17 and made a speech on October 20 during which he repeated his well-known position that a Great Power trusteeship for Korea was only a formula for increasing the Russian threat to a unified Korea and an encouragement to the most radical Korean Communists. On October 23 Rhee called a meeting of Seoul's political notables, including leaders of the Korean Democratic Party, Yo Un-hyong, and Pak Hon-yong. This group announced the creation of a new umbrella organization to advance Korean independence, the Central Council for the Rapid Realization of Korean Independence, to which the leaders of the provisional government would be added when they came to Seoul. The first sign of some movement came on November 11, when Yo Un-hyong announced that he would form a People's Party distinct from the Communists. Ten days later, the People's Republic met and announced that it would work with the military government and not attempt to function as a national government. Nevertheless, the leaders in Seoul declared that the local and regional People's Committees would continue to function and must be considered in any further negotiations. Rhee, however, compromised his own position by accepting financial support from prominent Korean Democratic Party bankers and still argued that the real menace was the subversion of Korean unity measures by the Russians and their agents among the leaders of the Korean Communist Party. Hodge's staff began to wonder if Rhee's real interest was in making money, not governing.[27]

The political tar pit in Seoul thickened with the triumphal return of Kim Ku and his closest associates, which included Shin Ik-hui and Yi Pom-sok of the Restoration Army, on November 23. The next month, Kim Kyu-sik, Kim Won-bong, and twenty associates reached Seoul. Hodge gave Kim Ku the treatment of a visiting U.S. senator: spacious quarters on the grounds of Doksu Palace, vehicles, and the privilege of keeping his private armed guards. Shin Ik-hui repaid the favor by publicly condemning the military government for employing collaborators and bureaucratic thieves. Kim Ku wanted the government purged of its "pro-Japanese" employees and the vacancies filled by his loyal followers. Kim Ku also expressed his opposition to any arrangement that favored the Russians.

Aware that the idea of trusteeship was very much alive within the State Department, Hodge and his two political advisers, Benninghoff and William L.

Langdon, attempted to persuade Rhee and Kim Ku to focus on the politics of Korea, not the Soviet Union. In Rhee's case, they supported his request that his old OSS contact, M. Preston Goodfellow, be continued on active duty and sent to Korea as Rhee's personal adviser. Goodfellow avidly sought this role not just to help Rhee but also to give himself the opportunity to work with Korean entrepreneurs who needed American contracts. Hodge accepted Goodfellow only because he hoped that the journalist–political organizer turned temporary army colonel might persuade Rhee to moderate his language about the Russians and the Korean Communists. Hodge had no comparable leverage on Kim Ku once "the Assassin" set up his organization in Seoul. Hodge himself despaired that Washington understood his problems in Korea and the unresolved economic crisis. Hodge wavered between establishing a separate government in the American zone and simply cutting the Koreans loose with immediate independence and accepting whatever regime emerged from the chaos. He argued that some Great Power trusteeship would never bring a unified Korea and would only unite the Koreans in their opposition to the military government.[28]

THE TRUSTEESHIP CRISIS

As the first winter of the Allied occupation of Korea approached, the asymmetry of political power between the two occupation zones widened. The U.S. military government now faced a crisis that threatened the program of relief and recovery initiated in a haphazard and hurried fashion by Hodge's occupation administrators and a large and confused civil bureaucracy staffed by too many Koreans tainted by their prior service in the Japanese government-general. The social confusion of liberation placed inordinate burdens on the military government for which no easy solutions existed. About 19,000 Japanese remained in Korea by the end of November 1945, but the repatriation program was a clear success. The southern zone's Korean population had increased by 1.3 million refugees from China, Manchuria, Japan, and the Soviet zone. Hodge's economic managers and analysts predicted a long, cold winter, made longer and colder by shortages of coal and electricity, both controlled by the Soviets. As a gesture, Hodge sent a trainload of rice to the Russians, who kept the rice and the train.

One bright spot, however, was that the annual rice crop had been abundant, largely because it had been planted and fertilized as part of the Japanese war effort. The surrender now seemed to ensure that the rice would be used to feed all Koreans before any of it would be shipped to Japan, under American distribution plans. In October 1945 the military government announced that the existing Japanese regulations on rice collection and pricing were null and void and that Korea's agricultural products would be sold at free-market prices. Landowners could collect no more than a third of the rice harvest from their tenants, a formula advocated by the Korean People's Republic. When coupled with land reform — which applied only to former Japanese-owned lands—the free pricing program promised to feed all Koreans and reduce the attraction of more radical rural communalism. The promise of more rice, however, turned out to be a forlorn hope. Autumn storms ruined part of the harvest, and another portion of it perished when free farmers refused to harvest the rice on abandoned Japanese land unless they could be guaranteed a rich return for their labor. Speculators rushed into the distribution vacuum and bought up tons of 1945 rice for sale to Japan. The military government reimposed price controls and a governmental purchasing program in less than a month, but the damage had been done.[29]

Other aspects of the military government's recovery program showed more heartening promise. By November, Governor Arnold reported that a Korean court system was functioning and that only crimes against American lives and property committed by Koreans would be tried by military tribunals. The Korean National Police, supervised by American-educated Cho Pyong-ok, a reformist member of the Korean Democratic Party, was undergoing expansion and retraining through a new American-directed police academy, which graduated thirteen hundred new officers. On the economic front, the limited renaissance of southern zone industry proceeded through the New Korea Corporation, a governmental agency with American and Korean directors that attempted to put the Japanese-owned businesses back in operation. In some cases, this meant displacing labor committees sponsored by the Korean People's Republic, which were better at making demands for fair labor practices than at running a factory. The military government accepted the creation of the National Council of Labor Unions (its abbreviated Korean name, *chonpyong,* emphasized struggle), which rapidly claimed more than a million members.

Some of the reforms reached heroic proportions. To restore the cultural integrity of Korean primary and secondary schools, the Department of Education, advised by Horace H. Underwood and his son Horace G. Underwood, employed Professor Choe Hyon-bae, a renowned scholar of Korean culture and education at Chosun Christian College, to prepare a new family of textbooks. Emerging from a Japanese prison in 1945 after three years of almost solitary confinement, Professor Choe brought with him his notes for new books that would eliminate not only Japanese cultural indoctrination but also two thousand Chinese characters. The mix of traditional Chinese ideograms and Korean *hangul* words had always been a barrier to popular education. In addition, Professor Choe, working with two Korean colleagues, prepared books that could be printed in Western fashion—front to back with pages turned to the left, pages read from left to right and from top to bottom—a reform that made the use of modern printing presses, typewriters, and writing instruments easier. Disposing of Japanese textbooks proved no problem; Koreans burned them for warmth. When the first new books were ready for distribution in November 1945, Professor Choe could not stop the book burning, which was sometimes abetted by book vendors who found that books-for-fuel paid more than government contracts for shipping books. Books sent to the major cities moved by train, but only with permits, escorts, and bonding agreements. Isolated rural areas could be reached only by truck, and the Department of Education used army trucks with American officers and enlisted men to move books throughout the country, accompanied by Korean representatives selected by Professor Choe. One such team, braving weather and bad roads, traveled over five thousand miles and delivered more than a million books between January and March 1946.[30]

General Hodge tolerated the organization of broadly based popular organizations, even those that looked suspiciously like Communist fronts. In December 1945 alone, the military government accepted the legitimacy of the National League of Peasants' Unions, the Korean Democratic Youth League, and the Women's League, as well as more than fifty groups claiming to be political parties. What Hodge would not tolerate was a parallel government. First, he eliminated the private armies sponsored by the Korean People's Republic and the Korean provisional government by outlawing all armed groups except for the U.S. Army and the Korean National Police. A small army that called itself the "Boy Scouts" numbered fifty thousand members, only fifteen thousand of whom were under the age of eighteen. The military government banned the wearing of "Boy Scout" uniforms and reorganized a true Scouting organization in 1946, starting with twelve-year-olds. At the same time, Hodge received approval from MacArthur and Washington to organize a "police reserve" or national constabulary, which would eventually replace American soldiers and Korean National Police officers on routine security duties and provide a cohesive riot-control force to reinforce the police. An incident at Namwon, a town in Chollanam-do, encouraged the process: during a riot over the occupation of some buildings, American military police fired into the mob and killed two Koreans and wounded sixty. Initially, Hodge's proposal—Plan Bamboo—assumed that the new force would absorb the private armies and provide jobs for unemployed veterans. Similar plans administered by the U.S. Army in the Philippines and Cuba almost fifty years before had helped weaken resistance to American occupation. Feeling relatively confident that he could now shape events rather than simply respond to recurring crises, Hodge issued a proclamation on December 12 that declared that any actions taken by Koreans in the name of the Korean People's Republic were unlawful and that those who attempted to exercise governmental authority would be subject to prosecution. Such actions also delayed progress toward Korean independence.[31]

The basic barrier to Korean unification and independence in December 1945, however, was not the harried remnants of the Korean People's Republic but Washington's conviction that any permanent "solution" to the "Korean problem" required a formal agreement among the United States, the Soviet Union, Great Britain, and Nationalist China. The British and Chinese governments faded from the issue of Korea's future by their own choice and by American design. The Soviet Union, however, waited to see what the United States would propose before it made any concessions on the economic issues that were so urgent to the military government, specifically, the availability of electric power and coal and the flooding of the southern zone with worthless currency. Hodge, Benninghoff, and Langdon concluded that the Russian generals in Pyongyang would remain uncooperative until Marshal Stalin directed them to behave otherwise—a sound evaluation. The State Department—from John Carter Vincent (director, Bureau of Far Eastern Affairs) to Undersecretary Dean Acheson to Secretary of State James F. Byrnes—clung to a concept dear to Franklin Roosevelt: that postcolonial nations should pass through some period of education on Western political values and practices and economic development before receiving international recognition as sovereign states. This trusteeship system might fall under the new United Nations organization, but in the short term, it would probably work best if established by the Allied victors and occupiers of World War II.[32]

In the autumn of 1945 the trusteeship idea appealed to almost no one outside of the State Department and its champions in the media and foreign policy elite. The Soviets had shown no interest in the concept, except when it might offer them greater leverage in some country where they had been excluded by American design, which meant Japan. Stalin certainly was not going to surrender his control of the Eastern European countries that the Soviet army had bled to liberate so that local Communists could form new pro-Soviet governments. Many aspiring new nations saw trusteeship as simply neocolonialism, however well-intentioned, and native leaders (certainly in Korea) regarded trusteeship as a new name for popular-front provisional governments that would soon commit suicide, assisted by local Communists. True Marxist-Leninists, as well as socialists and radical nationalists, thought that trusteeship was an international capitalist plot that would favor only a class of neocolonial native exploiters who would continue the enslavement of peasants and workers. Native leaders who accepted trusteeship as an expedient compromise qualified for a favorite English word: *lackey*. Even the Americans could not present a consistent approach in Asia, where they rushed the Philippines to independence in 1946, but not Korea. The only real difference between the Filipinos and the Koreans in terms of economic distress and social upheaval was that the Soviet army did not occupy Luzon forty miles above Manila or help the Communist Hukbalahap insurgents establish a government at Baguio.

The State Department, however, still regarded trusteeship as a potential path to a unified Korea, a position that John Carter Vincent made clear in a speech to the Foreign Policy Association on October 20, 1945. The speech and subsequent American press coverage alarmed Hodge and his advisers as well as every Korean political leader who could find a newspaper reporter or American official. The timing could not have been worse, since Secretary Byrnes was scheduled to meet the Soviets in Moscow in December to discuss a wide range of unresolved political issues left over from World War II. Hodge's expectation was that the Moscow conference might help him with the economic problems in his zone; he was less sanguine that the Russians would agree to any scheme that would move Korea toward independence and the withdrawal of all foreign troops. Hodge, MacArthur, and Langdon thought that the best option was to end both military occupations and let the Koreans fight it out. Hodge and MacArthur knew that despite their persistent reports that trusteeship was not going to please the Koreans, the State Department was unmoved. However, American officials and the Koreans found it more expedient to blame the Russians for the trusteeship proposal. Predictably, Syngman Rhee led the chorus of anti-Soviet political spokesmen in Seoul, and no other political leader found merit in the concept before Byrnes went to Moscow.[33]

Although Ambassador W. Averell Harriman warned the State Department that it should be cautious about appeasing the Russians, Secretary of State Byrnes arrived in Moscow for the foreign ministers' conference (December 16–27, 1945) convinced that he had one last chance to negotiate meaningful agreements with the Soviet Union that would advance the peaceful reconstruction of Europe and Asia. His initial proposals for an agreement that might produce a unified, independent Korea included the concept of a Great Powers trusteeship that could last as long as five years. The American and Soviet occupation authorities would organize a joint administrative structure that would unite the two occupation zones with a common economic and transportation system. Korean participation was not addressed, but it was not excluded either. Stripped of their complexities, the American proposals offered the prospect of nation-building reforms first and the creation of a single Korean government later. The Soviets wanted a provisional Korean government first and reforms second, which reflected their optimism that the Koreans north and south would find the American concept of trusteeship so objectionable that their outrage would accelerate their march on the road to socialism. The Soviets responded to Byrnes's proposals with a counterproposal: the United States and the USSR should establish a Joint Commission in Korea that would represent the occupation commanders. This commission would address the general issue of creating a unified interim Korean government, along with the specific issues of economic integration and human rights related to travel, political activity, interzonal communication and mail service, and religious freedom. The Joint Commission might consider proposals to preserve public order and the phased withdrawal of foreign troops. With minor changes in language, Byrnes accepted the Soviet proposal on December 21, and its terms leaked to the press before the final communiqué of December 27. Along with some concessions to the realities of power in Eastern Europe, the Korea agreement appeared to be a victory for renewed Allied cooperation and hardly seemed like a trusteeship for Korea at all—except to the Koreans and the military government.[34]

In the Soviet zone the Moscow agreement allowed the Soviets to disband Cho Man-sik's Democratic Party—and to do so with the justification that Cho and his middle-class Christian followers now endangered the prospect of a unified Korea by opposing a trusteeship. On January 2 Cho met with his central committee and won its approval of an anti–Moscow agreement statement. Choe Yong-gun and Kim Chaek conveniently missed the meeting. Three days later, the thirty-two members of the plenum of the People's Committee of Pyongyang and the Five Province Administrative Bureau met to discuss implementation of the Moscow agreement.

The vote swung toward approving the agreement, as the sixteen Communist delegates needed only one other vote to create an anti-Cho majority. Cho Man-sik again denounced the Moscow agreement and walked out with his party's delegates. Within days, Soviet military police arrested him on charges of treason and conspiracy with American and Japanese agitators and placed the dignified old patriot under house arrest in the Koryo Hotel. Months later, the Russians spirited him off to jail, where he lived in illness and isolation until his execution in 1950. Choe Yong-gun took over the chairmanship of the Democratic Party and turned it into a pro–Moscow agreement party.[35]

The reaction to the Moscow agreement in Seoul carried great import for General Hodge and the military government as well as all the major actors in the discordant southern Korean political arena. As soon as the Moscow agreement became common knowledge in Seoul, Hodge launched a major damage-control operation to ease Korean fears that the Russians were coming through the agency of the Joint Commission and some indefinite all-Korea provisional government. Rhee was no help, temporarily silent and watching the growing disarray. Hodge talked with Song Chin-u to ensure that the Korean Democratic Party would not rush to judgment. Hodge asked him to intercede with Kim Ku, whose anti-trusteeship obsession would surely lead to inflammatory words and might actually produce a coup attempt, however doomed. With the police under the control of Korean Democratic Party stalwarts Cho Pyong-ok and Chang Taek-sang, as well as the U.S. Army military police, the provisional government's underground militia, youth groups, and street mobs would have no chance. Hodge, however, wanted to avoid the use of force against a movement that he still regarded as the best hope for a strong, popular political base in southern Korea and the potential foundation of any future Korean government, unified or not. Song may have met Kim Ku during the night of December 29–30. What is certain is that Kim Ku refused to help Hodge, and in the early morning of December 30, assassins associated with Kim Ku murdered Song Chin-u, who became the first but not the last major political figure to die before 1950.

Hodge tried to distance himself from the Moscow agreement by explaining that the assumed "tutelage" and "trusteeship" provisions sounded worse than they were and that he had not abandoned the goal of a unified Korea and Korean involvement in the governing process. The State Department reassured the general that he could stress economic issues as the Joint Commission's highest priority, and its instructions gave Hodge wide latitude in setting economic priorities. In his public statements to the Koreans by press and radio, Hodge stated that the Korean People's Republic had become a barrier to independence, that the military government would overcome the existing economic problems, and that the Joint Commission would be the first step to independence. Protests would only prolong trusteeship and economic distress. Predictably, Kim Ku denounced Hodge and the agreement, but the demonstrations in Seoul by every political faction did not turn violent, in part because—for once—the Seoul metropolitan police did not attack the protesters. Korean participants in the military government did not come to work for several days, and some staged limited sit-ins and picketing. The protesters' signs and chants alternated between Korean and English, so the foreign media would get the anti-trusteeship message. Following Song's death, Kim Ku's public rhetoric escalated as he called for permanent work stoppages, demonstrations, disruptions of military government business, physical attacks on Korean employees of Hodge's regime and his "collaborator" supporters, and major economic strikes. Kim Ku even issued several proclamations announcing that he was taking over the government. His patience exhausted, Hodge called Kim Ku to his office and may have threatened him with arrest, trial, and execution for treason. Kim Ku countered with a threat to commit suicide on the spot. This droll exchange ended with Kim Ku pleading that he had been misunderstood and that he shared the American general's deep suspicion of the Russians and Communists of any nationality. The coup attempt—if that was what it was—ended January 1 with Kim Ku replacing Syngman Rhee on Hodge's list of untrustworthy politicians. The excitement, however, had not ended.[36]

While Hodge coped with Kim Ku's attempt to make the provisional government the only political power in Seoul, the factions of the Korean People's Republic also took to the streets to protest the Moscow agreement. Yo Un-hyong's People's Party and Pak Hon-yong's Communists marched arm in arm, banners and placards in bright array, chants against trusteeship and all forms of neocolonialism in full throat. On January 3, however, the Communists reversed their position on the Moscow agreement, probably on instructions from Pyongyang relayed through the Russian consul in Seoul. Quickly the banners and placards changed as the protesters painted out "Down with Trusteeship" and replaced it with "Up with Trusteeship." The reversal now aligned Pak Hon-yong with both the Russians *and* the military government, a shift that so outraged all the other Korean factions that one wonders if Pyongyang wanted to kill the Communist movement in the American zone. On the evening of January 3 the representatives of ninety-one protest groups held a conference in Seoul and passed a series of resolutions condemning the Communists. One resolution called for the military government to arrest Pak Hon-yong and try him for subversion and treason and then execute him. A rumor spread throughout the city that Pak Hon-yong hoped that the Soviet Union would annex Korea as one of its many race-based Asian republics. Pak's apostasy wrecked his credibility with many Koreans and made him and his disciples fair game for suppression by the military government, which was happy to cast Pak as the villain preventing independence, replacing General Hodge.[37]

Hodge's critics, however, especially the unfriendly media and the State Department, believed that the general had undermined the Moscow agreement, an act of indiscipline or a conscious act sanctioned by a "higher authority" that wanted to discredit Byrnes and the agreement. It is more likely that Hodge knew that President Truman and the War Department, as well as General MacArthur, had serious reservations about the Joint Commission. As early as December 30, the president openly questioned Byrnes's judgment. Byrnes himself admitted the same day that a Korean trusteeship might not be necessary. Undersecretary Dean Acheson immediately distanced himself from John Carter Vincent and his Asian specialists. MacArthur's own political adviser joined the critics of the Moscow agreement. Hodge discussed the issue with two important visitors, Secretary of War Robert Patterson and Assistant Secretary of War John J. McCloy. When Patterson came to Seoul in January 1946, Hodge offered to resign his post and retire, but the secretary reassured him that although he had to go through with the Joint Commission commitment, the War Department expected no miracles. Patterson, Ambassador Harriman, and the Joint Chiefs of Staff appreciated Hodge's strong leadership in Korea and understood his problems. In essence, Hodge was right back where he had been when he first stepped ashore at Inchon: he was still responsible for creating some sort of political leverage in Korea that would strengthen American negotiations with the Soviet Union for an independent, unified Korea. Privately, Hodge doubted that this faint hope was realistic. He believed that the only viable alternative was to build the foundation of an independent government for southern Korea regardless of Soviet protests and noncooperation.

3

Putting Korea Together Again: The Rise and Fall of the US-USSR Joint Commission, 1946–1947

With as much pomp and circumstance as his XXIV Corps could muster—and the military policemen outnumbered the bandsmen—Lt. Gen. John R. Hodge and his staff welcomed the Russians to Seoul on January 15, 1946, for the first meeting of the United States–Union of Soviet Socialist Republics Joint Commission. The first meeting would establish the commission's agenda and organization. The purpose of the Joint Commission was to put Korea back together. However, all the president's generals and all the premier's generals could not reassemble their separate Korean occupation zones. The negotiators produced no formula that their respective governments would accept, because neither Marshal Stalin nor President Truman wanted to risk even a small diplomatic defeat when there were greater stakes in China and Japan. The Koreans themselves did little to work with the four powers (Nationalist China and Great Britain abstaining) that had agreed to work toward an independent, unified Korea. After a year of futile negotiations, Korea marched a step closer to civil war.[1]

Whatever his reservations about the value of the conference, General Hodge played his role of host without a misstep. The Russians, seventy-three in number, traveled to Seoul in a nine-car armored train bulging with weapons and special communications gear. Two of the cars were gondolas filled with coal, a token gift and reminder of who controlled Korea's coalfields. Armed Russian guards surrounded the train as soon as it pulled into Seoul Station. Hodge had no comment. The Russians made the short drive to Doksu Palace in the heart of downtown Seoul without incident; the boulevards had been cleared of local traffic by the Seoul metropolitan police. The two delegations posed for pictures in front of the palace's Marble Hall, built in 1909 by King Kojong to receive Western visitors and hold important negotiations. The palace grounds could not produce a blaze of flowers in January, but the ornamental trees and shrubs gave some grace to the flow of uniformed officers and dark-suited diplomats that shuffled into the grand hall for the opening ceremonies. Col. Gen. Terentii F. Shtykov set the tone for media relations in his first and only statement at Doksu Palace: "I will not tell you anything." The Soviet delegation followed its chief, the political officer of the Soviet army in northern Korea. Shtykov brought two key members of his staff, Maj. Gen. G. I. Shanin and Maj. Gen. Alexei A. Romanenko. The Soviet foreign ministry sent one of its rising stars, S. K. Tsarapkin, head of the United States Division of the Foreign Ministry, a protégé of V. M. Molotov and Andrei Vishinsky and later the Soviet ambassador to the United Nations and to the United States.[2]

The American delegation understood its negotiating position. It surrendered nothing to the Soviets in ability, but its makeup must have impressed the Russians by the fact that the American participants were a long way from Washington in space and spirit. The chief of the American delegation was Maj. Gen. Archibald V. Arnold, U.S. Army, a Military Academy graduate (1912) too old to be a member of any army inner circle. Arnold shared wartime service in the Pacific with a close friend, MacArthur's invaluable operations officer Maj. Gen. Stephen J. Chamberlin, a West Point classmate. Arnold came to Korea in command of the Seventh Infantry Division, which he had led with distinction since 1943. Arnold's deputy was Maj. Gen. Archer L. Lerch, a graduate of the University of California–Berkeley (1917) and George Washington University (LLB, 1942), a reserve officer who became a career army judge advocate. For the last two years of World War II, Lerch served as the army's provost marshal general or chief policeman. He came to Korea as a key member of the occupation government and replaced Arnold as military governor in January 1946. The generals, however, depended on two foreign service officers, Howland H. Sargeant and Arthur C. Bunce, who provided expertise on the prior negotiations in Moscow and Cairo as well as a detailed knowledge of Korea's economic woes.[3]

The conference held fifteen sessions in Marble Hall between January 16 and February 5, 1946, and produced nothing that suggested any future agreement. General Hodge asserted that the American goals in the negotiations had not changed since the Moscow conference's official communiqué: (1) to eliminate the Thirty-eighth Parallel as a de facto boundary; (2) to organize a US-USSR commission that would work with the Korean political leadership to establish a unified and independent Korean nation; and (3) to draft a US-USSR plan to assist Korea in economic development, educational reform, transportation and communications restoration, and the creation of representative political institutions. The American delegation had instructions to avoid fundamental political issues—which looked intractable—and to concentrate on improving economic ties between the two occupation zones. Faced with growing shortages of fuel and electricity, the military government hoped that it could trade a small rice surplus to the Soviets for coal, raw materials, fertilizer, and hydroelectric power. The Russians made vague promises of economic cooperation and to open up rail and postal communications with southern Korea, but their interest was in creating a provisional government for all of Korea. The Russians believed that northern Korea's economic leverage over the

American occupation zone could be transformed into a formula for political participation in a transitional government that would work to the advantage of the Korean Communists. The Russian position from first to last left no room for misinterpretation: any political group that had publicly opposed the Moscow agreement had forfeited its right to be consulted on the timing and form of any future Korean government. This position would exclude every southern Korean political association except the Communists.[4]

Nevertheless, the delegations followed their instructions to convene the Joint Commission sometime in the near future. The two delegations agreed to hold wide consultations with Korean leaders in the two occupation zones and to examine the leadership and platforms of the hundreds of groups that claimed to be legitimate political parties. The Russians remained stubborn on economic issues, although they suggested that they had a rice shortage. They would not discuss reparations, capital goods issues, currency reform, the transfer of fertilizer and concrete for rice, or any other measure that would advance economic integration. The Russians also rejected any proposal that the occupation authorities allow parallel Korean negotiations on unification. The Americans concluded that the Russians feared the popularity of Kim Ku's provisional government coalition, the bedrock of anti-Soviet agitation.[5]

When the Joint Commission assembled for its official meetings in Seoul, March 20–May 18, 1946, the Soviet and American delegations returned to the issue of Korean representation in any future all-Korean constitutional process. The Russians did not retreat from their restricted definition of political legitimacy. In fact, they insisted that the anti-trusteeship parties were really antireform and pro-Japanese. As postcolonial parasites, these Koreans could not be allowed to participate in forming an interim government. The principal accomplishment of the Joint Commission's meetings was Joint Communiqué No. 5 (April 18, 1946), which allowed anti–Moscow agreement groups to recant their opposition to trusteeship and qualify for consultation about any future provisional government. The communiqué represented a modest tactical American victory, but it could be interpreted as a leftist coup.

The American delegation, headed by General Arnold but guided by State Department political officers in Washington and Seoul, informed the Russians that the military government had appointed its own advisory group, the Representative Democratic Council, composed of twenty-five prominent nationalist politicians including Syngman Rhee, Kim Ku, Kim Kyu-sik, and An Chae-hong. Though invited, Yo Un-hyong decided at the last minute not to cooperate, as did two other leaders of the People's Party. When the council called a rally to protest the work of the Joint Commission, a crowd of 200,000 filled the streets of Seoul in March 1946. Hodge's political advisers estimated the strength of the southern Communist party at only 15,000. They correctly predicted that southern Korean politics would become even more anti-Communist with the integration and mobilization of an estimated 1.5 million refugees from Manchuria, the Soviet zone, and Japan. With major land reform of some sort likely in the American zone, it appeared that the negotiating strength of the Americans and southern Koreans was in the ascendency.[6]

When the Joint Commission adjourned on May 8, 1946, still at an impasse over how to form a new Korean national government, General Hodge and his State and War Department directors in Washington had already begun a reevaluation of occupation policy in the southern zone. The issue was whether to proceed with the "Koreanization" of the military government, even to the point where a de facto Korean government might emerge. The nub of the problem was whether Hodge could or should hold some sort of election in the southern zone. Seoul and Washington had no illusions about the need for drastic economic action in southern Korea; all the economic indicators suggested that the 1945 rice crop would soon be exhausted and that the 1946 rice crop under government control would not meet the needs of a hungry population swollen with refugees. Ambassador Edwin Pauley reported to President Truman that unless the military government received more economic support, the Communists would hold the political initiative with their appeals for land reform, the redistribution of wealth, and the ruthless elimination of Japanese collaborators, broadly defined. Like his advisers, Truman approved of more aggressive administrative and economic reform in the American zone, with more "representative" Koreans moving ahead in the administrative departments. There would not, however, be a Korean government, because neither Kim Ku nor Syngman Rhee could govern without confusion and corruption. The Americans believed that Kim Kyu-sik had all the proper progressive values, but he had no power base and no talent for leadership. Yo Un-hyong and Pak Hon-yong were demagogues of the Left, probably under orders from Pyongyang, or so it appeared. In any event, the Truman administration would not quite give up on the Joint Commission, even though it admitted that the Moscow agreement appeared wounded.[7]

Hodge dispatched General Arnold to Washington in October 1946 to hammer out a political plan for southern Korea based on the assumption that the Soviet Union would never accept an elected, representative provisional government unless the Americans agreed to disenfranchise every political group in the south except the People's Party and the Communist Party. In any event, the growing economic crisis in the American zone needed immediate attention; linking Korean economic recovery with Japan's had caused all sorts of problems, including salt and soya shortages, trade barriers, the diversion of scarce consumer goods, and currency and credit problems. The Korean Left seemed committed to a position of permanent noncooperation and subversion, while the Right seemed content to build its popularity at the expense of the military government and to take its case to the mobs in the streets. Arnold admitted that too many Korean Democratic Party and provisional government veterans held office in the military government in Seoul, especially in the national police and financial agencies, but there was no pool of apolitical replacements for them. Honesty and efficiency seemed to be unknown in the Korean political lexicon. People who were living on less than fifteen hundred calories a day would not embrace Jeffersonian democracy, even if Soviet socialism eventually lost its theoretical appeal. The first task was to strengthen southern Korea, not push ahead with Joint Commission negotiations.[8]

GOVERNING TWO KOREAS

While its delegation fiddled in Seoul, the Russians and the Korean Communist coalition in Pyongyang burned with urgency to build socialism in one part of Korea. Before the dawn of the new year, General Chistiakov reduced the forced reparations program and ordered industrial facilities to be repaired and made operative, not packed off to the Soviet Union. The nationalization of factories and banks continued apace, along with the confiscation of land and property held by "class enemies," defined not just by collaboration with the Japanese but also by education, religion, and class status. Kim Il-sung played his role as ardent wrecker of the old order at party meetings and mass rallies. He preached that Sovietization was the only road away from Japanese colonialism. If the northern Koreans did not build a strong state quickly, they would fall prey to the Japanese and American capitalists, who planned to strip Korean wealth through an alliance with the new collaborators, Kim Ku and Syngman Rhee. The Russians and the "real Koreans" would triumph through sacrifice, industry, and a complete commitment to the immutable principles of socialism.[9]

After six months of hurried recruitment, thorough screening, and minimal training, the Russian and Korean administrative leaders formed the foundation of a national internal security organization that concentrated all police functions in the Security Bureau, later the Ministry of the Interior, headed by Choe Yong-gun. The Security Bureau forces included civil police, firefighters, prison guards and administrators, criminal investigators, intelligence operatives, a national constabulary, a border patrol, maritime police, and a railway constabulary. By July 1946, the Security Bureau forces may have numbered as many as ten thousand uniformed personnel. At the same time, the Communists organized a system of military training agencies, dominated from the first by Kim Il-sung and his Kapsan faction. The first agency, the Pyongyang Institute, started its initial class in January 1946 and graduated this class in April. At the institute's official opening ceremony, Kim Il-sung challenged the class to be the elite officers in a future People's Army. The institute, directed by Kim Chaek, provided military training and political indoctrination for the coming struggle against Japanese imperialism and Korean capitalism. In July 1946 the Pyongyang Institute took the mission of training military-political officers, while a new Central Security Officers School (also near Pyongyang) began training officers for operational and technical leadership in the combat and service units of a future army. At the same time, June–August 1946, the north Koreans established three Security Cadres Training Centers, which started basic military training for the rank and file of a future army. Although Kim Il-sung's faction held the majority of leadership positions in the training command, key members of the Yanan faction (Pak Hyo-sam and Kim Mu-chong) and the Soviet faction (An Kil) took assignments in the military bureaucratic structure. By the end of 1946, the Russians, who provided as many as eight hundred advisers and administrative personnel to the system, provided a steady flow of Russian weapons and equipment to the five training commands, replacing weapons seized from the Japanese. After a short period of ordnance largesse, the Russians demanded that the Koreans pay for their weapons with foodstuffs and raw materials. Although the Koreans received some light field guns, they did not get heavy artillery, self-propelled guns, tanks, or other types of armored fighting vehicles.[10]

The American-Korean military government in the southern occupation zone attempted to bring some order and public well-being to the Korean people—against the opposition of the Korean political elite. No doubt war-weariness, cultural insensitivity, indiscipline, ignorance, impatience, and the primitive living conditions made the soldiers of the U.S. XXIV Corps and the military government tiresome occupiers after the Japanese departed, but Korea's problems were more deeply rooted in the circumstances of liberation, decolonization, and the breakdown of public order in all its forms. Crimes against persons and property increased in 1946 until the reorganized Korean National Police (KNP) took back the streets with an enthusiasm for quick physical punishment and forced confessions that rivaled that of their Japanese predecessors. Inflation, the scarcity of food and consumer goods, and low pay encouraged the policemen to invent extortion schemes great and small, which outraged the public they were supposed to protect. American advisers curbed bad behavior by the police with increased training and indoctrination, but with limited success. The one success the KNP had was preventing any leftists from joining its ranks; its recruitment practices favored refugees from northern Korea, veterans of the Japanese-sponsored military and security services, Christians, and members of small-town property-owning families, however humble. The senior leadership of the KNP had close ties to the conservative Korean Democratic Party, but not the Kim Ku faction. The only potential armed rivals the police would tolerate consisted of a group of paramilitary youth associations, the most powerful of which was Yi Pom-sok's National Youth Corps.[11]

With the paramilitary and militia forces formed by the political parties outlawed and disbanded in early 1946, the military government found itself with a "security gap." Keenly aware of the potential civil affairs and media disaster that might occur if American troops killed Korean civilians as thieves or mass protesters, Hodge wanted some other force to guard high-value industrial and transportation facilities as well as back up the KNP on riot duty. Although the War Department approved Hodge's plan for a 45,000-man army, the State Department disapproved of the concept of a "military" force, which the Russians would condemn, and the proposed size of the force. The compromise scheme, Plan Bamboo, was to create a 25,000-man "police reserve." Plan Bamboo received State Department approval on January 6, 1946, and Hodge ordered Military Governor Lerch to recruit the first companies of what would become nine light infantry regiments of the Korean Constabulary, with one regiment stationed in each of southern Korea's eight provinces and one on Cheju island. The director of national defense, Col. Arthur S. Champeny, appointed Lt. Col. John T. Marshall as the Constabulary's first commander and charged him with recruiting Korean officers; U.S. Army officers transferred from the departing Fortieth Infantry Division formed up the first three companies at a Japanese barracks at Nowon, a small town northeast of Seoul on the road to Chunchon. The members of "private armies" had until January 21, 1946, to surrender their arms and apply for membership in the Constabulary. After that date, they became outlaws.[12]

Colonel Marshall took personal charge of selecting Constabulary officers, advised by an American major, a Nisei corporal, and two young Korean officer-aspirants who spoke English. The original plan envisioned granting sixty commissions (twenty each) to veterans of the Japanese Imperial Army, the Manchukuo army, and Koreans in the Chinese service, such as the Kwangbok ("restoration") army. The latter officers, aligned with Kim Ku's provisional government faction, boycotted the selection interviews. The "first class," or the first 110 officers of the Constabulary (less two), consisted of veterans of the Japanese army, all but two serving as officers. A major determinant in the selection process was educational level and potential utility in a force that would use U.S. Army manuals and be trained by American officers.

The selection process stressed rapid decisions. Officer-aspirants reported to either a Methodist seminary in Seoul or a Japanese army barracks at Taenung, just outside the city. The first twenty-nine candidates that satisfied Marshall assembled at the seminary, where the U.S. Army officers assigned to command the Constabulary regiments picked their Korean subordinates. As they awaited selection, the candidates practiced their English, which gave the seminary and the group the misleading title of "Military English Language School." There was no formal military or English-language training until the second recruitment campaign began in June 1946. Before the first 110 officers of the Constabulary took commissions, they did receive some military instruction, but that first class specialized in on-the-job training, with all its perils and irregularities.

The Constabulary officers had different military experiences. Twenty-two of the new officers had attended a Japanese or Manchurian military academy, really an officer candidate course rather than a school. The largest single group (seventy-two officers) had entered Japanese service as *hakpyong,* or university students under compulsory military training; this group had been called to active duty in 1944–1945 and attended screening courses before being given administrative assignments, since the Japanese army did not favor Koreans commanding Japanese soldiers. As a group, the *hakpyong* were young, well-educated Korean nationalists who became the most reform-minded (and pro-American) officers of the Constabulary. Of the entire first class, seventy-five became general officers of the Hanguk Gun, or Army of the Republic of Korea (ROKA). The fifteen most senior officers were veterans of the Japanese and Manchukuo armies. Of these fifteen senior Constabulary officers, four became chiefs of staff of the ROKA, two were chairmen of the Korean Joint Chiefs of Staff, and another a lieutenant general. One was discharged for cheating on an examination but returned to the army in 1950 and retired as a brigadier general, two more retired as colonels, three resigned their commissions before 1950, and two officers were imprisoned and discharged for Communist sympathizing.[13]

Although the first group of Constabulary officers was relatively young—most of them were in their twenties—their initial difficulties came not from inexperience but from their attachment to Japanese concepts. Japanese blouses, Sam Browne belts, and samurai swords did not suggest a new order, as the Russians complained. Corporal punishment and maladministration produced the first mutiny in March 1946, when twenty sergeants of the First Battalion, First Constabulary Regiment, presented their commander, a former military police captain in the Manchukuo army, with a petition of grievances signed in blood. The captain denounced the men as traitors and ordered their arrest, whereupon the sergeants assaulted their commander and other officers. The beatings were so serious that the battered officers required hospitalization. The Constabulary commander, Lt. Col. Russell D. Barros, a veteran of guerrilla warfare in the Philippines, discovered that the sergeants had also sent their petition to Kim Ku, who championed their protest against corruption and brutality. Barros discharged the sergeants without formal charges and sent the officers to other commands. The senior officer went to the new Fourth Regiment at Kwangju. He was Chung Il-kwon, later army chief of staff and a favorite of the American advisers.[14]

The First Regiment's mutiny only dramatized the difficulty of starting an instant army with uncertain personnel and only a handful of inexperienced American advisers, fewer than twenty-five during most of 1946. Barros, however, identified one adviser, Capt. James H. Hausman Jr., as an officer of exceptional interpersonal skills, sound infantry experience, abundant energy, and initiative. Tall, insouciant, and good-humored, Jim Hausman arrived in Korea in early 1946. He had already served in the U.S. Army for twelve years, having illegally enlisted at age sixteen to escape his father's domineering personality. James Sr. treated his second son like one of his New Jersey construction workers. In 1940, when the draft registration brought his fraudulent enlistment to light, First Sgt. Hausman, Fifth Infantry, managed to correct his service record and return to active duty as a reserve infantry lieutenant. His skill as a trainer doomed him to Stateside duty until 1944, when he went to Europe as the operations officer of an infantry battalion. Combat in the Battle of the Bulge put Captain Hausman in a shell hole for three days with a leg wound, gangrene, and frostbite. In 1945, however, he was just another reserve captain with a Combat Infantry Badge, a Bronze Star, a Purple Heart, and a limp, but he agreed to remain on active duty to attend the Advanced Infantry Officers Course at Fort Benning and the Military Government School, Carlisle Barracks, Pennsylvania. His willingness to accept a civil affairs assignment in Japan kept him in the army, but his orders took him to Seoul, not Tokyo. A thorough professional, Hausman so impressed Barros with his work with the Eighth Regiment, Korean Constabulary, that Barros brought Hausman to Seoul as his all-purpose executive officer for training and operations.[15]

Hausman arrived at Constabulary headquarters too late to influence the formation of the second class, a new group of candidates selected to attend a formal officer training school. The 263 candidates for the more structured eighty-day course were far more "representative" than the first class had been, and far more politicized. Thirty-five candidates had been officers in "foreign armies," which now included Chinese forces. Sixty more came from the enlisted ranks of the Constabulary to reward talented and meritorious noncommissioned officers. All the other candidates came from civil life, although some of them had served in the Japanese armed forces as enlisted men. By the time the second class graduated, it had shrunk to 196 men, 79 of whom eventually became generals. What could not be judged immediately was the new officers' political preferences; some of them came from the Kim Ku faction, while others were already Communists or would become so. Among the most radical candidates was a former Japanese army captain and left-wing nationalist from North Kyongsang Province (Kyongsangbuk-do) named Park Chung-hee, who would later serve as the general-president of South Korea from his coup in 1961 until his assassination in 1979 by Kim Chae-gyu, an associate from the second class and former director of the Korean Central Intelligence Agency. Lee Chi-op, deputy director of the officer training school, was convinced that Park tried to murder him during his tumultuous stay at the school. Park certainly used his participation in the second class to identify and recruit other revolutionaries for a Communist network within the Constabulary. Fleeing agents of the Korean National Police, members of the South Korean Labor Party found a refuge in the Constabulary, and the KNP refused to surrender any of its extensive dossiers on subversives to the Constabulary. Lee Chi-op later guessed that at least half the class had been either party members or sympathizers. Despite starting his own postwar career as a police commander, Lee received no aid from the KNP, even after he was almost beaten to death by several of Park's disciples.[16]

The Communists did not monopolize the flow of problem officers into the Constabulary, as Barros and Hausman knew. General Hodge did not pay much attention to the Constabulary, but Military Governor Archer Lerch, the optimistic lawyer-negotiator, saw the Constabulary as a home for the friends of Korea's political giants. Chae Pyong-duk, an amateur sumo wrestler and an arsenal supervisor in Seoul for the Japanese, had many local friends, as did Won Yong-dok, a Seoul society doctor who had served as a military surgeon and lieutenant colonel in the Manchukuo army. Members of the first class, "Fat" Chae and Doctor Won had favored access to Kim Ku and Syngman Rhee and flaunted the disciplinary sanctions against binge eating and drinking. The unreconstructed warlord of the second class was Song Ho-sung, a mysterious expatriate former colonel in a Chinese mercenary army as well as a Kwangbok army veteran who had close personal ties to Kim Ku and Yi Pom-sok. Other military figures with strange careers and interesting qualifications hovered in the background, unwilling to join the Constabulary while it remained under American control.[17]

The military government needed both a nonpartisan, professional national police force and an army, and it had neither as public unrest increased in 1946. Incidents of theft and violence involving Koreans and American troops reached such proportions that General Hodge cautioned his commanders that their continued service required better troop behavior; General Lerch complicated this situation by curbing the use of army provost-martial courts to punish Koreans, which almost guaranteed light sentences or acquittals for Korean suspects. Public health difficulties added to the tension. In January 1946 the southern occupation zone had a minor smallpox epidemic, which quite properly sent the army's medical establishment into an anti-plague mode of forced inoculation. In June 1946, with the start of the rainy season *(changma)*, the southernmost provinces were struck with a cholera epidemic. Despite a crash program of spraying, inoculations, quarantine, and travel restrictions—enforced by the Constabulary—cholera marched northward with the rains until the epidemic burned out in September. According to the military government's statistics, almost fifteen thousand Koreans had sickened and recovered, but more than nine thousand had died. The epidemic, however, did not prevent a crippling railroad strike or the increase of seaborne smuggling, which could not be stopped even by a special task force of U.S. Navy destroyer patrols.[18]

The military government saw its control of civic order in the American occupation zone attacked by nature. The fertilizer shortage had already cut rice production by 20 percent per hectare, and the 1946 rice crop suffered a further reduction of equal proportion owing to torrential summer rains. A three-day June deluge (twenty-five inches in the Han River watershed) swamped rice paddies and destroyed the delicate terraced irrigation systems. The harvest came a month later than usual. Faced with a famine following an epidemic, General Hodge ordered the Korean National Police to make lawful, forced rice collections for government distribution, but the policy looked like confiscation to the farmers, and the limited compensation smacked of a new colonialism. Only half of the military government's estimated rice needs—calculated to feed the urban population at reasonable prices—went into controlled public warehouses. Even Douglas MacArthur, usually inattentive to Korean affairs, reported to Washington that Korea needed 150,000 tons of rice immediately; he also stated that he would not be surprised if Soviet forces invaded southern Korea at the end of the disappointing rice harvest, when unrest would be at its peak. The peaceful occupation of Japan might even be affected by the impending disaster in Korea.[19]

THE AUTUMN HARVEST UPRISING

The lack of progress by the Joint Commission and the administrative trials faced by the military government set the stage for the first violent challenge to the American occupation in southern Korea. The general cause of unrest in the summer of 1946 was inflation (reflecting the power of the black market and the scarcity of consumer goods) and the increase in rice prices, fueled by Korean farmers' discontent over government rice collections and the stalled program of land reform. The effectiveness and duration of the Autumn Harvest Uprising (September–November 1946) also reflected the influence of the Korean Communist Party, principally directed by Pak Hon-yong. The Communists, however, still needed allies from the leftist oppositionist coalition, the Democratic People's Front, organized by Yo Un-yong in February. The Democratic People's Front brought leftist leaders together to challenge the popular appeal of the Emergency National Assembly, a rightist oppositionist coalition organized the same month and dominated by Kim Ku. Syngman Rhee refused to join the conservative Korean Democratic Party, whose sympathizers tried to buy his loyalty by paying his living expenses, and he rebuffed various overtures from Kim Ku to create a new coalition based on the Korean Independence Party.

Rhee distanced himself from both the American-sponsored Representative Democratic Council and the oppositionist Emergency National Assembly in order to strengthen his personal political organization, the National Society for the Rapid Realization of Korean Independence (NSRRKI). The society enjoyed some success in forming local groups all over the south as a counterforce to the Democratic People's Front. Embedded within and camouflaged by the "mass" political organizations were special action groups prepared to conduct urban riots and terrorist operations against both the military government (especially the KNP) and the political opposition. For the NSRRKI, the Korean Democratic Party, and the Korean Independence Party (the Kim Ku coalition), the political action groups centered on youth associations composed of rootless urban young men and northern refugees. Although the military government and the KNP attempted to place some of the youth associations—especially Yi Pom-sok's National Youth Corps—under government control as a paid police auxiliary, the youth associations could not be removed from the streets, where they confronted the Communist-dominated labor unions and other protest associations.[20]

General Hodge knew that suspension of the Joint Commission talks on May 8, 1946, would encourage the oppositionist parties that wanted to subvert the military government. He understood that the subversives included formidable clandestine groups of the Left and Right. He announced publicly that criticism of the military government and Joint Commission that encouraged political action would not be tolerated. The government's first target was the Chongpan-sa Printing Company, whose building also housed the headquarters of the Korean Communist Party and three Communist newspapers. The company's sin, however, was not just the editorial policies of its newspapers but also the use of its printing presses to produce counterfeit currency of the Bank of Chosun. Closing it down was not enough for the Right, however, which sent truckloads of youths to wreck the Chongpan-sa Printing Company, an act that brought about the suspension of the *Daedong-*

ilbo, a newspaper that supported Kim Ku. The summer campaign of the Korean National Police focused on the Communists. Three Communist papers were placed under permanent sanction, between twenty and thirty Communist leaders were either arrested or forced underground, and the Chongpyong (labor federation) headquarters was raided and its membership records impounded for intelligence purposes. When the surviving Communist leadership met to condemn Pak Hon-yong and the central committee for reckless adventurism, the military government raided a party assembly on September 29 and detained more than two hundred party leaders.[21]

In the meantime, Pak Hon-yong escaped the police sweeps of known Communist offices and homes and crossed the Thirty-eighth Parallel. He reached Pyongyang in early August, and that same month he and Kim Il-sung went to Moscow to confer with Stalin on increasing the aid to the southern Communists. The visit to the capital was the first for Pak and Kim, and they may have been part of an international trade delegation that toured Russian factories from August 24 to September 5. What is certain is that Stalin personally approved their request for filmmaking equipment, printing presses, and other technologies suitable for propaganda activities. General Shtykov endorsed the request, and the Soviet All-Union Society for Cultural Connections filled the order. The Soviets made no commitments to support an insurgency in the American zone if the Joint Commission made no progress.[22]

As the Joint Commission meetings limped to their inconclusive adjournment, the military government made a major political move after extended consultation with representatives from the State and War departments, who framed Hodge's guidance from Washington. The principal purpose of the political initiative in the American zone was to strengthen Hodge's hand in the next meeting of the Joint Commission, which the Americans assumed would occur. The Moscow agreement might be bleeding, but it was still alive. At the same time, however, any action that admitted Korean politicians to the military government raised the possibility that the United States would abandon the Moscow agreement's goal of unification and sponsor a new regime in its zone. After extended discussions in Seoul and Washington, the State Department published an interagency memorandum, "Policy for Korea," on June 6, 1946, that directed Hodge to attempt to form a Left-Right coalition led by Kim Kyu-sik and Yo Un-hyong. In Seoul, Hodge and his advisers accepted the proposition that a Moscow agreement settlement might still be a possibility, but they believed that their negotiations with Kim and Yo were the first step toward establishing a provisional government in southern Korea that would evolve toward an independent state.[23]

The military government proceeded with the delicate and complex task of pushing the Communists and Korean Independence Party (Kim Ku) to the margin of the political arena, aided inadvertently by Syngman Rhee, who resigned from the doomed Representative Democratic Council. William Langdon, Hodge's principal political adviser, believed that Kim Ku and Rhee, who flirted with the idea of southern Korean independence, had exhausted the popular appeal of opposing trusteeship and negotiations with the Soviets. Langdon and Second Lt.

Leonard Bertsch—a thirty-five-year old Akron, Ohio, lawyer turned civil affairs officer and a self-proclaimed constitutional law expert and political operative— spent much of the spring consulting with agents of the Representative Democratic Council, Korean Democratic Party, and People's Party on the issue of elections and a provisional government. Reforms in landholding and other economic issues dear to the Koreans would provide more leverage against the Soviets and address the deteriorating conditions in the American zone. On June 29, 1946, Langdon and Bertsch believed that the moderate coalition with Kim Kyu-sik and Yo Un-hyong at its head could provide the foundation for a future elected provisional government. The next day, General Hodge announced the formation of the Coalition Committee, which replaced the Representative Democratic Council, and charged it with designing the composition of an elected legislature, to be entitled the Interim Legislative Assembly. This assembly could develop programs for land reform, property sales, the purge of colonial collaborators, and political activity by the Koreans themselves. This process, which might lead to a separate Korean nation in the American zone, had President Truman's approval.[24]

Against the background of cholera, a torrential *changma,* rising prices, and food shortages, the military government faced another season of frustration in dealing with the Coalition Committee. Syngman Rhee remained officially aloof from any action that suggested compromise with the Soviets, but his NSRRKI built a following outside Seoul and attracted local organizers away from Kim Ku's Korean Independence Party and the People's Party. Rhee claimed that he stopped a potential coup organized by Shin Ik-hui (one of Kim Ku's closest associates and a patron of several unofficial intelligence organizations), the secret societies of the Right, the youth associations, and the Korean National Police. If Kim Kyu-sik and Yo Un-hyong fumbled their chance for national greatness, Rhee had to be considered a replacement, and he was certainly preferable to Kim Ku and his ilk or any of the Communists.[25]

The Democratic People's Front, the leftist coalition of ninety groups dominated by Communist leadership, did not let the military government search unchallenged for its "third force" of centrist organizations. The Communists made a number of charges against the Americans: that they sought to reestablish Japanese colonialism, rejected social and economic reform, corrupted all true nationalists who served them, and sought to remake Korea in some perverse Western image of the United States. In addition to the heat, floods, cholera, inflation, and food shortages, the Democratic People's Front capitalized on incidents of bad behavior by American troops and the inevitable friction between two groups of people of different cultural values; this friction was exacerbated by the military government's policy of nonfraternization and the provision of creature comforts, such as powered milk and scotch, only to Americans and their closest Korean associates. The immediate catalyst for the violence that struck the American zone in September–November 1946 was the protest marches by students and labor unions against rising prices, falling wages, and food shortages. The farmers marched against the

Korean National Police for its corrupt and heavy-handed collection of rice and rents.[26]

Just what role organizers of the Democratic People's Front played in provoking the 214 incidents of violence that constituted the Autumn Harvest Uprising of 1946 is uncertain, as is Soviet and north Korean involvement. The timing and location of the incidents, 140 of which occurred in the two Kyongsang provinces and their capitals, Taegu and Pusan, suggest a degree of coordination and cooperation that can be credited only to the Democratic People's Front. Small mobs (500 to 1,000 people) made almost 100 simultaneous attacks on separate police substations, assisted by the skilled use of prepared demolition and the cutting of telephone wires. The mobs contained small "action groups" that targeted the homes and businesses of prominent, affluent "rightists." Certainly the speeches and street bulletins rang with the rhetoric of Korean socialism.[27]

The uprising began in late September with a series of general strikes by railroad workers in Seoul, Pusan, and Taegu, the last city a hotbed of radicalism and discontent. After the first protest marches of September 23, industrial workers, farmers, students, and the urban underclass of the young and the unemployed joined the mobs that surged up and down the streets of most of Korea's southern cities and occupied police stations. The demonstrations turned violent when a policeman shot and killed a Taegu protestor on October 1, which set off a siege of Taegu's main police station. American intelligence officers estimated that the participants numbered 69,000 in the two Kyongsangs and 65,000 in the two Chollas. Between October 2 and 6, street mobs—modestly armed with farm tools and clubs—attacked stations and substations of the Korean National Police throughout North Kyongsang Province and the city of Taegu. The Taegu mob proved to be the most vicious, killing thirty-eight policemen. Fifteen more died in the province.

The pattern of violence in the Kyongsangs, in which 115 cities, towns, and villages became battlegrounds, pitted the rioters against the Korean National Police, small detachments of the Korean Constabulary, and American military policemen and infantry. The Constabulary commanders knew that they had Communists in their ranks and were thus reluctant to join the conflict. In the most prolonged and violent confrontations, American infantry in riot formations took the streets away from the rioters, in at least two cases by firing into the mobs with deadly effect. At Chinju and Masan on October 7, American soldiers killed 12 Koreans and wounded more than 100. The number of American troops committed to the fray in the Kyongsangs (the U.S. Twentieth Infantry Regiment and the Sixth Infantry Division Artillery) may have numbered 2,717 officers and men, but the Koreans (7,761 police and Constabulary members) carried the brunt of the battle. The targets of the riots were rice storage buildings, police stations and barracks, government offices, and the homes of prominent officials and property owners. If the police did not resist, they were often allowed to escape without their weapons and uniforms, but if the police fired on the mob and did not stop it, they died in battle or were tortured and executed in an orgy of murder. Policemen, youth auxiliaries, and officials were found impaled through the rectum, mutilated, burned, castrated, disemboweled, and buried alive. Deaths outside of Taegu among Korean security forces may have been as high as 82. The wounded and missing numbered between 100 and 250. The rioters suffered almost 200 dead and 260 wounded, and the security forces arrested 5,540 suspected Kyongsang rebels. The military government estimated that another 200 "rightists" had been killed, wounded, or captured. Of special concern to the security forces was the fact that about 300 military rifles and thousands of rounds of ammunition had disappeared, presumably into arms caches for some future uprising.

Although intelligence analysts disagreed about the level of organization that could be traced to Pak Hon-yong, they agreed that the Kyongsang mobs had shown more than bloodlust. One clue was the sabotage of bridges and roadways between cities; another was the reluctance of the rioters to engage American troops, an interesting demonstration of discipline that ran counter to the anti-Americanism of the leftist press. Additional evidence of planned events was the kidnapping of prominent citizens, the systematic destruction of police and tax records, and the use of disguises and ruses to dupe the Korean police. One cannot deny the existence of a popular Korean rage in 1946 that resurrected memories of the Tonghak rebellion of the 1890s, but the Autumn Harvest Uprising had too much structure to be dismissed as a spontaneous protest against the military government. American counterintelligence officers found sufficient documentary evidence to implicate the Korean Communist Party, its Young Men's Alliance auxiliary, and the local and regional People's Committees that had survived as clandestine organizations after 1945.[28]

As the uprising faded under military pressure in the two Kyongsang provinces, the revolt flared again in November 1946 in South Cholla Province (Chollanam-do) to the west. There were new outbreaks of bombings in Seoul and Inchon. With a month's experience in coping with the insurgency, the American intelligence officers in the region had little doubt that the underground People's Committees had organized the uprising. The two Cholla provinces were notorious for their resistance to any central authority, and the radicals of Cholla had always been at the strident edge of rabid Korean nationalism and revolutionary economic and social reform. If there was political polarization within the American occupation zone, it had divided the two Cholla provinces from the rest of the country. The network of Cholla revolutionaries ran into Seoul itself. Korean and American analysts placed 90 percent of the population of the two provinces in the oppositionist camp. However, the Autumn Harvest Uprising in South Cholla never took on the degree of violence that characterized the uprising in the Kyongsangs. The October riots made the uprising in November less surprising. The American troops, Korean police, and Constabulary required to stop the uprising numbered half those committed in the Kyongsangs. The number of riots mounted to only 59. The Korean security forces lost 10 killed, 33 wounded, and 11 captured or missing. In the attacks on police stations, 54 rebels died, 61 were wounded, and 357 were arrested. Civilian victims numbered fewer than 50, and the rebels captured and retained an insignificant number of military weapons. Although property damage was troubling, almost all of it fell on the police and the homes of policemen. Only three New Korea Company rice warehouses were damaged. In sum, the revolt in Cholla in November 1946 provided only a coda of futility to the more serious violence in the two Kyongsang provinces in October.[29]

The Autumn Harvest Uprising distressed General Hodge and his advisers— not to mention the American advisers to the Korean National Police and the Korean Constabulary—because it threatened the delicate negotiations with the Coalition Committee to establish a representative assembly in the American zone. Hodge conferred with his designated moderates. Kim Kyu-sik and Yo Un-hyong felt greater menace from Kim Ku's faction and the Korean Democratic Party than they did from the Communists, which Hodge thought naive. He was unwilling to act on their demand that he remove all the senior KNP officers (including Cho and Chang) and abolish the youth associations serving as KNP auxiliaries. Yo was especially sensitive to intimidation, since he had been kidnapped and held incommunicado for thirty-six hours; he had no idea who had abducted him or why, only that the police had shown no interest in the case. Yo guessed that the Right wanted him to break all contact with the Communists. Intelligence sources put Pak Hon-yong back in southern Korea after a trip to Pyongyang, suggesting Soviet involvement in the uprising. Yo Un-hyong, however, had also visited Pyongyang and returned with the impression that the Soviets and Kim Il-sung had not backed the revolt. Yo thought that Pak had made a pact with Kim Mu-chong and the "Chinese" Korean Communists, but that the "Russian" faction backed his (Yo's) effort to form a new leftist People's Democratic Front that would isolate the troublesome and ambitious Pak. Yo Un-hyong proved his cooperativeness with the military government by identifying Pak's closest allies in the party and union structure in Seoul and Kyonggi Province, thus allowing the Korean police and American agents to make some timely arrests that broke the back of the railway and industrial strikes.[30]

The uprising in the southern provinces could not be explained away as just a Communist plot, since Hodge's investigation, conducted by a committee of Korean and American notables, found that the grievances about rice collection, taxes, inflation, police corruption and brutality, and unemployment were rooted in fact. These factors, however, simply made the reform of the police and the enlargement of the Constabulary more urgent, and they strengthened Hodge's conviction that only a Korean solution for the zone's economic problems would be viewed as legitimate and not as Japanese-American neocolonialism. General MacArthur found the revolt more ominous, perhaps the beginning of a joint Soviet–north Korean strategy of forced unification. In addition to an emergency shipment of 150,000 tons of rice to Korea, MacArthur urged the doubling of the Korean Constabulary and the transfer of enough American troops to his theater to bring the U.S. Sixth and Seventh Infantry Divisions to full strength with wartime allowances of equipment and ammunition. MacArthur put his staff to work on three contingency studies—Baker Plans 61, 62, and 63—that focused on a national anti-American uprising in Korea. Baker Plan 61 proposed the deployment of two divisions from Japan to reinforce the XXIV Corps to suppress any uprising. Baker Plans 62 and 63 focused on the evacuation of American occupation forces and U.S. citizens if the Truman administration decided not to suppress a rebellion or counter an invasion from north Korea that would swing the balance to the Communists. Given the absence of modern airfields in Korea (Kimpo being the exception), the planners identified Inchon and Pusan as critical to any American troop movements in or out of Korea. They collected detailed information on the suitability of both ports for military operations; data were provided by both Korean and Japanese port administrators and survey teams of the U.S. Army Corps of Engineers. Along with their concern about the deployment of two American divisions to Korea, the planners also wondered how they would deal with all the Koreans who would flee to Japan if a Communist takeover of Korea appeared likely.[31]

Hodge, however, thought that it was an opportune time for dramatic political action. Even as the revolt flamed in the south, Hodge announced a plan to create an Interim Legislative Assembly of ninety Koreans, half of whom would be elected, half appointed by him. The elections would be held in November. Hodge believed that his Communist nemesis, Pak Hon-yong, had left his zone forever, even though the Communist Party had not been outlawed. He believed that he could reduce Kim Ku's power by rooting out his agents in the KNP and Korean Constabulary, a task Cho Pyong-ok and Chang Taek-sang would perform with enthusiasm, since they knew that all the subversives challenged their power over the police. Chang Taek-sang, who used his post as Seoul police chief as a stepping-stone to Cho's national directorship, had already survived three assassination attempts—with one more to follow. As for Rhee, the elderly demagogue departed for Washington in December 1946 to take his case to Secretary of State James F. Byrnes and the United Nations. Hodge still regarded him as a threat to the plans to reconvene the Joint Commission and establish the Kim-Yo Coalition Committee and the Interim Legislative Assembly. "Rhee is a nuisance in that he wants everything done his own impractical way and wants to head a separate Government of South Korea."[32]

Hodge could also take comfort from Pak Hon-yong's failure to rebuild the Korean Communist Party after the summer police raids and the suppression of the Autumn Harvest Uprising. Pak had returned to Seoul in July, just as the Coalition Committee was taking shape. Pak called for the restructuring of the Korean Communist Party, the People's Party, and the New People's Party, whose Leninist roots remained in Pyongyang. In September, Pak and Ho Hon set up a base at Haeju, just across the Thirty-eighth Parallel in Hwanghae Province on Korea's west coast, but they continued negotiations through their agents. In November, after his trip to Moscow, Pak announced that he and Ho Hon would now head the fusionist South Korean Labor Party (SKLP) and continue to work for the anti-Japanese revolution and a socialist division of land, wealth, and property among Korea's impoverished masses. The formation of the SKLP, however, ended Yo Un-hyong's flirtation with Pak's Communism; Pak did indeed inherit some of the People's Party, but Yo rescued most of his followers from apostasy by forming the Socialist Workers' Party, cleansed at least superficially of its association with the Communists and the radicals of the Democratic National Front. Yo Un-hyong even believed that his own conversion to support the Moscow agreement ensured that Pyongyang would not help Pak Hon-yong in his latest "adventurism." Yo's new party made no revision of its goals of social and economic justice.[33]

For Hodge, Pak Hon-yong's exile and Rhee's disgruntled departure represented another victory in a chain of triumphs achieved by December 1946. With Washington's approval, the military government had announced the plan for the Interim Legislative Assembly (on July 1) and then (on August 31) transferred all important executive posts in the government to Koreans, with the Americans retained as advisers. General Lerch, the military governor and a judge advocate of reformist bent, sought many ways to strengthen the jurisdictional domain of the Korean courts and their protection of individual rights. Although the elections of October 17–22 were marked by some fraud and coercion, administrative ineptness seemed to be the principal reason for a low and confused voter response that sent thirty-one conservatives and only fourteen moderate socialists to the first assembly. When Yo Un-hyong protested the election results in the name of the Coalition Committee, Hodge immediately appointed forty-five more liberal assemblymen, most of them from a list of candidates acceptable to Yo Un-hyong and Kim Kyu-sik. When the assembly convened on December 12, twenty conservative delegates immediately walked out to protest Hodge's compensatory appointment of moderates.

The general countered by decreeing that the Interim Legislative Assembly could pass laws by a simple majority vote rather than the two-thirds vote he had originally anticipated. With Rhee and Kim Ku in eclipse, Hodge was ready to accept a plan negotiated by Langdon in Pyongyang (October 3–7) with the two principal Soviet regional diplomats (and probable intelligence agents) Gerasim M. Balasanov and Anatolii I. Shabshin, the former Soviet vice-consul in Seoul. The main issue remained the acceptability of Korean political leaders. The Russians would not accept the participation of Syngman Rhee and Kim Ku, but they seemed less adamant in their opposition to the coalition patched together by Yo Un-hyong and Kim Kyu-sik. The Russians seemed less inclined to insist that all the anti-trusteeship factions be disqualified for their oppositionist past. If the Koreans endorsed the Moscow agreement now and behaved well in the future, some oppositionists might qualify for participation. In an exchange of letters between General Hodge and General Chistiakov (General Shtykov's superior in Vladivostok) in October–December 1946, the Americans and Soviets moved toward an agreement to reconvene the Joint Commission, with Hodge promising the good behavior of the Korean politicians on whom he staked his zone's political future.[34]

The shifting alignments were not limited to the Koreans. Still alarmed by the potential disaster the Autumn Harvest Uprising posed to the presence of American troops in north Asia, Douglas MacArthur called for a political and strategic review of a Korean policy linked to the Moscow agreement. He suggested that the State Department explore some arrangement by which the United Nations would assume responsibility for creating a transitional government for Korea and would oversee the mutual staged withdrawal of all foreign troops. MacArthur did not have to add that he wanted the two American divisions in Korea safely under his control in Japan. The general repeated his complaint that the Russians would never allow the Koreans to have a non-Communist government; the Soviets would continue to see themselves as anti-imperialists and paint the United States as capitalist villains in the service of Japan. In his view, the Truman administration should pass the Korean problem to the United Nations for some sort of neutralist, unaligned solution. The general himself remained a distant observer of Hodge's problems.[35]

Hodge had additional reasons to think that the military government had improved its control of nationalist politics in its zone. General Lerch named An Chae-hong the civil administrator in February 1947. A patron of Kim Kyu-sik and a key leader in the March First Movement, as well as one of the three founders of the Preparatory Committee of August 1945, An Chae-hong, a Waseda University graduate and YMCA activist, became de facto deputy military governor. One of An's responsibilities, supported by a budget of $5 million, became the supervision of a new coalition of youth groups, the Korean National Youth Movement (KNYM), that would prepare young men and women (aged eighteen to thirty) for "patriotic, orderly, useful, and democratic life and service." Although An Chae-hong's office had the assistance of eight U.S. Army officers and enlisted men, the real power over the KNYM rested with Yi Pom-sok, the former chief of the Kwangbok army in China and an associate of Kim Ku's in the provisional government and the Korean Independence Party. Envisioned as a national organization of at least thirty thousand members with chapters at the *gun* and *myon* levels by the end of 1947, the KNYM established a training center at Suwon in January 1947. The purpose of this training—organized by Korean educators—was to provide literacy and civics education, outdoor survival training "similar to Boy Scout work," and preparation for volunteer service projects in rural Korean towns that desperately needed improved roads, parks, water supplies, sanitation facilities, and schools. In assessing the KNYM, William Langdon admitted that its apolitical stance simply meant that Yi Pom-sok had not yet aligned himself with any faction, but he would probably use the movement to build an independent power base that would stress both reform and anti-Communism, with a strong emphasis on the authoritarianism Yi Pom-sok had admired in the Guomindang. Nevertheless, the movement might prove to be a useful counterforce to both the Communists and the grassroots associations that still aligned themselves with Syngman Rhee and Kim Ku. Langdon reassured the State Department that, for the moment, the KNYM was not a barrier to negotiations with the Russians or the work of the Interim Legislative Assembly.[36]

As the military government faced its second full year of de facto nation building, General Hodge had some reason to hope that his onerous assignment would come to an end in 1947. He had abolished the Japanese hold on Korea in terms of the police, property ownership, public services, education, landholding, and fishing rights. The military government had curbed an epidemic and a food shortage. The government had survived a nasty, violent protest movement that might have produced a rebellion. Through some blend of Korean politics and international agreement, the Koreans had a modest chance of avoiding a Soviet solution to the expedient division of 1945. What Hodge underestimated was the success of Korean oppositionists and American liberals in painting his administration as an unholy alliance of Korean fascists and American conservatives. Mark Gayn, a reporter for *Newsweek* and the *Chicago Sun,* visited Korea in October 1946. Despite Leonard Bertsch's effort to explain Hodge's problems, Gayn reported that southern Korea was a U.S.-created police state with a crippled economy and no hope of self-government. The Thirty-eighth Parallel was "a real frontier" between two deplorable regimes. Korea is "the most depressing story I have ever covered," Gayn wrote.[37] Many American officers disagreed with Gayn's conclusions, but not his mood.

4

The Moscow Agreement Is Abandoned, 1947

The discontented winter of 1946–1947 simply extended the global wreckage of World War II into a warmer season. While the spring weather thawed the soil, Soviet-American relations congealed into hostility and anxiety, remaining frozen for another forty years. As the cold war took on definitive shape in 1947, the issue of Korea's future became less important to American policy makers as the problems of postwar reconstruction in Europe and the turmoil in the Mediterranean–Middle Eastern world mounted. American newspaper coverage of Korea reflected the declining interest, as perceived by editors. In 1946, stories of the Joint Commission negotiations and Korean political maneuvering received byline coverage and forward placement in the news section; in 1947, if Korean news stories appeared in the *New York Times* at all, they were short notices in the rear of the paper. *Times* correspondent Richard Johnston, a sympathetic and knowledgeable reporter of General Hodge's dilemmas, wrote to the general about his December 1946 interview with President Truman, "I was shocked by his unfamiliarity with the problems." Johnston's interviews with responsible diplomats and army officers produced the same impression, "a consistent lack of knowledge as [to] what the Korean question is all about or as to how it is to be solved, except as a small part of the whole."[1]

The Truman administration faced more than its share of distractions, both foreign and domestic, that winter. In November 1946 the American electorate rejected the New Deal, wartime controls, government spending, and, perhaps, postwar internationalism by electing Republican majorities in the Senate and House of Representatives for the first time in almost twenty years. The polls identified Harry S. Truman as the next object of a protest vote in the presidential election of 1948. When the Eightieth Congress convened in early 1947, its Republican leadership took immediate action to cut taxes, curb government spending, roll back executive regulatory power, and eliminate internationalism in the State Department. Truman launched a preemptive strike to save the State Department by replacing Secretary James F. Byrnes with a national icon and his personal hero, General of the Army (Retired) George C. Marshall. Aware of his lack of popularity with Congress, Undersecretary Dean Acheson agreed to remain in office only six months, to be succeeded by Robert Lovett, Marshall's trusted protégé and a former assistant secretary of war. Like most of the senior officers at State, Marshall placed Western Europe and Latin America at the top of his priority list. His ill-fated efforts as a peace negotiator in China the preceding year had cooled him to anything Asian except for the reconstruction of Japan.[2]

Soviet pressure on Turkey to revise the international agreement that governed the use of the Turkish straits and the Communist insurgency against the Greek monarchy provided the immediate impetus to change policy. President Truman's declaration of containment before a joint session of Congress on March 12, 1947, might have used Asian examples, if the administration had so chosen. Besides the civil war in Greece and the Russian military intimidation of Yugoslavia and Turkey, there were other civil wars in China, the Philippines, Indochina, and Malaya. Russian forces massed in Manchuria, Korea, the Maritime Territory, Sakhalin Island, and the Kamchatka peninsula, surrounding Japan. The president called for a program of economic and military assistance for Greece and Turkey. Now the *New York Times* remembered Korea and demanded, editorially, that the Koreans be included in the administration's next foreign aid request to Congress. Speaking for Secretary Marshall, en route to a foreign ministers' meeting in Moscow, Acheson testified on March 20 that Korea required $400 million to $500 million in economic and military assistance.[3]

If the Truman administration had difficulty finding an answer to the Korean problem, it could still redefine what the problem was, and it began to do so in 1947. The vision of a unified, neutralist, and "democratic" (meaning nontyrannical) Korea dimmed as the months passed, but Washington would not yet abandon the Korea of its dreams. The least acceptable alternative was an authoritarian Communist state just across the Tsushima Strait from Japan. Where would the anti-Communist Koreans flee to next? Japan would hardly welcome them. The United States, where anti-Asian racism looked mild only by comparison with anti–African American racism, was no alternative. The only other imaginable alternative in 1947 was to accept the Thirty-eighth Parallel as an international boundary that divided Korea into two states. The diplomats and military planners believed that an independent south Korea would simply become a hostage to Communist aggression unless defended by American troops indefinitely—an unacceptable proposition to everyone, especially the War Department. Building a more robust economy in the American zone and giving the military government more legitimacy with the Koreans seemed obvious steps. Ironically, such nation-building success would make it inevitable that the American zone would become a truncated, strong, independent Korea; abject failure would bring a unified Communist Korea. Half measures would bring war.[4]

Whether Syngman Rhee, Kim Ku, Yo Un-hyong, or any of the other politicians who imagined themselves modern incarnations of the Chosun kings ever became president of Korea, any future regime would have to defend itself. The challenge to form an effective military force depended on two major institutional developments: (1) the creation of an intelligence system that would provide accurate assessments of enemy military capabilities and political intentions, and (2) a national defense force that would combine a conventional army with special operations forces and a national police force that could defeat a conventional invasion and suppress an insurgency. As a new phase of the power struggle in Korea developed in 1947, the Koreans and their patrons looked more to good arms than to good laws.

LEARNING AND GUESSING: INTELLIGENCE IN KOREA, 1945–1948

The widening rift between the United States and the Soviet Union in 1947 placed an increasing burden on the civilian and military intelligence officers on both sides of the Iron Curtain to know the enemy better and divine what his intentions might be. Although they had not completely ignored each other during World War II, the United States and the Soviet Union had directed their enormous intelligence efforts against Nazi Germany and Japan. Great Britain, which prided itself on its sophistication and wisdom in every aspect of intelligence operations, shared the Allied leadership role in assessing Nazi plans and operations and predicting future enemy strategic and operational moves. Unlike the United States, Great Britain and the Soviet Union did not demobilize their intelligence establishments after 1945; in the case of Great Britain, a thorough scouring of MI-6 (the foreign intelligence service) might have uncovered the unhappy fact that some of the most trusted and clever British operatives had become Soviet "moles." The Russian intelligence service used the chaos of the postwar world to build networks of agents within foreign governments, Soviet diplomatic and military missions, and Communist parties abroad. The Russians also pieced together a good picture of the Allied and Axis intelligence systems through the people and files they captured from the Germans and Japanese.[5]

During World War II, the United States attempted to create a wartime intelligence establishment that would meet civilian-political needs as well as military requirements. The collection and assessment of information were hardly new governmental functions, since diplomats and military and naval attachés stationed abroad had performed such duties for centuries. By the first half of the twentieth century, the United States—principally the central intelligence staffs of the U.S. Army and U.S. Navy—had developed the historical, cultural, organizational, and linguistic expertise to run a respectable intelligence organization. However, the Department of State and the other agencies it represented abroad took a bounded view of its intelligence responsibilities. Chided by the British early in World War

II, Franklin Roosevelt had created the Office of Strategic Services (OSS) to carry out missions of espionage, sabotage, psychological warfare, propaganda, and all sorts of "off-line" negotiations with enemies, allies, neutrals, and plenty of people who could not decide which side they were on.[6]

The American armed forces were not satisfied that the OSS would meet their needs, even at the political-strategic level, so the U.S. Army (including the U.S. Army Air Forces) and the Navy–Marine Corps headquarters and theater forces all created massive staffs to perform a wide range of intelligence missions. For the wartime army, intelligence activities were the responsibility of the assistant chief of staff (G-2) of the War Department (Army) General Staff. The G-2 advised the chief of staff and headed the Military Intelligence Division, whose members (permanent or temporary) were assigned to the Military Intelligence Service. The U.S. Army Signal Corps retained control of the Signal Intelligence Service, which controlled the encryption of friendly messages and intercepted, decoded, and translated all forms of enemy radio, telephone, and telegraph communications. The navy system started with the director of naval intelligence and his staff in the Office of the Chief of Naval Operations (OP-16), the Office of Naval Intelligence, and various fleet and naval district intelligence offices throughout the world. The navy's counterpart to the army's Signal Intelligence Service was OP-20-G, an organization of cryptographers, linguists, communications specialists, and analysts within the office of the director of naval communications. The field operating units for communications intelligence were designated fleet radio units, with the most famous one in Hawaii known as Fleet Radio Unit Pacific or HYPO. As the Army Air Forces developed toward organizational autonomy, it developed its own comprehensive intelligence staff.[7]

Stripped of its technical arcana and aura of mystery, the world of politico-military intelligence is not difficult to understand. However, the assessment of intelligence is difficult to do well and in a timely manner. Even the best predictions are useful to politicians and generals only if they have enough time to act on the analysis, provided they believe it in the first place. Intelligence is refined analysis based on masses of reliable information, and reliability is not easy to determine. An intelligence assessment starts with a requirement: someone in authority—a head of state or a general—needs to know something and defines that need well enough so that his intelligence officer can draw up an appropriate collection plan. Information comes, broadly, from five sources: (1) human beings who talk and write and whose words and actions provide significant observations and physical evidence, such as an interrogation report, a captured operations order, or an agent's observation of a troop movement; (2) electronic intelligence, which is data collected about enemy radar and other electromagnetic technologies used for military operations; (3) signals intelligence (SIGINT), or the interception and analysis of enemy communications, which provides information about the location of the sending station (presumably a headquarters), the content of the message itself, and the location of the recipient; (4) technical intelligence, which usually involves the capture and evaluation of enemy communications technologies, ordnance, and other instruments of war; and (5) photographic intelligence, which consists of taking photographs of and filming enemy-held terrain and forces from all sorts of aerial, surface, and undersea platforms. Depending on the requirements, any or all of these information sources may be applicable to a particular intelligence problem.

No nation warms to the idea of being the target of information collection by any other nation, so civilian and military organizations with information to control or hide carry out counterintelligence operations. The purpose of such operations is to ensure the secrecy of one's own intelligence operations or to allow the "escape" of false information to deceive an enemy. Because the type of information revealed can identify its source, often inadvertently, intelligence collection is frequently accompanied by a deception plan, designed to fool an enemy counterintelligence operation. For example, during World War II, the Anglo-American cryptological community went to great lengths to hide its ability to crack German and Japanese ciphering systems. Assuming correctly that the ULTRA-MAGIC systems might be exposed, the Allies shaped the ULTRA-based information to make it look as if it came from other sources, such as captured documents, traffic analysis, POW interrogations, and elsewhere. Making it appear that the analyses and predictions came from espionage also wreaked havoc within the Axis intelligence community, leading to charges of treason and conspiracy; it also meant that real agents, double agents, and many innocents were compromised, tortured, and executed without knowing that they were victims of a deception plan.[8]

The status of American and Soviet intelligence capabilities in the Asia-Pacific theater changed dramatically after August 1945, improving for the Russians and declining for the Americans. Confronting and fighting the Japanese along the borders of the Maritime Territory and Siberia for most of the century, the Soviets had an extensive information collection system in place even before the invasions of Manchuria and Korea in August 1945. In the 1930s the Soviets had built an extensive spy network in Japan under the direction of Richard Sorge. Even though the Japanese rolled up Sorge and many of his agents, some of the network remained intact, shielded by the Japanese Communist Party and anti-American elements of many nationalities that continued to survive in postwar Japan. In addition to obstructing the reforms of the Allied occupation in Japan, Japanese and Korean Communist agents infiltrated many of the civilian agencies employed by the occupation force, thus providing human intelligence to their Soviet contacts living in Japan. Despite the best efforts of the army's Counterintelligence Corps (CIC) and the assistance of its Japanese police and intelligence allies—many of them holdovers from the wartime military and police—American military activity in Japan remained transparent. The same condition applied to Korea. In addition, the Soviets benefited from the revelations provided by Japanese POWs taken in the August campaign. Essentially trading sensitive information (including testimony about Japanese bacteriological and chemical research and experimentation in China) for their lives, the Japanese POWs provided a wealth of information and records on Japanese and Korean personalities, facilities, economic assets, military research and development, and war crimes. The United States was hardly a laggard in mounting a comparable preemptive strike on Japanese intelligence assets in China and Japan (the first Japanese general MacArthur met in Tokyo was the army's chief of intelligence, who happened to speak English), but the Soviets had stolen a march on the Allied postwar intelligence network in Asia.[9]

As it went through the permutations of purges and war, the Soviet intelligence system grew and prospered through the malevolent and effective leadership of Laurentii Beria—next to Stalin, the most feared and powerful man in the Soviet Union in 1945. Beria's empire was the Narodnyi Kommissariat Vnutrennikh Del (NKVD), or People's Commissariat for Internal Affairs, renamed Narodnyi Kommissariat Gosudarstvennoy Bezopastnosti (NKGB), or People's Commissariat of State Security, but still under Beria's control. The First Division of the KGB conducted foreign intelligence operations. On foreign assignments, KGB representatives worked undercover as Soviet diplomats, trade representatives, newspaper correspondents, and even officers or members of the Glavnoye Razvedyvatelnoe Upravleniye (GRU), or Main Intelligence Directorate of the Red Army General Staff. The KGB dealt with foreign "assets," such as the British traitors known as the "Cambridge Five" and Klaus Fuchs and Alan Nunn May, the scientists who compromised the Allies' nuclear weapons development.[10]

The Soviet occupation army in north Korea brought a robust intelligence organization with it, including KGB and GRU operatives. In addition to developing ties with the Japanese and Korean Communists in Japan, the senior KGB officer in Pyongyang set about drawing Korean Communists in the American zone into a network that would support Korean agents sent south as refugees, businessmen, and fishermen. By 1947, the U.S. Army's 971st Counterintelligence Detachment, the senior CIC headquarters in Korea, estimated that the Russians maintained as many as one hundred highly trained agents in the American zone, who swam in the murky sea of a thousand more agents recruited by the Communist Party in the south. The supporting infrastructure of Communist sympathizers might have numbered as many as four thousand. No Korean organization was safe from penetration, although the Korean National Police (KNP) had become the most effective agency in ferreting out enemy agents because of its coercive methods and demand for anti-Communist ideological conformity. Since the U.S. Army Forces in Korea (USAFIK) hired so many Korean nationals to do its housekeeping and routine administrative and service tasks, CIC assumed that Communist agents were in daily contact with all American commands, especially those in Seoul. The most famous case was an army colonel who took a Russian agent for his mistress. The only advantage the Americans had was that Korean agents tended to defect when faced with the prospect of exposure or returning to Pyongyang.[11]

The Russians, of course, did not trust the Koreans and conducted their own intelligence operations in the American zone. One center of Soviet espionage and contact with the Korean Communists was the Russian consulate in Seoul, the only such diplomatic organization the military government had to deal with, since the Japanese had eliminated all other diplomatic missions in Korea in 1941–1942. General Hodge attempted to get the State Department to shut down the Russian consulate, but it did not. The consular staff and the Joint Commission's liaison mission in Seoul enjoyed diplomatic immunity, but not unfettered travel privileges. In addition, it appears that someone on the consular staff became an agent for the USAFIK intelligence staff. When the Russians closed their consulate and withdrew its Joint Commission liaison mission in 1948, the KGB left an agent, an American-speaking Mr. Zubin, as a caretaker, but he drew too much CIC attention. The center of Soviet intelligence operations shifted to the Greek Orthodox Church. The resident priest, P. K. Policarp, had come to Seoul in 1932 from Tokyo and immediately showed little concern for his White Russian parishioners, raising the flag of the USSR at his church. Although Policarp was not a Soviet citizen, the White Russians and the Koreans suspected that he represented the KGB and was working himself into the favor of the Communist Party. Part of the priest's congregation of spies included Russian-speaking Koreans who immigrated to the American zone from Manchuria and the Soviet Union itself and enjoyed the protection of being Soviet citizens. Late in 1948 the KNP arrested Policarp for contesting the takeover of his church by a Korean of the Greek Orthodox faith sponsored by the Greek Orthodox Church of the United States.[12]

The principal responsibility for all intelligence activities in Korea and Japan during the American occupation rested with General of the Army Douglas MacArthur, Supreme Commander Allied Powers (SCAP). Unlike his success in curbing the activities of the OSS in the Southwest Pacific theater during the war with Japan, MacArthur did not control intelligence activities outside Japan and Korea. This meant that army, navy, and civilian intelligence activities in China, the Philippines, and elsewhere (meaning Manchuria and the Soviet Union) were not under his control. MacArthur depended on intelligence analysis from agencies in Washington, about which he later complained mightily. He was not a passive victim of an "intelligence gap"; like many others, he paid little attention to Korean affairs. As he had throughout World War II, MacArthur depended on Charles A. Willoughby, a professional intelligence officer and the Far East Command (FECOM) G-2 until April 1951. Fifty-three years old in 1945, Willoughby enjoyed MacArthur's confidence to a degree shared only by other members of the "Bataan Gang" or other veterans of the Southwest Pacific theater. Willoughby used a ferocious combination of keen intelligence, linguistic ability, force of personality, professional competence, and physical intimidation to rule the FECOM intelligence community and became the sole interpreter of its estimates for MacArthur.[13]

During World War II, Willoughby developed some operating characteristics that did not serve MacArthur well in Japan and Korea. First, he was habitually skeptical of any sources not under his control, especially reports of agents. He also tended to ignore assessments made by the intelligence staffs of subordinate headquarters. He came to depend on communications intelligence for his most risk-free assessments. He frequently underestimated the strength and capabilities of Japanese forces because of his reluctance to accept anything but the most convincing sources. His temper and intemperate language made others reluctant to question any of his assessments, however erroneous. And Willoughby consciously or unconsciously shaped his intelligence estimates to fit MacArthur's preexisting operational plans. Willoughby also shared his commander's innate political biases against Democrats, the British, most Asians, Washington agencies in general and the navy in particular, army officers who might be critical of SCAP's infallible judgment, potentially unfriendly representatives of the press, civilian diplomats, and Communists, generously defined.

As his own FECOM G-2 staff shrank from 4,000 personnel to less than 1,000 by 1947, Willoughby had to look elsewhere for assistance, especially since his own force included Japanese-language interpreters of the Allied Translator and Interrogation Service, who were of limited use in intelligence missions focused on the Chinese Communists and the Russians. The theater force of 1,300 CIC agents represented one potential source of reinforcement. In December 1946 Willoughby met with the senior officers of the 971st CIC Detachment in Seoul and announced that it would henceforth focus on "positive intelligence," which meant collecting agent information on Russian and Korean military developments north of the Thirty-eighth Parallel. Willoughby then ensured that he saw all USAFIK G-2 reports to Washington. Although not at its full strength of 200 personnel, the 971st CIC Detachment still represented the single largest American intelligence agency in Korea. The G-2 staff of USAFIK numbered 42, the 315th Headquarters Intelligence Detachment (translators and interrogators) numbered 51, and the Civil Communications Intelligence Group (radio, telegraph, and telephone monitoring and censoring) had only 14 American and 190 Korean listeners. The American advisory groups to the Korean National Police and Korean Constabulary numbered around 80, and in the case of the police, the advisers received little information to share and could not curb police interrogation methods, which stressed beating confessions out of suspects. Willoughby looked elsewhere for new agencies to attach to his FECOM G-2 empire.[14]

The retasking of the 971st CIC Detachment probably reduced the military government's ability to assess political developments in the American zone and allowed it to ignore the signs of growing disaffection in southern Korea. Although the CIC had unusual investigative and arrest powers, it included only two Korean-speaking Americans and only twelve Korean-American agents. It was further plagued by constant infighting by Col. John E. Baird, the provost marshal for USAFIK and senior adviser to the KNP, and Capt. John P. Reed, the very able USAFIK assistant G-2 and manager of assessments. Reflecting Baird's priorities, the intelligence effort in the American zone focused on the leftists rather than the subversive activities of the nationalist Right. Reed, however, thought that the threat posed by the Communists was exaggerated. A cautionary analysis by Leonard Bertsch drew Reed's red pencil and a downgrading of the Communist threat.

Bertsch, however, had based his assessment of the South Korean Labor Party's underground organization on some very thorough research by agents of the military government's Public Opinion Bureau of the Department of Public Information (DPI). The DPI study of Korean politics stressed the fact that American CIC agents and military government officers did not have the language and cultural skills to make reliable assessments of local political developments. Even though the KNP remained a major barrier to political and economic reform, the DPI assessment of the Communist threat was far more realistic than the G-2 position that the South Korean Labor Party was doomed. The analysts for the DPI identified the two Cholla provinces, the two Kyongsang provinces, and Cheju-do island as the probable sites of additional protest and violence.[15]

As Communist control tightened in the Soviet occupation zone, USAFIK G-2 and the 971st CIC Detachment found it increasingly difficult to run agent networks north of the Thirty-eighth Parallel, known as Operation Blue. Their major sources remained refugee reports, which were often vague on military matters. Friendly Korean line-crossers (later dubbed "Blue Boys") seldom penetrated as far north as the Pyongyang-Wonsan line before they were captured or fled south to survive. Resistance groups in the north shrank and disappeared without external support. One asset was the agent network that had survived in Manchuria, jointly sponsored by the Guomindang's security service and the successors to the OSS, the Strategic Services Unit and the Central Intelligence Group (1945–1949). As the Chinese Communists rooted out this network, the flow of agents in and out of north Korea dwindled, although a handful of moles survived. American-run agents and their controllers fell back to restricted enclaves: the MI-6 station at the British embassy in Beijing, the Marine-occupied enclave at Qingdao, Shanghai, Nanjing, Hong Kong, and eventually Taipei, Taiwan. In-place agents could not be reached; international travelers could not move freely in Communist-controlled territories. Intelligence on Communist China depended on the Chinese Nationalists and the British, both of whose intelligence services had been penetrated and were not trusted by FECOM in any event.

The effort to collect information on the Russians, north Koreans, and Chinese Communists fell by default to Chinese and Korean intelligence entrepreneurs, some of whom had worked for the Japanese or the Korean provisional government in China, or both. One such network was called Paikyisa, or the White Clothes Society, sponsored by the Guomindang's spymaster Gen. Tai Li. Co-opted by Kim Ku's protégé Shin Ik-hui for "political action," the society became a private espionage agency in late 1945. Paikyisa members, who tended to be anti-Communist northerners, infiltrated the security agencies in the American zone and claimed to have moles in the north Korean Communist Party and security forces. The society worked "off line" for the KNP and, perhaps, the 971st CIC Detachment. It eventually provided agents to the Korean Research Bureau, the Korean intelligence service that replaced USAFIK G-2 in 1948, and the Korean Liaison Office, a special office established the same year by General Willoughby as the Korean arm of

FECOM G-2. Another unique intelligence unit grew from the U.S. Army Air Forces (soon to be the U.S. Air Force) District 8, Office of Special Investigations, stationed at Kimpo airfield. The "father" of this organization, which became Detachment 2, 6004th Air Intelligence Service Squadron, was Chief Warrant Officer Donald Nichols, a former army sergeant with all the piratical impulses of television's fictional "Sergeant Bilko," a special rapport with the Koreans, and a dark life of alcoholism and pedophilia. Nichols claimed to run a network of agents in the Soviet zone and to enjoy special contacts with Syngman Rhee. He almost certainly had many friends in the KNP. Nichols's bold claims as a spymaster covered his real and more useful accomplishment—the creation of a communications intelligence operation at Kimpo directed by a Russian-trained cryptanalyst defector from north Korea, Cho Yong-il, and a veteran of the Japanese communications security service, Kim Se-won. Nichols's group first complemented and then supplanted the only other USAFIK SIGINT asset, a detachment and then a company of the Army Security Agency's signals service group, which was withdrawn in 1948. Aware that only these sorts of agencies would replace the meager American assets, General Willoughby changed the mission of the Korean Liaison Office to be an active field agency for intelligence collection and analysis, working with the intelligence services eventually created by the South Korean armed forces. General Hodge welcomed a more active USAFIK-FECOM intelligence association. Directed by U.S. Army officers, the Korean Liaison Office numbered five Americans and sixteen Korean agents by the end of 1949.[16]

The communications intelligence effort in north Asia added another dimension of complexity to FECOM's collection effort. The Army, Navy, and Air Force believed that they had different SIGINT requirements, which at the operational level was true. Duplication of effort with scarce resources in terms of equipment, operators, cryptographers, and linguists was another matter. The Army Security Agency Pacific managed radio-intercept field units throughout the Japanese home islands, targeted at Russian stations; the U.S. Navy ran a facility at the naval base at Yokosuka and on Okinawa; the Air Force managed the First Radio Squadron (Mobile) at an air base in Japan. The collected Russian and Chinese intercepts went to Washington for processing, but Willoughby managed to get some of the transcripts distributed to his headquarters for analysis on a limited basis. Whether the analysis was done in Tokyo or Washington, MacArthur and fewer than ten of his staff saw the summaries. In a defense reorganization in 1949, Congress authorized the creation of an all-service Armed Forces Security Agency, but this agency went unfunded and had no impact on fusing the service SIGINT efforts before 1950.

The transformation of the Central Intelligence Group into the Central Intelligence Agency (CIA) in 1947–1949 provided FECOM with a jurisdictional victory without immediate benefit. General Willoughby's G-2 office had already mounted its own espionage effort against Russia and, secondarily, against north Korea through its Joint Special Operations Branch—joint mostly in name, since it was an army-dominated effort. Its operations reflected the dwindling information from returning Japanese POWs and refugees; agents now had to travel through Soviet lands and Manchuria for information. The CIA, however, wanted to start its own north Asia operation with the Field Research Unit, FECOM, the cover name for the agency's Office of Special Operations or espionage group. The next CIA agency to join the organizational potage was the Document Research Unit/G-2 FECOM, which was really a unit of the CIA's Office of Policy Coordination (OPC) or covert operations group. Both these CIA offices in Tokyo established small detachments in Seoul; their activities were coordinated by an army colonel on Willoughby's central staff—the price the CIA was willing to pay to set up shop in Tokyo. Colonels Richard G. Stilwell and Jay Vanderpool of the OPC were officers of high reputation and accomplishment in World War II and had experience in espionage and clandestine operations. Neither was eager to try Willoughby's patience, and between them, they had an agency operational group of fewer than twenty people. The civilian in charge of CIA intelligence analysis, George Aurell, had a Field Research Unit staff of four in Tokyo.[17]

For all its confusion and growing pains, the Central Intelligence Group made good use of FECOM's reports and those of USAFIK G-2 and provided accurate analysis in Washington on Korean political and military developments. Its major study before South Korean independence, "The Situation in Korea" (January 3, 1947), correctly assessed Korean unhappiness with the Joint Commission, the popularity of reform and wealth redistribution at the expense of the Japanese and their Korean collaborators, the growth of the Communist dominion in north Korea, and the Soviet fear of a non-Communist south Korea. The Central Intelligence Group reported the growing appeal of "Kim Il Sawng," but firm evidence on public opinion in Pyongyang did not exist. The analysis of the Autumn Harvest Uprising stressed economic causes but did not hide the unpopularity of the military government and the Joint Commission. It reported General Hodge's fear that a partisan revolt in his zone, supported by a conventional invasion, would occur as soon as USAFIK withdrew. Only some sort of concession from the Soviets could open the way for an all-Korea provisional government, an unlikely event. "There is therefore little prospect that the Moscow Decision may be carried out in the near future."[18]

An analysis in March 1948 by the CIA's Office of Reports and Estimates, "The Current Situation in Korea," offered even less hope for a unified, non-Communist Korea. The south Korean economy had continued to deteriorate due to the lack of access to power and raw materials in the northern provinces. Only by increasing its regional trade in finished goods could Korea find some form of economic relief. The country desperately needed an American economic aid program. The likely "Extreme Rightist" government of Syngman Rhee would not survive long without American support, and Rhee was "unpopular and unreliable." Improving the food supply and access to basic consumer goods for the south Koreans would be wise, but the supreme challenge remained the creation of a responsible, representative government. Syngman Rhee enjoyed great public acclaim, but his writ was broad rather than deep, and his people's lack of patience was legendary. Government police and youth association pressure had strengthened the Left. North Korea, in contrast, enjoyed popular support, Soviet aid, and the leverage of a real army. The departure of American troops would leave south Korea "threatened with military disaster." The future of Korea still hung in the balance. So did American influence in Asia.[19]

BUILDING THE SECURITY ESTABLISHMENTS FOR TWO KOREAS, 1947–1948

As the struggle over the reunification of Korea continued, the Soviet and American occupation forces transferred the responsibility for internal policing almost entirely to native Korean forces. These forces emerged not in the image of their official sponsors—the Red Army and the U.S. Army—but in a unique blend of Korean, Chinese, and Japanese military culture beneath their superficial adaptation to Russian and American norms. The two Koreas each had parallel security establishments—a national police force and a national military establishment of land forces and small air and naval forces. Neither force had much capability except for internal security duties against dissident guerrillas. The north Korean force, however, developed an institutional base to transform itself into a potent conventional army, fully capable of successful offensive operations against its southern counterpart. The south Korean forces remained hostage to the rivalry between the Korean National Police and the Korean Constabulary, the formation of secret political societies within both forces, and the reluctance of the U.S. Army and Department of State to commit money and advisers to a force that they did not fully trust.

Kim Il-sung maintained the facade of a coalition regime by allowing the Democratic Party (without Cho Man-sik) to exist, and he courted Chongwudang, the northern mutant of Chondogyo, the religious party. Kim followed a faux-accommodationist party line to confound his Communist rivals. Kim demonstrated his confidence at the Second Party Congress (March 1948). He drove through the candidacy of twenty-nine new members and retained thirty of the original forty-three Central Committee members, thus establishing a clear majority for his Kapsan faction of the Korean Workers' Party. He encouraged factionalism in Chongwudang until one leadership group betrayed another as anti-Communists, whom Kim then arrested. He did not put any pressure on the Yanan, Soviet, or southern Communist groups in the party structure.[20]

Although Kim Il-sung and his Russian advisers did not move to eliminate all non-Communist political groups in the northern zone, the Soviets ensured that the security forces remained under their close supervision. The most dedicated Korean Communists of all factions with any military experience took all the significant positions. When the north Koreans created military ranks in 1947, Choe Yong-gun became the only full general (one large star like a Soviet marshal), and Kim

Mu-chong, Nam Il, and An Kil became his three principal subordinates. In February 1948, Kim Il-sung, claiming no status other than party leader, announced the founding of the People's Army (In Min Gun) under the leadership of his closest Kapsan faction comrades—Kim Chaek as director of the National Defense Bureau, and Choe Yong-gun as the commanding general of the army. In mid-1947 the Security Officers Training Center changed its identity to become the First and Second Divisions and the Fourth Mixed Brigade; two of the three commanders were Kim Il-sung's protégés. Soviet-trained Korean officers dominated the headquarters staffs, schools, support agencies, and political department, while Chinese-trained officers held troop commands and high posts in the training establishment. Russian officers kept their counterparts under close supervision; each division (10,400 officers and men) included a Soviet mission of 150 officers for training and administrative duties until the end of 1948.[21]

The north Korean police establishment included four forces: the National Police, the Railway Constabulary, the Border Guard, and the Coast Guard. Following Soviet practice, these forces fell under the direction of a minister of internal affairs, who was Gen. An Kil, a veteran partisan and Manchurian comrade of Kim Il-sung's. An Kil, however, died of illness in December 1947 (age forty) and was replaced by Pak Il-u of the Yanan faction. Of the four security forces, the Border Guard received the most military training and heaviest weapons within the Bureau of Internal Affairs. The Border Guard evolved into a formidable paramilitary force deployed in brigades throughout the thickening defenses along the Thirty-eighth Parallel. By the end of 1948, the four police forces numbered 40,000, while the People's Army (150,000) had developed into three light infantry divisions, a mixed arms brigade, and a tank regiment on the Soviet model. Both the People's Army and the Border Guard accepted veterans of Japanese military service as enlisted men, provided they were not "class enemies."

Kim Il-sung faced only one potential armed challenge within his own borders—the southern Communists who rallied to Pak Hon-yong in the city of Haeju, only a few miles from the border in southern Hwanghae Province. Survivors of the Autumn Harvest Uprising drifted across the border and found a new home at the Kangdong Institute, a political-military training center for would-be agents and partisans. Kim Il-sung had no intention of allowing the South Korean Labor Party to develop its own army. With ample money and Soviet support, Kim moved the southern Communists into his own administrative and political structure with Pak Hon-yong eventually appointed deputy premier and minister of foreign affairs, positions of influence but not independence. Kim closed the Kangdong Institute in 1949 and strengthened his control of other partisan and espionage training centers under the control of his most trusted subordinates, including O Chin-u, a Kapsan stalwart. In September 1947, when the Soviets proposed that all foreign troops be withdrawn from Korea, the Russians felt confident that the north Korean army and police forces could, at a minimum, defend north Korea and could serve as the base of a larger and more heavily armed force capable of attacking the Korean forces in the American zone.[22]

General Hodge enjoyed no such surety that the Korean forces in the American zone could keep order, let alone fight another army. The KNP, enraged by the massacres of the Autumn Harvest Uprising, made the destruction of the South Korean Labor Party its first priority; although the party itself was legal, the KNP pursued its leaders for all sorts of conspiratorial offenses, real and imagined. Although 85 percent of the policemen had joined the force since 1945, the senior officers still reflected the police culture of the Japanese, as yet unmodified by law or American moral suasion. The rank and file reflected similar values, deepened by the addition of policemen who were refugees from the north, with limited means and large grievances. American military policemen, investigators from the Criminal Investigation Division, and officers of the military government detachments all reported police extortion rings, many linked to Kim Ku's Korean Independence Party and the Northwest Young Men's Association, which served as a police auxiliary. The existence of the officially sponsored Korean National Youth Movement did not reduce the appeal of the Northwest Young Men's Association and like-minded street gangs. When General Lerch ordered a crackdown on the most extreme groups, which had started a campaign of intimidation against the Korean court system, Yi Pom-sok and Yi Chong-chon, also a veteran of the Guomindang's paramilitary forces, reorganized the rightist splinter youth associations as the Taedong Youth Association, endorsed by both Kim Ku and Syngman Rhee. The terrorist attacks and street battles between the anti-Communist youth groups (still enjoying police protection) and the outlawed Communist Democratic Youth Association continued into 1948 and plagued every major Korean city. The unreformed KNP remained more interested in breaking the influence of labor unions and harassing leftist politicians such as Yo Un-hyong than in honest, impartial law enforcement. Its American advisers either shared its political prejudices or felt helpless to change police behavior.[23]

Hodge did not want his own forces to take on larger law enforcement responsibilities, since his provost marshal and division commanders did not consider the American tactical troops—and even some of their military policemen—as sufficiently experienced and disciplined to replace the KNP in handling civil disorders. Hodge's own troops—many of them new enlistees whose average age dropped rapidly from twenty-five to twenty—became a growing threat to public order; their complaints to their parents and the press focused on the condition of their old Japanese barracks, the quantity and quality of their mess-hall food, and the burden of housekeeping ("rock painting") that replaced field training as the army's budget for operational readiness shrank after 1946. General Hodge characterized his callow enlisted men as people who thought that the army should provide them "with a vacation with pay while they earned a free education." They expected Asian duty to be better than home: recreational facilities, beach resorts, nightclubs, "plus pin-up girls in the flesh at all times. We don't have those things here." Hodge got no comfort when the War Department directed MacArthur to investigate the low morale of XXIV Corps.[24]

The Korean Constabulary (still officially a "police reserve") showed some promise as an alternative to the Korean National Police and the U.S. XXIV Corps in the search for order. Although General Hodge may have viewed the Constabulary as the foundation of some future Korean army, the official policy was to transfer American weapons and vehicles to the KNP first and the Constabulary second. The American advisers to the Constabulary in 1946 and 1947 seldom numbered more than twenty, about half serving at the headquarters at Camp Sobinggo (now part of the Yongsan base) and half with the nine provincial regiments, which now included a regiment on Cheju-do. Hodge directed Lt. Col. Russell Barros, the Constabulary commander, to emphasize security duties; the general wanted American units to surrender their roving patrols and sentry posts that protected Korean buildings and facilities to the Constabulary. In early 1947 the military government authorized a transfer of 100,000 won ($6,600) a year for every U.S. Army sentry the Constabulary replaced. Guard duty, however, did not satisfy Colonel Barros or the Constabulary, so Capt. James H. Hausman, de facto operations and training officer, spent much of his time arranging for Constabulary companies to train with American weapons and American instructors from the U.S. Sixth and Seventh Infantry Divisions. The Koreans remained armed with cast-off Japanese rifles and light machine guns.[25]

Although the War Department vetoed a plan to assign each Constabulary regiment to an American counterpart for training, the U.S. Army approved Hodge's request to enlarge the Constabulary from 25,000 to 50,000, a strength reached in March 1948. General MacArthur supported this plan but vetoed a more ambitious scheme for a six-division army of 100,000 that Hodge preferred. The War Department staff estimated that a proper military advisory mission to Korea would require 600 officers and men and the funds for an equal number of Korean interpreters for a force of 50,000, or half the number Hodge recommended. The hurried and haphazard enlargement of the Constabulary in 1947 exacerbated the problem of political loyalty among the recruits. The KNP refused to provide personal information on recruits, and the small Constabulary staff could hardly screen all the applicants. In fact, most of the recruiting and recruit training occurred at the Constabulary regimental headquarters, where the commanding officers had every incentive to run their manning numbers up (for pay and logistics purposes) and to ignore loyalty questions. Although the National Youth Movement provided some volunteers, the Constabulary also accepted (accidentally, to be sure) hundreds of fugitives from the South Korean Labor Party and other harried leftist associations.[26] The perilous status of the Constabulary put a special strain on Barros and Hausman as they tried to build an efficient, professional, politically neutral officer corps. Their principal protégé, Maj. Yi Hyong-kun, a twenty-eight-year-old former captain in the Japanese Imperial Army, acted as the de facto Korean chief of the Constabulary, but his youth and prior service—and lack of political connections—prevented him or his equally able contemporaries, Chung Il-kwon and Paik Sun-yup, from becoming Constabulary chief in November 1946, when Hodge directed Barros to assume adviser status rather than command the Constabulary. Hodge appointed Maj. Song Ho-sung, the fifty-four-year-old commander of the Third Regiment, as Constabulary commander. A veteran of thirty-three years of Chinese service and a "general" of the Kwangbok army, Song Ho-sung was more warlord than modern general, and his lust for drinking parties made it difficult to keep him focused on decision making. His principal qualifications were his lack of experience in the Japanese service and his popularity with his patrons in the Korean Independence Party. Fortunately, most of the time, Song Ho-sung allowed Hausman and his most trusted Korean protégés to run the Constabulary for him.

Finding officers for the expanding Constabulary demanded much of Hausman's attention, and he worried that too many incompetents and potential troublemakers were still accepting commissions in the Constabulary. The graduates (387 of 459 applicants) of the third and fourth classes of the Officer Training School (January and May 1947) came from the ranks of the Constabulary or directly from civil life and were predominantly southern Koreans with military experience as conscripts in the Japanese service. Barros and Hausman took direct action to control the problem of self-inflicted subversion of the Constabulary when they formed the fifth class (380 graduates out of 400 candidates), which completed its ninety-day course in October 1947. Two-thirds of the fifth class consisted of refugees from the Soviet zone; they tended to be Christian, middle class, educated, and angry with the Communists. Members of the fifth class rooted out the Communists in their ranks, as did the subsequent sixth and seventh classes, the officer intake of 1948. Hausman hoped that this self-policing would spread to the Constabulary regiments in the field. He could do little about appointments at the senior level; Korean politicians pressured Hodge to appoint a host of favorites. When the Constabulary established three brigade headquarters in Seoul, Taejon, and Pusan in September 1947, Song Ho-sung assumed command of one (Seoul) and Col. Won Yong-dok, a Manchukuo army medical officer and Seoul socialite, took command of another (Taejon). The third brigade went to Col. Yi Ung-jun (aged fifty-seven), a former Japanese colonel who had refused a commission until late 1946. His son-in-law, Yi Hyong-kun, served briefly as a regimental commander in Taejon, then departed with the first group of Constabulary officers sent to the U.S. Army Infantry School at Fort Benning, Georgia, in 1948.[27]

The Constabulary's growth in numbers and rise in power put it in direct competition with the Korean National Police, some of whose officers aspired to lead a real Korean army. As the Constabulary assumed the protection of Korean businesses—such as the critical coal mines in the Cholla provinces—it endangered the KNP's protection rackets. The KNP and Constabulary vied for local favors and American support. In a growing number of incidents, policemen arrested members of the Constabulary for trivial offenses and harassed them on and off duty. The tension reached its peak in June 1947, when a Constabulary company attacked the KNP station in Yongam, Chollanam-do, to free an imprisoned soldier. Three men died in the gun battle, which ended only when senior officers finally regained control of the attackers and the ammunition on both sides ran low. Although both forces shared a common interest in battling the growing threat of Communist subversion, they viewed each other as enemies. Members of the Constabulary believed that they should be immune from civil arrest, and the KNP regarded the Constabulary as a nest of traitors and criminals.[28]

The Constabulary continued to defend its own reputation and interests in its own way. In August 1947 a squad of soldiers assaulted the regional headquarters of the Democratic Party in Chungju, Chollabok-do, kidnapping ten workers in revenge for anti-Constabulary statements and trashing the party headquarters. The KNP did not intervene. American officers and their Korean counterparts rescued the politicians and discharged the men. The next month, a young soldier, responding to insulting remarks made by an important government bureaucrat, assaulted the gentleman in his official car. The "victim" was none other than Chang Taek-sang, police chief of Seoul. Chief Chang chased the soldier into the Constabulary compound, shouting that the soldier should be arrested, but a Constabulary officer persuaded Chang that if he and his driver did not leave immediately, the rest of the garrison might become violent. He apologized to Chang and promised that his assailant would be disciplined; the chief, furious but rational, left the scene with two of his own officers for protection. Chang refused to retract his charge that the Constabulary was nothing but a haven for anarchists, thieves, and terrorists.[29]

On March 1, 1947, the Korean National Police fooled its foes and supporters by refusing to participate in a second abortive coup attempt by the rightist coalition of Kim Ku, Kim Sung-su, and Syngman Rhee. How serious the coup attempt was remains open to debate, but certainly the Kim-Kim-Rhee factions staged massive street demonstrations and issued all sorts of declarations that the defunct provisional government would soon supplant the military government. Rather than let the Sam-il demonstrations flower in Seoul and Pusan, however, the police immediately mobilized and curbed the demonstrations; in Pusan the KNP riot battalion fired into a mob of eight thousand and killed five people. Kim Sung-su and Syngman Rhee denounced the violence, again isolating Kim Ku in a crisis. Hodge's political advisers correctly reported that the rightist coalition had no mass base of support and that its leadership remained split by ambition and personality. Moreover, the Korean Democratic Party still nursed a grudge over Kim Ku's involvement in the murder of its chairman, Song Chin-u, the year before. The Korean Democratic Party still regarded Kim Ku as a serious threat and sometime ally, given his popularity as a "hero" of the anti-Japanese resistance movement. The key event, or so Hodge's advisers thought, was that Cho Pyong-ok and Chang Taek-sang had demonstrated their independence from the Korean Democratic Party and the propertied classes by opposing the Sam-il demonstrations. The KNP's strong response had saved the Constabulary and American troops from more unwelcome riot duty and warned the Right that it could not count on the KNP as its party army. The police interpreted the military government's surprised approval, however, as an invitation to take up its witch hunt against the Left, which included the "Communist" Constabulary Third Brigade in southeastern Korea. On a national level, the Constabulary remained untested as the sense of crisis and political polarization spread throughout the American occupation zone.[30]

TOWARD TWO KOREAS: WASHINGTON, 1947

The U.S. government could not get rid of Korea without risking more domestic discontent about the "appeasement" of Communism. The Russians saw no need to relent in their demand that the United States disenfranchise any person or party that opposed the Joint Commission. Soviet intransigence guaranteed conflict between the military government and its critics Right and Left, Korean and American. The Soviets had made one simple and dangerous proposal that amounted to assisted suicide: the two occupying armies should withdraw and allow Korean "self-determination." Between January 1947 and the next year, the political fortunes of Korea took another tragic turn with the final collapse of a negotiated unification guaranteed by the United States and the Soviet Union and the inevitable subsequent step, the creation of two Korean states.

Inside the Truman administration, the State Department and the War Department (the Department of the Army after July 1947) found that their conflicting perspectives on Korea produced nothing but inertia, because neither the president nor Congress would intervene to break the bureaucratic deadlock. The balance of power now rested slightly with the State Department, which immediately called for an interdepartmental study of Korean policy sponsored by its Civil Affairs Division, headed by Maj. Gen. John H. Hilldring, the principal agency monitoring occupation policy and disbursing Government Aid and Relief in Occupied Areas (GARIOA) funds. Knowing that he still had some influence with Secretary of War Robert P. Patterson, Hilldring, now the assistant secretary of state for occupied areas, allied himself with John Allison in the Far East Affairs Bureau. Patterson, Hilldring, and Allison recognized the threat to Korea if the Joint Chiefs of Staff listened to General MacArthur's pleas to transfer the two divisions in Korea to the U.S. Eighth Army in Japan. Assured of State Department concurrence, Patterson called for a full State-War-Navy Coordinating Committee (SWNCC) review of Korean policy, which Patterson already regarded as bankrupt at its present level of funding and commitment. The SWNCC created a special interdepartmental committee consisting of three members: Maj. Gen. Archibald V. Arnold, the former military governor and Joint Commission delegation head, represented the War Department and General Hodge; the other two members were civilians sympathetic to a policy revision. The interdepartmental committee reported that the U.S.

government needed to make a real commitment to improving the dire economic conditions in the American zone. GARIOA funds would not meet Korea's needs forever. Economic improvement, encouraged by a $600 million U.S. grant over three years, would strengthen any future negotiations through the Joint Commission and help blunt the call for immediate independence for a rump Korea based on the American zone. Conversely, a solution that would lead inevitably to an all-Communist Korea would be a triumph for the Soviet Union and "seriously impair the U.S. world position." A unified, independent Korea that allowed the withdrawal of American troops would be a "complete political defeat" for the Soviet Union.[31]

The special committee's report, endorsed by the State Department, headed into the interagency staffing process, but it had a competitor; an analysis by the Joint Strategic Survey Committee argued that America's future security did not require American military bases in Korea, Indochina, Taiwan, and Indonesia. American troops in Korea should be redeployed as soon as possible. The political fate that awaited Korea was not the Pentagon's problem. Secretary of War Patterson did not accept the joint committee's position. He called General Hodge to Washington to testify before Congress about the importance of a Korean aid bill and to educate the White House and senior officers in the Pentagon on Korean problems. Hodge was also encouraged to cultivate the media, in part to counter Syngman Rhee's ongoing lobbying.

Working from his suite in the Carlton Hotel in Washington, Syngman Rhee pursued his own dreams—as always, a mix of dizzy romanticism and hardheaded nationalist realpolitik. In private conversations with Americans, Rhee urged a direct military confrontation that would force the Russians to return to the Soviet Union. Rhee argued that nuclear weapons and MacArthur's theater forces would intimidate the Russians. The next best option was an independent south Korea, established, supported, and defended by the United States. Rhee remained vague about just what process would produce an independent Republic of Korea; he shifted from unilateral American action to United Nations sponsorship and back again. It was far easier to return to his old role of dedicated oppositionist and exiled politician, except this time, his target was Hodge and the military government. Yo Un-hyong feared that Rhee had discredited Hodge, the patron of the Coalition Committee and the Interim Legislative Assembly, but Military Governor Lerch assured him that the rumor of Hodge's recall was unfounded. Nevertheless, Rhee happily announced that *his* policy of dealing with the Russians as enemies had now been adopted by the United States.[32]

Hodge arrived in Washington in early February 1947 armed with his own study, fashioned by his deputy and the likely head of the next delegation to the Joint Commission, Maj. Gen. Albert E. Brown. Brown's study, "Development of a Political Program," stressed that American identification with the trusteeship concept was the single most important negative influence on Korean politics and allowed Rhee and Kim Ku to build a mass following with their "powerful, even potentially explosive appeal." Putting more moderates into the military government and sup-

porting the Coalition Committee would be fruitless unless the Korean people identified American policy with economic improvement. General Hilldring provided
some hope because he thought that he had a good aid bill that limited GARIOA
funds for Germany and Japan, which would be supported by a separate State Department appropriation. He would redirect the army's unspent occupation money
to Austria and Korea. With some promise of economic relief, Brown met with the
leaders of the Kim Ku faction (the provisional government–Korean Independence
Party group) and almost received a commitment not to stage mass protests against
the reconvening of the Joint Commission. Brown stressed that Kim Ku's past ties
with the Chinese Nationalists compromised him with the State Department and
gave Rhee an advantage, but Kim Ku (with Rhee isolated in Washington) now had
a chance to reestablish his position as a great patriot and leader. Since he had issued Proclamation No. 1, the 1945 call to oppose trusteeship, he could now denounce the proclamation. Kim Ku made no promises, but he got the point.[33]

Although Syngman Rhee and John Hodge had different agendas and limited
success in securing congressional appropriations for Korean economic reform and
revival, they managed to keep Korea in the media spotlight for about five weeks.
Rhee cultivated the Hearst and McCormick newspaper chains and other anti-
administration groups to spread rumors of General Hodge's recall. Hodge used his
contacts with the New York Times and other sympathetic newspapers and the Time-
Life empire to publicize his views. Hodge also profited from the KNP's suppression of the March 1 demonstrations, which illustrated the military government's
resolution to keep order. In the meantime, Rhee and his clique—including Louise
Yim and Ben Limb—worked in New York to spread the idea of United Nations intervention as a substitute for the trusteeship commitment and the Joint Commission. Rhee was, as usual, too clever by half, because he knew that John Allison and
other Asianists had started to consider this option but could not admit it, since the
State Department had just mounted one last offensive to persuade the Russians to
be more cooperative in the next meeting of the Joint Commission. Prepared to
dramatize his policy of noncooperation with the military government, Rhee returned to Seoul in late March 1947, determined to speak for independence now for
American-occupied Korea.[34]

When General Hodge returned to Seoul in April 1947, he sent General Lerch,
the military governor, to Washington to watch his exposed political flank in the
United States. Lerch found the highest officials uninterested in Korea; the midlevel
bureaucrats fully aware of the military governor's dilemmas, but paralyzed for lack
of guidance; and an active Korean Commission lobby still embarked on a concerted effort to discredit the military government, largely by criticizing the American officers for being pro-Japanese or pro-Communist and the troops for being
anti-Korean. Lerch's assignment was to ensure that Korea received all or part of
the $600 million that Hodge had requested and wanted incorporated into the as-
sumed largesse of the new Marshall Plan. The general was also supposed to counter
Syngman Rhee's strident call on March 22 for an independent Republic of Korea

in the American occupation zone. Lerch should explain the Interim Legislative Assembly and the Joint Commission as a dual track to unification. Another part of Lerch's mission was to develop a Korea lobby outside of the Korean Commission, based on a civic education program (the "Korean project") that Hodge had proposed to Princeton University, the Hoover Institution of Stanford University, and the Rockefeller Foundation. Neither Hodge nor Lerch thought that any of these multiple tasks would be accomplished without hard work, good luck, and the muzzling of Syngman Rhee.[35]

General Lerch found the War Department friendly and cooperative, the State Department dubious but not hostile, and the Korean Commission dedicated to Syngman Rhee's goal of eliminating the military government. The War Department, however, had washed its hands of Korea as an "occupied country" and gladly passed the Korea problem to the State Department, which had at least accepted the $600 million economic aid proposal. The Korean Commission would not accept any reform that challenged Rhee. Lerch had expected Ben Limb, Louise Yim, and Henry Chung to follow their master's voice, but he was surprised at the militancy of the American members, Robert T. Oliver, Jay Jerome Williams, and John Staggers, whose brother, Harley Staggers, was an influential Fair Deal Democratic congressman from West Virginia. The Korean Commission position, pushed relentlessly in the religious and popular press, was that Korea wanted independence *now,* with Syngman Rhee as president. In the face of such intransigence, Lerch feared that the State Department was in no hurry to replace the military government and had not done much thinking about the Korea problem—with the exception of General Hilldring's marginalized occupation policy office. He took solace from the fact that the diplomats understood that they had a problem and that an economic aid package was essential to maintaining the American position in Seoul.[36]

Despite some good news from Seoul, where the Interim Legislative Assembly passed a franchise bill in early July, Lerch watched Hodge's hopes for help from Washington fade in the growing conflict between the State Department and the hostile Eightieth Congress. Secretary Marshall had abandoned the Korean $600 million aid bill in his first effort to win congressional support for the Eurocentric Marshall Plan. The only comfort was that the War Department's GARIOA money earmarked for Korea should last until fiscal year 1949. The State Department had also postponed appointing a civilian proconsul (similar to John J. McCloy in Germany) to replace General Hodge, who desperately wanted to leave Korea. Another problem was the conviction in State that Hodge had allowed the antiunion forces in Korea (the KNP, for one) to destroy any hope of organizing Korean factory workers as a force for anti-Communist industrial democracy, an Asian version of the American policy of supporting the non-Communist socialist labor unions all over Europe. Lerch tried to explain that this was a lost cause. On a more positive note, the Korean Commission agreed to tell Rhee that his oppositionist, opportunistic tactics had helped kill the Korean aid bill. Robert Oliver and Ben Limb, however, refused to sign the radiogram at the last minute, which weakened its potential impact. Preston Goodfellow, who had resurfaced as a Korean Commission activist, agreed with Lerch that Rhee's hostility to Hodge and the military government had become a serious barrier to political change in Seoul. Washington opinion had started to shift toward abandonment.[37]

Syngman Rhee's reaction to the cautionary messages from Washington was complete denial that his oppositionism endangered Korea. Instead, Rhee saw all his opponents as pro-Japanese and pro-Communist. Lerch believed that "the old fellow has gone completely insane" and would soon talk himself into captivity for his subversion of the military government, the Joint Commission, and the Interim Legislative Assembly. Rhee's attacks on Hodge had taken their toll in Washington, where officials believed that Hodge ruled by dictatorial fiat without Korean participation or the advice of State Department experts. Lerch repeatedly told officials that Hodge made no economic decisions without the advice of his National Economic Board, a group of Korean and American economists headed by Dr. Arthur Bunce of State, a former YMCA worker in Seoul who spoke Korean. As for reining in Rhee, the best Lerch could do was to persuade the Korean Commission to advise Rhee to await the findings of the new Asia policy review, scheduled to be made by the army's Lt. Gen. Arthur C. Wedemeyer. Lerch and Hodge agreed that the Joint Commission solution for Korean unification would not work because of Soviet opposition to "reactionary" Korean participation in any successor government. The latest "solution," Lerch reported, was a vague suggestion that the United Nations solve the Korea problem. Lerch had difficulty explaining to the planners that this option would do nothing to assuage Korean fear of any American-sponsored solution. A United Nations trusteeship would be viewed as a sellout to the Russians and would be exploited by Syngman Rhee, who would characterize a United Nations trusteeship as not only pro-Soviet but also an opportunity for the "collaborationist" Koreans to strengthen their grip on the executive bureaucracy left behind by the Americans. Rhee saw no problem, however, in accepting money from the same privileged classes or admitting in private that Korea had no future without reconciliation with Japan. In the meantime, Archer Lerch died of a heart attack on September 11, 1947, arguably the first American officer to fall in the Korean War.[38]

TOWARD TWO KOREAS: SEOUL AND PYONGYANG, 1947–1948

Showing frustration and confusion, both foreign and domestic, the Truman administration edged away from negotiated cooperation with the Soviet Union and toward impatient confrontation. The issues were real: the reconstruction of Europe and the Soviet Union's efforts to draw Turkey and Iran into its informal empire, which extended into Germany and would soon include Czechoslovakia. Stalin showed growing irritation with Tito's independent socialism in Yugoslavia and contemplated replacing the leaders in Belgrade with compliant Communists.

Working through the Albanians and Bulgarians, as well as the untrustworthy Yugoslavs, the Soviets extended some arms assistance and moral support to the Communist-led Greek insurgents. Working with the concepts of containment developed by George Kennan, a favored adviser to Secretary of State George C. Marshall, President Truman decided to use the occasion of a meeting of the Council of Foreign Ministers to tell a joint session of Congress on March 12, 1947, that his administration would henceforth extend economic and financial aid to those "free, democratic" nations facing Communist-inspired insurgencies or external military threats. In Moscow, Marshall suggested to Foreign Minister V. M. Molotov that the Russians might use the next meeting of the Joint Commission to demonstrate Stalin's commitment to changing former colonies into independent nations by peaceful means. Molotov responded positively: the Soviet zone of Korea had captured the revolutionary spirit of the Korean people. He welcomed more negotiations on a democratic government. Let the talks begin![39]

A combination of diminished hope, growing anxiety, and increased urgency brought the Americans and Russians together again for the second extended negotiations of the Joint Commission from May 21 to October 18, 1947. The talks brought the problem of a unified Korea no closer to a solution. The key to reconvening the Joint Commission had been a slight concession by the Russians (or so it was perceived) on the question of consultation with Korean political groups that had opposed the Moscow agreement and did not abide by the terms of cooperative political behavior laid out in Joint Communiqué 5 (June 1946). Secretary Marshall and Foreign Minister Molotov exchanged letters (April–May 1947) that suggested the Soviets' new willingness to compromise on the issue of Korean participation in the formation of some sort of transitional government for all Korea. The Americans assumed that the Russians feared some success of the American-promoted Coalition Committee, increased economic assistance, and the possibility that the military government would cede more of its administrative powers to the Koreans themselves. The Americans certainly took the new negotiations seriously. When General Hodge returned to Korea, he brought with him an additional political adviser, Joseph E. Jacobs, an expert on Russian affairs. With Washington's approval, the military government also instituted a series of unilateral reforms designed to make it easier for Korea to do business with its Asian neighbors.[40]

In less than a month of meetings at Seoul's Doksu Palace, the U.S. delegation (headed by General Brown, Hodge's deputy commander) and the Soviet delegation (headed again by Gen. Terentii Shtykov) produced a formula for soliciting Korean opinion on the form and process of establishing a transitional government. The Soviets would determine which political groups in south Korea were fit to participate, excluding only those groups that still publicly and adamantly opposed the work of the Joint Commission. Adherence to the principles of Joint Communiqué 5 would now be enough to entitle a group to representation; past opposition to trusteeship would be forgiven. In return, the American commissioners, led by General Brown, would go to Pyongyang to screen the north Korean political groups.

Each group had to complete a membership and policy questionnaire to qualify for an interview. The Americans eventually collected information from 38 groups in north Korea, and the Russians screened 425 groups in the south. The Russians first omitted any group that claimed fewer than 10,000 members. They then reversed course and announced that any group that *at any time* had taken part in the actions of the Anti-Trusteeship Committee could not be included in future political activity, thus reducing the 425 potential participating groups to 118. Ultranationalists, principally the Kim Ku faction, refused to participate; Syngman Rhee's allies completed questionnaires but never surrendered their self-proclaimed right to demonstrate and speak against trusteeship.[41]

The Koreans helped subvert the Joint Commission's ill-conceived effort to get a sense of the popular will. Analyzing the 118 parties they accepted as potentially legitimate, the Soviets calculated that these parties had 38 million members (or nearly twice the total population of the American zone), almost evenly divided between moderate-to-left and moderate-to-ultraright. American analysis mirrored that of the Soviets: a polarized electorate of around 14 million that was almost evenly divided, with around 1 million supporters of the Democratic Party (Kim Sung-su) and Independence Party (Kim Ku) holding the balance of power. If the uncompromising Right (a claimed 12 million members) was disqualified, the National Democratic Front (the Communists and other socialists) and moderate-left groups would control any future government, even if it were formed only in southern Korea. In the meantime, Brown had discovered in Pyongyang—to no one's surprise—that no nationalist-moderate group dared participate in the political process; the 38 northern parties claimed a membership of more than 13 million (or about 50 percent more than the entire population of the Soviet zone). Even allowing for swollen membership claims, the proportional representation was likely to remain about the same; if the south Korean ultranationalists were banned from the political process, the Communist-leftist alliance would soon dominate the government of a unified Korea. However, any government formed with full south Korean representation would not be disposed to follow a line dictated by Moscow or Pyongyang. Once more, the political impasse hardened despite American efforts to find some formula acceptable to the Russians that would incorporate at least part of the nationalist-moderate alliance. Although the Joint Commission's work limped into the autumn of 1947, its work had limited influence on the political forces loose in Korea.[42]

The shifting rightist coalition of Rhee, Kim Ku, and Kim Sung-su could agree on no common policy except opposition to the military government and trusteeship. They could not shape a single position on land reform, distribution of Japanese vested property, or the issue of "collaborationism" and the use of Japanese technicians in the government except to block any measure that Hodge proposed. The only reform on which they agreed (temporarily) was to remove Cho Pyong-ok and Chang Taek-sang from their posts in control of the Korean National Police. Their alternative was to reorganize the police around Yi Pom-sok's Korean

National Youth Association and other (quasi-criminal) youth associations—an option that horrified the Americans, with good reason. Hodge could not wait for the Right, characterized by his advisers as "extremely nationalistic, prosperous, complacent, and self-righteous." The National Society for the Rapid Realization of Korean Independence (NSRRKI; Rhee), Korean Democratic Party (Kim Sung-su), and Korean Independence Party–Korean provisional government (Kim Ku) would not relent on their opposition to the Joint Commission, which they saw as a Soviet instrument of subversion. Rhee went so far as to claim that he and President Truman were in step on the wisdom of containment and that Hodge was not.[43]

The man in the middle—Kim Kyu-sik of the Coalition Committee and presiding officer of the Interim Legislative Assembly—fully appreciated that the polarization of the Korean political factions made any true democratic process impossible. Kim argued that the Koreanization of the military government, in the works for May 1947 and already functioning as a de facto "interim administration" under An Chae-hong, should include the complete reform of the Korean National Police and the elimination of corrupt, ineffective, and "Japanese" officials throughout the middle and lower levels of the bureaucracy. In the countryside, the failure to redistribute Japanese-owned and other abandoned and confiscated farmlands had given new life to the appeals of the Communists. The Kim-Yo coalition had made land reform a critical centrist policy. Even more distressing, there was no chance for free elections in Korea since the Korean Democratic Party and Korean Independence Party and their respective "youth associations" ruled the streets of the provincial cities and towns. The police did little or nothing to curb political violence. The prospect of national elections for a new provisional government— the goal of the Joint Commission—only exacerbated the problem of dealing with the "collaborators," who dominated the economy and the Korean National Police. Kim Kyu-sik despaired over the prospects for democracy in Korea. "Only after the police is reformed can we have a fair election."[44]

The Interim Legislative Assembly did little to strengthen the American bargaining position. The confrontational Right (represented by the Kim Ku and Syngman Rhee groups) blocked a reformist-accommodationist movement in which Kim Sung-su's Korean Democratic Party would form a moderate-right coalition with the Kim Kyu-sik and Yo Un-hyong's parties and their allies in the Right-Left Coalition Committee. The Kim Ku–Rhee forces, led by Shin Ik-hui, made "collaborationism" the litmus test of true patriotism and forced the Korean Democratic Party to take the defensive on matters of land reform and property distribution. Kim Sung-su bought off his xenophobic rivals by agreeing to attack Hodge. In January 1947 the assembly condemned trusteeship and the military government's policy of appeasing the Japanese and the Communists by a vote of forty-four to one. Kim Kyu-sik tried to resign as assembly chairman, but his peers rejected his resignation and proceeded to consider a new electoral law that would disenfranchise the Left and "collaborators," make some future president a potential dictator, and make it unlikely that anyone would enact economic reforms. The assembly's larger problems were those of omission. Even though General Hodge pressed it to come up with policies the military government could execute, the assembly failed to produce laws on land reform, economic regulation, rice production and distribution, business and banking reform, labor unionization, and a host of other pressing issues. The assembly spent a great deal of time and energy discussing the disposal of Japanese-owned assets and how to bar the worst collaborators from public employment and political participation.[45]

For much of its existence, the Interim Legislative Assembly also debated the structure of a future provisional government; this structure was described in two proposed constitutions, neither of which satisfied the military government. One constitution, championed by Shin Ik-hui, proposed that Korea have a strong presidential government, with the president elected by the legislature; much of the organization and powers of the new government mirrored those of the provisional government when it operated in China. Although Shin Ik-hui, known as a deft maneuverer among Korean politicians, enjoyed a strong reputation as a reformer-nationalist, his constitution (introduced on February 27, 1947) did not please the military government because it did not deal with fundamental issues of the franchise, civil rights, human rights protections, and the balance among the executive, legislative, and judicial branches. The proposed Korean government would be centralized and authoritarian, much like its Japanese predecessor. By tying this government to the provisional government, the Shin Ik-hui government looked like a coup in the making, with Kim Ku the savior-in-waiting. The assembly rejected the proposal on March 10. On March 3–11, 1947, the Interim Legislative Assembly debated another proposed constitution, this one endorsed by Kim Sung-su's Democratic Party and championed by that party's principal spokesman, Chang Dok-soo. This bill at least attempted to deal with the responsibilities of all three branches of government, but it also assigned great power to a future president. Military government analysts concluded that both bills had the same purpose: to replace the military government.[46]

In the meantime, Hodge completed the transfer of the civil departments of the military government to the control of Koreans—although they were certainly the "right sort" of Koreans, favored by Americans of the Progressive tradition. Of the eighteen most responsible administrators holding office in mid-1947, fourteen were university graduates (ten from American universities), ten were Christians or Christian educated, and six were refugees from north Korea. Almost all the officeholders had political ties to the Korean Democratic Party or the Korean Independence Party or had no political alignment. They all knew English, the official language. Almost all of them had been the target of Japanese suspicion and harassment, but not imprisonment. Only one—Cho Pyong-ok, director of the Department of Police—became a political force in South Korea after independence, based largely on his wide contacts within the Korean National Police.[47]

Responsive, honest, and efficient public administration by Americans and Koreans proved no cure for the internal political struggles in the American zone and the deepening Communist stranglehold on north Korea. Syngman Rhee kept expanding the reach of his NSRRKI within Korea and continued his criticism of Hodge as an incompetent appeaser, charges he spread in the United States through the reborn Korean Commission and its allies in the "Asia First" media. Lerch's death in September strengthened the pro-Rhee hard-liners in the military government, who thought that Lerch had been too kind to the Koreans and too soft on subversives and criminals. His replacement, Maj. Gen. William F. Dean, brought limited knowledge and limp convictions to the office of military governor. Kim Ku kept the provisional government–Korean Independence Party faction alive with conspiratorial plotting, demonstrations, street violence, and murder. Gunmen with ties to Kim Ku's supporters assassinated Yo Un-hyong in July 1947 and Chang Dok-soo in December 1947, the second leader of the Korean Democratic Party to be murdered by Kim Ku's loyalists. Political analysts within the military government saw a new upsurge in violence and the potential for civil war in the American zone that would dwarf the troubles of the autumn of 1946. The difficulty was determining whether the challenge would come from the rightists, disenfranchised by the Russians, or the leftists, suppressed and divided by the United States. Beset with the confusion and betrayals of the season—and Syngman Rhee stood first in the ranks of the betrayers—Hodge finally dissolved the Interim Legislative Assembly in December 1947, which set off another wave of protests.[48]

The lack of progress in the Joint Commission negotiations and the pallid performance of the Interim Legislative Assembly fed the growing pessimism within the military government and its embattled partner, the Coalition Committee. Kim Kyu-sik and Ahn Chae-hong thought that the Soviet-Korean factions on either side of the Thirty-eighth Parallel were on the ascent as they rallied to oppose the rightist factions of Kim Ku, Kim Sung-su, and Syngman Rhee. Hodge did not agree with their gloomy assessment in early 1947, but by midyear, he had joined the ranks of the despondent. The Koreans, Hodge reported, had been seduced by "rainbow promises of free land and share the wealth." Extremists on all sides were storing illegal arms and collecting war chests; the theft of American military property was on the rise. The Korean economy showed no signs of growth. Unless the Joint Commission produced a viable unification plan soon, "I expect to see terrorism by both factions begin on a scale that may approach an oriental style civil war."[49] By the end of July, Hodge reported that "anything may be expected, mostly unpleasant as far as we here are concerned."[50] Even the final passage of an electoral law in September and Marshall's stern talk to the Soviets about their resistance to any equitable Korean solution did not convince Hodge that his command no longer faced a potential insurrection.[51]

Within the State Department, which was supposed to assume the responsibility for governing Korea, and the Department of the Army, which was eager to end the military government and withdraw its two shrunken infantry divisions and their supporting units, support waned for the Joint Commission and a policy tied to the Moscow agreement. The reports from Seoul offered little optimism. Joseph Jacobs,

Hodge's senior political adviser, shared the general's fears. Unless someone produced a magic formula for Korean reunification, the military government would have to take action to destroy and divide the rightist coalition while holding the Communists at bay. "The only other safe alternative would be to arrange with the Soviet Union for mutual withdrawal of troops and let nature take its course which will eventually mean another Soviet satellite in Korea."[52] Syngman Rhee now made speeches that paired Hodge, Bunce, Bertsch, and Jacobs with Joseph Stalin and Kim Il-sung. Jacobs saw the distinct possibility of a Korean civil war that might match those in Greece and China in intensity and ferocity, fueled by subversives and partisans from the Soviet zone. "In order to control the situation the United States would probably be compelled to increase its armed forces in Korea and to station along the Thirty-eighth Parallel more or less permanently at least 1 division of well-trained American troops, not recruits, and we should have to train and equip a South Korean army of some considerable size."[53] General Brown, whose Joint Commission duties had taken him to Pyongyang twice in 1947, saw no way to break the Korean Communist–Soviet grip on the northern provinces. In his extended discussion with Lt. Gen. Albert C. Wedemeyer in August, Brown judged Korea to be on the brink of a civil war of revolutionary proportions. "Even the Right should be considered as Left." Brown thought that Communism per se had little appeal to Koreans as an ideology. It appealed to their anticolonialism and stubborn nationalism but not to their economic instincts, which were strongly entrepreneurial. Wedemeyer echoed Brown's concern over the lack of land reform and economic recovery and the growing polarization of Korean politicians. Korea might involve American troops in a civil war in Asia, the very thing the United States was attempting to avoid in China.[54]

Within the Washington bureaucracy, the problem of Korea received a full review in the summer of 1947, a review that produced a new policy statement by the State-War-Navy Coordinating Committee on August 4, 1947. The diplomats and generals proceeded on the assumption that the Joint Commission would make no breakthrough on a formula for establishing a provisional government for one Korea. At the same time, the military government had done all it could to foster a sound economy, a reformed educational system, wide political participation, and a legal liberation from Japanese colonialism. Although much more could have been done to strengthen the Korean economy, at least American policy had not restored Korean dependence on Japanese markets. On the political scene, Hodge had favored responsible domestic politicians, not expatriate dictators-in-waiting. The American military presence, however, was an irritant and not very effective since both American divisions were half strength, untrained, and afflicted with disciplinary problems.[55]

The Joint Chiefs of Staff provided a timely rationale for trimming the American commitment to a new Korea. Working on supporting studies for the Joint Emergency War Plan, the contingency plan for a war with the Soviet Union, the Joint Chiefs of Staff strategists finished Operation Plan Moonrise in August, timed

coincidentally with the issuance of the SWNCC policy statement. The plan outlined general war problems in Asia. The essential requirement was for the United
States to defend its air and naval bases in Japan from attacks from Vladivostok and
the rest of Soviet Asia. Against the likely American-Korean ground force opposition, five Soviet divisions could overrun Korea in a matter of weeks. One after
another, the army's senior generals, including Dwight D. Eisenhower, fell in line
behind the idea of withdrawing the XXIV Corps, even if it put Korea at risk. In late
September the Russians introduced the formal proposal for the immediate withdrawal of all foreign troops from Korea, which looked appealing until one read the
intelligence evaluations about the north Korean army-in-the-making and compared
its considerable combat capability with that of the Korean Constabulary. In the
meantime, civil unrest in the American zone threatened any sort of political reform
and made the military government the culprit for all of Korea's ills. It was determined that the United States should not, however, bear the onus of voiding the
Moscow agreement; it should make one more effort through the Joint Commission, while increasing economic assistance to southern Korea and enlarging and
transforming the Constabulary into a conventional army. The American public also
needed to know more about Korea, which was a "liberated" country, not a willing
part of the former Japanese empire. If the Russians continued to refuse to deal with
the Korean ultranationalists, the United States should plan to replace the Moscow
agreement formula with a political initiative in the General Assembly of the United
Nations. Desperate times required desperate measures.[56]

By October 1947, the meetings of the Joint Commission had become less fre-
quent and much less meaningful. From August to October, Secretary of State Marshall and Undersecretary Robert Lovett carried on a strained correspondence with
Molotov about the commission's lack of progress. The Soviet delegation spent
most of its time arguing for the proposal (advocated by both delegations at different times) that all foreign troops leave Korea according to a strict schedule. The
two Koreas, the Soviets said, could then negotiate with each other on how to unify
Korea. The Americans had already seen a hint of such "negotiations" in the low-
level espionage and sabotage activities in their occupation zone, and they watched
any sign of non-Communist political participation disappear in the Soviet zone.
There was no room for compromise. On October 18, 1947, the Joint Commission
met for the last time; again, the Soviets raised the issue of troop withdrawal and
announced that they would depart on a unilateral basis in 1948. The American delegation worked on a final communiqué that summarized the lack of agreement. On
October 21 the Russians left Seoul for the last time.

The U.S. government looked for a diplomatic rabbit hole in which to drop
the policy of a Korean trusteeship. It did not quite surrender the hope that some
sort of neutralization and unification might still be possible. Hodge and his advisers thought that there was only one choice: establish a separate republic in the
American zone. The Soviets would, of course, be stridently unhappy, but any
United Nations action on security issues could be addressed in the General As-

sembly, safe from any veto cast by the Soviet Union in the Security Council. The United States could introduce a resolution proposing that the United Nations take the responsibility for organizing an electorate and holding Korean elections, in both zones if possible, but in the American zone as quickly as possible. The State Department, not the army, would manage the process and provide Hodge with definitive guidance on assisting the United Nations. Both State and the army would provide funds for the reorganization of the south Korean government. As the American delegation guided the resolution through the approval process, the military government would transform itself into an interim national Korean administration governing for the benefit of the Korean people. Few thought that such a process would be simple, peaceful, and timely. The senior officers of the Department of State—Marshall, Lovett, George Kennan, Dean Rusk, W. Walton Butterworth, and John Allison—agreed with little enthusiasm that the United Nations might be the last, best hope for creating a Korea that would not be a pawn in the cold war.[57]

5

The United Nations Enters the Struggle, 1947–1948

The bright sunshine and the warmth of a late summer's day on Long Island made the opening of the Second Session of the General Assembly of the United Nations a celebration of nature over the work of man. With the temperature in the seventies, the air redolent of mowed grass and ripening apples, the delegates pushed into the General Assembly building, a deco monster saved from the World's Fair of 1939–1940. Some were anxious to prove the United Nations' ability to save the world from war. By September 17, 1947, the United Nations had two years of experience, but little accomplishment, in dealing with the turmoil of the postwar world. Since the adoption of the UN Charter at San Francisco in 1945, the United Nations had done little to develop an international common law for interstate behavior. More than fifty years and 8,000-plus General Assembly resolutions later, the issue is still in doubt, but optimism, however tempered, shaped the gathering of the assembly at Flushing Meadows that September. The assembly had a great issue of peace on its agenda. It was not Korea, but Palestine.[1]

Secretary of State George C. Marshall led the U.S. delegation to its front-row seats with his accustomed dignity and calm, but his outward manner belied deep reservations about the chances of a negotiated settlement between the Arabs and the Jews. Though uncomfortable at public speaking, Marshall did his duty in his opening address, which was most notable for its tilt toward the partition of Palestine. Although Marshall stressed the immediacy of the crises in Palestine and Greece, he also mentioned that Korea needed international attention. "The Korean people . . . are still not free," even though they had been liberated from Japanese colonialism. The division of Korea, the lack of progress by the Joint Commission, and the aspirations of the Koreans had created a situation that "cannot continue indefinitely." Perhaps the United Nations could find a road not taken to unification and independence. "We do not wish to have the inability of two powers to reach agreement delay any further the urgent and rightful claims of the Korean people to independence."[2]

On the same day that Secretary Marshall proposed that the General Assembly try its hand at peacemaking in Korea, Undersecretary of State Robert A. Lovett sent a message to Foreign Minister Andrei Vyshinsky about the failure of the Joint Commission. The State Department had already cleared the message with Great Britain and Nationalist China, the other partners in the Moscow agreement. In the best interests of the Korean people, Lovett asserted, the Moscow agreement approach should be modified or abandoned. "It is the intention, therefore, of my Government to refer the problem of Korean independence to the forthcoming sessions of the General Assembly of the United Nations."[3] The same phrase appeared in Marshall's speech. If the Korean issue were placed on the Security Council's agenda, the Soviet Union, as one of the council's five permanent members, would surely have vetoed any proposal. The Russians argued that the Korean impasse was the business of the Moscow agreement signatories and the Korean people, as defined by the Soviets, not the United Nations. The General Assembly, however, was veto-proof. Given the United States' leverage with the Western European and Latin American members, the assembly could reasonably be expected to approve an American proposal.[4]

As Secretary Marshall droned on about the challenges the United Nations faced in its mission of building a new world order out of the wreckage of European colonialism, the rest of the American delegation, freed from the strain of listening to simultaneous translation through heavy headphones, watched the secretary with dutiful intensity and admiration, real or feigned. In the pecking order of UN representation, the secretary of state served as the head of the American delegation, but in practice, the permanent representative and de facto head of the delegation was Warren R. Austin, a former U.S. senator (R-Vt.). A committed internationalist and protégé of Senator Arthur Vandenberg, Austin had served fifteen years in the Senate before President Truman appointed him to the United Nations as an ambassador. Austin's official position was to serve as the American "chief of mission" and Security Council representative. At age sixty-nine, Austin, a small-town lawyer and apple grower turned politician, had reached the point in his life when his attentiveness had become uneven. He was impatient and abrupt but altogether devoted to representing the United States in what he regarded as a noble experiment in global peacekeeping. He regarded the Soviet Union and Communism as enemies to be met with strength, but not suicidal confrontation. Austin had no special regional interests or expertise in the world of international politics, except for China, where he had once done business.[5]

Two other delegates would play important roles in shaping the future of Korea. One of them was Eleanor Roosevelt, the widow of FDR and high priestess of international human rights and American social reform. Among her many interests was the fate of Korean Christians, an interest cultivated by the Korean Commission and the several Protestant denominations with missionary headquarters in New York City. The other member, also a New York resident who moved in much the same elite social and political circles, was John Foster Dulles. Dulles's early adulthood had been shaped by World War I and the Versailles Peace Conference, which he had attended at age thirty-one as a minor functionary. As a protégé of Bernard Baruch and a key drafter of and negotiator for a failed plan for postwar reparations, Dulles became transformed from an indifferent New York corporation lawyer to a committed internationalist and public servant whose career ended with his death while serving as Dwight D. Eisenhower's secretary of state (1953–1959). In the autumn of 1947 Dulles had made a thirty-year career of international activism through his participation in nongovernmental associations, principally the World Council of Churches. The role came naturally to Dulles, the son of a Watertown, New York, Presbyterian minister and a Wilsonian idealist since his student days at Princeton University (class of 1908). He was a member of an extended family that included secretaries of state Robert Lansing and William Foster and several missionaries to China. Although his reserved manner and sparing use of words reinforced his image of probity and moral certitude, Dulles's commitment to Christianity, entrepreneurial economic development, improvement of the human condition, and innate individual liberties did not stop at the water's edge. Dulles preached the potential value of international organizations in constraining state lawlessness, and he wrote an important book on the subject of postwar reconstruction even before World War II began.

By 1945, Dulles had become the principal spokesman of the international wing of the Republican Party and Governor Thomas Dewey's shadow secretary of state, assuming that Dewey won the presidency in 1948. Dulles was also a confidant of Senator Vandenberg, the embattled foe of Senator Robert A. Taft and the party's unilateralist and isolationist wing. Dulles's association with Dewey and Vandenberg ensured that the Truman administration included him as an adviser to the American delegation to the San Francisco conference that created the United Nations. Given his experience at Versailles, Dulles felt that his advice should have been more influential in the drafting of the UN Charter. He predicted that the division of ultimate authority between the Security Council and the General Assembly would lead to paralysis in a crisis. Unlike many of his contemporaries, Dulles regarded the General Assembly as the ultimate voice of the international community in the search for peace, a view shared by Austin. He was equally sure that the challenge to peace came primarily from international, revolutionary Communism and its devil's pact with the Soviet Union. Unlike other of his contemporaries, Dulles regarded the Chinese, Korean, and Japanese test of containment to be as important as support for the nations of Western Europe. Like Eleanor Roosevelt, his New York City domain included pro-Korean activists. Although it is tempting to link the two old Princetonians John Foster Dulles and Syngman Rhee, there is no evidence that they had contact as students or had any continuing relationship. In 1947 Dulles had certainly made no specific commitments except that Korea should not be abandoned to Communism.[6]

With the Soviet delegation, led by the formidable Andrei A. Gromyko, in constant opposition, the Americans moved with all calculated haste to make Korea a United Nations responsibility, but as a foster parentage arrangement that could be directed by the State Department. The thirteen-member committee that controlled the agenda voted eleven to two to consider the Korean question. The issue then went to the First (Political and Security) Committee of the General Assembly, one of the seven committees of the whole that dealt initially with General Assembly agenda items. To refer an issue to the First Committee, however, required a General Assembly vote; in this case, the vote was taken on September 23, barely a week after the first official American proposal. The vote to refer the Korean question to the First Committee passed forty-one to six, with seven abstentions. The Russians cried "foul" in every imaginable way that denied jurisdiction and legitimacy.[7]

The First Committee debates on the Korea question soon revealed the same divisions that had stymied the Joint Commission half a world away. The American proposal reflected earlier concepts. First, the United Nations, the occupying powers, and the Koreans would create a provisional government for both zones through some sort of democratic process, preferably elections, which should be held no later than March 31, 1948. The Korean government, with UN assistance, would create its own security forces as soon as possible. When the Korean government and the United Nations agreed that the Koreans could defend themselves, all foreign forces would leave the peninsula. The instrument for UN participation would be a special nine-nation commission that would bear the responsibility of determining the extent of Korean participation and the legitimacy of the Korean participants. The UN commission would organize and supervise the electoral process by which the Koreans would adopt a constitution and establish a government. The Soviets found this plan as flawed on Long Island as it had been in Seoul. Gromyko offered a simpler solution: withdraw all foreign troops by the end of January 1948, and then let the Koreans form a government without foreign interference. The process of forming a Korean government in New York, the Russians argued, required Korean participation *now,* and the occupying powers should form delegations as they saw fit. Dulles could not let this plan stand, so he amended it to require that both sides hold elections for the Korean representatives to the United Nations.[8]

The First Committee first disposed of the Russian proposal—as amended by the United States—and accepted it by a vote of forty-one to zero, with seven abstentions. The aggravated Gromyko demanded another vote, this one on the original Russian proposal, which was rejected by a vote of six to thirty-five, with six abstentions. Since this division would probably be repeated when the General Assembly considered the American proposal in a plenary session, the First Committee went ahead and drew up a plan for a nine-nation committee with political and geographic balance. It had only one precedent: the formation of an eleven-nation special commission to investigate the Arab-Jewish conflict over the future of Palestine. This new group would be entitled the United Nations Temporary Commission on Korea (UNTCOK). With the Russians protesting at every step, Dulles recommended Australia, Canada, Nationalist China, France, El Salvador, India, the Philippines, Syria, and the Ukrainian Soviet Socialist Republic as UNTCOK members. The Ukrainians refused to serve, following Gromyko's nonparticipation policy. The First Committee accepted an eight-nation UNTCOK by a vote of forty-six to zero, with four abstentions. The UNTCOK solution completed the work of the First Committee.[9]

The First Committee's final draft resolution committed the United Nations to work toward the rapid creation of an independent Korea and the withdrawal of foreign troops. The Koreans themselves would play a major part in determining the process by which UNTCOK would supervise the creation of a Korean government by elections. The Koreans would establish their own governmental agencies and armed forces without the interference of any nation that belonged to the United Nations. The first step would be to hold elections on March 31, 1948 (with adult suffrage and a secret ballot), for representatives who would work with UNTCOK in forming a national assembly. All the elections would be supervised by UNTCOK to ensure the sanctity of polling places. The elected representatives would be apportioned by population. Whether the UN representatives realized it or not, this formula—for which the Russians had been fighting for almost three years—was likely to produce a regime unlike the Stalinist model growing under Pyongyang's control north of the Thirty-eighth Parallel. When a Korean national government had taken power, foreign troops would depart within ninety days, if not sooner.[10]

On November 13 the General Assembly, in its plenary session, considered Resolution 112 (II) as reported out by the First Committee. The debate lasted one day. The Soviets made a final effort to postpone action by insisting that a Korean delegation should be present to participate in the debate. Dulles pointed out that the resolution included ample opportunities for Koreans to participate and to do so in Korea, where representativeness would be more likely. When Gromyko insisted that troop withdrawal should precede the elections, not follow a completed political process, Dulles countered that such an arrangement would simply delay Korean independence. In sum, the cursory debate largely repeated the arguments heard by the First Committee and changed no one's position. On November 14 the General Assembly approved Resolution 112 (II) by a vote of forty-three to zero, with six abstentions, all members of the Soviet voting bloc. The United Nations would be going to Korea.[11]

ON THE BRINK, 1947–1948

Whether UNTCOK would eventually bring salvation or disaster to Korea, it did not address the plight of the Korean people or the immediate problems of the dual government administering the American occupation zone. By the autumn of 1947, the thrills of liberation had long since passed. At the personal level, problems of survival drove millions of Koreans to despair. Almost every province and major city had experienced a 30 percent increase in population as the refugees from Manchuria, the Soviet zone, and Japan looked for new homes and work, both of which were in short supply. Many Korean refugees became wards of their hard-pressed extended families. Seven-year-old Bryan Choe arrived in Kwangju, Chollanam-do, with his parents and younger brother after a harrowing flight from Manchuria through the Soviet zone; all the family's remaining wealth arrived in gold and gems sewn into the two brothers' winter coats. Bryan's father never quite recovered from losing his job as a store manager, but his mother took in laundry and taught school. They lived with relatives, split by politics. One uncle, a police supervisor, threatened to kill or imprison all Communists, including an aunt, who promised to lead the coming revolution. Other young refugees fared badly. For the bright, petite teenager Choi Pong-sun, also known as Matsuko Nagayama, her homecoming to Wonju was so bleak that she and her brother attempted to run away and return to Japan, from which they had fled with their family in 1945.[12]

For the 3,231 Americans who made up the U.S. Army Military Government in Korea (USAMGIK), each day became a recurring challenge to make some difference in building a new Korea. For the 2,594 military personnel, release from active duty or transfer provided hope; for the 637 civilians, the reconstruction of Korea often had greater implications. By August 1947, Christian missionaries (not Koreans) officially recognized by the USAMGIK numbered fewer than 100; this tally did not account for at least equal numbers of former missionaries and "mish kids" who returned to Korea to serve in the occupation government as Department of the Army civilian employees (or DACs) or later in the Korea mission of the U.S. Economic Cooperation Administration (ECA). Of the five adult males in the Underwood family—stalwarts of Korean Presbyterianism and Chosun Christian College—patriarch Horace H. and eldest son Horace G. worked in the Department of Education; John became the pastor of Seoul Union Church, while twin brother James remained in a church in America; Richard, leaving the army for Hamilton College, learned that his teenage classmates (he had turned twenty) neither cared for nor believed his stories about being a Counterintelligence Corps (CIC) agent in Korea. Born and raised in Pyongyang, William Hamilton Shaw, the son of Methodist missionaries, left the U.S. Navy, where he had commanded a PT boat, to become an instructor at the Korean Coast Guard Academy at Chinhae; he and his family then moved to Seoul, where he worked for the ECA.[13]

The challenge of building a new economy and political culture proved irresistible to some Americans. Demobilized as a temporary colonel while serving in Japan, economist Charles H. Donnelly went to Korea as a DAC and key member of the National Economic Board in January 1948. A disciple of the independent, charismatic Dr. Arthur A. Bunce, Donnelly remained in Korea until August 1948 and the termination of U.S. Army Forces in Korea. Donnelly found Korea's economic problems challenging and the Korean lack of civic virtue maddening. John C. Caldwell, the son of Shanghai missionaries and married to a Korean-born "mish kid," left the OSS group in China still in uniform to be the military government's head of "civil information," a mix of public education and psychological warfare. Alternating between the refugee debriefing station at Kaesong and Seoul, Caldwell sympathized with the refugees, who would always be suspect in the south. By 1948, Caldwell, now a DAC in what would become the U.S. Information Service, had established a set of cultural centers throughout Korea where Koreans could read English books and newspapers and stay warm. Caldwell also admired Bunce's dedication to agricultural revival, but he thought that the ECA should not have exported rice to Japan for hard currency. The mission also charged farmers for desperately needed fertilizer (500,000 metric tons by 1948) that had been earmarked as "gifts" from the United States, although the money went into a long-term agricultural development fund. Caldwell admired the American missionaries in the USAMGIK—the Underwoods, Bill Shaw, Harold Voelkel, Howard Moffett, and Charles Bernheisel—for their ability to mollify the Koreans and calm the Americans.[14]

For Rev. Charles A. Sauer, who served the Methodist Church in Korea from 1921 until 1962 except for his exile during World War II, the struggle against the Communists exposed the American churches as cowardly—just as they had been during the struggles against the Japanese in the 1930s. In his letters to the *Christian Advocate,* Sauer expressed his dismay that there had been attacks on the military government but none against Pyongyang from American churchmen. With no real protest, the United States had allowed the confiscation of five Methodist schools, three hospitals, nine primary schools, and fifteen major church complexes in the Soviet zone. Methodist and Presbyterian refugees numbered 200,000 among the million Koreans who had fled south. As for the southern Communists, Sauer thought that only 10 percent were hard-core Reds or "bricks." Another 20 percent were "tomatoes," weak but all Red. The majority were "radishes," Red only on the outside and ready to switch if sufficiently pressured to change loyalties.[15]

For General Hodge, the new year and the arrival of UNTCOK focused all his attention on closing down the military government, redeploying the XXIV Corps, and turning over the governance of Korea—at least below the Thirty-eighth Parallel—to the Koreans. Hodge thought that unification was a dead issue. His goal was to contain the southern Communists, reform the Korean National Police and expand the Korean Constabulary into a real army, and prevent disaffected Korean politicians of whatever persuasion from subverting the interim government and the security forces. Hodge had no illusions that democracy would come to Korea with elections. "I've never seen a people so politically minded and at the same time so ignorant of the political facts of life as viewed from the standpoint of representative government. Their sole idea is personal and individual power, by fair means or foul."[16] Hodge remained concerned that his own troops would only increase the tension. Maj. Gen. Orlando "Pinky" Ward, commanding the U.S. Sixth Infantry

Division, minced no words in describing his division as close to collapse. The division had gone from sixteen thousand officers and men in early 1947 to thirty-two hundred effectives a year later. Those remaining spent most of their time on house-keeping chores and combating thievery at seven posts in the four southernmost provinces and Cheju-do. On a good day, the division could mount three or four motorized patrols of platoon strength in an area of responsibility encompassing twenty thousand square miles. Without Korean police and Constabulary assistance, the Sixth Division could not even protect itself, let alone anyone else.[17]

General Hodge felt his key civilian advisers move away from the flagpole as they anticipated the shift of power in Korea. William Langdon remained the consul general in Seoul and focused on American civilian personal and business interests, a marginal problem. Clyde B. Sargent, a key political operative since 1946, resigned his position as head of a political advisory group in April. Sargent believed that his group, which identified and contacted Korean politicians, had become an embarrassing target of Communist propaganda. Sargent also believed that any Korean regime in the south would not survive an American withdrawal. Joseph E. Jacobs was slightly more optimistic, even though the guidance from Washington was "as topsy-turvy as ever." The Korean Commission's lobbying in Washington simply confused everyone; Syngman Rhee's representatives were as slippery as the Russians. Arthur Bunce conceded that Rhee now appeared to be the heir apparent to Hodge. UNTCOK would probably establish a process that would (unintentionally) favor Rhee. The current illusion in Seoul was that Rhee "will institute a whole series of necessary reforms which will so appeal to the North Koreans that their army will revolt, kill all the nasty Communists, and create a lovely liberal democracy to the everlasting credit of the U.S.A.!"[18]

For many of the American advisers to the interim government, the economy of the American zone would drive the politics of 1948. The economic indicators were mixed. The American zone had given up on coal shipments from the Soviet zone, although electricity still came from north Korea until May 1948. Coal for southern Korea factories and the power generators now came from Japan and the United States; the value of coal and oil imports almost doubled between 1947 and 1948. Half the coal went to the railroad system. The primary concern for the USAMGIK was agricultural production of rice and other grains, which increased 25 percent in 1946–1949 but still fell well short of the peak production years, 1941–1944. Heavy rains in 1946 destroyed 20 percent of the rice harvest, followed by a 1947 drought that reduced the harvest to half wartime levels. Cereal grain production remained a source of tension between Korean farmers and the government because the fear of grain shortages in the cities forced the government to continue rice collections and to extend this practice to the "summer grains"— barley, wheat, and rye. In 1948 the government planned to buy more than 15 percent of the estimated grain harvest (120,000 of 765,000 metric tons), but any plan for pricing crops that had previously been unregulated angered the farmers. Whether because of poor growing conditions or evasion, rice and grain collections for 1947 and 1948 were about one-third below quota in the two Cholla provinces and North Kyong-sang, hotbeds of political opposition from the South Korean Labor Party (SKLP). A July typhoon destroyed 28,000 metric tons of rice in the Chollas, as well as killing 75 villagers and injuring 254. Summer floods affected 250,000 people and damaged or destroyed 100,000 homes. The interim government's continued inde-cision on land reform provided the oppositionists with a cause that had wide appeal.[19]

Even if the Koreans had had more money to spend, they would have found little to buy. Imported consumer goods came from Japan and the United States and went to the U.S. Army and its civilian employees, Korean and American, includ-ing officials of the interim government. Consumer goods manufactured in Korea were also controlled and rationed to a wider group of consumers that included co-operative farmers, critical industrial and service workers, and the Korean security forces. In 1948 the favored consumers numbered 437,000 Koreans of a population estimated at over 20 million. The scarcity of goods and the government's efforts to check runaway inflation produced an illegal shadow economy that benefited any subversive organization (such as the rightist youth associations) but favored the Communists most because of their ties to the radical Choryon (the association of Korean residents in Japan) and the Japanese Communist Party. The Pyongyang regime also aided its southern comrades by licensing only companies and shippers that served as SKLP fronts. The level of smuggling remained a chronic source of crime, corruption, and disillusionment; the black markets in every major city served too many customers to disappear and enjoyed tacit Korean police protec-tion. American consumer goods, which were highly prized, disappeared at Pusan and Inchon, sometimes with GI collusion. Any U.S. Army installation looked like a great shopping center without checkout counters; the Korean attitude toward pub-lic property (Japanese or American) was that such property belonged to anyone clever enough to steal it and encouraged a "slicky boy" culture of young thieves with world-class skills. One of the most active sites of illicit Japanese-Korean trade and intense klepto-revolutionary organization was Cheju-do island, fifty miles off Korea's southwest coast.[20]

The deep economic uncertainty in southern Korea could be reduced through only two basic sources—American assistance and the disposition of Japanese prop-erty in Korea. Until the U.S. Economic Cooperation Administration established its Korean mission in 1949, the U.S. Army served as the principal conduit of economic assistance. Military surplus property valued at $141 million passed into Korean hands; an estimated 40 percent of the property went to the Korean police and army, but the rest went to the Korean government and private hands and represented im-portant contributions to the infrastructure of transportation, construction, medical aid, public sanitation, and communications. The second source of support—$301 million—came from the appropriated Government Aid and Relief in Occupied Areas (GARIOA) trust fund, administered first by the U.S. Army and then by the State Department until the program ended in 1949. This money provided immediate relief through the importation of food, agricultural supplies, raw materials (e.g., lumber, cotton), fuel and petroleum, medical supplies, and clothing and textiles. The peak assistance, $180 million, came in 1948. Very little of the GARIOA imports contributed to long-term capital investment ("reconstruction") in industry, mining, and fishing; from 1945 to 1949, such purchases of long-term durable goods amounted to only $70 million, or about 15 percent of GARIOA imports.[21]

The fate of Japanese-owned property and assets in Korea, valued at more than $2 billion, remained in limbo until 1948, a golden goose fattened for the many contesting potential butchers. A series of decisions in Washington and Tokyo in 1947, crafted by the State-War-Navy Coordinating Committee over General MacArthur's opposition, opened the door for a "Korea for the Koreans" distribution plan. Japanese property in Korea would not be used for Allied reparations; former Japanese owners would have no legal right to sue or to sell their confiscated property. Korea's uncertain political future, however, made Hodge, working through the New Korea Corporation, reluctant to auction off anything but farmland. At least he knew that the farmer-buyers were Korean and would eventually produce cash crops that would repay their government-backed loans. Businesses were another matter. Simply assessing the holdings and identifying the owners of 5,358 business enterprises took more than two years. The potential buyers with capital—avid bargain seekers—all brought political problems: Japanese, Chinese Nationalists, American fortune seekers, Korean "collaborators." The Interim Legislative Assembly liked the idea of using Japanese assets to build Korea. It even talked about additional claims for reparations against Japan, even after the United States pointed out that Korea was not eligible under law. Unlike Poland, for example, Korea was a victim without a recognized exile government. Hodge and his advisers preferred to pass the vested property problem on to some successor Korean government. Even a land reform bill could not clear the landholding bloc of the Korean Democratic Party (KDP) in the assembly. The reformers also wanted a law that would allow the prosecution of current large landholders for collaborationism. The prospect of some UN-sponsored solution allowed Hodge to dissolve the assembly and then announce on March 22, 1948, a plan to sell Japanese-owned farmlands (already cultivated under lease agreements) to some 500,000 tenant farm families. Within five months, the military government had sold off all but 15 percent of the vested farmlands. Ninety percent of other Japanese property remained in government hands, which would give a successor Korean government an enormous economic advantage in terms of patronage for anti-Japanese politicians such as Syngman Rhee and Kim Ku. In the meantime, American economic assistance would keep the southern Korean economy barely afloat.[22]

The Korean security forces reflected the desperation of the larger society south of the Thirty-eighth Parallel and offered little sense of security. For the Korean National Police (KNP), the turmoil started at the top. Director Cho Pyong-ok and Chang Taek-sang, chief of the Seoul metropolitan police, started a guerrilla war against each other. Cho decided that he could clean up his own image by attacking

Chang's division for corruption and police brutality; the real issue was probably Chang's growing power within the KDP. The Americans suspected Cho Pyong-ok's collusion with Kim Ku in the assassination of a second KDP chairman, Chang Dok-su, on December 2, 1947. Chang Taek-sang's secret agents reported that Kim Ku had a vendetta against the KDP. Cho unleashed two trusted lieutenants from his national detective bureau against Chang's own chief of detectives and senior captains, all veterans of Japanese service. The furor played out in the press: charges and countercharges, resignations, judicial actions, and a fourth assassination attempt on Chang Taek-sang. Syngman Rhee and Kim Sung-su tried to mediate, probably seeking new allies. The police corruption issue—and the KNP's Japanese heritage—was a national problem that proved intractable for the Americans. A policeman made less money than American-paid houseboys, and extortion in all forms characterized KNP stations in every province. Examining the KNP's accounts, Charles Donnelly found that the police controlled one-twentieth of south Korea's entire coal production. "The National Police have so many private rackets that NEB [National Economic Board] members thought it unnecessary to give them everything they said they need." Only Division G (Pusan) had a reputation for discipline, impartiality, and efficiency, largely because the division chief had developed a system of business enterprises that supported his police and gave their families jobs.[23]

Despite its own internal problems, the Korean Constabulary showed signs of organizational vitality and growing status at the expense of the Korean National Police. While American advisers to the KNP shrank to 10, advisers to the Constabulary reached 100 in early 1948 and grew to 248 by year's end. When General MacArthur and the Pentagon agreed to enlarge the Constabulary to 50,000 by July 1948, they authorized the transfer of not only American rifles and carbines but also light artillery, machine guns, M-2 half-tracks, M-24 light tanks, and M-8 "Greyhound" armored cars. The new arms made the Constabulary the firepower king of Korea—below the Thirty-eighth Parallel. A 50,000-man Constabulary was already close to a fact in March, the date of its new manpower authorization. In April 1948 General Hodge received specific orders to prepare for every military contingency except an invasion of north Korea. Hodge immediately ordered the creation of formal schools for the Constabulary, with American arms and instructors from the two American divisions. On May 20, 1948, Brig. Gen. William L. Roberts replaced Col. Terrill E. "Terrible" Price as senior adviser to the Department of Internal Security (DIS). Roberts immediately saw that having two headquarters (DIS and the Korean Constabulary) was a redundancy, and Hodge authorized him to cut the DIS staff and build up the Constabulary's headquarters. Roberts also approved the creation of a Military Police Command that would stamp out subversion and indiscipline within the Constabulary. The first two police commanders, Maj. Choi Sok and Lt. Col. Shin Sang-chul, were former Japanese officers and trusted members of the Constabulary's first class.[24]

Roberts's assignment to Korea sent signals to veteran advisers such as Jim Hausman that better times lay ahead. Roberts appeared to be just another fifty-seven-year-old balding, fleshy brigadier on the eve of retirement, which he was, but he was also much more. From a small town on the Ohio River, William L. Roberts (known as Lynn to his friends) had left Ohio for West Point (class of 1913) and a full life as a cavalry and progressive armored officer. Tested in five campaigns in France in 1918, Roberts held troop commands and attended schools that prepared him for the next war. Although a sound trainer and tactician, Roberts did not match the meteoric rise of many of his contemporaries. In late 1944 he was still a colonel commanding an armored combat command, one of three such combined arms task forces in an American armored division. In Bastogne, however, Roberts's Combat Command B, Tenth Armored Division found itself surrounded with the 101st Airborne Division, and Roberts's tankers provided the mobile firepower that the paratroopers sorely lacked. Roberts's own performance in a high-stress, high-visibility command earned him a Silver Star and a Legion of Merit and the respect of two future army chiefs of staff, Omar N. Bradley and J. Lawton Collins. He also enjoyed good relations with Maj. Gen. Charles L. Bolté, the personable army G-3, a decorated veteran of both world wars and the army's Korean "action officer." Collins characterized Roberts as "a man of integrity and high professional attainments," and Matthew B. Ridgway called him "keen [and] resourceful," if sometimes tactless. Douglas MacArthur reported that Roberts was "physically strong, mentally alert and of [the] highest moral character." An assessment of 115 combat arms brigadier generals in America's European army in 1945 rated Roberts twenty-eighth in value to the service. Roberts had a direct line to the Pentagon that did not depend on MacArthur's approval.[25]

General Roberts showed good sense in focusing his own efforts on capturing more resources from the shrinking U.S. XXIV Corps, whose commanders had more arms and equipment than they had men to maintain them. Roberts let Hausman take the lead on dealing with the Koreans, especially as counselor to the younger, more professional officers. Roberts established a Provisional Military Advisory Group–Korea (PMAG-K) with a table of organization that would provide American operational and training counterparts down to the Constabulary battalion level. He then let the Pentagon know that he needed more high-quality junior officers direct from the States, not XXIV Corps officers in the wrong specialties who had overseas tours to complete. While Roberts waited for more help, his staff culled the rifle companies of the U.S. Sixth Infantry Division, which was due to leave its area in the southernmost provinces, for capable captains and lieutenants who had already been training Constabulary companies. Few of the PMAG officers foresaw how exciting their assignments would become by the end of the year.[26]

The political confusion in the American zone reinforced the conclusion of the Communist elite in Pyongyang that they could continue building socialism in one zone without interference from any source, foreign or domestic. With much fanfare, the Red Army prepared to leave the Soviet zone in late 1948, comfortable with the arrangements for Russian and Soviet-Korean party officials and military officers to remain within the Korean Workers' (Communist) Party, the government, and the security forces. The regime squeezed its potential opponents harder and harder. In December 1947 it changed currency and gave the people one week to exchange old Japanese yen at devalued rates. Industrial collectivization continued, designed to support the Soviet Union's Asian provinces. In the meantime, the Communists tightened their control on the zone north of the Thirty-eighth Parallel; the flow of refugees declined dramatically early in 1948 and did not increase when the weather improved. Those who did escape reported more aggressive action by Border Guard patrols. Incidents of border violence increased, with seventy-four clashes in February alone. The Korean National Police reported 21 dead and 150 wounded (most of them civilians) along the border in the first three months of 1948.

Kim Il-sung's personal strength continued to grow. The Second Party Congress (March 1948) enlarged and reorganized the Central Committee to suit Kim as the new group tilted the balance toward Kim's Kapsan faction, allied with the Yanan fiction, and away from the domestic Communists and Pak Hon-yong's exiles from the SKLP. The Potemkin parties—the Democratic Party and the quasi-religious Chongwudang—survived as "popular front" facades because they attracted naive regime critics who could then be identified as dissidents and eliminated. Chongwudang members maintained contacts with their southern brethren of Chondogyo, which could provide an oppositionist cover for espionage and subversion. When Chondogyo's leaders shifted their support to Syngman Rhee, Chongwudang's hard-core Communists, led by Kim Tal-hyon and his Russian advisers, still supported a small Chongwudang faction in the Kyongsang provinces, which provided a minor alternative to the SKLP for subversion in the south.[27]

Supported by a clique of Russian party officials and KGB agents in Pyongyang—but not by the Red Army—Pak Hon-yong continued to argue that the underground cells and action groups of the South Korean Workers' Party would block elections in the south and mount a war of terrorism, guerrilla warfare, and sabotage. Pak predicted that any Korean "puppet" government that replaced the Americans—one most likely headed by Syngman Rhee—would topple from dual pushes coming from the SKLP and Rhee's "rightist" foes, who were well-established within the KNP and funded by the "collaborators" of the Korean Democratic Party or the youth associations affiliated with Kim Ku's provisional government–Korean Independence Party faction. In addition to the regular party cells, the SKLP had two critical new bases: the Korean Constabulary and the teachers and students of the urban high schools, protected from KNP raids by tradition and the naive Americans in the Bureau of Education. Given to romantic optimism about the moral rightness of Communism, Pak probably ignored any signs that the SKLP leadership had been penetrated by anti-Communist informers in the pay of the 971st CIC Detachment, the KNP, and varied rightist groups. The 971st CIC Detachment claimed to run 180 informants within the SKLP; one of the most effective agents was a north Korean Communist political officer who defected and started a new life (patiently and carefully) within the strategic Seoul "City Branch" of the SKLP.

The 971st CIC Detachment believed that its penetration had been so successful in 1947–1948 that the USAMGIK "has had adequate warning of impending disturbances and contemplated sabotage," an optimistic but not inaccurate assessment of its work. Given their prior experience with non-Soviet Communists, the Russians in Pyongyang probably saw the SKLP as a useful but weak reed in the swamp of Asian revolution.[28]

Kim Il-sung doubted that Pak's plans ("romantic deviationism") would liberate all Korea from the Americans and their "flunkies" and "puppets" in Seoul. In fact, he believed that the Americans themselves were no more than the "flunkies" of the imperialistic Japanese, who wanted Korea back in their economic thrall. In a major address on February 8, 1948, titled "On the Occasion of the Creation of the Korean People's Army," Kim announced the enlargement of the security forces and the creation of a regular north Korean army, by conscription if necessary. The United Nations would do nothing more than rubber-stamp the power of the southern reactionaries. The task of the People's Army would be to protect north Korea and then unite all Korea before the emerging imperialist coalition of the United States, south Korea, and Japan could rearm. There could be no compromise with imperialism, even in the guise of the United Nations.[29]

THE 1948 ELECTIONS: THE PRELIMINARIES

Between the arrival of the United Nations Temporary Commission on Korea in Seoul in January 1948 and the Republic of Korea's independence day on August 15, 1948, the creation of two antagonistic Korean states became an irreversible certainty. War between the two Koreas also became inevitable, with or without the intervention of allies. Indeed, the war that ravaged all Korea from 1950 to 1953 began in April 1948 as a classic people's war, the Phase II insurgency in Mao Zedong's formulation. The elections sponsored and observed by UNTCOK in the American zone in May 1948 became a casus belli as well as a fig leaf for the liquidation of the military government and the eventual withdrawal of all U.S. Army units (except the advisory group) by July 1949. The Russian Twenty-fifth Army also departed north Korea, but it left behind a political-training mission of 550 officers and men and a naval force of more than 30,000, as well as weapons intended for the Korean People's Army (KPA). This gave the north Koreans an immediate advantage in firepower that the KPA used to blast open partisan infiltration routes across the Thirty-eighth Parallel. Although the Republic of Korea, a nation born in war, survived the violent challenges to its very creation, the United States adopted a policy of disengagement that made a larger war a certainty.

For reasons that were self-serving and idealistic, the army officers and diplomats who handled Korean affairs in Seoul, Tokyo, and Washington tried to manage disengagement in such a way as to defend south Korea from the Communists within the policy framework stated in National Security Council Memorandum 8 (April 2, 1948), the definitive guidance for relations with Korea. The first order of business in the New Year was to ensure that UNTCOK came, saw, and did something to extract the United States from its Korean quagmire. UNTCOK arrived under a cloud created by Canadian prime minister Mackenzie King's threat to withdraw his nation from UNTCOK if the commission left the United States. According to Lester B. Pearson, King's ambassador to the United States, unless the Russians reversed their position and accepted the UNTCOK mission in Pyongyang, any UNTCOK inquiry would be futile and probably provocative. President Truman himself reassured King "that the Korean matter itself is of considerably less importance" than King believed, especially as a potential embarrassment for the United Nations. The Canadians should not take up the fears spread by the British government of Clement Attlee and Ernest Bevin, Laborite isolationists. At best, the Russians might cooperate; at worst, two-thirds of the Korean people would become an independent nation. King agreed that Canada would remain a participant, but only on the condition that Russian noncooperation would allow UNTCOK to refer the issue back to the General Assembly for reconsideration.[30]

The north Koreans, with Russian approval, rejected any contact with UNTCOK by means of radio broadcasts throughout January, and every effort to reach Pyongyang that month ended with silence or rejection. The south Korean leaders were anything but quiet. Before UNTCOK held its first formal consultative meeting with the south Korean political elite—from moderate right to ultranationalist right—a group led by Kim Ku, Kim Kyu-sik, Shin Ik-hui, and Syngman Rhee offered to reform the provisional government and hold either a national election or one in the American zone only. This unsuccessful preemptive strike simply dramatized that a March 31 election deadline was absurd, and Hodge could hardly allow a coalition party masquerading as a legitimate government (the Koreans claimed a lineage back to the constitution of 1919) to manage any election. Under the firm, courageous direction of its first chairman, Indian diplomat K. P. S. Menon, UNTCOK attended a rally of seventy-five thousand "students" and other youthful street politicians in a Seoul stadium on January 12. Menon asked for cooperation in finding a way to unify Korea through negotiations with Pyongyang. Rhee and Kim Ku stalked off the stage, leaving Cho Pyong-ok to urge UNTCOK to form a government before a war began. As UNTCOK's investigating subcommittees met over the next three weeks, the UN commissioners received a cram course on Korean revolutionary politics. The result was a hung commission that wanted more guidance from its master, the General Assembly, which was meeting in its legal but truncated form as the Interim Assembly at Flushing Meadows. The majority of five (Australia, Canada, India, Syria, and El Salvador) agreed only on the need for more time and thought. The minority members (abstaining) were no more unified. Nationalist China and the Philippines supported action to make south Korea independent, while France made no commitment of any sort. General Hodge and his advisers detected a taint of anti-Americanism and leftist anti-imperialism among the commissioners, but not in Ambassador Menon, whom the

Koreans condemned as a fellow-traveling pro-Communist neutralist. It is true that the commissioners worried about the lack of leftist Korean representation.[31]

UNTCOK's understandable procrastination set off another round of political realignment in south Korea. As UNTCOK perceived the situation, Kim Kyu-sik, even without the dead Yo Un-hyong, still appealed to the Americans and to Korea's dispirited moderates, some of whom had rallied to An Chae-hong. Sensing new opportunities, Kim Ku became more strident about the possibility of Korean-Korean negotiations for a unified Korea. Kim Kyu-sik followed his example, but Rhee urged immediate elections in the south. This new twist aligned Rhee with the conservative KDP (again), which was still well funded but intimidated by physical attacks on its leaders and the constant charges of "collaborationism." Rhee, however, kept up his attacks on Hodge and the military government, thus maintaining his claim to independence, while he encouraged UNTCOK to get on with southern elections. Rhee believed that the odd couple of Kim and Kim would not stay betrothed, especially if they actually tried to negotiate with Pyongyang. Rhee improved his status with Hodge when he remained quiet about a Japanese crackdown on Korean schools and associations throughout Honshu. Still no Rhee enthusiast, Hodge predicted that elections in southern Korea alone, even if the non-Communist Left participated, would produce a government dominated by Syngman Rhee, whatever the constitutional form of government.[32]

As the UNTCOK commissioners prepared to take their woeful report back to New York, the Koreans treated them to several examples of street demonstrations and mob violence Seoul style. Rightist groups and a leftist labor-student coalition formed a "General Strike Committee against the UN Korean Commission" and called for a nationwide shutdown of factories, the railroads, and communications. The strike committee, dominated by SKLP organizers, gave Hodge three days to reply to its demands: the withdrawal of UNTCOK, the withdrawal of all foreign troops, the free distribution of rice to working people, a threefold increase in salaries, uncompensated land reform, the nationalization of key industries, a wide purge of collaborators and freedom for political prisoners, and the transfer of power "to the People's Committee as in North Korea." Protest demonstrations outside Doksu Palace turned ugly, with riot battalions of the metropolitan police and youth association action groups surging around the city hall, hotel district, and commercial heart of the city. Hodge committed some U.S. infantry, military police, and Constabulary companies to back up the police. In 105 incidents between February 5 and 12, the military government reported 55 attacks on the railroads alone. Terrorists assaulted 21 KNP substations. The uncertain number of casualties included 12 policemen killed and 36 civilians injured; arrests numbered in the thousands. Hodge increased his security arrangements and awaited UNTCOK's next move.[33]

When Ambassador Menon and Victor Hoo, one of the two Chinese Nationalist commissioners, arrived at Flushing Meadows, they found the Interim Assembly prepared to fly in an unexpected direction—to hold elections in the American zone and direct UNTCOK to supervise them. One surprise was the news that Pyong-yang had released a draft constitution for a Democratic People's Republic of Korea for the Soviet zone, along with an appeal to southern Koreans to join this revolutionary triumph. Another was that the United States had circulated a resolution instructing UNTCOK to conduct an election that would produce a functioning government, not a consultative body, in the American zone. Menon gave a full, pessimistic report on Korean unification, democracy, economic development, and security. He discussed Korean leaders and political parties with no enthusiasm. In an Interim Assembly session that began on February 19, Menon reported the impossibility of holding elections by March 31, although he knew that the Koreans planned another round of demonstrations on Sam-il (March 1). The assembly then voted thirty-seven to three to adjourn for at least a week to study Menon's report. The renewed debate allowed one of the State Department's stars, Ambassador-at-Large Philip C. Jessup, an author-historian and international lawyer of global renown, to argue that elections in the American zone would free twenty million Koreans to determine their own political future. Jessup hit all the right notes that fused expediency with idealism. On February 24 Jessup introduced an American resolution for Korean elections *now* (defined as May 1948) that provided for some future negotiated unification. The recent Communist coup in Czechoslovakia added power to Jessup's argument. Although Canada and Australia remained unconvinced, all other member nations of UNTCOK supported the American resolution. On February 27 the assembly adopted the American election plan by a vote of thirty-four to two, with eleven abstentions. UNTCOK and USAMGIK immediately announced that elections would be held in May. In Korea the political factions reacted with a volatile combination of celebration and street violence.[34]

As the Interim Assembly approached a decision on Korean elections, the parties most concerned with the conduct and outcome of those elections rallied. For General Hodge, the chief concern was that the military government and the interim government, his Korean partner, would manage the election and define who was being elected and for what purpose. Hodge believed that UNTCOK, especially the Canadians and Australians, had shown an unhealthy interest in meddling in Korean politics, largely to stimulate a New Left in the Korean political arena. The only likely result of such meddling would be to encourage the immediate withdrawal of all American troops, which would be disastrous. Moreover, the New Left could join part of the Old Right in either disrupting the election or not participating. It was already hard enough to hold the political leaders to their private promises to cooperate. "Part of this fight against elections in South Korea is definitely Communist activity and part of it, including current opposition by many really patriotic Koreans, is due to a quirk of psychology that leads them to feel that if on their own initiative they demand an election in South Korea, they are demanding a permanent split of their nation and fall in the traitor category. This patriotic, nationalist class does not face the fact that their country is already split."[35]

After the Interim Assembly resolution sent UNTCOK back to Korea to hold an election, Hodge and the State Department made certain that everyone understood exactly what the election would do. First, there would be a voter registration period of roughly one month before the election. The Korean electorate (male and female) would choose 200 representatives—that is, roughly one for every 100,000 people and geographically distributed—to a new national assembly. The assembly would presumably draft and adopt a constitution for a republican form of government that would include executive, judicial, and legislative branches. This government would exercise full sovereignty, including the power to negotiate its future relationship with the United States. It would qualify for United Nations membership. Its immediate challenge would be economic development and security from internal revolt and external invasion. This government, however, would not represent the complete fulfillment of the General Assembly resolution of November 14, 1947, which asserted that a unified Korea was the ultimate goal of international policy and in the interest of peace. It was authorized, therefore, "to take over the functions of government from the military commands and civilian authorities of north and south Korea." All foreign troops would leave Korea as soon as this government took power, within ninety days if possible. The electoral process would begin "on or about" May 9.[36]

The Korean politicians needed no encouragement to begin electoral positioning, and Syngman Rhee stole a march on Kim Ku and Kim Kyu-sik, his strongest personal rivals. Once again Rhee used rallies, the press, and radio to claim credit for "forcing" the United Nations and Hodge to hold elections; he claimed that Korea needed his special skills as an international statesman to survive. Rhee's greatest victory, however, was to pull together a powerful coalition of his own National Society for the Rapid Realization of Korean Independence (NSRRKI), the KDP, eight special-interest parties (for example, one consisting of north Korean refugees), and much of the bureaucracy of the south Korean interim government, which was still dominated by An Chae-hong. Rhee's relationship with the KDP, however, was not completely collaborative, which worked to Rhee's benefit. KDP leaders still carried the onus of "collaboration" and use of the Korean National Police (Cho Pyong-ok) and youth associations (Yi Pom-sok) to attack the two Kims' followers and all leftists. Much to Hodge's annoyance, the KDP backed a new political paramilitary group, the Korean National Defense Army, headed by "General" Lee Chung-chon, a former Nationalist Chinese army officer and Kwangbok army leader in China, a defector from the Kim Ku faction, and a potential rival of Yi Pom-sok. Rhee encouraged the NSRRKI to work with Lee's Taedong Youth Association. Both of Lee's paramilitary groups attracted recruits by promising that they would be the nucleus of a "pure" future Korean army. Lee and his groups supported elections in the south and offered to provide "order" to the elections.[37]

In Pyongyang the prospect of UN-sponsored elections set off a wave of political actions designed to embarrass the Americans, confuse the Koreans, and discourage UNTCOK. In November 1947 key Soviet and Korean Communist leaders designed a plan to cripple any UN-American "puppet" political initiatives. The long and loud proclamation against foreign troops in Korea, whose withdrawal would be a first step before the formation of a national unification government, represented one part of the plan. Other parts included (1) to cut off electricity to the south, (2) to build up the revolutionary underground in the south, and (3) to prepare the People's Army to cross the Thirty-eighth Parallel and finish a war that the partisans would begin. In December the USAMGIK knew Pyongyang's plan, so it came as no surprise when the Russians complained in March 1948, that the Americans were not providing the food and consumer goods they had promised in a June 1947 exchange agreement. Hodge furnished a new delivery schedule that should have satisfied the Russians. Nevertheless, the Soviets threatened to cut power after April 15 because the USAMGIK wanted too many kilowatts and sent too little money. They did not respond to Hodge's offers to negotiate. Joseph Jacobs warned the State Department that a successful election would throw the switch on part of the American zone's electrical grid.[38]

Pyongyang's December 1947 announcement that it would adopt a new all-Korea constitution was a baited hook irresistible to the antielection politicians in Seoul. That the fragmented Left would respond came as no surprise, but others joined the rush to explore reconciliation, including Yo Un-hong (the younger brother and political heir of the murdered Yo Un-hyong), Kim Kyu-sik, and Kim Ku. When Pyongyang announced on February 10 that it would hold a March plebiscite on a new constitution, seven prominent leaders, including Yo and the two Kims, sent an appeal to Kim Il-sung and Kim Tu-bong to hold an emergency conference in Pyongyang. On March 25 Radio Pyongyang—without mentioning the southern initiative—called for a meeting of all antielection parties in Pyongyang on April 14, a date designed to disrupt any electoral registration in the south. Kim Il-sung then sent a formal invitation to fifteen southern leaders, including Syngman Rhee, to meet with the "progressive" leaders throughout all Korea. Yo and Kim Kyu-sik started to shrink from the trip, even though Kim Il-sung guaranteed their personal safety. Thirteen leaders agreed to go to Pyongyang, but Rhee did not. Hodge and Jacobs suspected that the antielection members of UNTCOK (especially the Australian and Canadian delegates) had encouraged the Pyongyang conference. Hodge refused to give the Pyongyang trip official approval, but he did nothing to stop this quixotic journey to political suicide. His immediate problem was prodding UNTCOK to authorize and supervise the registration of southern Korean voters, which he had scheduled for March 30–April 8 with the State Department's approval.[39]

In the meantime, the Washington civil-military bureaucracy plodded ahead with its own review of Korean policy and finally produced a new statement that combined incompatible ends and means with an act of faith. The staff of the new National Security Council (NSC) inherited the State–Army–Navy–Air Force Coordinating Committee (SANACC) 176/39 study of what the United States should do about Korea, whether one or two. At its ninth meeting, the National Security Council (Truman did not attend) approved SANACC 176/39, making it NSC 8 (April 2, 1948). The six principals or their representatives (State, Defense, Army, Navy, Air Force, and National Security Resources Board) approved UNTCOK-USAMGIK plans to register voters for a May 10 national election in the American zone. (The one-day change avoided an ominous solar eclipse.) Only Soviet intransigence would prevent an all-Korean unification election. The study reviewed all the efforts since 1943 to restore the independence of one Korea, violated in 1905–1910. It concluded that a Soviet Korea would menace China and Japan. It then presented an analysis of several basic conditions: (1) two-thirds of Koreans lived in the American zone and deserved an independent government of their choosing, (2) the southern Korean provinces were in disarray because of the country's division and the disruption of economic ties to Japan, and (3) the Soviet–north Korean security forces (170,000) enjoyed substantial military superiority over their American–south Korean counterparts (75,000). The Pyongyang regime had crushed all political dissent; the USAMGIK–interim government had not. The southern zone's economic condition would be further weakened when the Soviets turned off the electricity, a foregone conclusion. Examining all the imaginable options, the study concluded that only a representative government in south Korea, supported by the United States, would advance American interests in north Asia, where the futures of China and Japan were at stake. The study rejected, however, a clear "guarantee [of] the political independence and territorial integrity of South Korea, by force of arms if necessary, against external aggression or internal subversion." Instead, the United States should fashion a program of limited commitment, under which it would (1) help create a Korean army out of the Constabulary, (2) withdraw American troops, (3) expend $185 million in GARIOA funds for economic relief, and (4) work with UNTCOK to create an independent government in the American zone. No American commitment should be regarded as a casus belli, and further US-USSR negotiations should be investigated. The United States and the United Nations should cooperate to unify Korea by negotiation, if possible. The focus should be "to withdraw from Korea as soon as possible with the minimum of bad effects." Without much thought, President Truman approved NSC 8 on the same day, although his official endorsement was dated April 8. General Hodge was immediately sent a summary of NSC 8 and received the full text on April 26. Hodge understood that this constituted firm guidance on the holding of elections.[40]

In the turmoil, Syngman Rhee took his largest risk and announced without qualification that he supported elections conducted by UNTCOK-USAMGIK and would actually stand for election himself. He would no longer attack General Hodge and the entire USAMGIK–interim government bureaucracy. Rhee saw the prize—the presidency of a Korean republic. He assumed that the provisional constitution proposed to the UN Interim Assembly would be accepted, and he intended to make sure that the comprehensive powers of the presidency were not reduced.

To ensure his sort of constituent assembly, he had to enter the fray as a candidate, not an Olympian senior nationalist statesman. Rhee did not like his vulnerability, given his strained relationship with the Korean Democratic Party. The confusions on the Right and Left, complicated by the Pyongyang conference, offered some hope. Hodge had not become Rhee's admirer, but he used his power not only to make land reform a reality but also to pardon political prisoners and to issue a "Proclamation of the Rights of the Korean People" designed to limit arrest powers to the KNP. With the majority of UNTCOK now leaning toward the U.S. position on elections, Rhee and Hodge found a rare common victory in the registration process. Following procedures designed by the Americans, 7 million of 7.8 million eligible voters registered, despite the continuing threat of violence. The south Koreans and the Americans had survived the first phase of the new liberation. The general elections, however, would have to be conducted under the shadow of the Pyongyang conference, which began on April 19 with 695 attendees. More ominously, a full-scale guerrilla war had begun on Cheju-do.[41]

THE CHEJU-DO REBELLION

The Korean war began on April 3, 1948, on Cheju-do with widespread, orchestrated attacks by Communist-led partisans against the civil government, the rightist youth associations, and the island's detachment of the Korean National Police. Although the direct armed confrontation between the Korean security forces and the antigovernment guerrillas remained contained for a crucial six months, the American occupation zone became a continuing battlefield for an insurrectionary people's war until the North Korean invasion of June 1950. Before the first T-34/85 tank rolled across the Thirty-eighth Parallel, thousands of Koreans died in a war that is even less well known than the internationalized, conventional war of 1950–1953. The Koreans, of course, remember it all too well, and like most survivors of vicious civil wars of the twentieth century, they are more prone to denial and forgetfulness than to public remembrances that might lead to a new cycle of retributive violence.

Just how many Koreans died in the two-year insurgency will never be known with any precision. The government's security forces (the KNP, the Constabulary, and paramilitary groups) suffered 7,235 deaths in the pacification campaign. The number of dead among the armed partisans and terrorists, mutineers, leftist families, innocent bystanders, pro-government civil officials and their families, and targeted social groups such as the Christians and anti-Communist youth groups can only be estimated. The estimates themselves vary widely by source and range from 30,000 to 100,000 dead; the deaths attributed to the 1948–1950 war were and are a matter of intense political dispute in both Korea and Japan, a haven for antiregime refugees and political operatives. The low estimate of 30,000 deaths seems most plausible, given the nature of the revolt and its suppression and the limited firepower available to all the belligerents. That atrocities occurred on both sides is unquestionable, but the depopulation of much of Cheju-do's interior and parts of the mainland's four southernmost provinces appears to be a matter of flight, not murder. Even the loss of 30,000 lives is wretched enough in its political impact and human misery, but it became overshadowed by the horrors to come. Another statistic explains the lack of American interest in the partisan war: only three Americans died during the course of the conflict—a GI shot by guerrillas near the Thirtyeighth Parallel; an American army captain who perished in a jeep accident in the battle zone; and a missionary, Ethel van Wagoner Underwood, murdered by two Communist terrorists in her Chosun Christian College home on March 17, 1949.[42]

Cheju-do probably struck the Americans as an odd place for a civil war to begin. The island is blessed with awesome natural beauty. Fifty miles off the mainland in the warm waters of the East China Sea, Cheju-do is Korea's Hawaii, Ireland, and California folded into one island of seven hundred square miles. The island is really the above-water peak of a gigantic volcano; its topography is dominated by Halla-san, the highest mountain in southern Korea at sixty-five hundred feet and so vast from crater to base that it rivals Japan's Mount Fujiyama in dramatic beauty. The flora, fed by Korea's abundant rainfall, includes upland pines and oaks as well as the tropical plants and palms of the seaside flatlands. The island's agricultural products range from barley, wheat, corn, millet, and yellow rapeseed (used to make canola oil) to garden vegetables, bananas, pineapples, and the succulent Cheju-do oranges and tangerines. Chejudoans raise horses, introduced by the Mongols in the thirteenth century, and cattle and sheep, introduced by Westerners—including Irish-Catholic priests—in the twentieth century. Today, Cheju-do, blessed with grottoes and tumbling streams, is a vacation paradise for Koreans and Japanese, especially newlyweds, who must make the pilgrimage to Sunset Peak (Songsanpo) and the Chungmun bridge over one of the island's spectacular waterfalls. The dominant sound on Cheju-do is the buzz of cameras, both video and digital, for Korean reality is defined by family photographs. The island is not free of obscure reminders of its violent past, but the war memorials are much less interesting than the mysterious *tol-harubang,* or stone "grandfather statues" of volcanic rock that resemble the statuary of Easter Island. Knowledge of the *tol-harubang* has spread worldwide through the visitors to Cheju-do. The memorials remain hidden.

For all its visual beauty, the island's history of death and resistance made it a hothouse for revolution. Throughout the dynastic wars and foreign invasions of premodern Korea, Cheju-do was the actual and symbolic place of last resistance. The most notable example of suicidal resistance came in 1273, when the remnants of a Koryo army refused to obey an imperial decree to surrender and perished to the last man in a battle with the Mongols. Modern Chejudoans revolted in 1862, 1898, and 1901. Cheju-do's location made it a point of contact among Koreans, Japanese, and Dutch and Portuguese mariners who wandered into the East China Sea. At this flashpoint of intercultural contact, Chejudoans held on desperately to their local culture, a village society dominated by the affluent female pearl divers, fishermen, and farmers. World War II brought another in a long series of traumatic events to the island; it was converted into a heavily guarded Japanese air and naval base integrated into the defense of the home islands from American bombers and submarines. The Japanese presence reinforced the islanders' ardent nationalism and radical reformism. The Japanese commanders followed a live-and-let-live policy, and the islanders took supplies and stole a few weapons with an eye to the future. The surrender in 1945 allowed the Communists, working within the structure of the People's Committees, to store Japanese weapons and take possession of the abandoned Japanese caves and fortifications. In the meantime, the island's population climbed from 220,000 (1944) to 282,000 (1948), increasing the strain on housing and food supplies. A backwater to the U.S. Army Military Government in Korea, the island seemed of little importance once the Japanese had been disarmed and repatriated, a task undertaken and completed in October 1945.[43]

In the wave of resistance against the second round of Joint Commission negotiations and the appearance of UNTCOK, Cheju-do reached the level of "problem" status for the Department of Internal Security in 1947. The increased violence on Cheju-do in February and March 1948 grew from the political problems of the preceding eighteen months. After the departure of the Japanese from the island, the U.S. military government administered the island with an American army officer until a suitable Korean could be found. Appointed in 1946, the first Korean governor was Pak Kyong-hun, an islander. He did his best to meet the people's needs and did not break contact with members of the former People's Committee or other leftist reform groups. Pak, however, faced food shortages, high unemployment rates, a cholera epidemic, and police corruption. On March 1, 1947, the KNP shot eight peaceful marchers but went unpunished, while 400 protesting islanders were imprisoned. Governor Pak's problems became even more complicated when the interim government sent anti-Communist northern refugees to settle Cheju-do and appointed mainland senior officers to command the island's KNP, reinforced with rightist youth associations. With his own supporters under increasing police harassment, Pak resigned and tried to form a political party for the forthcoming elections. His temporary replacement was Lt. Col. Russell Barros, senior adviser to the Constabulary and sympathetic to the islanders' protests against the police. The timing was bad, however. Barros went south in April 1947, just as Hodge was ordering the Americans to move from command to advisory roles. Yi Pom-sok and Cho Pyong-ok persuaded Hodge to appoint one of their liege men, Ryu Hai-jin, to be the new governor. Barros became merely the senior American commander on the island, his authority limited to the Fifty-ninth Military Government Company, a CIC detachment, and a reinforced platoon of the U.S. Twentieth Infantry Regiment, rotated from the mainland for security duties.[44]

Governor Ryu initiated a yearlong reign of terror that ignored the Americans, harried the moderates (including ex-governor Pak and his followers), and drove the South Korean Labor Party into the role of underground movement and popular rallying point for the anti-Ryu islanders. Ryu's operatives were especially hard on Koreans associated with the Americans or any local Christian church; his control of food rationing, commerce licensing, law enforcement, and virtually every aspect of the islanders' daily life made Ryu a formidable opponent. Before he left the island for routine reassignment to the United States, Barros demanded an investigation of Ryu's administration. While Hodge weighed the problem, Barros accelerated the recruitment of a Constabulary regiment made up of islanders, designed to checkmate the police. This Ninth Regiment became a haven of oppositionists, including Communists, and resisted the firm hand of its commander, Lt. Col. Kim Ik-yol, a member of the Constabulary's first class, veteran of the Japanese army, and sympathizer with the Left. Colonel Kim even negotiated with the SKLP's most effective leader, an islander named Kim Tal-sam, also a Japanese veteran and a well-respected middle school teacher. Kim Tal-sam also served as the military organizer of the island's SKLP partisans. On Kim Tal-sam's recommendation, many young men flocked to the Ninth Regiment to escape police persecution and formed an SKLP cell in the regiment. An American investigating team came to the island in November 1947 and conducted a three-month inquiry. In February 1948 it reported that Barros's charges were absolutely justified. Ryu was a corrupt dictator surrounded by a private army of the police and paramilitary youth auxiliaries who were billeted in private homes, which they robbed and ruined. Governor Ryu lied, cheated, and stole with impunity. He would not work with the Constabulary or the Fifty-ninth Military Government Company. His style was violent, lawless, rapacious, incompetent, and megalomaniacal. His administration had alienated thousands of island farmers. He kept 365 prisoners—all Communists, he claimed—in a Cheju City jail designed for one-tenth that number. He had ruined the island's public health program by driving out competent, honest doctors and public health professionals on political grounds. He had incited two boys' schools to fight each other. In a society that was already left-leaning, he had polarized the people, but not in equal proportions, since the locals turned to the Left to outmatch the émigré Right. The investigators recommended that Governor Ryu and his senior police officials be replaced as soon as possible. Administrator An took no action.[45]

Following the general instructions of Pak Hon-yong and the Haeju party directorate, the Cheju-do branch of the SKLP participated in the February 1948 general strike with great ardor and indifferent results. A series of demonstrations, raids, and ambushes simply stirred the Korean National Police to retaliate with village sweeps, mass arrests, and a few summary executions. Governor Ryu believed that he had broken up the SKLP leadership, but he brought in more mainlander auxiliary policemen drawn from the Northwest Youth Association. The most immediate result of the KNP's repression campaign was to force younger SKLP guerrilla leaders such as Kim Tal-sam to assume the political direction of the rebels. The partisans—the five hundred to seven hundred hard-core members of the People's Liberation Army of Cheju-do—struck back on the night of April 3–4 with desperate fury, seeking a demoralizing assault on the KNP and the opportunity to seize

U.S. Army carbines from the police rather than depend on their bolt-action Japanese model 99 rifles. The partisans had excellent intelligence provided by Lt. Mun Sang-gil, an officer on the Ninth Regiment's staff. Instead of fighting along Cheju-do's south shore, the Communists simultaneously attacked a dozen police stations in and around Cheju City and outlying villages. The guerrillas cut telephone lines and set ambushes for police vehicles; in the initial battles, they killed as many as thirty policemen, police family members, paramilitary youths, and innocent bystanders, with total casualties estimated at almost one hundred. Guerrilla casualties were probably fewer than ten in the initial attacks but mounted to thirty or more in the forty-eight-hour melee that followed. Casualty counting was complicated by kidnappings, panicked flights, and defections. The guerrillas, stunned by the bloody enormity of their success, fell back to their base camps hidden on the slopes of Halla-san.[46]

Director Cho Pyong-ok and Governor Ryu reacted with vigor and reinforced the KNP on the island with almost a thousand more policemen and auxiliaries, and Constabulary headquarters dispatched a battalion (eight hundred officers and men) from Pusan's crack Fifth Regiment to bolster the Ninth Regiment. The Constabulary's lethargic response to the KNP's calls for help was an ominous sign, and the American soldiers had orders not to intervene. The guerrillas avoided both the Constabulary and the Americans. When the KNP took to the field on a great guerrilla hunt in mid-April, the police and partisans exchanged ambushes and atrocities with growing savagery. On April 29 the ultimate catastrophe occurred: some soldiers of the Ninth Regiment joined a rebel attack on a police station. The Fifth Regiment battalion rushed to the rescue and broke the attack, but it was now clear that the Ninth Regiment could not be trusted until its SKLP members had been identified and eliminated.[47]

Maj. Gen. William F. Dean, the military governor, flew into Cheju-do on April 29 with a Constabulary staff in tow to reorganize the government's counterinsurgency campaign. While his public-relations staff made a crude propaganda newsreel, the general made more important decisions. The Ninth Regiment would be reorganized and renumbered as the Eleventh Regiment; only soldiers whose loyalty was proven would be allowed into the field. Another trusted Fifth Regiment battalion from the mainland would be dispatched to Cheju-do. The new Eleventh Regiment would be commanded by Lt. Col. Pak Chin-kyung; Col. Kim Ik-yol was reassigned. The dynamic and handsome Pak Chin-kyung, ninety-first in Constabulary seniority, had already proved himself to be a soldier of remarkable talent. A *hakpyong* from the Foreign Language University of Osaka, Pak had served as an engineer officer in the Japanese army but immediately enlisted as a common soldier in "Speedy" Lee's company in the Fifth Regiment (Pusan). He had been commissioned as a first sergeant in mid-1946; two years later, he was considered a peer of the most promising officers, such as Paik Sun-yup and Chung Il-kwon. That he spoke excellent English no doubt helped his meteoric career, but his leadership skills and tactical deftness were real enough for General Dean to give him operational control of all the security forces, advised by Col. Rothwell Brown (USA). The KNP and Constabulary would reverse roles: the police would handle lowland population control and political screening, and the soldiers would go after the guerrillas on Halla-san.[48]

The continued skirmishing and occasional terrorist forays in the towns of Cheju-do discouraged Chejudoans from voting on May 10. The turnout, less than half of registered voters, was so low that UNTCOK and the USAMGIK agreed that the island's two seats should be declared vacant and elections held later. In the week before the vote, the Americans counted fifty "events" that killed thirty-four people, but after the election, the pace of operations slowed. Freed from protecting the polling places, Colonel Pak abandoned secret contacts with Kim Tal-sam, initiated with the encouragement of Lt. Mun Sang-gil and Maj. O Il-gyun, and mounted a careful, sequenced counterinsurgency campaign that began in mid-May. As Constabulary combat patrols moved inland around the entire circumference of Halla-san, the KNP and auxiliary militia (mainland youths and islanders) organized fortified villages and temporary camps for four thousand interior villagers who were forcibly resettled and thus severed from the guerrillas, who enjoyed the active support of perhaps six thousand islanders. Refugee interrogations produced six hundred hard-core SKLP members, who were put into high-security prison camps. American advisers accompanied the KNP and Constabulary, and their presence probably curbed summary executions. Light liaison aircraft flown by army pilots combed Halla-san for guerrilla bands. What First Lt. Charles Wesolowsky, a battalion adviser, remembered about the operation was the use of oxen to carry supplies, the blooming azaleas, the constant rain on the mountain, and the lack of contact with the guerrillas. By the end of May, the KNP reported sixty-four police dead and four hundred civilians of all political persuasions killed in rural sweeps. Other sources put the dead at six hundred. Within the all-Korea context, the Cheju-do rebellion concerned General Hodge and his advisers, but they assumed that the newly active, reformed Constabulary and the KNP would soon eliminate the Communist partisans. Police director Cho Pyong-ok dismissed the Chejudoan rebels as a harried, inept band of romantic malcontents who hardly understood Communism. Seoul awaited more good news from Cheju-do.[49]

The Cheju-do campaign, however, stalled in June 1948 with the coming of the summer rains (which hit the island first) and the shock of learning the true extent of Communist infiltration of the Constabulary. The catalyst for the crisis in the Constabulary was the murder of Pak Chin-kyung, newly promoted to colonel, on June 18, 1948. Returning to his quarters after a promotion party, Colonel Pak went to sleep and never awakened, killed by a rifle bullet fired by one of his headquarters corporals, a protégé of Lt. Mun Sang-gil. Quick action by the American advisers, CIC agents, and Korean military policemen prevented the escape of Mun and his two coconspirators, who were eventually tried for murder and executed. The two enlisted men, dedicated Communists, would not expose the SKLP cells in the Constabulary, but Lieutenant Mun named names, which led to more arrests.

Col. Choe Kyong-nok, a humorless, strict product of the Japanese army, and Lt. Col. Song Yo-chan, a tall, burly, gregarious former Japanese army sergeant who had trouble remembering that he was a senior officer, took command of the merged Ninth and Eleventh Regiments. Song's "work hard, play hard" approach to duty earned him the nicknames "Tiger" from his followers and "Rock Head" from his critics. Song Yo-chan, however, was a hard-case field soldier with warlord instincts who knew how to push troops through either charm or intimidation. His first task was to cleanse his regiment, a task he took up with enthusiasm.[50]

The Cheju-do revolt had not yet reached the level of a national crisis, but it did not fade away either. Instead, it revealed the persistent strength of the SKLP and its allies and their unbroken ability to challenge the creation of a new south Korean government by terrorism, partisan warfare, and subversion of the Constabulary.

A RUSH TO INDEPENDENCE: THE 1948 ELECTIONS

Between May and August 1948, the Korean people in the American zone had two chances to vote on their political future. Neither election would have met American and Western European standards for honesty and openness, but at least one had a decent claim to fairness and freedom from coercion. The first election was held by the U.S. military government and the Korean interim government, with the reluctant participation of the United Nations Temporary Commission on Korea. The second election was run by the underground South Korean Labor Party and its coalition of leftist oppositionists, as well as defectors from Kim Ku's Korean Independence Party, the remnants of the late Yo Un-hyong's Laboring People's Party, and dispirited members of Kim Kyu-sik's Alliance of Popular Sovereignty. The first election produced the Republic of Korea and allowed the American occupation force to depart; the second abortive election was another effort by an alliance of northern and southern socialist revolutionaries and other dissidents to accelerate the American withdrawal and undermine the successor regime. The regime in Pyongyang—a union of the Kapsan faction, the Yanan faction, and the Soviet Koreans—stirred the political tempest, eager to create so much confusion that the Communists could march into Seoul as peaceful liberators after the "puppet" government and its domestic opponents had ruined each other.

The conduct of the election in the American zone still reflected some hope that the Russians and north Koreans would relent and agree to an electoral formula for all of Korea. Few Koreans and Americans in the south believed that such a hope was realistic, but some Korean politicians either thought so or thought that opposition to the election would work to their advantage. They included Kim Ku and Kim Kyu-sik. The appearance of UNTCOK complicated the electoral process, since only three of the members (Nationalist China, El Salvador, and the Philippines) supported a south Korean election with complete conviction. The representatives of three influential countries in the United Nations (Canada, Australia, and India) wanted to sever the UN-Korean connection, in no small part because they intended to use the United Nations to oppose what they viewed as America's hysterical anti-Communism and simpleminded, moralistic neoimperialism. The remaining two members (France and Syria) wandered between the two camps. Quixotic France eventually joined the pro-election faction without equivocation, but Syria remained disengaged. Fear of establishing unhappy precedents for future UN peacemaking roles influenced UNTCOK's vacillations.[51]

For once, General Hodge and Washington agreed that the elections should proceed with all deliberate speed after the March 10 guidance to UNTCOK from the UN Interim Assembly. The antielection faction of UNTCOK interpreted this guidance to mean that UNTCOK could refuse to endorse the conduct or the results of the election, since it was responsible for judging whether conditions in the American zone met the generally understood definition of "free elections." As UNTCOK defined the issue, these conditions involved an assessment of voter registration, the selection of candidates, the education of the public on electoral issues, the degree of public peace in all aspects of the electoral process, and the actual conduct of the voting on election day. The potential for procrastination or eventual cancellation of the elections seemed endless unless the military government and the Koreans pushed the process along. The process might require an occasional compromise with the antielection faction, the "fullest possible participation" faction, which demanded the participation of the SKLP and the parties of the two Kims. UNTCOK became obsessed with the prominence of the "oligarchic" Korean Democratic Party of the "collaborators." This obsession worked to the benefit of Syngman Rhee, whose NSRRKI looked democratic by comparison, as long as it seemed to hold the youth associations at arm's length. From March until the eventual election day—May 10—the Americans, UNTCOK, and the Korean electoral officials and security forces bickered and compromised over issues that someone thought essential to an acceptable election.

UNTCOK's antielection faction, lead by Australia's S. H. Jackson and Canada's George S. Patterson, assumed the role of aggressive challenger to Hodge's early efforts to move toward a vote. The Interim Legislative Assembly's electoral law (August 1947) had too many restrictions for UNTCOK's taste, and Hodge, freed from the necessity of dealing with the now-defunct assembly, could modify the law by decree. His amnesty program was one of several "adjustments." The interim government screened 6,260 recently arrested protesters, and Hodge pardoned 3,140 dissidents. Hodge reduced the voting age from twenty-three to twenty-one. When UNTCOK questioned the fact that twelve of the thirteen members of the National Election Committee were associated with the Korean Democratic Party, Hodge reformed the committee. The law now required a candidate to have two hundred (previously one hundred) names on the nominating petition, to reduce the number of frivolous candidates. For reasons as much legal and administrative as political, the general would not change a provision under which any

Korean proscribed from candidacy for prior collaboration or subversive actions could not vote. Hodge also rejected the idea of a weeklong election period that would roll from south to north like the *changma* and might produce a week of rippling violence. There would be one national election day.[52]

Two working groups dominated by Patterson and Jackson, however, continued to find the general conditions for an election unsatisfactory. They complained about the repressive Korean National Police and its youth association auxiliaries, which forced Hodge to order the amalgamation of poll watchers into a citizens' Community Protective Corps, organized and supervised by officers of the U.S. Army and the Korean Constabulary. Hodge also issued detailed instructions to the police not to intimidate voters, especially through the granting or denial of food ration cards. Despite all the cautionary reforms, Hodge could not satisfy the Patterson-Jackson group, which reported that noncooperation by the Left and the ultranationalists put the election into question. The group admitted that conditions had improved, but UNTCOK would not endorse the election unless other changes occurred. The evidence from voter registration was heartening; between March 31 and April 9, more than 7.8 million of an estimated 8 million eligible Koreans registered to vote for members of a national assembly. For most of April, UNTCOK sent small observation teams (the whole UNTCOK mission numbered only about sixty) to the hinterlands to investigate political conditions. On April 28 the commission went on record that it would take the next step—observing the polling—because Korea was free enough for a meaningful election. This position still had three dissenters—the representatives of Canada, France, and Syria. The shift of Australia and India to a pro-election position was decisive.[53]

Though Korea could hardly qualify as a democracy in values and processes, the approaching election showed some signs of republicanism. Roughly half the southern Korean population of twenty million was aged twenty-one years or older. In the face of continued violence and intimidation throughout the rest of April and the first week of May, seven million Koreans turned out on election day, or about three-fourths of the potential electorate. UNTCOK reported that in the ten days preceding the election, 323 people (including 32 policemen) died, a report that does not square with the USAMGIK estimates. The Americans reported 327 dead and 316 wounded of all persuasions between February 7 and May 14, excluding Cheju-do losses. There is more agreement on election day violence: 44 dead and 62 wounded in attacks on polling places. Allowing for confused reporting, the broad picture is clear enough. Of the 13,000-plus polling places, fewer than 100 could not function because of violence. Of more than 900 candidates, fewer than 10 were murdered before or during the election. For a country on the verge of civil war, the election was a success for USAMGIK and the Korean people.[54]

The May 10 election felt the long shadow of the Pyongyang conference (April 19–29), which adjourned in time for the southern delegates to return home and speak against the electoral division of Korea. There had been no debate in Pyongyang; the delegates had been called together to approve Kim Il-sung's plan to preempt the southern elections. The Pyongyang conferees published resolutions that (1) condemned the holding of separate elections in the American zone, since these invalid elections would force the permanent division of the country; (2) demanded the immediate withdrawal of all foreign troops from Korea; (3) proposed a post-withdrawal conference of Koreans only, to work out a government for the whole country; (4) pledged noncooperation with any election held in the south and resistance to any government established by that election; and (5) promised that "progressive" leaders in both halves of Korea would never conduct a civil war against each other. The central theme needed little elaboration: foreign troops must go and let the Koreans decide their own future. Upon their triumphal return to Seoul, Kim Ku and Kim Kyu-sik announced that they had received a personal pledge from Kim Il-sung that Cho Man-sik would be released from jail, that no electricity would be denied to the south, and that the north Koreans would not establish a separate government. Kim Ku, however, returned from Pyongyang convinced that the Soviet zone was a Communist dictatorship, and he promised Hodge that he would not disrupt the election. The Pyongyang participants then arranged another surprise by publishing a model constitution for their version of a new Korea, which provided for an alternative set of elections without anyone's supervision. In the meantime, the southern elections proceeded, and on May 14 the Russians quit transferring electricity to the south, a move that embarrassed the two Kims, who had accepted the election in a desperate attempt to reenter the southern political arena. The May 10 election, however, had driven them to the political margin and removed them as Syngman Rhee's principal rivals.[55]

The election results in the American zone set the stage for another round of frantic political bargaining and realignments, since the new National Assembly's principal task was to draft and approve a constitution for the Republic of Korea. No single group had a working majority. Even the best-organized groups could claim only limited success. The NSRRKI offered 235 candidates in some 200 constituencies, but the voters returned only 55. The Korean Democratic Party fared no better; the 91 KDP candidates produced only 29 winners. The two youth groups of Yi Pom-sok and Lee Chong-chon offered 107 candidates, 18 of whom were elected. Sixty-five other organizations ran 103 candidates but produced only 13 winners. The largest single group—candidates who ran without any affiliation at all—produced 85 winners from 417 candidates. The demographic profile of the 208 members of the First National Assembly (subtracting Syngman Rhee but adding 9 winners in substitute and vacancy elections) gives a little more shape to the character of the assemblymen. They were "senior" statesmen, since 170 had been born before 1910; only 3 had been born in provinces that were now in the Soviet zone. The largest regional bloc came from Seoul and the four northern and central provinces (Kyonggi-do, Kangwan-do, and the two Chungchongs), which were strongholds of the NSRRKI and the independents. The percentage of NSRRKI, independent, and "third-party" assemblymen from the two southeastern Kyongsang provinces was about evenly divided at one-third of the 70 positions. The Korean Democratic

Party had the strongest regional association; almost half of the KDP assemblymen (54) came from the two southwest Cholla provinces, elected by the SKLP boycott. In every other region, the KDP ran fourth among the four political groupings.[56]

Other demographic characteristics establish the class basis of the First National Assembly. Although the politics of the American zone and the failure of the two-Kim faction and the Left to contest the election certainly influenced the profile, the Confucian deference to age, wealth, education, and social standing probably most influenced the electorate. More than half (121) of the assemblymen had attended or graduated from a college or university; 49 others were high school graduates, thus leaving only 38 with less than a high school education. Only 15 of the college men had been educated outside Korea, China, and Japan. The occupational profile clearly shows elitist representation: agricultural groups had virtually no representatives, although the 27 businessmen and others no doubt held some tenant-run farmlands. The two largest groupings were civil servants (71) and educators (38)—Confucianism in full. Twenty-two members listed "politics" as their profession, while lawyers (7) and doctors (10) were minority professions. Thirty-three members had no identifiable occupation. The KDP had the smallest percentage of civil servants but the second largest percentage of educators and the second largest percentage of businessmen. There was simply no dramatic occupational difference among the four groups. The available statistics give no data on wealth or religious preference, although education levels and occupations might suggest a slight bias toward Christians. What was more important for the future of Korea was that a largely rural and industrial working-class society chose elitist assemblymen who would either favor an authoritarian-bureaucratic administrative state or oppose any "government" party for personal and regional reasons. The concept of a "ruling party" and an "opposition party," still strong in Korean politics, can be found in the First National Assembly before the adoption of the constitution of the First Republic. The demographics also suggest that regime opponents were likely to come from the four southern provinces where the original People's Committees had flourished and the SKLP had a strong underground following, based on its opposition to KDP businessmen and landholders. North of Taegu, however, the "ruling" party of the NSRRKI, the independents, and the small parties had a strong base in the cities and countryside, a sociological barrier numbering in the millions between the Communists north of the Thirty-eighth Parallel and the dissidents in southern Korea.

From the American perspective, the May 10 elections created several new problems, but they paled in comparison to the consequences of not holding elections at all. The USAMGIK and the interagency group in Washington that guided Hodge thought that the election results were a decent reflection of Korean opinion. Boycotts and coercion, Right and Left, had not poisoned the process. Although Kim Kyu-sik had committed political suicide, he had at least taken Kim Ku along on the trip to oblivion. Unhappily, Syngman Rhee had survived again, and the Americans, military and diplomats alike, assumed from the first week after the election that he would now dominate the formation of a new government by building from his NSRRKI base to add in the independents and small-party representatives until his obvious "mandate of heaven" would bring in defectors from the KDP. Hodge relished the prospect of being persona non grata to the new government. He approved of Washington's judgment that he should turn over the office of Commanding General USAFIK to the next senior officer, his deputy, Maj. Gen. John B. Coulter, a model of decency and probity untouched by political controversy. Hodge's days in Seoul were numbered, much to his delight. UNTCOK decamped to Shanghai to write its report on the elections, which it still had not blessed, but returned to Seoul on June 9. The U.S. government cared about UNTCOK's actions, but not much. With its members still arguing among themselves, UNTCOK finally issued a series of statements (June 25–30) that bowed to the inevitable, which was that the United States and the southern Koreans would go forward with the transfer of power from the USAMGIK to the government of a new Republic of Korea. UNTCOK's grudging conclusion was that the elections expressed the Koreans' desire to be independent under a Korean government, even one that was less than democratic: "The results of the ballot of 10 May 1948 are a valid expression of the free will of the electorate in those parts of Korea which are accessible to the Commission and in which the inhabitants constitute approximately two-thirds of the people of all Korea."[57]

One challenge was to blunt Pyongyang's attempt to continue its own unification charade. In June 1948 Kim Il-sung invited the two Kims to Pak Hon-yong's Haeju headquarters for more unification discussions. Desperate to reestablish their influence in the new South Korea, the two Kims declined to participate. On July 5 the delegates to the Haeju conference declared the prospective South Korean government illegitimate and announced that Pyongyang would conduct another national election in both zones on August 25 for delegates to a Korean Supreme People's Assembly. The strange bedfellows of the two Kims' faction denounced this plan, but the SKLP and other leftist dissidents pledged their dedication to the sub rosa election. The Korean National Police then dedicated itself to ensuring that no such election occurred. From June into August, the police went on the offensive against leftist underground networks, making arrests without much discrimination or legality on the theory if they arrested enough people, they were likely to catch a few real Communists. The KNP arrested sixty suspected SKLP organizers in Taejon, Taegu, and Chongju. The result was clear enough. The jail population swelled by four thousand "detainees" and overwhelmed the meager penal system.[58]

The Communists put the best face on their electoral farce. Pyongyang claimed that 77.5 percent of a southern Korean electorate of 8.6 million voters had voted for 360 representatives to a 572-member Supreme People's Assembly. Radio Pyongyang crowed that "the South Korean people fought the enemies at gunpoint and elected 1,000 representatives in open and underground elections." A full delegation would attend the August 21–25 assembly at Haeju "in spite of the suppression of the reactionaries." The Supreme People's Assembly had one goal: demand that the United Nations and all foreign troops allow truly free all-Korean negotiations. Of course, 99.97 percent of the enlightened citizenry of northern Korea had voted as well. Socialist mathematics produced more leftist voters in the American zone than in the entire turnout of May 10. The reality was that there had been no protest election at all. Afraid that Syngman Rhee would treat them less gently than John Hodge, SKLP organizers headed for the Thirty-eighth Parallel. The KNP arrested 120 organizers in its August sweep and confiscated petitions (not votes) for representatives to the Supreme People's Assembly. Many of the million signatures were forged, but those that were not provided crucial intelligence for the police.[59]

The new National Assembly wasted no time transforming itself into a government, meeting for the first time on May 31 and electing Dr. Syngman Rhee, self-proclaimed all-knowing elder statesman and manipulator of the U.S. government, as its chairman. Rhee wasted no time opening negotiations with the USAMGIK on the transition process and appealing through Hodge and Jacobs for American diplomatic recognition and economic and military assistance. Rhee did not protest Hodge's suggestion that he open negotiations with UNTCOK and announce that he would reserve one hundred seats above the statutory two hundred for future assemblymen from the north, a sop to UNTCOK. Rhee was more interested in the new constitution, which drew on models considered by the Interim Legislative Assembly the year before. The drafting committee, chaired by Rhee but including KDP and other representatives, examined variants of a parliamentary system and a presidential system and chose an earlier draft written largely by Shin Ik-hui, a defector from the Korean Independence Party and a rising star since his return to Korea in 1945 with Kim Ku. Now one of the principal organizers and theoreticians of the NSRRKI, Shin knew what Rhee wanted in terms of constitutional powers, and he knew that Rhee shared a strong elitist, authoritarian bent with Kim Sung-su's KDP. Drafted by two respected jurists, Dr. Yu Chin-o and Kwon Sung-yol, the constitution included a British-style parliamentary system with cabinet accountability and assembly primacy, but fused it with a presidential office with wide powers. Under Rhee's influence and with KDP support, the drafting committee forwarded a constitution with broad executive powers and few limitations to the assembly at the end of June. The preamble was a statement of the natural rights of man, a Korean adaptation of Jeffersonian liberalism. The body of the constitution, 103 articles in ten chapters, provided the framework of a new government, including a bill of rights of twelve freedoms. The key difference with the U.S. Constitution was the president's power to govern by decree in times of crisis, as defined by the president. With no federalism to cloud his calculations, a Korean president was only an insurgency away from a dictatorship. The assembly adopted the constitution with intense but shortened debate on July 12. Eight days later, as provided for in the constitution, the assembly elected Syngman Rhee the republic's first president for a four-year term. Rhee received 180 of the 198 votes cast. Kim Ku received a pathetic thirteen votes, and the ultimate administrator, An Chae-hong, received two. As the rush to independence gathered speed, General Hodge announced that he would begin to transfer power to the Korean government on August 15, the day the Koreans had been liberated from the Japanese in 1945.[60]

Blessed with wide powers to rule by administrative fiat through his appointed cabinet, Rhee found the assembly unmoved by his initial candidates for appointment, which required assembly approval. Rhee chose Yi Si-yong as his figurehead vice president, but his nomination of the aggressive youth corps leader and former provisional government stalwart Yi Pom-sok for premier met immediate opposition. The KDP demanded six cabinet posts, which Yi opposed. Rhee eventually picked two KDP ministers, but he favored the men he needed most to hold his regime by force if necessary. Yi Pom-sok served as both premier and minister of defense; the other powerful youth leader, Lee Chong-chun, became minister without portfolio. Dr. Chang Taek-sang, the czar of the Seoul metropolitan police, became foreign minister; his rival, Cho Pyong-ok, went on an extended tour that eventually made him ambassador to the United Nations. The KNP was turned over to new professional policemen of limited ability and ambition, much to the initial relief of the Constabulary and its American advisers.[61]

The imminent abolition of the USAFIK-USAMGIK arrangement and the departure of XXIV Corps' two skeleton infantry divisions clearly shifted the responsibility of representing the United States in Seoul from the U.S. Army to the State Department and the Economic Cooperation Administration, headed in Seoul by Dr. Arthur C. Bunce, Hodge's principal economic counselor. As the State Department helped Rhee seek official recognition and open negotiations with the United Nations for membership and assistance, Secretary of State George Marshall (through Robert Lovett and Assistant Secretary William H. Draper Jr., an army general) organized an American mission in Seoul. The ambassador designate was John J. Muccio, a forty-eight-year-old career extrovert who had enjoyed the personal diplomacy of the party circuit throughout Latin America and the Mediterranean since his graduation from Brown University in 1921. Born in Italy and an army veteran of World War I, Muccio had never married and thus had no diversions from his full schedule of meetings and social events. He was not an Asian specialist, but he had expert help in Bunce, counselor Everett F. Drumright, and Dr. Harold J. Noble, a Korean missionary's son and wartime intelligence officer. The most important American diplomatic actions, however, occurred in Washington and Flushing Meadows—first to get the General Assembly to accept the creation of the Republic of Korea, and then to create a second United Nations Commission on Korea that was no longer temporary.[62]

Having argued that, based on law and international politics, the United Nations had the principal responsibility for Korea's future, the State Department believed that UNTCOK had outlived its usefulness. The General Assembly, in the face of Soviet hostility, should extend its influence through a successor mission. Basically, legal niceties aside, the United States wanted the United Nations to share the burden of creating a de facto trusteeship without calling it one. It would have to convince Syngman Rhee (or coerce him with economic and military assistance) that the United States and United Nations would not tolerate a dictatorship, especially one created in the aftermath of a controversial and divisive UN political intervention taken in the interest of the United States. The United States also wanted to withdraw its troops on its own schedule, not that of the United Nations or the Soviet Union. On the eve of Korea's new independence, Joseph Jacobs, in his last days as Hodge's political adviser, urged the department to pressure the army to reschedule its complete withdrawal for 1949, not 1948. With another session of the General Assembly approaching and relations with the Soviet Union in disarray, "I feel we should stand firm everywhere on [the] Soviet perimeter, including Korea, until we know more clearly what actions will be taken in [the] General Assembly and what will be [the] outcome of our present negotiations with respect to Berlin and [the] rest of Germany."[63]

For Syngman Rhee, the continued support of the United States and the United Nations seemed essential to the survival of the Republic of Korea—as long as he controlled that support. He needed more than security guarantees, military assistance, and an economic program of billions of dollars. He needed international legitimacy, which meant more recognition than that granted without grace in several muddy statements by UNTCOK. Rhee wanted the United Nations to declare that his regime was the only internationally recognized government in Korea, that it was the government of all Korea on either side of the Thirty-eighth Parallel. Without such recognition, Rhee saw no prospect of borrowing the $500 million needed to stop inflation and establish the government's credit. "We must make a formal request to the UN and the State Department to help at least in stabilizing the currency for the benefit of all concerned."[64] Rhee, in fact, believed that UNTCOK endangered his regime through its naive negotiations with Pyongyang. For once, he shared a fear with John Hodge. UNTCOK wanted the United States to stay close to the Korean government, but only if it operated under UN guidance as interpreted by UNTCOK.[65]

As the annual *changma* came to an end and the weather cleared and warmed over the Han River valley, the political atmosphere in the American zone also changed, but not with the certainty of the seasons. Some developments were clear and inexorable: the U.S. XXIV Corps was leaving and would be gone by 1949. This redeployment of the U.S. Sixth and Seventh Infantry Divisions in September 1948 did not mean that all American tactical units would depart. The composite Fifth Regimental Combat Team remained to support the Constabulary regiments on the Thirty-eighth Parallel north of Seoul. As American foot and motorized patrols continued along their routes, logisticians moved troops and thirty thousand tons of materiel through the port of Pusan and signed over weapons and supplies to the Constabulary. Neither task was without risk. On July 19 eight armed Koreans in civilian clothes ambushed an American patrol, killing one GI and wounding another, near the Thirty-eighth Parallel. On September 14 a train wreck killed thirty-six GIs and injured sixty-six; the crash was accidental, but the troops suspected that SKLP terrorists wanted to speed their departure. The members of Gen.

John Coulter's rump USAFIK, including Lynn Roberts's Provisional Military Advisory Group, had no illusions about the dangers inherent in their rearguard mission.[66]

The shift of power to a Korean government put the Americans and their staunchest allies, the pro-American officers and men of the Constabulary, at risk. American servicemen (e.g., CIC agents) could no longer arrest Koreans for crimes against American lives and property except on American bases. The Department of Internal Security claimed sole jurisdiction over its members charged with subversion but conceded that the KNP had initial jurisdiction over military personnel suspected of crimes against Korean civilians. This arrangement was immediately exploited by the KNP to continue its vendetta against the Constabulary as its competitor in graft and a refuge for SKLP fugitives. A continuing KNP-Constabulary guerrilla war within a new fragile government simply increased the likelihood of an eventual Communist takeover or a rightist coup by unhappy elements of the Korean Democratic Party and Kim Ku's die-hard followers. This conflict was part of the continuing war between the SKLP and rightist paramilitary terrorists. "Although each of these groups have their own particular, and sometimes peculiar, views as to the procedure and components for the formation of a new government, all fall under two main fronts, Left Wing and Right Wing, the Communistic against the anti-Communistic. Although feeling is divided into two categories, a predominating Korean racial and nationalistic spirit prevails."[67]

The South Korea that Syngman Rhee and his fractious cabinet proposed to govern in an uneasy alliance with the National Assembly had struggled upward from social chaos and economic beggary. It was hardly a promising experiment in free-market economics and political democracy. American economic aid—direct aid and U.S. Army local spending—had provided some stimulus for local industry. Government subsidies had encouraged food production, as had the distribution of Japanese-owned farmlands, but 1.2 million returning Koreans had kept food demand just beyond local production, which had been hurt by poor weather and fertilizer shortages. The success of public health programs and family formation indicated that Korea would soon have enough births to outstrip deaths; "natural increase" in 1947 numbered 625,000. In 1948 half the Korean population was younger than twenty-one. Average life expectancy was fifty years, compared with seventy in the United States. Korean industry showed signs of life, its electricity generated in South Korea with Japanese coal. Some Japanese-owned businesses in Korea (vested property) had moved into Korean hands, although more slowly than Korean politicians urged.

The signs of potential economic collapse were as ominous as the indicators of economic progress were hopeful. The interim government passed along a public debt almost equal to the estimated budget for fiscal year 1949 (30 million won); the new government had no credit rating or revenue-expenditure plan that would attract international bankers. The repair and expansion of roads, bridges, levees, water pipelines, schools, government buildings, public health facilities, railroads, and telephone lines had driven the debt, but the infrastructure development plan of the USAMGIK remained incomplete. The Americans' departure produced a wave of economic insecurity. Rice prices in the open market increased 100 percent between 1947 and 1948. Although the rate of inflation had slowed since 1945, it remained a threatening problem. Wholesale prices almost doubled in one year and included commodities such as all grains, firewood, meat, fish, soap, paper, cement, coal, all forms of cotton, and rubber shoes. Price controls and directed distribution still applied to many commodities, but these measures only slowed inflation. The most affected Koreans were also the most politicized: fixed-income government employees, urban professionals and corporate "salarymen," small merchants, and students from low-income families. The potential for political disaffection reached volcanic proportions as most of the American soldiers bade good-bye to the Land of the Morning Calm.[68]

Yosu is in flames while loyal ROK soldiers search a residential neighborhood for guerrillas, October 1948. (Lt. Col. Minor L. Kelso, USA [Ret.])

Brig. Gen. Paek Kim-il, ROK task force commander for the recapture of Sunchon and Yosu, poses with KMAG adviser First Lt. Minor Kelso, USA, October 1948. (Lt. Col. Minor L. Kelso, USA [Ret.])

Mutineers of the Fourteenth Regiment who surrendered at Yosu in October 1948 await transportation to prison and eventual execution. (Carl Mydans, *Life* [Colorific])

The ROK army executes its own. Mutineers of the Fourteenth Regiment pay the ultimate price for the Yosu-Sunchon rebellion at the military prison, Susaek-dong, west of Seoul, 1949. (U.S. Army)

Soldiers of the ROK Ninth Regiment close in on a guerrilla base camp in the Chiri-san mountains, January 1949. (Lt. Col. Charles L. Wesolosky, USA [Ret.])

The body of former lieutenant Kim Chi-hoe on display after the guerrilla leader died of wounds in the Chiri-san mountains, April 1949. Kim was a key leader of the mutiny of the Fourteenth Regiment in Yosu. (Col. H. S. Fischgrund, USA [Ret.])

Brig. Gen. Chung Il-kwon, commander of the Chiri-san Task Force, distributes a bounty of one million won to a company of the Third Regiment for killing guerrilla chieftan and former lieutenant Kim Chi-hoe, April 1949. At the right is KMAG adviser Capt. Harold S. Fischgrund. (Col. H. S. Fischgrund, USA [Ret.])

Happy ROK soldiers and an American sergeant parade two captured mutineers in southern Korea, August 1949. (Col. H. S. Fischgrund, USA [Ret.])

The ROK army invites U.S. diplomats and Western correspondents to see captured insurgent arms and guerrillas at Yongsan Army Base, Seoul, April 1950. In the foreground are Col. Kim Chong-yol, chief of staff, ROK air force; Maj. Gen. Chae Pyong-dok, chief of staff, ROK army; and Capt. James H. Hausman, USA, KMAG liaison and adviser to General Chae. (Col. H. S. Fischgrund, USA [Ret.])

Captured soldiers of the Korean Liberation Army, survivors of the two Tenth Infiltration columns at Yongsan base, Seoul, April 1950. (Col. H. S. Fischgrund, USA [Ret.])

Captured weapons and equipment of the Tenth Infiltration guerrilla columns from the DPRK, displayed at the KMAG compound, Yongsan base, April 1950. The weapons are of Japanese and Czech manufacture. (Col. H. S. Fischgrund, USA [Ret.])

Enlisted soldiers of the ROK Seventh Division prepare for a patrol at the Thirty-eighth Parallel, April 1950. Note the mix of Japanese and U.S. Army uniforms. The rifles are pure American, the .30-caliber Garand M-1. (Col. H. S. Fischgrund, USA [Ret.])

Brig. Gen. William L. Roberts, USA, chief of KMAG, conducts a light machine guns inspection at the ROK Military Academy, Nowon, 1950. (U.S. Army)

A lieutenant of the Cavalry Regiment mans a .50 caliber machine gun in the turret of a M-8 "Greyhound," an armored scout car, 1949. The 37 mm gun was no match for North Korean T-34 tanks. (Robert Shackleton)

A typical ROK army strong point along the Thirty-eighth Parallel, 1949–1950, manned by infantrymen with 81mm mortars and .50-caliber machine guns. (Col. H. S. Fischgrund, USA [Ret.])

Lt. Col. Han Shin, deputy chief of operations, ROK army, briefs distinguished visitors on defense plans. They are (left to right) Minister of Defense Shin Sung-mo; U.S. Ambassador John Muccio; Capt. James H. Hausman, USA, KMAG liaison to headquarters, ROK army; Brig. Gen. William L. Roberts, USA, chief of KMAG; and Huh Jung, mayor of Seoul (U.S. Army)

Brig. Gen. Paik Sun-yop, commander of the ROK First Division and future army chief of staff, 1950. General Paek became the ROK's most famous wartime general. (Gen. Paek Sun-yup)

At the Thirty-eighth Parallel, north of Uijongbu, June 1950, are (left to right) Col. W. H. Sterling Wright, USA, acting chief, KMAG; Col. Yun Chun-gun, commander, Ninth Regiment, ROK army; Brig. Gen. Yu Jae-hung, commander, Seventh Division, ROK army; John Foster Dulles; Minister of Defense Shin Sung-mo; Foreign Minister Ben Limb; and Maj. Joseph W. Bilello, USA, KMAG adviser to the Ninth Regiment. (National Archives)

6

The Republic of Korea Enters the World and Almost Dies Stillborn, 1948–1949

The government of the Republic of Korea (ROK) entered the world of ambivalent parentage, christened by the inconstant summer weather of Korea. When Syngman Rhee took the oath of office as president on July 24, the last rains of the *changma* drenched the crowd that had gathered in front of the capitol, the former headquarters of the Japanese colonial government at the head of Sejongno Boulevard. Rhee's speech, delivered in high-court Korean, bored and puzzled most of the curious onlookers but affirmed his reputation as "Yi Paksa" or "Rhee the Great Scholar." The president himself seemed lost in a large yellow slicker and intimidated by a microphone that sizzled with moisture. The president's theme, however, was clear enough: he would become president of a unified Korea, and the regime in Pyongyang had no legitimacy. The Communists were traitors who had sold their birthright as Koreans to another foreign power, the Soviet Union. They had replaced one kind of colonialism with another, and "their doom is unavoidable before man and God." The real Koreans would build the real Korea south of the Thirty-eighth Parallel and then absorb their captive brethren to the north. Rhee provided no details about how this unification would occur.[1]

Syngman Rhee had a second opportunity three weeks later to explain the goals of his Korea. Even though the transfer of power from the U.S. Army Military Government in Korea to the new administration was far from complete, General Hodge and President Rhee agreed that the formal declaration of national independence would be issued on August 15, exactly three years from the day that the Japanese had surrendered power to Yo Un-hyong and the Committee for the Preparation of Korean Independence.

The republic's cloudy birth did not immediately give way to sunny days for President Rhee, but at least the weather turned hot and clear by independence day. The political climate remained overcast, however. The assembly began a concerted power struggle against Rhee by rejecting his first nomination for prime minister,

Rev. Yi Yun-yong, a figurehead, on July 24. Five days later the assembly approved the nomination of Yi Pom-sok, the strongman of the youth associations, who enjoyed the confidence of the remnants of Kim Ku's Korean Independence Party and the newly assertive Korean Democratic Party (KDP) of Kim Sung-su. Part of the bargain with Rhee was that "General" Yi would also take the portfolio of defense minister. With one presidential aspirant placed in the cabinet, the assembly chose another challenger, the charismatic and persuasive Shin Ik-hui, as chairman of the assembly. Rhee received one bit of welcome news. The government of Nationalist China promised on August 12 to recognize the Republic of Korea; this instant recognition proved to be the exception, since other members of the United Nations, including the United States, postponed recognition until the General Assembly met in Paris that fall and acted on the report of the United Nations Temporary Commission on Korea (UNTCOK). Rhee understood the reason for the postponement of international approval: the other nations wanted to see if the transfer of power from the military government went smoothly and whether Rhee's executive departments showed any signs of life. Rhee viewed the wait-and-see policy as a personal affront.

The ceremonies to mark the transfer of power from the American military government and the administrative departments it had created in collaboration with the Interim Legislative Assembly were held as scheduled on August 15, under a blazing sun. President Rhee, dressed in the dark gray *hanbok* of a traditional Korean gentleman, welcomed his distinguished visitors to the dais. General Hodge appeared, counting the days until his return to the United States. Rhee welcomed a figure from the anti-Japanese past, a signer of the 1919 declaration of independence, O Se-chang. At eighty-four, Mr. O enjoyed a deserved reputation as a teacher, journalist, political activist, poet, and subversive. His greatest claim to recognition was as one of Korea's greatest Chinese calligraphers and the spiritual leader of Chondogyo. Mr. O had also served an obligatory prison term (three years) at the hands of the Japanese, but unlike President Rhee, he emerged from prison with his fingers still supple and his calligraphy improved by the long days of practice. Three other guests represented the champions of the new Korea: Dr. Rufino Luna, the Filipino chairman of UNTCOK, Ambassador Liu Yu Wan of Nationalist China, and Monseigneur Patrick J. Byrne, apostolic delegate of the Holy See.

The most honored guest, however, was none other than General of the Army Douglas MacArthur, making his first trip to Korea, along with his wife Jean. The MacArthurs and their court flew from Tokyo to Seoul only for the day. The security for the Commander in Chief Far East and Supreme Commander Allied Powers required more military policemen and infantry guards than did Seoul's liberation. At the reviewing stand at the capitol building, the sun burned down on the Koreans and Americans alike with a blanket of humidity that wilted the general's unadorned khaki cotton uniform (no tie, as usual) and melted the starch in Rhee's *yangban* costume and Mrs. Rhee's *hanbok*. The sun did not melt the rhetoric of the two elderly gentlemen who dominated the proceedings. President Rhee urged the crowd to remember that the continued division of Korea remained the unsolved challenge. He swore that his mission was to unify Korea. Until then, "our joy is clouded with sorrow." Rhee promised that his government would foster democracy, respect individual rights, stress the equality of all Koreans, and tolerate dissent. He would not tolerate, however, dissent that endangered his regime, since such traitorous acts represented a clear and present danger to the state. General MacArthur played the same theme in his own speech. The future would bring a unified Korea, since Koreans came from "too proud a stock to sacrifice . . . their noble cause to any alien philosophies of disruption." The artificial barrier of the Thirty-eighth Parallel "must and will be torn down," and all Korea would be united. In the meantime, vigilance and determination would be the watchwords. MacArthur pledged "to defend Korea as I would California."[2]

At the end of all the speeches, the Great Bell of Chongno pealed the glad tidings of Korean independence, answered by church, temple, and palace bells throughout the city. Umbrellas popped out to block the sun as a parade, heavy with police and military units, marched down the broad boulevard. Rhee enjoyed the parading of the army, still officially the Korean Constabulary. He clapped with special enthusiasm when the Constabulary's crack ceremonial unit, the Cavalry Regiment, passed in review. One squadron rode horses that had been bought, fed, and curried with great difficulty, but the troopers took pride in their appearance, if not their uncertain equestrian skills. Members of the other squadron had more confidence in their mounts, a small fleet of U.S. Army M-2 half-tracks and jeeps, bristling with .50-caliber machine guns. Rhee could not tell that the spit-shined troopers and their vehicles had virtually no training for field operations and that the vehicles had few spare parts.[3]

The sight of his army on parade gave President Rhee pause, for he already fretted about where the loyalty of the Constabulary rested. Rhee believed that men in uniform had difficulty serving republican governments created by democratic processes and led by politicians shaped by elections and patronage politics. Rhee expressed his anxiety in a conversation with Brig. Gen. Yi Ung-jun, whom Rhee promoted and then appointed as the army's first chief of staff. General Yi, a fifty-two-year-old graduate of the Japanese Imperial Military Academy and former Japanese colonel, had agreed with reluctance to serve in the Constabulary under American supervision and with younger officers of equal rank. He became the first general in the new Korean army. Rhee and Yi were, in fact, distant clansmen with family roots in north Korea. General Yi made sure that the president met the general's son-in-law, the boy-colonel (age twenty-eight in 1949) Yi Hyong-gun, also a graduate of the Japanese Imperial Military Academy. Rhee asked Colonel Yi whether his purported nicknames of the "Korean Napoleon" and the "Korean Tojo" were accurate. When Colonel Yi declined to answer, Rhee said that he hoped the colonel would be satisfied with military glory and would not try to overthrow the government.[4]

Whatever Rhee's generals might be or might become, the president himself had yet to prove whether he could be a legitimate national leader and executive administrator or was just another failed expatriate. The odds were not good. Rhee had shown little interest in coalition building, compromise, negotiation, or power sharing. His inability to grasp economic realities was legendary. He trusted no one except his wife Francesca, who disliked Americans, especially diplomats and officers. Rhee's uneven attention to administrative matters deepened with age and suspicion. Even if Rhee had been a heroic national leader of a small power struggling for independence—such as an Ataturk, a Pilsudski, or a Mannerheim—he would have found the future of the Republic of Korea daunting. When Rhee became president, only two nations—the Philippines and China—recognized the Republic of Korea. All the others awaited the UN General Assembly judgment on South Korea's legitimacy. In the meantime, the United States had started a liquidation process in terms of its military involvement that suggested a hasty end to direct American responsibility for the governance of Korea. The bureaucratic implications were significant. The Department of State—under a cloud for its perceived failure in China—would replace the Department of the Army as the American trustee of Korea's political future. And State had neither guns nor money.[5]

The transfer of power to the new Korean government began smoothly enough, since the U.S. Army was anxious to go home—or at least to Japan. On August 24, 1948, the Rhee government agreed to a Provisional Military Advisory Group (PMAG) plan, blessed by U.S. Army Forces in Korea (USAFIK), to transfer the custody of bases and organizational property from the U.S. Sixth and Seventh Infantry Divisions to the Korean Constabulary. On September 15, the remaining units of the two American divisions began their exodus. Two days later, the transfer negotiations produced a formula for passing control of bases and equipment to the Constabulary and ensuring that the Constabulary would be the foundation of a new Korean army. The American military withdrawal was real, but its timetable uncertain. The direction, however, was fixed—toward transportation at Inchon and Kimpo airfield. On September 17, USAFIK completed an agreement with the Constabulary over which equipment and real property would pass into Korean hands and which would remain in the hands of the USAFIK stay-behind forces and PMAG. The reckoning included Government Aid and Relief in Occupied Areas (GARIOA) funds destined for the Constabulary, the largest source of American money to support Rhee's government.[6]

While the military accountants worked on their spreadsheets, the Koreans had other kinds of accounts to settle. Dusting off an anticollaborator law passed by the Interim Legislative Assembly in July 1947 and vetoed by Maj. Gen. William F. Dean, the military governor, three Daehan Youth Corps representatives demanded that the National Assembly craft a new bill. Their motion passed 105 to 16. The drafting committee produced a bill with elastic definitions of pro-Japanese collaborationism and with loopholes so that compromised politicians could escape prosecution while they pursued traitors. The law included provisions for an inquisitorial system under a special investigating committee, special courts, and special prosecutors, since the assembly wanted to purge the senior officers of the Korean National Police (KNP) and Constabulary. Rhee opposed the bill but regarded a veto as futile. The assembly passed the law on September 7 by a vote of 103 to 6, and Rhee signed it on September 12, 1948. The Seoul press applauded the assembly's patriotism and wisdom. The assembly also enacted an amnesty law that forced Rhee to release five thousand "political prisoners" by October.[7]

The social and economic conditions in South Korea created a sea of popular discontent that nourished the subversive fish loose in the republic. Rhee's cabinet, which included only one interim government holdover (Min Hui-sik, minister of transportation), had little experience and, according to the Seoul press, was unqualified by virtue of its education (too much), fluency in English (too unpatriotic), political loyalty (too close to Rhee or the KDP), and age (too young—the cabinet's average age was fifty-two). Rhee had actually formed a cabinet with some talent and much independent political influence.

The two strongest ministers—Yi Pom-sok and Chang Taek-sang—were presidential aspirants. An Ho-sang (minister of education) was also a strongman with ties to the youth associations. Although Kim To-yon (minister of finance) and Lee In (minister of justice) were KDP protégés of Kim Sung-su, Yun Chi-yong (minister of internal affairs) had broken with the KDP, and Cho Pong-am (minister of agriculture and forestry) was a former Communist. Chun Chin-han (minister of social affairs) had emerged as a non-Communist labor leader. The subministerial appointees were holdover administrators from the interim government. For key representatives abroad, principally to the United States and the United Nations, Rhee dispatched Cho Pyong-ok (former police director and presidential aspirant), Chang Myon (aka John Chang, Korea's most prominent Catholic layman), Helen Kim (Ehwa Women's University president), and Chang Ki-yong (veteran expatriate lobbyist and a former American citizen).[8]

All the president's men and women faced staggering economic and political difficulties. Rhee flirted with open-market rice collection policies but quickly reverted to government-set prices and compulsory collection because half of South Korea's population depended on rationing and fixed prices. American withdrawal had already increased inflation and pinched the Korean economy. Special emissary Cho Pyong-ok insisted that the end of American economic aid would be Korea's death sentence. Secretary of State George C. Marshall and Robert Lovett, his deputy, agreed with the visiting Koreans that the immediate challenge was strengthening the KNP and the Constabulary to ensure that insurgents would be unsuccessful and that the north Koreans would not be tempted to flaunt their military superiority with an invasion. Ambassador Cho thought that the members of UNTCOK had modified their bias against Rhee's security forces, which helped make expansion and reform more likely. The State Department increased its insistence that some American troops remain behind after the general withdrawal early in 1949.[9]

The immediate burden of ensuring the security of the Republic of Korea fell on the KNP, the Korean Constabulary, and the American officers and enlisted men of PMAG. The American advisers were a mixed bag of veteran senior officers, experienced captains, and new lieutenants. In August 1948, when the Constabulary advisers switched from the Civil Affairs Section, USAFIK headquarters, to PMAG, the officer cadre included one brigadier general (William L. Roberts), one colonel (W. H. Sterling Wright), seven lieutenant colonels, five majors, thirty captains, and sixty-three lieutenants. By 1949, at General Roberts's insistence, the advisory group had tilted toward more experience: eighteen lieutenant colonels, forty-three majors, eighty-six captains, and twenty-four lieutenants. Counting enlisted personnel, PMAG ended 1948 with 240 officers and men; a year later it had reached a preinvasion peak strength of 495. The group was small, however, for an army growing beyond 60,000 and for the organization of eight division headquarters and a comprehensive system of schools and training bases. Operational units had the fewest advisers per soldier; each constabulary regiment had an advisory unit of one or two junior officers and three or four enlisted men. Senior officers who were accompanied by their families (permitted for two- to three-year overseas assignments) preferred Seoul, and the concentration of Constabulary bases in the Han River valley made such assignments possible. The result was that regimental advisers were captains or sometimes lieutenants, which made successful advising a miracle of personal diplomacy, often cemented in a common battle with *soju, kimchi,* and mystery meats and vegetables. General Roberts, however, issued new orders against off-duty fraternization, gift receiving, and interference with Korean law enforcement. The adviser's lot was sometimes not a happy one.[10]

The Korean security forces faced even greater challenges than PMAG did. The KNP remained deeply unpopular with all but affluent Koreans. The National Traitors Act put the entire KNP in a state of high anxiety and considerable vengefulness. Although the US-ROK agreement on the status of USAFIK and the Korean "security forces," signed on August 24, 1948, kept the police under nominal American operational control, Rhee directed that the KNP be transferred to the new Ministry of Home Affairs, headed by the president's longtime personal secretary, Yun Chi-yong. Minister Yun immediately announced his intention to clean up the KNP in the spirit of the National Traitors Act. A wave of protests and resignations followed, and the new senior officers paid even less attention to their American advisers. The exception was Lt. Col. Ernest E. Voss (USA), who built the Daehan Youth Association as a police auxiliary and a rival to the government-sponsored Korean National Youth, dominated and politicized by Yi Pom-sok. Voss's intentions were pure enough; he was a council member of the Boy Scouts of America and founder of the Boy Scouts in the Philippines. Daehan Youth served as a recruiting ground for new policemen, and it carried the enthusiasm for pursuing subversives to extralegal heights. The KNP and Daehan Youth went on the offensive in July 1948. Any critic of the KNP became an ascribed Communist. The detective bureau of the Seoul metropolitan police remained the spearhead of the antisubversive crusade, and in late September it arrested a South Korean Labor Party

(SKLP) cell of eight would-be assassins of Syngman Rhee, four of whom were Constabulary enlisted men. The KNP charged that USAFIK would not be able to clean up the Constabulary before it relinquished operational control in 1949. That the SKLP had created cells throughout the Constabulary was well known by its senior officers and American advisers, but Hodge and his successor, Maj. Gen. John B. Coulter, wanted no additional excitement with the 1948 elections and UNTCOK to manage. What they did not know was that the Kim Ku diehards had created another cancer in the Constabulary, the rightist Revolutionary Volunteer Army (RVA), organized by Maj. Oh Dong-gi and Choe Nung-jin, the former policeman who had tried to run against Rhee in May.[11]

Why the Fourteenth Regiment became the battleground for the soul of the Constabulary and the survival of the Rhee regime remains a mix of mystery and murky accident. Formed in South Cholla and stationed in the small port city of Yosu, the regiment was a known haven for SKLP fugitives. The initial regimental commander, Lt. Col. Yi Yong-sun, a distant clansman of the Korean imperial family and a former Japanese naval officer, had been a popular but not especially effective commander. The regimental adviser, First Lt. Joe W. Finley (USA), thought that Colonel Yi had been replaced for political reasons; his successor was Oh Dong-gi. As August drifted into September, Finley received a visit by an American Counterintelligence Corps (CIC) agent, who told him that the regiment had become a nest of conspirators. They assumed that the dissidents were Communists, but Major Oh may have made the regiment the cutting edge of the RVA, or the RVA may have been a front for the SKLP. With the agent's evidence, Finley went to Seoul to request help with a unit housecleaning. He argued his case with PMAG's intelligence staff, but to no avail, for reasons he never understood. Finley requested reassignment to the U.S. Seventh Infantry Division, and his request was granted — with a letter of reprimand. Jim Hausman, however, was the only officer who believed Finley's story that Major Oh was a Kim Ku loyalist. Hausman conspired with Col. Paik Sun-yup, the Constabulary G-2 and an experienced counterterrorist, and they had Major Oh recalled to Seoul for interrogation and exposure. The Fourteenth Regiment drifted toward disaster.[12]

The already suspect Fourteenth Regiment was not the only concern for Hausman, Paik, and the Constabulary staff. Major Oh's transfer had opened command of the Fifteenth Regiment (Masan) for Lt. Col. Choe Nam-gun, a charming former captain of the Manchukuo army and a suspected Communist. Choe had strong ties to the Sixth Regiment (Taegu), in which he had served for two years. Intelligence and CIC agents saw the possibility of a three-regiment (the Sixth, Fourteenth, and Fifteenth) mutiny that might also draw in the discontented and radical Fourth Regiment (Kwangju), a unit commanded by an ineffective and corrupt lieutenant colonel. The rebel force could isolate the anti-Communist Fifth Regiment and Division G of the KNP, both based at Pusan. A widespread mutiny could turn Korea's four southern provinces into a Communist-dominated battleground and kill UN recognition and American aid. An additional concern was the ongoing withdrawal of the U.S. Sixth Infantry Division from the same area; that division had been chosen to lead the American withdrawal because it was leaving Far East Command. Part of the Sixth Division–Constabulary transition plan was an ordnance turnover, consisting of U.S. Army M-1 rifles, Browning automatic rifles, carbines, machine guns, and mortars for the Constabulary. The Constabulary's Japanese weapons would go into storage. At turnover time, a Constabulary battalion would have twice as many weapons as men. Although Constabulary and PMAG headquarters saw the potential for trouble, Generals Song Ho-sung and Roberts would not authorize more than a quiet loyalty screening and the dispatch of more men and weapons to the most dependable regiments. For one thing, the Cheju-do rebels showed new signs of life. Worse still, the KNP's summer hunt for subversives, a city and town operation, had driven the SKLP survivors into the hills and into guerrilla bands; although these bands were not large and were poorly armed, they were a persistent security threat. In September 1948 Communist guerrilla bands had formed in six of the republic's eight mainland provinces. In only Kyongsangnam-do, in the Pusan area, had the Constabulary and KNP shown any real energy, detaining 709 suspects and holding 226 for prosecution. The peace of early October 1948 was a false season than would be shattered at Yosu.[13]

THE YOSU REBELLION AND ITS AFTERMATH

The new Korean government inherited a deteriorating security situation, not limited to Cheju-do. Although the Korean National Police continued its pursuit of leftist leaders, the arrests did not halt the raids and organizing activities of the oppositionists. The ominous signs of partisan activity now included Kangwon Province in east-central Korea, split by the Thirty-eighth Parallel. The partisans, estimated at five hundred to six hundred, were "local malcontents," but there were rumors that the bands included rebels from Cheju-do and cadres from north Korea. The members of the "People's Flying Column" appeared most interested in stealing arms and food, which they carried off to bases in the Taebaek mountains, the forested spine of steep ridges that runs the entire length of eastern Korea. Another characteristic of the partisan deployment suggested that rebel bands in North Kyongsang Province had moved north to join the Kangwon bands, a massing of guerrillas that indicated a major effort to dominate the eastern half of the border. This movement did not exhaust the concentration of partisans. Intelligence assessments by both Americans and Koreans found guerrillas, organized by the South Korean Labor Party, in every province. The arrests retarded but did not stop the Communists' organizational efforts. Agents from Pak Hon-yong's headquarters in Haeju appeared among the captives. "In every province, the South Korean Labor Party organized mobs, attacked police boxes, coerced farmers, and planned infiltrations of constabulary, police, and civil government offices." The KNP and Coast Guard made arrests that showed a constant flow of agents and money overland and by ship from the Kangdong Institute to SKLP organizers. Although Cheju-do had quieted, mounting evidence indicated that the Communists intended to wage subversive warfare throughout the Republic of Korea. The partisans' greatest weakness was their lack of firearms equal to the carbines and M-1s carried by the KNP and the Constabulary.[14]

For the forty-odd soldiers of the Fourteenth Regiment's Communist cell, the day of decision arrived at night. On October 19, 1948, Lt. Col. Pak Song-hun, acting regimental commander, received orders to send one of his battalions, which had just been rearmed with American weapons, to Cheju-do. The entire regiment now had two sets of rifles and ample ammunition. The conspirators, however, feared that Constabulary and KNP agents had penetrated their cell and that hesitation would spell disaster. While Colonel Pak and part of his staff went to the Yosu docks to see off the Cheju-do battalion, Sgt. Maj. Chi Chang-su and First Lt. Kim Chi-hoe led their rebels into regimental headquarters and seized it and the communications center in a sharp but short gun battle. The regimental executive officer died; twenty other officers and noncommissioned officers fell or surrendered. By radio and telephone, the mutineers called for a popular uprising against the police, government officials, and the landlord class; the rebel force soon swelled to 1,000 soldiers, Communists youths, hysterical students, and street looters. After a feeble attempt to fight its way back into the burning town, the fragmented Cheju-do battalion, reduced by desertion, fled on two Coast Guard ships. Colonel Pak escaped in ignominy by stripping off his uniform, a condition that the Constabulary later made permanent. Seizing Yosu, the rebels rounded up and executed 500 police, loyal soldiers, government officials, rightist youths, and unfortunate innocents. In addition to more than 2,000 weapons, the rebels captured 500,000 rounds of ammunition. Seizing a passenger train of five cars, 500 to 800 rebels headed for the city of Sunchon, about forty miles north of Yosu. The mutineers and the Yosu mob, shouting Communist slogans and believing that they had started a major campaign to depose Syngman Rhee, looted, robbed the Yosu banks, pillaged the bars, and chased suspected loyalists.[15]

Alerted by hysterical fugitives from Yosu, the Sunchon garrison—a KNP company and a Constabulary company from the Fourth Regiment—steeled itself for an attack by the maddened mob from the hijacked train. Three American advisers accompanied the Constabulary company. While two lieutenants deployed the company along a river that protected the police station—the KNP's castle keep—First Lt. Minor L. Kelso, a Fourth Regiment adviser, talked with the KNP company commander, who promised to hold out as long as possible. Kelso then left Sunchon to meet a second Constabulary company en route. The rebels arrived first and added perhaps another thousand rabid youths to their ranks as they swarmed toward the police station. Part of the Constabulary company found refuge in the post office. The rebels overran the police station and massacred more than sixty captive policemen and their families. Perhaps four hundred policemen escaped, but few rallied for a counterattack. An American aerial observer confirmed that Sunchon was in enemy hands. The rebel soldiers allowed the one trapped Constabulary company to withdraw, and some of its men joined the uprising. The next day a Fourth Regiment task force blocked the road west but lacked the strength to counterattack, having run short of ammunition. Inside Sunchon, the rebels celebrated with an orgy of murder and arson. Three days later, Lieutenant Kelso found the police captain's body wrapped in barbed wire and burned with gasoline in the town square. A lone dog gnawed at the charred corpse. The rebels did not stop with killing policemen; they slaughtered civilians who could not flee fast enough. Corpses of all ages choked the escape routes to a missionary compound and lay scattered beside roadside ditches.[16]

In Seoul, the Rhee government learned of the Yosu-Sunchon revolt on October 20 and suspected a rightist mutiny, until Yi Pom-sok convinced Rhee that the Communists were his most dangerous enemy and that inaction would only encourage more mutinies. Yi pledged that he would rally the KNP and trustworthy youth paramilitary groups. That afternoon, after a conference with General Coulter, Yi ordered General Song; his own chief of staff, Col. Chae Pyong-dok; Col. Chung Il-kwon, the Constabulary chief of staff; and Lt. Col. Paik Sun-yup, the G-2, to organize a campaign to break the revolt. The American advisory team included Capt. Jim Hausman, Constabulary headquarters adviser; Capt. John P. Reed, the PMAG G-2; Captain Frye, a field adviser; and Capt. Harold S. Fischgrund, Ninth Regiment adviser. The group added another member the next day, Lt. Col. Kim Paik-il, the Constabulary assistant G-3 and a courageous, experienced, professionally sound field commander from his days as a counterguerrilla officer in the Manchukuo army. His north Korean origins made him even more attractive as a loyalist. Hausman convinced Song and Rhee that Kim should take command of the Fifth Brigade for the relief of Sunchon and Yosu. Although Chung Il-kwon directed operations as task force chief of staff, Hausman made this request after he found the Fifth Brigade commander paralyzed by the fear that his Fourth Regiment would join the mutiny. Rhee approved Kim Paik-il's appointment as acting brigade commander, but only if Hausman promised to take command if the Korean officers proved incompetent or disloyal. Roberts approved this arrangement, but he and Hausman hoped that such a crisis would not occur.[17]

With appropriate haste, the Seoul command-advisory group issued orders for eleven battalions from six different regiments to encircle Sunchon and seal off the Yosu peninsula. The force of five thousand loyal troops significantly outnumbered the estimated rebel army of one thousand. The troop ratio was not as impressive as it looked, however, for the Fourth, Sixth, and Fifteenth Regiments were all suspect. The Fifth and Twelfth Regiment battalions were under proven and loyal commanders such as Paek In-gi and Paik In-yup. As the battalions deployed, General Song decided that he would take command of the entire task force through the Fifth Brigade's Kim Paik-il and the Second Brigade's Col. Won Yong-dok, the doctor turned infantryman. Col. Hurley E. Fuller thus launched an unsubtle distraction campaign aimed at General Song, spiced with many troop visits and social drinking. A veteran of two wars and commander of two infantry regiments against the Germans, Fuller knew how to handle troublesome generals and kept Song away from headquarters. The task force fell under the de facto command of a triumvirate of talent: Jim Hausman, Paik Sun-yup, and Chung Il-kwon. Kim Paik-il took the road east to Sunchon with two loyal Twelfth Regiment battalions and two suspect Fourth Regiment battalions, trailed by a KNP and youth battalion. The Third Regiment task force moved south into blocking positions. On October 22, Kim's brigade—with the Fourth Regiment battalions in the van—advanced cautiously under its own mortar fire against token resistance. Lieutenant Kelso gave his Korean gunners on-the-job training, since none had ever fired an 81mm mortar. With white cloths around their helmets and arms, the loyal troops moved with care among the heaps of corpses left behind by the rebels. The KNP battalion started a war of rage against anyone it found, whether captives or wandering civilians. Hausman demanded that Yi Pom-sok call off his vigilantes: "Police now in Sunchon out for revenge and are executing prisoners and civilians gathered for questioning without benefit of trial. Several loyal civilians already killed and people beginning to think we are as bad as the enemy. Personnel must be sent and a court set up to stop these executions."[18] Two American reporters watched police and Constabulary soldiers beat suspects in Sunchon and Yosu and intervened to save one young man who screamed for help in English. The battered youth claimed to be a Christian and a loyalist; he tried to prove his innocence by joining a loyalist militia unit, swathed in bandages. Who knew his loyalties? Did he even know himself? The reporters got a firm commitment from an elderly woman: "I favor who has the most guns."[19] The Constabulary stopped the atrocities with Seoul's approval, but this crisis did not end the campaign's viciousness.

Under pressure from Seoul to quash the revolt as quickly as possible, the collective leadership of the Yosu-Sunchon task force could not seal off the escape routes from Sunchon, and several hundred rebels slipped through a porous blocking position established by a Fifteenth Regiment battalion at Hadong. The regiment's commander, Choe Nam-gun, disappeared for four days. He claimed that he had tried to negotiate a surrender for the rebels and had been held hostage; given his SKLP connections, which were exposed the next year, Colonel Choe probably arranged for the rebels to escape into the Chiri-san mountains. "Friendly fire" problems between the loyalist Twelfth Regiment and elements of the Sixth and Fifteenth Regiments were likely more than accidents of poor coordination. The real problems, in the strategic sense, were in Seoul: the Republic of Korea had not yet been blessed by the United Nations and the United States. As an exercise in international politics, retaking a city was far more important than conducting a coordinated and careful campaign that would seal the Yosu peninsula and capture the rebels. "On to Yosu" ensured that hard-core Communist partisans would escape north to the mountains and a protracted Maoist war.[20]

On October 22, Col. Kim Paik-il's task force, now led by two effective Twelfth Regiment battalions, turned south toward Yosu. The recapture of Yosu was not a model operation. With no coordination with Colonel Kim, a battalion of the Fifth Regiment commanded by Capt. Kim ("Tiger") Chong-won, a fanatical anti-Communist, twice tried to seize the Yosu docks with an amphibious landing. Twice the Fifth Regiment force was driven back to sea on October 23 and 25. In the meantime, Kim Paik-il's brigade stalled, and the arrival of two Third Regiment battalions did not swing the balance. The Fifth Regiment's mad landings had not broken the resistance. The force that eventually crushed the inner-city rebels was a task force from the Cavalry Regiment, dispatched from Seoul with fifteen jeeps and ten M-2 half-tracks bristling with machine guns. There was no parade ahead for the inexperienced Korean motorized cavalry and its two advisers, First Lt. Robert M. Shackleton and Second Lt. Ralph Bliss. The two young lieutenants brought their unit by train to Sunchon, then made a motor march through the city, where they were appalled by the destruction and atrocities. They found Colonel Kim's infantry stalled outside Yosu, attacking the rebels with mortar fire. Hausman and Kim Paik-il quickly organized small task forces of jeeps, half-tracks, and infantry that plunged into the city against rebel roadblocks. The .50-caliber machine guns on the half-tracks tipped the balance toward the loyalist soldiers, but the Reconnaissance Troop (the formal unit name of the mechanized task force) lost thirty dead and wounded (25 percent of its combat strength) from rooftop fire and Molotov firebombs. The machine gunners blasted away without much fire discipline; the .50-caliber bullets chewed up whole blocks of buildings, rebel positions, and exposed civilians. The mortar fire turned downtown Yosu into an inferno. On October 27, after two days of mounted sorties into the center city, the last rebel holdouts surrendered or died fighting. The rebels' last stand endangered a girls' school and its students, but the loyalist troops finally worked patiently to free the young hostages and end the resistance with maximum persuasion and minimum firepower.[21]

The Yosu-Sunchon rebellion rocked the Rhee administration and the American mission in Seoul, but both struggled out of shock and denial to strengthen South Korea's security system. There was no question that the weeklong fighting had been a major political event, despite Yi Pom-sok's pitiful attempt to cast the revolt as simply Communist terrorism with no roots in the population. Yi blamed the Americans for allowing Communists into the Constabulary, one of many errors that led to his relief as defense minister in March 1949. Ambassador-in-waiting John Muccio and his staff, some of whom regarded the Constabulary as more dangerous than the Communists, praised Rhee for allowing PMAG to run the Constabulary and for forcing the Constabulary to purge its own ranks rather than accept a National Assembly witch hunt. By the end of November 1948, Col. Paik Sun-yup's investigators had arrested or discharged 1,571 Constabulary members. With Hausman's encouragement, Rhee refused to have the National Traitors Act applied to the Constabulary or to accept Communist-inspired atrocity stories, which were accepted as gospel by one of Muccio's key political advisers, Gregory Henderson. Muccio accepted Roberts's and Hausman's assessment that the reformed and expanded Constabulary could handle every security threat except an invasion from north Korea.[22]

The State Department's public position was that the rebellion did not influence the American disengagement policy. "No Americans, military or civilian, have been in any way involved," the department announced.[23] Of course, if one meant *units*, the press release was true, but correspondents of four major newspapers arrived from Tokyo to cover the recapture of Yosu and reported the presence of American advisers. They apparently did not notice or ignored U.S. Sixth Infantry Division soldiers providing aerial and jeep reconnaissance, ammunition resupply, radio intercept intelligence, communications, and transportation to the Constabulary. The State Department did not dwell on the scope of the week's violence. Yi Pom-sok released casualty figures that made the fighting seem to be a great regime victory; of the 2,533 dead, 1,984 were mutineers and rebel soldiers. The KNP, youth auxiliaries, and other loyalists had suffered only 682 deaths, although there were 833 people missing. The government held 1,571 rebels in custody. The American analysis, produced by PMAG and 971st CIC Detachment officers, produced less reassuring casualty assessments. Regime loyalists had died in distressing numbers: 286 policemen, 138 soldiers, and 672 civilians of "rightist" or unknown loyalties. The mutineer army had lost 228 dead. The exact number of other deaths was unknown but might be in the 500 to 800 range. The government held 847 prisoners, of whom 397 had been tried by year's end, resulting in 211 death sentences and 162 long prison terms. The most disturbing statistic received little publicity: an estimated 1,000 rebels and much of the captured arms and ammunition had disappeared into the mountains of two southern provinces, Chollabuk-do and Kyongsangbuk-do.[24]

Just who died and who did not in the Yosu-Sunchon rebellion indicated a consistency of behavior that put the Communists at the center of the conflict. The KNP and its youth association auxiliaries were the prime targets; the Fourteenth Regiment ringleaders incited the mobs with charges of police repression. Government officials and records were fair game, as were prominent followers of Rhee, Kim Ku, and Kim Sung-su. The Communists also targeted Christian congregations and leaders of all ages. The most famous case involved Pastor Son Yang-won, who had spent seven years in a Japanese prison for opposing Shintoism. After a people's court in Sunchon condemned and executed his two seminarian sons for not renouncing Christianity, Pastor Son saved his sons' betrayer, a fellow student, from execution by the KNP by pleading for his life and pledging to raise him as a Christian and adopted son. (In July 1950, the North Koreans reversed the propaganda error by executing Pastor Son and his adopted son.) In contrast, the two U.S. Army lieutenants trapped in Sunchon were ignored by the rebels, who could have killed or captured them with little effort. Another indication of some communication between the rebels and Pyongyang was the fact that Radio Pyongyang often broadcast accurate details of the fighting before reports came from task force headquarters in Kwangju. A U.S. Army signals intelligence unit monitored radio transmissions between Yosu and Pyongyang that included instructions to avoid incidents with Americans.[25]

The Rhee government could no longer avoid the issue of defense organization after the Yosu-Sunchon uprising. The president himself shrank from military affairs and feared soldiers. Therefore, he left negotiations on defense issues to Yi Pom-sok, whose negotiations with General Roberts in August–October 1948 had produced nothing but acrimonious disagreement. Yi wanted a military establishment built on an army numbering in the hundreds of thousands, based on conscription and designed for population and territorial control, extending in theory into north Korea. Yi's experiences in China shaped his concept. He also argued for an extensive but highly centralized Ministry of National Defense in which a single army officer and staff would control all the armed forces of Korea under the minister's supervision. The principal requirement for the army's leaders was a dedication to fighting leftist subversion. The Korean army "should fight to the last soldier against Communism."[26] Appointments of senior officers should be based principally on their political reliability, not professional qualifications. Yi also argued for a ten-regiment territorial reserve force of "ardent and patriotic" youths, preferably raised by volunteerism through the youth associations, but mustered by conscription if necessary. General Roberts challenged Minister Yi on every issue. He believed that Korea needed a relatively small (100,000-plus man) army with air and naval support forces officered and trained on the postwar American model. Yi's reserve schemes were politically motivated, fueled by patronage schemes. According to Roberts, the Korean military establishment should mirror the American system, organized as strong service departments coordinated by a defense ministry of modest size and limited powers. Roberts and his staff thought that Korea needed a law based on the American National Security Act of 1947 and two parallel laws that had established the postwar organization of the U.S. Army. As for the officers of the armed forces, they should be promoted and assigned based on professional merit alone. Roberts agreed that too many Constabulary officers already believed that personal politics transcended performance. Yi Pom-sok, however, had a whole list of potential senior commanders for the new army, a few of whom already served in the Constabulary and many of whom were affiliated with the youth associations and the KNP. A common thread was the candidates' ties to the China experience and the Korean provisional government, although not necessarily to Kim Ku. Roberts correctly believed that Yi Pom-sok, who had lost some of his influence in the police force, now wanted to build a new power base in the army, which he would tie to the youth associations as a source of dedicated anti-Communist recruits. Since Syngman Rhee would not break the deadlock—a position acceptable to Roberts for the moment—Roberts and Yi avoided both agreement and confrontation.[27]

The Yosu uprising, however, gave defense organization a much higher priority for Syngman Rhee. With his sponsorship, the National Assembly passed its first National Security Act on December 1, 1948, followed by the Army Organization Act two weeks later. The Constabulary became the Army of the Republic of Korea

(Daehan Mingukyukgun), and the Coast Guard became the Navy of the Republic of Korea (Daehan Mingukhaegun). The American advisers still used the term "Coast Guard" to emphasize the navy's inshore, counterguerrilla, countersmuggling missions. The fledgling aviation force of the army remained part of the ground forces until it became the air force in October 1949. The legislation established a Ministry of National Defense with a minister–cabinet officer, not necessarily a civilian, and a small staff. The basic responsibility for military policy making would rest with the army's chief of staff and his headquarters staff, assisted by PMAG. The army also received wide powers to police its own ranks for potential subversives, which resulted in the creation of a Counterintelligence Corps (ROK CIC) and Military Police Command, both of which developed as the power base for ambitious (and politically connected) generals who could challenge the authority of the chief of staff. The legislation also allowed the president to appoint senior officers who had no prior Constabulary service, even though the Constabulary was the army's linear predecessor and institutional foundation. As Hausman recognized in a study he did for General Roberts, the defects in the law for professionalizing the officer corps had to be accepted because of the problems facing the Korean army: the necessity of waging a nationwide counterinsurgency campaign, the imminent departure of the two American divisions, the uncertainty of military aid from the United States, the purge of Communists from the army, the need to bring financial discipline to the Korean armed forces, and the continued expansion and training of the army's six brigades, scheduled for expansion to six divisions in 1949. Moreover, all these urgent actions required constant negotiation with Yi Pom-sok and President Rhee as well as Minister Muccio and the State-Defense planers in Washington.[28]

As the Constabulary transformed itself into the Korean army, the faces became as important as the spaces. The PMAG advisers urged Rhee to replace Song Ho-sung as chief of staff. On a personal level, the Americans liked Song, who was a dedicated Korean patriot, personable, articulate, and willing. As a senior commander, however, Song became paralyzed by fatigue, anxiety, and professional ignorance. Rhee obliged Roberts and sent Song off to Taiwan as military attaché to Nationalist China. Brig. Gen. Yi Ung-jun, rehabilitated from his Japanese service in 1947, replaced Song while Rhee pondered a chief of staff for the army. A compromise candidate became chief of staff of the armed forces: Brig. Gen. Chae Byong-dok, a member of the first class and the second most senior Constabulary officer as well as a former ordnance major in the Japanese army. "Fatty" Chae, five feet five inches tall and 250 pounds—a binge eater and drinker of legendary proportions—was not a fathead or incompetent, but the American advisers did not consider him a field soldier (like the Paik brothers) or a skilled administrator (like Chung Il-kwon or Choe Duk-sin). On the upside, Chae was not one of the instant generals and colonels who had joined the army or been promoted after its creation in December 1948. One of the new generals, Kim Hong-il, had actually joined the Constabulary in late 1948 to command a new military academy. As a former division commander in the Chinese Nationalist army, he had combat experience as a large force commander and impressed the Americans. Although Rhee liked the aggressive, younger Constabulary officers favored by Roberts and Hausman based on professional criteria, especially if they were anti-Communist "northerners," the president could not resist promoting and commissioning officers who represented important rightist constituencies: Yi Ung-jun, the former Japanese railway troops colonel who saw himself as the patron saint of the army; Won Yong-dok, the Seoul socialite surgeon of Japanese service; Kim Sok-won, the "Kaiser Bill" with a memorable mustache, a murderous sociopath who had fought partisans in the Japanese service; Shin Tae-yong, a temperamental, stubborn former Japanese army lieutenant colonel; and Yi Chong-chan, a charismatic and handsome former Japanese army colonel who had lived in Buddhist solitude since 1945 as penance for his military "collaborationism." On the whole, the appointments could have been worse; they could have included "generals" such as Yi Chung-chun of the United Young Men's Party or KNP commanders. Rhee, however, feared that favoring the police and its auxiliaries strengthened Yi Pom-sok.[29]

The reform of the Coast Guard depended on personality, in this case, Capt. (later Adm.) Son Won-il, the Coast Guard commander and future chief of naval operations. A career mariner, Son had earned a captain's license in the Chinese and German merchant marine by 1935. On a trip to Korea, he had been arrested and tortured by the Japanese as a spy, probably because he was a Methodist from the Pyongyang area and a young March First Movement rebel. He returned to Korea from China in 1945 to help establish the Coast Guard. Like the Constabulary, the Coast Guard attracted dissidents—especially Communists from the radical sailors' unions—and suffered defections. In May and June 1948 mutineers seized two different small patrol craft and sailed north. Empowered to police his own ranks, Admiral Son established a way to corner subversives: make Protestant Christianity the official religion of the Korean navy. In November 1948 Son dictated that sailors stationed at his Seoul headquarters would attend chapel; this policy became common practice throughout the navy, and in November 1950, the navy established a Chaplains Office. In the meantime, navy recruiters sought out Christian refugees from north Korea fishing communities. When a formal U.S. training mission arrived in December 1949 to replace a small group of contract advisers supervised by PMAG, they found the Korean navy well trained and ardently anti-Communist. Admiral Son's investigators were tracking down the last Communists hiding in the navy's scattered patrol boats and small crews.[30]

The Yosu-Sunchon rebellion represented another milepost on the road to civil war in Korea. It almost certainly had not been orchestrated from either Haeju or Pyongyang, although Pak Hon-yong and Kim Il-sung embraced the rebels' cause. Communist broadcasts urged more Constabulary and dissident uprisings. Loyalist observers reported mysterious vessels off the coast of Cheju-do, but all the POWs taken by government troops were southern Koreans. The Cheju-do partisans had become more aggressive, but too late to distract the Constabulary from crushing the revolt. The revolt, in fact, had been the peak of the South Korean Labor Party's 1948 campaign to undermine the Republic of Korea. The SKLP's haphazard in-surgency—which was certainly not over yet—had passed the point where the op-positionists could increase their resistance—unless the Rhee regime killed itself with incompetence and factionalism, and the United States, by its failure to sup-port South Korea, assisted in the suicide. The other imponderable was Kim Il-sung's interest in fanning the flames of the southern uprising.

RED STAR, BLUE BANNER RISING: KIM IL-SUNG ASCENDANT, 1948–1949

While the Republic of Korea struggled with a devil's brew of political, military, social, and economic problems, Kim Il-sung's Kapsan faction, with the support of the Soviet Koreans, drew the puppet strings of power closer and redefined the relationship between the Democratic People's Republic of Korea and the Soviet Union. For all the trappings of autonomy and Koreanized Stalinism, North Korea remained a client state in all things that counted: military power and economic assistance. Nevertheless, Kim Il-sung enjoyed an expanding freedom to direct a war of subversion against South Korea. Whether he believed such a war would pro-duce a Communist victory is uncertain, but he used it to argue for more military assistance from the USSR and as a reason to move his own military forces into direct combat with the South Koreans along the Thirty-eighth Parallel. Even though the Red Army made its much-trumpeted withdrawal from Korea by early 1949, the Russians had not lost interest in the possibility of an all-Communist Korea, a strategic salient that protected both Communist China and Asian Russia and represented a dagger pointed at the heart of a reborn pro-American Japan.[31]

Although the Second Party Congress (March 1948) seemed to put the Kapsan-Soviet factions in a dominant position in Pyongyang, the success of the Chinese Revolution and the insurgency in South Korea temporarily strengthened the for-tunes of the Yanan and the southern domestic factions. The only permanent losers in North Korea were the domestic Communists and the pseudo-independent par-ties that had given North Korea the fig leaf of political toleration and "popular front" administration, to deceive both naive South Koreans and the United Nations. The Yanan faction maintained its influence in the party and security establishment; Pak Hon-yong's faction drew strength from the flood of Communist refugees from South Korea after the suppression of the March 1948 general strike and the failure to block the creation of the Republic of Korea in August. Ho Hon, second only to Pak Hon-yong among the leaders of the southern Korean Communists, came north to assume party and cabinet posts. Kim Il-sung and his supporters, however, en-sured that they did not lose their leverage. Just before the formal declaration of the creation of the Democratic People's Republic of Korea (September 9, 1948), the Central Committee held an emergency meeting; it made no dramatic leadership changes, but it appointed an organizational committee to develop plans for new party-government relations and Korean-Soviet association. The chair of the committee was Kim Il-sung, and its four other members were all Soviet Koreans.[32]

The Communist media bombardment of the North Korean people by radio, newspapers, and magazines stressed Kim Il-sung's growing status as the First Revolutionary, the all-wise party leader and heroic anti-Japanese guerrilla commander. Kim still had to share his mythic glories with such Communist stalwarts as Kim Tu-bong and Kim Mu-chong, but his cult of personality had the post position in the race for deification. When the Central Historical Museum of Pyongyang reopened in 1947 after a proper revolutionary refurbishing, the modern history section had a Kim Il-sung Room with 316 items. Kim's modest but real military credentials received special attention. In addition to the affectation of a guerrilla rank of "general," Pyongyang propagandists linked the creation of the *Inmingun*, or People's Army, to Kim Il-sung's campaigns against the Japanese. Like his hero, Marshal Joseph Stalin, Kim Il-sung enjoyed military poses and postures, and he dressed in a gray suit that was neither military nor Western-civilian; Kim's fashion sense seemed designed to link him with Mao Zedong. In 1948 Kim Il-sung posed with four of his closest Kapsan loyalists at the opening of a Pyongyang arsenal that manufactured the Soviet PPSh41 submachine gun. Three of the four new generals—Choe Yong-gun, Nam Il, and Kang Kon—wore Soviet-style uniforms as shiny as their "burp guns." The fourth, Kim Chaek, apparently went to the same tailor as his boss. Three years later, two of them would be dead in battle, and two would be in disgrace for the defeat of 1950. Kim alone in his gray Mao suit would still be in power, thanks to the assistance of the two masters of the cult of personality.[33]

Like Syngman Rhee, Kim Il-sung's political advantage depended on his ability to lift his Korea through foreign patronage. Of course, Kim's relations with Moscow rested in the capable hands of Gen. Terentii Shtykov, retitled Soviet ambassador to Pyongyang, and Col. Alexandre M. Ignatiev, Kim's personal adviser since 1945. As head of state and government, Premier Kim Il-sung asked Stalin for formal recognition in October 1948; Stalin's doting reply promised a wide range of new economic relations as well as diplomatic support. Kim immediately appealed to the United Nations and France for representation in any future discussions of Korea's unification. In the fall of 1948 Kim's government announced all sorts of development projects linked to Soviet largesse: railroad electrification, harbor improvements, arms manufacturing, engineering schools, public sanitation, modernization of the nationalized timber and mining industries, and growing availability of Soviet consumer goods. The Russian military managers and technocrats who remained in Pyongyang would ensure that the Democratic People's Republic of Korea would become a workers' and peasants' heaven and that Kim Il-sung would receive credit for the miracle.

Kim Il-sung cemented his alliance of convenience with the Soviet Union during his first official visit to Moscow as a head of state in March–April 1949. The North Korean delegation moved by train at a leisurely speed and in large numbers.

Besides Ambassador Shtykov and Pak Hon-yong, Kim also brought four key economic planners from his cabinet. Because not all of the six principal Korean delegates could speak Russian, the Koreans used an interpreter. Although most of the discussion of economic and cultural ties occurred at the ministerial level, the North Korean delegates met with Stalin for an hour and a quarter on March 5. Stalin quizzed Kim Il-sung at length about the Koreans' two-year plan. Kim Il-sung knew what kind of credit (quoted in American dollars) and industrial equipment he needed. Stalin agreed on a limited extension of credit ($40 million) and the acceptance of orders for machine tools to build automobiles, steam engines, and textile factories. Stalin inquired about Korean timber, electrical power, minerals, and coal. The Russians were not inclined to give money and durable goods to the Koreans as gifts.

The conversation turned to security issues. Pak Hon-yong described the ongoing insurgency and SKLP infiltration of the security forces with enthusiasm. Stalin cautioned the Koreans that subversion could work both ways. He questioned Kim and Pak about varied aspects of the People's Army's readiness and the South Korean threat. The Koreans reported that their army held the initiative in sporadic border clashes, but they judged their air and naval forces to be inadequate. The Koreans wanted more military schooling for their officers inside the Soviet Union. The talk returned to trade and possible ties to China, Japan, and the Philippines. There was no more talk of military issues. As a result of the Moscow mission, however, the Democratic People's Republic of Korea and the Soviet Union signed an eleven-part agreement on trade, technical training, financial arrangements, transportation ties, and cultural exchanges. No new policies on military arrangements were necessary, since the rearmament (from Japanese to Russian weapons) and reorganization of the People's Army were already well advanced.[34]

Satisfied with his Moscow mission, Kim Il-sung took more steps to concentrate power in himself and his most trustworthy lieutenants. In May 1949 he sent Kim Il, a Soviet Korean general of the People's Army's political department, to Beijing to conduct exploratory talks about military assistance from the People's Liberation Army, which had sent a military mission to Pyongyang the previous December. Although Kim Il did not return with a formal agreement, the Chinese generals assured the Koreans that the Sino-Korean soldiers in the Chinese army would soon be available for new missions. In the meantime, Kim Il-sung restructured the Central Committee and created a unified Workers Party of Korea, with himself as chairman of both groups; Pak Hon-yong became his deputy of both groups, along with Ho Ka-i, a Soviet Korean. Kim placed Pak in charge of another committee, the Democratic Front for the Unification of the Fatherland, created to direct the partisan war in South Korea and conduct political actions designed to undermine the authority of the Rhee regime. Kim, however, had no intention of allowing Pak to be the liberator of South Korea. He took over the direct training of the partisans at the Kangdong Institute, Haeju, and manned the posts along the border in the Ongjin peninsula, Hwanghae Province, with crack units of the Border Guard and People's Army.[35]

As the border war with South Korea waxed and waned in the summer of 1949, the Soviets enlarged and strengthened their armed forces in north Asia. The military buildup, followed with accuracy by Western intelligence agencies, went well beyond defensive requirements. In late 1948 U.S. and British intelligence analysts reported that the USSR had large and balanced forces based in China, Manchuria, and the Maritime Territory, including twenty-seven divisions, thirty-five hundred to four thousand aircraft of Frontal Aviation and the Air Defense Force, and one thousand aircraft and sixty-four submarines of the Soviet navy. This force was enough to take Korea and Taiwan and conduct an air-naval blockade of Japan. The analysts saw no need for the Russians to use this force, however, to attack Korea and Taiwan when the North Koreans and Chinese had ample forces to do so. The Korean People's Army could take Korea with five frontline divisions and five aviation regiments, all of which Kim Il-sung might have in 1949.[36]

"THE PRESENT WAS DARK, THE FUTURE MORE ENCOURAGING"

The haphazard suppression of the Yosu-Sunchon uprising and the more methodical pursuit of the remaining guerrillas and Communist cells in the Korean army gave the officers of the Constabulary and their American advisers a sense of mission that was unusual in the Rhee administration. The failure of their ministerial counterparts to take hold of Korea's political and economic problems put at risk the two essential conditions for the republic's survival: continued American military and economic assistance and General Assembly approval of UNTCOK's report on the 1948 elections, an action that would recognize the Republic of Korea as the only legitimate Korean state. In a crucial three-month period (November 1948–January 1949), the Rhee administration staggered into an indistinct future with few strong vital signs, but at least it was still breathing. The republic seemed destined for continued unrest. The gap between electrical power generation and the demand for power widened; blackouts and brownouts plagued Korean cities and factories. Commodity prices climbed, as did the government's indebtedness. The Rhee administration had neither the will nor the skill to collect taxes, cut spending, impose price controls, or take any of several actions that might have checked inflation. Instead, it simply printed and circulated more money.[37]

The growing rice shortage dramatized the Rhee government's ineffectiveness. The assembly performed its self-defined function, wailing like a Greek chorus about the impending disaster without providing any responsible solutions. The rice crisis was political, not natural. Imported American fertilizer, good weather, ample rains, energetic cultivation by the new landholders, and repair of the irrigation system produced a bumper crop of 5.8 million tons, which should have been ample to feed the republic's 20 million people. The estimated yield was as good as Korea's World War II highs—and it did not have to help feed Japan. Even a soaring birth rate and the arrival of almost 10,000 refugees a month from North Korea did not appear to make a rice shortage inevitable. The government stopped its food imports from the United States. The rice harvest was as abundant as predicted, but by December the rice under government control, collected in order to be rationed to feed city dwellers, was only about half the rice-tons held in January 1948 (720,000 tons). The government, fearing a farmers' noncooperation campaign and simply being incompetent and corrupt, had collected only one-third of its 1.1 million ton quota. When the press uncovered the emerging crisis, the government increased the individual grain ration by one-sixth. Free-market grain brought food prices down but did little to check the price inflation in other commodities. The economic roller coaster did not halt, but the rice shortage waned in 1949.[38]

The United States continued to subsidize Korea with economic assistance, but with fewer dollars and more demands for economic reform. On December 10, Minister Muccio and President Rhee signed an elaborate economic aid agreement. The plan required the Koreans to reduce government spending, halt inflationary-expansionist monetary policy, initiate a tax-not-borrow fiscal policy, reduce imports, increase exports, increase savings and domestic investment, and stimulate industrial and agricultural production. A major goal was to not only create more wealth but also provide a more equitable distribution of wealth for all Koreans. The plan required political courage, patience, persistence, sacrifice, and administrative skill. Unfortunately, none of these characteristics described the Rhee government. The plan anticipated close supervision of the Korean government by American economic advisers from the Economic Cooperation Administration (ECA), an arm of the State Department. Dr. Arthur C. Bunce, anathema to Rhee, continued his service as the primary American economic manager in his post as ECA-Korea director. Rhee's response was to try to hire his own set of American ministerial advisers. He employed Dr. Harold Lady, the son of missionaries, who became Bunce's nemesis. The Lady-Bunce rivalry would have been more disruptive if there had been more money to allocate, but dollars were in as short supply as good rice. On January 5, 1949, Harry Truman signed an executive order that transferred army-administered GARIOA funds to the ECA's Korea office; the transferred sum was $29.7 million, all that was left until the fiscal year ended on June 30. Then there would be no money at all unless Congress passed a new Korean aid bill. Yet the economic troubles still seemed manageable. An American analysis of Korea's economy found reasons to be hopeful: "The present was dark, the future more encouraging."[39]

Just as the lights never quite went out all over Seoul—the proliferation of U.S. Army generators pushed back the gloom—the Rhee government never quite flopped. Although the Korean economy needed inspired management, the armed resistance to the government remained the issue of the moment that might poison relations with the United States and United Nations. The Yosu-Sunchon revolt set off a wave of appeals in the Korean press, the assembly, religious and educational groups, trade associations, and political parties that the United States delay the

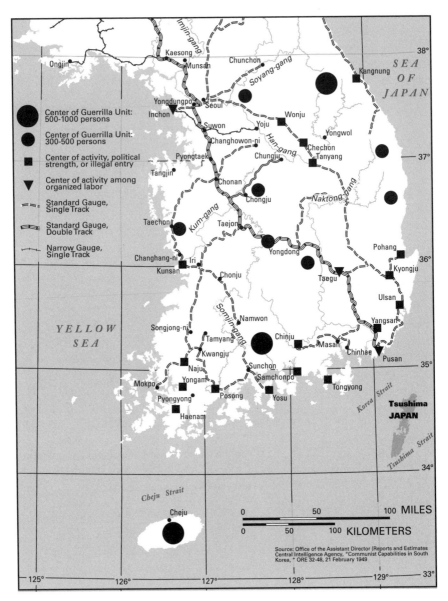

Legend

Center of Guerrilla Unit: 500-1000 persons

Center of Guerrilla Unit: 300-500 persons

Center of activity, political strength, or illegal entry

Center of activity among organized labor

Standard Gauge, Single Track

Standard Gauge, Double Track

Narrow Gauge, Single Track

Ongjin
Kaesong
Munsan
Chunchon
Soyang-gang
Kangnung
SEA
OF
JAPAN
38°
Yongdungpo
Seoul
Inchon
Wonju
Suwon
Yoju
Changhowon-ni
Han-gang
Yongwol
Pyongtaek
Chungju
Chechon
Tanyang
37°
Tangjin
Chonan
Chongju
Naktong-gang
Taechon
Kum-gang
Taejon
Yongdong
Pohang
36°
Changhang-ni
Iri
Chonju
Taegu
Kyongju
Kunsan
Ulsan
Somjin-gang
Namwon
Yangsan
Songjong-ni
Tamyang
Chinju
Masan
Chinhae
Kwangju
Sunchon
Samchonpo
Pusan
35°
Naju
Yongam
Tongyong
Korea Strait
Mokpo
Pyongyong
Posong
Yosu
Haenam
Tsushima
JAPAN
Tsushima Strait
34°
YELLOW
SEA
Cheju Strait
Cheju
33°

| 0 | 50 | 100 MILES |
| 0 | 50 | 100 KILOMETERS |

Source: Office of the Assistant Director (Reports and Estimates
Central Intelligence Agency, "Communist Capabilities in South
Korea," ORE 32-48, 21 February 1949

125° 126° 127° 128° 129°

Map 4. The Insurgency in Korea, 1949

withdrawal of its troops. On November 20 the assembly adopted a resolution (with ninety-eight sponsors) that requested the continued presence of American troops. State Department officers in Washington and Seoul joined the movement with cogent interdepartmental memoranda. The National Security Act gave all Koreans the responsibility for rooting out subversive groups; the Communists took pride of place as a target for suppression when the National Assembly outlawed the SKLP in early December 1948. The assembly approved the US-ROK aid agreement on December 13 by a vote of eighty-four to zero. The rightist parties (still championed by Kim Ku, Kim Sung-su, and Yi Pom-sok) encouraged the Korean National Police to apply liberal definitions of subversion in enforcing the National Security Act through a new Bureau of Public Peace. Subversives should be defined as current and former members of the SKLP and all its associated progeny, anyone who advocated unification, and anyone who advocated a Right-Left popular front coalition in South Korea. The government courts and prosecutors refused to enforce such sweeping definitions of subversion. The assembly, more interested in the National Traitors Act, did not resolve the deadlock between the police and the courts. As Muccio reported to Washington, the measure of Rhee's survival was "largely negative," meaning that the potential catastrophes never quite occurred and that muddling through worked.[40]

For the Constabulary—officially the South Korean army after December 1948—the counterinsurgency campaign required much more than avoiding defeat. The Chejudoan partisans remained a threat, harbored by a sympathetic population and hidden by the forests and cliffs of Halla-san. The partisans numbered at least 1,000, with an SKLP support structure twice or thrice as large. The Ninth Regiment, the island's garrison, numbered 2,700 officers and men. On the mainland, the partisan groups, organized as "brigades" on a provincial basis, mustered between 150 and 500 guerrillas. The most troublesome concentration of partisans, more than 1,000, were the bands roaming the Chiri-san mountains in Chollanam-do. The principal commander was Kim Chi-hoe, one of the Yosu revolt leaders and a former lieutenant. The major weakness of the rebels was their ordnance. About half the partisans carried Japanese and American rifles; the rest were armed with only sharpened sticks and farm tools.[41]

Some of the Communists remained hidden within the army. Col. Paik Sun-yup, the G-2, estimated that every regiment had taken in 10 to 40 Communist agents, and the rebel cells included officers from lieutenant colonels down through second lieutenants. The largest group came from the Fourteenth Regiment, but the Fourth Regiment (Kwangju) contributed about 50 disaffected soldiers to the Chiri-san bands and had its flag burned for treason, as the Fourteenth Regiment's had been. Two Fourth Regiment cells resisted arrest on October 29 and November 2 and shot their regimental and battalion commanders before fleeing or surrendering. The two regiments and Fourth Brigade received new numbers. When the trials of the Yosu rebels ended in January 1949, the Army of the Republic of Korea's judge advocates and military policemen had brought 2,817 suspects to trial and convicted all but about 600 of them. The courts sentenced 410 to death and 563 to life imprisonment. In November alone, the courts tried 1,714 and executed 67. No one in PMAG or army headquarters thought that four months of purges had cleansed the army.[42]

The war on Cheju-do shifted to the government's advantage through an accident and the determination of Song Yo-chan, the burly ex-sergeant, to crush the rebels before the Ninth Regiment rotated to the mainland at the end of December. "Tiger" Song picked up his headquarters phone on the night of October 28 and overheard two of his soldiers discussing a mutiny, which would start with Song's murder. Tapping the colonel's phone was clever; using it to plan a coup was not. Half buffoon, half charismatic field soldier, Song roared into action, sweeping up seventeen SKLP "moles" in his headquarters. The next day, Song loyalists tied six would-be mutineers to stakes and shot them to pieces; an American adviser had warned Song that Korean marksmanship and nerves were not up to a formal military execution, and they were not. In the meantime, the partisans massed for a raid-and-ambush operation on the KNP substation at Samyang. The raid was a draw, with three dead on both sides. The exploitation was a Ninth Regiment victory. Working on mutineer confessions, Song massed several patrols and encircled two hundred key rebel cadres on the afternoon of October 29. Half the rebels eventually broke out of the trap in an eight-hour battle, but the other half died or surrendered. The regiment's morale soared, and Song took his men to the field on a major sweep-and-clear operation.[43]

The Ninth Regiment and KNP companies scoured the villages and roamed the forests of Halla-san with relentless vigor that was uncharacteristic of the Korean army. To distract Song's troops, the rebels attacked a few villages, massacred some villagers and drove off the rest, and torched their thatch-roofed homes. The Communists also murdered five prominent rightists in early November. The army won the battle of burning and killing. Just how many rebels, SKLP supporters, and innocent villagers died in the autumn-winter suppression campaign will always be uncertain, but U.S. Army advisers and an intelligence team on the island provided estimates that did not depend entirely on Korean army and police reports. In eleven contacts, November 7–14, government forces killed 60 rebels; in twelve contacts, November 24–28, the soldiers claimed 337 killed and 322 taken prisoner. Another tally, November 20–27, claimed 576 killed and 122 captured. For the month of December, the claims were 600 dead and 106 captured. General Roberts's staff reported 1,625 captured, October 1–November 20. With some discounting for exaggerated claims, rebel deaths in the last three months of 1948 certainly exceeded 2,200, only a fraction of whom were hard-core Communist cadres and combat troops. The government forces captured few weapons (sixty—most of them Japanese rifles) and little military ordnance and supplies. The limited number of security force casualties (fewer than 100 dead and wounded) and the dearth of captured weapons suggested noncombatant deaths, probably field executions. About the number of rebel dead reported by the Koreans, USAFIK stated, "It is very doubtful that all of these were bonafide Guerrillas." American analysts believed that the SKLP leaders and fighters had suffered, but at least 300 survived to fight another day. For the moment, however, the Cheju-do partisans had been driven into lowland hiding or deep into the chill caves of Halla-san. They were still belligerent; Capt. Harold Fischgrund watched hundreds of fires flare on Halla-san's slopes to celebrate a Communist holiday.[44]

The insurgency on the mainland centered on the guerrilla bands that formed in the Chiri mountains of south-central Korea along the borders of the two Cholla and southern Kyongsang provinces. Although reinforced by SKLP fugitives and dissident youths, the fighting core of the guerrilla battalions (80 to 120 men) of the self-styled People's Liberation Army came from the mutineers of the Constabulary. Former Lt. Kim Chi-hoe, Fourteenth Regiment, provided skilled, inspired leadership for the 300 surviving rebels of his regiment, based in the Chiri-sans between Kwangju (Chollanam-do) and Masan (Kyongsangnam-do). In two separate incidents in November, about 50 mutineers from the Fourth Regiment joined Kim's battalion and brought their weapons. In two separate mutinies (November 2 and December 6), the Odae-san guerrillas gained more than 100 soldiers from the ranks of the Sixth Regiment (Taegu), although loyalist troops (at a cost of 9 dead) prevented the exodus of half the mutineers and most of their weapons, including mortars and machine guns. The Kangwon-do/Odae-san guerrillas were homegrown (SKLP cadres and deserters) and imported. A military police raid on the Tenth Regiment (Kangnung and Yongwol) netted 58 Communist soldiers, but others escaped into the mountains, where they joined a special operations battalion of SKLP-Haeju Communists that had crossed the Thirty-eighth Parallel in mid-November. The Odae force numbered around 400, and the infiltrators were well armed with rifles, pistols, and submachine guns—lethal against inattentive policemen and soldiers.

The Chejudoan guerrillas announced their survival by attacking the town of Odong-ni on December 19, surprising a newly arrived Second Regiment company. As a welcome to Cheju-do's new garrison, the attack could not have been more successful: thirty homes burned; ten soldiers and eleven police and auxiliaries killed at a loss of two guerrillas. Kim Chi-hoe's Chiri-san battalion did even better on a raid in Chollanam-do, killing thirty-four soldiers and eleven civilians and wounding eighteen. In a four-day running fight with an army-police rescue force, the guerrillas lost eighteen dead and fourteen captured. Almost trapped, Kim led a breakout that cost his force another twenty-five partisans, but the escape and subsequent attacks gave Kim Chi-hoe a reputation for heroic opposition that rivaled that of Kim Tal-sam of Cheju-do. The government forces did better in Kangwon-do in the same period (November 14–December 7, 1948) because the Kangdong Institute partisans crossed the border in small groups and did not know the Kangnung-Yongwol area. The purge of the Tenth Regiment had fractured their local support system. In a series of searches, roadblocks, and raids, the government forces killed or captured half the infiltrators before they could rendezvous; one of the dead was the Communist battalion commander, the only one who knew the details of the mission. The partisan actions in December, however, dramatized South Korea's perilous condition and desperate need for a diplomatic victory.[45]

Thousands of miles separated the misty Chiri-sans from France, but the stakes were just as high: the future of the Republic of Korea. In September 1948 the General Assembly met in Paris to honor the memory of the League of Nations. On its agenda was the report of the United Nations Temporary Commission on Korea on the election of a constitutional government in the American zone and the failure to find a formula to unify Korea by negotiation. Whatever their reservations about the report, the members of UNTCOK were happy to rid themselves of their mission. Russian intransigence—even with the promised Red Army withdrawal under way—made UNTCOK's dissolution easier; in fact, procedural issues raised by the Russians convinced some critics that UNTCOK had already ceased to function, making its report irrelevant. The Russians encouraged UN members to see the Korean elections as another American neocolonial charade designed to please Japan. The principal villains of the piece were John Foster Dulles, American representative to the First (Political) Committee and the puppet-president Syngman Rhee. Ambassador Jacob Malik, the Soviet delegate, urged the UN to abandon Korea. The first test went decisively against the Russians. The First Committee voted thirty-six to six to one to welcome the ROK representative, John Chang, to its debate and rejected similar representation for a North Korean delegation by a vote of six to thirty-six to eight. UNTCOK's report seemed destined for General Assembly acceptance when the First Committee passed an Australian-Chinese-U.S. draft resolution that would recognize the legitimacy of the Republic of Korea and extend the help of the United Nations for "the further development of a representative government based on the freely-expressed will of the people." The First Committee vote was forty-one to six.[46]

Although John Chang argued that South Korea did not require more UN supervision and that the United Nations needed to focus on North Korea, the Rhee government understood that further American assistance depended on its acceptance of a second UN commission to monitor its political development. On December 8, two days after receiving the First Committee's approval of UNTCOK's report and the draft resolution, the General Assembly voted forty-eight to six to one to recognize the Republic of Korea as the internationally sanctioned independent Korea. Further negotiations would explore future unification, but a new United Nations Commission on Korea (UNCOK) would investigate Communist "coercion, terrorism and violence" and apply pressure to reduce "the threat or use of force." UNCOK would observe the withdrawal of foreign troops, which should be completed by early 1949. After UN General Assembly Resolution 195 (III), "The Problem of the Independence of Korea," went into effect on December 12, the UN member nations were urged to extend full diplomatic recognition to the Republic of Korea. The United States promptly announced that it would extend such recognition on January 1, 1949. The new year would at least begin with the

U.S. government freed from its self-imposed burden of making American policy congruent with UN approval. The great uncertainly was the bellicosity of the Democratic People's Republic of Korea, which had replaced all the Soviet soldiers along the Thirty-eighth Parallel. The head of the North Korean army, Marshal Choe Yong-gun, had just announced in a speech to the candidates at the Pyongyang Political Officers School that his army would liberate South Korea as soon as the insurgency weakened the Rhee administration. The Communists had lost a campaign, but not yet the war.[47]

7

"We Are Fighting for Our Lives!"
1949–1950

The business of intelligence analysts is to spread doom and gloom among politicians and military commanders, men who are optimistic by nature and distrustful of intelligence analysts. In Washington, another review of National Security Council Memorandum 8 (NSC 8) produced a flurry of analysis that began in despondency and ended with cautious optimism. Foreign service officers Max Bishop and Niles Bond started the process with a December 1948 memorandum that called for a reexamination of Korea policy. Their own assessment from the Northeast Asian Affairs Division of the State Department concluded that the withdrawal of American troops from Korea would be a major watershed in the region. They argued with some success that a residual force should remain in Korea after XXIV Corps departed in early 1949. The army agreed to create the Fifth Regimental Combat Team (RCT) out of the Thirty-first Infantry Regiment (U.S. Seventh Infantry Division), the 555th Field Artillery Battalion, a motorized reconnaissance troop, and appropriate support units, in all about eight thousand soldiers stationed in the northwest corner of the Republic of Korea. The decision did not sit well with General MacArthur, but State and Defense believed that Bishop and Bond had a valid argument when they said that U.S. troops in Korea contributed to deterring a Soviet attack on Japan proper.[1]

The Fifth RCT decision (December 1948) did not end the debate on Korean defense. Gen. J. Lawton Collins, army chief of staff, asked General MacArthur just how long an American tactical unit should stay in Korea, now that the original NSC 8 goal of December 31 for complete withdrawal had passed. MacArthur repeated his previous position: an American unit in Korea of regimental size would not deter war and would serve only as a hostage in a general conflict with the Soviet Union. Although he could not judge the impact of complete withdrawal and doubted that anyone could make that prediction, MacArthur thought that the South Korean army could handle any contingency short of an invasion by the Russian army. MacArthur doubted, in any event, that security problems would topple the Rhee regime. The continuing food crisis would decide the fate of the Republic of Korea, which needed more rice and wheat, not guns. Now that the training of the Army of the Republic of Korea (ROKA) was "substantially complete," the Fifth RCT and the remnants of the U.S. Army Forces in Korea could be withdrawn.[2]

As the interagency review of NSC 8 progressed, the CIA's contributory evaluation stressed that the withdrawal of all American combat units from Korea "would probably in time be followed by an invasion, timed to coincide with Communist-led South Korean revolts." The ROK security forces could not stop a North Korean invasion, at least not in 1949. The withdrawal alone might lead to the collapse of the Rhee government, and its fall "would seriously diminish U.S. prestige and adversely affect U.S. security interests in the Far East." The CIA estimated that the South Korean Labor Party (SKLP) might have as many as 10,000 hard-core members and could claim 600,000 sympathizers and dissident supporters. Retaining the Fifth RCT in Korea would be a good hedge against revolt and invasion. The army's analysts disagreed. They argued that the Korean security forces had proved that they could crush a rebellion, and the North Korean army could not invade the ROK unless it received Stalin's permission and a major infusion of Russian arms. The G-2 dissenters considered the predictions of collapse, revolt, and invasion to be exaggerated. The plan to expand the ROKA and furnish it assistance, plus the moral protection of the United Nations Commission on Korea (UNCOK), should deter the North Koreans. The presence or absence of the Fifth RCT would not be much of a factor in preventing an invasion.[3]

Minister John Muccio and Maj. Gen. John B. Coulter, the second and last commanding general of U.S. Army Forces in Korea (USAFIK), agreed with the State-CIA pessimism. Muccio believed that the extension of economic and military assistance to Korea, approved by President Truman in Executive Order 10026-A (January 5, 1949), had improved the morale of the Rhee government, which had no clue how limited that monetary aid would be. The ROK government had developed all sorts of rivalries that made it weak and ineffective. There were personality clashes, presidential-legislative battles, Korean-American disagreements, civil-military tensions over conduct of the counterinsurgency campaign, police-army feuds, schisms between southerners and northern refugees, city-rural tensions, and an unsettled waxing and waning of coalitions of political parties and youth associations. The economy was plagued by inflation, rice shortages in the cities, a lack of consumer goods, and no capital accumulation and investment. In contrast, the news from North Korea—the flow of talkative refugees continued at about a thousand a month—suggested a firm bond between the Soviet Union and the Democratic People's Republic. After the Red Army's withdrawal, an invasion had to be considered a real possibility after all the American forces departed later in the year.[4]

The closer one worked to the raw data collected by the Korean-American intelligence community, the worse the future appeared. To the 971st Counterintelligence

Corps (CIC) Detachment, the Communists appeared to be building a firm foundation for a combined conventional invasion and mass uprising. The Kangdong Institute had collected a force of a thousand hard-core SKLP cadres and youthful partisans to send south; the partisans would punch holes in the security forces along the Thirty-eighth Parallel, which would allow agents free access to their contacts throughout South Korea. The contacts appeared to be concentrated in Seoul and the two Cholla provinces. Some of the agents had instructions to enlist in the ROKA to strengthen the surviving cells in the military. The Communists had abandoned any hope of subverting the Korean National Police (KNP) since the rightist youth associations had managed to dominate the police recruiting system and monopolize the training of auxiliary police. In the meantime, the socialist-populist parties in South Korea were in the process of further fragmentation, as their disheartened leaders attempted to escape the grip of their coalition with the SKLP. The SKLP's principal interest appeared to be in mounting a terrorism campaign directed at Korean government employees and civic leaders with close ties to the United States; this group produced the biggest and most dangerous advocates of anti-Communism. The SKLP had organized a terrorist group—the Righteous Blood Society—for special missions. The Communists saw an opportunity to enlist southern college students, radicalized by Yi Pom-sok's diktat in November 1948 that he would soon organize a program of compulsory military training for college students. The Communists also had plans to send reinforcements into the mountains to bolster the hard-pressed partisan units still active in the Chiri-san and Odaesan ranges. Quick action seemed necessary, since the new small farmers turned landowners showed more interest in fertilizer and seedlings than in revolution.

In North Korea, the government had introduced a number of programs to mobilize the people for war. It introduced general conscription for public service among males aged eighteen to thirty-five, with party members drafted first for military service. Political prisoners had been moved to coal mines, where they could be worked to exhaustion and not menace factories; all factory workers, now good Communists, between the ages of eighteen and thirty would begin basic military training. In the meantime, as many as three divisions of the new *In Min Gun* had deployed south of the Thirty-eighth Parallel. The 971st CIC Detachment had even obtained an invasion plan, which would become active when five basic conditions had been met: (1) American military intervention seemed improbable (i.e., after the last troops left South Korea), (2) the Chinese Communists won their civil war and could provide more assistance, (3) the Red Army had pulled its troops out and poured more weapons in, (4) the Rhee regime was "in extreme confusion," and (5) the United Nations lost interest in Korea. The general concept of operations involved four Communist armies. Two conventional forces launched from the Thirty-eighth Parallel would encircle Seoul from the northwest through Kaesong and Munsan-ni and from the north through Chunchon and Suwon. Partisan armies formed in Cheju-do and the two Cholla provinces would capture Mokpo, Kunsan, and Taejon. Another partisan army formed in the Taebaek mountains would capture Taegu. These two forces would then combine to capture the critical port of Pusan. One significant indicator of North Korean planning was the sudden short-age of quality paper, especially photographic paper, in South Korea; apparently, North Korean agents had bought paper that could be used for identification cards, military maps, photographs, and detailed operations orders. Another troublesome development was a major construction project to build military emplacements throughout North Korea.[5]

President Rhee sent Cho Pyong-ok, the former director of the KNP, but per-suasive and American educated, to Washington to ensure that the State Department understood the urgency of Korea's need for political reassurance, military support, and economic aid. On January 5, 1949, Special Envoy Cho and his party met with Undersecretary Robert Lovett to explain the precarious position of the Rhee gov-ernment. Ambitious members of the National Assembly might open their own ne-gotiations with Pyongyang to form a coalition government, and these negotiations, which could lead to a North-South coalition government, might topple Rhee and open the way for a Communist coup. Such deals in China had fatally weakened the Nationalists and displaced the true democrats in Czechoslovakia. Lovett told Cho that Rhee should reform his government, stamp out corruption, and quit depend-ing on intimidation and empty promises. Cho responded hotly that such accom-modation was "a luxury which could not [be] afforded by a government fighting for its very existence." Lovett simply repeated his advice for reform, reform, and more reform.[6]

To provide Rhee a public show of support, President Truman approved a State Department proposal to send a special mission to Seoul. Since the mission would also meet with General MacArthur to discuss his conduct of the occupation of Japan and its future defense, the principals should represent the Department of the Army. Secretary of the Army Kenneth Royall and Lt. Gen. Albert C. Wedemeyer received the call to visit the Far East in February 1949. The meeting with Rhee did nothing to resolve any of the standing issues involving the redeployment of the Fifth RCT. Muccio and his staff, including General Roberts, held firm to their po-sition that the ROK security forces were not ready to take full responsibility for Korea's defense. The presence of American troops, though sometimes an irritant and a political issue, provided tangible psychological reassurance to a political elite that was given to despondency and denial.

Rhee's own testimony reinforced Muccio's characterization of Korean politi-cians. The president railed against State as a nest of his enemies because Muccio, Roberts, and their advisers had conspired with the National Assembly to defeat his plans to create a larger army, a larger and militarized national police, and a reserve army of veterans of Japanese and Chinese service and the anti-Communist youth associations. Korea could have an army of 100,000 in six weeks if the United States would provide the funds for arms and order General Roberts to be more coopera-tive and less critical of the army's logistical management, accounting, training, and personnel policies. Rhee recommended that the Provisional Military Advisory

Group (PMAG) be abolished and a new military mission formed, since the United Nations had recognized the Republic of Korea as the only legitimate government of all Korea. Rhee believed that the United Nations had authorized him to form an army capable of invading North Korea before it became too militarily formidable. Muccio quickly corrected Rhee: neither the United States nor the United Nations would approve of a war of unification. Rhee and Gen. Chae Pyong-dok had been seduced by their own public rhetoric about *pukjin* ("march north") and their fanciful plans to form an army that "in a short time" could move on North Korea. Royall and Wedemeyer came away from the meeting with unbounded sympathy for Muccio and Roberts, but they believed that a complete withdrawal was justified. As long as the United States fashioned an economic and military assistance program that would strengthen the ROK armed forces and keep them under American influence, Rhee could not indulge his obsessive fear that the army would overthrow his government and his obsessive dream to invade North Korea.[7]

Leaving Rhee feeling abandoned and desperate, the Royall-Wedemeyer mission added its impressions to the continuing discussions, shaped by the tension between State and the Joint Chiefs of Staff over Korean policy and the liquidation of USAFIK. The first draft of a revision of NSC 8 predicted that the fall of Korea would compromise the American position in Asia. The problem was that a full-fledged invasion could probably not be stopped by the current ROKA, even with the help of the Fifth RCT. A defeat would discourage the formation of American alliances in the region. Yet the UN General Assembly had made it very clear that its attitude toward South Korea would depend on the prompt withdrawal of all foreign troops. The first draft memorandum (NSC 8/1) underwent so many alterations that it became NSC 8/2, "The Position of the United States in Respect to Korea," when approved by the NSC and President Truman on March 22, 1949. The final version made it clear that USAFIK would disappear forever by July 1 and would be replaced by the Korean Military Advisory Group (KMAG) with a strength of around 500 officers and men. There was a possibility that the American withdrawal would be misread by the Soviet Union and the Democratic People's Republic as an invitation to wage an accelerated war of subversion, perhaps aided by an invasion. The best way to disabuse the Communists was to conduct an aggressive program to improve the ROK armed forces and police. This force would number 114,000 soldiers, sailors, and national policemen; there was no need for a separate air force. This force would be adequate to defend South Korea from subversion, but it would not be capable of a sustained invasion of North Korea. Just how much aid Rhee would receive would depend not just on the nature of the North Korean threat but also on the improved performance of Rhee's government in addressing inflation, corruption, deficit spending, land reform, and the disposition of Japanese vested property, as well as its cooperation with the American diplomatic mission and KMAG. In sum, although the United States had a responsibility to see that the Republic of Korea survived, it would deal with Korea's security through a combination of bilateral negotiations with Seoul and its firm commitment to the principles and processes set forth in the UN General Assembly resolution of December 12, 1948.[8]

When the United Nations Commission on Korea, no longer temporary or temporizing, arrived in Seoul in February 1949, its members quickly learned that Syngman Rhee viewed them with suspicion and considerable dismay. The committee itself arrived with representatives from six nations: Australia, the Philippines, France, Nationalist China, Syria, and India. Demonstrating its independence, Canada refused to continue on the committee, thus eliminating the principal critic of the Republic of Korea. The policy of the Australian delegation had shifted to a more understanding position. The Rhee administration, reflecting the president's animus to UNCOK, insisted that the commission's mission was to investigate conditions in North Korea and pursue the dream of unification. It regarded this assignment as hopeless but less dangerous than UNCOK's other charge, which was to monitor the development of democratic, representative government in South Korea. UNCOK could thus become—and did become—a platform for all of Rhee's critics, which included Kim Kyu-sik and Kim Ku, both driven into the political wilderness in 1948 by their flirtation with Kim Il-sung and their noncooperation in the creation of the republic. Kim Ku remained dangerous because of his penchant for subversion, terrorism, and political assassination. The two Kims recognized that UNCOK provided an opportunity for their political resurrection, so they created the National Independence Federation (December 1948) to work with the United Nations for the unification of the two Koreas. UNCOK insisted that its charge to "consult" widely with Korean political leaders did not limit it to representatives of the Rhee government, but Rhee's principal officer for liaison with UNCOK, Dr. Cho Pyong-ok, demanded that the commissioners not recognize Kim Ku, who was a traitor. Rhee himself continued to harangue the UNCOK chairman, Australian Patrick Shaw, arguing that UNCOK should deal only with his administrators or, in extremis, members of the National Assembly. Shaw rejected Rhee's position. Although UNCOK attempted to collect information and opinion from a wide variety of sources, the Rhee administration harassed the commission with demonstrations and the arrest of its Korean employees, witnesses, and attached journalists under the terms of the National Security Act. By July 1949, UNCOK conceded that it could not continue its investigation and stated that it would file a report that criticized both Korean governments.[9]

Syngman Rhee may have frightened UNCOK on occasion, but he concerned U.S. diplomats even more, despite the fact that he had already reshuffled his cabinet to give it a more cooperative cast. Rhee sent Chang Taek-sang off to Great Britain as ambassador, a pleasant assignment for the University of Aberdeen doctorate, but one that took him out of the political mix. Ben Limb, a stalwart of Rhee's Korean Commission in Washington, became foreign minister. The minister of home affairs went to Manila, replaced by Capt. Shin Sung-mo, an honest, apolitical, vigorous, conscientious veteran with twenty years' experience as a licensed officer of the British merchant marine. Aged fifty-seven in 1949, Shin spoke English and enjoyed a reputation as a nationalist opponent of Japanese rule in the 1910–1919 years. His loyal work as home minister convinced Rhee to give him the portfolio of national defense in March 1949, even though Yi Pom-sok continued as prime minister. Shin's appointment did not calm the State Department, which began to warn Muccio that "reliable sources" elsewhere in the Far East were convinced that Rhee would order an invasion of North Korea in May or June 1949. The chief planner was Yi Pom-sok. Muccio forwarded Rhee's pledge to do nothing rash, but the president argued that the withdrawal of the last American troops created an opportunity for the "predatory aggressor nation" to the north to escalate its military pressure on the republic. South Korea required massive American military assistance that would produce a larger army as quickly as possible.[10]

On May 2, 1949, President Rhee and Prime Minister Yi met with senior American diplomatic representatives to discuss Korea's security crisis. At a minimum, they wanted the United States to double the number of military advisers and send more senior advisers to Korea. Rhee's principal concern was that his army was too small. He wanted a program that would turn the youth associations into a mass reserve force. The withdrawal of American troops and the likely collapse of Nationalist China made it essential that the United States keep some forces in Korea and make a public pledge to defend it in the event of an invasion. Rhee complained that Secretary of the Army Royall had made a public statement in Tokyo that excluded Korea from the defense of Japan. The end of the American occupation had discouraged the patriotic Koreans and encouraged appeasers such as Kim Ku and Kim Kyu-sik. In addition to a bigger army, the Koreans believed that they needed a bigger navy and a real air force. Another participant in the discussion, Carlos Romulo of the Philippines, representing the United Nations, sided with Rhee on the deterrent effect of American troops and promised to raise the issue in the General Assembly. Rhee stated that Korea would fight to the last man against an invader, but he admitted that the lack of an American security guarantee probably reduced the number of potential heroes. He needed more troops of his own *and* a mutual security treaty with the United States.[11]

The State Department remained unmoved by Rhee's latest pleas for help, even when supported by Muccio. The United States did not have enough money to provide ships and planes for Korea. President Truman had already decided that Korea would get no more than $11 million in military assistance. Korea played no role in defense planning, even for Japan. In any event, the Korean economy could not support a large army, and the money that went to the army would be lost to needy farmers and workers. The State Department wanted every spare dollar to go to its economic mission. The key to Korea's security was long-range economic development, and State had a good proposal for $100 million a year for three years to push the Korean economy ahead. Rhee would have to live with his current armed forces, because the Joint Chiefs of Staff would not back an ambitious military assistance plan. The best the U.S. Army would do was to increase the size of the advisory group and arrange for Korean officers to attend schools in Japan and the United States.[12]

BUILDING THE KOREAN PEOPLE'S ARMY, PREPARING THE PEOPLE FOR WAR

Facing no serious internal opposition to his plans to unify Korea, Kim Il-sung did not despair when Stalin rejected his proposal for escalating warfare and rapid rearmament in March 1949. He knew that Ambassador Terentii Shtykov, the erstwhile political directorate general turned diplomat, would denounce the Republic of Korea as a fascist warmonger bent on destroying the Democratic People's Republic of Korea. The critical event that had unleashed the South Korean police on the outposts of the North Korean border constabulary was the withdrawal of American troops. Shtykov bombarded Moscow with alarmist telegrams throughout February and March about clashes in which ROK police and soldiers penetrated the border and defeated the gallant border guards, who fought with inferior Japanese weapons and little ammunition. Shtykov studiously ignored the partisan penetrations of the Kangdong Institute guerrillas, and he often confused firefights in Kangwon-do with clashes in Kyonggi-do and Hwanghae-do on the western coast. He argued with conviction that the ROKA intended to make major cross-border raids, even an invasion, sometime in the spring of 1949. He reported that units of the regular South Korean regiments had concentrated in front of Haeju on the Ongjin peninsula, at Kaesong, at Chunchon, and at Hoengsong in central Korea. The puppet troops of the Third Division defended the eastern coastal corridor and the Taebaek mountains at Kangnung. Shtykov continued to report alarming tales of ROKA redeployments to the border areas and the movement of tanks and heavy artillery (of which the ROKA had none) to attack positions. South Korean deserters, Communist agents inside the ROKA, and spies provided mounting evidence of South Korean malevolence and soaring military capability, defined for Shtykov by the North Koreans.[13]

The Korean People's Army (KPA) had already jumped ahead of its southern rival in size and arms. As the Soviet Twenty-fifth Army started its redeployment from North Korea, Russian staff officers and their KPA counterparts prepared a plan in December 1948—and received promises of funding—for a formidable force. The KPA's projected six infantry and two armored divisions, with corps and supporting troops, would provide Kim Il-sung with a striking force of 100,000 officers and men when the organization was completed in 1950. This force would be supported by an aviation component of 150 Yak-9 and IL-10 combat aircraft, designed for ground-attack operations. Further study reduced the armored component to one tank brigade (the 105th) armed with the T-34/85 Russian medium tank of late World War II vintage. The tank's high-velocity 85mm gun could penetrate the frontal armor of any tank in the American inventory except the M-26 "Pershing," should U.S. tanks show up in the hands of the ROKA. The planners envisioned that each infantry division would have a Soviet-style artillery regiment of four battalions with twenty-four towed 76mm guns, twelve towed 122mm guns, and twelve self-propelled 76mm guns with ranges up to thirteen thousand yards. To match the forty-eight guns in a KPA division, the ROK infantry division had one artillery battalion of fifteen short-barreled M-3 105mm howitzers per division by 1950, but only three of eight divisions actually had artillery battalions.[14]

The Soviet agreement to arm the Korean People's Army—extended from an eight-division to a twenty-division program by 1950—did not include a manning plan. All the soldiers (with the exception of Soviet advisers) would be Koreans, but not necessarily Koreans then living within the borders of the Democratic People's Republic. Kim Il-sung quickly renewed his contacts with the Chinese People's Liberation Army. In January 1949 Kim sent a mission of two, Choe Yong-gun and Kim Mu-bong, to Harbin, Manchuria, to meet with Zhou Bao-zhong, an old comrade of the Northeast Anti-Japanese United Army and the provisional administrator of Manchuria. The three principals agreed to recruit Sino-Korean veterans for the North Korean army, provided their revolutionary credentials were in order. The Communist Party strongman for Manchuria, Gao Gang, approved the agreement. In May 1949 Kim Il-sung made a more dramatic recruiting effort by sending Kim Il, the KPA's chief political officer, to Beijing to fish for more Chinese support from the top leaders. Kim Il found the Chinese, savoring their approaching victory, in an expansive mood. In talks with Mao Zedong, Zhou Enlai, Gao Gang, and Gen. Zhu De, the North Korean delegation received encouragement, a concrete promise of manpower, and much advice on preparing for a war of attrition if the quick strike did not work. The Chinese warned that the Koreans should think about a war in which they faced the South Koreans, Japanese, and Americans, but the Chinese thought that if such a major regional war developed, they and the Russians would commit their forces to the fray. The most alarming development would be the return of Japanese troops to Korea, sponsored by General MacArthur. The Chinese Communists, however, would not commit their forces until the revolution was complete.[15]

The Chinese delivered on their promise of assistance before Kim Il-sung could say *kamsa hamnida* (thank you). Kim made sure that the Russians quickly learned what a splendid comrade Chairman Mao was in the cause of Korean unification. The Chinese provided the edge the KPA required to move into positions just north of the Thirty-eighth Parallel. In July 1949 the Korean 166th Division, People's Liberation Army, joined the North Korean army as its Sixth Division. The next month the 167th Division transformed itself into the Fifth Division, KPA. Only the senior officers changed positions. By the end of the year, the KPA had formed another division from Sino-Korean veterans in Manchuria. Conscription brought forty thousand young men into the People's Army; their physical condition received more attention than their politics. After they pulled off the Thirty-eighth Parallel in 1950, two Border Guard *(Boandae)* brigades went through retraining and expansion and became the Eighth and Ninth Divisions of the KPA. Throughout North Korea, political officers identified young men suitable and eligible for military service. Part-time military training became part of the routine on farms and in factories; failure to participate meant a trip to the mines and forced labor camps. The government used draft registration to ensure that all Christians had enrolled in the government's "Christian League," which gave the government a good inventory of its most dangerous group of subversives.

In June 1949, as advance units of the Korean People's Army occupied fortified outposts on the border, Kim Il-sung announced the formation of a new organization, the Democratic Front for the Attainment of the Unification of the Fatherland. The purpose of the Democratic Front was to provide a forum from which to confront Rhee and the Americans with their lack of legitimacy. The Democratic Front would work with anti-Rhee southern politicians to force another UN-supervised election—this time, one that was truly representative. Ho Hon, the Communist lawyer from Seoul (second only to Pak Hon-yong in the pantheon of southern Communists), assumed chairmanship of the Democratic Front. His goal was to arrange a national election, which the Communists would have carried by adding their great support in the north to that of the southern dissidents. There was no doubt in Ho Hon's mind that his public plea to work for unification would produce no important negotiations, but the Democratic Front's goal was to sow confusion and false hope within the South Korean electorate. For Kim Il-sung, the Democratic Front would show the Russians that he could play the subversion game with the best of revolutionaries, and if the Democratic Front produced no results, he could blame its failure on Pak Hon-yong and Ho Hon.[16]

In the meantime, shipments of arms and ordnance arrived at North Korea's east coast ports, principally Wonsan. In February 1949 a Soviet naval transport from Vladivostok brought a shipment of 2.5 million rounds of rifle ammunition, 15,000 shells, forty 82mm mortars, 100 heavy machine guns, and 400 pistols. To find men to match the weapons, the Korean Workers' Party and the Youth League provided or screened about a third of the recruits, the required proportion of representatives of the proletariat. The experience of Kim Chae-pil, a young farmer and landholder in Pyongannam-do, was illustrative. Having survived Japanese service in 1945 as a construction worker on Okinawa, Kim returned home to learn that he belonged to a proscribed social class, made worse by his membership in the Presbyterian Church. Banned from high school, Kim became a truck driver, hauling salt from the mines to west coast cities. Found guilty of harboring a fugitive schoolteacher, Kim served his three-year prison sentence on construction projects around the border town of Sinuiju. Kim's health failed when the police cut his rations and extended his work hours in 1949. Broken in body and nearly in spirit, Kim accepted sick leave to visit his family, who nursed him back to health. The local party officials in Namyang followed his recovery with interest until they judged him sufficiently strong to return to state service. A police officer visited his home to tell him that his past crimes and reactionary roots had been forgiven. He had just become a truck driver for the People's Army. Kim Chae-pil's nightmare returned as he became part of the military mobilization of the North Korean people.[17]

Kim Il-sung, acting with the supreme confidence of an isolated tyrant, opened new negotiations for offensive war. On September 3, 1949, he sent Mun Il, his Russian translator and a Soviet citizen, to see Ambassador Shtykov. North Korean agents reported that the South Koreans planned a punitive expedition against Pak Hon-yong's base camps at Haeju, Ongjin peninsula. The targets included an important cement plant. Kim Il-sung wanted approval to seize all of Ongjin and, perhaps, territory south of the Thirty-eighth Parallel all the way to Kaesong—a border town important in North Korean lore as the southern capital of the ancient Koryo Kingdom and a center of true "Koreanism," unlike its southern rivals Paekche and Shilla. The Russian embassy and military mission found documented evidence of intentions to bombard the cement plant, but only deserters' reports to verify the invasion plans. Shtykov reported Kim's plan the same day he heard it and put his deputy, Grigorii I. Tunkin, to work investigating the feasibility of Kim's Ongjin adventure. Despite Pak Hon-yong's enthusiasm for the plan, also endorsed by Ho Ka-i, Shtykov and Tunkin reported that the North Koreans were much too optimistic about their military prospects. Kim admitted that he was not prepared for a general civil war, but he argued that the South Koreans would not waste their inferior forces to hold Ongjin. American options would not be timely or effective: organize a Japanese–Chinese Nationalist expeditionary force for Korea, use the U.S. Air Force and Navy to aid "the puppet army," and take over the South Korean army with KMAG officers. Kim believed that a quick strike at Ongjin would bag two South Korean regiments and demoralize the rest of the ROKA. The operation could move eastward to Kaesong. If not, Ongjin could be easily held. Kim conceded that the KPA did not have sufficient supplies or air, naval, or armored forces for a protracted general civil war, but he insisted that Rhee had neither the will nor the capability to retake Ongjin or start attacks elsewhere.[18]

Now better informed and more cautious, Shtykov and Tunkin would not support Kim's plan because the KPA and the southern partisans could not win a general civil war quickly—and in their opinion, a civil war was exactly what the Ongjin-Kaesong operation would start. A more limited Ongjin operation might produce a moral victory, but it could also give Rhee the cause and time to build more American and international support. The Soviet mission in Pyongyang recommended that Stalin discourage Kim's plan because "a drawn out civil war is disadvantageous for the north both militarily and politically." For one thing, such a war would probably increase aid to Syngman Rhee, not reduce it, which was the current trend. The war would likely bring such death and destruction that "the military casualties, suffering and adversity may elicit in the population a negative mood toward the one who began the war." A Korean war, moreover, would not reap direct benefit for the Soviet Union, since it would allow the Americans to increase "agitation" against the Soviet Union and further encourage "war hysteria." The North Koreans could not guarantee a quick victory, and even a small partial success risked unhappy results. In this case, the northerners, though they might win strategically, would lose politically in many regards. Such an operation would be used to accuse the northerners of trying to inflame a fratricidal war. It would also be used to increase American and international interference in Korean affairs.[19]

Moscow did not require much time to accept its ambassador's advice to reject Kim Il-sung's plan. On September 24, 1949, the Politburo instructed Shtykov to meet with Kim Il-sung and tell him *nyet*. The military balance was not favorable enough, even if the southern Koreans awaited "liberation" and unification. Any move on Ongjin and Kaesong menaced Seoul itself and would surely bring a full military response by Rhee. A North Korean military "initiative" would likely give the Americans "cause for any kind of interference in Korean affairs." The Politburo's *nyet*, however, was not absolute. The Foreign Ministry ensured that Shtykov and Tunkin understood that Stalin expected them to reassure the North Koreans that only their timing was wrong. Kim must not begin operations "that will not lead to the defeat of the enemy but will create significant political and economic difficulties for North Korea, which, finally, cannot be permitted." The KPA did not yet enjoy the requisite superiority in arms and numbers for a swift victory, and the South Korean masses had not been adequately prepared to support an invasion with "a general uprising." Even a limited Ongjin peninsula operation could not be mounted without menacing Kaesong and thus Seoul, which would be the sure beginning of a general war. The Politburo supported the goal of a unified Korea by an insurgency, ultimately supported by the KPA, but the North Korean Communists still had much to do for the "development of a partisan movement, the creation of liberated regions, and the preparation of a general armed uprising in South Korea." The North Koreans would have to be patient and restrained.[20]

Stalin's conditional *nyet* had several implied messages not fully explained in the Politburo's message to Kim. The most telling correlation of forces to be sought was simply China in, America out. Stalin wanted the Chinese Communists, not the Soviet Union, to take up the yoke of Korean patronage, or at least share it. In early 1949 the People's Liberation Army held the strategic initiative and broke the Nationalist army into uncoordinated pockets of resistance in western and southern China. American military assistance had been too little, too late. Nevertheless, the Chinese civil war had not ended, and Stalin knew that Mao Zedong would resist another war at the wrong place and wrong time. As for the Americans, they still had a tactical ground force deployed across the roads to Seoul, and the Russians would shrink from a direct military confrontation with the United States, even in Asia. The American armed forces still occupied Japan, and although their naval and air forces might have limited influence on a land campaign in Korea, they could certainly pulverize the Soviet bases at Port Arthur and Vladivostok if they chose to intervene. Stalin even expressed concern that South Korea and the United States might provoke a war. The Americans had responded to the Berlin blockade with an awesome airlift of supplies, protected by tactical aircraft. It was wiser to let such vigilance wane.

Stalin's attention in 1949 faced westward, not to Asia. The Neo–Great Game focused on France, Italy, Germany, Eastern Europe, and the Balkans. The Soviets were in battle joined. They watched the Communist parties of France and Italy falter and fade. Tito of Yugoslavia remained intractable, and the Arab and Persian nationalists were difficult to mold into new Leninists. The new regimes in East Germany, Poland, and Czechoslovakia needed more nurturing. The Red Army had few resources for a major war; Stalin's military priorities were air defense and nuclear bombs and missiles. Wars of national liberation for Asians should be fought by Asians.[21]

"WE ARE FIGHTING FOR OUR LIVES!"

He could be querulous, dissembling, irrational, stubborn to a fault, self-righteous, an economic naïf, and antimilitary to the core, but President Syngman Rhee did not qualify as paranoid. There was little disagreement in Seoul that Rhee's government did not look like a good bet to last the year. If fighting Communists were not enough, Rhee met the challenge of the new assembly's National Traitors Act with a counterattack of his own, justified by inserting portions of the Peace Preservation Act (1948) into the National Security Act (1948). Having established a Special Investigating Committee (SIC) that had its own police and special court system to enforce the National Traitors Act, the hostile leadership of the assembly ordered a wave of arrests shortly before the end of 1948. Among the first hundred "collaborators" arrested by SIC agents were Rev. Yang Ju-sam, the first Methodist bishop of Korea and Rhee's close friend; Yi Yi-yong, an aged member of the royal family; Pak Hong-sik, a wealthy retailer and donor to the Korean Democratic Party; and Dr. Chang Taek-sang, the Seoul police chief turned foreign minister. Protected by law and its own internal policing system, the ROKA escaped the witch hunt (although the SIC presented Rhee with a list of collaborationist officers), but the Korean National Police remained a prime target of SIC investigators. Rhee used the Seoul police, aided by a sympathetic major and police chief, to conduct a reciprocal campaign of intimidation against the National Assembly. In addition to pure malice and political advantage, the presidential-legislative war had three issues: a land reform act that contained acceptable programs for owner compensation and equitable terms for rent and investment in seed and fertilizer, the sale of vested Japanese property in government hands, and Rhee's failure to negotiate a military and economic assistance agreement with the United States. These issues, however, were not resolved, and the Rhee-assembly feud raged on until the arrests of several assemblymen gave the president his Pyrrhic victory.[22]

The pursuit of dissident assemblymen became only a small (if highly visible) part of Rhee's war on the South Korean Labor Party, directed with enthusiasm by

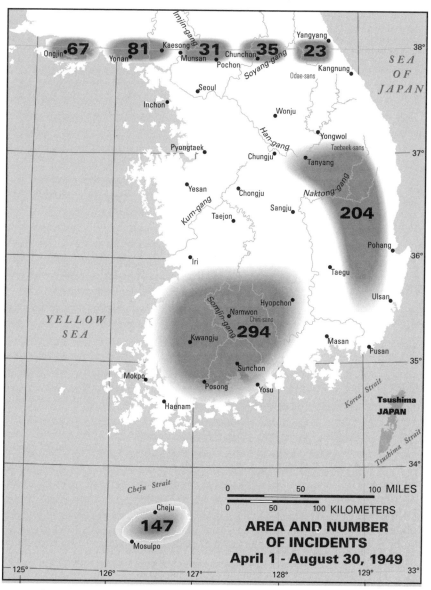

Map 5. The Partisan and Border War

Yi Pom-sok. The population of political prisoners in South Korea increased in 1949 from 12,500 to 40,000 convicted or detained dissidents and suspects. The minister of education, An Ho-sang, started an assault on schoolteachers whose criticisms of the government he interpreted as Communist; in fact, the SKLP *had* used the public schools as a fertile recruiting ground for teachers and students. The government also believed that the Communists in Seoul had begun a campaign of terrorism. On March 17, two Korean gunmen broke into the Chosun Christian College home of Dr. and Mrs. Horace H. Underwood and shot Mrs. Underwood to death as she attempted to block their entry. Under interrogation, the assassins, members of the Democratic Students League, claimed that their target had been Miss Mo Yun-suk, a prominent nationalist poet, apostate Communist, and liaison officer to UNCOK. The Underwood family and others believed that Ethel van Wagoner Underwood, one of the most esteemed women of the Protestant missionary community, had been the target from the start. The outpouring of public grief—thousands attended her memorial service in Saemunan Presbyterian Church and interment in Seoul Foreign Cemetery—made it politic, however, for the Communists to claim that they had made a mistake. The next victim, former captain of detectives Pak Il-won, also had strong ties to the Americans as an effective and prominent employee of the U.S. Office of Information; his murderers, SKLP stalwarts, confessed that they had shot the right person. Captain Pak had been a close friend of Chang Taek-sang, himself a perennial target. Yi Pom-sok unleashed the KNP and the soldiers of the First Brigade, and their raids in Seoul netted party chief Yi Chang-op and sixty other SKLP officers and key operatives; Yi confessed that he had received drugs and money from Pyongyang and Haeju to finance his operations. The government forces continued their sweep to wipe out the Communist infrastructure throughout Korea.[23]

The search for Communist cells in the army continued with a vengeance, mounted by the ROKA G-2 staff and its American advisers and assisted by the 971st CIC Detachment and the Koreans' own military police organization. Between January 1 and March 15, government agents arrested 78 officers and 174 enlisted men and convicted 225 of them of various crimes, including treason, subversion, and a host of criminal activities. The senior officers bore the brunt of the punishment: six were sentenced to death, and nine were given life imprisonment. Another 210 convicted defendants received sentences that varied from six months to twenty years. By December 1949, the army had jailed 38 officers and 835 enlisted men. Despite predictions that the ROKA had been purified, some 60 soldiers of the Sixth Regiment (Pohang) defected with their weapons and marched off to join the guerrillas in the Odae mountains, leaving behind two dead loyalists. This February 1949 embarrassment, however, was offset by the capture of several important Communist cells among officers stationed in the Seoul area.

The most senior officer arrested was Maj. Park Chung-hee, a dour, bright, dogged veteran of the Manchukuo army who had been identified by his peers as a revolutionary and a charismatic leader. Park Chung-hee despised politicians, policemen, and those fellow officers whom he identified as corrupt opportunists.[24] He also detested army officers with northern roots, Christian backgrounds, and conservative politics. A native of Kyongsangbuk-do Province and a graduate of the prestigious Taegu Teachers College, he resented the rising power of the refugee officers of the Constabulary's first class in the army. His political radicalism and *tonghak* prejudices made him hostile to American influence in Korea. Through one of his brothers, he was led to the SKLP and a conspiracy to unseat Syngman Rhee. The army judicial system made short work of Major Park; on February 8, 1949, a court-martial convicted him of treason and sentenced him to life imprisonment. Maj. Gen. Yi Ung-jun approved the court's judgment on April 18, 1949, and directed that the sentence be served at Sodaemun Prison. Ex-Major Park, however, agreed to reveal the identities of other SKLP members in the officers corps and help roll up the Communist agent network in South Korea, an agreement that made his sentence negotiable. He also had his champions in the army, including Won Yong-dok and Paik Sun-yup. By the end of 1949, Park, a civilian member of the army's intelligence staff, had begun the process of resurrection that eventually made him president of the Republic of Korea.[25]

The relentless search for Communists—or any other dissenters—in the armed forces set off the last surge of defections from the army and navy in May and June 1949. Although the Communists trumpeted the defections as further proof of the bankruptcy of the "puppet" forces, the mutinies also demonstrated the cohesiveness and determination of the loyalists in the armed forces. Whether they were inspired by a belief that a North-South war was imminent or by approaching exposure, the defectors rocked the Rhee administration. Buffeted by all his troubles and dismayed by the limited support from the United States, Rhee wrote a personal plea to General MacArthur for more arms for an enlarged security force built around the anti-Communist youth associations. Rhee would accept arms and money from any source, including private donors. "We are fighting for our lives!"[26] The naval defections occurred first on May 10–12 on the MCM/YMS 508 (harbor patrol boat and minesweeper) *Kanghwa,* whose captain and crew took their ship to Wonsan, North Korea. On May 21 two officers and three sailors from the crews of the YMS *Tong Yong* and YMS *Kangkyung* attempted to sail the *Tong Yong* from Pusan to North Korea, but loyalist crews captured the ship before it left the harbor. One mutineer committed suicide, and the other four surrendered to face trial and execution. The affair marked the end of SKLP influence in the navy and convinced General Roberts that Admiral Son's force had earned additional investment.[27]

The next army mutiny shook the Rhee regime, but it marked the last gasp of SKLP infiltrators trying to ruin army morale and discredit the KMAG advisers. The affair began with the arrest of Lt. Col. Choe Nam-gun, transferred for his inept performance in encircling and capturing the Yosu-Sunchon rebels and for suspected Communist sympathies. The transfer allowed Colonel Choe to take over the Communist cell in his new command, the Eighth Regiment, deployed along the border in western Kangwon-do Province and thus stationed across one of the corridors used by the Kangdong Institute guerrillas, now led by Kim Tal-sam, the Chejudoan partisan leader. That the Eighth Regiment's border patrols proved singularly inept was no surprise, since two of its battalion commanders, Maj. Kang Tae-mun and Maj. Pyo Mu-won, both part of the Constabulary's notorious second class, were members of the SKLP. On the evening of May 5 the two majors announced that they were taking the better part of their two battalions on a forced night march as a training exercise. Major Pyo, a skilled and respected commander, duped his men and marched them across the border into North Korea, where they were welcomed, much to their astonishment. Immediately, two companies broke and ran back to the border, pursued by fire from the North Korean *Boandae*. In the other battalion, where some junior officers suspected Major Kang's treason, two companies took unauthorized ammunition with them on the march. When Major Kang got his battalion across the border, he told his troops that they were surrounded and must surrender. The loyalists immediately opened fire and drove back their traitorous comrades and the *Boandae*. The loyalist companies fought their way back across the border, taking and inflicting casualties. When the stragglers and wounded could finally be collected, the two battalions had lost 4 officers and 363 enlisted men of the 9 officers and 796 soldiers who had left on the march. Subtracting the loyalist casualties in the two withdrawals, it appeared that the true defectors numbered 127. What impressed Jim Hausman and other American advisers was that the junior officers had shown unusual initiative, the loyalist companies had maintained their cohesion, and the soldiers had returned with their weapons. The Eighth Regiment, reinforced with quality officers and trustworthy troops, became one of the better regiments in the South Korean army.[28]

With the approaching departure of all U.S. combat troops and a growing uncertainty about American military aid, the Rhee government mounted three simultaneous counterinsurgency campaigns against the SKLP partisans. Desperate for some military success, the president permitted the American advisers more latitude in selecting commanders and designing operations, which allowed the professional officers of the first class to conduct field operations in cooperation with their American counterparts and the stay-behind elements of USAFIK, which provided essential intelligence and logistical services. By the summer of 1949, however, as the partisan threat slackened, the ROKA faced a growing border war with its North Korean counterpart along the Thirty-eighth Parallel. Nevertheless, by the end of the 1949 rainy season, the South Korean army had gained the upper hand in the counterinsurgency campaign and laid the organizational and operational foundation to deal a coup de grâce to the partisans by the spring of 1950.[29]

The counterguerrilla campaign had four territorial foci: Cheju-do island, the Chiri-san mountains of South Cholla Province, the Odae-san mountains of western Kangwon Province, and the Taebaek mountain ranges of the two Kyongsang provinces. The partisan bands in the last two regions had contact with Communist security forces along the border, received reinforcements, and could move between their operational areas with considerable freedom. The Chiri-san groups, which included the Yosu-Sunchon mutineers, and the Chejudoan guerrillas faced an inexorable war of encirclement and attrition, beyond the aid of the Kangdong Institute infiltrators. The operations on Cheju-do proved to be the most immediately successful at the greatest human cost: probably 7,000 guerrillas, SKLP cadres, innocent villagers of all or no political persuasion, and ROK security forces died in January–April 1949. The trend lines demonstrated the shrinking guerrilla threat. In March, partisan deaths in one week (347) outnumbered surrenders (92), but this trend reversed during two weeks in April (15 dead versus 172 surrendered, and 62 versus 316); by mid-May (2 versus 17), General Roberts reported that Cheju-do had ceased to be a military operational area. For the first time, captives (3,600) outnumbered partisan deaths.[30]

The Cheju-do campaign had a special urgency that was fully appreciated by Col. Yu Jae-hung, commander of the Second Regiment and the island's police-militia task forces. UNCOK wanted to conduct elections on the island (suspended in 1948), and Syngman Rhee wanted to visit the island and declare victory on the first anniversary of the Cheju 4.3 incident. The campaign benefited from Seoul's assistance and Colonel Yu's skilled command. Finally responding to the plight of the island's refugees, rural economic collapse, and widespread village destruction (an estimated twenty thousand buildings had burned down), the U.S. Economic Cooperation Administration (ECA) mission to Korea sent emergency food and medical supplies to the island. For the first time, the government offered an amnesty program and made a serious effort to curb indiscriminate killing. Colonel Yu received mainland reinforcements: more police and an additional infantry battalion. He also mobilized a loyalist militia force of government employees (including teachers) and youth association members; he put them through basic training but kept them under military command and armed them only with spears. Basically, these militia groups served as "beaters" in mass sweeps in the mountains and provided thick encirclements of mountain villages and guerrilla base camps. Soldiers and police did the fighting and close-in searches. The primary targets were caches of arms and food and guerrilla leaders—targets often exposed by new prisoners. The destruction of caches mounted, and the SKLP cadre shrank with the deaths of four key members and Yi Tok-ku, Kim Tal-sam's able successor as guerrilla commander. Colonel Yu and his advisers estimated that in April 1949 fewer than one hundred armed guerrillas remained at large, and two SKLP cadres who escaped the island admitted that the Cheju-do rebellion had been crushed.[31]

The most effective and stubborn partisans roamed in and out of the Chiri-sans, striking unwary army patrols and police stations. Led by Kim Chi-hoe, the Yosu rebel lieutenant and Kim Tal-sam's equal as a guerrilla commander, the Chiri guerrillas time and again eluded encirclement. On November 18, 1948, the rebels ambushed a Twelfth Regiment convoy and killed forty-nine soldiers, including the regimental commander, Col. Paek In-gi. Nine battalions from five different regiments—later increased to twelve battalions—pursued a well-armed, disciplined force of three hundred to five hundred guerrillas without much success. On December 15 the partisans attacked an army-police company encamped in a South Cholla village and killed forty-five loyalists, including eleven villagers. An army relief force cornered the raiders during their withdrawal and killed forty-three guerrillas before Kim Chi-hoe could organize a breakout. At best, the campaign had not yet been won or lost by either side. The army, however, could reinforce its Chiri-san brigade, whereas the guerrillas could not as they were pushed farther back into the mountains and away from the villages that provided food and new recruits. The police occupied one village after another and executed and beat suspected SKLP supporters into submission while army patrols ambushed supply columns and destroyed base camps throughout a cold, snowbound winter. In mid-March an army task force caught one part of the "Second Corps" of the People's Army and killed forty-three partisans and recaptured nineteen rifles, a disastrous loss for Kim Chi-hoe. He himself led more than one hundred guerrillas in an attack on Kanmun-ni to seize food and arms, but the army-police garrison (alerted by an informer) met the attack and killed thirty guerrillas at a cost of three dead and three wounded. The advantage shifted to the government forces.[32]

Further reinforced by an additional regiment, the Chiri-san Task Force (Col. Chung Il-kwon) conducted an encirclement campaign in March–April 1949 that reduced the Second Corps to a harried band of forty surviving partisans. At a cost of 5 dead and 21 wounded, the army claimed to have killed 234 guerrillas and to have taken 911 more SKLP suspects into custody by capture or amnesty-driven surrenders. More than 100 weapons—most of them Fourteenth Regiment rifles and carbines—returned to army custody. One death—Kim Chi-hoe—made the campaign an unqualified victory. Wounded in a skirmish on April 8, the key SKLP field commander died in camp sometime before an army patrol found his decomposing body on April 23. Lieutenant Kim's wife identified his corpse, but the army sent the feared mutineer's severed head to Seoul for final identification. Hausman protested to Army Chief of Staff Yi Ung-jun that such rebel-suppression practices smacked of the Japanese colonial period. In the meantime, air and infantry patrols scoured the Chiri-sans for the remaining guerrillas while army-police roadblocks and population checkpoints made the Kurye region difficult to escape.[33]

As government forces reduced the partisan threat in southern Korea, the ROK police and army faced an expanding war along the Thirty-eighth Parallel. By the end of 1949, the border war had become a direct and bloody confrontation between the South Korean army and the Korean People's Army, the Communist regulars. It revealed serious operational problems within the ROKA as well as tension between the Rhee government (especially Prime Minister Yi Pom-sok) and the U.S. Mission in Korea, meaning Ambassador Muccio and General Roberts. The Korean government used the border war to rally anti-Communist Koreans with tales of aggression and lurid promises to take the war into North Korea. "March north" became a meaningless threat in 1949, but it irritated the American diplomats and officers in Seoul, largely because they knew that such rhetorical aggressiveness did not sit well in Washington or in the United Nations. The border war gave Pyongyang good material for its propaganda campaign against Rhee and in support of the Democratic Front for the Unification of the Fatherland. Border operations allowed the KPA to test its "puppet" adversary and develop a defensive belt north of the Thirty-eighth Parallel while it planned and conducted limited operations into South Korea. The KPA's initial incursions supported cross-border expeditions by Kangdong Institute guerrillas, but these soon became an essential strategy for pressuring the Rhee regime, which deployed one-third of its police and army along the border. The conflict allowed Kim Il-sung and his Russian advisers to show Stalin what advantages the Communists were accumulating for a strategic showdown and what opportunities existed for an invasion once the American troops departed.[34]

The "Parallel War"—its geographic location and its relationship with the southern insurgency made it thus—developed in four general areas. From west to east, the conflict developed on the Ongjin peninsula, in the southern quarter of Hwanghae Province south of the Thirty-eighth Parallel, an isolated area that could be reached from the ROK only by ship from Inchon. The region was well developed by Korean standards, with rich farms, good roads, prosperous villages, and a political and commercial hub at Haeju. Although many of Hwanghae's farmers were landholders and Christians, Pyongyang had checkmated their potential rebelliousness with Communist refugees from the ROK, land reform, imprisonment of notables, and a heavy police and border constabulary presence. Ongjin was Kim Il-sung's preferred site for a Communist foothold south of the border. The ancient capital city of Kaesong provided the next locus to the east in the Parallel War. It rested in a topographical bowl north of the Imjin River along the direct rail line and highway between Pyongyang and Seoul. Kaesong remained a politicized and polarized city of fifty thousand inhabitants. It had nurtured a strong People's Committee in 1945 and an SKLP regional cell. Its dominant groups, however, were pro-government, or at least anti-Communist: Christian merchants and farmers, government officials, urban professionals, clergymen, and missionaries. The Rhee government made the city a police and army bastion because of its political and military importance. Although astride another corridor to the east, the city of Uijongbu also developed as a center of conflict in Kyonggi-do.

The other border province—Kangwon-do—was (and is) divided by the border east to west but also north to south by the formidable Odae and Taebaek mountain ranges, today the site of Mount Sorak National Park and associated resort areas. The western part of Kangwon Province is dominated by the Soyang and Pukhan rivers, part of the Han River watershed. The provincial capital, Chunchon, developed on an alluvial alley along the Soyang before the river joins the Pukhan to the south. Residents of the Chunchon region—with strong ties to Seoul—tended to be anti-Communist, but the steep mountains and deep river valleys made the area attractive for partisan operations astride the primitive, limited roads that led south to Hoengsong, Hongchon, and Wonju along the southern tributaries of the Han. Across the Taebaek range, the other populated region of Kangwon-do ran along a narrow coastal plain at the edge of the East Sea, also known to foreigners as the Sea of Japan, and focused on the fishing and commercial towns of Chumunjin, Kangnung, and Samchok. Steep, fast-flowing rivers cut the Taebaek range but did not provide enough alluvial plain for settlement off the coast, except at Yongwol, an interior mining town and SKLP stronghold in 1949. Yongwol's politics and isolation made it a natural region for partisan operations. The portion of Kangwon-do north of the Thirty-eighth Parallel was more populated and prosperous and included the coastal town of Yangyang and the interior towns of Hwachon, Inje, and Yanggu, astride the rivers and roads that led south between Chunchon and Kangnung, creating narrow parallel corridors to Yongwol.

No single dramatic clash marked the start of the Parallel War, but the phased reduction of American troops in January 1949 produced a series of incidents that, as they accumulated, made the border a war zone. After two months of relative quiet, the North Korean *Boandae* and mixed ROK police and army forces fought five major engagements (more than one hundred men on both sides) between January 23 and February 5. The American advisers reported that a cross-border raid by a KNP special operations company south of Haeju on January 19 started the new cycle of border clashes at the instigation of Yi Pom-sok, who increased the KNP border force from twelve hundred to eighteen hundred. While he was still minister of defense, Yi ordered the army to displace forward—three regiments from Ongjin to Tungduchon—to support the police. USAFIK staffers believed that the South Koreans initiated most of the skirmishes to justify more arms requests, but the *Boandae* counterattacked with enthusiasm and greater strength, showing an equal lust for engagement. The one skirmish on the east coast appeared to be a diversion to cover a guerrilla column infiltration. The Communists emphasized their bellicosity on February 26 by shooting down a U.S. Army light reconnaissance aircraft (L-5) a mile south of the border near Kaesong. The lull of April appeared to be only a pause in a continuing campaign.[35]

As General Roberts focused on the administrative chores of disestablishing USAFIK and organizing a sound ROKA training program, the Parallel War flared again in early May and raged for three months. The fighting brought on a war of words between Pyongyang and Seoul, a barrage of invasion promises and countercharges. The war of bullets and words produced no clear victor, with both Korean armies bloodied but still belligerent. If anything, Syngman Rhee irritated Muccio and Roberts more than the North Koreans did, since he alternated between bold, bellicose talk and pitiful cries for more arms, a bigger army, and a real navy and air force. Already well advanced in fielding a war-ready People's Army, Kim Il-sung talked less and fought more, moving regiments into the border defenses in June 1949, first to support the *Boandae* with heavy mortars and artillery and then to take on infantry battles, too. North Korean operations in Kangwon-do covered guerrilla infiltrations, but in Kyonggi-do, the engagements had less to do with operational objectives and more to do with "face," fear, and military fantasy.[36]

The Parallel War in Kangwon-do reflected the tension created by the expeditions of the Kangdong Institute partisans and the subsequent KNP-army search-and-kill operations against the guerrillas. This confrontation between the ROK Tenth Regiment, based at Kangnung, and the *Boandae*, based at Yangyang, also had a maritime dimension, since each side had a small fleet of coastal patrol boats capable of landing raiding parties beyond the border. Alerted to a partisan infiltration in early February 1949, the commander of the Tenth Regiment ordered one infantry company and one 105mm howitzer to go north and intimidate the North Koreans with a cross-border raid on February 3; the only things that violated the border were five howitzer shells fired into the village of Kisamun-ni, although the regimental commander reported "combat fiercely" and hits on a North Korean naval station. General Roberts complained to Yi Pom-sok about the "outrageous action" and demanded disciplinary action, to no avail. Far from KMAG's watchful eye, a South Korean partisan unit attempted to start operations in Kangwon-do north of the border, which set off a vigorous North Korean counterguerrilla campaign in late June; the Tenth Regiment retaliated with a raid on Yangyang, but it fell into an ambush and had to retire in haste and under fire to its border defense positions. The ROK defense minister, Shin Sung-mo, claimed a victory and cited the action as proof that his army could march to Wonsan if so ordered, a claim equally absurd as Radio Pyongyang's parallel claim of victory.[37]

Operations around Chunchon focused on restoring the disaffected Eighth Regiment and counterpartisan operations in western Kangwon-do, but in early August, after a long period of patrol skirmishing in the mountains north of the city, a North Korean battalion occupied some defensible terrain south of the border near the Soyang River. The North Korean goal was likely to draw ROK soldiers into an artillery kill zone since the South Korean Sixth Division commander could not allow the Communists to hold their enclave. After two weeks of desultory battle, the Sixth Division's Seventh Regiment and the division's lone artillery battalion finally convinced the North Koreans to cut their losses (reported as fifty) and withdraw. KMAG did not regard this skirmish as either a major threat or a significant triumph.[38]

The westernmost areas of border confrontation—the Ongjin peninsula, Kaesong, and the Uijongbu corridor—developed as the principal sector of the Parallel War of 1949. Kim Il-sung made the conquest of Ongjin his first goal in proving to the Russians that his army could crush the South Koreans in 1950—or whenever he received the heavy arms an invasion would require. Kaesong might be an easy conquest because of its proximity to the border and vulnerability to fire from the dominant hills to the north. For the South Koreans, Ongjin had to be defended for national honor; across the border, Haeju and the SKLP's Kangdong Institute were just as attractive an objective as Kaesong was to the Communists. The lines of communication for both sides allowed the deployment of large land and naval forces, compared with the mountainous regions of eastern Kyonggi-do and Kangwon-do.

The ROKA assigned three divisions to the Ongjin-Kyonggi sector. A special task force garrisoned the Ongjin border, which grew to two reinforced infantry regiments, usually from the four-regiment Capitol Division. The division had regiments of proven loyalty and good combat performance in 1948, including the Second, Seventeenth, and Eighteenth Regiments, the First Provisional Artillery Regiment, and the Cavalry Regiment. The Kaesong–Munsan-ni corridor was the responsibility of the First Division, two of whose regiments (the Eleventh and Twelfth) had combat experience in the southern provinces. The three regiments garrisoned their sector in depth with the regiments in column (Kaesong, Munsan-ni, Inchon, Susaek) west of Seoul. The Seventh Division deployed its three regiments in column from the front north of Tongduchon through Uijongbu to Seoul.[39]

The first shots of the escalating Parallel War cannot be identified, since both sides sniped and shelled each other sporadically from winter into spring, especially in the Hill 292 sector north of Kaesong. Hill 292, officially south of the border, was a southern spur ridge of Songak-san, or Hill 488, north of the border. Before soldiers of the Eleventh Regiment (Lt. Col. Choe Kyung-rok) could complete an outpost on Hill 292, a North Korean battalion occupied the ridge and built five heavy bunkers along its southern military crest; Colonel Choe, his staff, and advisers observed the position on May 1 and confirmed that the Eleventh Regiment should drive the KPA off the ridge. The attack, planned for May 4, was approved by the First Division commander, Brig. Gen. Kim Sok-won, the former Manchukuo army colonel and ally of Yi Pom-sok and Yi Chong-chon. General Kim, whose bristling mustache and loud promises of "march north" made him the darling of the Seoul press and Radio Pyongyang, had little to do with the operation except to approve it. The KMAG advisers considered Kim a windbag warlord who would avoid responsibility for any operations until they were "victories." Notorious for selling tires and gasoline to any buyer, including North Korean smugglers, "Kaiser Bill" led KMAG's list of 1948 "instant generals" who would be replaced as soon as Roberts and Hausman could convince President Rhee to act. Kim had created his own vulnerability by deploying almost all of his eight infantry battalions along the border, holding only one company in reserve. His advisory team and subordinates protested that the KPA could not resist an opportunity to penetrate a sketchy defense backed by no counterattack force and limited artillery.[40]

Although the Eleventh Regiment's attacks of May 6–8 eventually cleared Hill 292, the ROKA could not drive the Communists off Hill 488 with only mortar and artillery fire. The rules of engagement prohibited operations over the border except for limited artillery counterbattery fire. North Korean artillery and mortars made closing with Hill 292 dangerous, even killing civilian onlookers and scattering a platoon of officer-observers. The Eleventh Regiment received more artillery support, but it was too light and erratic to swing the engagement. In desperation, a battalion commander organized an all-out assault on May 8. Nine noncommissioned officers (NCOs) from the Eleventh Regiment and the NCO School training cadre, led by the school commander, strapped mortar shells and other explosives to their bodies and plunged into the key bunkers to destroy them. The "ten human bomb soldiers" became hallowed heroes to the Koreans, but the Americans doubted that an army using "Japanese tactics" had much future. After a follow-up consolidation action around Hill 292, in which a well-liked battalion commander died, Colonel Choe halted the infantry attacks, having lost thirty-nine dead and twice as many wounded. Full of undiminished bluster, General Kim ordered more assaults directly on Songak-san after a KPA battalion attacked nearby Paechon and bloodied two more Eleventh Regiment companies. Kim's July attacks actually reached Songak-san but could not hold it for more than four days under a deluge of artillery fire. A single KPA company made the final assault on July 29 to retake the peak. The KPA remained safe behind the border in its artillery observation posts and continued its harassing fire on Kaesong.[41]

The fighting on the Ongjin peninsula produced the most sustained, lethal campaign of the Parallel War, but it, too, faded by early autumn. The peninsula had great symbolic importance for both Koreas, especially for the southern Communists at Haeju. In February two ROKA scout planes flew over Haeju without American knowledge. Roberts grounded all aircraft so that he could check rumors that the Koreans were preparing rocket racks for their L-4s.[42] On May 21–26, raiding companies of the *Boandae* struck the outpost line of the Mobile Police Unit, the field combat battalion of the Korean National Police, and seized five hilltops at least three miles below the border. The KNP company could not match the North Koreans' mortars and machine guns. The resident ROKA garrison, the new Eighteenth Regiment from Pohang, manned a fallback defense line and asked for help. Total casualties for both sides were probably around thirty. Reorganized as the Ongjin Task Force when joined by the Twelfth Regiment from Inchon, the ROKA garrison, commanded by Lt. Col. Choe Sok of the Eighteenth Regiment, counterattacked on May 31 and retook two of the contested hills. The North Koreans, reinforced by an entire *Boandae* brigade of perhaps two thousand soldiers, counterattacked and by June 7 had established a new line anchored on Torak-san, the westernmost of the five positions. Although they were low on ammunition, the ROK defenders repelled the attacks. ROKA losses since May 31 were thirty-eight killed, eighty wounded, and thirty-eight missing. The American advisers put Communist casualties at seventy but conceded that Colonel Choe's claim of three hundred might have some merit. The operational situation, assessed by an observer team led by Col. Kim Paik-il of Sunchon fame, was clear enough: the Communists were winning.[43]

Army Chief of Staff Maj. Gen. Chae Byong-dok came to Ongjin to evaluate the situation and ordered a concentrated attack on Torak-san by the Twelfth Regiment, the newly arrived Thirteenth Regiment, and the First Independent Battalion, a unit of northern refugees and KPA deserters. With reinforcing artillery, the Ongjin Task Force now numbered 2,800 officers and men. General Chae, accompanied by Col. Paik Sun-yup (ROKA G-2) and Capt. John Reed (USAFIK G-2), told task force officers that the forthcoming attack might cross the border, but as it turned out, that was not a concern. In three days of attacks, the South Korean soldiers managed to retake half of Torak-san, but they could not drive off the Third *Boandae* Brigade's six battalions. On June 15 the battle stalled again. The ROK security forces had now suffered 88 killed, 242 wounded, and 43 missing for the period May 19 to June 14. The worst single loss came from a "friendly" mortar barrage that stopped a promising Twelfth Regiment attack on Torak-san's peak, killing 8 and wounding 42 soldiers, including a battalion commander. A weeklong KMAG assessment found glaring errors in fire support coordination, communications, reconnaissance, and lateral attack planning. And the Communists remained entrenched inside South Korea.[44]

Defense Minister Shin and General Chae insisted to General Roberts that the republic's national honor and morale required an Ongjin victory. Simply frustrating the Communist plan to take the whole peninsula was not enough. The battle must go on or new attacks would be mounted against North Korea elsewhere. The Second Regiment, fresh from Cheju-do, came to Ongjin and completed the recapture of five of the seven hills taken by the Communists. The ROK soldiers also captured two Soviet advisers, but one committed suicide; a Haeju hospital admitted eight wounded Red Army officers and enlisted men on June 24.[45] On August 3 the reconstituted Third *Boandae* Brigade, commanded by Choe Hyun, a former Red Army officer and future KPA corps commander, attacked two Eighteenth Regiment companies and killed or wounded 210 ROK soldiers. The North Koreans seized three hills, but the counterattacking Second Regiment retook one of them the next day. The South Koreans claimed to have inflicted 300 more casualties on the enemy. Now the *Boandae* held two positions south of the border, and the ROKA held one hill north of the border. In another lull—as both sides rotated battalions and improved their strong points and artillery positions—General Roberts urged his counterparts to reduce shell expenditures and thin out the number of troops at the front. The Ongjin Task Force suffered more hard blows: another 53 killed and 121 wounded after August 4. With the force reorganized, Colonel Choe commanded his own regiment, one Twelfth Regiment battalion, the First Independent Battalion, and six artillery pieces, facing an enemy force of about equal size. Once again, almost the complete force held frontline positions.[46]

In September the South Koreans strengthened the Ongjin force to two full regiments (the Twelfth and Eighteenth) and supporting units under a new commander, Col. Lee Hyun-suk. Colonel Lee immediately impressed Roberts with his aggressiveness and operational ineptness. Instead of training his units and holding the front with outposting forces, Lee kept all his infantry forward to menace Torak-san. Roberts warned Minister Shin that Ongjin was a costly diversion from defending Seoul and killing guerrillas. Lee's two American advisers, two captains with World War II combat experience, had trouble keeping Lee from attacking Torak-san.[47] Commander Choe Hyun proved Roberts right by attacking the neglected garrison on Eunpa-san with two battalions of his Third Brigade on October 14. The Second Regiment defenders lost the hill and could not retake it as heavy artillery barrages broke up their hasty counterattacks. Under pressure from Roberts and his staff, Colonel Lee finally cut his losses and stopped his attacks. The Communists now held key terrain south of the border, so they also let the conflict revert to artillery sniping and night patrols. The Ongjin campaign ended—for the moment—with the whimper of an odd shell.[48]

The Kyonggi-do–Ongjin battles had a maritime component that suggested that "march north" really meant "sail north" to the South Koreans. Stung by coast guard defections, Minister Shin and Admiral Son, the ancient and vengeful mariners, gathered their limited flotilla of patrol craft, manned with new ROK marines, and embarked off Ongjin City on August 11. They attacked an unwary North Korean gunboat squadron celebrating Liberation Day (August 15) inside Monggum-po harbor, twenty miles beyond the border on the north side of the Changson-got peninsula. The raiders captured one small craft and sank three others while the marines destroyed some harbor facilities. The entire ROK naval force was back to Pusan by August 18.[49]

The growing military confrontation with the Communists in 1949 gave the Rhee administration and the American diplomats and military advisers in Seoul ample reason to focus increased attention on defense policy. Although their shared urgency did not take them in a common direction, General Roberts believed that the ROK-US partnership was improving. President Rhee remained suspicious of the army, but Roberts found the president much less likely to be swayed by Yi Pom-sok and more likely to follow Shin Sung-mo's advice, which almost always reflected KMAG's views.

Rhee became tired of Yi Pom-sok's aggressiveness and ambition, so he heeded Roberts's and Hausman's advice to reform the military command system. The office of Chief of Staff to the Minister of National Defense was abolished (to KMAG's delight), so Maj. Gen. Chae Pyong-dok became simply army chief of staff until he was replaced by Brig. Gen. Shin Tae-yong in October 1949. General Shin, a political favorite of Rhee's supporters, proved disinterested in hard policy choices, but the Americans worked well with his deputy, the eager Chung Il-kwon. Rhee's interests were guarded by Brig. Gen. Won Yong-dok, general staff secretary. The most objectionable of the other generals, Kim Sok-won, lost the First Division. (Radio Pyongyang loved to identify "March North" Kim by his Japanese army name, "Colonel Kanayama.") General Chae took charge of "the Arsenal program," a KMAG initiative to make Japanese rifle parts, ammunition, mines, and grenades in Korea, a job much like "Fat" Chae's ordnance work for the Japanese army. He also became director of the Military Mobilization Board. Other generals of limited expertise and potential, such as Song Ho-sung, moved to marginal posts; more promising commanders, such as Paik Sun-yup, Yu Jae-hung, Kim Paik-il, and Kim Hong-il, received more challenging assignments. Roberts believed that the Korean officer corps would require much training, much patience, and much pressure to abandon their "new" army, ex-colonial military culture. "Officers . . . are difficult. At times it seems their only desire is to get the original position. Many

times we've heard: 'you can't tell me—I'm a commissioned officer.' They love parades, the great preparation for parades—they love lining up whole battalions to welcome or send off some stuffed-shirt colonel or general at the expense of a whole or
half-day's training; they love to talk and to listen to speeches; they love to chase down
alleged subversives; they seem to abhor thinking a thing through, or working."[50]

General Roberts thought the Korean common soldier deserved better tactical
and administrative leadership: "The soldier is fine. He can be molded into a reasonably good soldier in six months, in my opinion. He has many qualities I'd like to
transfer to American soldiers, viz attentiveness, stoicism, a desire to learn, a ready
willingness to die if ordered, tenacity. His weaknesses are his desire to kick civilians
around like his Jap predecessors used to do, his sadistic tendencies, and his leaders. These soldiers actually seem to revel in disagreeable weather and hardships."[51]

Although the counterinsurgency campaign and the Parallel War had retarded
field training and administrative reform, General Roberts believed that the ROKA
could stop a North Korean invasion of three divisions, but he wondered whether
unmatched North Korean tank, artillery, and air forces might soon tip the balance.
A great deal of work remained to be done to improve the ROK security forces.
Whether KMAG would have the time and resources was anyone's guess.

THE MILITARY ASSISTANCE QUESTION

The first eight months of South Korean independence proved that the republic had
only a fair chance of surviving its infancy, especially if its wet nurse lost interest.
Syngman Rhee had come to office in part because he claimed to be a genius at ex-
tracting aid from the Americans without compromising his goal of a free, unified
Korea. His strident calls for more arms—required to defend his own republic or to
wage a preemptive war on the Democratic People's Republic—alarmed Ambassador Muccio, who reported that Rhee was obsessed with expanding and arming the
ROK security forces. The president was "feverishly eager" for more arms. Rhee
knew that his calls for unification by force did not please Washington. As a new fiscal year opened with no aid in sight, a desperate Rhee promised President Truman
that "the Republic of Korea will not attack territory north of the Thirty-eighth Parallel." The American mission in Seoul saw no immediate threat of invasion, but
the Koreans thought otherwise. The People's Army had deployed behind the border,
only waiting orders to strike south, "and if they do, it is we the Koreans, civilian
and military, who will pay the price, not the good-willed American advisors." Rhee
would not surrender his great quest "to liberate our enslaved fellow countrymen in
the north."[52]

Although Rhee recognized that the American mission could withdraw its advisers and stop the meager flow of aid if he really ordered a "march north," he gam-
bled that he could enlarge his security forces and pressure the Americans to increase their assistance. Officially, the United States had agreed to support an army

of 65,000, a national police of 35,000, and a coast guard of 4,000. There was no provision for a separate air force. In July 1949, however, the ROKA numbered 100,000 officers and men, the national police 53,000 (10,000 in field combat units), and the coast guard 6,200. Minister Shin announced the creation of the ROK Marine Corps (April 15) and Air Force (October 1) to an unhappy American mission. The army expansion plan, announced June 6, came during the negotiation of a detailed ROK-US military assistance program, a bit of a coup for Rhee. He then doubled the quick strike by getting a mobilization law passed by the National Assembly (September 1) that introduced conscription for Korean males at age twenty-one. The military service law would ensure adequate recruits (half the volunteers were medically unfit) and a reserve land force of 100,000 built on the youth associations, if someone could find the money for arms and training.[53]

The expansion of the ROKA did not reduce Rhee's concern about the naval and air defense of his nation. He argued that American assistance for his ground forces did nothing to provide a complete defense system, which was "unfortunate for Korea." The president bombarded General MacArthur with requests for U.S. Air Force surplus aircraft—especially propeller-driven F-51s that were being replaced with jets—and naval patrol craft. Rhee sent Shin Sung-mo to Tokyo with a list of requirements, to no avail. He sent air intelligence reports to MacArthur that stressed the shipment of Russian aircraft to North Korea through the port of Wonsan; the South Koreans, presumably using intelligence collected by the industrious Donald Nichols (see chapter 4), accurately reported the Russian program to create a North Korean air force of more than one hundred aircraft. Rhee complained to MacArthur that he could not recruit Gen. Claire Chennault's choice as a senior adviser to the nonexistent ROK air force—Air Force Brig. Gen. Russell E. Randall, an "Old China Hand" in Chennault's U.S. Fourteenth Air Force. Randall could not take foreign employment unless he retired from active duty and received official permission to take foreign military employment, an unlikely event. Rhee reported that he knew 106 qualified Korean pilots, trained by either the Chinese or the Japanese, but he could not create an air force unless the United States provided him with aircraft.[54]

The American military presence to advise and support the Korean security forces increased less dramatically and rapidly, and it was never large enough to perform all its missions. When the final agreement on the status of the troops left behind by USAFIK was signed (January 1950), the existing provisional advisory group retroactively became KMAG, or "Kiss My Ass Good-bye" to the cynics. General Roberts received his request for a minimum group of five hundred officers and men, which he quickly judged inadequate to advise an expanded coast guard and a new air force. The organizational plan assumed that KMAG would staff six ROK divisions "within [the] limitations of the Korean economy." The ROKA formed eight divisions. General Roberts also underestimated the requirement for Americans in the army's ambitious school system. Given the inability of Korean commanders to conduct unit training, Roberts had no choice but to become an enthusiastic military school master and assign his best officers and NCOs to training duties. He insisted that KMAG's principal mission was training the ROKA officers to train their units, especially in marksmanship. One result of this choice was that American advisory teams remained regimental, not at the battalion level, as planned. Roberts initiated a program to send promising officers to U.S. Army schools in the United States—twelve were sent in 1948 and 1949—so they could return to key training billets. The Rhee government, especially Mrs. Rhee, complained about the foreign currency cost of such assignments, the per diem for travel, housing, and food. Roberts then proposed a plan to send groups of thirty officers to train with their U.S. Army counterparts in Japan. Although Ambassador Muccio and General MacArthur finally approved the concept, the wrangling over issues of security, cost, unfavorable precedents, and the selection process delayed the program until May 1950. In the meantime, KMAG had negotiated twenty-seven school slots in the United States.[55]

Another critical adjustment the American mission faced was building an integrated intelligence system in Korea that profited from Korean sources but did not become captive to quixotic operations or analysis. At the military level (ROKA and KMAG G-2) the problems were few, since Col. Chang Do-yong and Capt. John P. Reed worked well together. The internal security problems of the ROKA remained the domain of the provost marshal general's department—consisting of 186 officers and 2,487 men in 1949—and, later, the Counterintelligence Corps, both usually led by Rhee loyalists of rabid anti-Communist bent. At the politico-strategic level, the reorganization had more significance. At the initiative of Gen. Charles Willoughby (Far East Command G-2), Col. Jay Vanderpool, representing the CIA, went to Seoul and established the Korean Liaison Office (KLO) in June 1949. He immediately went to work with the Korean Research Bureau, which was nominally civilian, and Detachment 2, Office of Special Investigations (headed by Nichols), to run agents into North Korea, "turn" officers of the People's Army, and do radio interception and analysis. Besides running Korean signals intelligence, the KLO worked with the navy's Fleet Radio Unit, Far East Command, which monitored Chinese Communist and Russian radio transmissions. Even though Willoughby focused on Russian threats to Japan and, secondarily, the military activities of the Chinese Communists, the KLO produced current and accurate intelligence assessments; outside of Seoul and Tokyo, however, few intelligence officers—let alone decision makers—took them seriously.[56]

General Roberts certainly appreciated good intelligence, but his major problem was putting the ROK security forces' logistical house in order and preparing a workable request for fiscal year 1950 funds under the provisions of the Mutual Defense Assistance Act of 1949. His proposal had to be coordinated with the ECA economic programs sent to Washington by Dr. Arthur Bunce's staff. For one thing, Bunce's analysts saw the ROKA as an unstable consumer of scarce Korean money, foreign exchange, and American aid. The mission economists were correct. The Korean army and navy were financial management disasters, and KMAG knew it. The extent of the problems can be understood by relevant examples. In 1949, 60 percent of all motor vehicles in the ROKA were "deadlined," or inoperative. Poor maintenance had led to cannibalization; although the lack of spare parts had been a problem, the Korean soldiers simply had no experience or even the language necessary to help them fix the vehicles. At one point, an inspection of the half-tracks and M-8 "Greyhound" wheeled reconnaissance vehicles of the Cavalry Regiment proved so disastrous that the inspectors recommended that the mechanized squadron be converted to horse cavalry. Another proposal was that southern counterpartisan units surrender all their vehicles for pack mules and oxcarts. If nothing else, such measures would reduce the ECA's expensive importation of gasoline for the ROKA, which seemed to "lose" around 2,000 of the 5,500 barrels imported each month. The ordnance situation was no better. General Roberts wanted to train Korean soldiers to shoot straight with American weapons, but ammunition shortages curtailed formal marksmanship training. Between July 1 and December 31, 1949, Korean soldiers reduced the stockpiles of rifle and carbine ammunition by one-third, with no resupply in sight. Similar shortages of spare parts and ammunition also plagued the coast guard, which had trouble keeping half of its twenty-five "combat" ships operational.[57]

Any military assistance funding from the United States required stringent fiscal and monetary controls that the Rhee administration could not and would not impose. That more than a quarter of the Korean budget went to defense spending—wasted and misapplied—did not improve the American mission's bargaining position with Washington. By comparison, the State Department's request for Korean economic assistance, $150 million for fiscal year 1950, was more than ten times larger than the companion military assistance plan. General Roberts found the imbalance striking, since he considered military aid a good investment in American security: "The cheapest thing big industrial America can do is to furnish other peoples the product of our factories and resources in order that they may shoot for us and may shoot first, consequently 1 or 2 billions of dollar value is but a drop in the bucket and the finest bit of preparation we can make. I feel this way about this South Korean Army, my work is to make them capable of shooting first and well for Uncle Sugar."[58] Economic assistance, however, was more controversial in Washington. It was also tardy. By late June 1949, Congress had not moved on the Korean economic aid proposal, and Government Aid and Relief in Occupied Areas (GARIOA) funds would expire on June 30. The State Department urged President Truman to back the $150 million plan to improve power generation, fertilizer production, and coal mining. An economically weak Korea would be a prime target for a Communist takeover, an unacceptable blow to American prestige and the security of Japan. The president's personal intervention did nothing, however, to speed up the economic assistance package.[59]

The Truman administration had no better luck with its military assistance program, since the president himself wanted defense spending reduced from the Pentagon's proposed $16.5 billion (fiscal year 1951) to $13 billion, a ceiling imposed on July 1, 1949, by the Bureau of the Budget and the National Security Council. In fact, Truman refused to spend $615 million in fiscal year 1950 that Congress had added to the defense budget for the air force. The administration viewed military assistance to other nations as defense on the cheap and sent a bill to Congress to create a program.

The administration's proposal went to Congress on August 5 and, with some predictable alterations, became law when Truman signed the Mutual Defense Assistance Act of 1949 on October 6. The process of creating a military assistance program for America's formal allies and other military wards started with the interdepartmental Foreign Assistance Steering Committee, consisting of the secretaries of state and defense and the administrator of the ECA. The real work, however, went to a working group, the Foreign Assistance Correlation Committee (FACC), dominated by the armed forces; it was chaired by Maj. Gen. Lyman L. Lemnitzer (USA) and largely influenced by Maj. Gen. Alfred M. Gruenther, the representative of the Joint Chiefs of Staff (JCS). The FACC established criteria for military assistance determined by JCS contingency plans; priority went to members of the North Atlantic Treaty Organization (NATO), nations nearest the Soviet Union, and those with firm, preexisting American commitments. The FACC established three classes of aid recipients: Category I or "substantial"; Category II or "limited"; and Category III or "token" assistance. Korea fell into Category III.[60]

When the JCS sent a formal military aid plan to the White House in April 1949, the Republic of Korea's share of the $1.7 billion was $20 million. Truman directed the JCS to cut the entire package to $1.4 billion but to keep Korea and the other Category III nations at their proposed levels. The JCS did not like the president's decision on the total package and tied military assistance in Korea to the continuing discussion of troop withdrawal. In June 1949 the JCS completed its review of Korean policy and reported its conclusions, which became Truman's as well: "From a strategic point of view, the position of the Joint Chiefs of Staff concerning Korea summarized briefly is that Korea is of little strategic value to the U.S. and [the] commitment by the U.S. of U.S. military forces in Korea would be ill-advised and impracticable in view of our heavy international obligations as compared with our current strength."[61]

The appropriations act that followed the Mutual Defense Assistance Program (MDAP) authorization ran into immediate trouble in Congress. The Truman administration, in great haste to have a program of some sort, worked on a marked-up bill that contained many compromises. Truman asked for broad discretion to move funds between and within categories, but Congress granted him only a 5 percent discretionary authority to reallocate funds. Congress did not like the internal assignment of monies and categories, especially the omission of Nationalist China from the plan. Category III nations, to which the Pentagon planners now added Iran, had their total aid capped at $28 million; Congress added $75 million for "the general area" of China but did not specify Korea as falling within that area. The Truman administration, however, saved most of its spending plan for the members of NATO. Only twelve days after it received the Defense Department's revised assistance plan (October 8, 1949), Congress passed the MDAP appropriations act of $1.3 billion. The "token" nations of Iran, the Philippines, and Korea received $27.6 million. In accompanying actions taken during the congressional review, the JCS reduced Korea's share of Title III funds to $10 million, in consultation with Ambassador Muccio and General Roberts, neither of whom welcomed the news. The Korean allocation did not change when Congress passed the MDAP appropriations act on October 20 and Truman signed the bill into law on October 28. All that remained was for someone to decide how Korea's "token" aid of $10 million should be spent.[62]

The legislative process related to Korean aid brought two congressional visitors to Seoul, followed by a Defense Department assessment team. The visitors gave the Rhee government a chance to plead its case to someone outside the American mission. Much to Rhee's dismay, Shin Sung-mo's impassioned presentations made no difference to the economy-minded Americans, but it did encourage the formation of a small "Korea lobby" led by Congressmen A. L. Miller (R-Neb.) and Harley O. Staggers (D-W.V.). The issue was the relationship of military aid to economic assistance: why spend $100 million on a country that could not defend itself from invasion, given the low level of military assistance? The House Committee on Executive Expenditures went to Seoul in September 1949 to find out, followed in November by Senator William F. Knowland (R-Calif.), a powerful member of the Senate Foreign Relations Committee and a leader of the "China lobby." The congressional visitors got the proper briefings from the American mission, but they also received Shin Sung-mo's own appraisal (drafted by Gen. Won Yong-dok and Gen. Chae Pyong-dok) of Korea's immediate needs. KMAG was as surprised as the congressmen by Shin's "Present Situation of the Korean Army," which predicted an invasion in early 1950 (probably March) and stressed the urgent need to provide the ROK armed forces with 100 M-26 "Pershing" heavy tanks; an air force of 350 aircraft, built around F-51 "Mustang" fighter-bombers and B-26 "Invader" light bombers; enough standard 105mm and 155mm howitzers to give each Korean division a four-battalion artillery group, like American infantry divisions; twenty days of ammunition for every weapon; enough rifles and carbines to arm a reserve force of more than 100,000; double or triple the existing number of mortars and antitank guns; and a naval force of thirty patrol craft, more heavily armed than the coast guard's current ships. As the Department of the Army had feared, the Koreans learned how little MDAP funding they would receive. Minister Shin's request, however, carried a higher price tag—$58 million to procure and $29 million to maintain—than Congress would accept. The only immediate worry was that Rhee would not agree to bear any of the costs of supporting the KMAG personnel. The army staff awaited a congressional response, but there was none. The same process applied later for Senator Knowland's visit and an aborted tour by Army Chief of Staff Gen. J. Lawton Collins.[63]

The official MDAP survey team—Niles W. Bond from the State Department and Lt. Col. Richard H. Lawson (USA) from the Defense Department—came to Seoul on December 14, 1949, to negotiate the military aid program for fiscal year 1950, which still had six months to run. Bond and Lawson, both of whom had been Korean affairs officers in Washington, knew that the negotiations would be pro forma since Muccio and Roberts had fashioned the original request to reflect the dollar limits imposed by Washington. Muccio, for example, had urged a patrol craft fleet of thirty vessels in April 1949 but learned that no one had the $30 million required for such a purchase. Roberts had an optimal request, fully staffed with Minister Shin, that included more and better artillery pieces, machine guns, three kinds of mortars, more scout aircraft, engineering equipment, and several radio and wire communications systems. The cost—along with the minimum purchase of ammunition and replacement parts—was $75 million, another pipe dream. For three days Bond and Lawson reviewed the Korean "request" (i.e., an American request for Korea that the Koreans would not endorse) with the Muccio team and modified the program by reducing the number of howitzer shells and adding more M-1 rifles and carbines. The Americans then met on December 17 with the Korean defense principals: Syngman Rhee, Shin Sung-mo, Chae Pyong-dok, Shin Tae-yong, Kim Chung-yol (ROK Air Force), and Kim Yung-chol (ROK Coast Guard). The Americans pointed out that combat aircraft, naval patrol ships, tanks, and heavy artillery were too costly and not necessary for fighting insurgents. The Koreans insisted that they were at war and faced a heavily armed People's Army. If a "march north" mania concerned the Americans, it did not emerge as an issue. Only younger, liberal members of Muccio's staff feared such ROK adventurism. Muccio, Everett Dumright, and Harold J. Noble did not worry about a preemptive offensive since Roberts and his advisers controlled the flow of ammunition and supplies and operated the only effective military radio system in Korea. The only real capital investment in the final plan of $10.23 million was five light aircraft. The list simply provided more small arms, ammunition, communications equipment, and spare parts. The Koreans, though unhappy, approved the plan the same day they saw it.[64]

The American mission and the Bond-Lawson team had done their duty, driven by economy, but they agreed that the ROK armed forces could use an additional $10 million in aid. They substituted two L-5 aircraft for the L-4s in the plan, with the full knowledge that the ROK Air Force intended to arm them. Although they shared KMAG's doubts about the Koreans' ability to maintain artillery and vehicles, they shared Muccio's view that the psychological support was more important, and they discussed such purchases for the fiscal year 1951 program, already in the drafting stage. KMAG focused especially on the growing North Korean artillery capability, demonstrated by the use of Soviet 122mm howitzers and 120mm mortars in the Parallel War. Captain Reed also believed that U.S. M-5 light tanks and M2A2 105mm howitzers, captured from the Chinese Nationalists, would soon enter the North Koreans' inventory. As for air support, KMAG recommended the F-51 and stressed that the ROKA had no antiaircraft guns to protect it from the

North Koreans' Yak-9 fighter-bombers, estimated at thirty. Except for the obvious need for more coastal patrol craft, Muccio would not challenge the financial limitations imposed by Washington.[65]

The Bond-Lawson military assistance program, slightly modified, became the official plan for Korea until the end of fiscal year 1950. The process of review in Washington further slowed the action. President Truman did not authorize actual purchases (Executive Order 10099) until January 1950. A final review of the Korean program by the interagency Foreign Military Assistance Coordinating Committee was not completed until March 29, 1950. Further adjustments brought the dollar value up to nearly $12 million, but the reviewing committee showed more interest in French Indochina and the Philippines than in Korea. The regional emphasis on Europe never changed, with $1.1 billion earmarked for European countries and $28 million for the Title III countries outside "the general area of China." France, for example, received $695 million in military sales and $725,000 in training support, compared with Korea's $12 million and $33,000 in the same two categories. The same proportions reappeared in early drafts of the fiscal year 1951 program: military sales (i.e., transfers) of $500 million for France and $10 million for Korea. Under the fiscal year 1950 program, the ROK armed forces received actual ordnance and equipment, contracts signed, and spare parts purchased and shipped valued at $1.3 million, with other deliveries meted out until fiscal year 1952. The real aid program did little to strengthen the ROK armed forces by June 1950.[66]

In desperation, the Rhee administration looked for aircraft and warships outside the American military aid system. Using their scarce foreign currency, the South Koreans went shopping for weapons, much to the dismay of the State Department economists. Their efforts to buy a primitive air force made no difference in 1950, but the one vessel they added to their fleet of small warships made a critical contribution to the republic's survival in the summer of 1950. The purchase of ten AT-6 "Harvard" aircraft—a twin-seat, single-engine World War II American trainer manufactured by North American Aviation—required a national fund-raising crusade in Korea. The Rhee administration appealed for citizen donations through the schools. Schoolchildren gave money, too, for the *kongukki* ("national endorsement") aircraft. Women contributed gold and silver jewelry. The Korean air force thus received 350 million won, or $389,000, for its new planes. The Koreans found a seller in the Air Carrier Corporation's Canadian subsidiary, which provided the aircraft complete with bomb racks and machine guns. The American mission supported the purchase after the fact and appealed to the Department of Defense to provide air force advisers, aerial ordnance, and ground support equipment since the Koreans had a good nucleus of Japanese-trained pilots and faced a serious North Korean air threat. The requests for advisers and aviation ordnance and equipment went unanswered, although the ten aircraft finally arrived in Seoul in May 1950.[67]

From its formal creation in late 1948, the ROK Coast Guard enjoyed the strong support of the American mission, if not the State Department and the U.S. Navy. Ambassador Muccio monitored KMAG's attention to the coast guard and championed Admiral Son's many projects for better training and materiel readiness. Muccio supported Son's request for real patrol craft, not worn-out U.S. Navy yard minesweepers (YMS) and Japanese minelayers, which MacArthur wanted returned anyway. Instead of the requested fifteen patrol craft, the Rhee government purchased one ship, the *Ensign Whitehead* (PC 701), from the U.S. Maritime Commission in October 1949. To build and outfit a new patrol craft would have cost about $900,000; the final payment for PC 701 was $60,000. The money was raised by the Korean Coast Guard by private subscription, most of it from the sailors' own pockets. The money was also used to buy three more YMS patrol craft. Renamed *Paektusan*, the ROK's one real warship underwent refitting in an American yard, including the mounting of one three-inch .50-caliber main battery gun and six .50-caliber machine guns. It also took on adequate spare parts and ammunition. The arms and ammunition cost $56,161.40, reimbursed by the United States under Section 408(e) of the Mutual Defense Assistance Act of 1949. Under the same provision, the United Stated paid $20,000 for outfitting the AT-6 aircraft and $177,000 for arms and ammunition for three small naval patrol craft.[68]

Attempting to enlarge his unofficial arms-purchasing venture, President Rhee enlisted the aid of his wartime partner in haphazard resistance operations, M. Preston Goodfellow. Having failed to recruit American investors for Rhee, Goodfellow visited Seoul and found his prospects for deal-making slim. He acted on Rhee's plea to use all his Washington contacts to make deals for heavy weapons and a ship to carry them to Korea. Rhee also asked him to chart the course of the Korean economic aid bill in Congress. Assuming that Korea would eventually spend American dollars for "self-liquidating projects," Goodfellow teased Rhee with visions of construction and arms but could produce no surplus weapons bonanza—not even M-1 rifles. In the meantime, Goodfellow wandered the West Coast looking for patrol craft for sale. He did find a freighter for sale for $550,000, which Rhee did not have. He also found two American shipping companies that would carry fertilizer to Korea. Rhee eventually concluded that Goodfellow had no idea how to avoid the stern supervision of the ECA.[69]

Until Congress acted on the State Department's request for economic aid for Korea, no one could spend any American-appropriated money for anyone's schemes, sound or fantastic. As Goodfellow warned Rhee, Washington knew one word: economy. He might have added a second word: China. The Bureau of the Budget did the first trimming, reducing the request from $100 million to $60 million. As the legislation snaked its way through the committee review process in both houses of Congress, Secretary of State Dean Acheson learned that there would be little aid for Korea unless the administration spent more money on Nationalist China. The State Department, however, tried to convince Rhee that his economic mismanagement and lack of land reform had made Congress skeptical of Korea's investment potential. Ambassador Philip Jessup, Korea's champion in the United Nations, visited Seoul to lecture Rhee on reform and Muccio on overidentification with client states. Acheson and Jessup could have saved their sermons. The problem was Truman's China policy, with a subdued chorus of secondary complaints about the paltry military aid for Korea. After Truman announced on January 5, 1950, his intention of disengaging from the Chinese civil war, Acheson had to explain that the president did not mean that the United States would abandon its Asian interests. On January 19, 1950, the House rejected the Korean aid bill (HR 5330) by a vote of 192 to 191, with 170 Democrats and 21 Republicans voting for the bill, and 61 Democrats, 130 Republicans, and 1 Communist voting against it.[70]

The timing and dollar amounts of military and economic assistance for Korea represented their low priority in American foreign policy in 1949–1950. As Korea's needs increased, the Truman administration and Congress became the victims of self-inflicted denial about the growing crisis in Asia. The Communist victory in China only encouraged the spread of socialist, anti-imperialist revolutions in French Indochina, Malaya, Indonesia, the Philippines, and Korea. Even Japan was not immune to leftist populism. If not directly fomented by the Soviet Union, the Asian upheaval nevertheless served Stalin's purpose, which was to reduce American influence in Eurasia and disrupt any postfascist, neoimperialist war on Communism and its homeland, the Soviet Union. As an Asian power, Russian influence in Manchuria and Korea predated the revolution by a century. That interest had precipitated the Russo-Japanese War of 1904–1905, which involved aid to competing Korean military factions. Now the military assistance battle had been joined again.

THE RHEE GOVERNMENT WINS THE WAR AGAINST THE SOUTH KOREAN LABOR PARTY

Although the government's obsession with arming itself against a North Korean invasion dominated much of its dialogue with U.S. officials in Seoul and Washington, the most immediate threat the ROK faced was the continuing insurgency in its eastern and southern provinces. Between October 1949 and April 1950, the South Korean regime won the counterinsurgency campaign against the partisans of the SKLP, belatedly reinforced by guerrillas sponsored by the North Korean government and trained by the People's Army. The victory was neither complete nor permanent, but it was sufficient to persuade Rhee that he could risk National Assembly elections in May 1950. The president increased his pressure on the assembly to change the constitution, which he devoutly believed should be amended to allow his reelection in 1952 by popular, not assembly, vote. He also received some encouraging signs that the Korean economy might improve, although the American analysts of the ECA doubted that Rhee had the political courage to curb government spending and reduce the rate of inflation. Nevertheless, Rhee had shown survival skills that exceeded the expectations of the United States and the Democratic People's Republic of Korea.[71]

Rhee's personal stature as president climbed and dipped with events, but on balance, he had strengthened his grip on the executive branch and outlasted one generation of exiles and resisters, the venerable survivors of the March First Movement, the People's Republic, and the provisional government. On June 26, 1949, An Tu-hui, an undercover organizer of the Korean Independence Party who also happened to be a lieutenant in the South Korean army, ambushed Kim Ku on a Seoul street corner. Lieutenant An blasted "the Assassin" into oblivion with his .45-caliber Colt automatic pistol. Though convicted of murder and sentenced to life imprisonment, An Tu-hui survived to be reinstated into the army in 1950 and completed his military career as a lieutenant colonel; American investigators believed that Kim Ku's lethal punishment for his flirtation with Pyongyang had been encouraged by agents who worked for Yi Pom-sok. Many Koreans thought that the trail of responsibility would end with Syngman Rhee. Certainly, Kim Ku's death removed the only Korean politician who enjoyed public admiration for his rabid nationalism and terrorist attacks on the Japanese. Nevertheless, Kim Ku had reduced his politics to forming conspiracies with the most xenophobic and greedy officers of the KNP and the army. Kim Ku's death ended the immediate underground threat from the Right.[72]

The threats to the Rhee government now came almost entirely from the Left as the president himself moved farther to the Right and co-opted or marginalized other ultranationalist threats to his personal power. Rhee's war against the SKLP continued on many fronts with increased vigor and effectiveness. His pursuit of the SKLP also matched the parallel assault on Communists in Japan, which produced twenty-two thousand arrests and firings and the suppression of the Choryon. The KNP, still assisted by the "battalions" of the Northwest Youth Association, tightened its grip on the provincial cities and towns; to defend itself and progovernment villagers, the KNP formed small tactical battalions of "combat police" for local operations and, with the army's reluctant blessing, armed itself with machine guns and light mortars. American influence on the KNP almost disappeared and opened the way to new abuses and extortion. The KNP detectives and special branch pursued the SKLP urban-based leadership with Javert-like intensity, and the KNP formed alliances of convenience with the army's CIC and G-2 staffs and the government's independent intelligence agency, the Korean Research Bureau. Colonel Choe Yong-hui, a favorite of General Roberts, became the ROKA provost marshal general in November 1949. The army continued its internal investigation of subversives among its own ranks; in January 1950 the Military Police Command made its last major raid into army headquarters and barracks, arresting thirty-six officers and sixteen enlisted men of dubious loyalty. The raids were the last purge of the ROKA's ranks before June 1950.[73]

The insurrection on Cheju-do faded away into a Carthaginian peace as the surviving rebels and their network of supporters lapsed into cautious inactivity. President Rhee himself visited the island in April 1949 to declare victory and participate in government-sponsored photo opportunities designed to show how peaceful Cheju-do had become. A subcommittee of UNCOK came to the island with Rhee's blessing to conduct elections for the two vacant seats in the National Assembly;

the elections were peaceful, but the voter turnout was limited by the war-weariness of the islanders. The insurgent Chejudoans never completely disappeared, but the KNP continued to whittle away the partisan infrastructure, arresting several local SKLP leaders, while the First Separate Battalion (militantly anti-Communist) of the army and the KNP combat police patrolled the Halla-san hinterland. Imprisoned rebels took their war to the mainland prisons, where they staged a prison riot and mass jailbreak in Mokpo. Rhee still held the upper hand, since the KNP held around 2,000 islanders as hostage-prisoners, of whom 249 were executed en masse in October. The one useful change that KMAG demanded for its support was the elimination of the Northwest Youth "special action units" from the KNP and their withdrawal from the villages. The first great battlefield of the insurgency became the first site of success for the government forces.[74]

The Parallel War on the Ongjin peninsula flared one more time before winter, and mutual prudence froze the fighting to isolated patrol actions by the eve of the new year. Still smarting from the autumn pummeling the army had received at the hands of the *Boandae,* Gen. Chae Pyong-dok replaced the war-weary Second Regiment with the crack Seventeenth Regiment, commanded by the charismatic and fearless Lt. Col. Paik In-yup, the younger brother of Paik Sun-yup. Assigned to the Capitol Division for administrative purposes, the regiment had formed and trained the year before with considerable autonomy. Colonel Paik had used his influence and reputation to fill his ranks with refugees from northern Korea, the embittered sons of displaced and persecuted Christian landholders and businessmen. Although Colonel Paik probably received no specific orders to attack the Communist border outposts astride the Thirty-eighth Parallel, he knew that a tactical victory would be welcome in Seoul. In December 1949 the Seventeenth Regiment attacked the dominant outpost on Unpa-san and surprised the North Koreans; Paik had turned the tactical tables on the North Koreans, who discovered that the attack had been bait for an ambush that ruined a KPA battalion sent to reinforce the defenders on Unpa-san. A subsequent KNP attack on another outpost set off another battalion night engagement that ended in a standoff after two hours of fighting and twenty casualties on both sides. Paik decided to horde his luck and put his regiment on the defensive for the rest of the winter. The North Koreans followed suit.[75]

With the Parallel War in perilous equilibrium, the army and KMAG decided to concentrate on eliminating the Communist partisans in the southern and eastern mountain regions of South Korea. President Rhee happily endorsed the joint planning, largely supervised by Chung Il-kwon and Jim Hausman. On October 1, 1949, Maj. Gen. Shin Tae-yong, new chief of staff of the ROKA, announced that President Rhee had ordered him to destroy all the guerrillas in the Republic of Korea. The campaign would be waged by three task forces named for their operating areas: Honam, Chiri-san, and Taebaek-san. The three task forces would receive the first priority in weapons and supplies and would be officered by the most successful antipartisan commanders of the 1948–1949 campaign. The three commanders were

Paik Sun-yup, Kim Paik-il, and Yu Jae-hung. The campaign reflected renewed partisan activity, which was embarrassing to the Rhee regime and its armed forces. For the first time in five months, partisans raided police substations and other isolated security detachments, especially the hated youth battalions of police auxiliaries. The Chiri-san partisans, estimated at three hundred fighters, struck two county seats in Chollanam-do and made off with weapons, ammunition, and released prisoners after killing ten policemen and soldiers. Encouraged by this success, the Chiri-san partisans struck the Chinju base of the newly formed First Battalion, ROK Marine Corps, and overran the city's key offices, police stations, storehouses, barracks, and depots. Although the marines fought with elan, they received little help from the police and scattered army detachments, and the partisans held the city into the morning of October 28, when they drove off (in captured trucks) with six thousand sacks of flour and an assortment of military equipment, weapons, and ammunition. On the east coast, Kim Tal-sam, the Communists' most feared partisan commander, led three hundred well-trained, well-armed guerrillas in an early-morning raid on Andong in Kyongsangbok-do. Kim's band also made off with a large supply of weapons, food, ammunition, and equipment and left behind ten dead policemen and soldiers. On November 7 a motor launch from North Korea, the first reported maritime infiltration, landed Japanese weapons and ammunition for the guerrillas near Yongdok. The ROKA Twenty-second Regiment flooded the area with combat patrols and caught up with one guerrilla column on November 24 and fought a running battle for three days. The army killed thirty partisans and caught twenty more with thirty-six rifles (most Model 99 IJA) and one U.S. Army machine gun. The pursuit stalled with the death of Lt. Col. Chun Jong-gun in one skirmish that also killed five other soldiers. A fresh regiment picked up the trail and killed or captured another two hundred partisans, but the key SKLP leaders and core groups escaped. With ample supplies for a larger band, Kim Tal-sam called in the remnants of Yi Ho-jae's Kangwon-do guerrilla column. The unified brigade of about five hundred fighters rallied in the mountains north of Pohang in early November. Part of their purpose was to receive two more shiploads of munitions from North Korea, accompanied by two hundred more fighters.[76]

Not conforming to the Communist Chinese theory of people's war, the rash of partisan attacks and the massing of scattered columns had little to do with rallying the peasants. Expediency, not theory, forced the SKLP guerrillas into action. Without more weapons and food—and a few more good partisans—the People's Liberation Army could not survive the oncoming winter in the mountains. The sum of their actions suggests that the partisans knew that their mission was to survive long enough to participate in a far larger operation in 1950. Few guerrilla leaders would have *known* of any invasion plans, but they would have recognized the signs of an approaching conventional operation. The partisans made few efforts to win the hearts and minds of the rural villagers, since their mission was intelligence collection and rear-area ambushes and sabotage. Special intelligence operatives under the control of O Chin-u, one of Kim Il-sung's closest comrades and the future

North Korean minister of defense for life, began to appear in the field, suggesting something far more ominous than a few raids in the isolated mountain areas. The combined Kim-Yi group kidnapped recruits, massacred POWs, publicly executed government representatives and policemen, and took what they wanted from the helpless villagers. The Communists' abandonment of their precepts for cultivating a rural population worked to the ROKA's advantage; local guides, informants, and temporary militia became easier to recruit. In fact, the good behavior of the government forces—though opportunistic—gave the counterpartisan campaign a momentum it had lacked in its early stages.[77]

After a one-week general amnesty expired, the three counterpartisan task forces began continuous operations in October 1949. The weight of the ROKA's effort came against the guerrillas in the Chiri-sans. The headquarters of the Fifth Division served as the task force headquarters, but Paik Sun-yup could call on infantry battalions from the Second and Third Divisions, the other two southern divisions. The Third Division (Taegu) also had the responsibility of dealing with the Taebaek partisans; the two-regiment Eighth Division, stretched thin along the Thirty-eighth Parallel and the East Sea coastline, had the mission of containing any guerrillas moving in its area; and the pursuit mission went to the Honam Task Force. Navy patrols increased along the inshore waters of the East Sea. All the task forces used the same proven operational concepts of partisan eradication. Auxiliary forces under KNP field battalion supervision set up roadblocks, checkpoints, and roving patrols to control population movement; isolated villages that could not be garrisoned were burned, and the villagers were forced into lowland refugee camps. Regular army battalions, assisted by scout aircraft, roamed the mountains with company-sized patrols armed with nothing heavier than light machine guns and light 60mm mortars, searching for guerrilla base camps and caches. The task force headquarters rotated battalions to keep the troops fresh and the reaction to current intelligence rapid. There were no big engagements, just the inexorable pressure of ambush, pursuit, entrapment, and annihilation. In the ROKA's first "big week" (October 14–21), army headquarters claimed 201 guerrillas killed and 23 captured. Some weeks produced mixed results. The week of October 28 to November 4 ended with claims of 227 guerrillas killed and 65 captured, but the army lost 53 soldiers when the partisans ambushed a company of the Twenty-second Regiment. The key to the ROKA's eventual triumph was its ability to stay in contact with the partisans. Even if the South Korean army exaggerated its kills, it was whittling down the guerrillas day by day, week by week; its own losses were not prohibitive, at between 10 and 20 soldiers a week. Captures and surrenders started to increase to more than 50 a week, and the army even began to seize weapons, which were more valuable to the guerrillas than lives. The weather turned worse in late December, with snow and subfreezing temperatures in the mountains. In the last week of December, 8 ROK soldiers froze to death in the Chiri-sans, and 191 soldiers were hospitalized with severe frostbite.[78]

The Chiri-san campaign ground along into January and continued for another month before Paik Sun-yup reported that the guerrillas had shrunk to a harried, divided set of bands that might total 500 fighters. As the partisan main force shrank, it became more dangerous. In the first week of January 1950, it cost the ROKA 25 killed and 30 wounded to kill 134 guerrillas and capture 30 wounded. The chances of massacre also increased. On December 24, 1949, a patrol from the Twenty-fifth Regiment entered the mountain village of Suktal-ni in Kyongsangbok-do and murdered 86 inhabitants of all ages (23 under the age of fifteen) and both sexes, all "convicted" of aiding the Communists. The troops burned the village. Twelve villagers survived the mass shootings to complain to the police, who tried unsuccessfully to cover up the atrocity by accepting an army report that the guerrillas had committed the massacre. The leader of the massacre, Second Lt. Yu Chin-gyu, argued that the villagers were Communist sympathizers; the KNP captain who investigated the murders knew better but had no desire to expose an ROKA lieutenant and his errant company. The incident could not be concealed, however; members of the National Assembly learned about the affair and demanded an investigation, probably with the encouragement of Gregory Henderson, civil rights monitor of the army and police for the American embassy. The ROKA court-martialed Lieutenant Yu and two sergeants, convicted them, and packed them off to a military prison.[79]

The campaign to clear the Chiri-sans reduced partisan activity in the Cholla provinces and Kyongsangnam-do at a high cost to both belligerents. In the months of December 1949 and January 1950, the Ministry of Defense (with mild agreement from KMAG headquarters) claimed the deaths of 1,713 guerrillas at a cost to the security forces and assorted friendly civilians of more than 200 dead. The "guerrilla" body count undoubtedly included villagers impressed into partisan service and those unlucky enough to be caught in the crossfire at some "Communist village." The Chiri-san Task Force conducted its operations with 5,000 to 6,000 soldiers and combat police continuously in the field. Despite its successes, the nationwide count of Communist partisans remained stable at about the same number, presumably through local impressment and recruitment and the infiltration of partisans across the Thirty-eighth Parallel. The Korean and American planners directing operations from Seoul recognized the urgency of shifting the army's operational focus to Kangwon-do and Kyongsangbuk-do and the annihilation of the combined Taebaek partisan columns commanded by the skilled and relentless Kim Tal-sam, Yi Hyon-sang, and Yi Ho-jae. The Chiri-san survivors would have to be contained while the ROK counterguerrilla battalions moved in strength into the eastern mountain ranges for a decisive engagement with the most menacing and active Communist partisans.[80]

The Taebaek-Odaesan counterpartisan campaign of 1950 developed into a great engagement as the Communists rushed reinforcements south and the ROKA massed more than half of its infantry battalions against the partisans. From the government's perspective, the race against time meant that the ROKA had to intercept and break up the guerrilla columns before they established a support system of agents, caches, and base camps. The Communists added deception to their operations by dressing as ROKA soldiers or KNP field companies, so that their extortions and massacres would be blamed on the government forces. The ROKA and combat police handled captured guerrillas with hard hearts and heavy hands; POWs who refused to cooperate (thus losing any negotiating advantage) were summarily executed in the field, in part to intimidate the villagers. The presence of American advisers probably inhibited the atrocities, as did the investigations of Walter Sullivan of the *New York Times,* who may have been coached by Gregory Henderson. Jim Hausman continually warned Korean officers about the trouble that executions and torture caused the U.S. embassy and their negative effect on American audiences. He also stressed that effective operations required live informants and guides, not corpses to terrorize the villagers.[81]

As the weather improved in the late winter of 1949–1950 and the government's control over the population of the two northeastern provinces tightened, the Taebaek-san Task Force increased its pressure on the guerrillas, who had again scattered in order to forage and survive. Accepting the risk that widely separated combat patrols of company strength might be ambushed, Paik Sun-yup ordered saturation patrols of small mobile units moving along routes that would allow rapid concentration when a patrol made contact. In February the task force reported that it had killed 569 guerrillas and that the general pattern of partisan movement was north toward the border. In April the army struck one of the partisan columns recently dispatched from North Korea, encircled it, and killed or captured virtually all of its 300 members. In the first two weeks of April the ROKA made 88 contacts, killed 390 guerrillas, and captured 83 more; for the first time its count of captured weapons reached significant numbers—almost 200 weapons of all kinds, including machine guns and mortars. Another series of engagements in the last week of April added another 237 partisans to the score of dead, with 37 captured. The government forces lost 104 dead and missing and 200 wounded in April alone. The government even believed that Kim Tal-sam was among the dead, but he was not. The most dangerous guerrilla column still roamed Kangwon-do and engaged the government forces in raids and ambushes throughout April 1950. At a cost of 200 troops, the Sixth Division killed or captured 198 partisans in four battles. A more puzzling development was the low number of refugees headed south—only 400 in April 1950, compared with 3,600 who crossed the border in April 1949. The nationwide pattern of contacts, however, showed a dramatic decline—only 43 in May 1950, compared with 200-plus in April.[82]

As the Korean mountains turned blue-green with the buds of oaks, maples, and ginkgoes, the hopes of the South Korean army also blossomed after the warm success of the winter campaign to suppress the guerrillas. Good intelligence pictured the remaining Communists as demoralized and fragmented into small groups of nuisance value that could be hectored by the KNP field battalions. Infiltration of partisans from the north appeared to have ended, even if border skirmishes had not. Instead, groups of surviving partisans (including the elusive Kim Tal-sam) had crossed the border into North Korea. The army planners estimated that the biggest threat from the north was now raiders who entered the republic by ship, another reason to strengthen coast guard patrols and marine raiding forces. A government-sponsored program to organize former SKLP members into informants, agents, propagandists, and security force members had begun to pay dividends in rooting out party cadres and intelligence agents. In late May, ROK counterintelligence agents captured two leading Communists in Seoul, and they carried lists of some two hundred SKLP members in the government and the army. Radio Pyongyang even joined the campaign to destroy the SKLP by broadcasting political commentary that attacked the southern Communists for all sorts of apostasy: romantic deviationism, insufficient socialist ardor, military ineptness, and failure to mobilize the masses for resistance in the best Maoist style. For once, it appeared that the Communists were on the defensive, that the threat of subversion had ended in the republic, that the new year might bring new political stability and economic development. It was a false spring.

8

The Once and Future Invasion, 1949–1950

If Kim Il-sung had used a Marxist-Leninist astrologer to shape policy, he would have watched the correlation of forces meet the stars in their courses in the winter of 1949–1950 to create the preconditions for invading the Republic of Korea. The suppression of the South Korean Labor Party and its People's Liberation Army was a disappointment, not a strategic defeat. Kim Il-sung and his Russian advisers, Ambassador Terentii F. Shtykov and Col. Alexei M. Ignatiev, did not believe in Pak Hon-yong's passionate promises that the insurgents would push the Rhee administration to the edge of collapse. The hopeful omens came from other political developments. The American troops departed South Korea and left nothing behind that could stop a brigade of T-34/85 tanks covered by Soviet artillery and accompanied by tough, veteran Korean infantry. The "puppet army" might be able to chase guerrillas and abuse villagers, but it was ill prepared to stop tanks with its small arms and limited numbers of antitank artillery.

The other ordnance that mattered had pushed a large mushroom cloud, reeking radiation, above the barren steppes north of Semipalatin, Kazakhstan, on August 29, 1949. The Soviets had exploded their nuclear device, rated at twenty kilotons and modeled on the American Nagasaki plutonium bomb. Known as "First Lightning" to the Russians and "Joe 1" to the Americans, the nuclear device had beaten the predicted Western schedule by three or four years. As the cloud blossomed upward, Lavrentii Beria, the secret policeman Stalin had made his nuclear chief, crowed with excitement. "Is it like the American bomb?" the jubilant Beria asked two Russian engineers who had observed the American tests in 1946 at Bikini atoll. All the happy engineers and scientists assured Beria that their bomb was better; they were ecstatic about the explosion, since they assumed that Beria would have shot them if the bomb had fizzled.

The news of the blast came first from the United States. On September 3 an American intelligence "sniffer" aircraft picked up radioactive dust drifting east

across Asia. On September 23 President Harry S. Truman confirmed press specu-
lation that the Soviets had indeed developed an atomic bomb. Truman reassured
the American people that one atomic explosion did not mean that the United States
had lost its nuclear supremacy. The Soviet news agency TASS shouted two days
later that the USSR had developed an atomic bomb. As the radioactive dust settled, Stalin gloated over his newfound nuclear equity—more perception than reality—and dreamed of a future when American threats of atomic preemption and
punishment would be meaningless. On October 10 Truman approved an ambitious
program of nuclear weapons development that would produce small fission
weapons in the thousands for tactical targets and enough hydrogen "superbombs"
to turn the entire populated Soviet Union into a glowing steppe.[1]

Although October brought no joy to Pennsylvania Avenue, crowds of ecstatic
Chinese flooded Tiananmen Square, Beijing, to hear Chairman Mao Zedong pro-
claim victory in the civil war and the establishment of the People's Republic of
China on October 1, 1949. After more than twenty years of civil war, the Chinese
Communists felt confident enough to celebrate their triumph at the gates of the imperial Forbidden City. The cause of the celebration—the collapse of Chinese Nationalist military resistance from Shanghai to Nanjing in the valley of the
Yangtze—was real enough. Moreover, the summer campaign of 1949 had been
marked by reassuring American passivity. The marine brigade at Qingdao held its
enclave and then sailed away; the U.S. Navy patrol squadron based at Shanghai
took away the refugees with claims to American protection and headed to the
Yangtze bar and the open sea. By October 1, Mao Zedong had ordered the People's
Liberation Army, especially his crack Third and Fourth Field Armies of one million men in 132 divisions, to keep moving south against the remnants of the Nationalist armies. With many new U.S. Army weapons confiscated from the Nationalists, the People's Liberation Army headed for the Formosa Strait and the
border of French Indochina, ready to put the last revolutionary nails in the coffin
of colonialism.

Although the Russians had claimed Korea as part of their Asian sphere of interest, the Chinese Communists were also interested parties in Kim Il-sung's revolution. Already supplicants for Soviet military assistance, the Chinese could
hardly match the flow of heavy weapons from Russia into North Korea. Yet Mao's
generals could and did release Korean veterans of the People's Liberation Army
for service in the Korean People's Army (KPA). The Chinese had a debt. In 1946,
facing a good Chinese Nationalist army and two U.S. Marine Corps divisions in
north China, the People's Liberation Army had used North Korea as a sanctuary
and base camp; it had shifted forces to its embattled armies in northern Manchuria
through North Korea; and it had used Korea as a refuge and a hospital. Asian anticolonialism and the fraternal bonds of socialist revolution, however, were not
enough to cement Sino-Korean relations. As they had for centuries, the Chinese
and Koreans cautiously adjusted their national interests to form an association of
mutual advantage that allowed them to look to Russia as a counter to Japanese im-

perialism that had now been reborn, the Communists believed, as American interventionism.[2]

MAO ZEDONG GOES TO MOSCOW

The son of a smallholding farmer, librarian and minor poet, Mao Zedong had ridden a revolution from Hunan Province to the great northern capital itself, Beijing. As the Guomindang and regional warlords fled or changed sides in 1949, Chairman Mao brought his considerable entourage to Beijing and moved into a spacious Ming dynasty pavilion deep in the recesses of the Forbidden City. A new dynasty had embraced the mandate of heaven under the inspiration of Sun Yat-sen and V. I. Lenin. Mao gloried in the view from his suites of the South and Center lakes, a pastoral park of fish, birds, and willows. Mao had a great rite to perform: the formal announcement of the revolution's triumph and the proclamation of a new Middle Kingdom, the People's Republic of China.

On the afternoon of October 1, 1949, Mao Zedong, fifty-six years old and starting to bloat, mounted the lower balcony of the Gate of Heavenly Peace, still surrounded by an entourage of aging revolutionaries and the stalwarts of his court, the comrades of the Long March and the years in the Yanan caves. The gate shimmered with red banners, red silk lanterns, and the new red flag with six gold stars. A portrait of Mao Zedong dominated the real speaker, who read his speech behind a bank of antique radio microphones in an abrasive Hunan dialect. A crowd of 100,000 true believers heard the chairman promise a future "infinitely bright." Mao reviewed Chinese history since the First Opium War and repeatedly promised that "nobody will insult us again." The parade that followed Mao's speech made his point even more forcefully. Following the ranks of the tough infantry of the People's Liberation Army rolled abandoned tanks and trucks that had once belonged to the U.S. Army.[3]

Two months after he called the People's Republic of China into being, Chairman Mao boarded a train for Moscow and his first trip outside China. He had been invited to the Kremlin to celebrate Marshal Stalin's seventieth birthday on December 21, 1949. Mao had more on his mind than a Communist gala. In the waning days of World War II, the Soviets had negotiated another unequal treaty with the Nationalist regime that took a giant step toward reversing Russia's losses to Japan in the Treaty of Portsmouth (1905). In territorial terms, the Chinese wanted to roll back the new Soviet imperialism in Mongolia, Xinjiang (Sinkiang), and Manchuria. The Chinese wanted the Soviets to set limits on their development of the port of Lüshun (Port Arthur) and the Liaodong peninsula, held as a ten-year leasehold. The Chinese wanted to ensure that Xinjiang and Mongolia were neutralized in a strategic sense, whether by demilitarization or annexation or as spheres of interest or protectorates. Manchuria was another matter. It was a land of rich minerals and bountiful food as well as great symbolism, and a China that held Manchuria was a China that controlled its own destiny. Simply allowing the Soviets to replace the Japanese as masters of Manchuria was no victory for the revolution. The symbol of new Russian imperialism was Soviet control of the Zhongdong Railroad and the military base at Lüshun. Preliminary negotiations by the Chinese Communists, represented by Liu Shaoqi, and the Soviets, represented by Anastas Mikoyan, produced no resolution of the matter of treaty revision, one of Mao's high-priority goals and Stalin's least favorite subject. Mao was determined to make the unequal treaty issue a test of the new partnership between Moscow and Beijing.[4]

Although the Soviet leaders wined and dined Mao Zedong upon his arrival in Moscow on December 16, the chairman cooled the negotiating atmosphere by stating that one of Stalin's great accomplishments was abandoning the unequal treaties of the czars. He then pressed Stalin to make good on hints made to Liu Shaoqi that a new treaty might help cement relations between the world's two great revolutionary powers. Stalin did not reject this possibility, but he refused to discuss specifics, and he certainly told Mao that he would not surrender the concessions granted in 1945 by the Nationalists. After their meeting on December 16, the two principals did not see each other until Stalin's birthday party five days later. On December 20, however, Mao talked with I. V. Kovalev, Stalin's personal representative and transportation minister, and stated frankly that he and Stalin needed to agree whether they were negotiating a new treaty or just holding general discussions. If a new treaty was the goal, Mao would summon his best negotiators, led by Zhou Enlai, to Moscow. Mao also lobbied several of Stalin's fellow Politburo members. The impasse continued, and it included several poisoned moments when Stalin cold-shouldered Mao in public. After this chilly display, Stalin agreed to talk treaty if the Chinese would publicly state their goals. Mao did so in a TASS interview on January 2. He sought a new agreement that revised the current treaty, provided a Soviet loan to China, and produced a long-term trade agreement between the two nations. Mao's reference to the onerous 1945 treaty marked the first time that issue had been brought up.

The Soviets decided that they could live with a revised treaty if that was Mao's price for strategic cooperation in Asia and a willingness to work out understandings on Xinjiang, Mongolia, and Manchuria. There was much unfinished business in Asia in which Russia and China had a common interest: accomplishing the complete destruction of the Guomindang and its new refuge on Taiwan, ensuring that Japan remained crippled and isolated, curbing American imperialism, and assisting the people's wars in the Philippines, Indochina, and Malaya. Mao and Stalin agreed on at least one thing: the Chinese Revolution would rewrite the future of great power relations in Asia.

On January 2, 1950, the Soviet leadership met with Stalin to frame a new formal agreement with the Chinese that would allow Mao to take the offensive against his domestic enemies and regional competitors, but without surrendering the advantages of the 1945 treaty. Even before Zhou Enlai arrived in Moscow—a prospect that cut both ways, since Zhou skillfully balanced Russian and Chinese interests—the Soviets gave Mao a set of light concessions and 1945 reassertions: (1) defense against Japan and its allies, (2) the independence of Mongolia, (3) $300 million in credits (in U.S. dollars), and (4) a series of aviation and trade agreements to be drafted in detail later. The status of Xinjiang and the presence of Soviet forces in Manchuria remained at issue, but Mao Zedong felt that the tides were now running in his favor.

With Zhou Enlai's help after January 20, Mao and the Soviets hammered out the provisions of the Treaty of Friendship, Alliance, and Mutual Assistance, signed on February 14, 1950, in Moscow. In a series of meetings, January 22–February 10, the Chinese and Soviets formed a revolutionary alliance that lasted three decades. They also drafted an additional agreement (not published) related to security issues, principally noninterference accords that neutralized the Asian-Muslim borderlands between the Soviet Union and China and prohibited either party from using foreign nationals to exploit the region's rich natural resources. Western intelligence sources guessed correctly that the Chinese would insist that some protocols remain secret, but they guessed wrong about the arrangements for military assistance, which were unaddressed. The entire negotiations avoided military issues, including the Korean situation, except for vague plans to phase out the Russian forces in Manchuria in less than ten years and to dispose of Japanese POWs still in Russian hands who might be tried as war criminals by China.

The Sino-Soviet treaty of 1950 reflected the strengths and vulnerabilities of both parties, domestically and internationally, and it was hard for Western analysts to know which was which. Stalin certainly needed a foreign policy victory since he had presided over limited defeats and no decisions for three years: the decline of the Communist parties in France and Italy; the apostasy of Tito's Yugoslavia and a losing people's war in Greece; the failure of the blockade of Berlin; and the formation of the North Atlantic Treaty Organization, bolstered by the Marshall Plan and the Mutual Defense Assistance Program (MDAP). The coup in Czechoslovakia and the formation of the Warsaw Pact helped keep the Kremlin optimistic, but the Soviet bomb and Mao's victory in China suggested new opportunities to regain the global political initiative and put the United States and its allies on the defensive. An alliance with China brought added strength to the Soviet position vis-à-vis the United States and Japan, especially since Mao's plans for revolutionary reconstruction, self-defense, and southern expansion required Soviet military assistance and economic ties as well as a secure northern frontier. Noticeably understated in the Sino-Soviet discussions was the subject of unifying the two Koreas by bolder military action. Mao and Stalin agreed to let the issue ride.[5]

KOREA IN AMERICAN POLICY

For the American policy makers in Washington, burdened by the weight of challenges unmet and programs unfunded, Korea became a country that would not go away. Whenever certain subjects arose—coping with Communist China, making peace with Japan, dealing with the remnants of the Guomindang on Taiwan, or deterring Russia—the Korea problem popped up as an unwelcome complication better dealt with by denying its existence. Of all the organizations that handled Korean issues, the Department of Defense had the clearest vision: Korea did not count. Secretary of Defense Louis Johnson, who had replaced the stricken James V. Forrestal in March 1949, had a single mandate from President Truman, who wanted to run the government like his failed clothing store—on the cheap. Johnson's imperious style and naked ambition, plus a vindictiveness notable even in Washington, made it easy to blame him for every problem that arose in defense planning. Johnson's economy measures—and the ruthless power he exercised over the armed forces—originated in the White House with a president who feared the postwar depression that had not yet occurred.[6]

To be sure, Truman and Congress were dueling economizers, but Truman consistently issued guidance that set budget ceilings at less than half the funding that the Joint Chiefs of Staff (JCS), through the service departments, requested. In July 1948 the JCS approved the first joint war plan for a conflict with the Soviet Union, known as Halfmoon or Joint Emergency War Plan 1, and asked the services to provide forces for its execution. The war plan envisioned a conflict in which the Strategic Air Command carried on a nuclear air assault on the Soviet Union while the other services and the tactical wings of the air force battled Soviet forces in Europe, the Middle East, and north Asia. Although Halfmoon went through several subsequent variations and altered strategic assumptions, the recommended force structure of seventy air force wings, twelve army divisions, two marine division–aircraft wing amphibious forces, and a 900-ship navy (300-plus combatants) did not change, nor did its price tag of more than $30 billion a year. Truman and Congress battled over the difference between $14.2 billion and $13.9 billion, both driving the budget for fiscal year 1951 down toward $12 billion or even $11 billion, despite the explosion of the Soviet bomb and the victory of the People's Republic of China.[7]

With the fall of the Chinese Nationalist regime almost certain, the American intelligence community assessed the strategic importance of Asia to the United States and the Soviet Union and concluded that north Asia—meaning Japan and Korea—remained assets worth controlling or at least denying to a potential enemy. America's interests, however, could be protected with military forces stationed outside the Asian mainland on a system of island bases that ran from the Aleutians through Japan and Okinawa to the Philippines; the Mariana Islands of Guam, Saipan, and Tinian offered strategic depth for the air and naval forces (with nuclear weapons) with which the United States could control the Pacific and influence Asia. The explosion of the Soviet atomic bomb set off a sympathetic blast within the intelligence agencies, with the Central Intelligence Agency at odds with the State Department and all the service intelligence staffs. The CIA analysts did not believe that one demonstration bomb would encourage the Soviet Union to sponsor military adventures of its own or through proxies such as China and North Korea. The majoritarian dissenters thought the CIA's optimism excessive and dangerous. Even if the Soviets could not reach targets in the United States, the rich number of targets in Europe and Asia gave the Soviets a credible deterrent to American nuclear weapons. Given the dismal state of America's conventional forces, the Soviets risked little in a proxy war.[8]

Within the box of austerity and strategic acrimony, military planners found Korea bobbing up again and again as the State Department opposed a complete, precipitous troop withdrawal. The army staff completed one study, "Implications of a Possible Full Scale Invasion from North Korea Subsequent to Withdrawal of United States Troops from South Korea," in June 1949 and examined several options for responding to an invasion, in concert with an uprising or not. One option included an extension of the Truman doctrine to Korea, with a mutual defense alliance. Another option was to evacuate American nationals and take the problem to the UN Security Council. This might produce "a police action with U.N. sanction by the introduction of a military task force into Korea composed of U.S. units and units of other member nations of the United Nations with the objective of restoring law and order and restoration of the Thirty-eighth Parallel boundary inviolability." The JCS, however, was uninterested in taking action on any of the options, which might have set off another review of National Security Council Memorandum 8/2 (NSC 8/2).[9]

Under intolerable budgetary restraints, the JCS could not avoid a continuing reassessment of its strategic challenges. Its review of Asian perils in February 1950 did not include Korea as a pressing issue. The planners had a full agenda of real and potential crises: the likely Chinese invasions of Hainan and Taiwan islands, the war in Indochina, the impact of the Sino-Soviet treaty, the insurgency in the Philippines, the security of Japan, and the likely war between India and Pakistan. The agenda might have included the insurgency in Malaya, instability in Indonesia, the Chinese threat to Tibet, and the war in Korea. In the hierarchy of strategic concerns, Asia ranked third, behind Europe and the Middle East.[10]

The view of strategic priorities differed in headquarters, Far East Command (FECOM), Tokyo, but Korea did not advance in the hierarchy of problems. Gen. Douglas MacArthur used two groups for long-range planning and policy analysis, the Joint Strategic Plans and Operations Group (JSPOG) and the Joint Committee. The three key staff members of the Joint Committee were Maj. Gen. Edward N. Almond, FECOM chief of staff; Maj. Gen. Doyle O. Hickey, deputy chief of staff; and Brig. Gen. Edwin K. Wright, deputy chief of staff for operations and planning. None of these army generals had long-term relations with MacArthur, but all three shaped FECOM positions more surely than the "Bataan Gang" of legend. Almond and Hickey had commanded divisions in the war with Germany, and Wright had served as armored planner for the U.S. Twelfth Army Group. All enjoyed the confidence of Gen. Omar Bradley (chairman of the JCS) and Gen. J. Lawton Collins (army chief of staff), and they understood the JCS's problems.

When they took on the mission of developing a theater strategy to support the Joint Emergency War Plan, they focused on using uncommitted Government Aid and Relief in Occupied Areas funds to build a wartime base structure on Okinawa and to reduce the facilities in Japan, Korea, Guam, and Saipan. They accepted the reality of Clark Air Force Base and Naval Base in Subic Bay, the Philippines, but stressed that these facilities defended Taiwan, not Japan. Like the JCS, they viewed mainland bases in Asia as indefensible hostages in a general war. Even bases in Japan proper ran the risk of attack or siege from hostile mobs and terrorist saboteurs.[11]

As chief of JSPOG, Wright held the central position in FECOM planning and was the only general in the group; the rest of JSPOG, by MacArthur's fiat, consisted of four navy captains, four army colonels, four marine colonels, and four or five air force colonels. Wright had another qualification that interested MacArthur: he had just finished a tour as deputy director of the CIA. MacArthur regarded Hickey and Wright as loyal FECOM advocates who also enjoyed the confidence of the JCS, the CIA, and the army staff. Hickey and Wright supported the Korean Military Advisory Group (KMAG) within the boundaries set by MacArthur, but they did not challenge the JCS position that Korea was an expendable outpost.

The State Department regarded the Republic of Korea as a grand experiment in nation building in Asia, no matter how cynical the foreign service officers sounded or how much they disliked Rhee and his grasping cronies. The State planners, however, expected more than a humanitarian award for supporting the ROK. Korean security contributed to Japanese security. An anti-Communist Korea showed that the American influence in Asia would not disappear with Nationalist China. The Asianists at State also had good reason to prove their opposition to Communism. Frustrated and opportunistic members of Congress, led by Senator Joseph McCarthy (R-Wis.), discovered in early 1950 that chasing "Reds" in State (and there were some) made good media coverage. Men who lived abroad and spoke foreign languages were easy victims. Nevertheless, the men handling Japanese and Korean affairs enjoyed reputations for probity and for progressive, pragmatic Victorian liberalism, which made them difficult targets for the McCarthyites and attractive allies of Secretary of State Dean Acheson, Undersecretary of State James Webb, Ambassador Philip Jessup, Ambassador-at-Large W. Averell Harriman, and Paul H. Nitze, who had replaced George Kennan as head of the policy planning staff. The key figure among the "new Koreanists" was none other than Dean Rusk, the assistant secretary for Far Eastern affairs and one of the army colonels who had drawn the line at the Thirty-eighth Parallel in 1945. Rusk enjoyed equally cordial relations with Acheson and the Republican "shadow" secretary of state, John Foster Dulles, just appointed special envoy to negotiate a peace treaty with Japan. Rusk also served as State's ambassador to the Department of Defense.[12]

As he watched the Republicans use the China issue to attack President Truman and the armed forces move toward a nuclear weapons–only strategy, Secretary of State Acheson looked for an opportunity to recast American declaratory policy for Asia. An interservice missions and budget battle in Congress in the autumn of 1949 put Truman and the JCS on record as believing that Korea played no role in American strategic planning. Taiwan, in contrast, appealed to the JCS as an island base to deter Communist China's march south, a view anathema at State. In an effort to draw the distinction between contingency planning by the JCS and national interest as defined by State, Acheson also wanted to provide a rationale for halting economic aid to the Guomindang. He and George Kennan, who wrote an early draft of Acheson's speech, saw little threat of Soviet military action but ample openings for subversion in Asia. Kennan even saw Korea as an example of "non-strategic" importance and hopeful development: "Korea has come along surprisingly and shows signs of being able to hold its own with our help."[13]

In his January 12, 1950, address to the National Press Club, Acheson emphasized that strategic planning for the use of offshore bases on Formosa did not define America's interests in Asia. The fate of potential and actual allies had to be decided on a case-by-case basis, but the United States would oppose Communism as a new kind of imperialism encouraged by the Soviet Union, which had now enlisted a new proxy for subversion, Communist China. The United States had a firm commitment to Japan, Korea, and the Philippines that it would exercise alone or in concert with the United Nations or its wartime allies, in the case of Japan. In other areas, Acheson proposed to work with the new nations to advance their independence and economic development. No hostile power should misunderstand America's commitment to the Republic of Korea as the foundation for a future free, unified Korean nation.[14]

The National Press Club speech, later interpreted by Truman's critics as an invitation to invade South Korea, actually stirred Acheson and his Asia advisers (Rusk, Walton Butterworth, John Hickerson, and Howland H. Sargeant) to approach the president about conducting another review of Asia policy. Truman had no objections to an interagency review as long as it focused on the effect of the Soviet Union's possession of nuclear weapons. Acheson gave the study assignment to Nitze's policy planning staff. As Acheson anticipated, Secretary of Defense Louis Johnson wanted no part of the review, since he saw the possibility of a State-JCS alliance to increase conventional forces, a disaster in an era of strict budgetary restraint. Although Nitze recruited State's best and brightest for his study, Johnson sent only Maj. Gen. James H. Burns, his foreign aid action officer, and Burns's assistants to the drafting sessions and interviews. Johnson and General Bradley met Acheson only once for fourteen minutes to discuss the study, and they spent most of the meeting criticizing Nitze and Burns. When "The Report to the President Pursuant to the President's Directive of 31 January 1950" took shape in March–April, Johnson did not object to continuing the policy review through the National Security Council—the paper was now christened NSC 68—because he was confident that its price tag for the armed forces ($221 billion over five years) represented fiscal fantasy. As Johnson predicted, the JCS-State champions of rearmament made no headway with Truman or his budget advisers, champions of the

Democratic Party's "Freedom Budget," which would fix the entire federal fiscal year 1951 budget at 15 percent of the gross national product, or around $35 billion.[15]

As a companion piece to the NSC 68 strategic analysis, Rusk and his Asian specialists addressed Syngman Rhee's alarm over Acheson's National Press Club speech. In fact, NSC 68 included an Annex 8 on regional challenges, and its Part II, "The Conditions of Success of the U.S. Programs in Asia," included Korea as one of the Asian nations at risk from anticolonial Communism, championed by China. The State Department's principal instrument for combating subversion was economic development without industrialization; the developing nations from India to Indonesia need maximum food production, clean water, controlled extractive industries to produce valuable raw materials, manufacturing of light consumer products, birth control, and investment in roads, railroads, and power grids. Military spending, local or American, would divert scarce funds from development. Rhee knew State's agenda only too well, and he complained loudly and often to Acheson that only a dramatic surge in military assistance and an American security guarantee would compensate for excluding Korea from America's "strategic perimeter."[16]

In his meetings with Ambassador John Chang, Assistant Secretary Rusk stressed the firmness of the American commitment, but aid remained conditional. The ROK had to get its defense spending in hand, curb inflation, and complete its land reform program. The government needed to get its rice distribution plan under control, and it had to solve the problem of redistributing vested Japanese property. In addition, the May election had to go off exactly on schedule and satisfy the United Nations Commission on Korea (UNCOK) for its lack of violence and obvious honesty. Rhee continued to stress his military requirements and to stall on political and economic reforms. Rhee bombarded State with requests to give him a real navy and air force, to no avail, since the Defense Department would not support the requests. Muccio advised Washington to postpone the requirements for economic reform, since Rhee had agreed to conduct the May 1950 elections under the unchanged 1948 constitution and with UNCOK observation. In fact, Rhee seemed persuaded that changing ministers did not improve administration, and Muccio's staff actually saw some improvement in the economic indicators, as well as in the ROKA's counterguerrilla campaign, by April 1950.

Acheson agreed to a major internal review of Korea policy even though he knew that Johnson would never consent to a revision of NSC 8/2. Acheson told Ambassador Chang that he would conduct the review anyway, since the secretary sensed a slightly elevated interest in the White House and Congress in Asian security, even if it were only a response to McCarthyesque ranting about abandoning Taiwan. Nevertheless, the review might produce a recommendation to reduce economic aid, especially since Korean intransigence had alienated Economic Cooperation Administration chief Paul Hoffman. A one-day "Far East" interdepartmental conference did indeed debate Korea's economic woes, not its security problems. Only two army representatives attended, both civilian managers. The impasse continued on revising NSC 8/2. In fact, the threat of reduced economic aid produced an uproar in the National Assembly and gave Radio Pyongyang an excuse to gloat over Rhee's problems.[17]

The U.S. government continued to accept a strained status quo in its relations with the Rhee government. At the State Department, official interest in security problems waned as the counterguerrilla war shrank to noncrisis proportions. Rhee became ill and deeply depressed by Washington's inability to share his sense of impending disaster. He had expressed his vision of doom to his American public affairs adviser, Professor Robert T. Oliver, in a letter the previous September. Unless the United States supported Asian nationalists, the Soviet-supported Communists would win the war of propaganda, subversion, economic aid, and partisan and conventional war. The new nations "cannot keep fighting," he wrote, and Korea was at the center of "this losing battle." The ROK needed arms, not more soldiers. His forces could join "our loyal Communist army in the north to clean up the rest of them in Pyongyang," driving out the Soviet-puppet clique of Kim Il-sung, "gangsters . . . terrorists, assassins and robbers." Most North Koreans would welcome liberation, but without American assistance, South Korea would be the victim, not the liberator.[18]

Rhee had managed to maintain his faith and determination through the winter of 1949–1950, buoyed by military success and some economic improvements. But Washington's failure to support his enlarged army and newborn navy and air force sent him spinning off into despondency. The threat of reduced economic assistance put him abed, while his wife Francesca managed his care and the affairs of state. The American embassy dispatched Harold J. Noble, its third senior officer ("counselor") and most senior Korean-speaker to the Kyongmudae, Rhee's residence, at the president's request. Raised in Korea in a Methodist missionary family, Noble had earned three degrees at American universities, served as a Marine Corps intelligence officer and Japanese linguist during World War II, and covered Asian politics as a journalist before joining the foreign service. He had known the Rhees for years. Rhee unburdened himself to Noble about his trials with the fractious conservatives of the Korean Democratic Party, which had been retitled the Democratic National Party (DNP) but was still dominated by Kim Sung-su. The DNP wanted to control the cabinet and run the National Assembly. It also wanted Rhee to shift senior police officers to electoral districts where it faced real opponents. Rhee appealed for American support for a free election, and the embassy staff went into action with a vengeance to see that the Republic of Korea worked its way into the American conscience as an example of the new, free postcolonial Asia.

The American political activism in Seoul had another dimension—the improved US-UNCOK relationship and Rhee's tardy realization that UNCOK's approval strengthened his bargaining position for increased aid. UNCOK had no chance of influencing North Korea, but it could use its partnership with the United States to influence the assembly election and, through it, remake the Rhee government in Trygve Lie's image while the UN secretary-general coped with the

Soviet Union's revenge on the Security Council. The council had stalled after Ambassador Jacob Malik walked out (January 13, 1950) over the United Nations' failure to replace the Nationalist Chinese with a Communist delegation. UNCOK's electoral mission had another dimension—the parallel discussion of forming a regional alliance system under UN sponsorship, to be called the Pacific Union. The idea came from Ambassador Wellington Koo of Nationalist China and found special champions in President Elpidio Quirino of the Philippines and Carlos Romulo, his UN chief of mission and a confidant of Lie's. The heart of the union would be the anti-Communist trio of Taiwan, the Philippines, and South Korea. It was hoped that Japan would also be a partner, silent or not, as its eventual peace treaty allowed. Rhee supported the movement with enthusiasm in 1949, but not in 1950, since the United States thought that the Pacific Union was only a Guomindang survival ploy and an unwanted complication in moving Japan into the Western world. Rhee stayed home when delegations of the potential members met in the Philippines in May 1950. It may have been the high point in Rhee's new cooperativeness, but it did nothing to change his growing anxiety.[19]

The president would not have been reassured by the first Korean-American general defense plan for the Republic of Korea, drafted by his army's operations staff and the KMAG advisers. As the plan was being developed in December 1949, the enemy situation was not yet too ominous; the North Koreans had three Border Guard *(Boandae)* brigades deployed along the Thirty-eighth Parallel, backed by two infantry divisions and two artillery divisions of the KPA. The next line of deployment (Chinampo-Pyongyang-Wonsan) was manned by two divisions, a tank regiment, an independent brigade, two marine raiding regiments, security and construction units, and naval forces. Two former divisions of the People's Liberation Army and seven *Boandae* battalions were stationed along the border with China and Russia. The deployment of the South Korean army placed three divisions and a separate regiment in Kyonggi Province to defend Seoul, with two more divisions deployed along the border to the east. Three divisions garrisoned the rest of the country and pursued the guerrillas, and one marine battalion held Cheju-do.[20]

Based on a traditional estimate of the situation endorsed by General Roberts as the chief of KMAG, the plan stressed the defense of the road-river corridors that converged on Seoul and the Han River valley. The concept of defense was based on the use of combined arms strong points at the natural choke points in the corridors. If the KPA remained at its current strength, estimated at around 77,000, it probably could be stopped, but if it expanded according to its own plans (reported by agents) to almost 200,000, with the addition of mobilized manpower and veterans of the Chinese Communist army, the Republic of Korea probably could not be defended without the commitment of American forces in Japan. The South Koreans would be outnumbered, outgunned in artillery and armor, fighting without air defense, and operating on a fragile system of supply and transportation. Only four South Korean army divisions had a single artillery battalion by 1950. Fourteen of twenty-one infantry regiments had an assigned antitank artillery company.

Neither the national police nor a seven-division reserve force (the latter a paper army) added much combat capability. Under the circumstances, offensive options for the ROKA were not realistic; the only hope was to train, expand, and reequip the South Korean army for a decisive battle north of the Han River, even if the rear areas were plagued by guerrillas.[21]

As explained by one of its authors, Lt. Col. Ralph W. Hansen, the G-3 adviser, the defense plan depended on the integration of barrier engineering, mining, timely artillery fire, and the opportunistic use of infantry task forces to trap the North Koreans on the narrow roads to Seoul. "Close cooperation and coordination between Korean Army Headquarters and lower units is imperative. Upon the shoulders of commanders and their staffs, the fate of Korea rests." A war would be won or lost along the three corridors that led to Seoul: the Kaesong-Munsan axis, the Uijongbu axis, and the Chunchon axis. The ROKA would concede the Ongjin peninsula and Kaesong and defend the "western corridor" along the line of the Imjin River. The Chunchon axis could be closed by the ROK Sixth Division. Any attacks farther east would be diversionary actions that other forces would have to meet, which meant the two-regiment Eighth Division. The strategic reserve would have to be the ROK Second Division (Taejon) and the Third Division (Taegu), which also held Pusan with a regiment. The Fifth Division, deployed against the guerrillas in the Cholla provinces, was the last and most distant reserve force. Colonel Hansen's assessment did not soar into unwarranted optimism or plunge into defeatist despondency, but it did communicate a concern that could not be camouflaged.[22]

The Korean Military Advisory Group had another plan, which it did not share officially with the Koreans, that placed the success of the general defense plan in doubt. No sooner had KMAG acquired official status in July 1949 than its staff wrote Operation Cruller. With KMAG the only army presence in Korea after the reassignment of the army's stay-behind subunits and the redeployment of the Fifth Regimental Combat Team to Hawaii, General Roberts assumed responsibility for preparing an evacuation plan for KMAG and Ambassador Muccio's diplomatic mission. The plan was not just a scheme for evacuating American citizens and diplomatic officials; Operation Cruller also provided for the departure of the ROKA's American advisers. At a time of crisis—an uprising, an invasion, or both—the American advisory group would depart, along with its expertise in operational planning, communications, logistics, and fire support coordination. Just who would order the execution of Operation Cruller—and under what conditions—was unclear, since General MacArthur and the State Department both had a clear interest in and divided responsibility for any American response to a future crisis in Korea.[23]

THE DEMOCRATIC PEOPLE'S REPUBLIC PREPARES FOR WAR

During January 1950, Joseph Stalin reduced his opposition to an invasion of South Korea and encouraged Kim Il-sung to believe that he would lead a victory parade

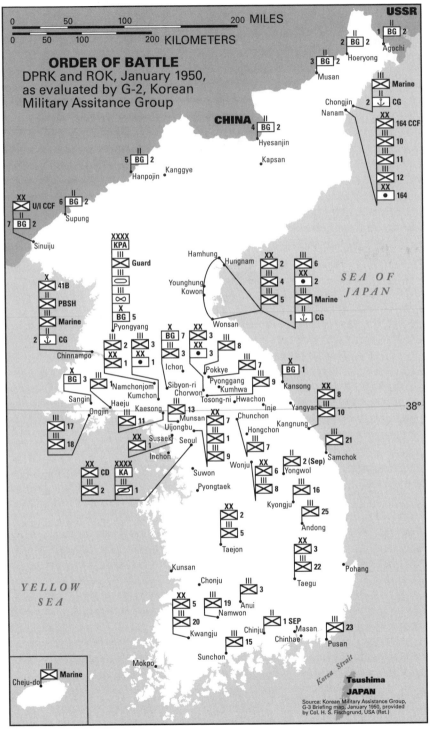

ORDER OF BATTLE
DPRK and ROK, January 1950, as evaluated by G-2, Korean Military Assitance Group

Map 6.

in Seoul sometime that year. No senior Soviet, Chinese, or North Korean official set a specific date, but the South Korean government believed that Stalin had made the decision for war on January 5 and set the date for April—or August at the latest. No single statement by Stalin or Kim Il-sung revealed the great design; no single document has been discovered that describes the core assumptions or operational concepts behind what became Operation Preemptive Strike. The flow of men and materiel that strengthened the Korean People's Army (and its air and naval components) could not be hidden, even if Korean intelligence agents and analysts could not quite get it right. The stark facts were correct enough: between November 1949 and May 1950, the KPA doubled in size (90,000 to 180,000) and completed its transformation from a light infantry force to a combined arms force of tanks, mobile heavy artillery and mortars, tough infantry, and effective special operations forces. The North Korean air force, built around forty-eight YAK-9 fighters and IL-10 light bombers, faced no comparable air capability in South Korea. The KPA navy of twenty to thirty fast patrol boats equaled or exceeded the operating speed and armament of the ROK navy. Many of the North Korean servicemen were veterans of the Russian, Chinese, and Japanese armed forces. Their officers had wartime experience and enforced the disciplinary standards of their unforgiving parent armies. In terms of operational capabilities, the North Korean armed forces, matched against their South Korean counterparts, had operational and tactical advantages that could be enhanced by strategic surprise.[24]

Kim Il-sung welcomed the Year of the Tiger by asking the Soviets for more guns and the Chinese for more men. At a dinner in Pyongyang on January 7, Kim again asked for Soviet support for his invasion plans. Ambassador Terentii Shtykov sent a North Korean request for 112 million rubles worth of military equipment to Moscow. He also told Stalin that Kim's ardor for an invasion had reached new heights, no doubt encouraged by Mao Zedong's trip to Moscow. The Chinese had already agreed to redeploy another sixteen thousand Korean veterans of the People's Liberation Army for military service closer to home. Kim insisted that he needed another Moscow visit to argue his case. Shtykov corroborated Kim's claim to have Beijing's support for a unification campaign. He and Kim also had a reliable report from Seoul that Rhee had reached the point of desperation because the United States would not intervene to save him or Taiwan, and the British recognition of the People's Republic of China was the crack of doom. Stalin wired Shtykov that another audience could be arranged. "Tell this to Kim Il Sung and stress that I am ready to help him in this matter." Such is the language that launched two hundred tanks.[25]

Stalin had reservations about Kim Il-sung's military judgment, so he sent another military mission to Pyongyang, a group of operational specialists, planners, and trainers led by Lt. Gen. Ivan V. Vasiliev, a proven World War II field commander. Kim Il-sung agreed to use his most recent loan to arm three new infantry divisions, and, under pressure, the North Koreans agreed to pay for their new weapons with a shipment of gold, silver, and monazite, a black sand that yields radioactive thorium for use in nuclear weapons. The value of the minerals was 120 million rubles, and Kim's quid pro quo produced a real loan of 70 million rubles. Kim still wanted a Moscow meeting, and he had paid his way, so Shtykov made the travel arrangements for Kim and Pak Hon-yong to make their third trek to Russia. The fellow travelers worked on the agenda for their talks, but the agenda items had nothing to do with the conduct of the forthcoming campaign. The topics all dealt with the economic development of the new Korea and the emerging Russian-Korean-Chinese alliance. Kim's leisurely trip to and from Moscow (March 30–April 25) led the Korean Liaison Office (U.S.) and the Korean Research Bureau (ROK) to conclude that the threat of an April invasion had passed. On March 10, they estimated that the next likely invasion date would be in June. In the meantime, Stalin held a strategic review session for Kim and Pak. Would the Americans intervene? Did the Chinese support the invasion? No and yes, answered Kim. Stalin urged Kim to plan carefully because, if he was wrong about the American reaction, the Chinese would have to march to the rescue. The USSR would not risk a general war with the United States over Korea. Kim promised a weeklong campaign at worst. Pak promised a partisan uprising of 200,000. The happy warriors agreed that their forces would be ready, the advisers' work done, in June 1950.[26]

Stalin still thought that he should spread the risks of Kim Il-sung's invasion by involving the Chinese. He told Kim that the Koreans needed a firm commitment of approval and support from Mao Zedong, who had withheld such a commitment in 1949. Stalin essentially gave Mao a veto over a Korean war, which surprised and concerned Mao, since his strategic vision remained focused southward. Upon returning to Pyongyang, Kim Il-sung discussed a trip to Beijing with his Korean and Russian advisers and the likely response from Chairman Mao. The omens were excellent. Mao had told the Korean mission in Beijing that the United States had withdrawn troops from China and Korea and seemed reluctant to do much to aid the French in Indochina. Encouraged by this news, Kim Il-sung and Pak Hon-yong flew to Beijing on May 13 for a night and day of discussions. Mao remained skeptical, unimpressed with Kim and Pak's optimism. He asked Stalin for his personal views, expressed directly, not interpreted by the Koreans. Stalin responded with a full and accurate description of his talks with the Koreans. Mao continued his discussions with the Koreans through May 14 and 15, probing their assumptions and critiquing their operational concepts. Although Mao warned the Koreans that the People's Liberation Army had unfinished business on Taiwan, he conceded that he could send an expeditionary force to Korea if the Americans intervened with their own troops or sent a new Japanese army into the fray. The Koreans heard *would*, not *could*, and Kim stubbornly insisted that the Americans would not intervene or would come too late to save the South Koreans. By the evening of May 15, Kim Il-sung believed that the Chinese had agreed to his planned campaign, and Stalin encouraged that optimism with his approval of a Chinese-Korean alliance after the Communist victory.[27]

Although US-ROK intelligence did not collect all the details of the talks in Moscow, Pyongyang, and Beijing, the Korean-American intelligence community in Seoul at least saw tangible signs of military preparations for war in North Korea. The South Korean intelligence establishment (army G-2 and the Korean Research Bureau) believed that an invasion was certain and would come soon. Gen. Chae Pyong-dok ordered a wave of agents into North Korea—so many that Shin Sung-mo thought Chae might be opening secret negotiations with the Communists. The more reliable sources were agents who had joined the KPA and the Communist government in 1946. The Korean Liaison Office (KLO) sided with the Koreans: the KPA stood poised for an invasion. The KMAG G-2 agreed with the KLO's analysis of the changes in the North Korean force structure and deployments but questioned the likelihood of a June invasion—at the start of the rainy season—when August would be hot but dry. The Koreans insisted that June would be the month; they had studied the transcripts of a March 10–15 meeting of the senior officers of the *Boandae* brigades in Pyongyang. These officers had received missions that involved moving civilians away from the border, starting new fortification projects and road building, moving supplies and ammunition forward to protected dumps, establishing new traffic and population control points, and conscripting youths for military service and labor projects. The March prediction of a June invasion looked better all the time.[28]

The sense of impending doom that grew in Seoul did not spread to Tokyo and Washington. The first filter was Gen. Charles Willoughby, the FECOM G-2 and KLO's sponsor. Willoughby did not accept the Koreans' predictions, for several reasons. First, he did not trust Asian sources, especially planted agents, who were a notable source of misinformation and deception as double agents. Second, signals intelligence did not provide convincing corroboration. Third, Willoughby believed that Stalin would issue a definitive attack order, and Anglo-American intelligence would know of Stalin's "execute" directive and inform MacArthur. Finally, he believed that there would be no Korean war because such a conflict would be "contingent upon the success or failure of Communism in [the] Southeast Asian countries."[29] Nevertheless, Willoughby sent the KLO reports forward to the army staff (G-2), along with his own analysis. The KMAG G-2 sent its reports to Washington, too, through the State Department's military attaché reporting system, which provided reports to the army G-2 and the CIA.

The impact of the invasion predictions became softer with distance from the Thirty-eighth Parallel. The CIA's new Asian operations were undermanned and underfunded and focused on China and Southeast Asia. The signals intelligence effort—meager by World War II standards—targeted the Soviet Union. The CIA's analysts depended largely on military collectors and staff analysts, so its evaluations reflected the military penchant for capabilities evaluation and a reluctance to predict intentions. The CIA analysis of North Korea's military buildup, published on June 19, 1950, received interdepartmental concurrence. The CIA's review of the KPA's readiness was accurate enough, but it shied away from predicting an invasion.

The continued debate in Washington over the CIA's mission and management guaranteed that the director of central intelligence, Adm. Roscoe H. Hillenkoetter, would be unable to run his own agency, much less coordinate the efforts of at least ten other intelligence empires within the federal government. Every issue, large and small, set off a bureaucratic turf battle. The military intelligence staffs with fifty years' experience wanted to either run the CIA or force it into irrelevance. No one wanted another rogue Office of Strategic Services under presidential patronage. The National Security Council added nothing but more interagency debating. Either the secretary of state or the secretary of defense had to force an issue, dominate the analysis process, and then convince the president that there was a problem only he could address. Harry Truman, despite bold talk about the "buck stopping here," had not made a clean foreign policy decision that carried serious risk since George C. Marshall had forced him to face the Russian threat in Europe in 1947–1948. Certainly, Truman would not consider a war threat in Korea unless Douglas MacArthur, Dean Acheson, and the JCS persuaded him that American interests were imperiled. Such warnings had not reached the Oval Office by June 1950.[30]

IN SEOUL, TOKYO, AND WASHINGTON, 1950

The American mission in Seoul and KMAG shrugged off the paltry MDAP allocation for fiscal year 1950 and went to work on another military assistance proposal for fiscal year 1951. Neither Muccio nor Roberts would relent in their argument that the South Korean army must be changed from an internal security force into a real army capable of deterring or defeating a North Korean invasion. They would not endorse Rhee's scheme for a larger army, however; they reported that sixty-five thousand officers and men would be adequate if they were properly armed and trained. The army should improve its firepower with 4.2-inch mortars and the standard U.S. direct-support artillery piece, the M2A2 105mm howitzer. Roberts doubted that the ROKA could maintain and employ medium tanks without long and intensive training; he also concluded that Korea (like Italy) was too mountainous for the efficient use of armor, a costly acquisition that would bring limited firepower improvements. Any investment in tanks might endanger a more pressing need: more small warships such as the PC 703, more patrol boats, and an air force of forty F-51 fighter-bombers. KMAG was alive to the KPA's armor threat. The American advisers preferred an antitank defense based on blocking corridors with antitank minefields, covered by towed 57mm antitank guns. Even with an austere proposal, the projected fiscal year 1951 military assistance program would cost $20 million or twice Korea's 1950 allocation.[31]

In January 1950 General Roberts made his case for more military assistance at a conference on the future security needs of Asia. The meeting brought the Joint Chiefs of Staff to Tokyo for consultations with General MacArthur, the air force and navy commanders in the Far East, and the commanders of the American forces

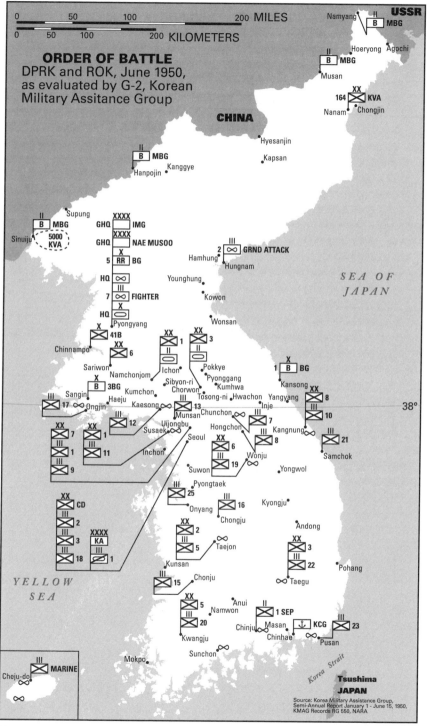

ORDER OF BATTLE
DPRK and ROK, June 1950,
as evaluated by G-2, Korean
Military Assitance Group

Map 7.

on Okinawa, in the Philippines, and in Korea. In his presentation, Roberts chose the high road in praising the ROKA for "genuine progress," enough progress, in fact, that it could stop a North Korean invasion unless "Russia furnished actual troops." Roberts felt "confident" that the South Koreans would prove steady defending their country. The ROKA "could handle any possible invasion by North Korean forces." He expressed concern, however, about reports that the North Koreans were receiving more heavy Russian weapons, especially tanks and aircraft. For the ROKA to become "a deterrent to external aggression," it would certainly need all he had asked for in the fiscal year 1951 military assistance proposal. And any reduction in the size of KMAG—a Pentagon pet project—would have to wait a year, which would allow the establishment of a training system and combat certification of every existing ROKA division. Roberts repeated his position that the ROKA did not need to be larger, just a great deal better.[32]

The Tokyo review revealed that the Pentagon and General MacArthur had two pressing issues that took much higher priority than the readiness of the ROKA and the growing menace of North Korea. From Washington's perspective, the most pressing issue was Japan's future—linked to that of the United States—and the development of a base system that would be guaranteed as part of the final peace treaty with Japan. With China now a hostile power, the urgency for a new relationship with Japan grew for both the State Department and the JCS. MacArthur was fully cognizant of this issue, but he added another: the security of Formosa. The concept of an offshore defense system for Asia and the western Pacific had no greater champion. State and the JCS might be most concerned with the Chinese march into Tibet and the anticipated assistance of the People's Liberation Army to the Vietnamese Communists, but the defense of Formosa—even governed by the discredited Guomindang—ensured the American position in the Philippines, the British hold on Hong Kong and Malaya, and Western influence in the newly independent Indonesia. MacArthur needed no tutorials on strategic vision, but he maintained special contact with two leading pro-American Chinese Nationalist generals, Ho Shili, the Nationalist representative in Tokyo, and Sun Liren, the head of the Ground Forces Combat Command on Taiwan. Although he kept the most rabid "Asia Firsters" at bay, MacArthur conducted his own tutorials on Taiwan for Arthur Hays Sulzberger, the editor-publisher of the *New York Times*.[33]

General Roberts continued to plead for greater training support while he waited for news of the fiscal year 1951 military assistance request. He received little encouragement on the latter, since the JCS had already committed the $75 million assigned to "areas around China" to the Philippines and the French expeditionary force in Indochina, with Taiwan a potential consumer as well. The U.S. Army, however, could arrange for officer training, and the army staff approved a plan to send twenty-three officers to schools in the United States and twenty-six to FECOM schools in Japan. The U.S. Air Force agreed to take three officers for training, and the U.S. Navy opened its fleet training centers in Japan to three different groups of Korean seamen. Although Roberts and Muccio welcomed the expanded training opportunities, they feared that all the signals from the Pentagon were for more heavy weather, a reduction of KMAG's advisory strength, and another "token" military assistance program for the next fiscal year.[34]

The Rhee administration did its best to shock the Americans into a more generous military assistance program. On May 10, 1950, Defense Minister Shin Sung-mo called a conference for the foreign press in Seoul and briefed them on the threat posed by the Korean People's Army. With its reinforcements from China, the KPA had six divisions, one tank brigade, three *Boandae* brigades serving as light infantry, and support units prepared for offensive operations — 183,000 officers and men. The KPA had 173 tanks, 30 armored cars, 609 76mm and 122mm artillery pieces, 1,162 medium and heavy mortars, 627 antitank guns, and almost 10,000 machine guns. Its air force had 195 aircraft, and its navy had 32 patrol boats. In reporting Minister Shin's briefing, Everett Drumright explained to General MacArthur that American analysts put the numbers at slightly lower levels, but they did not contest the presence of medium tanks, superior artillery, heavy mortars, and modern attack aircraft. Syngman Rhee wanted ominous estimates to support his requests for more military assistance. KMAG did an independent analysis and found the arms inventory of the KPA rapidly increasing. If the trend continued, the North Koreas would soon have the right combination of trained manpower and superior firepower to make a bid for unification by force, and most of the officials in the embassy and KMAG knew it.[35] The situation, however, had an awkward dimension. In March, General Roberts had sent a memo to the KMAG advisers with his personal assessment that the South Korean army could defeat its northern Communist rival if and when the KPA invaded. Roberts's assessment for the army staff was not quite the same: "If South Korea were attacked today by the inferior ground forces of North Korea, plus their Air Corps, I feel that South Korea would take a bloody nose." When briefing visiting VIPs, Roberts continued to emphasize the great strides the ROKA had made and how well it had used its American weapons for training and in fighting the Communist guerrillas. As Muccio and Roberts agreed, a certain amount of optimism increased the chances that Congress would provide the Koreans with more and better arms.[36]

While others argued about his views, Brig. Gen. William L. Roberts packed his bags in preparation for the trip home to California. Due to retire for age (sixty for brigadier generals) in September, the chief of KMAG qualified for reassignment after two years in Korea. He had taken a posting to a low-stress administrative assignment in California, near his home in Redlands. Satisfied that he was leaving behind a better South Korean army than he had found in 1948 — which was certainly true — Roberts enjoyed his last two months in Korea, with all the predictable "hail and farewell" events that pushed an aged commander toward his plane home. He attended a gala parade in April to celebrate Syngman Rhee's seventy-fifth birthday and heard the president tell Jim Hausman that the army belonged to its American advisers, not Rhee. Hausman responded that the army belonged to the government and the people of Korea. Rhee still insisted that KMAG commanded the army, that it was an Asian version of the U.S. Army. Roberts knew better. In a final message to the officers of the South Korean army, Roberts praised them for their patriotism, attention to duty, industry, and bravery. However, the general also provided a list of weaknesses to be corrected: lax security, misuse of terrain, too many frontal attacks without fire support, lack of quick and honest reporting, poor personal initiative, poor utilization of the best officers and men, brutality to civilians, lack of teamwork, poor care of equipment and vehicles, corruption, and too much interest in politics. Roberts stressed that the ROKA "will endure great hardship if properly led." Roberts was not going to use Korea as a platform to voice his criticisms. He attended the obligatory parties—most held in the *Piwon,* the "secret garden" of Kyongbok Palace—without comment. In dry, sunny weather, with the azaleas in bloom, Roberts and his staff hoped that each day of April and May that passed without an invasion made the Republic of Korea that much safer.[37]

On June 15 Roberts departed with great fanfare from Kimpo airport, headed for Tokyo and a rendezvous with General Bradley, chairman of the JCS, who was making an inspection tour of his Asia-Pacific outposts. Before he left Seoul, Roberts had discussed the condition of the ROKA with two respected international reporters, Frank Gibney of *Time* and Marguerite Higgins of the *New York Herald-Tribune*. He praised the ROKA for its improvement, its loyalty, its enthusiasm for hard training, and its use of the weapons in its possession. On the basis of the Roberts interview and discussions with other Americans in Seoul, Gibney reported that the ROKA was "the best [army] of its size in Asia," but its lack of an air force was its worst problem. Higgins praised KMAG for its insistence on weapons training, tactics, and physical fitness. She quoted Roberts as saying that the ROKA provided "maximum results at minimum cost." Neither Roberts nor the reporters predicted that the South Korean army could defeat its northern brethren. In fact, South Korean officers told them that their potential foe also trained hard and had better weapons.[38]

Secretary of State Acheson wondered why Roberts and the embassy seemed at odds with KMAG's official reports on the South Korean armed forces. The army staff had just received a KMAG analysis that new air and artillery shipments had made the KPA "capable of successful operations against [the] South." Muccio told Acheson exactly what he later said in congressional testimony. Although the ROKA had defeated the insurgent Koreans, particularly by killing five thousand dedicated guerrillas between September 1949 and April 1950, it was not prepared to stop a KPA invasion, which was now likely. Muccio explained that a report on May 4 had correctly assessed the ROKA's morale, physical conditioning, marksmanship skills, and small unit tactical training. Another report a week later had also been accurate. For all its splendid qualities, the ROKA could not stand before the aircraft, artillery, and tanks massing above the Thirty-eighth Parallel.[39]

On June 20 General Roberts spent forty minutes with General Bradley in Tokyo and discussed the condition of the ROKA. Bradley and Army Chief of Staff

Table 8.1. Estimates of Armed Forces, Korean People's Army, Democratic People's Republic of Korea, May–June 1950

	USSR Military Mission[a]	U.S. Embassy[b]	KMAG[c]
Manpower in combat units	130,000	183,000	103,000
Tanks, T-34	151	155	64
Antitank guns	113	380	356
76mm and 122mm howitzers and guns (self-propelled and towed)	286	609	296
82mm and 120mm mortars	748	1,162	637
Machine guns	3,118	9,728	6,032
Aircraft	211	195	100
Naval ships and patrol/landing craft	30	24	12

[a] USSR Military Mission, Democratic People's Republic of Korea, June 1950.
[b] U.S. Embassy report of Ministry of Defense, Republic of Korea, press briefing, May 11, 1950, Radiograms, 1950, MacArthur Papers.
[c] Korean Military Advisory Group (KMAG), *Semi-Annual Report,* June 15, 1950; U.S. Embassy to CINCFE, May 21, 1950, MacArthur Papers.

J. Lawton Collins later claimed that Roberts had called the Koreans "the best dog-gone shooting army outside the United States," an army that could stop the North Koreans. "Roberts was completely reassuring . . . we had no cause for concern in Korea." The South Koreans had "the best little army in Asia." A week earlier, William C. Foster, deputy administrator of the Economic Cooperation Administration, testified before Congress, drawing on what he called expert advice, that the South Korean army was "prepared to meet any challenge by the North Korean forces." Whatever wishful thinking occurred before June 25, 1950, and whatever scapegoating occurred afterward, Roberts and Muccio had consistently warned Washington that the ROKA had serious shortcomings in the weaponry and training necessary to blunt a North Korean invasion. Roberts's weapons request in the 1951 military assistance program reflected the Korean armed forces' pressing needs. Secretary of State Acheson and Secretary of State Johnson later admitted to a congressional joint committee probing the conduct of the Korean War that they knew in June 1950 that the South Korean army was probably not good enough to prevent the North Koreans from taking Seoul.[40]

Had Generals Bradley and Collins bothered to examine the status of the South Korean army, they would have concluded that it was ill prepared to face a North Korean invasion. The evidence was at hand: KMAG's semiannual report, January 1–June 15, 1950, completed to coincide with General Roberts's departure. The five principals who guided the report were Col. W. H. Sterling Wright (KMAG chief of staff), Lt. Col. Lewis D. Vieman (schools adviser), Lt. Col. Ralph W. Hansen (G-3 adviser), Capt. James H. Hausman (liaison officer to the chief of staff, ROKA), and Capt. John P. Reed (G-2 adviser). The KMAG planners had no delusions. In a conference with Muccio in April, the planners agreed that the ROKA had done well in defeating the guerrillas and holding fast along the Thirty-eighth

Parallel. The Korean National Police remained a problem, but the army, for all its turmoil, looked like a positive force for stability. In terms of sheer numbers, the opposing armies were balanced, with approximately 100,000 soldiers each, but the KPA had just "officially" joined three divisions from the Chinese army. In fact, army G-2 staffs in Korea, Japan, and Washington had a good grasp of the North Korean order of battle in terms of units, manpower, and armaments—better than the CIA's June 19 assessment. Time and again, KMAG had reported to FECOM G-2 that the KPA's armored force (whether 151 T-34 tanks or 64, as in the US-ROK estimate), air force, and mobile field artillery gave the KPA a decisive advantage in offensive operations mounted with any degree of surprise.

The South Korean army had fought guerrillas, battled border raiders, purged dissidents, doubled its numbers, and tried to train. KMAG's plan was to complete battalion-level training by July 31, 1950, which culminated cycles of individual, platoon, and company training. In June KMAG certified sixteen infantry battalions as trained, although they were still underequipped. Thirty battalions were still in the company training phase, and seventeen battalions remained in platoon training. For individuals, the emphasis had been on rifle marksmanship; for infantry squads, the training focused on tank hunting-killing with mines and demolitions. The M3 howitzer batteries and 57mm antitank cannon companies remained in the Seoul area for centralized instruction. Largely because of equipment shortages and the lack of trained leaders and technicians, KMAG rated only four infantry battalions as even 70 percent combat-ready, while all the rest were only 45 to 50 percent ready on average. Some of the unit personnel shortages reflected the assignment of twenty thousand soldiers to schools in Korea and Japan. In the summer of 1949 the two Korean armies had rough parity, but after January 1950 that balance was upset by an infusion of Russian weapons, vehicles, and equipment. The imponderable was whether the Russians would allow Kim Il-sung to unify Korea by conquest.[41]

The State-Defense debate on the threat to Korea and the status of the ROK armed forces made no difference in the fiscal year 1951 military assistance appropriations. The allocation for the Philippines and South Korea, still regarded as Category III or "token aid" nations, was $16 million out of a $1.2 billion authorization. In an interview for *U.S. News and World Report,* Senator Tom Connally (D-Tex.), an administration spokesman, again stressed that Korea was a nonstrategic nation and did not require increased weapons purchases. The Seoul embassy reported another bout of anger and despair in Rhee's household and proposed that State at least persuade Defense to turn loose the F-51s in Japan that the U.S. Air Force no longer wanted. The request disappeared into a bureaucratic void.[42]

The confusing assessments of June 1950 reflected something more substantial than General Roberts's offhand cheerleading, the shared inattention of three senior army generals who had some responsibility for Korean security, imprecise media reporting, and bureaucratic bungling. The Muccio-Roberts arms request for fiscal year 1951 required the Department of Defense and Congress to believe that

South Korea faced certain invasion soon, but also that Syngman Rhee's army had already put its $56 million of direct military assistance to good use. Congress needed to ignore the cost of stationing American troops in Korea and the value of Japanese vested property transferred to the Ministry of National Defense. Judgments about military assistance remained hostage to other factors: the failure of military aid to improve the Chinese Nationalist army, the May 1950 decision to make direct military equipment transfers to the French colonial army fighting in Indochina, the effectiveness of more than $100 million in economic aid to Korea, and the inadequate fiscal and monetary controls of the Rhee regime. In any event, the withdrawal of the U.S. Fifth Regimental Combat Team from the approaches to Seoul in June–July 1949 sealed Korea's fate. This action, not careless or careful words uttered in Washington or Seoul, heartened the Communists. The year of lost preparedness (1949–1950) could not be recovered by a sudden flood of tanks, artillery, and aircraft to ROK armed forces that were ill prepared to ingest American military technology—even World War II vintage. The South Korean officer corps had no equivalents to the Soviet Koreans who had fought the Germans in World War II. In addition, the Russians had trained thousands of KPA soldiers in Korea, Manchuria, and the Asian Soviet Union for four years. From Pyongyang's perspective, the end of the Rhee regime was a matter of timing, not strategy.

Epilogue and Prologue, June 1950

The enormity of the diplomatic task that faced John Foster Dulles, former member of the American delegation to the United States and former U.S. senator from New York, did not dismay the stern internationalist. He welcomed President Harry Truman's invitation to become an ambassador-at-large in Dean Acheson's State Department in May 1950. The president recognized that he needed to revive foreign policy bipartisanship since the Taft-McCarthy-Knowland pack in the Senate had come to full howl over the "loss" of China and the growing commitment to the North Atlantic Treaty Organization. Whatever their crusading impulses to attack Communism, the Taft-McCarthy-Knowland Republicans preferred isolationism to engagement, unilateralism to collective internationalism, and the low-cost pursuit of domestic Communists to the costly containment of Soviet imperialism. Still convinced that Communism was an international problem that could be conquered with political liberalism, collective security through the United Nations, Christian virtues, and free-market economics, Dulles, supported by Senator Arthur Vandenberg, braved the carping of oppositionist Republicans to stay in the fight. Against his better judgment, he accepted an interim appointment to the U.S. Senate in 1949 to fill a vacancy created by the resignation of Robert Wagner. He entered electoral politics at the urging of Vandenberg and another patron, Governor Thomas E. Dewey. He stood for a special election to the Senate in early 1950 and proved a poor campaigner; his defeat by Herbert Lehman surprised no one. With Vandenberg dying of cancer and Dewey virtually killed by the presidential election of 1948, Dulles felt an even greater need to build an independent political position, much like his fellow New Yorker, W. Averell Harriman, a Democrat and already a counselor to Truman. Acheson and Assistant Secretary Dean Rusk urged the president to use Dulles to fend off the Republicans. Dulles made Truman no promises in terms of supporting every policy, but he pledged his willingness to help the administration rescue its Far East policy. China might be a lost cause for bipartisanship, but Japan and Formosa were not. With Vandenberg's and Lehman's approval, Truman (with some doubts) appointed Dulles to the secretary of state's staff, much to the unhappiness of the Taftites.[1]

Acheson had a perfect assignment for Dulles: persuade Douglas MacArthur that the time had come to phase out the occupation of Japan, negotiate a peace treaty with the Yoshida government, and arrange for the permanent conversion of Okinawa and other sites on the home islands into permanent American bases. As far as anyone could tell, the mission would be easy since MacArthur had announced that the Supreme Commander Allied Powers should be scrapped and Japanese sovereignty restored. Dulles also knew of a plan to rearm Japan, a policy that MacArthur did not welcome. Dulles correctly assumed that he would become the principal negotiator when the United States and Japan opened discussions about their new relationship. He had no intention of touching the Formosa issue. Peace with Japan was a goal that Dulles thought worthy of his talents and tenacity.

Acheson had an additional assignment: go to Seoul and reassure Syngman Rhee that the United States and the United Nations would not abandon him to his enemies foreign and domestic. Ambassador John Muccio correctly reported that Defense Department officials had visited Tokyo, but never Seoul, and the Koreans viewed these snubs as a sign of abandonment. A longtime champion of the Republic of Korea, Dulles decided to go to Seoul first. In addition to the reassurance mission, Dulles would make sure that Rhee would not challenge the treaty negotiations with Japan, which would exclude him and probably produce little immediate benefit for Korea. Rhee needed even more, however. Acheson wanted Dulles to make as many public statements as possible that the United States did not define its relationship with Korea simply by the calculus of militarily defined strategic plans but by many other criteria embodied in the UN General Assembly resolutions that Dulles himself had crafted. To a degree, Rhee had earned some respect because he had accepted (however reluctantly) the demands of the United States and the United Nations Commission on Korea (UNCOK) that he hold elections for the National Assembly on May 30, 1950. With invasion scares, battles over amendments to the constitution of 1948, cabinet shuffles, and continuing economic woes, the assembly election had been uncertain. Rhee had accepted with bad grace the criticisms of the original arrangements for the balloting and the security of polling places. He had, however, again bowed to an American threat of nonrenewal of economic assistance and accepted a plan for monitoring the polls and counting the results that produced a freer election than the one held two years earlier. The superficial monitoring conducted by seven small UNCOK observation teams discovered no serious electoral abuses.[2]

The results of the National Assembly election of 1950, with 86 percent of registered voters participating, made the Republic of Korea appear more democratic than ever. The Korean voters rejected the "traditional" parties and voted for assemblymen who ran as independents and had held no prior office. Of the 218 candidates elected, only 35 had served in the First Assembly. The largest single group of assemblymen, the independents, numbered 133; 72 independents had never held office of any kind. Rhee's National Society for the Rapid Realization of Korean Independence elected only 18 members, 17 of whom were newcomers. The Democratic National Party (the reorganized Korean Democratic Party) sent 24 members to Seoul, all but 5 of them newcomers. More than half of the 43 third-party assemblymen were new to officeholding. Although the Second Assembly did not produce any other sort of demographic or sociological revolution, the assembly appeared to be a hopeful step away from the personalism and cronyism of the past. The political challenge was whether Rhee and his ministers could work with an assembly that could not be easily controlled or predicted.[3]

With expectations soaring, Ambassador John Foster Dulles and his entourage, which included John M. Allison as political adviser and two friendly newspaper editors, deplaned at Kimpo airport at 11 A.M. on Saturday, June 17, 1950. President Rhee and the ROK army band greeted the visitors with enthusiasm. Dulles came armed with speeches written with the help of Rusk, Paul Nitze, and Allison. The aircraft had stopped in Japan only to refuel. President Rhee could not have been more pleased: "Mr. Dulles comes direct to Korea. We love him all the more for coming here first. We have been playing second fiddle so long we are getting tired of it."[4] The Seoul press praised Dulles as Korea's greatest friend at the United Nations, the "midwife at the birth of Korea." The Seoul newspapers urged all Koreans to remain peaceful and show proper respect for "the supreme advisor to the US Department of State." Even Allison, the harried chief of the Office of Northeast Asia Affairs, was impressed with the Koreans' enthusiastic sincerity. Dulles hit the right note in his first public remarks at Kimpo; he had been invited to Korea in 1938 by the Japanese, but he had refused to visit a captive nation. Now he could come to a free Korea that would remain free.[5]

The Dulles mission saw the embattled border on Sunday, June 18, on a trip to the defense sector of the ROK Seventh Division at Uijongbu. Dulles had begun to get a sense of Korea's peril the day before in a two-hour embassy briefing and a short visit with Rhee. He then attended a dinner reception at the home of the secretary of the Presbyterian mission board. A delegation of Protestant missionaries had outlined the financial and political barriers confronting their medical and education programs; they also raised concerns about a war. The trip to the "front" at the Thirty-eighth Parallel the next day gave Dulles a chance to see the ROKA demonstrate its tactical skills and hear Minister of Defense Shin Sung-mo, Chief of Staff Chae Pyong-dok, and Brig. Gen. Yu Jae-hung, the division's new commander, describe the challenges of opposing an enemy that had aircraft, tanks, and superior artillery. General Yu emphasized his lack of land mines and antitank shells. Col. W. H. Sterling Wright, acting chief of the Korean Military Advisory Group (KMAG), and Maj. Joseph W. Billelo, a division senior adviser, stressed the high morale and skill of the ROK soldiers. The American officers told the visitors that the South Koreans could stop an invasion. The entire group advanced to an observation post for a photo opportunity—a memorable picture of Dulles, homburg on tight, staring into North Korea. Dulles told the accompanying press and officials present that superficial materiel superiority should not dismay the Koreans. "The deterrent to open military aggression is the existence of a central protecting power." Everyone assumed that he meant the United States, not the United Nations. Dulles added that Korea proved that an Asian nation could "contain the tide of Communism in the East."[6]

Dulles knew his approved message well: Korea was not alone. He stressed this theme in a private meeting with Rhee the next morning (June 19), then addressed the first meeting of the Second National Assembly that afternoon. Dulles welcomed Korea to the universal struggle against tyranny, a war in which the United States had "enlisted" during its revolt against Great Britain. Now the war on despotism pitted the free world against Communism, and Korea was at the front. Despite the skeptics' predictions of disaster, the Republic of Korea had made great strides in two years: held two elections, defeated an insurgency, widened individual liberty, and reshaped its economy. All these tasks had barely begun, to be sure, but showed true promise. "You are conducting what may go down in history as the Great Korean Experiment, an experiment which, in its way, can exert a moral influence in the 20th century as profound as that which, in the 19th century, was exerted by what was then called the Great American Experiment. That is why the eyes of the free world are fixed upon you. You carry the hopes and aspirations of multitudes." Korea now enjoyed the support of the American people and of the United Nations, which could not officially admit Korea, for technical reasons, but viewed free Korea as "spiritually, a part of the United Nations." The United Nations required "all nations to refrain from any threat or use of force against your territorial integrity or political independence." The free world had a moral obligation to protect Korea as long as it pursued the goals of prosperity and liberty. "You are not alone. You will never be alone so long as you continue to play worthily your part in the great design of human freedom."[7]

While Dulles made his appointed rounds, William R. Mathews and Carl McCardle, the attached newsmen, met with Colonel Wright for a briefing on KMAG and the South Korean army. Wright praised the Korean soldiers for their bravery and zeal. All they needed were a few tanks, a small air force, and better artillery to be the best army in Asia. Wright showed the editors a map of the North Korean army's positions and pointed out its offensive posture. Mathews noted: "He says positively that he will get twenty-four hours' notice of any impending attack by North Koreans; expressed absolute confidence in the thoroughness of his intelligence." Wright said that he had received three earlier, accurate attack warnings for the Uijongbu sector and assumed that the system would provide adequate warning in the future.[8]

Dulles took his message to two more meetings with President and Mrs. Rhee, a conference with Korean educators organized by Yonsei University's George L. Paik (minister of education), UNCOK, committees of Korean businessmen and government economic planners, foreign diplomats, and Korean religious leaders.

On June 20 Dulles made another major speech at Seoul National University, where he received an honorary degree for his efforts in the United Nations to create a free, unified Korea. He stressed that liberty and education combined to defeat tyranny. In two press conferences with Western journalists and the Korean press that afternoon, Dulles stressed that no peace treaty with Japan would be drafted that did not reflect Korea's interests. He added that he did not believe Korea needed a "Pacific Pact" to ensure its security. In a final communiqué issued after his early-morning flight to Tokyo on June 21, Dulles returned to his primary message. The Republic of Korea in two years had emerged from its captive colonial past and proved its potential to defend itself, feed and shelter itself, and govern itself. The Communist propaganda line that no one would defend Korea, hawked with stridency by Radio Pyongyang, was "silly." Abandonment was not Korea's future. "I hope that the days I have spent here . . . will be one more evidence of the fact that, as I said to the National Assembly, Korea does not stand alone."[9]

If words could stop tanks, Dulles had done his best to build the Koreans' resolve to resist whatever challenge Kim Il-sung mounted next. Whether he truly spoke for more than the Department of State remained to be tested.

Appendix

The Romanization of Korean and Chinese

Since the creation of a written Korean language in the sixteenth century by linguistic savants in the employ of King Sejong, the romanization of Korean—that is, changing the Korean phonetic alphabet into a Western alphabet—has defied consistency in written and pronounced form. It still does. Despite a "Koreanized" romanization system produced by the National Academy of the Korean Language for the Ministry of Culture and Tourism in 2000, written Korean still confounds Western authors and readers. There is a similar but much less severe problem with Chinese. Since this book is written for a non-Asian audience, I should explain my system. It too is inconsistent, but it is less likely to cause confusion for readers who have only a passing acquaintance with Korean and Chinese and need to see consistent words but not necessarily pronounce them. I have attempted to honor Korean pronunciation whenever possible.

This book uses elements of the McCune-Reischauer system of romanizing Korean, developed in the 1930s. This system has been modified in practice by Korean-published, English-language newspapers in Seoul. The essence of the changes instituted by the *Korea Times* and *Korea Herald* is that they dropped the diacritical marks (the breve and apostrophe) used to distinguish unaspirated consonants from aspirated consonants and simple vowels from compound vowels (diphthongs), which have no easy English rendering. The *Times-Herald* system, of course, simplifies electronic typesetting, although Korean-capable typewriters and computers can produce McCune-Reischauer diacritical marks. But dropping the marks can produce misleading pronunciations. For instance, some aspirated and unaspirated consonants can be romanized as one of two letters (e.g., *B* or *P*) that certainly sound and look different in Korean. In addition, romanized letters can represent two possible pronunciation choices (e.g., *R* or *L*) that usually (but not consistently) can be divined by their position in syllable order within a single word. A further complication is the irregular romanization of Korean family names; the

259

most perplexing (for Westerners) is ol, which becomes Yi, Lee, or Rhee, depending on the person's preference. For example, the name of prominent nationalist politician Yŏ Un-hŏng appears in American reports as Lyuh Woon Hyung, and Yi Pom-sŏk was Lee Bum Suk in his own usage.

The new Korean romanization system will eventually bring greater consistency and close the gap between written, Westernized Korean and spoken Korean, but its short-term effect is to introduce a new level of confusion for Anglophones. Therefore, I have spelled names of Korean people and places as they were romanized between 1945 and 2000, but using the *Times-Herald* system of eliminating the diacritical marks. Whereas the new Korean system attempts to use different English letters to differentiate between unaspirated and aspirated consonants and combinations of English vowels that produce (or might produce) vowel sounds indicated by the McCune-Reischauer diacriticals, I have used the romanization forms that *look* the most familiar to Anglophones.

Thus, Taegu remains Taegu, not Daegu. Pusan remains Pusan, not Busan. Pyongyang is Pyongyang, not P'yŏngyang, as it is in the McCune-Reischauer system. In the case of the vowel ŏ, I have romanized it as o, for visual consistency, even though *dŏk* is pronounced "duck," more or less. Although my choices may be inconsistent with other romanization systems, I hope they are consistent enough in a visual sense for Westerners. Koreans will know who and where I mean anyway, given their long familiarity with the romanization problem and their own alphabet. When a specific romanization has been sanctified by history, such as the names Syngman Rhee and Paik Sun-yup, I have not changed that usage. I have, however, adopted Yo Un-hyong, not Lyuh Woon Hyung, and Pak Hon-yong, not Park Hon-young, in two other important renderings. In another area of Korean linguistic confusion, I have romanized Sin, when used in a family name or place name, as Shin when it is the first syllable, but not when it is the last, as in Shin Sung-mo. I apologize to the *hangul* (written Korean alphabet) and *hanguk mal* (spoken Korean) purists—Koreans and others alike—but as my patient instructors at the Korean Language Institute, Yonsei University, once said, few Anglophones ever get Korean right in any form, and it is all "contexty" anyway.

Modernized, romanized Chinese presents a somewhat different problem, since Chinese ideographic symbols were never transformed into a native phonetic alphabet. The standardized twentieth-century system was Wade-Giles, which attempted with modest success to change spoken Chinese (Mandarin dialect) into a written form using the Western alphabet. Since the Chinese Revolution, a native Chinese romanization system has replaced Wade-Giles, not just in the People's Republic of China but also among millions of overseas Chinese of all political persuasions. The difficulty is that Anglophones unfamiliar with the "new" Chinese find some of the current renderings confusing. That Peking became Peiping and is now Beijing is not too difficult since the current usage is common in the West. The same phenomenon applies to Mao Zedong, who was once Mao Tse-tung; Zhou Enlai, who was once Chou En-lai; and Lin Biao, who was once Lin Piao. But what is one to make of Jiang Jieshi, who was once known as Chiang Kai-shek? (Chiang Kai-shek is the romanization from the Cantonese dialect.) Again, I have made a usage compromise, but one that leans toward present and future use, not, as in the case of Korean, toward past forms. Except when the historic (Wade-Giles) form seems more appropriate because of prior Western usage, I have used the modern Chinese romanization, as in Mao Zedong.

Following are two tables that show recurrent names of Korean people and places in three forms: *Times-Herald* (modified); National Academy of the Korean Language (2000), which is closest to spoken Korean; and McCune-Reischauer.

Korean People

Times-Herald (modified)	National Academy of the Korean Language (2000)	McCune-Reischauer
An Ho-sang	An Ho-sang	An Ho-sang
Ben C. Limb	Im Byeong-jik	Im Pyŏng-jik
Chae Pyong-dok	Chae Byeong-deok	Ch'ae Pyŏng-dŏk
Chang Do-yong	Jhang Do-yeong	Chang Do-yŏng
Chang Myon (John Chang)	Jang Myeon	Chang Myŏn
Chang Taek-sang	Jang Taek-sang	Chang T'aek-sang
Cho Pyong-ok (Chough Pyung Ok)	Jo Byeong-ok	Cho Pyŏng-ok
Choe Dok-sin	Choe Deok-sin	Ch'oe Dŏk-sin
Choe Yong-gon	Choe Yeong-geon	Ch'oe Yŏng-gŏn
Chung Il-kwon	Jeong Il-gwon	Chŏng Il-gwŏn
Kang Kon	Gang Geon	Kang Kŏn
Kim Chaek	Gim Chaek	Kim Ch'aek
Kim Chong-won	Gim Jeon-gwon	Kim Chong-wŏn
Kim Il-sung	Kim Il-seung	Kim Il-sŏng
Kim Mu-chong (Mu-Chong)	Kim Mu-jeong	Kim Mu-chŏng
Kim Paik-il	Kim Baek-il	Kim Paek-il
Kim Sung-su (Kim Sung-soo)	Kim Seong-su	Kim Sŏng-su
Kim Tae-sun	Kim Tae-seon	Kim Tae-sŏn
Louis Yim	Im Yeong-sin	Im Yŏng-sin
Paik In-yup	Baek In-yeop	Paek In-yŏp
Paik Sun-yup	Baek Seon-yeop	Paek Sŏn-yŏp
Pak Hon-yong (Park Hon-young)	Bak Heon-yeong	Pak Hŏn-yŏng
Shin Ik-hui (Shinicky)	Sin Ik-hui	Sin Ik-hŭi

Shin Sung-mo	Sin Seong-mo	Sin Sŏng-mo
Shin Tae-yong	Sin Tae-yeong	Sin Tae-yŏng
Son Won-il	Son Weon-il	Son Wŏn-il
(Sohn Won-il)		
Song Yo-chan	Song Yo-chan	Song Yo-ch'an
Syngman Rhee	Syngman Rhee	Yi Sŏng-man
Won Yong-dok	Won Yong-deok	Wŏn Yong-dŏk
Yi Hong-gun	Yi Hyeong-geun	Yi Hyŏng-gŭn
(Lee Hyung-Keun)		
Yi Pom-sok	Yi Peom-seok	Yi Pŏm-sŏk
(Lee Bum-suk)		
Yi Sang-cho	Yi Sang-cho	Yi Sang-ch'o
(Lee Sang-cho)		
Yi Ung-jun	Yi Eung-jun	Yi Ung-jun
(Lee Ung-joon)		
Yo Un-hyong	Yeo Un-hyeong	Yŏ Un-hyŏng
(Lyuh Woon Hyung)		
Yu Jae-hyung	Yu Jae-heung	Yu Jae-h'yung

Korean Places

Times-Herald (modified)	National Academy of the Korean Language (2000)	McCune-Reischauer
Cheju-do	Jeju-do	Cheju-to
Chiri-san	Jirisan	Chirisan
Chollabuk-do	Jeollabuk-do	Chŏllabuk-to
Chollanam-do	Jeollanam-do	Chŏllanam-to
Chunchon	Chuncheon	Ch'unch'ŏn
Chungchongduk-do	Chungcheongbuk-do	Ch'ungch'ŏngbuk-do
Chungchongnam-do	Chungcheongnam-do	Ch'ungch'ŏngnam-do
Han-gang	Hangang	Han-gang
Imjin-gang	Imjingang	Imjin-gang
Inchon	Incheon	Inch'ŏn
Kaesong	Gaeseong	Kaesŏng
Kangnam	Gangnam	Kangnam
Kangnung	Gangneung	Kangnŭng
Kangwon-do	Gangwon-do	Kangwon-do
Kimpo	Gimpo	Kimp'o
Kunsan	Gunsan	Kunsan
Kwangju	Gwangju	Kwangju
Kyonggi-do	Gyeonggi-do	Kyŏnggi-do
Kyongsangbuk-do	Gyeongsangbuk-do	Kyŏngsangbuk-to

Kyongsangnam-do	Gyeongsangnam-do	Kyŏngsangnam-to
Mokpo	Mokpo	Mokp'o
Paektusan	Baekdusan	Paektusan
Pohang	Pohang	P'ohang
Pusan	Busan	Pusan
Pyongyang	Pyeongyang	P'yŏngyang
Sokcho	Sokcho	Sokch'o
Taebaek-san	Taebaeksan	T'aebaeksan
Taegu	Daegu	Taegu
Taejon	Daejeon	Taejŏn
Tongduchon	Dongducheon	Tongduch'ŏn
Uijongbu	Uijeongbu	Uijŏngbu
Wonju	Wonju	Wŏnju
Yongdungpo	Yeongdeungpo	Yŏngdŭngp'o
Yongsan	Yongsan	Yongsan
Youido	Yeouido	Yŏŭido

Notes

INTRODUCTION

1. For an evaluative discussion of Korean War historiography, see Lester Brune, ed., *The Korean War: Handbook of the Literature and Research* (Westport, Conn.: Greenwood Press, 1996); Rosemary Foote, "Making Known the Unknown War: Policy Analysis of the Korean Conflict in the Last Decade," *Diplomatic History* 15 (Summer 1991): 411–31; Hakjoon Kim, "International Trends in Korean War Studies," *Korean War Studies* 14 (Summer 1990): 326–70; Judith Monroe-Leighton, "A Post-Revisionist Scrutiny of America's Role in the Cold War in Asia, 1945–1950," *Journal of American–East Asian Relations* 1 (Spring 1992): 73–98; Callum MacDonald, "Rediscovering History—New Light on the Unknown War," *Bulletin of Concerned Asian Scholars* 24 (October–December 1992): 62–69; and Philip West, "Interpreting the Korean War," *American Historical Review* 94 (February 1989): 80–96.

2. Foreign scholars have been most perceptive in identifying the shortcomings of Western treatment of the war: Man Ha-heo, "From Civil War to International War," *Korea and World Affairs* 14 (Summer 1990): 303–25; Yasuda Jun, "A Survey: China and the Korean War," *Social Science Japan Journal* 1 (1998): 71–83; Akagi Janji, "A Select Bibliography on the War," *Gunji Shiyaku* 36 (June 2000); Alexandre Y. Mansourov, "Korean War Studies in the United States" (paper presented at the Korean War Conference, Yonsei University, Seoul, ROK, July 14, 2000).

3. I have already proposed this framework of interpretation in shorter, earlier works: Allan R. Millett, "Understanding Is Better Than Remembering: The Korean War, 1945–1954," Seventh Dwight D. Eisenhower Lecture in War and Peace (Department of History, Kansas State University, 1997); Allan R. Millett, "The Korean War: A 50-Year Critical Historiography," *Journal of Strategic Studies* 24 (March 2001): 188–224; and Allan R. Millett, "The Korean War," in *Encyclopedia Britannica* (forthcoming).

4. For an introduction to modern Korean history, see Andrew Nahm, *Korea: Tradition and Transformation—A History of the Korean People,* 2d ed. (Elizabeth, N.J.: Hollym International, 1996); Yi Jyu-tae, *Modern Transformation of Korea* (Seoul: Sejong Publish-

ing Company, 1970); Carter J. Eckert, Ki-baik Lee, Young Ick Lew, Michael Robinson, and Edward W. Wagner, *Korea Old and New: A History* (Cambridge: Korea Institute, Harvard University, 1990); Bruce Cumings, *Korea's Place in the Sun: A Modern History* (New York: W. W. Norton, 1997); Donald N. Clark, *Living Dangerously in Korea: The Western Experience 1900–1950* (Norwalk, Conn.: East Bridge, 2003); and Shin Yong-ha, *Modern Korean History and Nationalism* (Seoul: Jimoondang Publishing, 2000).

5. Don Oberdorfer, *The Two Koreas: A Contemporary History* (Reading, Mass.: Addison-Wesley, 1997).

6. Andrew C. Nahm, "U.S. Policy and the Japanese Annexation of Korea," in *U.S.-Korean Relations 1882–1982,* ed. Taehwan Kwak, John Chang, Soon Sung Cho, and Shannon McCune (Seoul: Institute for Far Eastern Studies, Kyungnam University, 1982), 34–53. The Chemulpo or Shufeldt Treaty of 1882, Article I, contained that "good offices" clause. This article was interpreted by the Chinese and Korean courts as a pledge to help check Japanese intrusions in Korean politics, an interpretation immediately and consistently rejected by the State Department but taken seriously by American medical, educational, and religious missionaries in Korea after 1885. The American policy of "absolute neutrality" favored Japan and did so consciously. Even the Open Door policy (1900) did not apply to Korea.

7. The Peter Kim story is reconstructed from the documents in the Kim Papers, donated by Gen. Marshall Carter to the General George C. Marshall Library, Lexington, Va. The basic sources are Capt. Peter Kim, USAR, "Statement of Personal History," DD398, October 12, 1953, and T-5 Peter Kim, AUS, to Col. Paul J. B. Murphy, CE, USA, August 11, 1945.

8. Kim to Murphy, August 11, 1945.

9. Col. Marshall Carter, GS, USA, to C/S, U.S. Forces, China Theater, December 6, 1945, Kim Papers.

10. Kim DD398 (1953) with attached statements. Recalled to active duty in October 1950, Peter Kim served on the U.S. Eighth Army's intelligence staff until June 1952 as a Chinese language interpreter-translator and specialist in security issues and POW rescues. The army awarded him two Bronze Stars and a coveted Soldier's Medal for lifesaving during the Korean War. His postwar career included serving as a special assistant to Lt. Gen. Marshall Carter, deputy director of the CIA, and as a Chinese language instructor at the Defense Language Institute. He retired as a major in the infantry in 1964, having completed twenty years of satisfactory federal service.

11. Wanne J. Joe with Hongkyn A. Choe, *Traditional Korea: A Cultural History,* rev. ed. (Seoul: Hollym, 1997), 75–107, 212–19, 257–64, 330–53.

12. Kenneth M. Wells, ed., *South Korea's Minjung Movement: The Culture and Politics of Dissidence* (Honolulu: University of Hawaii Press, 1995); Tae-hung Ha, *Guide to Korean Culture* (Seoul: Yonsei University Press, 1968), 147–72; Keith Pratt and Richard Rutt with James Hoare, comps., *Korea: A Historical and Cultural Dictionary* (Richmond, Surrey, U.K.: Curzon, 1999).

13. Donald Stone Macdonald, *The Koreans,* 2d ed. (Boulder, Colo.: Westview Press, 1990), 113–77.

14. On the relationship of the Pacific war to Asian anticolonialism and postwar conflict, see Christopher Thorne, *The Far Eastern War: States and Societies, 1941–45* (London: Unwin, 1985); D. M. Condit et al., *Challenge and Response in Internal Conflict,* vol. 1, *The Experience of Asia* (Washington, D.C.: American University of the Department of

the Army, 1968); Anthony Clayton, *The War of French Decolonization* (London: Longman, 1994); and Michael Carver, *War since 1945* (New York: G. P. Putnam's, 1980). For the revolutionary impact of World War II on China and the course of the continued civil war that followed, see Edward L. Dreyer, *China at War, 1901–1949* (London: Longman, 1995), and James C. Hsiung and Steven I. Levine, eds., *China's Bitter Victory: The War with Japan, 1937–1945* (London: M. E. Sharpe, 1992).

15. J. Bowyer Bell, *On Revolt: Strategies of National Liberation* (Cambridge: Harvard University Press, 1976); Eric Wolf, *Peasant Wars of the Twentieth Century* (New York: Harper and Row, 1968); John Shy and Thomas W. Collier, "Revolutionary War," in *Makers of Modern Strategy,* ed. Peter Paret (Princeton, N.J.: Princeton University Press, 1986), 815–62; Samuel B. Griffith, ed., *Mao Tse-tung on Guerrilla Warfare* (New York: Praeger, 1961); Chalmers Johnson, *Autopsy on People's War* (Berkeley: University of California Press, 1973); George K. Tanham, *Communist Revolutionary Warfare* (New York: Praeger, 1961); Michael McClintock, *Instruments of Statecraft: U.S. Guerrilla Warfare, Counterinsurgency and Counter-terrorism, 1940–1990* (New York: Pantheon, 1992); and Liu Jikun, *Mao Zedong's Art of War* (Hong Kong: Hai Feng Publishing, 1995).

1. THE YEARS OF DIVISION, 1919–1945

1. This account of the March First Movement is based on Dae-yeol Ku, *Korea under Colonialism: The March First Movement and Anglo-Japanese Relations* (Seoul: Royal Asiatic Society–Korea, 1985); Frank P. Baldwin, "The March First Movement: Korean Challenge and Japanese Response" (Ph.D. diss., Columbia University, 1969); Lee Chong-sik, *The Politics of Korean Nationalism* (Berkeley: University of California Press, 1963); Shin Yong-ha, *Essays in Korean Social History* (Seoul: Jisik-Sanup Publications, 2003), 313–450; and Andrew C. Nahm, ed., *Korea under Japanese Colonial Rule* (Kalamazoo: Center for Korean Studies, Western Michigan University, 1973). Participant-observer accounts of special value are F. A. McKenzie, *Korea's Fight for Freedom* (New York: Revell, 1920); the reporting of the *London Daily Mail*'s correspondent in Japan; and Henry Chung (Chang Han-gyong), *The Case for Korea* (New York: Revell, 1920), an account by Syngman Rhee's personal secretary. See also *The Independence Movement through Pictures,* 2 vols. (Seoul: Seomundang, 1988); vol. 2, chs. 6–8, is a collection of photographs and captions based on the exhibits of Independence Hall, Chonan, which I visited three times from 1991 to 1998.

2. This discussion of Chondogyo and Christianity in Korea is based on Donald Baker, "Christianity," and John K. C. Oh, "Political Tradition and Contemporary Politics in Government," in *An Introduction to Korean Culture,* ed. John H. Koo and Andrew C. Nahm (Seoul: Hollym, 1997), 179–99, 221–43. See also Wi Jo Kang, *Christ and Caesar in Modern Korea: A History of Christianity and Politics* (Albany: State University of New York Press, 1997).

3. "Declaration of Independence (March 1, 1919)," appendix E in Andrew C. Nahm, *Korea: Tradition and Transformation: A History of the Korean People* (Seoul: Hollym, 1988), 538–39. See also Shin Yong-ha, "Re-evaluation of the March First Independence Movement," in *Essays in Korean Social History,* 422–39.

4. Ku, *Korea under Colonialism,* 65–132.

5. John Kie-chang Oh, "Political Tradition and Contemporary Politics and Govern-

ment," in Koo and Nahm, *An Introduction to Korean Culture*, 219–29; James B. Palais, *Politics and Policy in Traditional Korea* (Cambridge: Harvard University Press, 1991); Homer B. Hurlbert, *The History of Korea*, 2 vols. (Seoul: Methodist Publishing House, 1905); Shin Yong-ha, *Modern Korean History and Nationalism* (Seoul: Jimoondang Publishing, 2000); Shin, *Essays in Korean Social History.*

6. Kenneth M. Wells, *New God, New Nation: Protestants and Self Reconstruction in Korea, 1896–1937* (Honolulu: University of Hawaii Press, 1990); Donald N. Clark, *Christianity in Modern Korea* (Lanham, Md.: University Press of America, 1986); George L. Paik, *The History of Protestant Missions in Korea* (Pyongyang: Union College Press, 1929); Samuel Hugh Moffett, *The Christians of Korea* (New York: Friendship Press, 1962). Biographical sketches of the leading European and Korean churchmen of pre-1945 Korea—written by one of their contemporaries—is J. Earnest Fisher, *Pioneers of Modern Korea* (Seoul: Samsung Printing, 1977). See also Fred Harvey Harrington, *God, Mammon and the Japanese: Dr. Horace Allen and Korean-American Relations, 1884–1905* (Madison: University of Wisconsin Press, 1944).

7. Ku, *Korea under Colonialism*, 1–35; Wells, *New God, New Nation*, 47–81. The pre–World War II course of Korean-American diplomatic relations, government to government, is traced in John Edward Wilsz, "Encountering Korea: American Perceptions and Policies to 25 June 1950," in *A Revolutionary War: Korea and the Transformation of the Postwar World*, ed. William J. Williams (Chicago: Imprint Publications for the U.S. Air Force Academy Military History Symposium, 1993), 13–82; and John Chay, "The First Three Decades of American-Korean Relations, 1882–1910: Reassessments and Reflections" and Andrew C. Nahm, "U.S. Policy and the Japanese Annexation of Korea," in *U.S.-Korean Relations 1882–1982*, ed. Tae-hwan Kwak, John Chay, Soon Sung Cho, and Shannon McCune (Seoul: Institute for Far Eastern Studies, Kyungnam University, 1982), 15–53. See also Andre Schmid, *Korea between Empires, 1895–1919* (New York: Columbia University Press, 2002).

8. In addition to Fisher, *Pioneers of Modern Korea*, whose biographical essays are rich in anecdotes, the evangelical reformers are described in Richard Saccone, *Koreans to Remember* (Seoul: Hollym, 1993). Syngman Rhee receives the most biographical attention. His "official" biography was written by Robert T. Oliver, a Pennsylvania State University communications professor who served as Rhee's public-relations director in the United States: *Syngman Rhee: The Man behind the Myth* (New York: Dodd, Mead, 1955). The counterbiography is Richard C. Allen, *Korea's Syngman Rhee* (Rutland, Vt.: Charles E. Tuttle, 1960). See also Lee Chong-sik, *Syngman Rhee: The Prison Years of a Young Radical* (Seoul: Yonsei University Press, 2001). I also used the extensive Syngman Rhee Subject File, M. Preston Goodfellow Papers, Hoover Institution for War, Peace and Revolution, Stanford, Calif. Rhee's papers written in languages other than English are collected in the Syngman Rhee Papers Editorial Committee, Institute for Modern Korean Studies, Yonsei University, *Syngman Rhee Papers*, 18 vols. (Seoul: Yonsei University Press, 1998).

9. Kim Ku is profiled in Saccone, *Koreans to Remember*, 209–12, but a more perceptive analysis may be found in Chong-sik Lee, "The Personality of Four Korean Political Leaders: Syngman Rhee, Kim Ku, Kim Kyu-sik, and Yo Un-hyong," reprinted in Mark C. Monahan, *Korean Studies Reader* (Seoul: Yonsei University, 1998). Among the general compilations of Korean biographical information, the best is Keith Pratt and Richard Reutt with James Hoare, *Korea: A Historical and Cultural Dictionary* (Richmond, Surrey, U.K.: Curzon Press, 1999). Telling sketches by a political contemporary can be found in Louise Yim, *My*

Forty Year Fight for Korea (Seoul: Chung-ang University, 1967). See also Jongsoo Lee, *Pack-pom Ilchi: The Autobiography of Kim Ku* (Lanham, Md.: University Press of America, 2000).

10. Suh Dae-sook, *The Korean Communist Movement, 1918–1948* (Princeton, N.J.: Princeton University Press, 1967); Robert Scalapino and Chong-sik Lee, *Communism in Korea*, vol. 1, *The Movement* (Berkeley: University of California Press, 1972). I also benefited from a thorough American investigation of Yo Un-hyong: Maj. Charles P. O'Riordan, USA, Investigating Officer, "Report of Investigation: Lyuh Woon Hyung," January 11, 1947, found in the personal files of Leonard M. Bertsch, a key member of Headquarters, U.S. Army Forces in Korea, 1945–1948, as an army lieutenant and civil-political affairs specialist. An Akron, Ohio, attorney, Bertsch applied his skills as a Summit County civil service commissioner (Democratic member) to Korean politics. His papers, held by his family, were made available by David P. Bertsch (Akron) and Susan Bertsch Cull (Columbus).

11. Lee, *The Politics of Korean Nationalism*, 237–56. The Korean entrepreneur-reform perspective is evident in Carter J. Eckert, *Offspring of Empire: The Kochang Kims and the Colonial Origins of Korean Capitalism 1876–1945* (Seattle: University of Washington Press, 1991).

12. Platform of the Korean Communist Party, 1921, reprinted in Suh, *The Korean Communist Movement*, 30–33.

13. Ku, *Korea under Colonialism*, 199–291. See also Michael Edson Robinson, *Cultural Nationalism in Colonial Korea, 1920–1925* (Seattle: University of Washington Press, 1903).

14. Ku, *Korea under Colonialism*, 267–91.

15. Yim, *My Forty Year Fight for Korea*, 198–245; Oliver, *Syngman Rhee*, 156–70; Nahm, *Korea: Tradition and Transformation*, 308–12; Wayne Patterson, *The Korean Frontier in America: Immigration to Hawaii, 1896–1910* (Honolulu: University of Hawaii Press, 1988).

16. Lee, *The Politics of Korean Nationalism*, 201–33. Full biographies and personality assessments may be found in Lee, "The Personality of Four Korean Political Leaders," as well as G-2, HQ, USAFIK, "Who's Who in Korea," October 15, 1947, copy in Charles H. Donnelly Papers, U.S. Army Military History Institute, Carlisle Barracks, Pa.

17. Suh, *The Korean Communist Movement*, 4–52.

18. "Programs, Manifesto, and Platform of the North China Korean Independence League," August 15, 1942, in Dae-sook Suh, *Documents of Korean Communism, 1918–1948* (Princeton, N.J.: Princeton University Press, 1970), 412–21.

19. Ibid., 480–82; "Pak Hon-yong," in G-2, USAFIK, "Who's Who in Korea."

20. Dae-sook Suh, *Kim Il Sung: The North Korean Leader* (New York: Columbia University Press, 1988), 1–57.

21. For the experience of the Korean people in World War II, see Nahm, *Korea: Tradition and Transformation*, 223–60; and Choong Soon Kim, *Faithful Endurance: An Ethnography of Korean Family Dispersal* (Tucson: University of Arizona Press, 1988). For some of the many personal accounts, see Taiwon Koh, *The Bitter Fruit of Kom-Pawi* (New York: Holt, Rinehart and Winston, 1959); Richard Kim, *Lost Names* (Berkeley: University of California Press, 1988); Sunny Chae, *Forever Alien: A Korean Memoir, 1930–1951* (Jefferson, N.C.: McFarland, 2000); Peter Hyun, *Man Sei!* (Honolulu: University of Hawaii Press, 1986); and Hildi Kang, ed., *Under the Black Umbrella: Voices from Colonial Korea, 1910–1945* (Ithaca, N.Y.: Cornell University Press, 2001). See also Andrew J. Grajdanzev, *Modern Korea* (New York: John Day Company for the Institute of Pacific Relations, 1944).

22. Rhee-Goodfellow correspondence, 1944–1945, Rhee File, Goodfellow Papers; Goodfellow personnel file, CIA Historical Office; Richard Dunlap, *Donovan: America's Master Spy* (Chicago: Rand McNally, 1982), 395–96; Richard Harris Smith, *OSS: The Secret History of America's First Central Intelligence Agency* (Berkeley: University of California Press, 1972), 26, 52; Bradley F. Smith, *The Shadow Warriors: OSS and the Origins of the CIA* (New York: Basic Books, 1983), 91, 131, 170–72, 408.

23. Lee, *The Politics of Korean Nationalism,* 180–213; Kim Kook-hun, "The North Korean People's Army: Its Rise and Fall, 1945–1950" (Ph.D. diss., University of London, 1989). For profiles of Korean Communist leaders drawn from Russian archives, see Andrei Lankov, *From Stalin to Kim Il-sung: The Formation of North Korea, 1945–1950* (New Brunswick, N.J.: Rutgers University Press, 2002).

24. Suh, *The Korean Communist Movement,* 212–51; Koon-woo Nam, *The North Korean Communist Leadership, 1945–1965* (Tuscaloosa: University of Alabama Press, 1974), 1–53.

25. Col. Miraji Yano, "Seventeenth Area Army Operations," July 1956, Japanese Monograph No. 22, Headquarters, USAFE and Eighth Army (Rear), copy, U.S. Eighth Army Historical Reference Files, Dean Heritage Center, Yongsan, Seoul, ROK; Saburo Hayashi with Alvin D. Coox, *Kogun: The Japanese Army in the Pacific War* (Quantico, Va.: Marine Corps Association, 1959).

2. DEFEAT AND DIVISION

1. Col. Miraji Yano, "Seventeenth Area Army Operations," July 1956, Japanese Monograph No. 22, Headquarters, USAFE and Eighth Army (Rear), copy, U.S. Eighth Army Historical Reference Files, Dean Heritage Center, Yongsan, Seoul, ROK; Col. Kenneth C. Strother, USA (Ret.), "The Occupation of Korea, September–December 1945," with diary and notes by the Acting C/S, XXIV Corps, 1984, Kenneth C. Strother Papers, Manuscripts Division, U.S. Army Military History Institute, Carlisle Barracks, Pa. Korean demographics, economics, and physical data may be found in Shannon McCune, *Korea's Heritage: A Regional and Social Geography* (Rutland, Vt.: Charles E. Tuttle, 1956), and *Korea Today* (New York: Institute of Pacific Relations, 1950). See also Andrew J. Grajdanzev, *Modern Korea* (New York: Institute of Pacific Relations, 1944).

2. Statistical Research Division, Office of Administration, Military Governor, U.S. Army Military Government in Korea, "History of United States Army Military Government in Korea, September 1945–June 1946," 2 vols., ms. history, copy, USFK Historical Files, Dean Center, Yongsan, Seoul, ROK (hereafter cited as USAMGIK, "History, 1945–1946"); "Political Developments in Korea," 1946, Bertsch Papers.

For the background of the Japanese surrender, see John W. Dower, *Embracing Defeat: Japan in the Wake of World War II* (New York: W. W. Norton, 1999), 33–64. Conditions in Korea are described in C. A. Sauer, *Methodists in Korea, 1930–1960* (Seoul: Christian Literature Society, 1973), 112–13, and *When the Wolves Came: The Passing of a Pacifist in Korea* (Seoul: Yonsei University, 1973), 41–52.

3. An account and analysis of the Abe-Yo negotiations may be found in "Korea and the Provisional Government," with supporting documents in Far East Section, Research and Analysis Branch, Office of Strategic Services (OSS), "Korea" Files, 1942–1945, William J. Donovan Papers, U.S. Army Military History Institute, Carlisle Barracks, Pa.; C. Leonard

Hoag, "American Military Government in Korea," 1970, ms. history, U.S. Army Center of Military History, Washington, D.C.; E. Grant Meade, *American Military Government in Korea* (New York: Columbia University Press, 1951), 40–73. See also Won-sul Lee, *The United States and the Division of Korea, 1945* (Seoul: Kyung Hee University Press, 1982), and Michael C. Sandusky, *America's Parallel* (Alexandria, Va.: Old Dominion Press, 1983).

4. Bruce Cumings, *The Origins of the Korean War*, vol. 1, *Liberation and the Emergence of Separate Regimes, 1945–1947* (Princeton, N.J.: Princeton University Press, 1981), 68–100; Gregory Henderson, *Korea: The Politics of the Vortex* (Cambridge: Harvard University Press, 1968), 113–47; Chi-Young Pak, *Political Opposition in Korea, 1945–1960* (Seoul: Seoul National University Press, 1980), 28–55; Dae-suk Suh, *The Korean Communist Movement, 1918–1948* (Princeton, N.J.: Princeton University Press, 1967), 294–329.

5. Lee, *The United States and the Division of Korea*, 136–55. The activities of the Korean People's Republic were covered in detail in the *Haebang Ilbo*, September–December 1945, translated and annotated in Chong-sik Lee, ed., *Materials on Korean Communism, 1945–1947* (Honolulu: Center for Korean Studies, University of Hawaii, 1977), 21–114.

6. In addition to the sources listed earlier, I relied on the fusion of analyses from American foreign service officers and army intelligence officers in the weekly *Review of the Far East (RFE)*, a publication of the War Department's Military Intelligence Division, September–December 1945, especially "Korea," November 26, 1945, in *RFE*, II-5, copies in the Air Force Historical Research Agency Library, Air University, Maxwell Air Force Base, Ala.

7. Henry Chung, *The Russians Came to Korea* (Seoul: Korean Pacific Press, 1947), 39–78. A longtime associate of Syngman Rhee, Chung had every reason to demonize the Russians, but his book, even though it is designed to discredit the Soviet Union, is based on the stories of hundreds of refugees and the eyewitness reporting of three respected American newsmen: Harold Isaacs *(Newsweek)*, Richard J. H. Johnston *(New York Times)*, and Walter Simmons *(Chicago Tribune)*. Another description based on eyewitness testimony and his own experiences in North Korea is Richard F. Underwood, "Memories and Thoughts" (ms., 2000), 38–68, in the author's possession. A third-generation Presbyterian missionary in Korea, Underwood served as a U.S. Army intelligence agent in North Korea, October 1945–June 1946.

After the capture of Pyongyang in October 1945, the State Department's Office of Intelligence and Research conducted a five-month study of the Soviet occupation, based on captured documents and Korean interviews, entitled, "North Korea: A Case Study of a Soviet Satellite," April 2, 1951, copy, Korean War File, President's Secretary's Files, 1951, Presidential Papers, Harry S. Truman Library, Independence, Mo. Department of State, *North Korea: A Case Study in the Techniques of Takeover* (Washington, D.C.: Government Printing Office, 1961), is the unclassified, sanitized version.

The best secondary accounts are Charles K. Armstrong, *The North Korean Revolution, 1945–1950* (Ithaca, N.Y.: Cornell University Press, 2003); Erik Van Ree, *Socialism in One Zone: Stalin's Policy in Korea, 1945–1947* (Oxford: Berg, 1989), 85–186; Andrei Lankov, *From Stalin to Kim Il-sung: The Formation of North Korea, 1945–1950* (New Brunswick, N.J.: Rutgers University Press, 2002); and Kathryn Weathersby, "Soviet Aims in Korea and the Origins of the Korean War, 1945–1950" (working paper no. 8, Cold War International History Project, Woodrow Wilson Center, 1993).

8. Underwood, "Memories and Thoughts"; CINCAFPAC to War Dept., September 28, 1945, Foreign Affairs—Korea, Subject Files, Truman Papers.

9. Armstrong, *The North Korean Revolution*, 62–64; Koon-woo Nam, *The North Korean Communist Leadership, 1945–1965* (Tuscaloosa: University of Alabama Press, 1974), 43–53; Suh, *The Korean Communist Movement*, 294–329; Dae-sook Suh, *Documents of Korean Communism, 1918–1948* (Princeton, N.J.: Princeton University Press, 1970), 489–93, which reprints Pyongannamdo Committee, "Action Platform of the Korean Communist Party," October 6, 1945; Sydney A. Seiler, *Kim Il-sŏng: The Creation of a Legend, The Building of a Regime* (Lanham, Md.: University Press of America, 1994), which includes as appendix 5, "Yu Sŏng-Ch'ol's Testimony," the riveting personal account of a Soviet Korean who served as Kim Il-sung's Russian translator and became a lieutenant general and director of the Korean People's Army's operations bureau, covering Yu's service in 1945–1950 and his banishment in 1959; and Andrei N. Lankov, "The Demise of Non-Communist Parties in North Korea (1945–1960)," *Journal of Cold War Studies* 3 (Winter 2001): 103–25. Kim Il-sung has two major biographies: Baik Bong, *Kim Il Sung*, 3 vols. (New York: Guardian Books, 1970), the official biography from Pyongyang, and Dae-sook Suh, *Kim Il-sung*, rev. ed. (New York: Columbia University Press, 1988). Kim Il-sung's 1945–1946 speeches and public papers can be found in Kim Il-sung, *Selected Works*, 6 vols. (Pyongyang: Foreign Languages Publishing House, 1972), 1:1–73. See also Adrian Buzo, *The Guerrilla Dynasty: Politics and Leadership in North Korea* (Boulder, Colo.: Westview Press, 1999).

10. Communiqué, Cairo Conference, November 22–25, 1945, copy, Office Files, 1945, Office of the Commanding General, U.S. Army Forces in Korea/XXIV Corps, Historical Files/U.S. Army Pacific, Records of U.S. Army Pacific, Record Group (RG) 550, National Archives and Records Administration; Briefing Book papers, "Korea," in *The Conference of Berlin 1945*, 2 vols. (1967), 1:309–15, in Historical Office, Department of State, *Foreign Relations of the United States 1945*, 9 vols. (Washington, D.C.: Government Printing Office, 1967–1969); hereafter cited as *FRUS 1945*.

11. Charles M. Dobbs, *The Unwanted Symbol: American Foreign Policy, the Cold War, and Korea, 1945–1950* (Kent, Ohio: Kent State University Press, 1981), 2–28.

12. Policy Paper, Department of State, "An Estimate of Conditions in Asia and the Pacific at the Close of the War in the Far East and the Objectives and Policies of the United States," June 22, 1945 in *FRUS 1945*, 6:556–80.

13. Joint Post-War Committee, JCS, draft memo, "Unconditional Surrender of Japan," December 27, 1944; SWNCC, "Statement of Policy . . . 58/5," May 18, 1945; SWNCC 150/2, "United States Post-Defeat Policy Relating to Japan," August 12, 1945; drafts of "Proclamation No. 1" and "General Order No. 1"; SWNCC memo 21/5, August 11, 1945; General Order No. 1, August 15, 1945, as approved by President Harry S. Truman and accepted by Premier Joseph Stalin, August 16, 1945, with implementing guidance in SWNCC 58/9, September 4, 1945, all in *FRUS 1945*, 6:507–639.

14. JCS 1380/15 and SWNCC 150/4, "U.S. Initial Post-Surrender Policy for Japan," August 30, 1945, reprinted in Theodore Cohen with Herbert Passin, *Remaking Japan: The American Occupation as New Deal* (New York: Free Press, 1987), 14–18; Proclamation No. 1 from CINC USAFPAC to People of Korea, September 7, 1945, *FRUS 1945*, 6:1043–44.

For foreign service officers' evaluation of MacArthur, see John K. Emmerson, *The Japan Thread: A Life in the U.S. Foreign Service* (New York: Holt, Rinehart and Winston, 1978) and William Sebald, *With MacArthur in Japan* (New York: W. W. Norton, 1965). See also Sandusky, *America's Parallel*, 73–98, 172–97, 239–48.

15. "John Reed Hodge," June 11, 1946, CG USAFIK Office Files; "John R. Hodge," in Spencer Tucker et al., *Encyclopedia of the Korean War,* 3 vols. (Santa Barbara, Calif.: ABC-CLIO, 2000), 257.

16. CG XXIV daily journal, September 1945, USAFIK Office Files, 1945; USAMGIK, "History, 1945–1946," vol. 1; CG XXIV Corps to All Commanders, "Indoctrination," August 25, 1945, quoted in ibid.; Maj. Gen. A. V. Arnold, personal notes, XXIV Corps Op O B-40 and 7th Inf Div Field Order 45, September 1, 1945, with diary notes, Sept–Oct 1945, Archibald V. Arnold Papers, Special Collections, USMA Library, West Point, N.Y. The Department of State history of the occupation is "Korea, 1945–1948" (publication 3305, October, 1948), supported by documents in U.S. Department of State, "Korea's Independence" (publication 2933, Office of Public Affairs, 1948).

17. Strother, "The Occupation of Korea."

18. Political adviser (H. Merrell Benninghoff) to Secretary of State, September 15, 1945; CG USAFIK to SCAP, September 24, 1945, both in *FRUS 1945,* 6:1049–57; HQ Far East Command (FECOM), "History of the U.S. Army Forces in Korea," 1947, copy in Historical Reference Files, EUSAK History Office; HQ 40th Infantry Division, "Evacuation and Repatriation in Korea," 1946, ms. history, USFK Historical Files.

19. USAMGIK, National Economic Board, "South Korean Interim Government Activities" (SKIGA), Report No. 34 (July–August 1948), 6–10; CG USAFIK to Major Commanders, December 8, 1945, and their responses, December 12–15, CG USAFIK Office Files, 1945; Lt. Gen. John R. Hodge to Maj. Gen. Richard J. Marshall, C/S, AFPAC, December 28, 1945, CG USAFIK Office Files, 1945.

20. USAMGIK, notes for first report, September–December 1945, and "Resources of Korea," December 1945, Arnold Papers; USAMGIK, "History, 1945–1946," vol. 2, pt. 2; "Land Reform in Korea, 1950," in Shin Yong-ha, *Essays in Korean Social History* (Seoul: Yonsei University Press, 2003), 174–94.

21. SWNCC 176/8, "Basic Initial Directive to the Commander in Chief U.S. Army Forces Pacific for the Administration of Civil Affairs in Those Areas of Korea Occupied by U.S. Forces," October 17, 1945, *FRUS 1945,* 6:1049–50, 1073–86.

22. Statement from the Commanding General USAFIK, December 12, 1945, CG USAFIK Office Files, 1945.

23. Central Intelligence Group, Situation Report No. 2, "Korea," January 1947, Intelligence Files, President's Secretary's Files, Truman Papers; "Coalition Trends in Korean Politics," 1946, Bertsch Papers.

24. Lt. Gen. John R. Hodge to William Randolph Hearst, January 1948, CG USAFIK Office Files, 1948; FECOM, "History of the U.S. Army Forces in Korea," 1947; Louise Yim, *My Forty Year Fight for Korea* (Seoul: Chung-ang University, 1967), 201–44; Far East Section, R&AB, OSS, "Korea and the Provisional Government," September 28, 1945, Donovan Papers.

25. Karl Lott Rankin, *China Assignment* (Seattle: University of Washington Press, 1964); E. J. Kahn Jr., *The China Hands: America's Foreign Service Officers and What Befell Them* (New York: Viking Press, 1972); Dorothy Borg and Waldo Heinrichs, eds., *Uncertain Years: Chinese-American Relations, 1947–1950* (New York: Columbia University Press, 1980).

26. Robert T. Oliver, *Syngman Rhee and American Involvement in Korea, 1942–1960* (Seoul: Panmun Book Company, 1978), 1–24; Underwood, "Memories and Thoughts," 41–44.

27. Lee, *The United States and the Division of Korea,* 111–55; memorandum, "Syngman Rhee," 1947, Bertsch Papers.

28. Lt. Gen. John R. Hodge to Asst. Sec. of War John J. McCloy, December 6, 1945, Hodge Office Files; Gordon Walker, "Rhee Still Shuns Leftist Majority," *Christian Science Monitor,* filed December 13, 1945, copy, CG USAFIK Office Files, 1945.

29. Edward S. Mason, Mahn-je Kim, et al., *The Economic and Social Modernization of the Republic of Korea* (Cambridge: Harvard University Press for the Council on East Asian Studies, 1980), 167–81; McCune, *Korea Today,* 114–39; Hdqs., USAMGIK, "Resources of Korea," 1946, Arnold Papers.

30. "Education," in USAMGIK, "History, 1945–1946"; SKIGA no. 21 (June 1947), 86.

31. "Directorate of National Defense," in USAMGIK, "History, 1945–1946," pt. 2, 69–106.

32. SWNCC 101/4, "Korea: The Problem," October 24, 1945, *FRUS 1945,* 6:1096–1103; W. Langdon to Secretary of State, November 20, 1945, ibid., 1130–33.

33. Dobbs, *The Unwanted Symbol,* 2–83; Office of the Political Advisor to Secretary of State, December 30, 1945, *FRUS 1945,* 6:1152–53; Gen. of the Army Douglas MacArthur to JCS, December 16, 1945, ibid., 1144–48; Oliver, *Syngman Rhee and American Involvement in Korea,* 24–45.

34. War Department to CINCAFPAC, advance copy, communiqué, Moscow Conference, December 26, 1945, CG, USAFIK Office Files, 1945.

35. Lankov, "The Demise of Non-Communist Parties in North Korea," 103–25.

36. War Dept. to Political Advisor, CG USAFIK, JCS instructions on negotiations, December 4, 1945; Hdqs. USFK, "Statement from the Commanding General USAFIK," December 12, 1945; text of radio broadcast delivered by General Hodge on Moscow agreement, December 29, 1945; statements of Lt. Gen. John R. Hodge to the Korean people, January 2 and 3, 1946, all in CG USAFIK Office Files, 1946; "Korea," Annex B, MID, WDGS, *RFE,* January 28, 1946.

37. Lee, *The United States and the Division of Korea,* 214–35; Richard J. H. Johnston, "Party Rift Widens in Korea Dispute," *New York Times,* January 18, 1946.

3. PUTTING KOREA TOGETHER AGAIN

1. The documentary evidence on which this chapter is largely based is found in Commanding General's Office Files, U.S. Army Forces in Korea (USAFIK) and XXIV Corps, 1946 and 1947, Records of the General Headquarters, Far East Command, Supreme Commander Allied Powers, and United Nations Command, 1945–1957, RG 554, National Archives and Records Administration; and the documents reprinted in Historical Office, Bureau of Public Affairs, Department of State, *Foreign Relations of the United States 1946,* 10 vols. (Washington, D.C.: Government Printing Office, 1969–1972), vol. 8, *The Far East,* and *Foreign Relations of the United States 1947,* 8 vols. (Washington, D.C.: Government Printing Office, 1971–1977), vol. 6, *The Far East* (hereafter cited as *FRUS 1946* and *FRUS 1947*). See also Department of State, "Korea 1945–1948" (publication 3305, Office of Public Affairs, October 1948), and "Korea's Independence" (publication 2933, 1948).

In addition to the secondary sources cited in previous chapters, see also Soon-sung Cho, *Korea in World Politics, 1940–1950* (Berkeley: University of California Press, 1967); Bonnie B. C. Oh, ed., *Korea under the American Military Government, 1945–1948* (Westport, Conn.: Praeger, 2002); and E. Grant Meade, *American Military Government in Korea* (New York: Columbia University Press, 1951).

The arrangements for the first meeting of the Joint Commission are described in JCS to SCAP, January 5, 1946, *FRUS 1946,* 8:607–8; Lt. Gen. J. R. Hodge to State, January 12, 1946, ibid., 608–9.

The description of the Russian arrival is based on Richard J. H. Johnson, "U.S., Soviets Begin Discussion," *New York Times,* January 16, 1946, and contemporary still and motion picture photographs.

2. Hodge to SecWar, January 22, 1946, and Benninghoff to SecState, January 23, 1946, both in *FRUS 1946,* 8:611–12, 615–16. The Seoul meetings were covered in detail by Richard J. H. Johnston for the *New York Times;* see, for example, "Party Rift Widens in Korea Dispute," January 18, 1946.

3. The descriptions of Generals Arnold and Lerch are based on their official army biographical files, U.S. Army Center of Military History, and descriptions by Dr. Horace G. Underwood of Seoul, as well as the papers and an unpublished memoir of Maj. Gen. Albert E. Brown, "The Joint Commission on Korea," 1949, General Albert E. Brown Papers, U.S. Army Military History Institute, Carlisle Barracks, Pa. On the foreign service officers, see also James I. Matray, "Bunce and Jacobs: U.S. Occupation Advisors in Korea, 1946–1947," in Oh, *Korea under Military Government,* 61–78.

4. Benninghoff to SecState, January 23 and February 15, 1946, *FRUS 1946,* 8:615–16, 633–38; SecState to CINCFE, February 28, 1946, ibid., 645–46; CG USAFIK, press release, "Results of U.S.-U.S.S.R. Conference," March 7, 1946, CG USAFIK Office Files, 1946.

5. Benninghoff to SecState, March 19, 1946, *FRUS 1946,* 8:648–52; Hodge to Maj. Gen. Stephen J. Chamberlin, DC/S FECOM, April 3, 2003, CG USAFIK Office Files, 1946.

The economic conditions in the American zone are described in detail in Meade, *American Military Government in Korea,* 90–108, 190–224; Donald S. Macdonald, "The First Year of Military Government in Korea," ms. history, 1946, copy, USFK Historical Reference Files, Dean Center, Yongsan, Seoul, ROK; and Hdqs., USAMGIK, "Resources in Korea," 1945, Arnold Papers. Macdonald, later a foreign service officer and dean of Korean studies in the Department of State, served as an officer in the 101st Civil Affairs Group, Korea, 1946–1947;

6. Joint Communiqué No. 5, April 18, 1946, reprinted in Department of State, "Korea's Independence," 19–20; memo, meeting, SecState, SecWar, SecNav, "Korea," May 27, 1946, *FRUS 1946,* 8:681–82; Hdqs., USAMGIK, "Opinion Trends #10," May 10, 1946, Arnold Papers.

7. This analysis of the Joint Commission's first session is based on Joint Commission minutes and reports, March 20–May 6, 1946, copies in Bertsch papers. The assessment of Korean politics is in Leonard Bertsch, "U.S. Efforts to Unify Korean Political Factions," 1947, Bertsch Papers. The administration's assessment is Amb. E. W. Pauley to Pres. Harry S. Truman, June 22, 1947, and Truman to Pauley, July 16, 1946, *FRUS 1946,* 8:706–9, 713–14.

8. Conference notes and memo, Maj. Gen. A. V. Arnold, October 9, 1946, *FRUS 1946,* 8:741–43; USAMGIK, "Political Developments in Korea," 1946, Arnold Papers.

9. Kim Il-sung, "Nationalization of Major Industries—The Foundation for Building an Independent Sovereign State," August 10, 1946, in *Selected Works,* 6 vols. (Pyong-

yang: Foreign Languages Publishing House, 1971–1972), 1:68–73; Charles K. Armstrong, *The North Korean Revolution, 1945–1950* (Ithaca, N.Y.: Cornell University Press, 2003), 71–106.

10. Military Intelligence Service, General Staff, FECOM, *History of the North Korean Army,* July 1952, in File 330.008, USFK Historical Reference Files; Kim Kook-hun, "The North Korean People's Army: Its Rise and Fall, 1945–1950" (doctoral diss., King's College, University of London, 1989), 16–78.

11. "National Police: Organization and Activities in 1946," 1947, with appended notes and interviews, Historical Files, Historical Section, G-3, XXIV Corps/USAFIK, Records of U.S. Army Pacific, RG 550, National Archives and Records Administration; "Korean National Police," USAFIK/ USAMGIK, National Economic Board, "South Korean Interim Government Activities," Report No. 27 (December 1947), RG 10, Douglas MacArthur Papers, MacArthur Library and Memorial, Norfolk, Va.

12. Hdqs. USAMGIK, "The Organization of the Korean Constabulary," memo to all provincial governors, January 9, 1946, copy, Arno P. Mowitz Papers, U.S. Army Military History Institute, Carlisle Barracks, Pa.; Office of Administration, Military Governor, USAMGIK, "History of United States Military Government in Korea, September 1945–June 1946," 2 vols., 2:69–74, copy in USFK Historical Reference Files; HQ KMAG, "Narrative Report of the United States Advisory Group to the Republic of Korea," 1950, copy furnished by Col. Harold S. Fischgrund, USA (Ret.), assistant adviser, G-3, KMAG, in 1950; Headquarters, Korean Military Advisory Group, "History of the Department of Internal Security to 1 July 1948," 1948, copy furnished by the late Lt. Col. James H. Hausman, USAR (Ret.).

13. The portrait of the Constabulary officer corps is drawn from Huh Nam-sung, "The Quest for a Bulwark of Anti-Communism: The Formation of the Republic of Korea Army Officer Corps and Its Political Socialization, 1945–1950" (Ph.D. diss., Ohio State University, 1987); and Brig. Gen. Lee Chi-op, ROKA (Ret.), with Lt. Col. Stephen M. Tharp, USA, *Call Me "Speedy Lee"* (Seoul: Won Min, 2001), which has biographical sketches of the first 110 Constabulary officers. I profited from reading a longer and more candid list of biographies in draft. See also Lee Young-woo, "The United States and the Formation of the Republic of Korea Army, 1945–1950" (Ph.D. diss., Duke University, 1984), and Sejin Kim, *The Politics of Military Revolution* (Chapel Hill: University of North Carolina Press, 1971), 36–73. The official history of American-Korean military relations is Robert K. Sawyer, *Military Advisors in Korea: KMAG in War and Peace* (Washington, D.C.: U.S. Army Center of Military History, 1988), but I referred more often to the longer unpublished version by Major Sawyer and others, "The U.S. Advisory Group to Korea," 3 vols., 1950–1954, copies in the Center of Military History and USFK Historical Reference Files. Maj. Gen. Lim Sun-ha, one of the two Koreans who assisted Colonel Marshall, corrected errors in the standard references in a memo to the author, January 1, 2004.

14. Interviews with Lt. Col. James H. Hausman, USA (Ret.), and Maj. Gen. Lim Sun-ha, 1994–1995, Seoul, Korea, and Austin, Tex. The incident is mentioned in passing in an interview with Gen. Chung Il-kwon by John Toland, transcript and tapes furnished by the Franklin D. Roosevelt Library with Toland's permission. Gen. Lee Chi-op also recalls the incident, and it is alluded to in General Chung's memoir, *Chonjaeng-gwa Huejon* [War and Truce] (Seoul: Dong-a Ilbo, 1986), translated for me by Maj. Park Il-song, Korean Military Academy.

15. In addition to my own interview with Colonel Hausman on March 21, 1995, and subsequent correspondence and phone conversations, my description of Hausman depends on another interview by John Toland, 1988, tape and transcripts, Roosevelt Library; U.S. Army 201 File, Lt. Col. James H. Hausman, USAR (Ret.), National Personnel Records Center, St. Louis, Mo.; "Military Record of Capt. James H. Hausman, 0372397," copy in Hausman Papers, Korea Institute, Harvard University; Brig. Gen. W. L. Roberts [CG KMAG] to Maj. Gen. H. B. Lewis, March 7, 1949, Hausman Papers; Jung Il-wha, *Taeongryongul umjin migun taewi* [The American Captain Who Moved Presidents] (Seoul: Hankuk Moonwon, 1995); and Allan R. Millett, "James H. Hausman and the Formation of the Korean Army, 1945–1950," *Armed Forces and Society* 23 (Summer 1997): 503–39.

While undergoing minor surgery, Colonel Hausman died of a heart attack in Austin, Texas, on October 5, 1996.

16. Interviews with Brig. Gen. Lee Chi-op, Seoul, July 2000; Lee, *Call Me "Speedy Lee,"* 57–65, confirmed in subsequent conversations with Maj. Gen. Lim Sun-ha, 2000.

17. In addition to my interviews with Colonel Hausman and Generals Lee and Lim, I discussed the officers of the Constabulary with other members of the first class: Gen. Paik Sun-yup (January 6, 1995), Gen. Kang Yong-hoon (December 23, 1994), and Maj. Gen. Kim Ung-soo (May 7, 2000). For perceptive characterizations of the politicians and officers of 1945–1950, see especially Louise Yim, *My Forty Year Fight for Korea* (Seoul: Chungang University, 1967). Another important witness of the Constabulary officers is Col. Harold G. Fischgrund, USA (Ret.), G-3 adviser for Constabulary operations, 1948–1950.

18. On Hodge's concerns about his occupation force, see CG USAFIK, "To Members of the American Forces in Korea," March 3, 1946; CG XXIV Corps to All Commanders, Personal Message in re: Criminal Acts American Forces, March 3, 1946; Commanding General USAFIK, memo to all commands, June 3, 1946; CG USAFIK Office Files, 1946; and CG XXIV Corps, "Responsibilities of a Commissioned Officer," July 20, 1946, AG File 210.4, RG 338. The description of U.S. Army operations in Korea in 1946 is based on the weekly operations reports, G-3, HQ, USAFIK, Records of Headquarters, Far East Command, RG 554.

19. SCAP to C/S USA, October 28, 1946, *FRUS 1946*, 8:750–51; HQ, FECOM, "History of the U.S. Army Forces in Korea," 1947, copy, USFK Historical Reference Files; CINC USAFPAC, *Summation of United States Army Military Government Activities in Korea*, nos. 9–12 (June–October 1946), copies in U.S. Army Military History Institute; George McCune, "Korea—The First Year of Liberation," *Pacific Affairs* 20 (March 1947): 3–17.

20. For a comprehensive analysis of Korean politics, 1946–1947, see "Political Situation as of 31 December 1947," in Hdqs., 971st Counterintelligence Corps Det.—Korea, USAFIK; "Annual Report Progress Report for 1947," 110–34, copy in USAFIK Historical Files, 1947, RG 550. See also Robert T. Oliver, *Syngman Rhee and American Involvement in Korea: 1942–1960* (Seoul: Panmun Book Company, 1978), 46–71; and Justin Sloane, "The Communist Effort in South Korea, 1945–1948" (master's thesis, Northwestern University, 1949), written by a former army officer fresh from duty in the USAMGIK.

21. Special press release, Hdqs. XXIV Corps, "American-Soviet Commission Adjourns," May 8, 1946, CG USAFIK Office Files, 1946; Hdqs. USAFIK, "Statement of General Hodge Suspending the Dai-dong Press," May 14, 1946, CG USAFIK Office Files, 1946; *Dong-a Ilbo*, September 29, 1946, October 4, 1946, reprinted in translation in Chong-sik

Lee, ed., *Materials on Korean Communism, 1945–1947* (Honolulu: Center for Korean Studies, University of Hawaii, 1977), 219–20; "Police and Public Security," ch. III in Hdqs., FECOM, "History of the Occupation of Korea," copy in USFK Historical Reference Files.

22. Kathryn Weathersby and James Person, memo, "First Meeting, Kim Il-sung and Stalin," 2002, based on an April 1947 Soviet Foreign Ministry memorandum, RGASPI, Fond 17, Opis 128, delo 1119, list 93.

23. SWNCC, "Policy for Korea," *FRUS 1946*, 8:693–99; Langdon to SecState, April 10 and May 8, 1946, ibid., 658–59, 667–68; Bonnie C. Oh, "Kim Kyu-sik and the Coalition Effort," in Oh, *Korea under Military Government*, 103–22.

24. Langdon to State, May 8, 1946, *FRUS 1946*, 8:667–68; George M. McCune, "Postwar Government and Politics," *Journal of Politics* 9 (November 1947): 605–23; Donald S. Macdonald, "Korea and the Ballot: The International Dimension in Korean Political Development as Seen in Elections" (Ph.D. diss., Massachusetts Institute of Technology, 1977), pt. 2; Leonard Bertsch, "Coalition Trends in Korean Politics," 1947, Bertsch Papers.

25. Oliver, *Syngman Rhee and American Involvement in Korea*, 24–25; Cho, *Korea in World Politics*, 123–27; Langdon to SecState, August 26, 1946, *FRUS 1946*, 8:731–32.

26. Langdon to SecState, November 1, 1946, *FRUS 1946*, 8:753–56; Thomas H. Lee, "The Origins of the Taegu Insurrection of 1946" (history honors paper, Harvard University, 1990), copy in USFK Historical Reference Files; Kang Han-mu, "The United States Military Government in Korea, 1945–1948" (Ph.D. diss., University of Cincinnati, 1970); American Delegation, US-USSR Joint Commission, "Riots and Disorders 6th Infantry Division Area, Korea, Oct 1–10, 1946," October 14, 1946, Bertsch Papers.

27. The comprehensive narrative is Hdqs., FECOM, "The Quasi-Revolt of October, 1946," pt. 2, ch. 3 of "History of the Occupation of Korea," 1948, copy in USFK Historical Reference Files.

28. Hdqs., Sixth Infantry Division, G-2 Summary #1, "Kyongsang Communist Uprising of October, 1946," December 1, 1946, with statistical summaries and incident reports, copy in Records of the USAFIK, RG 550; Maj. Gen. Alfred E. Brown, USA, "Disorders Occurring at Taegu," October 4, 1946, copy, Bertsch Papers; IG USAFIK, report, "Investigation Disturbances at Taegu, Korea," November 12, 1946, USAFIK, "History."

29. Hdqs., Sixth Infantry Division, G-2 Summary #2, "Cholla-South Communist Uprising of November 1946," December 31, 1946, copy in File 720.009, USFK Historical Reference Files.

30. Joint Korean-American Conference, "Conclusions and Recommendations," November 26, 1946, appendix A to USAFIK, "History"; Lt. Leonard M. Bertsch, "Lyuh Abduction," October 19, 1946, Bertsch Papers; Langdon to SecState, November 14 and 24, 1946, *FRUS 1946*, 8:766–68, 770–71; Gen. D. MacArthur to C/S USA, October 28, 1946, ibid., 750–51.

31. SCAP to C/S USA, October 28, 1946, and Lt. Gen. J. R. Hodge to SecState, October 18 and December 31, 1946, *FRUS 1946*, 8:749–86; Lt. Gen. J. R. Hodge to MilGov, October 31, 1946, CG USAFIK Office Files, 1946; FEC Staff Study Files 429–431, Baker Plans 61–63, 1946–1948, with attachments, JSPOG Top Secret Control File, 1946–1953, J-3 Far East Command General File, 1946–1953, Records of Joint Commands, RG 349, National Archives and Records Administration.

32. Lt. Gen. J. R. Hodge to M. P. Goodfellow, January 28, 1947, Goodfellow Papers; Lt. Gen. J. R. Hodge to SecWar, November 5, 1946, CG USAFIK Office Files, 1946; Macdonald, "Korea and the Ballot."

33. Hdqs., USAFIK, memorandum, interview with Cho Pong-am, Korean Communist Party, October 31, 1946, CG USAFIK Office Files, 1946; Langdon to SecState, January 17, 1947, *FRUS 1947*, 6:596–600.

34. The Hodge-Chistiakov correspondence, October 26–December 24, 1946, is reprinted in Department of State, "Korea's Independence," 23–32. The link between the creation of the Interim Legislative Assembly and the second round of meetings of the Joint Commission is described in Director Office of Far Eastern Affairs (John Carter Vincent) to SecState, January 27, 1947, *FRUS 1947*, 6:601–3.

35. CG FECOM to JCS, January 12, 1946, *FRUS 1946*, 8:608–9; CG FECOM to JCS, ibid., 750–51; Arthur C. Bunce to Amb. George Atcheson (SCAP adviser), January 23, 1947, CG USAFIK Office Files, 1947, Headquarters, Records of Far East Command, Supreme Command Alllied Powers, and United Nations Command, RG 554; Vincent to SecState, January 27, 1947, *FRUS 1947*, 6:601–3.

36. W. Langdon to SecState, memo, "Korean National Youth Movement," January 21, 1947, CG USAFIK Office Files, 1947.

37. Mark Gayn, *Japan Diary* (New York: Sloane, 1948), 351–443. The considerable achievements of the USAMGIK are summarized in "List of Accomplishments by Military Government in Korea," 1946, Arnold Papers.

4. THE MOSCOW AGREEMENT IS ABANDONED, 1947

1. R. J. H. Johnston to CG USAFIK, January 27, 1947, Commanding General's Office Files, 1947, Headquarters, USAFIK, Records of U.S. Army Pacific, RG 550, National Archives and Records Administration.

2. Melvyn P. Leffler, *A Preponderance of Power: National Security, the Truman Administration, and the Cold War* (Stanford, Calif.: Stanford University Press, 1992), 141–81; Forrest C. Pogue, *George C. Marshall: Statesman, 1945–1959* (New York: Viking, 1987), 144–67.

3. *New York Times,* March 13–21, 1947.

4. SecState to CG FECOM, February 7, 1947, in Department of State, *Foreign Relations of the United States 1947,* 7 vols. (Washington, D.C.: Government Printing Office, 1972), vol. 6, *The Far East,* 605–6 (hereafter cited as *FRUS 1947*); J. C. Vincent to SecState, January 27, 1947, ibid., 601–3; SecWar to SecState, April 4, 1947, ibid., 625–28.

5. Herbert Romerstein and Eric Breindel, *The Venona Secrets: Exposing Soviet Espionage and America's Traitors* (Washington, D.C.: Henry Regenry, 2000).

6. Among the vast literature, see David Alvarez, ed., *Allied and Axis Signals Intelligence in World War II* (London: Frank Cass, 1999); Robert Louis Benson, *A History of U.S. Communications Intelligence during World War II* (Fort Meade, Md.: National Security Agency, 1997); David Alvarez, *Secret Messages: Codebreaking and American Diplomacy, 1930–1945* (Lawrence: University Press of Kansas, 2000); Wyman H. Packard, *A Century of U.S. Naval Intelligence* (Washington, D.C.: Department of the Navy, 1996); F. H. Hinsley, *British Intelligence in the Second World War,* 3 vols. (London: HMSO, 1979–1984); Joseph E. Persico, *Roosevelt's Secret War and World War II Espionage* (New York: Random House, 2001); Bradley F. Smith, *The Shadow Warriors: O.S.S. and the Origins of the C.I.A.* (New York: Basic Books, 1983); Marc B. Powe and E. E. Wilson, *The Evolution of American Military Intelligence* (Fort Huachuca, Ariz.: Department of the Army, 1973).

7. The American intelligence experience in the Pacific war can be found in John Winton, *ULTRA in the Pacific* (Annapolis, Md.: Naval Institute Press,1993); John Prados, *Combined Fleet Decoded: The Secret History of American Intelligence and the Japanese Navy in World War II* (New York: Random House, 1995); Ronald Lewin, *The American Magic: Codes, Ciphers and the Defeat of Japan* (New York: Farrar Straus Giroux, 1982); Edwin T. Layton with Roger Pineau and John Costello, *"And I Was There": Pearl Harbor and Midway—Breaking the Secrets* (New York: William Morrow, 1985); W. J. Holmes, *Double Edged Secrets: U.S. Naval Intelligence Operations in the Pacific during World War II* (Annapolis, Md.: Naval Institute Press, 1979).

8. Anthony Cave Brown, *Bodyguard of Lies* (New York: Harper and Row, 1975).

9. Richard J. Aldrich, Gary D. Rawnsley, and Ming-yeh Rawnsley, eds., *The Clandestine Cold War in Asia, 1945–65* (London: Frank Cass, 2000). See also Michael Schaller, *The American Occupation of Japan* (New York: Oxford University Press, 1985); Howard B. Schonberger, *Aftermath of War: Americans and the Remaking of Japan, 1945–1952* (Kent, Ohio: Kent State University Press, 1989); John W. Dower, *Embracing Defeat: Japan in the Wake of World War II* (New York: W. W. Norton, 1999); and Takemae Eiji, *Inside GHQ: The Allied Occupation of Japan and Its Legacy,* trans. Robert Ricketts and Sebastian Swann (New York: Continuum, 2002).

10. Christopher Andrew and Oleg Gordievsky, *KBG: The Inside Story of Its Foreign Relations from Lenin to Gorbachev* (New York: HarperCollins, 1990); Christopher Andrew and Vasili Mitrokhin, *KBG: The Sword and the Shield* (New York: Basic Books, 1999).

11. This description in drawn from Hdqs. 971st CIC Detachment, *Annual Progress Report for 1947* (1947) and *Annual Progress Report for 1948* (1948), Historical Files, XXIV Corps/USAFIK, Records of U.S. Army Operational, Tactical and Support Organizations, RG 338, National Archives and Records Administration.

12. 971st CIC Detachment, *Annual Progress Report for 1947,* 28–38, and *Annual Progress Report for 1948,* 34–37; memorandum for the record, "Conference between Russian Consul and General Hodge," April 27, 1946, CG USAFIK Office Files, 1946; Leonard Bertsch, "Soviet Agent in Seoul," October 25, 1947, Bertsch Papers.

13. The MacArthur-Willoughby relationship is described in Edward J. Drea, *MacArthur's ULTRA: Codebreaking and the War against Japan, 1942–1945* (Lawrence: University Press of Kansas, 1992), and D. Clayton James, *The Years of MacArthur,* 3 vols. (Boston: Houghton Mifflin, 1970–1985), vol. 3, *Triumph and Disaster,* 35–66, 354–84, 693–94.

None of his staff saw much of the reclusive MacArthur, who avoided meetings, inspection tours, and social events with obsessive determination. Supposedly a confidant, Willoughby saw the SCAP only fifty-one times in sixty-seven months, 1945–1951. Lt. Gen. Edward N. Almond, who held three senior staff posts in 1947–1951, saw MacArthur only forty times in fifty-two months, even though he served three years as FECOM chief of staff. These meetings were both individual and group sessions.

14. Historical Section, Hdqs. XXIV Corps, "History of G-2 Section, USAFIK," Historical Files, XXIV Corps, RG 338; 971st CIC Detachment, *Annual Progress Report for 1947,* 6–19; CG FECOM (G-2) to CG XXIV Corps, "Intelligence Reporting," October 25, 1947, CG USAFIK Office Files, 1947.

15. U.S. Army Intelligence Center, "CIC during the Occupation of Korea," ch. 30 in *History of the Counterintelligence Corps,* 30 vols. (1954–1959), printed in the "CIC Series" (1945.9 to 1949.1) of documents, copied and bound in three volumes by the Institute of

Asian Culture Studies, Hallym University, 1995, with a set held by the library of Yonsei University, Seoul; Leonard Bertsch, "Political Summary, February–March 1947," and memo, Political Analysis Section, Bureau of Public Opinion, Department of Public Information to CG USAMGIK, "Korean Political Organizations and Leaders," March 22, 1947, both in Bertsch Papers.

16. The pre-1950 intelligence story for Korea retains many mysteries, but I depended on the following (with caution): a CIC report of *Paikyisa* (1950) posted on www.pajooyom.com/eungtaek.htm (2002); Donald Nichols, *How Many Times Can I Die?* (Brooksville, Fla.: Brownsville Printing, 1981); memos and historical reports, 6004th AISS, 1951–1952, copies in USAF Organizational Archives, Air Force Historical Research Agency, Maxwell Air Force Base, Ala.; Tom Johnson, "The Korean War—The Cryptologic Story," June 2000, and David A. Hatch and Robert Louis Benson, "The Korean War: The SIGNIT Background," June 2000, Center for Cryptologic History, National Security Agency; Lt. Col. Leonard J. Abbott, memo from G-2 FECOM, "Korea Liaison Office Report," May 15, 1951, Willoughby Papers; CG USAFIK to AC/S G-2 FECOM, November 20, 1947, CG USAFIK Office Files, 1947.

The best "fusionist" account is Matthew M. Aid, "US Humint and Comint in the Korean War: From the Approach of War to the Chinese Intervention," in *The Clandestine Cold War in Asia*, 17–63.

17. History Office, Central Intelligence Agency, *CIA in Korea, 1946–1965*, 3 vols. (Washington, D.C., 1973), vol. 1; Arthur B. Darling, *The Central Intelligence Agency: An Instrument of Government to 1950* (University Park: Pennsylvania State University Press, 1990), 118–38, 273–81; Gen. Richard G. Stilwell, oral memoir (1979), pp. 72–90, Senior Officer Oral History Project, U.S. Army Military History Institute, Carlisle Barracks, Pa.; Col. Jay Vanderpool, oral memoir on Korea/Intelligence, ibid., 134–37.

Colonel Stilwell's team had talent. His deputy was the legendary Desmond FitzGerald. His "station chiefs" were Cols. Edward G. Lansdale, USAF (the Philippines), William Depuy, USA (China), Robert H. Cushman Jr., USMC (Micronesia), William R. Peers, USA (Taiwan), and Jay Vanderpool, USA (Korea). Hans Tofte (Japan) was the weakest link, but he influenced Korean special operations most.

18. ORE 5/1, CIG, "The Situation in Korea," January 3, 1947, copy, National Security Archive, Gelman Library, George Washington University, Washington, D.C.

19. ORE 15-4B, Assistant Director for Reports and Estimates, CIA, "The Current Situation in Korea," March 18, 1948, ibid.

20. Dae-sook Suh, *Kim Il-Sung* (New York: Columbia University Press, 1988), 74–105; Adrian Buzo, *The Guerrilla Dynasty: Politics and Leadership in North Korea* (Boulder, Colo.: Westview Press, 1999), 1–30; Erik Van Ree, *Socialism in One Zone: Stalin's Policy in Korea, 1945–1947* (Oxford: Berg, 1989), 149–86; Andrei Lankov, "The Demise of Non-Communist Parties in North Korea (1945–1960)," *Journal of Cold War Studies* 3 (Winter 2001): 103–25; AC/S G-2, USAFIK, "North Korea Today," 1947, Bertsch Papers.

21. Kim Kook-hun, "The North Korean People's Army: Its Rise and Fall, 1945–1950" (Ph.D. diss., University of London, 1989), 74–78. I also consulted MND ROK, "Military History of Korea," 1952, ms. history translated by members of 500th Military Intelligence Service Group, Far East Command, September 1952, copy in U.S. Army G-2 historical records, 1952, RG 319.

22. Suh, *Kim Il-sung*, 101–5.

23. Historical Section, Hdqs., FECOM, "History of the U.S. Army Forces in Korea,"

1948, pt. III, "The Police and National Events, 1947–48," pp. 7–16, copy in USFK Historical Research Files; Department of Public Information, "Korean Political Organizations and Leaders."

24. CG XXIV Corps to CGs 6th Inf Div, 7th Inf Div, and Korean Base Command, January 16, 1947, with a personal note to each XXIV Corps general officer, January 7, 1947; memo, CG 6th Inf Div, to Maj. Gen. E. N. Almond DC/S FECOM, March 31, 1947; Historical Section, Hdqs. (G-2) XXIV Corps, "History of Provost Marshal Section XXIV Corps, September 1945–July 1948," copy in RG 550; CG USAFIK to Maj. Gen. F. Parks (Ch Info), June 8, 1947, CG USAFIK Office Files, 1947, RG 338; Lt. Gen. J. R. Hodge to Cecil Brown, Mutual Broadcasting Company, June 10, 1947, CG XXIV Corps Office Files, 1947; C/S USA to CG FECOM, March 24, 1947, CG XXIV Corps Office Files, 1947. The quotations are in the Hodge-Brown letter.

25. Capt. Robert K. Sawyer, "United States Military Advisory Group to the Republic of Korea," pt. I (1945–1949), ms. history, U.S. Army Center of Military History, Fort McNair, Washington, D.C.; Young-woo Lee, "The United States and the Formation of the Republic of Korea Army, 1945–1950" (Ph.D. diss., Duke University, 1984), 88–119; interviews with Lt. Col. James H. Hausman, USAR, by John Toland (1988) and the author (1995).

26. Hausman inteview and interviews with Gens. Paik Sun-yup, Kang Yong-hoon, and Lim Sun-ha in 1994–1995 by the author; Col. W. S. Biddle USA to Director, Plans and Operations (G-3), Army Staff, File 091 (Korea) 1947, November 20, 1947, and Lt. Col. J. R. Dean Jr. to Lt. Col. T. Conway, November 18, 1947, File 091 (Korea) 1947, Records of the War Department/Department of the Army General Staff, RG 319, National Archives and Records Administration.

27. Huh Nam-sung, "The Quest for a Bulwark of Anti-Communism: The Formation of the Republic of Korea Officer Corps and Its Political Socialization" (Ph.D. diss., Ohio State University, 1987), 115–62; Se-jin Kim, *The Politics of Military Revolution in Korea* (Chapel Hill: University of North Carolina Press, 1971), 36–63.

28. National Economic Board, "South Korean Interim Government Activities," Report No. 25 (October 1947); Hausman oral history (1988).

29. G-2, 7th InfDiv, Periodic Intelligence Report (PIR) No. 190–191, August 18 and 19, 1947, and G-2/Historical Section, Hdqs., XXIV Corps—USAFIK PIR No. 640, September 23, 1947, Records of XXIV Corps and USAFIK, Records of Headquarters Far East Command, RG 554.

30. Hdqs. FECOM, "The Police and National Events, 1947–48"; CINC FECOM, "Summation of United States Army Military Government Activities in Korea," Nos. 18 and 19 (March and April 1947); Department of Public Information, "Korean Political Organizations and Leaders"; Leonard Bertsch, "Rightist Activity," September 19, 1947, Bertsch Papers.

31. SecState to CG FECOM, February 7, 1947, notes, *FRUS 1947*, 6:605–6; memorandum, "Korea," Special Inter-Departmental Committee on Korea, February 25, 1947, ibid., 608–20.

32. Maj. Gen. A. L. Lerch to Maj. Gen. T. Herren C/S USAFIK, February 15, 1947, CG USAFIK Office Files, 1947; Robert T. Oliver, *Syngman Rhee and American Involvement in Korea, 1942–1960* (Seoul: Panmun Book Company, 1978), 46–71; Maj. Gen. Albert E. Brown to Lt. Gen. J. R. Hodge, February 24–March 10, 1947, CG USAFIK Office Files, 1947; Minister Arthur C. Bunce to SecState, "Proposed Three Year Program for the

Rehabilitation of South Korea," February 25, 1947, CG USAFIK Office Files, 1947; M. P. Goodfellow to Lt. Gen. J. R. Hodge, January 16, 1947, M. Preston Goodfellow Papers, Hoover Institution for War, Revolution and Peace, Stanford, Calif.; William Stueck, "Syngman Rhee, the Truman Doctrine, and American Policy toward Korea," in *Studies on Syngman Rhee*, ed. Young Ick Lew (Seoul: Yonsei University, 2000), 639–66.

33. Maj. Gen. Albert E. Brown, USA, "Development of a Political Program," February 4, 1947, *FRUS 1947*, 6:607–8; transcripts, Maj. Gen. A. E. Brown interviews, March 5–7, 1947, Lt. Gen. Charles Herren Papers, U.S.Army Military History Institute.

34. Syngman Rhee, "A Solution of the Korean Problem," March 22, 1947, *FRUS 1947*, 6:604–5; SecWar to Acting SecState, April 4, 1947, ibid., 625–28. Much of Rhee's political action is also documented in Rhee File, M. Preston Goodfellow Papers, and Robert T. Oliver's book notes and document files, Robert T. Oliver Papers, Library, Pennsylvania State University.

35. My account of the Lerch mission is based on the Lerch-Hodge correspondence June 27–July 22, 1947, and other documents, all from the CG USAFIK Office Files, 1947, RG 338. Lerch stated the issues in a press conference in Seoul on March 27, 1947, transcript in USAFIK Office Files, 1947, as well as Brig. Gen. G. A. Lincoln, Hodge's chief planner, to Mr. Wilbur Denious, March 11, 1947, ibid. The Korea Project is described in H. H. Fisher (Hoover Institute) to Roger F. Evans (Rockefeller Foundation) and Alger Hiss (Carnegie Endowment), March 25, 1947, with attached memo, "Korean Project," as well as CG USAFIK to H. H. Fisher, May 3, 1947, with attached "Proposed Plan for Publicizing Korea in the United States," ibid.

36. Maj. Gen. A. L. Lerch to CG USAFIK, June 27, July 1 and 2, 1947, CG USAFIK Office Files, 1947. The Rhee faction account of the Washington discussions can be found in Oliver, *Syngman Rhee and American Involvement in Korea*, 92–118.

37. Maj. Gen. A. L. Lerch to CG USAFIK, July 2, 7, and 14, 1947, text of Korean Commission radiogram to Syngman Rhee and Rhee's reply, July 8 and 12, 1947, CG USAFIK Office Files, 1947.

The USAMGIK problems with labor unions are discussed in CG USAFIK to Maj. Gen. F. L. Parks, May 5, 1947; priority msg., Mr. Stewart Meacham to Labor Department, May 12, 1947; report, Mr. Stewart Meacham, "Labor Policy in Korea," September 11, 1947; and CG USAFIK to Chief, Civil Affairs Division, War Dept. Special Staff, January 8, 1948, all in CG USAFIK Office Files, 1947 and 1948, RG 554.

38. Maj. Gen. A. L. Lerch to CG USAFIK, July 15, 16, 18, 20, and 22, 1947, CG USAFIK Office Files, 1947. See James I. Matray, "Bunce and Jacobs: U.S. Occupation Advisors in Korea, 1946–1947," in Bonnie B. C. Oh, ed., *Korea under the Military Government, 1945–1948* (Westport, Conn.: Praeger, 2002), 61–78.

39. SecState Marshall to D. Acheson, April 2, and Acheson to Marshall, April 5, 1947, *FRUS 1947*, 6:624–25, 628–29; Molotov to Marshall, April 19, 1947, ibid., 632–35.

40. CG USAFIK to American Delegation to Joint Commission, April 28, 1947, CG USAFIK Office Files, 1947, RG 550; CG USAFIK to Maj. Gen. Albert E. Brown, June 9, 1947, ibid.

41. Soon-sung Cho, *Korea in World Politics, 1940–1950* (Berkeley: University of California Press, 1967), 143–58; the periodic reports of the activities of the Joint Commission can be found in W. Langdon to SecState, June 1, 1947; Hodge to SecState, June 26, 1947; J. E. Jacobs to SecState, June 28 and July 4, 1947, all in *FRUS 1947*, 6:658–61, 679–82, 688–89.

42. The authoritative accounts of the Joint Commission's experience in 1947 are transcript and notes of a conference held by Generals Hodge and Brown with Lt. Gen. Albert C. Wedemeyer, August 27, 1947, Brown Papers, U.S. Army Military History Institute; "US-USSR Joint Commission," transcripts and summaries, July–August 1947, USAMGIK, "South Korean Interim Government Activities" (SKIGA) Report No. 1, U.S. Army Military History Institute; and Political Advisory Group, American delegation, US-USSR Joint Commission, "Notes on Korean Politics," September 1, 1947, Bertsch Papers.

43. Maj. Gen. Albert E. Brown, "Political Situation as of May 19th," May 19, 1947, transcript and notes of meeting with Korean political leaders, Doksu Palace, Bertsch Papers; Department of Public Information, "Korean Political Organization and Leaders."

44. Kim Kyu-sik to J. R. Hodge, confidential memorandum with enclosures, April 14, 1947, CG USAFIK Office Files, 1947.

45. The proceedings of the Interim Legislative Assembly (also called the Korean Interim Legislative Assembly, or KILA) can be sampled in the daily summaries and supporting memos and intelligence reports in CG USAFIK Office Files, 1947. I also profited from memoranda for the CG USAFIK by Leonard Bertsch, "The Korean Interim Legislative Assembly," 1947; "Legislative Land Reform," October 16, 1947; Maj. T. E. Campbell and First Lt. L. M. Bertsch, "Political Survey: Cholla Namdo, Cholla Bukdo, Chungchong Namdo—September 10–26, 1947," September 29, 1947; "Rightist Activity," September 19, 1947; and "Election Law—Comment," September 20, 1947, Bertsch Papers.

46. Both proposed constitutions and accompanying analyses can be found in CG USAFIK Office Files, 1947. See MilGov to Acting CG USAFIK, March 20, 1947; translation and explanation, Interim Constitution in South Korea, February 28, 1947; draft, "Constitution for South Korea Interim Administration," February 27, 1947; G-2 USAFIK, periodic reports on the Interim Legislative Assembly, February 26–March 19, 1947; selected press reports, seven different Seoul newspapers, March 2–13, 1947; Office of the Korean Affairs Adviser, USAMGIK, daily summaries, Korean Interim Legislative Assembly, March 10–28, 1947; "Interim Constitution of South Korea," March 11, 1947; "Examination of the Interim Constitution and Administration of Government Bills before the Legislature," March 1947, all in CG USAFIK Office Files, 1947.

47. Office of Intelligence Collection and Dissemination, Department of State, OIR Report No. 4490, "Prominent Korean Officials in the United States Military Government in Korea," July 15, 1947, copy in CG USAFIK Office Files, 1947.

48. "Political Situation as of 31 December 1947," in 971st CIC Detachment, *Annual Progress Report for 1947,* 110–28; report, Special Squad, ibid., 135–40; Lt. Gen. John R. Hodge to W. R. Hearst, January 1948, CG USAFIK Office Files, 1948, RG 550; periodic (weekly and monthly) reports, no.1 (August 1947) to no. 27 (December 1947), National Economic Board (USAFIK/USAMGIK), RG 10, MacArthur Papers, MacArthur Library.

49. Lt. Gen. J. R. Hodge to SecState via CINCFE, July 2, 1947, *FRUS 1947,* 6:682–84. See also Jacobs to SecState June 20, 1947, ibid., 676–77.

50. Hodge to JCS via CINCFE, July 18, 1947, copy in CG USAFIK Office Files, 1947.

51. V. Molotov to SecState George C. Marshall, August 22, 1947, copy in USAFIK Office Files, 1947; "U.S. Sharp in Note to Russia on Korea," *New York Times,* August 14, 1947, and "Korean Voting Law Gets U.S. Approval," *New York Times,* September 5, 1947; Jacobs to SecState, August 12, 1947, *FRUS 1947,* 6:749–51.

52. Jacobs to SecState, September 8, 1947, *FRUS 1947,* 6:783.

53. Jacobs to SecState, September 19 and October 22, 1947, ibid., 6:803–7, 843–46.

54. Lt. Gen. Albert C. Wedemeyer, USA, "Resume of United States Policy toward Korea," appendix E to pt. III, "Korea—Political," in "Report to the President on China-Korea," ibid., 6:796–803; transcript of Wedemeyer-Brown discussions, Seoul, August 27, 1947, Brown Papers. See also William Stueck, *The Wedemeyer Mission* (Athens: University of Georgia Press, 1984).

55. SWNCC 176/29 (July 24, 1947) and SWNCC 176/30 (August 4, 1947), "Policy for Korea," *FRUS 1947,* 6:714–31, 738–41.

56. SecDef to SecState, September 29, 1947, ibid., 6:817–18; Kenneth W. Condit, *The History of the Joint Chiefs of Staff: The Joint Chiefs of Staff and National Policy,* 2 vols. (Wilmington, Del.: Michael Glazier, 1979), 2:179; Steven T. Ross, *American War Plans, 1945–1950* (New York: Garland, 1988), 25–101.

57. Memo, "Presentation of Korean Problem to the United Nations," October 1947, *FRUS 1947,* 6:832–89; State Dept. to Jacobs, November 3, 1947, ibid., 851; CG USAFIK to JCS, November 3, 1947, ibid., 852–53; SecArmy Kenneth Royall to SecState, November 19, 1947, and CG USAFIK to Undersecretary of the Army William H. Draper Jr., December 29, 1947, both in CG USAFIK Office Files, 1947.

5. THE UNITED NATIONS ENTERS THE STRUGGLE, 1947–1948

1. My description of the United Nations in September–November 1947 is based on Department of Public Information, Secretariat, United Nations, *UN Weekly Bulletin,* vol. 3, and coverage in the *New York Times,* September 17–30, 1947. The scholarly account is Leon Gordenker, *The United Nations and the Peaceful Unification of Korea: The Politics of Field Operations, 1947–1950* (The Hague: Martinus Nijhoff, 1959), 1–25. See also William J. Durch, ed., *The Evolution of UN Peacekeeping* (New York: Macmillan, 1993).

2. George C. Marshall, "A Program for a More Effective United Nations," State Department *Bulletin* 17 (September 28, 1947): 618–22. The principal American representatives were Secretary Marshall, Warren R. Austin, Herschel V. Johnson, Mrs. Franklin D. Roosevelt, and John Foster Dulles.

3. Acting SecState to Embassy USSR, September 17, 1947, in *Foreign Relations of the United States 1947,* 8 vols. (Washington, D.C.: Government Printing Office, 1971–1977), vol. 6, *The Far East,* 790 (hereafter cited as *FRUS 1947*); "Russia Informed on Move on Korea," *New York Times,* September 18, 1947.

4. Forrest C. Pogue, *George C. Marshall,* 3 vols. (New York: Viking, 1987), vol. 3, *Statesman, 1945–1959,* 336–54, 441–46; "Excerpt from a Speech by A. Y. Vyshinsky . . . ," September 23, 1947, in Foreign Ministry, USSR, *The Soviet Union and the Korean Question* (London: Soviet News, 1950), 33–34.

5. George T. Mazuzan, *Warren R. Austin at the U.N., 1946–1953* (Kent, Ohio: Kent State University Press, 1977). Austin spent ten months in China, 1916–1917, as a counsel for the American International Corporation, a transportation development company.

6. Richard H. Immerman, *John Foster Dulles* (Wilmington, Del.: SR Books, 1999); Frederick W. Marks III, *Power and Peace: The Diplomacy of John Foster Dulles* (Westport, Conn.: Praeger, 1993); Townshend Hoopes, *The Devil and John Foster Dulles* (Boston: Little, Brown, 1973).

7. "Korea before Assembly," *UN Weekly Bulletin,* September 30, 1947.

8. "Assembly Takes up Question of Korea," ibid., November 4, 1947; "Statement of

A. A. Gromyko . . . ," October 28, 1947, in Foreign Ministry, *The Soviet Union and the Korean Question*, 41–44.

9. "Committee Approves Korean Commission," *UN Weekly Bulletin*, November 11, 1947.

10. "Assembly Establishes Korean Commission," ibid., November 25, 1947.

11. Dietrich Rauschning, Katia Wiesbrock, and Martin Lailach, eds., *Key Resolutions of the United Nations General Assembly, 1946–1996* (London: Cambridge University Press, 1997), 190. See also Office of Public Information, United Nations, *Everyman's United Nations: The Structure, Functions and Work of the Organization and Its Related Agencies during the Years, 1945–1958*, 6th ed. (New York: United Nations, 1959).

12. Bryan Choi interview, October 13, 1996, summarized in Allan R. Millett, *Their War for Korea* (Washington, D.C.: Brassey's, 2002), 18–22. Sunny Che [Choe Pong-sun and Mrs. Charles Allen], *Forever Alien: A Korean Memoir, 1930–1951* (Jefferson, N.C.: McFarland, 2000), 171–75.

13. Horace G. Underwood with Michael J. Devine, *Korea in War, Revolution and Peace: The Recollections of Horace G. Underwood* (Seoul: Yonsei University Press, 2001), 102–30. Richard F. Underwood, "Memories and Thoughts" (ms., 2000), 67–79; "Fighting for the Koreans," in Millett, *Their War for Korea,* 192–98; CINC FECOM, *Summation of United States Army Military Government Activities in Korea,* no. 23, August 1947 (hereafter cited as *USAMG Activities*), USAFIK/USAMGIK Papers, MacArthur Papers, RG 10, and copies, U.S. Army Center of Military History.

14. Col. Charles H. Donnelly, USAR (Ret.), "Autobiography," 1979, with diary notes, 1948, 903–1015, Charles H. Donnelly Papers, U.S. Army Military History Institute, Carlisle Barracks, Pa.; John C. Caldwell, *The Korea Story* (Chicago: Henry Regenery, 1952).

15. Rev. C. A. Sauer, *When the Wolves Came: The Passing of a Pacifist in Korea* (Seoul: Yonsei University, 1973), 41–52.

16. CG USAFIK to C/S U.S. Army, June 17, 1948, CG USAFIK Official Files, 1948, Historical Files, Records of U.S. Army Pacific, RG 550, National Archives and Records Administration.

17. CG USAFIK to All Major Commands and Staff Sections USAFIK/XXIV Corps, January 3, 1948; CG 6th InfDiv to CG XIV Corps, March 30, 1948, CG USAFIK Official Files, 1948. The structure and condition of USAFIK can be verified in Hdqs. XXIV Corps G-3 Operations Reports, submitted on a weekly basis, January–March 1948, RG 554.

18. Clyde B. Sargent to Lt. Gen. J. R. Hodge, April 9, 1948, CG USAFIK Official Files, 1948; Joseph E. Jacobs to Lt. Gen. J. R. Hodge, December 18, 1947, ibid.; Arthur C. Bunce to J. Penfield, Associate Director, Division Far Eastern Affairs, January 20, 1948, Files 895.00/1-2048, State Department Central Files, 1948, General Records of the Department of State, RG 59, National Archives and Records Administration.

19. Shannon McCune, *Korea Today* (New York: Institute of Pacific Relations, 1950), 114–39; National Economic Board, "South Korean Interim Government Activities" (SKIGA), Report No. 34 (June and July 1948), 31–42, 228, MacArthur Papers; Office of the Economic Adviser to SecState, "Food Report for South Korea as of March 1948," May 10, 1948, reprinted in Cheju 4.3 Research Institute, *Migukmusong Chejudogwankyu munsoo* [U.S. Records Related to Cheju-do Internal Affairs, 1945–1950], 2 vols. (Cheju City, ROK: Cheju 4.3 Research Institute, 2000), furnished to me by the institute.

20. 971st CIC Detachment, *Annual Progress Report for 1948,* 30–34, 41–45; National

Economic Board, SKIGA, Report Nos. 28–30 (January–March 1948); Hdqs. FECOM, "History of the U.S. Forces in Korea," pt. III, "The Police and National Events, 1947–1948," ms. history, copy, USFK Historical Reference Files; National Economic Board, SKIGA, Report No. 32 (May 1948), 507.

21. CJCS-091 (Korea) memo, "U.S. Aid to Korea since Close of World War II," June 26, 1950, copy, Korea Subject Files, U.S. Army Military History Institute; Edward S. Mason, et al., *The Economic and Social Modernization of the Republic of Korea* (Cambridge: Harvard University Press for the Council on East Asian Studies, 1980), 167–81.

22. Arthur C. Bunce to R. N. Whitman, Division of Occupied Areas (Economic Affairs), Department of State, January 20, 1948, File 895.00/1-2048; National Economic Board, SKIGA, Report Nos. 28–34 (January–July 1948); Hdqs. FECOM, "History of the U.S. Forces in Korea," vol. 2, ch. 2; Sung-hwa Cheong, *The Politics of Anti-Japanese Sentiment in Korea* (Westport, Conn.: Greenwood Press, 1991), 47–56.

23. Donnelly diary entry, March 31, 1948, "Autobiography," p. 943; Political Advisory Group, memo, "Assassination of Chang Duk Soo," December 12, 1947, Bertsch Papers; "National Police," National Economic Board, SKIGA, Report No. 32 (May 1948); Hdqs. USAFIK, "History of Korean Department of National Police from 1 July 1948," 1948, with attached reports, USAFIK Historical Files, RG 550.

24. Robert K. Sawyer, "United States Military Advisory Group to the Republic of Korea," pts. I and II, 1945–1950, ms. history, 1955, copy, U.S. Army Center of Military History Library; Hdqs. ROKA, *Sabyon Hubang Chonsa* [The History of the Korean War in the Rear Area] (Seoul: Ministry of National Defense, 1956), 316–17.

25. William L. Roberts file, Records of the Association of Graduates, U.S. Military Academy, West Point, N.Y.; William L. Roberts 201 File, access granted by the Roberts family, 1998; William L. Roberts clippings file and memorabilia, Meigs County Historical Society, Millersport, Ohio.

26. Lt. Col. James H. Hausman interviews (1988 and 1994), in author's possession; narratives and diary entries provided to me by Col. Joe W. Finley, USA (Ret.); Lt. Col. Minor L. Kelso, USA (Ret.); Col. F. Foster Cowey Jr., USAR (Ret.); and Lt. Col. Charles L. Wesolowsky, USA (Ret.), all collected in 1995 and 1996.

27. National Economic Board, SKIGA, Report No. 31 (April 1948), 156–62; Adrian Buzo, *The Guerrilla Dynasty: Politics and Leadership in North Korea* (Boulder, Colo.: Westview Press, 1999); Andrei N. Lankov, "The Demise of Non-Communist Parties in North Korea (1945–1960)," *Journal of Cold War Studies* 3 (Winter 2001): 103–25; Erik Van Ree, *Socialism in One Zone: Stalin's Policy in Korea, 1945–1947* (Oxford: Berg, 1989), 175–86.

28. Hdqs. 971st CIC Detachment, *Annual Progress Report for 1948*, 17–56; the quote is on p. 56.

29. "On the Occasion of the Creation of the Korean People's Army," February 8, 1948, in Kim Il-sung, *Selected Works*, 6 vols. (Pyongyang: Foreign Languages Publishing House, 1971–1972), 1:195–203; MIS, G/S, FECOM, *History of the North Korean Army*, July 1952, File 330.008, USFK Historical Reference Files.

The best insider's view of Pyongyang, 1947–1948, remains "Yu Sŏng-ch'ol's Testimony," installments 5–8, originally part of 19 installments, November–December 1990, in the *Hanguk Ilbo* and reprinted and translated as appendix 5 in Sydney A. Seiler, *Kim Il-*

Sŏng: The Creation of a Legend, the Building of a Regime (Lanham, Md.: University Press of America, 1994).

30. Memorandum of Conversation: "Canada's Decision to Withdraw from the UN Korean Commission," January 3, 1948; Pres. Harry S. Truman to Prime Min. Mackenzie King, January 5, 1948; SecState to Acting Political Adviser (W. Langdon), January 6, 1948; and Memorandum, Chief Division of British Commonwealth to Under Secretary of State, January 9, 1948, all in Historical Office, Bureau of Public Affairs, Department of State, *Foreign Relations of the United States 1948*, 8 vols. (Washington, D.C.: Government Printing Office, 1973–1976), vol. 6, *The Far East and Australia*, 1079–84 (hereafter cited as *FRUS 1948*).

The UNTCOK's first visit to Seoul is analyzed by Gordenker, *The United Nations and the Peaceful Unification of Korea*, 26–69.

31. The UNTCOK experience, January–April 1948, is recorded in *First Part of the Report of the United Nations Temporary Commission on Korea*, 3 vols. (Lake Success, N.Y.: General Assembly, United Nations, 1948). See also Acting Political Adviser to SecState, January 15, 1948; Political Adviser (J. Jacobs) to SecState, January 24 and January 29, 1948; Political Adviser to SecState, February 2, 4, 5, 6, 8, and 12, 1948, all in *FRUS 1948*, 6:1084–85, 1087–97, 1105–9.

32. Memorandum of Conversation, Korea Affairs, Department of State, February 4, 1948, *FRUS 1948*, 6:1092–93; National Economic Board, SKIGA, Report No. 29 (February 1948); 971st CIC Detachment, "Political Activity," in *Annual Progress Report for 1948*, 57–84; Dr. Arthur C. Bunce to E. Martin, Dept. of State, January 17, 1948, File 895.00/1-2048, State Department Central Files, 1948; Robert T. Oliver, *Syngman Rhee and American Involvement in Korea, 1942–1960* (Seoul: Panmun Book Company, 1978), 119–39.

33. National Economic Board, SKIGA, Report No. 29 (February 1948); Political Adviser to SecState, February 10, 1948, *FRUS 1948*, 6:1097–98; 971st CIC Detachment, *Annual Progress Report for 1948*, 37–46; General Strike Committee against the UN Korean Commission to Lt. Gen. J. R. Hodge, February 7, 1948, Bertsch papers.

34. Gordenker, *The United Nations and the Peaceful Unification of Korea*, 56–76; "Elections Authorized for South Korea," *United Nations Bulletin* 4 (March 15, 1948): 214–18; Philip C. Jessup, *The Birth of Nations* (New York: Columbia University Press, 1974), 30–42.

35. CG USAFIK to SecState, February 22, 1948, *FRUS 1948*, 6:1125–27.

36. CG USAFIK Proclamation, "Elections," March 1, 1948, with administrative guidance, CG USAFIK Office Files, 1948; National Economic Board, SKIGA, Report No. 30 (March 1948); SecState to Political Adviser, February 27, 1948; U.S. Rep. to UN to SecState, March 1, 1948; SecState to Acting Political Adviser, March 3, 1948; and Memoranda, "Withdrawal of U.S. Occupation Forces from Korea," Office of Far Eastern Affairs, March 4 and 5, 1948, all in *FRUS 1948*, 6:1134–41.

37. 971st CIC Detachment, *Annual Progress Report for 1948*, 75–76.

38. "Future Soviet Tactics in Korea," excerpt, CIA Daily Summary, December 9, 1947, in Woodrow J. Kuhns, ed., *Assessing the Soviet Threat: The Early Cold War Years* (Washington, D.C.: Center for the Study of Intelligence, CIA, 1997), 159; CIA, ORE 15-48, "The Current Situation in Korea," March 18, 1948, National Security Archive; Jacobs to SecState, *FRUS 1948*, 6:1158–60.

39. Reports from Hodge, Langdon, and Jacobs to State Department, February 20–26, 1948; Hodge and Langdon to SecState, March 12–17, March 29, April 5–6, 1948. *FRUS 1948*, 6:1122–33, 1153–58, 1162, 1169–74.

40. NSC 8 with transmittal letters, April 2, 1948, *FRUS 1948*, 6:1163–69. I, however, depended on the record of proceedings of the NSC, ninth meeting, April 2, 1948, in NSC Records, 1948, President's Secretary's Files, Harry S. Truman Presidential Files, with annotations by Rear Adm. Sidney W. Souers and James S. Lay Jr., NSC executive directors.

41. Jacobs to SecState, April 7–14, 1948, *FRUS 1948*, 6:1175–79; Hdqs., USAFIK, "Summary and Conclusions: Technical Report of Elections of 10 May 1948," May 1948, Herren Papers; "Proclamation of the Rights of the Korean People," April 5, 1948, in *First Part of the Report of the United Nations Temporary Commission on Korea*, 2:60; National Economic Board, SKIGA, Report No. 31 (April 1948).

42. The only adequate account of the "Korean War before the Korean War" is John Merrill, *Korea: The Peninsular Origins of the War* (Newark: University of Delaware Press, 1989).

43. Park Chan-sik, "Island of Wind: A History of Misfortune, Banishment and Suffering," *Koreana* 13 (Summer 1999): 4–11. My family and I visited Cheju-do in 1991, 1992, and 1994.

44. Hausman interviews (1988, 1994) with Toland and Millett; Maj. Gen. Lim Sun-ha interviews, December 1998; Hdqs., FECOM, "History of U.S. Army Forces in Korea," pt. 3. For a detailed account of the Cheju-do affair, see John Merrill, "The Cheju-do Rebellion," *Journal of Korean Studies* 2 (1980): 139–97.

45. Lt. Col. Lawrence A. Nelson, USA, Special Investigator, Hdqs. USAMGIK, report, "Cheju-do Political Situation," 1948, copy in USAFIK Historical Files, RG 550, with appendices and endorsements.

46. Hdqs., FECOM, "Police and National Events, 1947–1948," in "History of the Occupation of Korea," 1948, pt. 3; National Economic Board, SKIGA, Report No. 31 (April 1948), 178–79.

The best single source on Cheju-do is Col. Rothwell H. Brown, USA, "Report of Activities on Cheju-do Island, 22 May 1948 to 30 June 1948," the investigative report prepared by a U.S. Army team commanded by Colonel Brown, CO, U.S. Twentieth Infantry and acting governor, Chollanam-do, copy in Rothwell H. Brown Papers, U.S. Army Military History Institute. The Brown report covers the background of the revolt as well as combat April 3–June 30, 1948. The Brown team interviewed the Korean National Police, Korean Constabulary, Northwest Youth members, islanders detained and free, and South Korean Labor Party captives.

47. Brown, "Report of Activities on Cheju-do"; XXIV Corps, G-3 Periodic Operations Reports for April 1948, Historical Files, Records of U.S. Army Pacific, RG 550.

48. Maj. Gen. W. F. Dean, CG, USAMGIK, memo, "Communist Activities on Cheju-do," August 10, 1948, USAFIK/USAMGIK Historical Files, RG 332. The portrayal of Pak Chin-kyung is based on Brig. Gen. Yi Chi-op ("Speedy" Lee), "The Korean Army Founders Association," a list of and biographical information on the first class, Korean Constabulary in the author's possession, as well as interviews with Maj. Gen. Lim Sun-ha and Maj. Gen. Kim Ung-soo (2000). Superintendent Cho Pyong-ok, "Opinion on the Settlement of the Cheju Situation," July 23, 1948, appended to Nelson, "Cheju-do Political Situation."

49. Hdqs., Korean Constabulary, weekly reports, May 1948, copies in the library, Korean Military History Research Institute, Korean War Memorial, Seoul; National Economic Board Report, SKIGA, Report No. 32 (May 1948); Lt. Col. Charles Wesolowsky, USA (Ret.), to the author, September 16, 1995, with attached reports.

American participation was directed by Lt. Col. John Mansfield, USA, commanding officer of the Fifty-ninth MG Company under the direction of Colonel Brown, who instructed Marshall to use the KNP to protect the towns and "to stop killing and terrorizing . . . innocent civilians."

50. The details of the murder are in Colonel Brown's "Report of Activities on Chejudo," but I benefited from a review of the case by Maj. Gen. Kim Ung-soo (2000), who served as defense counsel for the accused. Generals Lee and Lim provided characterizations of Choe Kyong-nok and Song Yo-chan, as did Colonel Wesolowsky, who served as regimental adviser.

51. Soon-sung Cho, *Korea in World Politics, 1940–1950* (Berkeley: University of California Press, 1967), 184–209; Gordenker, *The United Nations and the Peaceful Unification of Korea,* 49–85.

52. Langdon to SecState, March 12, 1948, and Hodge to SecState, March 17, 1948, *FRUS 1948,* 6:1150–54, 1155–57; Hodge to Maj. Gen. W. F. Dean, March 24, 1948, Official File, 1948; National Economic Board, SKIGA, Report No. 30 (March 1948), 188–90.

53. UNTCOK, *First Part of Report,* 3:1–60 and annexes III and X; Jacobs to SecState, April 14 and April 27, 1948, *FRUS 1948,* 6:1177–78, 1182–83.

54. National Economic Board, SKIGA, Report No. 32 (May 1948); UNTCOK, *Second Part of Report of the United Nations Temporary Commission on Korea,* 2 vols. (Paris: 3d Session, General Assembly, 1948), vol. 1; Hdqs., USAFIK, "Summary and Conclusions: Technical Report on Elections of 10 May 1948," Herren Papers; Donald S. Macdonald, "Korea and the Ballot: The International Dimension in Korean Political Development as Seen in Elections" (Ph.D. diss., Massachusetts Institute of Technology, 1977), pt. 2; Hdqs. Eighth Army, "The Police and National Events, 1947–48," in USAFIK, "History," vol. 2, pt. 3, pp. 16–31.

55. First Lt. Leonard Bertsch, "Report of Contacts," May 3, 1948, and "Interview with Kim Koo," May 7, 1948, Bertsch Papers; Jacobs to SecState, April 7 and 30, 1948, *FRUS 1948,* 6:1175–76, 1184–86; Jacobs to Sec State, May 3, 1948, ibid., 1188–91; Hodge to Chm JCS (Bradley) June 17, 1948, CG USAFIK Official Files, 1948; "North-South Conference," National Economic Board, SKIGA, Report No. 31 (April 1948), 156–62; Ministerstvo inostrannykh del. [Ministry of Foreign Affairs] USSR, "Message of the United Conference of Representatives of Northern and Southern Korea to the Governments of the USSR and USA . . . ," April 23, 1948, in Foreign Ministry, USSR, *The Soviet Union and the Korean Question* (London: Soviet News, 1950), 53–54; TASS communiqué, "Elections in South Korea," April 30, 1948; Margaret Carlyle, ed., *Documents on International Affairs, 1947–1948* (London: Oxford University Press, 1952), 701–2.

56. This analysis is based on data from Chi-young Pak, *Political Opposition in Korea, 1945–1960* (Seoul: Seoul National University Press, 1980), 64–78.

57. Excerpt, UNTCOK, *Second Part of Report,* ch. 6, cited by Jacobs to SecState, July 25, 1948, *FRUS 1948,* 6:1260–61; Gordenker, *The United Nations and the Peaceful Unification of Korea,* 110–29; Jacobs to SecState, May 26, 1948, *FRUS 1948,* 6:1207–10; JCS to CG FECOM, and memo for C/S USA, May 12, 1948, ibid., 1192–95; Hodge to C/S USA, June 17, 1948, CG USAFIK Official Files, 1948.

58. Cho, *Korea in World Politics,* 202–3; National Economic Board, SKIGA, Report No. 33 (June 1948); Hdqs. USAMGIK, "The Police and National Events, 1947–1948."

59. "Message of the United Conference of Representatives of Northern and Southern Korea to the Governments of the USSR and USA . . . ," September 10, 1948, in Foreign Ministry, *The Soviet Union and the Korean Question,* 57–59; 971st CIC Detachment, *An-*

nual Report for 1948; National Economic Board, SKIGA, Report No. 34 (July–August 1948). The quoted material is from 971st CIC Detachment, *Annual Report for 1948,* 14.

60. Constitution of the Republic of Korea, reprinted in UNTCOK, *Second Part of Report,* 2:23–31; National Economic Board, SKIGA, Report No. 34 (July–August 1948), 188–91; Pak, *Political Opposition in Korea,* 50–53.

61. 971st CIC Detachment, *Annual Progress Report for 1948,* 57–64; National Economic Board, SKIGA, Report No. 34 (July–August 1948).

62. Rodney J. Ross, "John J. Muccio," in *Encyclopedia of the Korean War,* 3 vols., ed. Spencer Tucker (Santa Barbara, Calif: ABC-CLIO, 2000), 1:461–62; SecState to Pres. H. S. Truman, April 27, 1948, *FRUS 1948,* 2:1183–84; Jacobs to SecState, May 26, 1948, *FRUS 1948,* 6:1207–10; Hodge to SecState, June 20, 1948, ibid., 1219–22.

63. Jacobs to SecState, August 12, 1948, *FRUS 1948,* 6:1272.

64. Syngman Rhee to M. P. Goodfellow, May 23 and July 17, 1948, Goodfellow Papers; Oliver, *Syngman Rhee and American Involvement in Korea,* 167–86.

65. Jessup (Acting U.S. Rep UN) to SecState, July 20, 1948, *FRUS 1948,* 6:1249–51.

66. July–September 1948 Record of Events, Enclosure 1, G-2, Hdqs. XXIV Corps Intelligence Summary No. 167 (October 1948); 971st CIC Detachment, *Annual Progress Report for 1948,* 39; *New York Times,* July 24, 1948.

67. Hdqs. USAFIK to Adviser, DIS, "Arrest of Korean Constabulary and Korean Coast Guard Personnel by National Police," memos and correspondence, August–November 1948, File 091.411, Classified Correspondence, 1948, Records of the Deputy C/S (G-3), Army Staff, Records of the U.S. Army Staff, RG 319, National Archives and Records Administration. The quote is from 971st CIC Detachment, *Annual Progress Report for 1948,* 17.

68. National Economic Board, SKIGA, Report No. 34 (July–August 1948), 1–86, which served as a final assessment and statistical analysis of Korea under the USAMGIK, 1945–1948.

6. THE REPUBLIC OF KOREA ENTERS THE WORLD AND ALMOST DIES STILLBORN, 1948–1949

1. Richard J. H. Johnston, "Dr. Rhee Becomes Korean President," *New York Times,* July 24, 1948. An excellent source on Rhee's presidency, 1948–1953, is the Syngman Rhee File in Korea, Miscellaneous Files, 1948–1953, White House Records Office Files, Harry S. Truman Presidential Papers, Truman Library. The file contains detailed information on Rhee, much of it hostile and sent by Koreans, as well as confidential letters from anonymous Korean sources—perhaps Chang Myon (John Chang) and Shin Ik-hui, American favorites among Korean political leaders. The file also includes copies of Rhee's speeches, newspaper articles, press releases, transcripts of meetings, and magazine articles. The Rhee file was maintained by William D. Hassett, presidential secretary and speechwriter.

In addition to printed descriptions of the events of July 24 and August 15, 1948, I used the C. H. Donnelly diary entries, July 24 and August 15, 1948, in "Autobiography," pp. 1000–1009, and the eyewitness account of Robert G. Shackleton, former senior adviser to the Cavalry Regiment. In addition, I watched contemporary motion picture footage.

2. "MacArthur Attends Korea Republic Fete" and "SCAP Sees Reunited Korea," *Pacific Stars and Stripes,* August 15 and 16, 1948; Syngman Rhee, "President's Address on August 15, 1948," program, "National Celebration," Capitol Grounds, August 15, 1948, all

in Personal Correspondence, August 1948, RG 10; and CINCFE to Chm. JCS, August 17, 1948, RG 9, MacArthur Papers.

3. Robert Shackleton to the author, March 7, 2003.

4. Lee Hyung-kun, *Gun-pun 1: Pun-hui Oi-kil Insaeng: Lee Hyung-kun Huigorok* [Serial Number 1: A Lonely Military Life: Memoir of Lee Hyung-kun], 100.

5. Chong-sik Lee, "The Personality of Four Korean Political Leaders," in *Korean Studies,* comp. M. C. Monahan (Seoul: Yonsei University, 1994).

6. House Report No. 2495, "Background Information on Korea," House of Representatives, 81st Congress, 2d Session, 1950.

7. National Economic Board, "South Korean Interim Government Activities" (SKIGA), Report No. 27 (December 1947), 152–54; Sung-hwa Cheong, *The Politics of Anti-Japanese Sentiment in Korea: Japanese–South Korean Relations under American Occupation, 1945–1952* (Westport, Conn.: Greenwood Press, 1991), 8–12.

8. National Economic Board, SKIGA, Report No. 34 (July–August 1948), 196–98.

9. Acting SecState R. A. Lovett, memorandum of conversation, September 23, 1948, in *Foreign Relations of the United States 1948,* 8 vols. (Washington, D.C.: Government Printing Office, 1973–1976), vol. 6, *The Far East and Australia,* 1309–11 (hereafter cited as *FRUS 1948*); SecState G. C. Marshall, memorandum of conversation, October 13, 1948, ibid., 1314–15.

10. Hdqs. USAFIK, Special Order No. 176, August 17, 1948, from Col. J. W. Finley, USA (Ret.); KMAG Roster 1949, copy from Col. H. G. Fischgrund, USA (Ret.); Hdqs., U.S. Eighth Army, KMAG Strengths, 1948–1952 and 1964–1969, File 200.408, USFK Historical Reference Files; "You and Korea," Gen. Thomas Herren Papers, U.S. Army Military History Institute, Carlisle Barracks, Pa.; KMAG, "Advisor's Handbook," 1949, Fischgrund Collection; Hdqs., PMAG, Information Bulletin No. 1, "Cooperation with Korean Law Enforcement Agencies," August 31, 1948, Mowitz Papers.

11. 971st CIC Detachment, *Annual Progress Report for 1948,* 47–48; Hdqs. USAFIK, "History of Korean Department of National Police for Period from 1 July 1948," October 1948, USAFIK Historical Files, RG 332; National Economic Board, SKIGA, Report No. 34 (July–August 1948), 247–51; Rhee to CG USAFIK, August 11, 1948, in Rosalyn Higgins, comp., *United Nations Peacekeeping, 1946–1967: Documents and Commentary,* 4 vols. (London: Oxford University Press for the RIAA, 1970), vol. 2, *Asia,* 151–309.

12. Col. J. W. Finley, USA (Ret.), to the author, July 23, 1995, and October 15, 1996; Col. J. W. Finley, "Experiences in Korea during the August 1947–December 1948 Period," furnished to the author; interview with Lt. Col. Hausman (1995); interview with Gen. Paik Sun-yup (1995); G-2, Hdqs., "History of the Rebellion of the Korean Constabulary at Yosu and Taegu, Korea," November 10, 1948, File TFGCT 091.411, copy furnished by Colonel Finley but also available in USAFIK Historical Files, RG550.

13. The events that preceded the Yosu rebellion are drawn from Hdqs. XXIV Corps, G-3 Operations Reports Nos. 42–54 (August 20–October 29, 1948), USAFIK Historical Files, RG 332; USAFIK, "History of Korean Department of National Police"; 971st CIC Detachment, *Annual Progress Report for 1948;* Hausman interviews (1988 and 1995); interview, Maj. Gen. Lim Sun-ha, Seoul, November 1994; G-2, USAFIK, Periodic Intelligence Report, October 1, 1948, USAFIK Historical Files, RG 332; PMAG, weekly reports, August–October 1948, copies on file in the research library, Korean Military History Compilation Committee, Korean War Memorial, Seoul; diary entries, July–September 1948, by Col. (then First Lt.) F. Foster Cowey Jr., USA (Ret.), former adviser to the Twelfth Regi-

ment, Korean Constabulary, 1948–1949, provided to the author; interview with Gen. Paik Sun-yup, January 5, 1995, Seoul; Gen. Chang Do-young, ROKA (Ret.), *Manghyang* [Nostalgia] (Seoul: Changmuri, 2001), 161–92, translated by Maj. Park Il-song; Col. John Lloyd, USA (Ret.), adviser, Sixth Regiment, Korean Constabulary, memoir (1996), furnished by his daughter, Mrs. Laura Prescott.

14. Maj. Millard Shaw, Acting Adviser, Police Department, "Police Comments on Guerrilla Situation," August 6, 1948; Joseph E. Jacobs to SecState, "Political Summary, July, 1948," August 16, 1948; and CG USAFIK to Intelligence division, Army Staff, Weekly Intelligence Summary (Week) No. 34, August 14–20, 1948, submitted August 21, 1948, all reprinted in Cheju 4.3 Research Institute, *Migukmusong Chejudogwankyu munsoo* [U.S. Records Related to Cheju-do Internal Affairs, 1945–1950], 2 vols. (Cheju City, ROK: Cheju 4.3 Research Institute, 2000), 1:562–71 (hereafter cited as CRI, *Cheju-do Internal Affairs*).

15. This account of the Yosu-Sunchon revolt is based on Lim Sun-ha, "Yosu-Sunchon Rebellion" (n.d., copy furnished by author); Capt. James H. Hausman, "The Yosu Rebellion," 1948, Hausman Papers; Hausman interviews (1988 and 1995); Gen. Paik Sun-yup, *Chiri-san* (Seoul: Koryowon, 1992), 147–93; Hdqs. USAFIK and PMAG, G-3 journals, October 20–27, 1948, with supporting messages and supplementary reports, USAFIK Historical Reports, RG 332; G-2 Hdqs., USAFIK, "Short History of the Yosu Campaign," November 1948, Hausman Papers; Maj. John P. Reed, "The Truth about the Yosu Incident," n.d. [1949], copy, Reference Files, Office of the Chief of Military History (OCMH).

16. Lt. Col. Minor L. Kelso, USA (Ret.), to the author, October 12, 1995, and January 9, 1996, with Sunchon photographs; Hdqs., Fifth Brigade "A Summary of Events," October 20–27, 1948, with supporting messages, Office of the Commander, PMAG Historical Files, RG 332.

17. Hdqs., Fifth Brigade, "Summary of Events," October 20 and 21, 1948; Hausman interviews (1988 and 1995).

18. Capt. J. H. Hausman to Cmdr. PMAG, 1048H, October 25, 1948, Hausman Papers.

19. Keyes Beech, *Tokyo and Points East* (Garden City, N.Y.: Doubleday, 1954), 139–41.

20. Chief PMAG to Capt. J. H. Hausman, 2210H, October 21, 1948, Hausman Papers; Hdqs., PMAG, letter of instruction to CG/Commander of Troops in Field (Brig. Gen. Song Ho-sung), October 21, 1948, Office of Commander, PMAG; Col. W. H. S. Wright to Hausman, October 22, 1948, attached to Hdqs., Fifth Brigade, "Summary of Events."

21. Robert G. Shackleton to the author, Korean War questionnaire (1997), letters July 1, 1996, and April 13, 2001, memorandum, "Korean Service, 1948–1949," April 11, 1997; Lt. Col. Ralph Bliss, USA (Ret.), to the author, February 13, 1997; Carl Mydans, "Revolt in Korea," *Life,* October 1948, furnished by Colonel Bliss; Col. F. F. Cowey Jr., diary entries, October 21–28, 1948, copies provided to the author.

22. Special Rep (Muccio) to SecState and U.S. delegation, United Nations General Assembly, October 28, 1948, *FRUS 1948,* 6:1317–18; Muccio to SecState, December 3, 1948, ibid., 1334–35; KMAG weekly reports, November–December 1948; memo, Roberts to Muccio, October 7, 1948, KMAG weekly report, copies in library, Korean Institute for Military History Compilation, Seoul.

23. Department of State, *Bulletin* 19 (October 31, 1948): 562.

24. 971st CIC Detachment, *Annual Progress Report for 1948,* 49; G-2, USAFIK, Intelligence Summary, No. 166, November 19, 1948, and G-2, USAFIK, Periodic Intelligence

Report (PIR) No. 1022, December 27, 1948; American Mission to Secretary of State, "Reviews of Observations of the Yosu Rebellion," November 4, 1948, in CRI, *Cheju-do Internal Affairs*, 2:646–53.

25. G-2, USAFIK, PIR No. 1022, December 27, 1948; G-2, USAFIK, "Short History of the Yosu Campaign," November 1948; Allen D. Clark, *History of the Korean Church* (Seoul: Christian Literature Society, 1960), 246–47.

26. Notes from conference, General Roberts and Yi Pom-sok, August 9, 1948, USAFIK/PMAG Historical Files, Series E11007, Records of the U.S. Army Pacific, RG 550.

27. This analysis is based on the Roberts-Yi conferences held between August 9 and September 20, 1948, with transcripts from the document collection cited in note 26, and additional analysis based on James H. Hausman, "The Korean Constabulary," n.d. [1949], Hausman Papers; and Lee Young-woo, "The United States and the Formation of the Republic of Korea Army, 1945–1950" (Ph.D. diss., Duke University, 1984).

28. Hausman interviews (1985 and 1995); Lim Sun-ha interviews (1994–1998); Capt. James H. Hausman to Chief, PMAG-K, memo, "Staff Study of Plans to Increase Present Strength of Korean Constabulary," November 6, 1948, Hausman Papers; interview with Gen. Chung Il-kwon, ROKA (Ret.), by John Toland, September 1987, Seoul, Toland Papers, Franklin D. Roosevelt Presidential Library, Hyde Park, N.Y.; Hdqs., PMAG, "An Examination into the Position and Functions of a Supreme Chief of Staff," August 26, 1948, with enclosed drafts of PMAG-proposed organization of Ministry of National Defense, PMAG Historical Files, RG 550; memo, "Proposed Organization and Functions of the Department of National Defense," November 26, 1948; Chief PMAG to Minister of Defense, memo, "Military Police," December 23, 1948; Director PMAG to Minister of Defense, September 29, 1948; Chief PMAG to CG USAFIK, December 1, 1948; Col. W. H. S. Wright, memo, "Difficulties Confronting PMAG," December 6, 1948, all in RG 550 or 554.

29. Director PMAG to President ROK, November 12, 1948, Weekly Reports, PMAG, November 1948; G-2, USAFIK, PIR No. 1011, December 13, 1948, and PIR No. 1022, December 27, 1948, a compilation printed by the Institute of Asian Culture Studies, Hallym University, 1989, copies in library, Korean Institute for Military History Compilation; Hausman, "Korean Constabulary."

30. "Coast Guard Historical Report," August 1–December 31, 1949, appended to KMAG Command and Historical Report, 1949, U.S. Army Pacific Command Reports, 1949–1954, RG 429; "Sohn Won-il," G-2, USAFIK, PIR No. 1022, December 27, 1948; Hakjoon Kim, "Sohn Won-il," in James I. Matray, ed., *Historical Dictionary of the Korean War* (Westport, Conn.: Greenwood Press, 1991), 427–28.

31. G-2, Hdqs., USAFIK, "North Korea," Intelligence Summaries No. 161 (October 15, 1948) and No. 167 (November 26, 1948), RG 338; Central Intelligence Agency, ORE 15-48, "The Current Situation in Korea," March 18, 1948, and ORE 44-8, "Prospects for Survival of the Republic of Korea," October 28, 1948, National Security Archive. See also Russell D. Buhite, *Soviet-American Relations in Asia, 1945–1954* (Norman: University of Oklahoma Press, 1981), 139–85. My analysis of Soviet-Korean relations is based on Evgeniy P. Bajanov and Natalia Bajanova, "The Korean Conflict, 1950–1953" (Institute for Contemporary International Problems, Russian Foreign Ministry, [1998]), furnished to me by the Department of Military History, Korean Military Academy. See also Charles K. Armstrong, *The North Korean Revolution, 1945–1950* (Ithaca, N.Y.: Cornell University Press, 2003), and Andrei Lankov, *From Stalin to Kim Il-Sung: The Formation of North Korea, 1945–1950* (New Brunswick, N.J.: Rutgers University Press, 2002).

32. Dae-sook Suh, *Kim Il-Sung* (New York: Columbia University Press for the East Asia Institute, 1988), 74–123.

The official names of the two Koreas present an interesting contrast in historical symbolism. South Korea is the *Daehan Minguk*, with *Daehan* being an imperial (1897–1910) title rooted in Korean prehistory that rejects *Chosun*, a name associated with Chinese dominance. North Korea, however, is the *Chosŏn Inminguk*, or Democratic People's Republic of Chosŏn (Korea), with *Chosŏn* being a historical name used as an alternative to *Korea*, a bastardized European name that began as the French *Corée*.

33. David A. Hatch, "The Cult of Personality of Kim Il-song: Functional Analysis of a State Myth" (Ph.D. diss., American University, 1986), 72–137.

34. "Stalin's Meeting with Kim Il Sung, Moscow, 5 March 1949," with notes and commentary by translator Kathryn Weathersby, in "Korea, 1949–50," Cold War International History Project *Bulletin* 5 (Spring 1995): 1–6, 9; text, "Agreement on Economic and Cultural Cooperation between the USSR and the KPDR," March 17, 1949, in Foreign Ministry, USSR, *The Soviet Union and the Korean Question* (London: Soviet News, 1950), 84–85; Installment No. 8, "Yu Song-ch'ol's Testimony," *Hanguk Ilbo*, November 9, 1990, in Sydney A. Seiler, *Kim Il-sung: The Creation of a Legend, the Building of a Regime* (Lanham, Md.: University Press of America, 1994), 133–37; Alexandre Y. Mansourov, "Communist War Coalition Formation and the Origins of the Korean War" (Ph.D. diss., Columbia University, 1997).

35. Suh, *Kim Il-Sung*, 83–105.

36. Joint Intelligence Committee, *American-British Agreed Intelligence, Soviet Intentions and Capabilities*, November 9, 1948, CNO Command File N2 TSC-000951, Operational Archives, Naval Historical Center, Washington, D.C., Navy Yard.

37. Civil Affairs Section, USAFIK, *Republic of Korea Economic Summation*, No. 36 (November–December 1948), 1–2, copy at U.S. Army Military History Institute.

38. Ibid.

39. Ibid., 1; USA-ROK Protocol on Economic Assistance, December 31, 1948, in Department of State, *Background on Korea*, 22–27; Syngman Rhee to M. P. Goodfellow, February 2, 1949, Goodfellow Papers.

40. American Mission in Korea to Secretary of State, "Political Summary for November 1948," December 7, 1948; "Political Summary for December 1948," January 10, 1949; and "Political Summary for January 1949," February 9, 1949, reprinted in CRI, *Cheju-do Internal Affairs*, 2:678–80, 705–11, 715–18; CG USAFIK, Weekly Intelligence Summaries Nos. 47, 48, 49, 51, and 52, November 20, 1948–December 31, 1949, in ibid., 665–67, 668–71, 673–74, 675–77, 681–84, 685–87, 688–90.

41. CG USAFIK (G-2) to CINCFE (G-2), memo, Communist underground forces, November 21, 1948, ibid., 668–71.

42. PMAG G-2, PIR No. 49, December 4, 1948, and PIR No. 1035, January 12, 1949; CG USAFIK (G-2) to Dept. Army, Week No. 45, November 6, 1948, in CRI, *Cheju-do Internal Affairs*, 2:658–61.

43. Capt. F. V. Burgess, USA, senior adviser, Ninth Regiment to PMAG, "Summary of the Situation on Cheju-do," October 30, 1948, PMAG Historical Files, RG 550.

44. Chief PMAG to CG USAFIK, December 1, 1948; Situation Report, CO, Ninth Regiment, Cheju-do, December 1, 1948; Chief PMAG, Current Activity Report, November 24, 1948, RG 338; Hdqs. USAFIK, G-2 Periodic Report No. 1015 (December 17, 1948); CG USAFIK to Dept. of Army, Week 46 (November 7–14), November 13, 1948; CG

USAFIK to Dept. of Army, November 21, 1948; CG USAFIK to Dept. of Army, December 24, 1948; American Mission Korea to Sec State, "Report of Minister of National Defense, Lee Bum Suk, on Internal Insurrections after April, 1948," January 10, 1949, with report attached; CIR, *Cheju-do Internal Affairs*, 2:662–704; Hdqs., USAFIK, PIR Nos. 1015, 1022, and 1025, December 17, 27, and 30, 1948; "Report of Minister of National Defense, Lee Bum Suk, on Internal Insurrections after April, 1948," January 10, 1949; American Mission Korea to Sec State, December 7, 1948. Government casualties were also loosely reported, but it appears that at least four hundred policemen and three hundred soldiers were killed throughout Korea, October–December 1948.

45. CG USAFIK (G-2) to Dept. of Army (Intel Div), December 31, 1948, in CIR, *Cheju-do Internal Affairs*, 2:688–90; Hdqs. USAFIK, PIR No. 1021, December 24, 1948.

46. Y. A. Malik, "Falsification of Elections in Southern Korea under the Cloak of the U.N.O. Commission," December 8, 1948, in Foreign Ministry, *The Soviet Union and the Korean Question*, 66–77; Acting US Rep to UN J. F. Dulles to SecState, December 6, 1948, *FRUS 1948*, 5:1334–35; statement of John Foster Dulles, "U.S. Urges Continuation of Temporary Commission on Korea," and "Joint Resolution," Department of State *Bulletin* 19 (December 19, 1948): 758–60.

47. General Assembly Resolution 195 (III) of December 12, 1948, in Higgins, *United Nations Peacekeeping*, 2:158–59; *Key Resolutions United Nations General Assembly*, 190–91; American Mission to Korea to Sec State, "Political Summary for December 1948," in CIR, *Cheju-do Internal Affairs*, 2:705–11.

7. "WE ARE FIGHTING FOR OUR LIVES!" 1949–1950

1. Director (Bishop), Northeast Asian Affairs Division to Director (W. W. Butterworth) Office of Far Eastern Affairs, December 17, 1948, in *Foreign Relations of the United States 1948*, 9 vols. (Washington, D.C.: Government Printing Office, 1972–1976), vol. 6, *The Far East and Australia*, 1337–40; Niles W. Bond, oral history interview (1973), pp. 26–35, Oral History Collection, Harry S. Truman Library, amplified by a telephone conversation with the author, March 2, 2000; W. W. Butterworth to R. Lovett, January 10, 1949, in *Foreign Relations of the United States 1949*, 9 vols. (Washington, D.C.: Government Printing Office, 1974–1978), vol. 7, *The Far East and Australia*, pt. 2, "Korea," 942–43 (hereafter cited as *FRUS 1949*).

2. C/S USA to CINC FE, January 14, 1949, and CINC FE to DepArmy, January 19, 1949, CSGPO JCS, File 091 (Korea), 1953, Records of the Chairman Joint Chiefs of Staff, RG 218, National Archives and Records Administration.

3. CIA, ORE 32-48, "Communist Capabilities in South Korea," February 21, 1949, and CIA, ORE 3-49, "Consequences of US Troop Withdrawal from Korea in Spring, 1949," February 28, 1949, with dissent, Department of the Army, National Security Archive.

4. CG USAFIK (for Muccio) to State Dept., November 12, 1948, General Correspondence, August 1947–January 1949, Records of the Undersecretary of the Army, RG 335; Special Rep. J. Muccio to SecState, January 27, 1949, *FRUS 1949*, vol. 7, pt. 2, 947–52; CG USAFIK to G-3, Army Staff, memo, January 10, 1949, File P&O 091 (Korea), 1949, General Records of the Army Staff, RG 319.

5. Hdqs. XXIV Corps, 971st CIC Det., CIC Monthly Information Report 7 (December 20, 1948) and Report 8 (January 12, 1949), XXIV Corps and USAFIK, Historical

File, 1949, RG 338; Alexandre Y. Mansourov, "Communist War Coalition Formation and the Origins of the Korean War" (Ph.D. diss., Columbia University, 1997), 1–122.

6. Memo of conversation, Undersecretary of State R. Lovett and Director, Office of Far Eastern Affairs (Butterworth) with Special Envoy Cho Pyong-ok, January 5, 1949, *FRUS 1949*, vol. 7, pt. 2, 940–41.

7. Memo of conversation, Pres. Syngman Rhee with Secretary of the Army K. Royall and Lt. Gen. A. Wedemeyer, USA DC/S (Plans and Operations), February 8, 1949, *FRUS 1949*, vol. 7, pt. 2, 956–58.

8. Thirty-sixth Meeting, National Security Council, March 22, 1949, Minutes, NSC Records, President's Secretary's Files, 1945–1953, Truman Library; NSC 8/2, "The Position of the United States with Respect to Korea," March 22, 1949, *FRUS 1949*, vol. 7, pt. 2, 969–78.

9. Leon Gordenker, *The United Nations and the Peaceful Unification of Korea: The Politics of Field Operations, 1947–1950* (The Hague: Martinus Nijhoff, 1959), 144–66; Robert T. Oliver, "Perspective on Asia," No. 82, "Korea," April 1949, reprinted in Cheju 4.3 Research Institute, *Migukmusong Chejudogwankyu munsoo* [U.S. Records Related to Cheju-do Internal Affairs, 1945–1950], 2 vols. (Cheju City, ROK: Cheju 4.3 Research Institute, 2000), 842–46 (hereafter cited as CRI, *Cheju-do Internal Affairs*); American Embassy, Seoul to Dept. State, "Operations of the United Nations Commission on Korea," April 26, 1949, ibid., 781–83; statement, Dr. P. O. Cho to UNCOK, May 16, 1949, ibid., 804–7; notes of discussion, Dr. Hur Kyang-duk (editor-publisher, *Seoul Sinmun*) with three members, UNCOK, March 27, 1949, ibid., 750–53; memo of conversation, Pres. Rhee with J. Muccio and E. Drumright, April 4, 1949, ibid., 755–60; American Embassy to State Dept., memo, "Draft Outline of UNCOK Report to General Assembly," July 23, 1949, ibid., 914–17.

10. SecState to American Mission, Seoul, April 13, 1949, and Muccio to SecState, April 13, 1949, *FRUS 1949*, vol. 7, pt. 2, 987–88; Pres. S. Rhee to Muccio, April 14, 1949, ibid., 990–91.

11. Memoranda of conversations, May 2, 1949, between Syngman Rhee and Yi Pomsok and J. Muccio, Brig. Gen. W. L. Roberts, and E. Dumwright, Seoul, *FRUS 1949*, vol. 7, pt. 2, 1000–1005.

12. SecState to Embassy, ROK, May 9, 1949, *FRUS 1949*, vol. 7, pt. 2, 1014–16; Acting SecState to Director, Bureau Budget, ibid., 1024–29.

13. The 1949 Shtykov-Tunkin correspondence with Moscow was translated by Kathryn Weathersby and printed in "Korea, 1949–1950," *Cold War International History Project (CWIHP) Bulletin* 5 (Spring 1995), with direct quotations also from the Soviet embassy, Pyongyang, and cables to the Foreign Ministry, Moscow, January 17–July 13, 1949, cited in Eugeniy P. Bajanov and Natalia Bajanova, "The Korean Conflict, 1950–1953" (Institute for Contemporary International Problems, Russian Foreign Ministry, [1998]). I also read another Soviet account of DPRK-USSR relations, 1949–1950, presented to ROK president Kim Young-sam by Russian president Boris Yeltsin in June 1994 and subsequently printed in Korean in *Chosun Ilbo*, July 26–August 4, 1994, translated for me by Dr. Kim Taeho. See also Mansourov, "Communist War Coalition Formation," 195–207.

14. Kim Kook-hun, "The North Korean People's Army: Its Rise and Fall, 1945–1950" (Ph.D. diss., University of London, 1989), 95–104; MIS, G/S FECOM, *North Korean Army* (Tokyo: GHQ, FECOM, August 1950); MIS, G/S, FECOM, *History of the North Korean Army* (Tokyo: GHQ, FECOM, July 1952), File 330.008, USFK Historical Files.

15. Kim, "The North Korean People's Army," 95–104; telegram, Shtykov to Vyshinsky, January 19, 1950; *CWHIP Bulletin* 5 (Spring 1995): 8; Bajanov and Bajanova, "The Korean Conflict," 43–47.

16. Charles K. Armstrong, *The North Korean Revolution, 1945–1950* (Ithaca, N.Y.: Cornell University Press, 2003), 219–31; Amb. T. Shtykov to Foreign Ministry, June 6–July 3, 1949, "A Prelude to Conspiracy," *Chosun Ilbo,* July 27, 1994.

17. Gen. S. S. Biryuzov to Foreign Ministry, February 4, 1949, reprinted in *Chosun Ilbo,* July 27, 1994; Kim Chae-pil, "One Measure of Freedom," in *Six Insides from the Korea War,* ed. Henry Chang (Seoul: Daedong Munhwasa, 1959), 143–219.

18. Telegram, Shtykov to Vyshinsky, September 3, 1949, translated and reprinted in Weathersby, "Korea," 6.

19. Telegram, Gromyko to Tunkin, September 11, 1949, and Tunkin to Soviet Foreign Ministry, September 14, 1949, ibid., 6–7.

20. Politburo message to Kim Il-sung via Amb. Shtykov, September 24, 1949, ibid., 7–8.

21. Gen. Dimitri A. Volkoganov, "Origins and Background of the War," June 23, 1994, International Symposium on [the] Korean War in Defense of Freedom on 44th Anniversary, Seoul; excerpts, weekly summaries, November 5, 1948–December 14, 1949, in Woodrow J. Kuhns, ed., *Assessing the Soviet Threat: The Early Cold War Years* (Washington, D.C.: Center for the Study of Intelligence, CIA, 1997), 255–345; David Holloway, *Stalin and the Bomb: The Soviet Union and Atomic Energy, 1939–1956* (New Haven, Conn.: Yale University Press, 1994), 234–93.

22. USAFIK, G-2 Periodic Intelligence Report (PIR) No. 1096, March 30, 1949; Ass't SecState to SecState, December 16, 1949, *FRUS 1949,* vol. 7, pt. 2, 1110–12; Sung-hwa Cheong, *The Politics of Anti-Japanese Sentiment in Korea: Japanese-Korean Relations under American Occupation, 1945–1952* (Westport, Conn.: Greenwood Press, 1991), 8–16.

23. USAFIK, G-2, PIR No. 1090, March 18, 1949, and PIR No. 1102, April 13, 1949; Horace G. Underwood with Michael Devine, *Korea in War, Revolution and Peace: The Recollections of Horace G. Underwood* (Seoul: Yonsei University Press, 2001), 117–20; Horace H. Underwood, "Dear Friends of Ethel's," March 17, 1949, Underwood Family Papers.

24. USAFIK, G-2, PIR No. 1102, April 13, 1949, PIR No. 1093, March 23, 1949, and PIR No. 1108, April 27, 1949; CG USAFIK to Dept. Army, February 4, 1949, USAFIK "Messages Out," January 1949–July 1950, RG 9, MacArthur Papers.

25. High Court-Martial Order No. 18, April 18, 1949, Office of the C/S, ROKA, copy and summary provided by Maj. Park Il-song, KMA, ROKA; MOD ROK *Hanguk Chonchaengsa* (Seoul: MOD, 1967), 1:749.

26. Pres. S. Rhee to Gen. D. MacArthur, May 22, 1949, RG 7, MacArthur Papers; memorandum of conversation, "Military Aid for Korea; Withdrawal of U.S. Troops," [Syngman Rhee with Mr. Muccio, Mr. Drumright], April 4, 1949, CIR, *Cheju-do Internal Affairs,* 2:755–58.

27. USAFIK, G-2, PIR No. 1115, May 12, 1949; FECOM, Joint Weekly Summary No. 33, May 21, 1949, General Records (Korea, 1949), Records of the Dept. of State, RG 59; Office of the Chief, KMAG, *Semi-Annual Report Period Ending 31 December 1949,* pp. 6–7, copy from File P&O 091 Korea, 1949–1950, RG 319; American Embassy to SecState, "Political Summary for May, 1949," copy in CRI, *Cheju-do Internal Affairs,* 2:847–53.

28. Amb. Muccio to SecState, June 11, 1949, *FRUS 1949,* vol. 7, pt. 2, 1041–43; USAFIK, G-2, PIR No. 1112, May 6, 1949, PIR No. 1113, May 7, 1949, PIR No. 1114, May

11, 1949, and PIR No. 1115, May 13, 1949; James H. Hausman, "The Korean Constabulary," n.d. [1949], Hausman Papers.

29. Chief PMAG, situation reports, December 1 and 3, 1948, PMAG Historical Files, RG 338; USAFIK, G-2, PIR No. 1015, December 17, 1948; oral memoir, James H. Hausman (1988), transcript, John Toland Papers, Roosevelt Library.

30. USAFIK, G-2, PIR No. 1108, April 27, 1949; Brig. Gen. W. L. Roberts to Lt. Gen. A.C. Wedemeyer, May 2, 1949, Correspondence, Chief PMAG, 1949, RG 554.

31. USAFIK, G-3, Operations Reports Nos. 2–19 (January 15–May 13, 1949), USAFIK Historical Files, RG 550.

32. USAFIK, G-2, PIR No. 1021, December 24, 1948; USAFIK, G-3, Operations Reports Nos. 2–19 (January 15–May 13, 1949); Lt. Foster Cowey, diary entries, November 17, 1948–January 5, 1949, provided by Lt. Col. Foster Cowey, USA (Ret.).

33. USAFIK, G-2, PIR No. 1108, April 27, 1949, and PIR No. 1115, May 13, 1949; Brig. Gen. W. L. Roberts to Lt. Gen. A. C. Wedemeyer, May 2, 1949; CG USAFIK to CINCFE, April 15, 1949, USAFIK msgs, January 1949–July 12, 1950, RG 9, MacArthur Papers.

34. Mansourov, "Communist War Coalition Formation," 148–86.

35. USAFIK, G-2/G-3, "Number and Intensity of Incidents along the 38th North-South Parallel," February 1949, USAFIK Historical Records, 1949, RG 550; USAFIK, G-3, Operations Reports No. 6 (February 12, 1949) and No. 8 (February 26, 1949), RG 550; CG USAFIK to DA (G-2), February 4, 1949, USAFIK "Messages Sent," 1949–1950, RG 9, MacArthur Papers; CG USAFIK to CINCFE, April 15, 1949, ibid.; personal journal entry, February 19, 1949, Col. F. Foster Cowey, USA (Ret.). The pilot was Capt. Keith French, USA.

36. My reconstruction of the Parallel War is based on USAFIK, G-2, PIR Nos. 1112–29, May 6–June 17, 1949), and USAFIK, G-3, Operations Reports Nos. 18–25 (May 1949), Records of the U.S. Army, Pacific, RG 550. The situation on May 1, 1949, is from Brig. Gen. W. L. Roberts to Lt. Gen. A. C. Wedemeyer, May 2, 1949, USAFIK Historical Files, Records of the U.S. Army, Pacific, RG 550; the best assessment is Col. Jay Vanderpool, USA, to Maj. Gen. C. L. Mullins, USA, July 28, 1949, Vanderpool Papers. Colonel Vanderpool was CIA representative in Seoul.

37. Memo for Chief, KMAG, February 7, 1949, and Brig. Gen. W. L. Roberts to Prime Minister Yi Pom-sok, February 10, 1949, Hdqs. KMAG, Historical Files, 1949, RG 554.

38. Chief, KMAG to Dept. Army, August 12, 1949, and August 19, 1949, KMAG "Messages Sent," 1949 file, RG 9, MacArthur Papers; Chief KMAG to Minister National Defense Shin Sung-mo, August 1, 1949, KMAG Historical Files, RG 554.

39. Hausman, "Korean Constabulary"; Brig. Gen. W. L. Roberts to Maj. Gen. Charles L. Bolte, DC/S (G-3), August 19, 1949, File P&O 091 (Korea) 1949, RG 319; KMAG to Dept. Army, July 2 and 22, 1949; USMILAT (Attaché) to Dept. Army, July 12, 1949, all in KMAG Files, RG 9, MacArthur Papers.

40. Lt. Charles L. Wesolowsky, USA, Eleventh Regiment adviser to Chief KMAG, May 15, 1949, furnished by Lt. Col. Wesolowsky; Col. Jay Vanderpool to Maj. Gen. C. L. Mullins Jr., Vanderpool Papers; USAFIK, G-2, PIR No. 1112, May 6, 1949, and PIR No. 1114, May 11, 1949; USAFIK, G-3, Operations Report No. 18 (May 6, 1949) and No. 19 (May 13, 1949); USAMILAT to Dept. Army, USAMILAT-28, August 2, 1949. The War Memorial, Seoul, has a memorial to the ten suicide bombers, and they have a prominent place in Ministry of Defense, ROK, *The Brief History of ROK Armed Forces* (Seoul: Ministry of National Defense, Information and Education Bureau, 1986).

41. The Parallel War is also described in Staff of the Korean Institute of Military History, *The Korean War,* 3 vols. (Seoul: Ministry of National Defense, 1997–2000), 1:57–62.

42. Chief KMAG to Premier Yi Pom-sok, February 4, 1949, Chief KMAG Historical Files, RG 550.

43. My reconstruction of the First Battle of Ongjin (May 19–June 14, 1949) is based on the contemporary notes, diary entries, and attached reports lent to me by Col. J. Foster Cowey Jr., USA (Ret.), the senior adviser to the Twelfth Regiment. Colonel Cowey, then a first lieutenant, observed the fighting from June 1 until his evacuation on July 19 with hepatitis.

44. Cowey notes and diary entires, June 13–23, 1949; USAFIK, G-2, PIR No. 1129, June 17, 1949; Col. Jay Vanderpool to Maj. Gen. C. L. Mullins Jr., July 28, 1949, Vanderpool Papers.

45. U.S. Embassy, Seoul, to Sec State, July 6, 1949, KMAG messages sent, 1949, RG 9, MacArthur Papers.

46. Brig. Gen. W. L. Roberts to Maj. Gen. E. M. Almond, C/S, FECOM, August 5, 1949, Chief KMAG Historical File, RG 554; Chief KMAG to Dept. Army, August 1 and 6, 1949; USAMILAT ROK to Dept, Army and Dept, State, August 3 and 9, 1949, MacArthur Papers.

47. Chief, KMAG to Minister of National Defense, September 30, 1949, Chief KMAG Historical File, 1949, RG 554.

48. Chief KMAG to Dept. Army, October 21 and 29, 1949, Chief KMAG Historical File, 1949, RG 554.

49. "Korean Coast Guard Historical Report," in Hdqs., KMAG *Historical Report 1949;* Ministry of Defense, ROK, "Military History in Korea," 1952.

50. Brig. Gen. W. L. Roberts to Maj. Gen. C. L. Bolté, August 19, 1949; USAMILAT Seoul to Dept. Army (G-2), October 5, 1949, MacArthur Papers.

51. Ibid. See also Chief KMAG to Min. Shin Sung-mo, "Political Appointments in the Korean Army," September 10, 1949, File P&O, 091 Korea.

52. Amb. J. Muccio to Ass't Chief, Division of North Asian Affairs, July 13, 1949; *FRUS 1949,* vol. 6, pt. 2, 1066–61; S. Rhee to H. S. Truman, August 20, 1949, ibid., 1075–76.

53. Brig. Gen. W. L. Roberts to Maj. Gen. C. L. Bolté, August 19, 1949; Brig. Gen. W. L. Roberts to Lt. Gen. A. C. Wedemeyer, May 2, 1949; Col. W. M. S. Wright to Gen. J. L. Collins, October 28, 1949; Office of the Chief, USMAG-Korea, "Historical Report, 1 July–31 December 1949," KMAG Historical Reports, Command Reports, U.S. Army, 1949–1954, Records of the Adjutant General's Office, 1917, RG 407.

54. S. Rhee to D. MacArthur, September 19 and December 2, 1949, with ROK MOD memorandum on the air forces of the DPRK, September 16, 1949, all in FECOM Official Correspondence, 1949, RG 9, MacArthur Papers.

55. Office of the Chief, USMAG-Korea, "Semi-Annual Report Period Ending 31 December 1949," DC/S DA (G-3), File P&O 091 Korea, 1949, RG 319; Chief KMAG to Dept. Army, November 12, 1949; AMEMB Seoul to CINCFE, December 23, 1949; KMAG to Dept. Army, January 30, 1950; Chief KMAG to CINCFE, February 14, 1950; CINCFE to Chief KMAG, March 17, 1950, all in KMAG messages, RG 9, MacArthur Papers; Chief KMAG to Maj. A. P. Mowitz Jr., July 11, 1949, Mowitz Papers.

56. Lt. Col. Leonard Abbott, USA, "Korea Liaison Office Report," May 15, 1951, RG 23, Maj. Gen. Charles Willoughby Papers, MacArthur Library.

57. "History of the G-4 Section," in KMAG Historical Report, July 1–December 31, 1949; USAFIK, G-2, PIR No. 1095, March 28, 1949; Chief KMAG to Min. of Def. Shin Sung-mo, October 4, 1949, File P&O 091 Korea.

58. Brig. Gen. W. L. Roberts to Lt. Gen. A. C. Wedemeyer, May 2, 1949.

59. James E. Webb (Under SecState) to Harry S. Truman, memo, meeting with congressional leaders, June 18, 1949, with enclosure, "Essential Points Concerning Korean Aid Bill," and SecState Dean Acheson to Pres. H. S. Truman, July 8, 1949, "Support for Korean Aid Program," both from Korea Aid Subject File, President's Secretary Files, Harry S. Truman Library. See also SecState to US Embassy, ROK, December 30, 1949, *FRUS 1949*, vol. 5, pt. 2, 1112–14.

60. Department of Defense, "U.S. Aid to Korea since Close of World War II," June 26, 1950, copy, Korea Aid Subject File; Director, MDAP, "Steps in United States Military Activities in and Aid to the Republic of Korea," June 25, 1950, Korea File, John H. Ohly Papers, Truman Library; oral history transcript, John H. Ohly (1971), Oral History Collection, Truman Library. I also relied on two studies done by my graduate research assistants: Mark Jacobson, "Notes on Congressional Discourse on the Arming of Korea, 1945–1950" (1998), and Michael B. Nelson, "Congressional Action on Military Aid for Korea, 1949–1950" (2000); both studies were based on congressional documents and the *Congressional Record*. The administration's aid priorities are clearly stated in Office of the President, memorandum of conversation, conference, the President, Secretary of State, and Secretary of Defense with the Atlantic Pact foreign ministers, April 3, 1949, President's Secretary's Files, 1949, and memo, "The 1951 Budget for the Department of Defense," 1949, Correspondence File, Frank Pace Papers, Truman Library.

61. The JCS endorsement of JCS 1776/4, "Korea," is found in its entirety in Chairman JCS, "Chronological Sequence of Events toward Korea," June 26, 1950, G-3, Army Staff, File P&O 091 Korea, 1950, copy in Records of the Joint Chiefs of Staff, RG 218. A detailed account of the history of the Mutual Defense Assistance Act, fiscal year 1950, can be found in Doris Condit, *The History of the Joint Chiefs of Staff: The Joint Chiefs of Staff and National Policy, 1947–1949,* 2 vols. (Wilmington, Del.: Michael Glazier, 1979), 2:423–36.

62. Steven L. Rearden, *History of the Office of the Secretary of Defense: The Formative Years, 1947–1950* (Washington, D.C.: Historical Office, OSD, 1984), 489–519.

63. Brig. Gen. W. L. Roberts to Maj. Gen. C. L. Bolté, September 13, 1949, and Maj. Gen. C. L. Bolté to Brig. Gen. W. L. Roberts, October 10, 1949, with "Present Situation of the Korean Army" attached, File P&O 091 Korea, 1949, RG 319; Col. W. H. S. Wright to Gen. J. L. Collins, October 28,1 949, File P&O 091 Korea, 1949–1950, RG 319.

64. MDAP Korea Survey Team, memo, "MDAP Negotiations," December 20, 1949, and Foreign Military Assistance Coordinating Committee," Report of MDAP Survey Team to Korea," February 8, 1949, both in MDAP Files, John H. Ohly Papers, Truman Library; "Fiscal Year 1950 Proposed Military Assistance Program for the Republic of Korea," December 17, 1949, copy in Chief KMAG Personal Correspondence, 1949, RG 338; Muccio to SecState, April 26, 1949, *FRUS 1949*, vol. 7, pt. 2, 995–97; Lee Young-woo, "The United States and the Formation of the Republic of Korea Army, 1945–1950" (Ph.D. diss., Duke University, 1984), 175–83; oral memoir, Miles Bond (1973), 26–39; Oral History Collection, Truman Library, confirmed in a telephone conversation, March 2, 2000.

65. Acting Chief KMAG to J. Muccio, October 6, 1949, File P&O 091 Korea, RG 319; Chief KMAG to Dept. Army, December 20, 1949, Chief KMAG Personal Corre-

spondence, 1949, RG 338; Foreign Military Assistance Coordinating Committee, "Report of MDAP Survey Team to Korea," February 8,1 950, Ohly Papers.

66. "U.S. Aid to Korea since Close of World War II," June 26, 1950; MDAP Administrator, OSD, "Report on Operations, Mutual Defense Assistance Program," August 28, 1950, Mutual Defense Assistance Program Subject Files, White House Confidential Files, Truman Papers.

67. SecState to USEmb Seoul, August 8, 1949; Chief KMAG to Dept. Army, September 21, 1949; Chief KMAG to Dept. Army, October 7, 1949; USMILAT ROK to CINCFE, May 24, 1950, all in KMAG Correspondence, 1949–1950, RG 9, MacArthur Papers. See also Headquarters, ROKAF, *Republic of Korea Air Force in the Korean War, 1950–1953* (Seoul: ROKAF, MOD, 2000), 31–36.

68. Memo, W. Galbraith to J. H. Ohly, June 27, 1950, "Acquisition by the Republic of Korea of Military Equipment on a Reimbursable Basis under Section 408(e) of MDAA," June 27, 1950, Ohly Papers; KMAG review of Coast Guard for Amb. Muccio, April 23, 1949; Muccio to SecState, July 26, 1949; Muccio to SecState August 19, 1949; Adviser ROK CG to Chief KMAG, September 26, 1949; Chief KMAG to Amb. Muccio, September 29, 1949; Amb. Muccio to SecState, October 7, 1949; all copies in File P&O 091 Korea, DC/S (P&O) Army Staff, RG 319.

69. M. P. Goodfellow to Pres. and Mrs. Syngman Rhee, January 3, 9, 10, 17, 24, and 31 and March 27 (2), 1950; Pres. Syngman Rhee to M. P. Goodfellow, January 19 and April 5, 1950, all in Goodfellow Papers.

70. SecState Dean Acheson to Charles Ross, January 20, 1950, and Dept. of State memo, "Analysis of Revised Korea-China Aid Bill," February 1950, Korean War File, President's Secretary's Files, Truman Papers; trip memorandum, Dr. Philip C. Jessup, January 14, 1950, in *Foreign Relations of the United States 1950,* 7 vols. (Washington, D.C.: Government Printing Office, 1976–1980), vol. 7, *Korea,* 1–7 (hereafter cited as *FRUS 1950*).

71. Memo of conversation, "Economic and Political Situation in Korea," March 15, 1950; Robert T. Oliver, *Syngman Rhee and American Involvement in Korea, 1942–1960* (Seoul: Panmun Book Company, 1978), 238–65; E. Drumright to SecState, February 10, 1950; and Bureau of Far Eastern Affairs, memo, interdepartmental meeting on the Far East, April 27, 1950, *FRUS 1950,* 7:26–28, 30–33, 48–52.

72. Amb. J. Muccio to SecState, June 27, 1949, *FRUS 1949,* vol. 7, pt. 2, 1045–46; interview with Ambassador James T. Laney by the author, July 1996, Seoul, about his duties as an investigator in the U.S. Army Counterintelligence Corps in 1949.

On October 22, 1996, an elderly Kim Ku disciple murdered An Tu-hui in his Seoul apartment. Colonel An, who had just returned to the ROK after living in the United States, was seventy-nine years old when he died.

73. FECOM G-2 Intsum No. 2723 (February 22, 1950), Willoughby Papers; Takemae Eiji, *Inside GHQ: The Allied Occupation of Japan and Its Legacy,* trans. Robert Richetts and Sebastian Swann (New York: Continuum, 2000), 480–85.

74. Notes, conference, DefMin Shin Sun-mo and Brig. Gen. W. L. Roberts, April 16, 1949, Chief KMAG, Personal Correspondence, 1949, RG 338; UNCOK, report on Cheju-do, May 17, 1949, in CRI, *Cheju-do Internal Affairs,* 2:350–51, 371; U.S. Embassy, memo On Cheju-do, May 1949, ibid., 855–56; UNCOK, report on "Provinces Affected by Recent Disturbance," ibid., 859–66; MILATTACHE Seoul ROK to Dept. Army, *JW* (Joint Weekly Summary) 17 (October 7, 1949), ibid., 867–68. Capt. H. S. Fischgrund, memo, "Tour of Cheju-do," November 22, 1949, ibid., 1022–24.

Casualty estimates for Cheju-do remain controversial and are exaggerated by anti-Rhee historians in Korea, Japan, and the United States. The government claimed that it killed 3,560 rebels, but the revisionists insist that the actual number, including the massacre of villagers, could be at least 30,000. The census figures suggest losses of less apocalyptic proportions: 233,445 (1946) and 253,164 (1949).

For a recent anti-Rhee, anti-U.S. statement, see Dr. Ko Chang-hun, "The Jeju Sasam (April Third) Uprising and Asian Peace" (paper presented at Cheju-do Conference, Harvard University, April 2003). See also John Merrill, *Korea: The Peninsular Origins of the War* (Newark: University of Delaware Press, 1989), 122–35.

75. G-2, KMAG, Periodic Reports No. 229 (December 13, 1949) and No. 234 (December 22, 1949), vol. III, USAMGIK, *Periodic Reports;* Capt. H. S. Fischgrund, USA, Ass't G-3 KMAG, "Resume of Korean Army Operations Prior to 25 June 1950," May 1951, and "Summary of Operations, Korean Army," 1950; Hausman interview with author (1995); Lt. Gen. Paik In-yup interview with John Merrill, Inchon, ROK, May 1978; Chief KMAG to Dept. Army, October 21, 1949, Chief KMAG Personal Correspondence, RG 338; U.S. Embassy, "Summary of Political Affairs of the Republic of Korea," September 1949, in CRI, *Cheju-do Internal Affairs,* 2:965–68.

76. U.S. Embassy, "Summary of Political Affairs of the Republic of Korea," October 1949, in CRI, *Cheju-do Internal Affairs,* 2:1002–6; Chief KMAG to Dept. Army, October 29, 1949, Willoughby Papers, MacArthur Library; Chief KMAG to Dept. Army, November 12 and 19, December 9 and 17, 1949, ibid.; MILAT to Dept. Army, December 16, 1949, in CRI, *Cheju-do Internal Affairs,* 2:1027–30; G-2 KMAG. Periodic Report No. 219 (November 22, 1949), No. 221 (November 29, 1949), and No. 225 (December 6, 1949), vol. II, USAMGIK, *Periodic Reports.*

77. G-2 KMAG Periodic Report No. 244 (January 6, 1950), vol. II, USAMGIK, *Periodic Reports;* Hausman interviews (1988 and 1995) and ms., "Korean Constabulary"; Fischgrund, "Resume of Korean Army Operations," 1950; FECOM Intsum No. 2683 (January 13, 1950), Willoughby Papers; G-2 (MIS), HQ FECOM, "A Brief History of MacArthur's Intelligence Service, 1941–1951," 1952, Willoughby Papers; "O Jin U, the Defense Minister of North Korea Is Dead at 77," *New York Times,* February 26, 1995; Kim Chom-kon, *The Korean War* (Seoul: Kwangmyong Publishing, 1973), 197–211.

78. Chief KMAG, weekly intelligence reports for October 21–December 30, 1949, Willoughby Papers; Paik Sun-yup, *Chiri-san* (Seoul: Koryowon, 1992), 215–55; FECOM Intsum No. 2698 (January 28, 1950), Willoughby Papers.

79. HQ KNP, report, "Incident at Suktal Village," January 1950, and report, CG ROK 3rd Division to KMAG, December 25, 1949, Chief KMAG Personal Correspondence, 1949, RG 338; USMILAT to Dept. Army, January 11, 1950, Willoughby Papers; Chief, KMAG, memo to U.S. Ambassador, "Report of Gregory Henderson," October 7, 1949, Office Chief of KMAG, Personal Correspondence, 1949, RG 338. Henderson is described in Harold J. Noble, *Embassy at War* (Seattle: University of Washington Press, 1975), 254–55.

80. G-2 KMAG Periodic Report No. 273 (March 3, 1950) and No. 284 (March 23, 1950), USAMGIK, *Periodic Reports;* Fischgrund, "Resume of Korean Army Operations," 1950; FECOM Intsums 2757 (March 26, 1950) and 2759 (March 28, 1950), Willoughby Papers.

81. Joint Intsums No. 11 (March 17, 1950) and No. 12 (March 24, 1950), in CRI, *Cheju-do Internal Affairs,* 2:1044–46, 1067–68; Hausman interviews (1988 and 1995); Walter Sullivan, "South Koreans in the Grip of Terror," *New York Times,* March 6, 1950;   Fich-

grund, "Summary of Operations, Korean Army," 1950. Hausman, for example, discouraged the ROKA from sending the heads of slain partisan leaders to Seoul for identification — with less than complete success. A detailed personal account of the campaign can be found in Gen. Yu Jae-hung, *Kyoktong-ui Sewol* [Years of Turbulence] (Seoul, 1994), 84–110, translated for me by Maj. Park Il-song.

82. G-2 KMAG Weekly Summaries No. 1 (April 1, 1950), No. 3 (April 20, 1950), No. 7 (May 18, 1950), FECOM Intsums No. 2772 (April 12, 1950), No. 2778 (April 18, 1950), and No. 2792 (May 2, 1950); Chargé E. F. Drumright to SecState, April 25, 1950, *FRUS 1950*, 7:47–48.

8. THE ONCE AND FUTURE INVASION, 1949–1950

1. David Holloway, *Stalin and the Bomb: The Soviet Union and Atomic Energy, 1939–1945* (New Haven, Conn.: Yale University Press, 1994), 273–93; Richard Rhodes, *Dark Sun: The Making of the Hydrogen Bomb* (New York: Simon and Schuster, 1995), 364–74.

2. Shen Zhi Hua, "The Sino-Soviet Treaty of Friendship, Alliance and Mutual Assistance and the Origins of the Korean War" (Association of Chinese Historians, 2000), copy sent to author; Chen Jian, "The Sino-Soviet Alliance and China's Entry into the Korean War" (working paper no. 1, Woodrow Wilson Center for International Scholars, 1992); Sergei N. Goncharov, John W. Lewis, and Xue Litai, *Uncertain Partners: Stalin, Mao, and the Korean War* (Stanford, Calif.: Stanford University Press, 1993), 36–109; Niu Jun, "The Origins of the Sino-Soviet Alliance," in *Brothers in Arms: The Rise and Fall of the Sino-Soviet Alliance, 1945–1963,* ed. Odd Arne Westad (Stanford, Calif.: Stanford University Press for the Woodrow Wilson Center, 1998), 47–89; Alexandre Y. Mansourov, "Communist War Coalition Formation and the Origins of the Korean War" (Ph.D. diss., Columbia University, 1997), 255–324.

3. This description is based on accounts by Philip Short, *Mao* (New York: John McLean, 1999), 416–21, and Ross Terrill, *Mao* (New York: Harper and Row, 1980), 195–99. I visited all these sites in 1996 and 1998.

4. Chen Jian, Vojtech Mastny, Odd Arne Westad, and Vladislav Zubok, trans. and commentators, "Stalin's Conversations with Chinese Leaders," *CWIHP Bulletin* 6–7 (Winter 1995–1996): 409, 420–29; Odd Arne Westad, "Fighting for Friendship: Mao, Stalin and the Sino-Soviet Treaty of 1950," in *Brothers in Arms,* with twenty-six translated telegrams and memoranda, December 18, 1949–February 20, 1950, including communications between Mao Zedong and the Central Committee, Chinese Communist Party; Chen Jian, *Mao's China and the Cold War* (Chapel Hill: University of North Carolina Press, 2001), 49–84.

5. Goncharov, Lewis, and Xue, *Uncertain Partners,* 110–29, including the text of the treaty and associated documents (259–64). See also Mansourov, "Communist War Coalition Formation," ch. 5.

6. Steven L. Rearden, *History of the Office of the Secretary of Defense,* vol. 1, *The Formative Years, 1947–1950* (Washington, D.C.: Historical Office, Office of the Secretary of Defense, 1984), 361–422, 537–50.

7. Kenneth W. Condit, *The History of the Joint Chiefs of Staff: The Joint Chiefs of Staff and National Policy,* vol. 2, *1947–1949* (Washington, D.C.: Historical Division, Joint Chiefs of Staff, 1979), 213–79, 288–309, 493–521, 523–60.

8. ORE, CIA, "The Strategic Importance of the Far East to the US and USSR," ORE

17-49, May 4, 1949, National Security Archive; ORE, CIA, "Estimate of the Effects of the Soviet Possession of the Atomic Bomb upon the Security of the United States and upon the Probabilities of Direct Soviet Military Action," ORE 91-49, April 6, 1950, in Woodrow J. Kuhns, ed., *Assessing the Soviet Threat: The Early Cold War Years* (Washington, D.C.: Center for the Study of Intelligence, CIA, 1997), 336–79.

9. Army Staff, "Implications of a Possible Full Scale Invasion from North Korea Subsequent to Withdrawal of United States Troops from South Korea," June 27, 1949, in *Foreign Relations of the United States 1949*, 9 vols. (Washington, D.C.: Government Printing Office, 1974–1978), vol. 7, *The Far East and Australia*, 1046–57.

10. JCS, "Review of Current World Situation and Ability of the Forces Being Maintained to Meet U.S. Commitments," February 1950, Omar N. Bradley Book Files, Clay Blair Papers, U.S. Army Military History Institute, Carlisle Barracks, Pa.

11. Minutes, Joint Committee, FECOM, Meetings 1–11 (August 1, 1949–June 6, 1950), Korea Files, RG 9, MacArthur Papers; oral memoir, Maj. Gen. E. K. Wright, USA (Ret.), 1971, D. Clayton James Papers, MacArthur Library.

12. This interpretation is based on a "Princeton seminar" on China and Korea conducted on February 13–14, 1954, under Secretary of State Acheson's sponsorship and designed to record material for Acheson's memoir, *Present at the Creation* (1969). The participants were Acheson, Herbert Feis, Kennan, J. Robert Oppenheimer, Nitze, George Perkins, Jessup, and Harriman, as well as three Princeton faculty who served as rapporteurs and questioners. The transcripts are available in Dean Acheson Papers, Truman Library. See also Dean Rusk, *As I Saw It* (New York: W. W. Norton, 1990), 154–77; Warren I. Cohen, *Dean Rusk* (Totowa, N.J.: Cooper Square Publishers, 1980), 6–76; and John M. Allison, *Ambassador from the Prairie* (Boston: Houghton Mifflin, 1973), 116–39.

13. Secretary of State Dean Acheson, "Crisis in Asia—An Examination of U.S. Policy," Department of State *Bulletin* 22 (January 23, 1950): 111–18.

14. Amb. J. Muccio to SecState, January 18, 1950; Chargé E. Drumright to SecState, January 28, 1950; Chargé E. Drumright to SecState, February 10, 1950; Amb J. Muccio to SecState, March 29, 1950; and conference notes, Assistant Sec. Rusk with Ambassador Chang, April 3, 1950, all in *Foreign Relations of the United States 1950*, 7 vols. (Washington, D.C.: Government Printing Office, 1977–1980), vol. 7, *Korea*, 8–11, 18–23, 26–28, 37–38, 40–43 (hereafter cited as *FRUS 1950*).

15. For the odyssey of NSC 68, see the documents in *FRUS 1950*, vol. 1, *National Security Affairs*; *Foreign Economic Policy,* 126–324, especially G. Kennan to SecState, January 6, 1950; record of meeting NSC State Committee, March 2, 1950; record of principals' meeting, March 22, 1950; NSC 68, April 7, 1950. NSC 68 and its neglected annexes 1–11 can be found in NSC Files, 1950, Records of the National Security Council, RG 273, National Archives and Records Administration, with additional copies in the NSC Files, Truman Library. Annex 1, "Military Programs," provides the JCS-approved force structure and budget estimates. I have followed Rearden, *History of the Office of the Secretary of Defense,* 521–36. The unsuccessful pitch for NSC 68 can be found in a panel discussion, "Why National Defense and International Cooperation Are Good Investments," May 15, 1950, Democratic National Convention, Speech File, Frank Pace Papers, Truman Library.

16. S. Rhee to R. T. Oliver, September 30, 1949, reprinted in Robert T. Oliver, *Syngman Rhee and American Involvement in Korea, 1942–1960* (Seoul: Panmun Book Company, 1978), 251–52; U.S. Embassy, ROK, memo, "Situation in Korea," April 3, 1950, *FRUS 1950*, 7:40–43.

17. E. Drumright to SecState, May 2, 1950 (two messages), and May 3, 1950, *FRUS 1950*, 7:59–63, 66; annex 8, pt. II, "The Conditions of Success of the U.S. Programs in Asia," NSC 68; SecState to Amb. J. Muccio, April 13, 1950; SecState to Amb. J. Chang, ROK, "Aide Memoire," April 3, 1950; "Inter-departmental Meeting on the Far East," April 27, 1950; Chargé E. Drumright to SecState, April 28, 1950, all in *FRUS 1950*, 7:43–44, 45–46, 48–52.

18. S. Rhee to R. T. Oliver, September 30, 1949.

19. Chargé E. Drumright to SecState, May 5, 1950, 68–74; Acting Chairman UNCOK (Jamieson) to UN SecGen T. Lie, April 28, 1950, *FRUS 1950*, 7:75–76; Leon Gordenker, *The United Nations and the Peaceful Unification of Korea: The Politics of Field Operations, 1947–1950* (The Hague: Martinus Nijhoff, 1959), 186–210; File, "Chiang-Quirino Proposal for a Pacific Union," documents, July 1949–May 1950, John Melby Papers, Truman Library.

20. G-2, KMAG Order-of-Battle Situation Map, January 1950, copy furnished by Col. Harold S. Fischgrund, USA (Ret.).

21. G-3, KMAG, "Korea," an estimate of the situation, January 1, 1950, copy furnished by Colonel Fischgrund.

22. Conference briefing, Lt. Col. Ralph W. Hansen, USA, January 1950, copy furnished by Colonel Fischgrund.

23. Operation Cruller, July 14, 1949, G-3 Army Staff, File 381, P&O Decimal Files, 1949, Records of the Army Staff, RG 319.

24. MIS, G/S, FECOM, *History of the North Korean Army,* July 1952, File 330.008, Eighth Army Historical Files, Dean Heritage Center, Yongsan, Seoul; MIS, G/S, FECOM, *History of North Korean Army Units: Corps and Divisions,* 1952, File 330.008; 500th MIS Group, translation, "Military History in Korea," 1952, Doc. No. 74969, copy in File 091, "Korea," G-3 P&O Files, 1952, RG 319 (a translation of a history done for the Ministry of Defense, ROK); Lt. Col. Leonard Abbott, USA, "Korea Liaison Office Report," with attached samples of 417 KLO reports, January 1–June 25, 1950, Charles Willoughby Papers, RG 23, MacArthur Papers.

25. J. Stalin to Amb. T. Shtykov, January 30, 1950, quoted in Evgeniy P. Bajanov and Natalia Bajanova, "The Korean Conflict, 1950–1953" (Institute for Contemporary International Problems, Russian Foreign Ministry, [1998]), 36. The North Korean–Soviet exchanges, January–March 1950, can be reconstructed from the Stalin-Vishinsky-Shtykov cable traffic, January 30–March 24, 1950, translated and printed in three collections: Bajanov and Bajanova, "The Korean Conflict," 36–42; pt. E, "Three Devil's Provocation," the Soviet account, with documents published in *Chosun Ilbo,* July 27, 1994, and translated by Dr. Kim Taeho; and Kathryn Weathersby, ed. and trans., "New Documents on the Korean War," *CWHIP Bulletin* 6–7 (Winter 1995–1996): 30–39.

26. Mansourov, "Communist War Coalition Formation," 255–324; Bajanov and Bajanova, "The Korean Conflict," 40–42.

27. A. Ignatieff to Vishinsky, April 10, 1950, and Shtykov to Vishinsky, May 12, 1950, in Weathersby, "New Documents on the Korean War," 38–39; Bajanov and Bajanova, "The Korean Conflict," 47–52; Abbott, "Korean Liaison Office Report," May 1951.

28. Abbott, "Korean Liaison Office Report," May 1951; G-2, MIS, Hdqs., FECOM, "A Brief History of MacArthur's Intelligence Service, 1941–1951," 1951, Willoughby Papers; Louise Yim, *My Forty Year Fight for Korea* (Seoul: Chung-ang University, 1967), 297–307; Gen. Chang Do-young, ROKA (Ret.), *Manghyang* [Nostalgia] (Seoul: Chang-

muri, 2001), 181–92; KLO #490A, May 10, 1950, and KLO #498C, May 15, 1950, appended to Abbott, "Korean Liaison Office Report."

29. FECOM Daily Intelligence Summary 2754, March 25, 1950, quoted in "A Brief History of MacArthur's Intelligence Service," 2; G-2, FECOM, "The North Korean Pre-Invasion Build-up," 1951, Willoughby Papers.

30. Office of Research and Estimates, CIA, "Current Capabilities of the Northern Korean Regime, June 19, 1950," ORE 18-50, National Security Archive. The CIA's problems are described in oral memoir, Gen. Richard G. Stilwell, USA (1979), Senior Officer Oral History Collection, U.S. Army Military History Institute; in March 1950, Stilwell was head of the Far East Division, OPC, CIA. See also Arthur B. Darling, *The Central Intelligence Agency: An Instrument of Government, to 1950* (University Park; Pennsylvania State University Press, 1990), 193–332.

31. Amb. Philip Jessup to SecState, January 14, 1950; Amb. J. Muccio to SecState, January 25, 1950; Brig. Gen. W. L. Roberts to Amb. J. Muccio, January 7, 1950; all in *FRUS 1950,* 7:1–7, 15–16, 16–18.

32. Brig. Gen. W. L. Roberts, chief, KMAG, briefing for the Chairman JCS, January 24, 1950, appended to CJCS, "Notes on the Visit of the Joint Chiefs of Staff to the Far East," February 16, 1950, Decimal File 091 (Japan), Office of the Chairman, Records of the Joint Chiefs of Staff, 1950, RG 218.

33. Undersecretary of the Army Tracy Voorhees to Gen. D. MacArthur, February 27, 1950, Official Correspondence 1950, MacArthur Papers; CINCFE to Dept. Army, May 29, 1950; CINCFE, "Memorandum on Formosa," June 14, 1950; CINCFE, "Memorandum on the Peace Treaty Problem," June 14, 1950, both in Formosa File, 1948–1950, FECOM General Files, MacArthur Papers. The influence of Formosa on strategic planning for Asia is summarized in Condit, *History of the JCS,* 2:493–521.

34. Chief, KMAG to G-3 (P&O), Army Staff, March 25, 1950, FECOM radiograms, January–March 1950, RG 9, MacArthur Papers; Hausman memoir (1985); G-3 to Chief, KMAG, "Reduction of Personnel Strength KMAG," April 17, 1950, and Chief, KMAG to Dept. Army (G-3), April 21, 1950, G-3 P&O File 091 (Korea) 1950, RG 319.

35. Am Embassy Seoul to SecState, May 11, 1950, and Am Embassy Seoul to CINCFE, May 11, 1950, RG 9, MacArthur Papers.

36. Brig. Gen. W. L. Roberts to Maj. Gen. C. L. Bolté, March 8, 1950, P&O G-3 File 091 (Korea), RG 319; Amb. J. Muccio to Asst Sec D. Rusk, June 1, 1950, *FRUS 1950,* 7:96–98.

37. Chief, KMAG to the ROKA, June 1, 1950, File 300.6, KMAG Historical Files, 1950, RG 554; Hausman interview with author (1994); Bond oral history (1973); Roberts 201 File; clippings in Roberts file, USMA Association of Graduates; Dorothy House Vieman, *Korean Adventure: Inside Story of an Army Wife* (San Antonio, Tex.: Naylor Company, 1951), 85–94—a collection of Mrs. Vieman's letters and diary entries, Seoul, May 4–June 16, 1950.

38. Frank Gibney, "Progress Report," *Time,* June 5, 1950; Marguerite Higgins, "U.S. Army Mission Called Success in South Korea's Fight on Reds," *New York Herald-Tribune,* June 5, 1950. Neither of these articles quotes Roberts as saying that the ROKA was "the best doggone shooting army outside the United States" or that it was "the best little army in Asia," as is often attributed to Roberts.

39. SecState to Am Embassy, June 13, 1950, and Amb. J. Muccio to SecState, June 14, 1950, *FRUS 1950,* 7:104–5; Amb. J. Muccio, "Military Aid to Korean Security Forces,"

June 9, 1950, in State Department *Bulletin* 13 (June 26, 1950): 1048–49; *FRUS 1950*, 7:321–322.

40. Capt. R. K. Sawyer, "United States Military Advisory Group to the Republic of Korea," pt. II, July 1, 1949–June 24, 1950, manuscript history, 1954, copy USFK Historical Files; testimony, Sec State D. Acheson and Sec Def L. Johnson, U.S. Senate Committees on Armed Services and Foreign Relations, *Hearings: Military Situation in the Far East*, 82d Congress, 1st Session, 1951, 5 vols. (New York: Arno, 1979), 3:2009–13, 2647; U.S. House, Committee on International Relations, "United States Policy in the Far East," pt. 2, "Korea Assistance Acts, Far East Portion of the Mutual Defense Act of 1920," 82d Congress, 1st Session, 1951; Gen. Omar N. Bradley and Clay Blair, *A General's Life* (New York: Simon and Schuster, 1983), 526–27, 529–30; Gen. J. Lawton Collins, *War in Peacetime: The History and Lessons of Korea* (Boston: Houghton Mifflin, 1969), 41–44. Roberts paid for his alleged enthusiasm for the ROKA by being denied a Distinguished Service Medal (usually awarded to a general officer upon retirement) when he left active service on September 30, 1950.

41. Headquarters, KMAG, *Semi-Annual Report*, January 1–June 15, 1950, copies in archives, Korean Institute for Military History Compilation, Seoul, and in G-3, Army Staff (P&O), File 091 Korea, Decimal File, 1950, RG 319; summary, "Interdepartmental Meeting on the Far East," April 27, 1950, *FRUS 1950*, 7:48–52.

42. Connally interview and E. Drumright to SecState, May 5, 1950; U.S. Embassy ROK, "Military Assistance to Korea," May 10, 1950; J. Muccio to SecState, June 14, 1950, all in *FRUS 1950*, 7:66–67, 78–81, 105; presidential message to Congress, "Continued Military Assistance: A Protection against Enslavement," June 1, 1950, in State Department *Bulletin* 23 (June 12, 1950): 938–40.

EPILOGUE AND PROLOGUE, JUNE 1950

1. John Foster Dulles, memorandum of conversation with President Truman, April 28, 1950, John Foster Dulles Papers, Seeley G. Mudd Manuscript Library, Princeton University. The scholarly account is Laurence A. Yates, "John Foster Dulles and Bipartisanship, 1944–1952" (Ph.D. diss., University of Kansas, 1981), 321–51.

2. Howard B. Schonberger, "John Foster Dulles," in *Aftermath of War: Americans and the Remaking of Japan, 1945–1952* (Kent, Ohio: Kent State University Press, 1989), 236–78; memorandum of conversation, John Allison, June 19, 1950, in *Foreign Relations of the United States 1950*, 7 vols. (Waashington, D.C.: Government Printing Office, 1977–1980), vol. 7, *Korea*, 107–9 (hereafter cited as *FRUS 1950*); Donald S. Macdonald, "Korea and the Ballot: The International Dimension in Korean Political Development as Seen in Elections" (Ph.D. diss., Massachusetts Institute of Technology, 1977); Leon Gordenker, *The United Nations and the Peaceful Unification of Korea: The Politics of Field Operations, 1947–1950* (The Hague: Martinus Nijhoff, 1959), 174–85; Amb. J. Muccio to Asst. Sec. State Far East Affairs D. Rusk, June 1, 1950, *FRUS 1950*, 7:96–98.

3. Chi-Young Pak, *Political Opposition in Korea, 1945–1960* (Seoul: Seoul National University Press, 1980), 64–87.

4. Quoted in Everett F. Drumright, memo, "Visit to Korea of John Foster Dulles," U.S. Embassy Seoul No. 658, June 23, 1950, with ten enclosures, copies, Korea Trip File 1950, Dulles Papers. In addition to Drumright's thorough report, see Allison's trip report,

June 23, 1950, *FRUS 1950*, 7:107–9, and William R. Mathews (editor of the *Arizona Daily Star*), diary, "Korea with John Foster Dulles Mission, June 24 to June 29, 1950," William R. Mathews Papers, Library, University of Pennsylvania. Allison also discusses the Dulles mission in his autobiography, *Ambassador from the Prairie* (Boston: Houghton Mifflin, 1973), 140–72, as well as the Japan treaty negotiations.

5. Mathews diary entry, June 17, 1950; the quotes are in Drumright's memo on the Dulles mission (and he was there); other details are from Elmer M. Lowry, "Korean Idyl: Then Came War" (Brandon, Ore.: self-published, 2001). On June 18, 1950, Lowry was an army captain and adviser to the ROK Ninth Regiment, Dulles's host. I also used a description from Gen. Yu Jae-hung, ROKA (Ret.), transcript and tape of interview by John Toland, Seoul, 1987, Toland Papers, FDR Library.

6. "Statement of the Honorable John Foster Dulles, before the National Assembly of the Republic of Korea," June 19, 1950, enclosure 2 to Drumright memo, "Visit to Korea of John Foster Dulles"; Mathews diary entry, June 18, 1950.

7. "Address of John Foster Dulles at Seoul National University," June 20, 1951, Dulles Trip File.

8. Mathews diary entry, June 19, 1950.

9. John Foster Dulles, final communiqué, June 21, 1950, Dulles Trip File. The Trip File contains translations of Seoul newspapers and Dulles's detailed itinerary.

Bibliographical Essay

To exploit all the documentary sources that reconstruct the war for Korea, 1945–1954, would require a multilingual team of international historians blessed with the highest security clearances, official approval, superlative investigative skills, patience without exhaustion, and years to do the research and then the writing. Of the major participants, only the United States and Great Britain have opened their archives; the Russian Federation of States (the former Union of Soviet Socialist Republics) and the People's Republic of China have allowed limited and carefully monitored access to their own and foreign scholars. The Republic of Korea and the Democratic People's Republic of Korea lost much of their government archives to each other in 1950, but both destroyed or now hide their most sensitive and revealing documents covering 1945–1950, and they restrict access (if they even admit the existence of records) for documents covering 1951–1954. The 1990s saw some expansion of the documentary evidence opened in Moscow and Beijing, but hardly any of that evidence deals with the events before 1949. The same national and periodization patterns apply to private papers as well.

Like its predecessors, this book is largely dependent on the records of agencies of the U.S. government, 1945–1950, and the civilian officials and military officers who dealt with Korean affairs during the administration of President Harry S. Truman. The principal agencies were the White House, which means Truman's presidential staff and the National Security Council; the War Department (Department of the Army after July 1947); the State Department; the Office of the Secretary of Defense and the staff of the Joint Chiefs of Staff, the former from 1949 and the latter in continuous existence since World War II; the Economic Cooperation Administration; and the Central Intelligence Agency (CIA) and its predecessors. In the pre–June 1950 period, the air force and navy played minor roles in Korean affairs. For Congress, whose interest in Korea was limited, the *Congressional Record* (1945–1950) provides some primary source material, and the hearings and reports of the Senate and House committees on the armed forces, foreign affairs, and appropriations provide some useful material. Much of the evidence, however, comes from executive agencies called to furnish data and analysis to congressional committees and subcommittees. The study of Congress and Korean affairs, 1945–1950, is not exhausted. It is ironic that much Korean War history published in Korean, Chinese, Russian, and Japanese is dependent on materials found in official records in the United States and Great Britain.

An essential source of material, especially for non-American perspectives, comprises the records, published and archival, of the United Nations, which sent two different missions to Korea in 1948–1950. The United Nations Temporary Commission on Korea (UNTCOK, 1947–1949) made two different investigating and monitoring trips to Korea, which, for practical purposes, meant the American occupation zone. UNTCOK collected extensive data and testimony from Koreans as well as American officials. After August 1948, UNTCOK had to deal with Syngman Rhee's government and the First and Second National Assemblies, but it also maintained close contact with the American mission, which became the American embassy in 1949. In 1949–1950 the UN was represented by the United Nations Commission on Korea.

The resources of the Harry S. Truman Library, Independence, Missouri, are the key portal to the White House's irregular attention to Korean affairs before June 1950. There are subject files with 1945–1950 documents in the major record groups on the Truman presidency: the President's Secretary's Files, 1945–1953, which include National Security Council records (there are also distinct National Security Council Files) and material furnished by the CIA, as well as classified and sensitive personal correspondence; the Official File, 1945–1953; the President's Personal File, largely of personal correspondence; a General File of nonsensitive subject files; a Confidential File of classified subject matter reference files; and a Staff Member and Office Files. One of the critical collections is "off line," the Korean War File, 1947–1952, created for Truman by the Departments of State and Defense and used by the president and Secretary of State Dean Acheson in writing their memoirs. The President's Secretary's Files include an extensive subcollection, "Korean War File." The president also directed the collection of key documents, "Selected Records Relating to the Korean War," in eight volumes (1945–1953). Volume 1 covers 1945–1949. The private papers donated to the Truman Library are equally important: Secretary of State Dean Acheson; George M. Elsey, the president's administrative assistant and Mutual Security Agency official, 1949–1953; John H. Ohly, a special assistant to the secretary of defense, 1947–1949, and thereafter an eighteen-year veteran in the foreign assistance field; Frank Pace Jr., Bureau of the Budget director, 1949–1950, and thereafter secretary of the army; and copies of the papers of Robert A. Lovett, undersecretary of state, 1947–1949, taken from the New York Historical Society. The library holds an extensive oral history collection and microfilms of essential agency records. There is a printed directory by Raymond H. Geselbracht and Anita M. Smith, *Guide to Historical Materials in the Harry S. Truman Library* (April 1995).

As Republican shadow secretary of state, John Foster Dulles became a figure of considerable influence in Korean affairs before he actually took office with President Eisenhower in 1953. He worked for a free Korea as part of the U.S. delegation to the United States, 1947–1949, and then as ambassador-at-large, 1950. His historic trip to Korea and Japan in June 1950 is documented in the Personal Papers of John Foster Dulles, Princeton University Libraries, Princeton, New Jersey. Part of this collection is available on microfilm from Scholarly Resources, Inc.

President Syngman Rhee's personal papers have been collected and preserved in the Institute for Modern Korean Studies, Yonsei University, Seoul, Korea. The most important documents, selected by a committee of scholars, have been published in an eighteen-volume collection in Korean. Rhee's most loyal English-language correspondents were Millard Preston Goodfellow (papers at the Hoover Institution for War, Peace and Revolution) and Robert T. Oliver, a professor of communications and public relations (papers at the library, Pennsylvania State University). Oliver's two most important books, *Syngman Rhee: The Man behind the Myth* (Dodd Mead, 1955) and *Syngman Rhee and American Involvement in Korea, 1942–1960* (Panmun Books, 1978), contain direct quotes from Rhee's letters. See also Lee Chong-sik, *Syngman Rhee: The Prison Years of a Young Radical* (Yonsei University Press, 2001).

Syngman Rhee's ability to communicate in English gave him a political advantage and an edge in winning the historiographical battles. The number of memoirs in translation has increased and gives a more balanced picture of Korean nationalist politicians: Jongsoo Lee, trans. and ed., *Paekpom Ilchi: The Autobiography of Kim Ku* (University Press of America, 2000), which is limited for the 1945–1949 period; Louise Yim, *My Forty Year Fight for Korea* (Chung-ang University, 1967); and Henry Chang, *Korea and the United States through War and Peace, 1943–1960* (Yonsei University Press, 2000). There are untranslated memoirs of Yi Pom-sok, Yo Un-hong (brother of Yo Un-hyong), and Kim Kyu-sik.

Great Britain's official documents are held in the Public Record Office, Kew, London. Korean materials can be found in the 1945–1950 (and 1950–1953) papers of the Cabinet Office, Ministry of Defense, Foreign Office, and Prime Minister's Office. Some of the key documents appeared in the annual review compiled by the Royal Institute of International Affairs: Margaret Carlyle, ed., *Documents on International Affairs, 1947–1948* (Oxford University Press, 1952), and *Documents on International Affairs, 1949–1950* (Oxford University Press, 1953).

Although the Dwight D. Eisenhower Presidential Library, Abilene, Kansas, is a major repository of Korean War documentation, the papers deal primarily with Eisenhower the presidential candidate and president, 1952–1953, and the years of postwar adjustment. Nevertheless, Eisenhower the general, serving as de facto chairman of the Joint Chiefs of Staff (JCS) and adviser to the Truman administration, 1947–1950, had an interest in Korea as an element of American strategic planning, so there are references to Korean issues in Eisenhower's personal correspondence. The guide is David J. Haight, comp., *The Korean War and U.S.-Korean Relations: A Guide to the Historical Holdings in the Eisenhower Library* (Dwight D. Eisenhower Library, 2000).

The U.S. Department of State General Records (Record Group [RG] 59) held at National Archives II, College Park, Maryland, contain files from the U.S. mission/embassy in Seoul, the Division of Northeast Asian Affairs, the Office of Far Eastern Affairs, the Policy Planning Staff, the Secretary's Office, and varied internal and interdepartmental boards, committees, and study groups. Many of the same documents, plus Korean materials, can be found in Records of Foreign Service Posts, Department of State (RG 84). The department publishes the abridged and sanitized historical record in the well-known *Foreign Relations of the United States* multivolume series, and the 1945–1950 editions contain extensive collections of Korea-related documentation, mostly Seoul-Washington correspondence and interagency studies. The most relevant volumes are *1943 Cairo Conference* (1961); *1945 Berlin Conference* (2 vols., 1967); *1945 Conferences at Malta and Yalta* (1955); *1946 The Far East*, vol. 3 (1971); *1947 The Far East*, vol. 6 (1972); *1948 The Far East and Australia*, vol. 6 (1974); *1949 Far East and Australasia*, vol. 7 (1974); and *1950 Korea*, vol. 6 (1976). There are Korean references in other collections that deal with U.S. relations with the Soviet Union, China, the United Nations, and Japan. Scholarly Resources, Inc., Wilmington, Delaware, has microfilmed much of RG 59 for World War II and the cold war. The Institute of Asian Cultural Studies, Hallym University, Chunchon, ROK, produced a multivolume bound, photocopied version of the microfilmed documents, 1989–1996, in various sets: *Records of the Policy Planning Staff, 1947–1954*, 13 vols., including country and area files and chronological files and documents related to the Policy Planning Staff–State participation in the National Security Council; *Internal Affairs Korea, 1949–1953*, 14 vols.; *Historical Policy Research: Korea Project File*, 26 vols.; and Office of Chinese Affairs, *Korean*

War. The same collection provides printed copies of CIA documents in eight volumes of Korea-relevant reports from the Office of Research and Estimates, Office of National Estimates, Joint Atomic Energy Intelligence Committee, and Office of Current Intelligence for 1948–1954. Even more useful are three volumes (1945–1949) of Counterintelligence Corps (CIC) field reports from Korea (1995) and the thirty-volume U.S. Army Intelligence Center, *History of the Counterintelligence Corps,* which includes a volume on "CIC during the Occupation of Korea." I used the set of these documents held by Yonsei University library, Seoul.

In addition to the *Foreign Relations of the United States* series, which appears twenty to thirty years after the events it documents, the U.S. Department of State, Office of Public Information produces open-source analysis and documentation on a time-urgent basis. The urgency is determined by a perception that a policy (and the president and secretary of state) is in trouble, usually defined by the media and the opposition party in Congress. U.S.-Korean relations, 1945–1950, was one of those issues. For "news," the department published a *Bulletin,* a weekly newsmagazine equivalent begun in 1939. Volumes 13–23 (1945–1950) carry many items on Korea and the United Nations. The other publications can be found in the department's Far Eastern Series publications, consisting of pamphlets and reports with accompanying documentation similar to legal briefs or institutional special reports. The issuing agency is the Government Printing Office. For the conduct of the Korean occupation and the preinvasion history of the Republic of Korea and the Democratic People's Republic of Korea, the most important publications are *A Historical Summary of the United States–Korean Relations with a Chronology of Important Developments, 1834–1962* (1962), *Korea: 1945–1948* (1948), *Korea's Independence* (1947), *North Korea: A Case Study in the Techniques of Takeover* (1961), *The Record on Korean Unification, Narrative Summary with Principal Documents, 1943–1960* (1960), *The Problem of Peace in Korea* (1952), and the infamous *United States Relations with China: With Special Reference to the Period 1944–1949* (1949).

The publications of the U.S. Congress sometimes include executive branch material already placed in the public domain by the committees of Congress through their hearings process. Although hearings and investigations are supposed to produce legislation, Congress interprets its informational, educational role broadly since there are always elections ahead that define a very wide political domain indeed. For Korean affairs, 1945–1950, the most interested congressional monitors were the House and Senate committees on the armed forces, foreign relations, and appropriations. The most famous congressional review of Korean policy was the "MacArthur Hearings," conducted jointly by the Senate Armed Services and Foreign Relations Committees and known more formally as "Military Situation in the Far East," Hearings, May 3–August 17, 1951, U.S. Senate, 82d Congress, 1st Session, in five parts (1951), commercially published by Arno Press (5 vols., 1979). In addition to hearings testimony, such publications normally include executive branch documents or congressional studies of some relevance to the subject of the hearings. For Korean policy analysis before the invasion of South Korea, the best Korean affairs information can be found in the publications and hearings of the House of Representatives on the Mutual Defense Assistance Act of 1949 and the subsequent annual review and appropriations process. These proceedings eventually produced House of Representatives Report No. 2495, 81st Congress, 2d Session, *Background Information on Korea* (1950). The same pattern can be found in the hearings and reports of the same committee and its Senate counterpart on the issue of economic aid to the Republic of Korea. The most relevant documents are U.S. Senate, Committee on Foreign Relations, *Aid to the Republic of Korea,* 81st Congress, 1st Session, and *Economic Assistance to China and Korea: 1949–1950,* 81st Congress, 1st and 2d Sessions, published in 1974. The military aid counterpart of this publication is *United States in the Far East: Korean Assistance Acts, Far East Portion of the Mutual Defense Assistance Act of 1950: Selected Documents, 1943–1950* (1976).

The second research cornerstone for the study of Korean affairs from an American perspective is the archival material preserved for the War Department (1945–1947), Department of the Army (1947–), Organization of the Joint Chiefs of Staff (1945–), Department of Defense (1949–), National Security Council (1947–); and CIA (1947–). The most relevant record groups are RG 218 (Records of the Joint Chiefs of Staff), RG 263 (Records of the Central Intelligence Agency), RG 273 (Records of the National Security Council), RG 319 (Records of the Army Staff), and RG 330 (Records of the Office of the Secretary of Defense, including the Office of Military Assistance). Until mid-1949 the U.S. Army was the principal "action agency" for Korean affairs, at which point the army shared responsibility with a full U.S. embassy and a mission from the U.S. Economic Cooperation Administration. Almost every general and special staff section of the postwar army had some business with the Korean command, which had three major elements in 1945–1949: U.S. Army Forces in Korea (USAFIK), U.S. XXIV Corps, and U.S. Army Military Government in Korea (USAMGIK). One general officer, first Lt. Gen. John R. Hodge (1945–1948) and then Maj. Gen. John B. Coulter (1948–1949), headed a dual headquarters for USAFIK and XXIV Corps, while another general served as military governor. Their principal contact in Washington was the army's assistant chief of staff, plans and operations (G-3), who served as the Pentagon "action officer" for Korea. The G-3's office kept various Korean reports and other documents in a Decimal File, P&O, G-3, File 091 (Korea), but other reports went to G-1 (Personnel), G-2 (Intelligence), and G-4 (Logistics), including, after July 1949, documentation from the successor unit, the Korean Military Advisory Group (KMAG). The army G-2 staff preserved books and other items in the Intelligence Library but filed the G-2 weekly and periodic reports and intelligence summaries. These records are in RG 319, Records of the U.S. Army Staff. Before its transfer to the State Department, another army staff agency, the Civil Affairs Division, War Department General Staff (renamed the Army Staff in 1947), supervised occupation policy, especially financial matters, and maintained File 014 (Korea) for its documents dealing with USAFIK and USAMGIK.

Since USAFIK, XXIV Corps, and USAMGIK began the occupation in 1945 as a major subordinate command of U.S. Army Forces Pacific and Supreme Commander Allied Powers (Gen. Douglas MacArthur), the Korean occupation forces' reports, correspondence, and other documentation became part of the original holdings in the Records of U.S. Theaters of War, World War II, RG 332. MacArthur's command then became a joint agency, Far East Command (FECOM). These records included historical files, manuscript histories, special document collections such as the G-3 USAFIK Yosu-Sunchon revolt collection, and important records such as the Provisional Military Advisory Group (PMAG) G-3 journals, September–December 1948. RG 332 became so unmanageable for archivists and researchers that the National Archives and Records Administration broke it up to form several new record groups, the immediate successor being RG 338, Records of Army Operational, Tactical and Support Organizations (World War II–), which still holds XXIV Corps records. One of the new record groups, RG 554, is Records of General Headquarters, Far East Command, the Supreme Commander Allied Powers (SCAP), and the United Nations Command, 1945–1957. The records of USAFIK, USAMGIK, and KMAG are now in RG 554. Some USAFIK, XXIV Corps, and USAMGIK reports may still be found in RG 550, Records of U.S. Army Pacific, Military History Office. These records contain G-2 and G-3 periodic reports and summaries, special studies, the 971st CIC annual progress reports, and the essential but underutilized Official Files, Commanding General (CG), USAFIK and XXIV

Corps, which is essentially a collection of John Hodge's private correspondence. There are portals to these records outside the archives: a microfilm series by Scholarly Resources; Hallym University's photocopied volumes of USAFIK G-2 *Periodic Reports* (1945–1950; 7 vols.) and USAMGIK G-2 *Periodic Reports* (1945–1948; 7 vols.); and the FECOM-USAFIK-USAMGIK manuscript histories copied and filed by Dr. Stanley Katz, indefatigable archivist and command historian, U.S. Eighth Army, in the research library, USFK-UNC-CFC-EUSAK historical offices, Gen. William F. Dean Heritage Center, U.S. Army Base, Yongsan, Seoul. The Katz files were expanded by one of his predecessors, Thomas Ryan, and are described in the UNC-CFC-USFK and EUSA Command History Office, *Historical Archives Index* (July 1, 1994). The library-archives at the Korean Institute for Military History Compilation, War Memorial, Yongsan, Seoul, which funded a decades-long U.S. document acquisition program, is another source; the collection is described in an English-Korean *Guide* (1994). Another archival source for organizational histories is the command histories collection in RG 407, Records of the Adjutant General's Office (1917–).

One part of USAFIK's written legacy deserves special attention. As soon as the USAFIK headquarters was up and running, General Hodge's office started submitting information and analysis for a publication by MacArthur's headquarters, Commander in Chief Far East (CINCFE), *Summation of United States Army Military Government Activities in Korea,* issued monthly beginning in October 1945 (no.1). The consecutive numbering of the monthly reports continued, even though the issuing headquarters changed; the first issue published without FECOM editing was no. 23 (August 1947), which was USAFIK, "South Korea Interim Government Activities 1947" (no. 1), compiled by one of General Hodge's key advisory groups, the National Economic Board. The NEB, composed of Americans and Koreans, provided news, statistics, and analysis of political and economic conditions in Korea in the "South Korean Interim Government Activities" series from August 1947 (no. 23) until July–August 1948 (no. 34). There are sets of this publication in various archival record groups, but they are most accessible at the U.S. Army Military History Institute, Carlisle Barracks, Pennsylvania; the U.S. Army Center of Military History, Fort Leslie J. McNair, Washington, D.C.; and the MacArthur Library and Memorial, Norfolk, Virginia.

The private papers and official documents of senior American civilian and military officials are often more easily accessible and revealing than are the records of their commands, especially since the highest commanders (that is, their libraries) draw the papers of their principal subordinates, usually staff officers. For example, Gen. J. Lawton Collins, army chief of staff, 1948–1953, placed his papers in the Eisenhower Library. The largest collection of Korean War–related documents of a military commander is General of the Army Douglas MacArthur Papers, MacArthur Memorial and Library, Norfolk, Virginia, available on microfilm from Scholarly Resources, Inc. MacArthur had general supervisory authority over USAFIK and USAMGIK until the JCS (at State's urging) assumed direct supervision for 1947–1948. As both CINC FECOM and SCAP in Japan, MacArthur retained a passing interest in Korea throughout 1945–1950, and his RG 5 (SCAP), RG 6 (CINCFE), and RG 9 (message collection) are full of important Korean materials. The Maj. Gen. Charles A. Willoughby Collection (RG 23) is just as valuable because Willoughby, G-2 FECOM, maintained extensive files for reference, postwar analysis, and old-fashioned dissimulation, a Willoughby specialty. Although they had only a tangential interest in Korea before June 1950, MacArthur's staff included Maj. Gen. Edward N. Almond (chief of staff), Maj. Gen. Doyle O. Hickey (deputy chief of staff), Maj. Gen. Edwin K. Wright (G-3), and others who gave extensive interviews and contributed papers to Dr. D. Clayton James, MacArthur's most thorough and careful biographer; Professor James, in turn, gave his research collection to the MacArthur Library. The extensive Almond Papers are actually held at the U.S.

Army Military History Institute, as are the papers of Gen. Matthew B. Ridgway, who monitored Korean affairs in 1949–1950 as deputy chief of staff (operations and administration), U.S. Army. As secretary of state (1947–1948), General of the Army George C. Marshall had Korean moments and left relevant documents, but his papers from his tour as secretary of defense (1951–1952) produced far more significant documentation. Also at the Marshall Library are the papers of Gen. James A. Van Fleet, who commanded the U.S. Eighth Army, 1951–1953, with distinction. Gen. Mark W. Clark, who succeeded Ridgway as CINCFE in 1952, left his papers to The Citadel; as commanding general, Army Field Forces, 1949–1952, Clark monitored U.S. Army training in Korea and Japan. The widest selection of U.S. Army officer interviews, memos, and donated letters and diaries may be found in the research files of three authors of Korean War books: Clay Blair, *The Forgotten War: America in Korea, 1950–1953* (Times Books, 1987); John Toland, *In Mortal Combat: Korea 1950–1953* (William Morrow, 1991); and five books by Roy Appleman, the most significant being *Ridgway Duels for Korea* (Texas A&M Press, 1990). Blair and Appleman placed their files (including Blair's material for a book on Gen. Omar N. Bradley) in the U.S. Army Military History Institute, and Toland's extensive interview tapes and transcripts are held at the Franklin D. Roosevelt Presidential Library, Hyde Park, New York.

Although the army as a whole regarded Korea as a punitive assignment in 1945–1950, U.S. Army officers, many of them nonregulars desperate to remain on active duty as the wartime army shrank, organized the Korean Constabulary and served first as its commanders, then as its advisers. Their administrative home was first USAMGIK, then PMAG (1948–1949), and finally KMAG (1949–). Two PMAG-KMAG officers, the late Lt. Col. James H. Hausman, AUS, and Col. Harold S. Fischgrund, USA (Ret.), became the institutional memory of KMAG and started a collection of documents on US-ROK military relations at the Korea Institute, Harvard University, under the direction of Professor Carter Eckert. Colonel Hausman, who died in 1996, served almost continuously in Korea between 1946 and 1959 as an army officer and then served as a civilian political adviser to the U.S. Army theater senior commander until 1981. As a captain and major, Hausman became the KMAG principal liaison officer to the commanding generals of the Constabulary and ROK army, 1946–1950. As a lieutenant and captain, Fischgrund was a regimental adviser and G-3 assistant adviser. Both made their personal files available to me and helped me make contact with former KMAG advisers and their families. Those unsung heroes in the victory over the Communist partisans provided me with interviews, documents, letters, photographs, books, and operations reports (1946–1950). These officers of the preinvasion KMAG are (in their retirement or separation ranks): Lt. Gen. W. H. Sterling Wright, USA; the late Brig. Gen. William L. Roberts, USA; Brig. Gen. Harold F. Mooney Jr., USA; Lt. Col. Charles L. Wesolowsky, USA; Col. F. Foster Cowey Jr., USA; Capt. Elmer M. Lowry, USA; Lt. Col. Ralph H. Bliss, USA; Lt. Col. Minor L. Kelso, USA; Lt. Col. Edwin M. Joseph, USA; Lt. Col. Joe W. Finley, USA; Col. James D. Holland, USA; Capt. Robert G. Shackleton, USA; and the late Col. Carl B. Nerdahl, USA. The KMAG portal study is Capt. Robert K. Sawyer, USA, et al., "United States Military Advisory Group to the Republic of Korea," 2 pts., 1945–1949 and 1949–June 1950, copy, U.S. Center of Military History. Another KMAG source is the Maj. Arno P. Mowitz Jr. Papers, 1946–1949, U.S. Army Military History Institute.

The personal papers of participants in USAFIK and USAMGIK proved more difficult to identify and use. The most useful—and unexploited—were the files kept by the late Leonard Bertsch, an army reserve civil affairs officer (lieutenant and captain) who joined USAFIK in 1946 and served in Korea until late 1948. An attorney in civil life and an active Democratic Party official in Akron (Summit County), Ohio, Bertsch became a key political operative and adviser to the USAFIK and USAMGIK generals, the Joint Commission, and the Korean Interim Legislative Assembly. Bertsch's papers remain in his family's hands and were made available to me by David Bertsch of Akron, Ohio, and Susan Bertsch Cull of Columbus, Ohio. Two of Bertsch's clients left more limited but useful papers: the Maj. Gen. Archibald V. Arnold, USA, Papers in the Special Collections, U.S. Military Academy Library, and the Maj. Gen. Albert E. Brown, USA, Papers, U.S. Army Military History Institute.

The Korean occupation received occasional attention from the Department of Defense, especially the Joint Chiefs of Staff. The JCS maintained some of its World War II committee structure and added new studies, including position papers for National Security Council documents, to RG 218, Records of the Joint Chiefs of Staff. The JCS benefits from a very detailed, heavily annotated history of the Korean War: James F. Schnabel and Robert J. Watson, *The Joint Chiefs of Staff and National Policy, 1950–1951: The Korean War,* 2 vols. in the larger series *History of the Joint Chiefs of Staff,* published in 1998 by the Office of Joint History, Office of the Chairman, Joint Chiefs of Staff. Only one chapter, however, deals with the 1945–1950 period. The historical office of the secretary of defense has a similar series under way; the first volume of *History of the Office of the Secretary of Defense* is Steven L. Rearden, *The Formative Years, 1947–1950* (1984), which is excellent on budgeting, strategic planning, weapons acquisition, alliance formation, and military assistance programs, all of which affected U.S. relations with Korea. Two books are especially sound in their use of relevant Office of the Secretary of Defense, JCS, and service records on the Military Defense Assistance Program: Lawrence S. Kaplan, *A Community of Interests: NATO and the Military Assistance Program, 1948–1951* (Office of the Secretary of Defense, 1980), and Chester J. Pach Jr., *Arming the Free World: The Origins of the United States Military Assistance Program, 1945–1950* (University of North Carolina Press, 1991).

The Korean perspective on the American occupation and the founding of the Republic of Korea can be found in the books of Korean and American academics with deep roots in Korea: Chong-sik Lee, *The Politics of Korean Nationalism* (University of California Press, 1963); Won-sul Lee, *The United States and the Division of Korea, 1945* (Kyung Hee University Press, 1982); Lee Young-woo, "The United States and the Republic of Korea Army, 1945–1950" (Ph.D. diss., Duke University, 1984); Joungwon A. Kim, *Divided Korea: The Politics of Development, 1945–1972* (Harvard University Press, 1975); Huh Nam-sung, "The Quest for a Bulwark of Anti-Communism: The Formation of the Republic of Korea Officers Corps and Its Political Socialization, 1945–1950" (Ph.D. diss., Ohio State University, 1987); Pak Chi-young, *Political Opposition in Korea, 1945–1950* (Seoul National University Press, 1980); Ohn Chang-il, "The Joint Chiefs of Staff and U.S. Policy and Strategy Regarding Korea" (Ph.D. diss., University of Kansas, 1983); Cho Soong-sung, *Korea in World Politics, 1940–1950* (University of California, 1967); Kim Gye-dong, *Foreign Intervention in Korea* (Dartmouth Publishing, 1993); Chung Too-woong, "The Role of the U.S. Occupation in the Creation of the South Korean Armed Forces, 1945–1950" (Ph.D. diss., Kansas State University, 1985); Sejin Kim, *The Politics of Military Revolution* (University of North Carolina Press, 1971); Kim Chull-baum, "U.S. Withdrawal Decision from South Korea, 1945–1949" (Ph.D. diss., State University of New York–Buffalo, 1984); Sung Hwa Cheong, *The Politics of Anti-Japanese Sentiment in Korea: Japanese–South Korean Relations under American Occupation, 1945–1952* (Greenwood Press, 1991); George McCune, *Korea Today* (Institute of Pacific Relations, 1950); Donald N. Clark, *Living Dangerously in Korea: The Western Experience in Korea, 1900–1950* (East Bridge Press, 2003); Carter Eckert, *Offspring of Empire: The Kochang Kims and the Colonial Origins of Korean Capitalism, 1876–1945* (University of Washington Press, 1991); and Donald S. Macdonald, "Korea and the Ballot: The International Dimension in Korean Political Development as Seen in Elections" (Ph.D. diss., Massachusetts Institute of Technology, 1977). The late Dr. Macdonald began his distinguished career as a Koreanologist as an army civil affairs officer (1945–1947) and made his early reputation by single-handedly stopping a "revolt" on Hai-do island and writing "The First Year of Military Government in Korea," 1946, copy, Dean Historical Research Center, U.S. Army Base, Yongsan, Seoul. Two other analyses of the USAMGIK that lead the field are E. Grant Meade, *American Military Government in Korea* (Columbia University Press, 1951), and Bonnie B. C. Oh, ed., *Korea under the American Military Government, 1945–1948* (Praeger, 2002).

The records of the government of the Republic of Korea remain elusive for 1948–1950, since some of them fell into Communist hands in July 1950 and then may have been recovered in Seoul or Pyongyang in September–October. The only records opened to researchers since the establishment of the ROK Government Archives and Records Service (GARS) are from the Ministry of Foreign Affairs, which has declassified and opened some documents annually since 1994. The GARS is organizing the official papers of Syngman Rhee's office. If the ROK Ministry of National Defense opens any records, it may be a significant opportunity for new discoveries about the role of the South Korean army in the pre–June 1950 counterguerrilla campaign. Korean National Police reports would also be welcome. The first volume of the revised ROK official history, *The Korean War* (3 vols., 1997–1999), includes a chapter on the 1945–1950 period but cites either open U.S. sources or earlier Korean studies of uncertain original research beyond interviews with participants and fragmentary reports, plus first-person published narratives of senior ROK officers. The only memoirs in English are Gen. Paik Sun-yup, *From Pusan to Panmunjom* (Brassey's, 1992), and Gen. Lee Chi-op, *Call Me "Speedy Lee": Memoirs of a Korean War Soldier* (Won Min Publishing, 2001). Although they are of varied quality and usefulness, Gens. Chung Il-kwon, Yu Jae-hung, Chang Do-yong, Yi Hyong-gun, and Yi Chong-chan have written their memoirs (in Korean).

From 1947 until the June 1950 invasion, the United Nations was closely involved in the issue of Korean independence and unification, and its investigations and reports from 1948–1950 are an essential source of analysis independent of USAFIK and the ROK government. The *Official Records: General Assembly,* available on microfilm and in printed form, include the consideration of Korean affairs by the Second, Third, and Fourth General Assemblies (1947–1950), as well as proceedings of the First Committee (Political) and Interim Committee. Even more relevant are the reports of the United Nations Temporary Commission on Korea (UNTCOK I and II, 1949–1950). Although not all the documentation is readily available, there are ample sources in UNTCOK, *First Part of the Report of the United Nations Temporary Commission on Korea* (3 vols., Second General Assembly, 1948), Doc. A/575 with appendices 1 and 2, and UNTCOK, *Second Part of the Report of the United Nations Temporary Commission on Korea* (2 vols., Third General Assembly, 1948), Doc. A/575 with appendices 3 and 4. These reports are followed by United Nations Commission on Korea (UNCOK I and II), *Reports 1949* (2 vols., Fourth General Assembly), Doc. A/936, and *Reports 1950* (Fifth General Assembly, 1950), Doc. A/1350.

The best introductions to United Nations' activities, 1945–1950, are the *United Nations Weekly Bulletin* (1945–1948), replaced by the bimonthly *United Nations Bulletin* in 1948, and the *Yearbook of the United Nations,* published by the UN Department of Public Information for 1947–1948, 1948–1949, and 1950. In addition, the president of the United States was required by law to report US-UN activities in a series, *United States Participation in the United Nations,* which Truman did for 1948, 1949, and 1950; thereafter, there were publications in the International Organization and Conference Series (Government

Printing Office, 1948–1950). The portal books for the United Nations in Korea are Leon Gordenker, *The United Nations and the Peaceful Unification of Korea: The Politics of Field Operations, 1947–1950* (Martinus Nijhoff, 1959), and Rosalyn Higgins, ed., *United Nations Peacekeeping, 1946–1967: Documents and Commentary* (4 vols., Oxford University Press for the Royal Institute of International Affairs, 1970), vol. 2, *Asia*.

The American scholarship on the occupation and division of Korea and the escalating civil war in 1948–1950 reflects the broader concern about the cold war and US-USSR conflict and accommodation. The most formidable defender of American policy (but not an apologist) is John Lewis Gaddis, whose corpus of scholarship culminated with *We Know Now: Rethinking Cold War History* (Oxford University Press, 1997), an extension of his *The United States and the Origins of the Cold War, 1941–1947* (Columbia University Press, 1972) and *Strategies of Containment* (Oxford University Press, 1982). Ironically, Gaddis's first book took the United States to task for its poor appreciation of Russia's legitimate security concerns. His position now is that the Soviet Union presented a serious challenge to long-term and legitimate American interests abroad and could not be "contained" without a strategy of nuclear deterrence and forward, collective defense that carried the risks of a nuclear World War III and the support of authoritarian allies. The Gaddis position, of course, reflected the declaratory policy of every presidential administration from Truman to George H. W. Bush and drew much of its ideological force from the work of George Kennan, Dean Acheson, Paul Nitze, Walter Lippman, Hans Morganthau, and Herbert Feis.

If Gaddis tends to tilt toward the "official" or "traditional narrative" of cold war history, Melvyn P. Leffler, *A Preponderance of War: National Security, the Truman Administration, and the Cold War* (Stanford University Press, 1992), and Michael J. Hogan, *Cross of Iron: Harry S. Truman and the Origins of the National Security State, 1945–1954* (Cambridge University Press, 1998), do not. Leffler and Hogan follow different roads of cold war revisionism, but they share a predisposition to doubt official explanations, to stress domestic economic and political imperatives, to hold American officials and policies to higher intellectual and ethical standards than their foreign contemporaries, and to judge the participants by retrospective criteria. Like Gaddis, they have earlier models, principally Henry Wallace, I. F. Stone, William Appleman Williams, and Walter LaFeber, and they share similar views with contemporary historians Thomas G. Paterson, Barton Bernstein, Martin Sherwin, and Arnold A. Offner, author of *Another Such Victory: President Truman and the Cold War, 1945–1953* (Stanford University Press, 2002). Both groups are, however, Eurocentric in most of their fundamental research and tend to slight regional and local exceptions to their global interpretations. Among the many guides to the cold war context of Korean issues are Michael Kort, *The Columbia Guide to the Cold War* (Columbia University Press, 1998); Burton I. Kaufman, *The Korean Conflict* (Greenwood Press, 1999); and Lester H. Brune, ed., *The Korean War: Handbook of the Literature and Research* (Greenwood Press, 1996). See also Daniel J. Meador and James Monroe, eds. *The Korean War in Retrospect* (University Press of America, 1998).

British and American historians of postwar Asia—or, more precisely of American diplomacy and postwar Asia—have insisted that the cold war globalists are not global at all and do not properly understand the two great developments rooted in World War II: the simultaneous collapse of the traditional European empires and Japan's parvenu Greater East Asia Co–prosperity Sphere, and the revolutionary changes in postwar China and Japan. For Korea, the pride of place belongs to Bruce Cumings, *The Origins of the Korean War*, vol. 1, *Liberation and the Emergence of Separate Regimes, 1945–1947* (Princeton University Press, 1981), and vol. 2, *The Roaring of the Cataract, 1947–1950* (Princeton University Press, 1990). Cumings, a historian of Korean-American relations and modern Korea with the requisite cultural and linguistic expertise, is also an iconoclastic contrarian, but not a Communist apologist. His eagerness to cast America's officials and policy in the worst possible light, however, often leads him to confuse chronological cause and effect and to leap to judgments that cannot be supported by the documentation he cites or ignores. Nevertheless, his grasp of Korean nationalism and oppositionism must be taken seriously, especially because it is supported by other accounts written by Korean and regional specialists: James I. Matray, *The Reluctant Crusade: American Foreign Policy in Korea, 1941–1950* (University of Hawaii Press, 1985); Peter Lowe, *The Origins of the Korean War* (Longman, 1986); Steven Hugh Lee, *Outpost of Empire: Korea, Vietnam and the Origins of the Cold War in Asia, 1949–1950* (McGill-Queens University Press, 1995); and John Merrill, *Korea: The Peninsular Origins of the War* (University of Delaware Press, 1989). The intellectual "fathers" of this group are the late Gregory Henderson, author of *Korea: The Politics of the Vortex* (Harvard University Press, 1968), and James Palais and Frank Baldwin, eds., *Without Parallel: The American-Korean Relationship since 1945* (Random House, 1973). These authors share an aversion for Japanese imperialism, the Park Chung-hee regime in South Korea, and much of American foreign policy in Asia. Much of their work is summarized in Bruce Cumings, ed., *Child of Conflict: The Korean-American Relationships, 1943–1953* (Washington University Press, 1983).

Never comfortable with the Leffler-Hogan school or Koreanized enough to be admitted to the Cumings school, Professor William W. Stueck Jr. followed a path away from his original critique, *The Road to Confrontation: American Policy toward China and Korea, 1947–1950* (University of North Carolina Press, 1981), to write *The Korean War: An International History* (Princeton University Press, 1995) and *Rethinking the Korean War: A New Diplomatic and Strategic History* (Princeton University Press, 2002), both of which are welcome correctives to some of Cumings's fulsome condemnations of American policy and Korean politicians. Stueck's most recent work is an anthology of essays, *The Korean War in World History* (University of Kentucky Press, 2004), that stresses the war's international dimensions. More conventional studies sympathetic to American confusions but less knowledgeable about Asian history are Charles M. Dobbs, *The Unwanted Symbol: American Foreign Policy, the Cold War and Korea, 1945–1950* (Kent State University Press, 1981), and Lisle Rose, *Roots of Tragedy: The United States and the Struggle for Asia, 1945–1953* (Greenwood Press, 1976).

Research from the documents preserved by the Russian Federation of States, the People's Republic of China, and the Democratic People's Republic of Korea has been the scholarly surprise attack of the last fifteen years. The Russians again organized the assault when President Boris Yeltsin sponsored some historical perestroika on the Korean War by releasing key documents on the Russian role in the war, 1948–1953. The purpose of the release — which came during a dramatic meeting in 1994 between Yeltsin and ROK president Kim Young-sam — was to place the responsibility for the war on Joseph Stalin, Kim Il-sung, and Mao Zedong. The documents came from four collections: the Presidential Archive, which included Soviet Central Committee Political Bureau (Politburo) records; the Communist Party Central Archives for materials prior to 1952; a second set of Politburo records for post-1952 documents; and the Central Military Archive of the Ministry of Defense. The selection process was managed by the Foreign Ministry, which meant that the contributions of the Ministry of Defense were minimal. The first collection of documents released came with a running narrative written by Foreign Ministry historians, the best known being Alexandre Mansourov, a junior officer who had learned Korean for assignments in Pyongyang and Seoul and translated some of the documents into Korean. The documents were published (with the narrative) in Korean in the mass-circulation Seoul newspaper *Chosun Ilbo* in July–August 1994 and reappeared in Korean, English, and Russian in a wide range of popular and academic publications.

The principal portals to the Russian perspective on Korean history after World War II are Evgeniy P. Bajanov and Natalia Bajanova, "The Korean Conflict, 1950–1953: The Most Mysterious War of the 20th Century," a Foreign Ministry history written in English, presumably in the mid-1990s, and circulated (for a price) outside Russia in various forms, valuable for its citations and direct documentary quotations; the translation of Russian documents by Kathryn Weathersby and Mark A. O'Neill, published with explanations and annotations in the *Cold War International History Project Bulletin* (1992–), especially issues 5–9 and 11 (1995–1998), Woodrow Wilson Center for International Scholars; Alexandre Mansourov, "Communist War Coalition Formation and the Origins of the Korean War" (Ph.D. diss., Columbia University, 1997); and Kathryn Weathersby, "Soviet Policy toward Korea, 1944–1946" (Ph.D. diss., Indiana University, 1990).

Prior to the Yeltsin release, the availability of Soviet documentation on the war was limited, largely in an effort to influence Western views. Perhaps the first was Foreign Ministry, USSR, *The Soviet Union and the Korean Question* (Soviet News, 1950). The scholarly studies that use Russian sources continue to grow: Sergei N. Goncharov, John W. Lewis, and Xue Litai, *Uncertain Partners: Stalin, Mao, and the Korean War* (Stanford University Press, 1993); Vladislav Zubok and Constantine Pleshakov, *Inside the Kremlin's Cold War* (Harvard University Press, 1996); Dmitri Volkogonov, *Stalin: The Triumph and Tragedy* (English-language version, Weidenfeld and Nichols, 1991); and Andrei Lankov, *From Stalin to Kim Il Sung: The Formation of North Korea, 1945–1950* (Rutgers University Press, 2002).

Perhaps the most important contribution of Russian archival material is the access it provides to the North Korean perspective, previously available only in super *juche* propaganda form. One notable work in this category is Sydney A. Seiler, *Kim Il-song: The Creation of a Legend, the Building of a Regime* (University Press of America, 1994), which includes the memoir of Gen. Yu Song-chol, Korean People's Army (purged), director of the KPA operations bureau in 1950 and a Soviet citizen, first published in 1990 in *Hanguk Ilbo*. Adrian Buzo, *The Guerrilla Dynasty: Politics and Leadership in North Korea* (Westview Press, 1999), and Charles K. Armstrong, *The North Korean Revolution, 1945–1950* (Cornell University Press, 2003), use Korean-language materials captured in 1950, as well as Russian documents. The newer works extend but do not replace Robert R. Simmons, *The Strained Alliance: Peking, Pyongyang, Moscow, and the Politics of the Korean War* (Columbia University Press, 1975), and Eric Van Ree, *Socialism in One Zone: Stalin's Policy in Korea, 1945–1947* (Oxford University Press, 1988).

The major influences on the scholarship on Korean affairs, 1945–1950, from a Chinese perspective have been the partial political liberalization of the People's Republic, an ongoing dialogue with Russia (the USSR) about responsibility for the 1950 invasion, a movement to demythologize Mao Zedong, an effort to improve relations with the Republic of Korea, and celebration of the Communist victory in the Chinese civil war, 1949–1950. The best single review of these developments and their historiographical influence is Yasuda Jun, "A Survey: China and the Korean War," *Social Science Japan Journal* 1 (1998): 71–83. Although the literature on the Chinese role in the war is voluminous—and untranslated—it is short on original and independent archival research, pays little attention to the 1945–1950 period, and reflects the Communist Party's view of history as an instrument of unchallengeable political indoctrination. The military historians of China (those of the Academy of Military Sciences and others) focus on operational issues, not the international and domestic politics that made the People's Republic of China a junior partner in the unification of Korea until October 1950. Most of the actual scholarship is accessible only in Chinese, Japanese, and Korean. There is also a continuing conspiratorial cast to the Chinese literature (and Korean and Japanese analysis of that literature) that ignores the legal dicta, which simply means that those who profit from events may not have planned and executed them.

Several essential collections have been translated from the Chinese and quoted at length in English and thus qualify as portal scholarship: *Selected Military Writings of Mao Zedong* (1981); *Mao Zedong's Writings since the Founding of the Republic* (1949.9–1950.2) (1987); *The Military Writings of Mao Zedong* (1993); CCP Central Archives, *Selected Documents of the CCP Central Committee*, 32 vols. (1983–1987, 1989–1992); Central Institute of CCP Historical Documents, *Selected Important Documents since the Founding of the PRC* (1991); People's Press, *Selected Documents of the Korean Problem* (1954); People's Press, *Selected Works of Leu Shaoqi* (1985); Chen Yun, *Selected Manuscripts* (1984) and *Selected Works* (1984); Liu Wusheng et al. for the CCP Central Press of Historical Documents, *Selected Collection of Important Historical Documents since the Founding of the PRC* (1991); People's Press, *Selected Works of Li Xiannian 1935–1988* (1989); CCP Central Archives, *Selected Telegrams and Letters of Zhou Enali* (1988) and *Selected Works of Zhou Enali* (1984); and the memoirs of People's Liberation Army generals Peng Dehuai (1981–1984), Chai Chengwen (1987), Deng Hua (1989), Du Ping (1989), Hong Xuhi (1990), Nie Rongzhen (1988, 1992), Xie Fang (1987), Yang Dezhi (1992), Yang Di (1998), and Zhu De (1983). The best sources for English translations of Chinese documents are Zhang Shu Guang and Chen Jian, eds., *Chinese Communist Foreign Policy and the Cold War in Asia: New Documentary Evidence, 1944–1950* (Imprint Publications, 1996), and the documents, annotations, and introductory essays in the *Bulletin* of the Cold War International History Project.

The English-language scholarship that reflects research into Chinese sources by historians starts with the last stages of the Chinese civil war and includes Zhang Shu Gang, *Mao's Military Romanticism: China and the Korean War, 1950–1953* (University Press of Kansas, 1995); Chen Jian, *China's Road to the Korean War: The Making of the Sino-American Confrontation* (Columbia University Press, 1994); Harry Harding and Yuan Ming, eds., *Sino-American Relations, 1945–1955* (Scholarly Resources, 1989); Odd Arne Westad, ed., *Brothers in Arms: The Rise and Fall of the Sino-Soviet Alliance* (Stanford University Press, 1998) and *Decisive Encounters: The Chinese Civil War, 1946–1950* (Stanford University Press, 2003); Thomas Christensen, *Useful Adversaries: Grand Strategy, Domestic Mobilization and Sino-American Conflict, 1947–1958* (Princeton University Press, 1996); and Dorothy Borg and Waldo Heinrichs, eds., *Uncertain Years: Chinese-American Relations, 1947–1950* (Columbus University Press, 1980).

The Russian scholarship has an important role in providing insight into the unique political culture of North Korea. First, last, and always, Kim Il-sung stands center stage in his self-made world of historical worship: Kim Il-Sung, *Selected Works* (6 vols., Foreign Languages Publishing House, 1971–1972), and Baik Bong, *Kim Il Sung* (3 vols., Miraisha, 1969). The beloved leader's approved version of the Korean War is Ho Jong-ho, Kang Sok-hui, and Pak Thae-ho, *The U.S. Imperialists Started the Korean War* (Pyongyang Foreign Languages Press, 1993). Russian, American, Korean, and Japanese records allow more balanced accounts of Communism in Korea that do not necessarily place Kim Il-sung at the heart of the Korean revolutionary cosmos. The pioneering work is Suk Dae-sook, *The Korean Communist Movement, 1918–1919* (Princeton University Press, 1967) and *Kim Il Sung: The North Korean Leader* (Columbia University Press, 1981); Robert A. Scalapino and Lee Chong-sik, *Communism in Korea* (University of California Press, 1973); Lee

Chong-sik, *The Politics of Korean Nationalism* (University of California Press, 1961); Kim Hak-joon, *The Korean War* (Parkyongsa, 1989); Kim Jom-kon, *The Korean War* (Kwangmyong Publishing, 1973); Koon Woo Nam, *The North Korean Communist Leadership, 1945–1965* (University of Alabama Press, 1974); and Chong-sik Lee, trans. and ed., *Materials on Korean Communism, 1945–1947* (Center for Korean Studies, University of Hawaii, 1977).

The conventional way to date the Korean War is to start the historical clock on June 25, 1950 (Sunday in Korea) and measure events from that date as a "war" with political causes, strategic goals, and operational and tactical difficulties. All the violence, political maneuvering, development of competitive revolutionary regimes, and occupation policies of the United States and the Soviet Union become "causes" rather than a war of unconventional means for unsurprising postcolonial ends. Prologues to war seldom stir historiographical and bibliographical musings, and the Korean War is no exception for the 1945–1950 years. The best guides are the seminal monographs on this period, described in this essay. There are, however, review essays and bibliographical guides that deal sufficiently with the 1945–1950 period to warrant portal status: James I. Matray, "Korea's Partition: Soviet-American Pursuit of Reunification, 1945–1948," *Parameters* 28 (Spring 1998): 150–62; Philip West, "Interpreting the Korean War," *American Historical Review* 94 (February 1989): 80–96; Rosemary Foot, "Making Known the Unknown War," *Diplomatic History* 15 (Summer 1991): 411–31; Allan R. Millett, "The Korean War: A 50-Year Critical Historiography," *Journal of Strategic Studies* 24 (March 2001): 188–224; Research Center for the Peace and Unification of Korea, "Selected Bibliography of the Korean War," *Korea and World Affairs* 8 (Summer 1984): 442–73; Hong-Kyu Park, "America and Korea, 1945–1953: A Bibliographical Essay," *Asian Forum* 3 (January–March 1971): 57–66; and William J. Williams, ed., *A Revolutionary War: Korea and the Transformation of the Postwar World* (Imprint Publications, 1993). Of all the Korean War bibliographies and encyclopedias that focus on 1950–1953, the most useful for 1945–1950 are Lester H. Brune, ed., *The Korean War: Handbook of the Literature and Research* (Greenwood Press, 1996), and Steven Hugh Lee, *The Korean War* (Longman, 2001).

The only way to learn Korean politics and culture is on the streets of Seoul, but there are books that help: Korean Overseas Information Service, *A Handbook of Korea* (Hollym, 1990); John H. Koo and Andrew C. Nahm, *An Introduction to Korean Culture* (Hollym, 1997); Keith Pratt and Richard Rutt, *Korea: A Historical and Cultural Dictionary* (Curzon, 1999); Andrew C. Nahm, *Korea: Tradition and Transformation: A History of the Korean People* (Hollym, 1988); Peter Hyun, *Koreana* (Korea Britannica, 1989); and Donald Stone Macdonald, *The Koreans* (Westview Press, 1988).

Index

First Battalion, First Constabulary
  Regiment, 79
First Battalion, ROK Marine Corps, 224
First Brigade (ROKA), 200
First Division (KGB), 97
First Division (KPA), 104
First Division (ROKA), 208, 211
First Independent Battalion (ROKA), 209,
  210, 223
First Provisional Artillery Regiment,
  Capitol Division, 208
First Radio Squadron (Mobile) (U.S.), 101
First Route Army (PLA), 35–36
Second Corps (KPA), 204
Second Division (KPA), 104
Second Division (ROKA), 225, 241
Second Regiment, Capitol Division, 208, 210
Second Regiment, Korean Constabulary,
  183, 203, 223
Third *Boandae* Brigade (DPRK), 210
Third Brigade, Korean Constabulary, 109,
  210
Third Division (ROKA), 193, 225, 241
Third Field Army (PLA), 230
Third Regiment, Korean Constabulary,
  107, 169, 170
Fourth Field Army (PLA), 12, 230
Fourth Mixed Brigade (KPA), 104
Fourth Regiment, Korean Constabulary,
  79, 181, 183
Fifth Brigade, Korean Constabulary, 168

Fifth Division (KPA), 194
Fifth Division (ROKA), 225, 241
Fifth Infantry (U.S.), 79
Fifth Regiment, Korean Constabulary, 146
  Yosu Rebellion and, 169–70
Fifth Regimental Combat Team (U.S.),
  156, 186, 190, 241, 253
  redeployment of, 189
  withdrawal of, 187
Sixth Division (KPA), 194
Sixth Division (ROKA), 207, 227, 241
Sixth Infantry Division (U.S.), 59, 85, 87,
  128–29, 133
  Korean Constabulary and, 162
  redeployment of, 156
  training by, 106
  withdrawal of, 165–66
  Yosu Rebellion and, 171
Sixth Regiment, Korean Constabulary,
  165, 183, 200
  Yosu Rebellion and, 168, 169
Seventh Division (ROKA), 208, 256
Seventh Infantry Division (U.S.), 58, 59,
  73, 87, 165, 186
  Korean Constabulary and, 162
  redeployment of, 156
  training by, 106
Seventh Regiment (ROKA), 207
Eighth Army (U.S.), MacArthur and, 109
Eighth Division (KPA), 195
Eighth Division (ROKA), 225, 241

Eighth Regiment, Korean Constabulary,
    80, 201
  border patrols by, 202
  restoration of, 207
Eighth Route Army (PLA), 33
Ninth Division (KPA), 195
Ninth Regiment, Korean Constabulary,
    145, 146, 181, 182, 309n5
  Eleventh Regiment and, 148
Tenth Regiment, Korean Constabulary,
    183, 207
Eleventh Regiment, First Division, 208–9
Eleventh Regiment, Korean
    Constabulary, 146
  Ninth Regiment and, 148
Twelfth Army Group (U.S.), 235
Twelfth Regiment, First Division, 208,
    209, 210
Twelfth Regiment, Korean Constabulary,
    203
  Yosu Rebellion and, 168, 169
Thirteenth Regiment, First Division, 209
Fourteenth Air Force (U.S.), 213
Fourteenth Regiment, Korean
    Constabulary, 165, 171, 181, 204
  Yosu Rebellion and, 2, 167, 168, 169
Fifteenth Regiment, Korean
    Constabulary, 165
  Yosu Rebellion and, 168, 169
Seventeenth Area Army (Imperial Japanese
    Army), 41, 44, 45, 58
Seventeenth Regiment (ROKA), 208, 223
Eighteenth Regiment, Capitol Division,
    208, 209, 210
Twentieth Infantry Regiment (U.S.), 85, 144
Twenty-second Regiment (ROKA), 224, 225
XXIV Corps (U.S.), 52, 56, 88, 120, 128,
    133, 156, 186
  departure of, 155
  Hodge and, 57, 58, 72, 106
  morale of, 106
Twenty-fifth Army (Red Army), 45, 48, 49,
    135, 193
Twenty-fifth Infantry Division (U.S.), 57
Twenty-fifth Regiment (ROKA), 226
Twenty-seventh Infantry Division (U.S.), 57
Thirty-first Infantry Regiment (U.S.), 186
Fortieth Infantry Division (U.S.), 7, 59, 78
Forty-third Infantry Division (U.S.), 57

Fifty-ninth Military Government Company
    (U.S.), 144, 145
Sixty-first Infantry Regiment (U.S.), 57
Eighty-eighth Special Operations Brigade
    (Red Army), 39
101st Airborne Division (U.S.), 133
105th Tank Brigade (KPA), 193
160th Infantry Regiment (U.S.), 7
166th Division (PLA), 194
167th Division (PLA), 194
315th Headquarters Intelligence
    Detachment (U.S.), 99
442d Regimental Combat Team (U.S.), 4
555th Field Artillery Battalion (U.S.), 186
971st Counterintelligence Corps (CIC)
    Detachment (U.S.), 97, 99, 100, 134,
    135, 171, 187–88, 200
6004th Air Intelligence Service Squadron
    (U.S.), 101

Abe Nobuyuki, 42, 43, 58
  Yo Un-hyong and, 44–45, 270n3
Acheson, Dean, 39, 67, 93, 221, 246,
    251, 254
  Bradley and, 237
  Dulles and, 255
  economic aid and, 220
  KMAG and, 250
  Princeton seminar and, 305n12
  Rhee and, 238, 255
  Vincent and, 71
Adams, Samuel, 48
Air Carrier Corporation, 219
Air Defense Force, 178
Allen, Horace N., 21–22, 23
Alliance of Popular Sovereignty, 148
Allied Intelligence Bureau, 39, 53
Allied Translator and Interrogation
    Service, 99
Allison, John M., 109, 111, 121, 256
Almond, Edward N., 235, 280n13
American Association of Shanghai, 7
American National Security Act (1947), 172
American Revolution, 14
An Chae-hong, 74, 118, 137, 139, 145
  KNP reform and, 116
  vote for, 154
  youth groups and, 90
An Chang-ho, 29

An Ho-sang, 29, 47, 48, 163, 200
An Kil, 40, 77, 104
Anti-Americanism, 5, 86, 136
Anticollaborator law, 162
Anticolonialism, 16, 23, 28, 119, 266n14
Anti-Communists, 11, 100, 103, 134, 142,
    149, 188
Anti-Fascist People's Freedom League, 12
Anti-imperialists, 13, 90, 136
Anti-Japanese Military and Political
    College, 41
Anti-Trusteeship Committee, 115
An Tu-hui, 222, 302n72
Appenzeller, Ella Dodge, 22
Appenzeller, Henry G., 22
Armed forces, estimates of, 251 (table)
Armed Forces Security Agency, 101
Army civilian employees (DACs), 127, 128
Army of the Republic of Korea (ROKA),
    78, 79, 172, 181, 196
    aid for, 219
    assessment of, 204, 248, 250, 251, 256
    border war and, 193, 202
    Communist agents in, 193
    counterguerrilla campaign of, 238
    growth of, 190, 213
    G-2 of, 200
    guerrillas and, 225, 226, 251
    intelligence and, 214
    KNP and, 227
    offensive options for, 241
    operational problems for, 204
    policing, 198
    purge of, 222
    training for, 187, 206, 212, 214
    weapons for, 253
Army Reorganization Act (1948), 172
Army Security Agency, 101
Army Signal Corps, 95
Arnold, Archibald V., 58, 59, 65, 73,
    75, 275n3
    Joint Commission and, 74
    Korea policy and, 109
Asia Firsters, 118, 248
Asia-Pacific war (1937–1945), 36–42
    revolutionary conditions from, 12
AT-6 "Harvard" aircraft, 219, 220
Attlee, Clement, 136
Aung San, 12

Aurell, George, 102
Austin, Warren R., 123, 285nn2,5
Autumn Harvest Uprising, 81–91
    analysis of, 102
    Hodge and, 87
    SKLP and, 105
    survivors of, 104

Baguio, 67
Baird, John E., 99
"Baker Forty," 58
Baker Plans, 88
Balasanov, Gerasim M., 89
Bank of Chosun, 82
Barros, Russell D., 79, 106, 144
    Hausman and, 80
    Korean Constabulary and, 107
    Ryu and, 145
Barsdel, Leonard F., 50
Baruch, Bernard, 124
"Basic Initial Directive to the Commander
    in Chief U.S. Army Forces
    Pacific for the Administration of Civil
    Affairs in Those Areas of
    Korea Occupied by U.S. Forces, 60
Bataan Gang, 98, 235
Benninghoff, H. Merrill, 61, 62, 63, 67
Beria, Lavrentii, 97, 229
Berlin Blockade, 197–98, 233
Bernheisel, Charles, 128
Bertsch, Leonard M., 84, 91, 269n10,
    275n7
    criticism of, 119
    intelligence and, 99–100
Bevin, Ernest, 136
Billelo, Joseph W., 256
Bill of Rights, 27
Bishop, Max, 186
Bliss, Ralph, 170
"Blue Boys," 100
Boandae brigades, 195, 202, 223, 240,
    245, 249
    Parallel War and, 206, 207, 209, 210
Bolshevik Revolution, 10, 40
Bolsheviks, 16, 25, 28
Bolté, Charles L., 133
Bond, Niles W., 186, 217–18, 219
Bonesteel, Charles H., III, 45
Book burning, 65–66

Border Guard (*Boandae*), 104, 177, 193,
    195, 240
  refugees and, 134
Border war, 178, 193, 202, 205, 206
Boys Clubs of America, 39
Bradley, Omar N., 235
  Acheson and, 237
  Roberts and, 133, 250–51
Brown, Albert E., 110, 111, 114–15, 119
Brown, Rothwell, 147
B-26 "Invader" light bombers, 217
Buddhism, 9, 11, 17, 18, 20
Bunce, Arthur, 73, 113, 127, 128, 155, 214
  criticism of, 119
  Lady and, 179
Bureau of Education, 134
Bureau of Far Eastern Affairs, 67, 109
Bureau of Internal Affairs, 104
Bureau of Public Peace, 181
Bureau of the Budget, 215, 220
Burns, James H., 237
Butterworth, W. Walton, 121, 237
Byrne, Patrick J., 160
Byrnes, James F., 67, 71, 88, 93
  Joint Commission and, 70
  trusteeship and, 68

Cairo Conference, 52
Caldwell, John C., 128
Cambridge Five, 97
Camp Sobinggo, 106
Capitol Division (ROKA), 208, 209,
    210, 223
Carlton Hotel, Rhee at, 110
Carter, Marshall, 8–9, 266n10
Castro, Fidel, 14
Catholics, 17, 21, 24, 38
Cavalry Regiment, Korean Constabulary,
    161, 208, 215
  Yosu Rebellion and, 170
Central Committee, 134, 175–76, 177
Central Council for the Rapid Realization
    of Korean Independence, 63
Central Historical Museum, 176
Central Intelligence Agency (CIA), 214,
    236, 245, 307n30
  analysis by, 102, 187, 234, 235
  FECOM and, 101
  mission/management of, 246

Central Intelligence Group, 100, 101, 102
Central Security Officers School, 76
Chae Pyong-dok, 80, 168, 173, 209, 210,
    217, 218, 223, 245, 256
  pukjin and, 190
  replacement of, 211
Chamberlain, Stephen J., 73
Champeny, Arthur S., 78
Chang, John (Chang Myon), 29, 47, 184,
    291n1
  aspirations of, 163
  commitment and, 238
Changan faction, 46, 47
Chang Dok-soo, 117, 118, 132
Chang Do-yong, 214
Chang Ki-yong, 163
Changma, 81, 84, 150, 156, 159
Chang Myon. See Chang, John
Changsung, 14–15
Chang Taek-sang, 29, 47, 69, 87, 88,
    131–32, 155, 191, 198, 200
  aspirations of, 163
  KDP and, 132
  Korean Constabulary and, 108
  removal of, 115
Chang Tok-su, 31, 47
Chang Tso-lin, 26, 28
Cheju-do rebellion, 2, 142–48, 202
  casualty estimates for, 303n74
  end of, 166–67, 203, 222
  Hodge and, 144
  Roberts and, 203
Chemulpo Treaty (1882), 266n6
Chennault, Claire, 213
Chiandae, 45
Chiang Kai-shek, 52, 62
Chicago Sun, 91
Chi Chang-su, 167
Chien-tao incident, 28, 29
China Lobby, 52, 217
Chinese, romanization of, 259–63
Chinese civil war, 93, 197, 221, 267n14
Chinese Communists, 26, 33, 35, 41, 62,
    188, 197, 232, 240
  Nationalists and, 12–13
"Chinese" Korean Communists, 87
Chinese Nationalists, 7, 26, 31, 32, 33, 40,
    62, 100, 111, 131, 137, 196, 232, 234,
    240, 253

collapse of, 230
Communists and, 12–13
Japanese surrender to, 8
weapons from, 218
Chinese Revolution, 175, 232
Chin Peng, 12
Chiri-san campaign, 202, 203, 225–26
Chiri-san Task Force, 183, 204, 226
Chistiakov, Ivan M., 45, 51, 76, 89
Choe, Bryan, 127
Choe Duk-sin, 173
Choe Hyon, 40
Choe Hyon-bae, book burning and, 65–66
Choe Hyun, 210
Choe In, 18
Choe Kyong-nok, 148, 290n50
Choe Kyung-rok, 208, 209
Choe Nam-gun, 165, 169, 201–2
Choe Nam-son, 17, 18, 19
Choe Nung-jin, 165
Choe Sok, 209
Choe Yong-dal, 47
Choe Yong-gun, 39, 50, 51, 68, 103,
      176, 194
   Interior and, 76
   speech by, 185
Choe Yong-hui, 222
Choe Yong-jin, 40
Choi Pong-sun, 127
Choi Sok, 132
Cholera epidemic, 50, 81, 84
Cho Man-sik, 29, 46, 47, 50, 51, 52, 63, 103
   KDP and, 68
   Kim Il-sung and, 151
   Moscow agreement and, 69
Chondogyo, 18–19, 23, 26, 47, 51, 103,
      134, 160
   independence movement and, 17
   politics and, 11
Chongpan-sa Printing Company, 82–83
Chongpyong, 65, 83
Chongwudang, 103, 134
Cho Pong-am, 34, 35, 163
Cho Pyong-ok, 29, 47, 69, 87, 88, 108,
      131, 139, 144, 147, 155
   economic aid and, 163
   Kim Ku and, 132
   KNP and, 65, 117, 146
   removal of, 115

State Department and, 189
UNCOK and, 191
UNTCOK and, 136
Choryon, suppression of, 222
Chosen Army, 28, 41
Chosun Christian College, 29, 65, 127,
      143, 200
Chosun dynasty, 4, 20, 21, 22, 48,
      49–50, 94
Cho Yong-gun, 69
Cho Yong-il, 101
Christian Advocate, 128
Christian Democrats, 2
Christian League, 195
Christians, 9, 18, 27, 29, 48, 77, 117,
      123, 142
   bias toward, 152
   Dulles and, 124
   independence movement and, 17
   massacre of, 44
   politics and, 11
   protest by, 22
   refugee, 174
   sacrifices for, 38
Christian Socialists, 2
Chun Chin-han, cabinet post for, 163
Chunchon axis, 241
Chung, Henry, 31, 112, 271n7
Chungang Preparatory School, 18, 29
Chung Il-kwon, 79, 107, 146, 168, 173,
      204, 211, 223
   Yosu Rebellion and, 169
Chungking coalition, 41
Chungmun bridge, 143
Chun Jong-gun, 224
Churchill, Winston, 52
Church of Canada, 22
CIA. *See* Central Intelligence Agency
CIC. *See* Counterintelligence Corps
Civil Affairs Division, 109
Civil Affairs Section, 164
Civil Communications Intelligence
      Group, 99
Civil rights, 29, 117
Civil unrest, 17, 105, 120
Civil wars, 12, 16, 72, 93, 119, 142,
      143, 151
Clark Air Force Base, 236
Club Hwabang, 50

Coalition Committee, 87, 89, 111, 114, 116, 118
  Hodge and, 84, 110
  Rhee and, 84
Cold War, 1, 121
Collaboration, 27, 29, 42, 47, 48, 70, 75, 76, 113, 115, 131, 137, 162, 174, 198
Collins, J. Lawton "Lightning Joe," 57, 58, 217, 235
  Roberts and, 133, 251
  ROKA and, 251
  withdrawal and, 186
Colonialism, 5, 25
  Japanese, 9, 11, 13, 14, 46, 48, 76, 84, 122
  struggle against, 9, 27–29, 31–36
Comfort women, 36–37
Comintern, 26
Committee for the Preparation of Korean Independence, 45, 159
Communist Democratic Youth Association, 105
Communist Youth International, 34
Community Protective Corps, 150
"Conditions of Success of the U.S. Programs in Asia, The" (NSC 68/8, Part II), 238
Confucianism, 9, 17, 20, 152
Connally, Tom, 252
Constitution
  DPRK, 138
  ROK, 139, 151
  U.S., 154
Containment, 1, 93, 114, 116, 235
Corps for the Advancement of Individuals, 29
Corruption, 85, 130, 144, 190
  Rhee and, 132
Coulter, John B., 153, 157, 168, 187
Council of Foreign Ministers, 114
Counterinsurgency campaign, 202–3, 207, 212, 221, 225
Counterintelligence, 96, 228
Counterintelligence Corps (CIC), 96, 97, 98, 99, 100, 127, 144, 157, 165, 222
  creation of, 173
  intelligence and, 214
Criminal Investigation Division, 105
Cult of the personality, 176

Culture, 65, 84, 144
  economic, 127
  Korean, 29, 37
  policy, 27
  political, 127
  popular, 11
  preserving, 4
  "slicky boy," 130
"Current Situation in Korea, The" (CIA), 102
Cynn, Hugh, 31

DACs. See Army civilian employees
Daedong-ilbo, 82–83
Daehan Youth Association, 164
Daehan Youth Corps, 162
Dean, William F., 118, 146–47, 162
Defense, Department of, 234, 236, 248, 252, 255
  aid from, 219, 238
  defense spending and, 216, 217
Defense plan, 211, 240, 241
Defense spending, 215, 216, 217
De Gaulle, Charles, 4
Democracy, 9, 11, 161
Democratic Front for the Unification of the Fatherland, 177, 195, 205
Democratic National Front, 89
Democratic National Party (DNP), 239, 256
Democratic Party, "Freedom Budget" of, 238
Democratic People's Front, 82, 84, 85
Democratic People's Republic of Korea (DPRK)
  bellicosity of, 185
  order of battle of, 242 (map), 247 (map)
  Soviet Union and, 177, 187
Democratic Students League, 200
Department of Education, 65, 66, 127
Department of Internal Security (DIS), 132, 144, 157
Department of Police, 117
Department of Public Information (DPI), 100
Department of the Army, 109, 217
  military government and, 118
  security and, 162
"Development of a Political Program" (Brown), 110
Devil posts, 14–15
Dewey, Thomas E., 124, 254

DIS,132, 144, 157
Disengagement policy, 135, 171, 221
DNP, 239, 256
Document Research Unit/G-2 FECOM, 102
Doksu Palace, 72, 73, 114, 137
Donnelly, Charles H., 127–28
Donner, Francesca. *See* Rhee, Francesca
    Donner
Donovan, William "Wild Bill," 38
DPI, 100
DPRK. *See* Democratic People's Republic
    of Korea
Draper, William H., Jr., 155
Drumright, Everett F., 155, 218, 249
Dulles, John Foster, 236, 285n2
    career of, 124–25, 255
    criticism of, 184
    diplomacy by, 254
    Rhee and, 124, 256, 257
    speech by, 258

ECA. *See* Economic Cooperation
    Administration
Economic aid, 73, 112, 114, 157, 163, 187,
    190, 215, 220, 221, 237, 239, 253, 255
    Rhee and, 179, 189
    Russian, 177
Economic Cooperation Administration
    (ECA), 127, 128, 155, 203, 216, 220,
    238, 251
    GARIOA and, 179
    gasoline imports and, 215
    mission of, 130
    Rhee and, 179, 221
Economic development, 26, 27, 29, 67, 73,
    74, 75, 111, 129, 138, 141, 157–58,
    192, 221, 228, 237, 239, 244
    elections and, 139
    funds for, 110
    military aid and, 217, 238
Economic problems, 64, 67, 84, 130,
    157–58, 163, 175
Economic reform, 86, 100, 111, 117,
    238, 257
Eisenhower, Dwight D., 120, 124
Elections, 89, 121, 165, 221, 222, 238,
    240, 255–56, 257
    criticism of, 151, 184
    independence, 148–58

Kim Il-sung and, 150–51
    noncooperation in, 151
    preliminaries to, 135–42
    Rhee and, 139, 142, 152–53, 154
Electricity, 151, 178
Endo Ryusaku, 44
Epidemics, 50, 81, 84, 91
"Estimate of Conditions in Asia and the
    Pacific at the Close of the War in the
    Far East and the Objectives and
    Policies of the United States, An"
    (State Department), 54
Executive Order 10099 (1950), 219

FACC, 216
Far East Area Committee, 34
Far East Command (FECOM), 100, 166,
    235, 236, 280n13
    G-2 of, 98, 99, 101, 245, 252
    intelligence and, 101
    map of, 54
    research by, 102
    training by, 248
F-51 "Mustang" fighter-bombers, 213,
    217, 218, 246, 252
Field Order 55, 58
Field Research Unit (FECOM), 102
Finley, Joe W., 165
First Committee, 125–26, 184
First Far Eastern Front, 43
First Opium War, 231
Fischgrund, Harold, 168, 183, 277n17
Five Province Administrative Bureau, 50,
    51, 68
Fleet Radio Unit Pacific (HYPO), 95, 214
Food shortages, 37, 84, 91, 187
Forbidden City, 230, 231
Foreign Assistance Correlation Committee
    (FACC), 216
Foreign Assistance Steering Committee, 216
Foreign Military Assistance Coordinating
    Committee, 219
Foreign policy, 1, 221
Foreign Policy Association, 67
Formosa, 230, 234, 255
    annexation of, 16
    Nationalists in, 12–13
    security of, 248
    strategic planning and, 237, 307n33

Forrestal, James V., 234
Foster, William C., 124, 251
"Freedom Budget," 238
Frontal Aviation, 178
Frye, Captain, 168
Fuchs, Klaus, 97
Fuller, Hurley E., 168, 169

Gannett, Frank, 39
Gao Gang, 194
GARIOA. *See* Government Aid and Relief
    in Occupied Areas
Gasoline, importing, 129, 215
Gate of Heavenly Peace, 231
Gayn, Mark, 91
General Strike Committee Against the UN
    Korean Commission, 137
Gibney, Frank, 250
Glavnoye Razvedyvatelnoe Upravleniye
    (GRU), 97
Goodfellow, Millard Preston, 53, 64, 113
    Rhee and, 38, 39, 220
Government Aid and Relief in Occupied
    Areas (GARIOA), 60, 236
    ECA and, 179
    end of, 130
    funds from, 109, 110, 111, 131, 141, 215
    Korean Constabulary and, 162
Great Bell of Chongno, 161
Great Korean Experiment, 236, 257
Great Powers, 5, 53, 60
    trusteeship and, 63, 64, 68
Greek civil war, 93, 122, 233
Greek Orthodox Church, Soviet
    intelligence and, 98
Gromyko, Andrei A., 125, 126
Ground Forces Combat Command, 248
GRU, 97
Gruenther, Alfred M., 216
G-2
    of FECOM, 98, 99, 101, 214, 245, 252
    of KMAG, 214, 245, 252
    of ROKA, 200, 214,
    of USAFIK, 99
    of U.S. Army Staff, 95, 252
Guerrillas, 36, 103, 131–32, 143, 166, 183,
    204, 206, 223, 227, 229, 240, 241,
    250, 252
    casualties for, 182, 203
    KNP and, 146, 147, 207

Korean Constabulary and, 146, 147
    ROKA and, 225, 226, 251
    Yosu Rebellion and, 178
Guerrilla war, 26, 29, 142–48, 157
Guevara, Ché, 14
Guomindang, 13, 100, 105, 231, 232,
    234, 240
    economic aid to, 237

Hakpyong, 78, 146
Halfmoon, 234
Halla-san, 143, 146, 147, 181, 182, 183,
    223
Hanguk Gun, 78
Hanguk Min-judang, 47
Han River, 21, 22, 45, 81, 156, 164, 205,
    240, 241
Hansen, Ralph W., 241, 251
Harriman, W. Averell, 45, 68, 71, 236, 254
Hausman, James H., Jr., 106, 165, 202,
    204, 223, 227, 249, 251
    arrival of, 79–80
    death of, 277n15
    Korean Constabulary and, 80, 174
    Rhee and, 208, 211
    Roberts and, 132–33
    ROKA and, 304n81
    self-policing and, 107
    study by, 173
    Yosu Rebellion and, 168, 169, 170
Hearst, William Randolph, 31, 39
Henderson, Gregory, 170, 226, 227
Hermit Kingdom, 4, 5, 20
Hickerson, John, 237
Hickey, Doyle O., 235, 236
Hideyoshi Toyotami, 42
Higgins, Marguerite, 250
Hill 292 sector, 208–9
Hill 488 sector, 208
Hilldring, John H., 60, 109, 111, 112
Hillenkoetter, Roscoe H., 246
Hirobumi, Marquis Ito, 24
Hirohito, 44, 55, 62
Hiss, Alger, 283n55
Ho Chi Minh, 4, 12, 14
Hodge, John R., 67, 81, 101, 114, 128,
    131, 132, 140, 145, 156
    advisers to, 129
    agenda of, 109, 111, 112, 149
    anti-Americanism and, 136

career of, 57–58
criticism of, 69, 119
elections and, 121, 138, 139, 142, 149, 150, 153, 154–55, 165
Japanese civil government and, 59
Kim Ku and, 69, 70, 151
leadership of, 71
MacArthur and, 56–57, 90
military government and, 117
national government and, 75, 91
occupation and, 60
partisans and, 102
police reserve and, 66
popular organizations and, 66
provisional government and, 61, 62
Rhee and, 62, 63, 110, 111, 113, 118, 137, 142, 154, 159, 160
Right and, 116
Russian consulate and, 98
security issues and, 105
trusteeship and, 68, 69
Hoffman, Paul, 238
Ho Hon, 35, 47, 88, 175, 195
Ho Ka-i, 40, 177, 196
Honam Task Force, 225
Hoo, Victor, 137
Hoover, Herbert, 39
Hoover Institution, 112
Ho Shili, 248
House Committee on Executive Expenditures, 217
Hukbalahaps, 12, 67
Human rights, 117, 123
Hungsandan, 29
Hungson Taewongun, 20
Hyon Chun-hyok, 51
HYPO, 95, 214

Identity, 4, 5, 9, 11, 60
Ignatiev, Alexandre M., 176, 229
IL-10 light bombers, 193, 243
Imjin River, 205, 241
Immigration, 6, 36–37
Imperialism, 5–6, 13, 135, 254
    American, 232
    Japanese, 5
    Soviet, 232, 254
Imperial Japanese Army, 29, 41, 42, 78
    Koreans in, 37
    nationalism and, 35

"Implications of a Possible Full Scale Invasion from North Korea Subsequent to Withdrawal of United States Troops from South Korea" (U.S. Army), 235
Independence, 12, 13, 29, 36, 110, 123, 126, 161, 237
    declaration of, 18, 19, 159
    delay in, 66, 69
    elections and, 148–58
    issue of, 59–60
    movement, 16–17, 28
    Korean, 5, 31, 38
    political, 141
    Rhee and, 111–12, 160, 162
Independence Army, 28
Independence Club, 23
Independence Gate, rally at, 19
Independent, 23
Inflation, 37, 130, 158, 178, 187, 190, 221
    halting, 156
Inmingun, 104, 176, 188
Intelligence, 178, 187–88, 202, 224, 227, 243
    analysis of, 186
    capabilities for, 96–97, 214
    concerns about, 94–103
    electronic, 95
    Japanese, 97
    photographic, 96
    politico-military, 95–96
    signals, 95, 101, 245
    Soviet, 97, 98
    technical, 95–96
    U.S., 229–30, 245
Interim Legislative Assembly, 84, 90, 112, 113, 116, 136, 141, 149, 154, 160
    anticollaborator law and, 162
    constitution and, 117
    dissolution of, 118
    elections and, 137–38, 139
    Hodge and, 88, 89, 110, 118
    Joint Commission and, 279n34
Interim People's Committee, 51
Internationalism, 92, 254
Interventionism, 43, 231
Irkutsk faction, 34
Isaacs, Harold, 31, 271n7
Isolationism, 136, 254

Jackson, S. H., 149, 150
Jacobs, Joseph E., 114, 118–19, 140
  criticism of, 119
  Rhee and, 154
  withdrawal and, 156
Jaisohn, Philip, 23
Japanese Communist Party, 26, 96, 130
Japanese empire, collapse of, 4–5, 11–12
Japanese Imperial Military Academy, 161
JCS. *See* Joint Chiefs of Staff
Jessup, Philip C., 138, 220, 236, 305n12
Johnson, Louis A., 234, 237, 251
Johnston, Richard J. H., 92, 271n7, 275n2
Joint Chiefs of Staff (JCS), 55, 109,
      119–20, 236, 248
  consultation with, 246
  defense spending and, 216, 217
  funding and, 234, 235, 237
  Hodge and, 71
  MacArthur and, 246
  military aid and, 192
  State Department and, 190
  strategic planning and, 237
Joint Commission. *See* United States-
  Union of Soviet Socialist Republics
  Joint Commission
Joint Communiqué No. 5 (1946), 74, 114
Joint Emergency War Plan, 119, 234, 236
Joint Special Operations Branch, 101
Joint Strategic Plans and Operations Group
  (JSPOG), 235, 236
Joint Strategic Survey Committee, 110

Kaesong-Munsan-ni corridor, 208, 241
Kangdong Institute, 104, 177, 183
  guerrillas from, 188, 193, 202, 203,
      205, 207
  SKLP and, 166
Kang Kon, 39–40, 176
Kang Tae-mun, 202
Kapsan faction, 40, 103, 104, 134
  Yanan faction and, 50, 51, 76–77, 175,
      176, 148
KDP. *See* Korean Democratic Party
Kelso, Minor L., 167, 168, 169
Kempeitai, 7
Kennan, George, 114, 121, 236, 237
Kil Sun-ju, 17
Kim, Betty Marie, 6, 7
Kim, David, 6, 7

Kim, Helen, 163
Kim, Herbert, 29
Kim, James, 6, 7
Kim, Peter, 6–8, 266nn7,10
Kim, Richard, 7, 8
Kim Chae-gyu, 80
Kim Chaek, 40, 51, 68, 104, 176
Kim Chae-pil, 195–96
Kim Chang-sei, 6
Kim Chi-hoe, 167, 181, 183, 204
Kim Chong-suk, 40
Kim Chong-won ("Tiger"), 170
Kim Chung-yol, 218
Kim Hong-il, 173, 211
Kim Ik-yol, 145, 146
Kim Il, 40, 194
Kim Il-sung
  address by, 135
  Chinese assistance for, 194, 243
  coalition regime and, 103
  cult of the personality of, 176
  leadership of, 39–40
  Mao and, 176, 230, 244
  Rhee and, 176
  rise of, 175–78
  Stalin and, 83, 176, 177, 205, 241, 243–44
  strength of, 134
Kim Il-sung Room, 176
Kim Jong-il, 40
Kim Ku, 24, 26, 33, 46, 48, 61, 63, 74–76,
      78, 80, 82, 87–90, 94
  assassination of, 222
  coup and, 108, 157
  elections and, 139, 149, 151
  failure of, 152, 191
  Hodge and, 69, 70, 151
  patronage for, 131
  petition by, 79
  politics and, 64
  Rhee and, 70, 151
  support for, 40–41, 83, 111, 154
  unification and, 153
Kim Kyu-sik, 46, 48, 61, 63, 74, 84, 87,
      90, 118, 136, 140, 192
  Alliance of Popular Sovereignty and, 148
  appeal of, 137
  elections and, 89, 139, 149, 151
  failure of, 152, 191
  Left-Right coalition and, 83
  military government and, 116

Rhee and, 151
unification and, 153
Unification League and, 32
Kim Mu-bong, 194
Kim Mu-chong, 33, 41, 50–51, 77, 87,
    103–4, 176
Kim Paik-il, 168, 209, 211, 223
Yosu Rebellion and, 169, 170
Kimpo airport, 88, 250, 256
Kim Se-won, 101
Kim Sok-won, 174, 208, 209, 211
Kim Song-ju, 35–36
Kim Sung-su, 29, 46, 47, 48, 116, 118,
    154, 171, 181, 239
cabinet post for, 163
corruption and, 132
coup attempt by, 108
KDP and, 160
supporters of, 115
Kim Tal-hyon, 51, 134
Kim Tal-sam, 145, 147, 183, 202, 203,
    224, 226, 227
Kim To-yon, 163
Kim Tu-bong, 32–33, 41, 50–51, 140
private army of, 51
status of, 176
Unification League and, 32
Kim Ung, 41
Kim Won-bong, 33, 34, 63
Kim Yung-chol, 218
King, Mackenzie, 136
Kingdom of Korea, independence of, 18
KLO. See Korean Liaison Office
KMAG. See Korean Military Advisory Group
Knowland, William F., 217, 254
Knox, Frank, 38
Knox, John, 13
KNP. See Korean National Police
KNYM, 90, 105, 106
Kojong, King, 17, 20, 21, 23–24, 31, 72
Koo, Wellington, 240
"Korea for the Koreans," 131
Korea lobby, 217
Korean, romanization of, 259–63
Korean aid bill (HR 5330), 112, 221
Korean Anti-Japanese Front Unification
    League, 32
Korean Army Founders Association, 289n48
Korean Army Headquarters, 241
Korean Bureau, 34

Korean Central Intelligence Agency, 80
Korean Coast Guard Academy, 127
Korean Commission, 118, 123, 129, 191
establishment of, 29
military government and, 111, 112, 113
Rhee and, 38, 52
Korean Communist Party, 25, 35, 46, 61,
    75, 133
Autumn Harvest Uprising and, 86
influence of, 82
joining, 34
recognition for, 51
reestablishment of, 50, 88
Rhee and, 63
Korean Communists, 26, 27, 31, 32, 97, 140
participation by, 73–74
Shanghai/Irkutsk divisions of, 34
Korean Communist Youth Association, 34
Korean Constabulary, 88, 120, 129, 137,
    142, 144, 145, 150, 155, 156, 171
army from, 141
dissidents in, 170, 174, 182, 183
formation of, 78–80
funds for, 162
guerrillas and, 146, 147
Hodge and, 80, 107
intelligence and, 99
KNP and, 80, 85, 103, 106–9, 132, 157
leadership of, 107
name change for, 172
rebellion and, 169
refugee officers of, 201
Rhee and, 161, 165, 174
security and, 163–64
SKLP and, 80
strengthening, 87, 106, 163, 164, 165, 228
subversion of, 148, 182, 183
weapons for, 132, 166, 167
withdrawal and, 165–66
Korean Democratic Party (KDP), 48, 51,
    61, 65, 68, 69, 75, 84, 87, 108–9, 116,
    117, 118, 134, 149, 154, 160, 198
cabinet and, 155, 163
coalition regime and, 103
coup and, 157
creation of, 47
elections and, 139, 151–52, 153
KNP and, 77
Rhee and, 63, 82, 137, 142, 239
supporters of, 115, 152, 256

Korean Democratic Youth League, 66
Korean Independence League, 46
Korean Independence Party, 82, 83, 84, 90,
    107, 154
  An and, 222
  elections and, 148
  Kim Ku and, 84, 105, 134, 148, 160
  provisional government and, 116, 117, 118
  supporters of, 115
Korean Joint Chiefs of Staff, 79
Korean Liaison Office (KLO), 100, 101,
    214, 244, 245
Korean Methodist Church, 38
Korean Military Advisory Group (KMAG),
    196, 201, 207, 212, 213, 219, 226,
    236, 240, 248, 251, 252, 256, 257
  analysis by, 210, 249, 250
  defense plan by, 241
  G-2 of, 214, 245
  Kim Sok-won and, 208
  KNP and, 223
  MDAP allocation and, 246
  praise for, 250
  reform and, 211
  Rhee and, 217, 249–50
  training and, 214
  USAFIK and, 190
  weapons and, 218
Korean National Association, 29
Korean National Defense Army, 139
Korean National Police (KNP), 60, 65, 81,
    82, 84, 87, 88, 97, 104, 112, 117, 128,
    131, 139, 157, 174
  arrests by, 153, 154, 166
  casualties for, 134
  Cheju-do and, 142, 144
  Communists and, 83, 188
  coup attempt and, 108
  elections and, 150
  Fourteenth Regiment and, 167
  guerrillas and, 146, 147, 207
  intelligence and, 99
  Kim Ku and, 77, 222
  Korean Constabulary and, 80, 85, 103,
    106, 107, 108, 109, 132, 157
  leadership of, 115
  partisans and, 223
  political/economic reform and, 100
  private armies and, 66

  problems with, 85, 164, 252
  raid on, 145, 182
  reform of, 77, 116, 155, 162–63
  Rhee and, 223
  ROKA and, 227
  security and, 163–64, 181
  SIC and, 198
  SKLP and, 105, 165
  strengthening, 163, 167
  USAFIK and, 165
  Yosu Rebellion and, 167, 168, 169, 171
Korean National Security Act (1948), 172,
    181, 191, 198
Korean National Youth Movement
    (KNYM), 90, 105, 106
Korean People's Army (KPA), 40, 51, 76,
    140, 204, 208, 209, 218, 245, 252, 253
  creation of, 104, 176
  estimates for, 251 (table)
  growth of, 104, 193–98, 243
  intelligence and, 214
  Kim and, 104, 206
  PLA and, 230
  readiness of, 177, 178, 212, 245, 246, 249
  SKLP and, 221
  strength of, 197, 240, 250
  weapons for, 135, 193, 194, 197
Korean People's Army (KPA) navy, 243
Korean People's Party, 61, 70, 74, 75, 84,
    88, 89
Korean People's Republic, 58, 61, 271n5
  creation of, 46–47
  non-Communist members of, 48
  political platforms of, 47
  private armies of, 66
  Rhee and, 63
Korean People's Socialist Party, 25
Korean Preparatory Army, 45
Korean Research Bureau, 100, 214, 222,
    244, 245
Korean Restoration Army, 25, 41, 63
  Kim Ku and, 32
Korean Section, Russian Communist
    Party, 25
Korean Supreme People's Assembly,
    153, 154
Korean Volunteer Army, 33, 41
Korean Volunteer Corps, 33
Korean Workers' Party, 103, 133, 195

Korean Youth Association, 31–32
Koryo Communist Party, 25
Koryo Hotel, 69
Koryo Kingdom, 196
Kovalev, I. V., 232
Kozuki Yoshio, 58
KPA. *See* Korean People's Army
Kwangbok army, 63, 78, 90, 107, 139
Kwangtung army, 36, 41, 43
Kwon Sung-yol, 154
Kyongbok Palace, 250

Laboring People's Party, 148
Labor unions, 45, 117
Labour Party, withdrawal and, 13
Lady, Harold, 179
Land reform, 64–65, 82, 84, 117, 119, 130,
     137, 238, 142, 190
Langdon, William L., 63–64, 67, 83–84,
     89, 90, 129
Lansing, Robert, 124
Lawson, Richard H., 217–18, 219
League of Nations, 184
Lebedev, Nikolai G., 50
Lee, Grand Price. *See* Yi, Grand Price
Lee Chang-op. *See* Yi Chang-op
Lee Chi-op ("Speedy"), 80, 146, 276n14
Lee Chong-chan. *See* Yi Chong-chan
Lee Chong-chon. *See* Yi Chong-chon
Lee Chung-chun. *See* Yi Chung-chun
Lee Chung-jon, 139
Lee Chung-sil, 6
Lee Ha-ung. *See* Yi Ha-ung
Lee Ho-jae. *See* Yi Ho-jae
Lee Hyong-gun. *See* Yi Hyong-gun
Lee Hyong-kun. *See* Yi Hyong-kun
Lee Hyon-sang. See Yi Hyon-sang
Lee Hyun-suk, 210, 211
Lee In, 163
Lee Kwon-mu. *See* Yi Kwon-mu
Lee Paksa. *See* Yi Paksa
Lee Pom-sok. *See* Yi Pom-sok
Lee Sang-cho. *See* Yi Sang-cho
Lee Sang-hun. *See* Yi Sang-hun
Lee Sang-jae. *See* Yi Sang-jae
Lee Si-yong. *See* Yi Si-yong
Lee Song-sun. *See* Yi Song-sun
Lee Sung-man. *See* Yi Sung-man
Lee Tok-ku. *See* Yi Tok-ku

Lee Tong-hwi. *See* Yi Tong-hwi
Lee Ung-jun. *See* Yi Ung-jun
Lee Yi-yong. *See* Yi Yi-yong
Lee Yong-hwi. *See* Yi Yong-hwi
Lee Yun-yong. *See* Yi Yun-yong
Leftists, 10, 11, 75, 157
Lehman, Herbert, 254, 255
Lemnitzer, Lyman L., 216
Lenin, V. I., 231
Lerch, Archer, 73, 81, 89, 90, 105, 110, 111
     death of, 113, 118
     mission of, 112, 283n35
     police reserve and, 77–78
     Rhee/Hodge and, 113
Liberalism, 9, 23, 27, 254
Liberation, struggle for, 27–29, 31–36, 64
Lie, Trygve, 239
Limb, Ben C., 29, 31, 111, 112, 191
Lim Sunha, 276nn13,14, 277n16, 282n26,
     290n50
Lin Biao, 12
Liu Shaoqi, 232
Liu Yu Wan, 160
Long March, 33, 231
Lovett, Robert A., 93, 120, 121, 123, 155
     Cho and, 189
     KNP/Korean Constabulary and, 163
Luce, Henry, 31
Luna, Rufino, 160

MacArthur, Douglas, 5, 12, 50, 53, 58, 59,
     67, 73, 81, 101, 106, 110, 132, 189,
     194, 241, 245
     arrival of, 160, 161
     assessment by, 235, 236, 249
     distribution plan and, 131
     Dulles and, 255
     Formosa and, 248
     intelligence and, 97, 98, 186–87
     Joint Commission and, 70
     Moscow agreement and, 71
     police reserve and, 66
     political/strategic review and, 90
     provisional government and, 61
     revolt and, 87–88
     Rhee and, 62, 160–61, 201
     Roberts and, 133
     training and, 214
     trusteeship and, 68

MacArthur, Jean, 160
Mackinder, Halford J., 13
Magsaysay, Ramon, 12
Main Intelligence Directorate, 97
Maintenance, problems with, 215
Malik, Jacob, 184, 240
Manchukuo army, 165, 168
Manchurian Koreans, 4, 24–25, 33, 49, 74
    population of, 37
    return of, 43, 127
Manse Revolution. *See* March First
    Movement
Mao Zedong, 29, 33, 40, 194, 197
    Kim and, 176, 230, 244
    in Moscow, 231–33, 243
    people's war and, 14
    Stalin and, 232–33
Marble Hall, 72, 73
March First Movement (Sam-il [3.1]
    Movement), 17, 18, 26, 44, 48, 51,
    52, 90, 174, 221–22
    impact of, 19, 20
    Japanese colonialism and, 27
Marshall, George C., 93, 118, 120, 121,
    122, 155, 246
    KNP/Korean Constabulary and, 163
    Korean aid bill and, 112
    Molotov and, 114
    speech by, 123
Marshall, John T., 78, 276n13
Marshall Plan, 111–12
Marx, Karl, 14
Marxists, 25, 27, 39
Masatake, Terauchi, 16, 22
Mass demonstrations, 34–35, 108,
    111, 138
Mathews, William R., 257
May, Alan Nunn, 97
McCardle, Carl, 257
McCarthy, Joseph, 236, 254
McCloy, John J., 71, 112
McCune, George, 22
MDAP. *See* Mutual Defense Assistance
    Program
Meiji Restoration, 4
Menon, K. P. S., 136–37, 138
Methodists, 21, 22, 31
M-5 light tanks, 218
Mikoyan, Anastas, 232

Military aid, 187, 190, 192, 202, 246,
    248, 251
    economic development and, 217, 238
    questions about, 212–21
    Rhee and, 196, 212, 213, 215, 218,
        219, 249
Military English Language School, 78
Military government, 116, 117, 118
    civic order and, 81
    order/public well-being and, 77
    police force for, 81
    reunification and, 119
Military Intelligence Division, 95
Military Intelligence Service, 95
Military Mobilization Board, 211
Military Police Command, 173, 222
Miller, A. L., 217
Min, Queen, 21
Minami Jiro, 37
Min Hui-sik, 163
Ministry of Defense, 226
Ministry of Education, 37
Ministry of Home Affairs, 164
Ministry of National Defense, 172, 173
    abolition of, 211
    Japanese property and, 253
Ministry of the Interior, 76
Minjung ideal, 9, 10
Min Myong-song, 21
MI-6, 94, 100
Missionaries, 23, 31, 38, 124, 127, 128
    Dulles and, 256
    protestant, 21–22, 24
Mobile Police Unit, 209
Modernization, 21, 22, 26
    Korean, 4, 26, 27
Moffett, Howard, 128
Moffett, Samuel A., 22
Molotov, V. M., 73, 114
Mongols, 143, 233
Moranbong Hill, 52
Moscow agreement, 68–69, 71, 74,
    90, 118
    Hodge and, 69, 70
Moscow Decision, 102
Mount Fujiyama, 143
Mount Sorak National Park, 205
Mo Yun-suk, 200
M-26 "Pershing" tanks, 194, 217

Muccio, John J., 155, 170, 173, 187, 192, 204, 249, 250, 252
  economic aid and, 179, 219, 238
  KMAG and, 219
  military aid and, 217, 218, 220
  mission of, 241
  on politicians, 189
  Rhee and, 190, 206, 255
  on ROKA, 246, 251
  training and, 214
Mun Il, 196
Mun Sang-gil, 146, 147
Muslims, 4, 49
  Hindu conflict with, 12
Mutual Defense Assistance Act (1949), 214, 216, 220, 301n61
Mutual Defense Assistance Program (MDAP), 216, 233, 246
  survey team of, 217–18

Nagayama, Matsuko, 127
Nam Il, 40, 104, 176
Namwon, incident at, 66
Narodnyi Kommissariat Gosudarstvennoy Bezopastnosti (NKGB), 97, 98, 104, 134
Narodnyi Kommissariat Vnutrennikh Del (NKVD), 97
National Assembly, 162, 170, 189, 213, 226, 258
  economic aid and, 239
  elections for, 221, 222, 255–56
  Emergency, 82
  First, 255
  Rhee and, 157
  Second, 256, 257
  security/military reorganization and, 172–73
  SKLP and, 181
  task of, 151
  transformation of, 154
National Congress, 19
National Council of Labor Unions, 65
National Defense Bureau, 104
National Democratic Front, 115
National Economic Board, 113, 127
National Election Committee, 149
National Guard, 57, 59
National Independence Federation, 191

Nationalism, 13, 17, 24, 35, 86, 119, 144
Nationalist Chinese, 52, 148, 139, 216
  economic aid for, 220
  PLA and, 197
  ROK and, 160
Nationalists, 11, 12, 26, 27, 34–35, 38, 44, 239
  Asian, 9
  Korean, 16, 29
  rebellion by, 23–24
  trusteeship and, 67
National League of Peasants' Unions, 66
National Press Club, Acheson at, 237, 238
National Security Council (NSC), 140–41, 215, 246
National Security Council Memorandum 8 (NSC 8), 135–36, 141, 186, 187, 190, 235
National Security Council Memorandum 68 (NSC 68), 237, 238, 239
National Security Resources Board, 141
National Society for the Rapid Realization of Korean Independence (NSRRKI), 82, 84
  elections and, 139, 149, 151, 153
  expansion of, 118
  Rhee and, 116
  support for, 152, 256
National Traitors Act, 164, 181, 198
National Youth Association, 116
National Youth Corps, 77, 82
NATO, 1, 216, 233, 254
Navy of the Republic of Korea, 172–73, 211, 243
NCO School, 208
NEAJUA, 35–36, 39, 194
Neocolonialism, 13, 53, 67, 87, 149, 184
New Korea Corporation, 65, 87, 131
New Korea Youth Party, 25
New Left, 138
New People's Association, 23, 24
New People's Party, 51, 88
New Shoot Society, 35
Newsweek, 31, 91, 271n7
New York Herald-Tribune, 250
New York Times, 92, 93, 111, 227, 248, 271n7, 275n2
Nichols, Donald, 101, 213, 214
Nimitz, Chester W., 53

Nitze, Paul H., 236, 237, 256, 305n12
NKGB, 97, 98, 104, 134
NKVD, 97
Noble, Harold J., 155, 218, 239
North American Aviation, 219
North Atlantic Treaty Organization
    (NATO), 1, 216, 233, 254
North China Korean Independence
    League, 33
Northeast Anti-Japanese United Army
    (NEAJUA), 35–36, 39, 194
Northeast Asian Affairs Division, 186
North Korean air force, 243
North Korean Workers' Party, 51
North Star Society, 26
Northwest Young Men's Association, 105
Northwest Youth Association, 145, 222,
    223, 289n46
NSC, 140–41, 215, 246
NSRRKI. See National Society for the
    Rapid Realization of Korean
    Independence
Nuclear weapons, 110, 229, 230, 235

Occupation, 45, 58, 60, 64, 88, 189
    policy on, 75
    zones, 2, 64, 68
O Chin-u, 51, 104, 224
Office of Naval Intelligence, 95
Office of Northeast Asian Affairs, 256
Office of Policy Coordination (OPC), 102
Office of Reports and Estimates (CIA), 102
Office of Special Investigations (U.S. Air
    Force), 101
Office of Special Operations, 102
Office of Strategic Services (OSS), 62, 98,
    100, 128
    creation of, 95
    Korea and, 38, 39, 49, 53
    MacArthur and, 246
Office of the Chief of Naval Operations
    (OP-16), 95
Officers Training Center, 104
Officer Training School, 107
Oh Dong-gi, 165
O Il-gyun, 147
Oil, importing, 129, 215
Old Right, 138
Oliver, Robert T., 112, 239

Ongjin peninsula, 207, 208, 210–11
    fighting on, 209, 300n43
Ongjin Task Force, 209, 210
"On the Occasion of the Creation of the
    Korean People's Army" (Kim), 135
OP-16, 95
OP-20-G, 95
OPC, 102
Operation Blacklist, 56
Operation Blue, 100
Operation Cruller, 241
Operation Plan Moonrise, 119
Operation Preemptive Strike, 243
Oppenheimer, J. Robert, 305n12
Order of battle, map of, 242, 247
Oriental Missionary Society, 22
O Se-chang, 160
OSS. See Office of Strategic Services

Pacific Pact, 258
Pacific Union, 240
Paejae Boys School and Debating
    Society, 23
Paek, George, 47
Paekche, 5
Paek In-gi, 168, 203
Pagoda Park, rally at, 19
Paik, George L., 257
Paik In-yup, 51, 168, 223
Paik Sun-yup, 51, 107, 146, 165, 168, 181,
    201, 209, 211, 227
    Chiri-san campaign and, 225–26
    Yosu Rebellion and, 169, 170
Pak Chin-kyung, 146, 147
Pak Hon-yong, 35, 46, 47, 48, 61, 70, 75,
    82, 83, 87, 104, 145, 166, 174, 175,
    176, 195, 196, 229, 244
    exile of, 89
    Kim and, 135
    Korean Communist Party and, 88
    Korean Communist Youth Association
        and, 34
    Kyongsangs and, 86
    Rhee and, 63
    security issues and, 177
    SKLP and, 134
    unification and, 153
Pak Hong-sik, 198
Pak Hyo-sam, 77

Pak Il-u, 41, 104
Pak Il-won, 200
Pak Kyong-hun, 144
Pak Song-hun, 167
Pang Ho-san, 41
Parallel War, 208, 209, 212, 218, 223
    described, 205, 206
    Kim and, 207
Paramilitary groups, 105, 139, 142, 146, 157
Paris Peace Conference, 16, 17
Park Chung-hee, 80, 200–201
Partisans, 14, 42, 44, 102, 143, 166, 167, 174,
        177, 181, 188, 196, 197, 204, 227, 239
    Anti-Japanese, 39
    campaign against, 202, 203
    Cheju-do and, 142
    decline of, 225, 226
    KNP and, 223
    PLA and, 224
    raids by, 224
Patronage, 29, 31, 131, 176, 197
Patterson, George S., 149, 150
Patterson, Robert P., 71, 109, 110
Pauley, Edwin W., 49, 75
Peace Preservation Act (1948), 198
Peace Preservation Law (1925), 34
Pearson, Lester B., 136
Peng Dehuai, 33
People's Commissariat for Internal
        Affairs, 97
People's Committees, 48, 49, 68, 144,
        152, 205
    Autumn Harvest Uprising and, 86
People's Committees, continued
    control of, 50
    described, 11
People's Flying Column, 166
People's Liberation Army (PLA), 40, 41,
        145, 183, 229, 231, 240
    assistance from, 177
    Formosa and, 230, 244
    Kim Il-sung and, 194
    Korean veterans in, 243
    KPA and, 230
    Nationalist army and, 197
    partisans and, 224
    Vietnamese and, 248
People's Republic of China, 13, 230
People's wars, 14, 142

Peter and Richard Kim Act, 8, 9
Pilsudski, Marshal, 162
Pius XII, Shintoism and, 38
Piwon, 250
PLA. See People's Liberation Army
Plan Bamboo, 66, 77
"Pledge of the Imperial Subjects," 37
PMAG. See Provisional Military
        Advisory Group
PMAG-K, 113
Policarp, P. K., 98
Police, 81
    colonial, 44
    combat, 222
    reserve, 66, 77–78
    ROK, 204, 206
    See also Korean National Police
"Policy for Korea" (State Department), 83
Politburo, 197
Political participation, 14, 27, 47, 117,
        239–40
Political philosophies, 10, 11
Political prisoners, 163, 188, 200
Political reforms, 100, 238
Popular front, 134, 175, 181
Potsdam Declaration (1945), 44
POWs. See Prisoners of war
Preparatory Committee, 46, 90
Presbyterians, 17, 21–22, 31, 32, 49–50,
        127, 195
    Dulles and, 256
    Shintoism and, 38
"Present Situation of the Korean Army"
        (Shin), 217
Price, Terrill E. "Terrible," 132
Price controls, 65, 158, 178
Prisoners of war (POWs), 2, 174, 266n10
    execution of, 225, 227
    interrogation of, 96–97
    Japanese, 45, 49, 102, 233
    Korean, 49
    returning, 55, 58
Private armies, 66, 78
Private Law 808 (1946), 9
Proclamation No. 1 (1945), 56, 111
"Proclamation of the Rights of the Korean
        People," 142
Progressives, 26, 117
Propaganda, 83, 129, 176, 205, 239

Protectorate, Japanese, 23–24
Provisional government, 44, 61, 75, 118
    Kim Ku and, 62, 74
Provisional Military Advisory Group
    (PMAG), 133, 157, 164, 165, 166,
    171, 173, 174
    plan of, 162
    purges and, 182
    Rhee and, 170, 189–90
Provisional Military Advisory Group-
    Korea (PMAG-K), 133
Public Opinion Bureau (DPI), 100
Pyo Mu-won, 202
Pyongyang conference, 142, 150, 151
Pyongyang Institute, 76
Pyongyang Political Officers School, 185

Quirino, Elpidio, 240

Radio Pyongyang, 140, 153, 208, 211,
    239, 258
    Parallel War and, 207
    SKLP campaign and, 228
    Yosu Rebellion and, 171
Railway Constabulary, 104
Randall, Russell E., 213
Recognition, 51, 160, 162, 165, 184
Reconnaissance Bureau, 39
Reconnaissance Troop, Korean
    Constabulary, 170
Reconstruction, 53, 56, 93
Red Army, 33, 34, 40, 50, 51, 67, 133, 134,
    188, 198, 210
    U.S. Army and, 103
    withdrawal of, 175, 184, 187
Red Army General Staff, 97
Reed, John P., 168, 209, 218, 251
    intelligence and, 99, 214
Refugees, 134, 174, 201
    antiregime, 142
    arrival of, 178–79
    Chinese, 230
    Christian, 128
    Communist, 205
    flow of, 134
Religion
    boycotting movement, 27
    freedom of, 27, 47

Repatriation, 44, 45, 55, 59
"Report to the President Pursuant to the
    President's Directive of 31 January
    1950," 237
Representative Democratic Council, 74,
    82, 83, 84
Republican Party, Dulles and, 124
Resistance movements, 11, 12, 43, 108
Restoration Army, 63, 78, 90, 107, 139
Review of the Far East (RFE), 271n6
Revolutionary movements, 13–14, 15,
    27, 48
Revolutionary Volunteer Army (RVA), 165
Revolutions, creation of, 20–27
RFE, 271n6
Rhee, Francesca Donner, 31, 160, 162,
    214, 239, 257
Rhee, Syngman, 23, 26, 46, 48, 75, 76, 80,
    82, 83, 88, 90, 94, 101
    cabinet of, 155, 157, 163
    coup attempt by, 108
    crises for, 178–79
    criticism of, 118, 184, 188, 191, 198
    fund raising by, 38
    Kim and, 176
    Kim Ku and, 70, 151
    leadership of, 29, 53, 111, 112, 239, 240
    lobbying by, 110
    MacArthur and, 62, 160–61, 201
    Moscow agreement and, 69
    opposition to, 113, 201
    patronage and, 31, 131
    politics and, 64, 256, 283n34
    popularity of, 102–3, 221–22
    presidency of, 2, 141, 159–60, 291n1
    provisional government and, 61, 62
    return of, 62–63
    Truman and, 116, 189, 212
Rhodes, Cecil, 13
Rice, 75, 87, 129, 158
    distribution of, 238
    problems with, 64, 65, 81, 82, 163
    shortage of, 37, 74, 117, 129–30, 178,
    179, 187
Ridgway, Matthew B., 133
Righteous Army, 24, 25, 26
Righteous Blood Society, 188
Righteous Movement, 28

Rightists, 10, 11, 29, 157
Right-Left Coalition, 116
Roberts, William L., 168, 170, 173, 182,
    189, 190, 204, 207, 210, 211, 222, 249
  career of, 132–33
  defense plan by, 240
  departure of, 250
  evacuation plan by, 241
  intelligence and, 214
  Korean Constabulary and, 174
  law enforcement and, 164
  on leadership, 212
  MacArthur and, 133
  military aid and, 215, 217, 218, 246
  PMAG and, 157
  Rhee and, 208, 211
  ROK-US partnership and, 211
  on ROKA, 246, 248, 250, 251, 252,
    307n38, 308n40
  screening and, 166
  training and, 213, 214, 215, 248
  USAFIK and, 206
  Yosu Rebellion and, 172
Rockefeller Foundation, 112
ROKA. See Army of the Republic of Korea
ROK Air Force, 213, 218, 219
ROK Coast Guard, 104, 167, 174, 218
  aid for, 219, 220
  arrests by, 166
  dissidents in, 174
  name change for, 172–73
ROK Marine Corps, 211, 213, 224
Romanenko, Alexei A., 50, 73
Romulo, Carlos, 192, 240
Roosevelt, Eleanor, 123, 124, 285n2
Roosevelt, Franklin D., 38, 53, 55, 67, 123
  Cairo Conference and, 52
  OSS and, 95
  Yalta and, 52
Roosevelt, Theodore, 5
Royall, Kenneth, 189, 190
Rusk, Dean, 45, 121, 236, 237, 254, 256
  commitment and, 238
  NSC 68 and, 238
Russian faction, 87
Russians
  Korean Communist coalition and, 76
  return of, 48–52

Russo-Japanese War (1904–1905), 4, 221
RVA, 165
Ryu Hai-jin, 144–45

Saemunan Presbyterian Church, 32, 38, 200
Saito Makoto, 28, 35
Salvation Army, 22
Sam-il, demonstrations on, 108, 138
Sam-il (3,1) Movement. See March First
    Movement
SANACC, 140–41
Sargeant, Howland H., 73, 237
Sargent, Clyde B., 129
Sauer, Charles A., 128
SCAP. See Supreme Commander of
    Allied Powers
Second Party Congress, 103, 134, 175
Second War Powers Act (1942), 8
Security, 77, 162, 163–64, 177, 190,
    192, 214
  building, 103–9
  elections and, 139
  Rhee and, 185
Security Bureau, 76
Security Cadres Training Center, 76
Security forces, 103, 141, 142, 187, 189,
    212, 213
  casualties for, 203
Self-determination, 5, 16, 53, 55, 109
Senate Bill No. 1607 (1946), 9
Senate Foreign Relations Committee, 217
Seoul Foreign Cemetery, 200
Seoul Foreign School, 6
Seoul National University, Dulles speech
    at, 258
Seoul Station, 28, 72
Seoul Union Church, 127
Seventh Day Adventists, 22
Shabshin, Anatoli I., 89
Shackleton, Robert M., 170
Shamanism, 17
Shanghai faction, 32, 34
Shanghai-Nanjing Koreans, 33
Shanghai Public School for Boys, 6
Shanghai Volunteer Corps, 6
Shanin, G. I., 73
Shaw, William Hamilton, 127, 128
Shilla, 5

Shinganhoe, 35
Shin Ik-hui, 46, 61, 63, 84, 100, 116, 117,
　136, 154, 160
Shin Sang-chul, 132
Shinminhoe, 23, 24
Shin Sung-mo, 191–92, 207, 210, 213,
　218, 245, 249, 256
　presentations by, 217
　Rhee and, 192
　ROK marines and, 211
Shin Tae-yong, 174, 211, 213, 218, 223
Shintoism, 11, 17, 37, 38, 171
Shtykov, Terentii F., 73, 89, 114, 176, 193,
　196, 197, 229, 243, 244
SIC, 198
Signal Intelligence Service (OP-20-G), 95
Signals intelligence (SIGINT), 95, 101, 245
"Situation in Korea, The" (USAFIK
　G-2), 102
SKLP. See South Korean Labor Party
Smallpox epidemic, 81
Smith, Adam, 13
Smuggling, 81, 208
So Chae-pil, 23
Socialism, 11, 46, 76, 85
Socialist Workers' Party, 89
Social reform, 86, 123
Social upheaval, 12, 14, 37, 67
Sodaemun Prison, Park at, 201
Song Chin-u, 18, 29, 44, 47, 48
　assassination of, 69, 70
Song Ho-sung, 80, 107, 166, 211
　Yosu Rebellion and, 168, 169
Song Yo-chan ("Tiger"), 148, 182, 290n50
Son Pyong-hui, 17, 18
Son Won-il, 174, 211
　military aid and, 220
　Roberts and, 201
　training and, 219
Son Yang-won, 171
Sorge, Richard, 96
South Korean Communist Party, 2
South Korean Labor Party (SKLP), 2, 106,
　135, 146, 147, 156, 157
　assessment of, 100, 187
　campaign of, 174–75, 177, 188
　City Branch of, 134
　elections and, 148, 149, 152
　formation of, 88–89

guerrillas of, 166, 224
Kim and, 104
KNP and, 105, 165
Korean Constabulary and, 80
KPA and, 221
opposition from, 130, 137
Park and, 201
rebellion and, 169
Rhee and, 198, 200, 222
suppression of, 153, 164–65, 166, 181, 182,
　183, 202, 203, 204, 205, 221–28, 229
as underground movement, 144–45, 152
Southwest Pacific Command, 12, 98
Soviet All-Union Society for Cultural
　Connections, 83
Soviet faction, 77
Soviet Far East Military District, 39
Soviet Navy, 178
Special action units, elimination of, 223
Special Activities Group, 39
Special Investigating Committee (SIC), 198
Staggers, Harley O., 112, 217
Staggers, John, 112
Stalin, Joseph, 67, 97, 187, 197, 231, 272n13
　attack order by, 245
　foreign policy and, 233
　Japanese repatriation and, 45
　Joint Commission and, 72
　Kim and, 83, 176, 177, 205, 241, 243–44
　Mao and, 232–33
　Marxism-Leninism and, 39
　military priorities of, 198
　nuclear weapons and, 230
　socialism of, 40
　Tito and, 113
　Yalta and, 52, 55
Stalinism, Koreanized, 175
State-Army-Navy-Air Force Coordinating
　Committee (SANACC) 176/39 study,
　140–41
State Department, 58–59, 93, 110, 123,
　125, 140, 155, 181, 189
　appeasement and, 68, 103
　China Lobby and, 52
　disengagement policy and, 171
　economic issues and, 69, 192, 215,
　220, 238
　elections and, 121, 139
　funding and, 111

GARIOA and, 130
Hodge plan and, 77
intelligence and, 94
internationalism in, 92
JCS and, 190
Joint Commission and, 74, 83
Kim and, 7
Korea and, 53, 109, 236, 256
military aid and, 192, 219
Moscow agreement and, 70, 90
occupation and, 75
provisional government and, 8, 61
Rhee and, 62, 111, 113, 239
Russian consulate and, 98
security and, 162
trusteeship and, 63, 67
UNTCOK and, 155
withdrawal and, 163
State-War-Navy Coordinating Committee
  (SWNCC), 45, 55, 119
  distribution plan and, 131
  Memorandum 176/8, 60
  policy statement by, 109, 120
Stevens, D. W., 24
Stilwell, Richard G., 102, 281n17, 307n30
Strategic Air Command, 234
Strategic Services Unit, 100
Strikes, 52, 137
  general, 2, 85, 137
  railroad, 81
Subic Bay, 236
Sukarno, Acmet, 12
Sullivan, Walter, 227
Sulzberger, Arthur Hays, 248
Sunjong, Crown Prince, 21
Sun Liren, 248
Sunset Peak, 143
Sun Yat-sen, 231
Supreme Commander of Allied Powers
  (SCAP), 56, 62, 98, 99, 160
SWNCC. *See* State-War-Navy
  Coordinating Committee

Taebaek mountains, 202, 205, 206
Taebaek-Odaesan counterpartisan
  campaign, 226
Taebaek-san Task Force, guerrillas and, 227
Taedong Youth Association, 105, 139
Taewongun, 21

Taft, Robert A., 124, 254, 255
Tai Li, 100
Taiwan. *See* Formosa
Taoism, 17
Taruc, Luis, 12
TASS, 230, 232
"Teaching of the Heavenly Way," 17
Terrorism, 14, 42, 142, 156, 157, 188
Textbooks, disposing of, 65–66
Tiananmen Square, 230
Time, 111, 250
Tito, 4, 113, 198, 233
Tong-a Ilbo, 29
Tonghak rebellion, 17, 24, 86
Training, 106, 187, 206, 212, 213–14, 215,
  219, 248
Treaty of Friendship, Alliance, and Mutual
  Assistance (1950), 233
Treaty of Kanghwa (1876), 21
Treaty of Portsmouth (1905), 231
Treaty of Versailles, 16
Truman, Harry S., 59, 88, 114, 234, 254
  China issue and, 220–21, 236
  containment and, 93, 116, 235
  defense budget by, 216
  Dulles and, 255
  ECA and, 179
  economic support and, 75
  Executive Order 10026-A and, 187
  foreign policy and, 246
  GARIOA and, 215
  Interim Legislative Assembly and, 84
  Japanese repatriation and, 45
  JCS and, 216
  Joint Commission and, 70, 72
  Korea and, 1, 53, 93, 109, 237
  military aid and, 192, 215–16, 219
  NSC and, 141, 190
  nuclear weapons and, 230
  protest vote and, 92
  Rhee and, 116, 189, 212
  surrender and, 56
Truman doctrine, 235
Trusteeship, 63, 113, 120, 155
  crisis, 64–71
  Kim Ku and, 69
  opposition to, 67, 70, 71
  Rhee and, 68, 115
Tsarapkin, S. K., 73

T-34 tanks, 193, 252
Tuesday Society, 34–35
Tunkin, Grigorii, 196

Uijongbu corridor, 207, 241
ULTRA-MAGIC, 96
Ultranationalists, 115, 120, 150, 222
UNCOK. *See* United Nations Commission
    on Korea
Underwood, Ethel van Wagoner, 143, 200
Underwood, Horace Grant, 22, 32, 65,
    127, 275n3
Underwood, Horace Horton, 38, 65, 127, 200
Underwood, John, 127
Underwood, Lillias Horton, 22
Underwood, Richard F., 49–50, 62, 127,
    271n7
Unification, 5, 103, 119, 120, 138, 141,
    153, 190, 197, 212, 243
    Communists and, 2
    Kim and, 193
    negotiations on, 74
    Rhee and, 191
United Nations, 122, 149, 169, 237, 258
    assistance from, 156, 184
    creation of, 124
    DPRK and, 175
    elections and, 139, 154
    imperialism and, 135
    initiatives by, 140
    Korea and, 110, 125–26, 136, 188, 205,
        256, 257
    Moscow agreement and, 90
    recognition and, 160, 162, 165
    Rhee and, 156, 163, 190, 255
    Soviet Union and, 121
    trusteeship and, 67, 113
United Nations Charter, 122, 124
United Nations Commission on Korea
    (UNCOK), 200, 203, 257
    arrival of, 191
    creation of, 155
    elections and, 238, 240, 255
    investigation by, 184
    moral protection of, 187
    Rhee and, 191, 222
United Nations General Assembly,
    120–21, 122, 123, 156, 190
    approval by, 178
    Dulles and, 124, 125

elections and, 139
Korea and, 136, 155, 184
resolutions by, 126, 184, 191, 255
UNTCOK and, 178
United Nations Security Council, 123
    Dulles and, 124
    Soviet Union and, 121, 240
United Nations Temporary Commission on
    Korea (UNTCOK), 137, 140,
    141, 147, 160, 163, 165
    approval of, 178
    Cheju-do and, 144
    dissolution of, 184
    Dulles and, 126
    elections and, 135, 138, 139, 142, 148, 149
    Hodge and, 156
    Kim Ku and, 136
    members of, 150
    power transfer and, 153
    recognition and, 160
    report of, 184
    Rhee and, 129, 136, 154, 156
    State Department and, 155
U.S. Air Force, 101, 196
    surplus from, 213
    training by, 248
U.S. Army, 6, 7, 49, 61, 62, 150, 155, 231
    intelligence for, 94, 95
    Kim brothers and, 8
    Korean Constabulary and, 78
    occupation and, 60
    postwar organization of, 172
    private armies and, 66
    Red Army and, 103
    training by, 214, 248
    withdrawal of, 187
U.S. Army Air Forces, 95, 101
U.S. Army Corps of Engineers, 88
U.S. Army Forces in Korea (USAFIK),
    97, 98, 153, 157, 162, 164, 182,
    187, 213
    disestablishment of, 190, 206
    G-2 of, 99, 100, 102
    intelligence and, 101, 202
    KMAG and, 190
    KNP and, 165
    structure/condition of, 286n17
    USAMGIK and, 155
U.S. Army Military Government, 144, 159
U.S. Information Service, 128

U.S. Marine Corps, 12, 62, 230
U.S. Maritime Commission, 220
U.S. Military Government in Korea
    (USAMGIK), 129, 135, 140, 147,
    152, 158
  elections and, 138, 150
  interim government and, 141
  makeup of, 127, 128
  power transfer and, 153
  Rhee and, 154
  USAFIK and, 155
U.S. Navy, 7, 12, 196
  aid from, 219
  Chinese refugees and, 230
  intelligence for, 94
  training by, 248
U.S. News and World Report, 252
U.S. Office of Information, 200
U.S.S. *Ensign Whitehead*, 220
U.S.S. *General Sherman*, 20
U.S.S. *Missouri*, 56
U.S.-Soviet relations, 1, 92, 94
United States-Union of Soviet Socialist
    Republics Joint Commission, 68–71,
    76, 89, 109, 110, 113, 114, 118, 119,
    120, 123, 125
  adjournment of, 75, 83
  Cheju-do and, 144
  economic issues and, 69
  Hodge and, 72, 74, 82, 83
  Interim Legislative Committee and,
    279n34
  negotiations of, 92
  organization of, 72, 73
  popular will and, 115
  problems for, 74, 81–82, 102, 109, 111,
    116, 122
  Russian consulate and, 98
United Young Men's Party, 174
UNTCOK. *See* United Nations Temporary
    Commission on Korea
USAFIK. *See* U.S. Army Forces in Korea
USAMGIK. *See* U.S. Military
    Government in Korea

Vandenberg, Arthur, 123, 124, 254, 255
Vanderpool, Jay, 102, 214, 281n17
Vasiliev, Ivan V., 243
Versailles Peace Conference, 124
Vieman, Lewis D., 251

Vietminh, 12
Vietnam Doc Lap Dong Minh, 12
Vietnam Quoc Dan Dong, 12
Vietnam War, 1
Vincent, John Carter, 67, 71
Voelkel, Harold, 128
Voss, Ernest E., 164
Vyshinsky, Andrei, 73, 123

Wagner, Robert, 254
Ward, Orlando "Pinky," 128–29
War Department, 56, 71, 93, 109, 112
  General Staff G-2 of, 95
  Hodge and, 57, 77
  Joint Commission and, 70, 83
  Kim brothers bill and, 9
  Korean Constabulary and, 106
  occupation and, 75
  provisional government and, 61
  Rhee and, 62
Warsaw Pact, 233
Wars of national liberation, 13, 198
Washington Koreans, 52
Webb, James, 236
Wedemeyer, Albert C., 8, 113, 119, 189, 190
Wesolowsky, Charles, 147, 290n50
White Clothes Society (*Paikyisa*), 100,
    281n16
White Guards, 25
White Russians, 16, 98
Williams, Jay Jerome, 112
Willoughby, Charles A., 100, 101, 102, 214
  analysis by, 245
  MacArthur and, 98, 99, 280n13
Wilson, Woodrow, 16
Women's League, 66
Won Yong-dok, 80, 107, 168, 174, 201,
    211, 217
Workers Party of Korea, 177
World Council of Churches, 124
Wright, Edwin K., 235, 236
Wright, W. H. Sterling, 164, 251, 256

Xinjiang, status of, 233

Yak-9 fighter-bombers, 193, 218, 243
Yalta, 52, 55
Yanan faction, 33, 41
  Kapsan faction and, 50, 51, 76–77, 175,
    176, 148

Yangban, 11, 20, 23, 24, 27, 32, 160
Yang Ju-sam, 198
Yi (or Lee), Grand Price, 20
Yi (or Lee) Chang-op, 200
Yi (or Lee) Chong-chan, 174
Yi (or Lee) Chong-chon, 105, 151, 208
Yi (or Lee) Chong-chun, 155
Yi (or Lee) Chung-chun, 174
Yi (or Lee) Ha-ung, 20
Yi (or Lee) Ho-jae, 226
Yi (or Lee) Hyong-gun, 161
Yi (or Lee) Hyong-kun, 106, 107
Yi (or Lee) Hyon-sang, 226
Yi (or Lee) Kwon-mu, 41
Yim, Louise, 29, 111, 112
Yi (or Lee) Paksa, 159
Yi (or Lee) Pom-sok, 32, 61, 63, 80, 82,
    115–16, 139, 144, 151, 169, 170, 171,
    174, 181, 192, 200, 204, 206, 207,
    208, 222
  aspirations of, 163, 164, 188
  KNYM and, 90
  National Youth Corps and, 77
  nomination of, 160
  opposition to, 155
  Rhee and, 168, 211
  Yosu Rebellion and, 172
  youth association and, 105
Yi (or Lee) Sang-cho, 41
Yi (or Lee) Sang-hun, 17
Yi (or Lee) Sang-jae, 17, 18
Yi (or Lee) Si-yong, 155
Yi (or Lee) Song-sun, 165
Yi (or Lee) Sung-man, 23
Yi (or Lee) Tok-ku, 203
Yi (or Lee) Tong-hwi, 25–26
Yi (or Lee) Ung-jun, 107, 161, 173, 174,
    201, 204
Yi (or Lee) Yi-yong, 198
Yi (or Lee) Yong-hwi, 34
Yi (or Lee) Yun-yong, 160
YMCA, 17, 23
YMS *Kanghwa,* 201
YMS *Kangkyung,* 201

YMS *Paektusan,* 220
YMS *Tong Yong,* 201
Yongsan base, 106
Yoshida, peace treaty with, 255
Yoshimichi, Hasegawa, 16
Yosu-Sunchon Rebellion, 166–75, 179,
    201, 203
  impact of, 174–75
  Rhee and, 167, 168, 170, 171–73
  suppression of, 178
Yo Un-hyong, 25, 31, 33, 46, 48, 58, 70,
    74, 75, 82, 84, 87, 94, 116, 118, 137,
    140, 159
  Abe and, 44–45, 270n3
  elections and, 89
  harassment of, 105
  Laboring People's Party and, 148
  Left-Right coalition and, 83
  People's Party and, 61
  popularity of, 47
  Rhee and, 63, 110
Young Men's Alliance, Autumn Harvest
    Uprising and, 86
Youth associations, 77, 103, 139, 201,
    213, 224
  anti-Communist, 142, 189
  elections and, 150
  as reserve force, 192
  Rhee and, 105
  Yosu Rebellion and, 171
Youth League, 195
Yuan Shi-kai, 21
Yu Chin-gyu, 226
Yu Chin-o, 154
Yu Jae-hung, 203, 211, 223, 256
Yun Chi-yong, 163, 164
Yu Song-chol, 40, 272n9

Zhongdong Railroad, 232
Zhou Bao-zhang, 194
Zhou Enlai, 194, 232, 233
Zhu De, 33, 194
Zubin, Mr., 98